# JAPANESE
## LEARNER'S DICTIONARY

**JAPANESE-ENGLISH / ENGLISH-JAPANESE**
Revised and updated

# LIVING LANGUAGE®

# JAPANESE
## LEARNER'S
## DICTIONARY
**JAPANESE-ENGLISH / ENGLISH-JAPANESE**
Revised and updated

**Revised by Hiroko Storm, Ph.D.**

University of Arizona

Assistant Professor of Japanese
Lafayette College

Based on the original by Ichiro Shirato

This work was previously published under the title *Living Language™ Common Usage Dictionary—Japanese* by Ichiro Shirato, based on the dictionary developed by Ralph Weiman.

Published in the United States by Living Language, an imprint of Random House, Inc.

www.livinglanguage.com

ISBN: 978-1-4000-2448-3

This book is available for special discounts for bulk purchases for sales promotions or premiums. Special editions, including personalized covers, excerpts of existing books, and corporate imprints, can be created in large quantities for special needs. For more information, write to Special Markets/ Premium Sales, 1745 Broadway, MD 6-2, New York, New York, 10019 or e-mail specialmarkets@randomhouse.com.

PRINTED IN THE UNITED STATES OF AMERICA

10  9  8  7  6  5  4  3  2  1

# CONTENTS

# INTRODUCTION

The *Living Language® Japanese Dictionary* lists more than 15,000 of the most frequently used Japanese words, gives their most important meanings, and illustrates their uses. This revised edition contains updated phrases and expressions, as well as many new entries related to business, technology, and the media.

1.  More than 1,000 of the most essential words are capitalized to make them easy to find.

2.  Numerous definitions are illustrated with phrases, sentences, and idiomatic expressions. Where there is no close English equivalent for a Japanese word, or where the English equivalent has several meanings, the context of the illustrative sentences helps to clarify the meanings.

3.  Because of these useful phrases, the *Living Language® Japanese Dictionary* also serves as a phrase book and conversation guide. The dictionary is helpful both to beginners who are building their vocabulary and to advanced students who want to perfect their command of colloquial Japanese.

4.  The Japanese expressions (particularly the idiomatic and colloquial ones) have been translated to their English

equivalents. However, literal translations have been added to help the beginner. For example, under the entry **TE,** *hand,* you will find: "**te ga aite iru** to be free; to have no work on hand." This dual feature also makes the dictionary useful for translation work.

# EXPLANATORY NOTES

NOUNS, VERBS, AND ADJECTIVES. The designation of nouns (*n.*), verbs (*v.*), adjectives (*adj.*), and adverbs (*adv.*) given in this dictionary refers to the word class (part of speech) of the English equivalent and *not* to the Japanese word.

Many nouns in Japanese can be converted into verbs simply by adding *suru*: (e.g., *benkyoo suru* = to study).

A verb that is translated in English in the infinitive form appears in the "plain present affirmative" in Japanese. Beginners are reminded that when such a verb is used as a predicate verb in sentences, it can be changed to the appropriate *-masu* (polite) form: *-masu, -mashita, -masen deshita, -mashoo,* etc.

Adjectives (*i* = adjectives) are listed in their "plain present affirmative" form. When they are used a predicate adjectives, an appropriate form of *-desu* (*desu, deshita, -ku arimasen, -ku arimasen deshita,* etc.) can be used.

PERSON AND NUMBER. An arbitrary choice has been made for the person (i.e., I, you, he, she, it, we, you, they) and number (singular or plural) used in the English translation of a Japanese sentence. Usually a Japanese sentence can be translated in several other ways.

HOMONYMS. In Japanese, there are many words that sound and are spelled alike but that have different meanings.

In the traditional Japanese writing system, however, such words may be written with different symbols (*kanji*).

COLLOQUIAL AND HONORIFICS. Very colloquial words, phrases, and sentences are marked either *colloq.* or *vulgar.* *Respect* and *humble* designate honorifics. *Respect* is an expression that can be used only in talking about someone else (not about oneself: speaker); and *humble* is used only in talking about oneself (the speaker or the speaker's in-group).

# Japanese-English

# A

**a** *(interj.)* O! oh! look! **a to iwaseru** to astonish, surprise. **A taihen.** Oh! heavens! Good Lord!

**AA** *(interj.)* O! oh! ah! alas! dear me! *(adv.)* in that way; like that; so; **aa suru** to do so (like that); **aa iu** to say so; like that; **aa iu hito** a person like that; **aa iu koto** a thing like that; **aa iu fuu na hito** that sort of person; **aa iu fuu ni** in that way; like that. **Aa kirei da!** Oh, how beautiful! **Aa omoshirokatta.** Oh, it was so interesting! **Aa soo?** Really? Is it? Did you?

**aachi** arch.

**aa iu = aa yuu** that sort of; **aa iu koto** that sort of thing; **aa iu hanashi** that sort of story.

**aasu** ground wire.

**abaku** to disclose, to reveal *(a secret);* to expose; to bring to light.

**abara** ribs; side; **abara bone** rib; side of the chest.

**abaraya** crumbling house; poor hut.

**abare-** prefix denoting: rough; rowdy; unruly; **abareuma** runaway horse.

**abaredasu** to get rowdy, riotous; to break loose; grow restive; to start to behave violently.

**abaremawaru** to rave, to riot.

**abaremono** *(n.)* rowdy; hooligan.

**abareru** to act (behave) violent; to rage; to be riotous.

**abekobe** being topsy-turvy; **abekobe no** opposite; inverse; **abekobe ni** in a contrary manner; upside down.

**abiru** to pour on oneself; to bathe in; to be under fire; **hitofuro abiru** to have a bath; **chuumoku o abiru** to receive attention.

**abisekakeru** See **abiseru.**

**abiseru, abisekakeru** to pour on; to shower; to lay (something) on; to heap reproaches on.

**abu** horsefly; gadfly.

**abuku** See **awa.**

**abunage na** insecure (in appearance).

**ABUNAI** dangerous, risky, precarious; critical; **abunai me ni au** to have a terrible experience. **Abunai!** Look out! Watch out!

**abunakkashii** insecure, unsteady; unstable; unreliable; **abunakkashii tetsuki de** in a clumsy manner.

**ABUNAKU** nearly; barely; **abunaku naru** to get dangerous. **Abunaku okureru tokoro deshita.** I almost missed the train.

**abunasa** danger, risk, peril.

**abunasoo na** dangerous-looking.

**ABURA** oil; fat; **aburadarake** covered with grease; oil-stained; **abura de ageru** to fry in oil; **abura ga noru** to become interested in; **aburaase** greasy sweat; **aburaase o nagashite** by the sweat of one's brow; **aburake no aru** oily, fatty, rich (food); **aburake no nai** lean; light; **aburakkoi** greasy, fatty, oily (food). **Aburakkoi mono ga suki desu.** I like greasy foods.

**aburaage = age** bean curd fried in oil (popular food item).

**aburae** oil painting; **aburae o kaku** to paint in oils.

**aburagusuri** liniment; ointment.

**aburami** fat; fatty part of meat.

**aburamushi** cockroach; aphid.

**aburu** to place over a fire; to grill; to warm; to dry; **te o aburu** to warm one's hands at a fire.

**achikochi** *(adv.),* **achira kochira** here and there; to and fro.

**ACHIRA** *(n.)* that direction; other side; over there; yonder; overseas; **achira no shuukan** customs of a foreign country. **Achira e ikimashoo.** Let's go that way.

**ACHIRA KOCHIRA** *(n., adv.)* here and there; various places; to and fro; up and down; **achira kochira kara** from far and near; **achira kochira o sagasu** to look for (something) here and there; **achira kochira inaka o ryokoo suru** to travel about the country.

**ada** enemy; revenge; vengeance; resentment; harm.

**adana** nickname.

**adokenai** innocent, artless; naïve *(used when speaking of a child)* **adokenai yoosu** naïve manner; innocent air.

**aegi** pant; gasp; **aegi aegi** gaspingly; out of breath.

**aegu** to pant; to gasp.

**aen** zinc.

**aenai** untimely; sad; pitiful; **aenai saigo** pitiful end (death); **aenai saigo o togeru** to come to a sad end.

**aenaku** sadly; unexpectedly; flatly; **aenaku kotowaru** to refuse flatly; **aenaku naru** to die.

**aete** *(adv.)* boldly; without hesitation; by any means; **aete suru** to dare, venture; **aete iu** I presume; I venture to say.

**afureru** to overflow, run over.

**agaku** to paw; to struggle.

**agameru** to revere; to worship; to respect; to glorify.

**aganai** atonement; redemption; compensation.

**aganau** to buy, purchase, atone, expiate, redeem.

**AGARIGUCHI** entranceway in a Japanese-style house.

**agariori** *(n.)* ascent and descent; **kaidan no agariori** going up and down the staircase.

**agarisagari** rise and fall; fluctuation; **nedan no agarisagari** fluctuation of prices.

**AGARU** to go up, come up; to rise; to ascend, climb (up); to rise in rank; to improve; to come to an end; to visit *(humble);* to go ashore; to eat, drink *(respect);* to become nervous; **chu ga agaru** to be promoted. **ude ga agaru** to become more skillful; **ame ga agaru** to stop raining; **riku ni agaru** to go ashore. **Mata agarimashoo.** I will call again. **Okashi o oagari kudasai.** Help yourself to a sweet, please. **Pitchas ga agaru.** The pitcher *(baseball)* is getting nervous.

**age** tuck (in Japanese clothes).

**ageashi** fault-finding; hypercriticism; **ageashi o toru** to trip (a person) up.

**ageku** *(adv.)* = **ageku ni; ageku no hate ni** the end; finally, at last; on top of all this; to make matters worse. **Shigoto o nakushita ageku ni byooki ni natta.** He lost his job, and on top of that (to make matters worse), he became ill.

**agemono** fried food.

**agenabe** frying pan.

**ageoroshi** = **agesage** loading and unloading; raising and lowering; **hashi no ageoroshi ni mo kogoto o iu** to find fault with everything [to make comments even on how the chopsticks are handled].

**AGERU** to raise, elevate, lift (up); to give, present (honorific; used when the speaker gives something to someone else). **Okane o ageta.** I gave her some money.

**agesage** = **ageoroshi** raising and lowering; praise and blame; **hashi no agesage ni mo kogoto o iu** to be (too) particular about trifles.

**ageshio** flood (rising) tide.

**AGO** jaw; chin.

**-agumu** suffix denoting to grow tired of, get (become) weary; **machiagumu** to grow tired of waiting.

**agura o kaku** to sit cross-legged.

**ahen** opium.

**ahiru** duck, drake; **ahiru no ko** duckling.

**ahoo** fool; idiot; blockhead; **ahoo na** foolish, stupid; **ahorashii** foolish; silly; ridiculous; **ahoo na koto** foolish affair.

**AI** love; affection; attachment; **ai suru** to love; care for; **fukaku ai suru** to love tenderly (deeply).

**ai** indigo, blue; **ai-iro no** blue, bluish.

**ai-** prefix denoting: mutually; with each other; **ai-mukatte** face to face; **ai-narande tatsu** to stand shoulder to shoulder.

**aibiki** secret meeting (of lovers); rendezvous.

**aiboo** partner; accomplice.

**aibu** caress; fondling; **aibu suru** to caress, fondle, pet.

**aichaku** deep attachment; passion; **-ni aichaku suru** to love passionately.

**AIDA** space (between); time (between); distance; interval; **sono aida** in the meanwhile; **nagai aida** for a long time; **hitotsuki no aida ni** in the course of a month; **watakushi ga ikite iru aida wa** as long as I live; **roppun no aida o oite** at intervals of six minutes.

**aidagara** relationship; terms; **shitashii aidagara de aru** to be on very friendly terms.

**aidoku suru** to read for pleasure; **aidokusha** subscriber; reader; reading public; **aidokusho** one's favorite book.

**aifuku, aigi** lightweight suit.

**aijin** lover, sweetheart; **aijoo** love, affection; **aijoo no aru hito** affectionate, warmhearted person.

**aikagi** passkey.

**AIKAWARAZU** as usual; as always; **aikawarazu isogashii desu** as busy as ever.

**aiko** a tie, even game, draw; **aiko ni naru** to end in a tie. **Kore de aiko da.** This makes us even.

**aikoku** love for one's country, patriotism.

**aikotoba** password.

**aikyoo** charm; amiability; **aikyoo no aru hito** charming, amiable person; **aikyoo no nai hito** disagreeable person; **aikyoo o furimaku** to have a smile for everybody.

**aima** interval; leisure; **aima ni** at intervals; **shigoto no aima ni** in one's spare time.

**aimai** obscurity; ambiguity; **aimai na** obscure; ambiguous; vague.

**AINIKU** unluckily; unfortunately; **ainiku na** unfavorable; unfortunate. **Oainiku sama.** I am very sorry (that I do not have it). **Ainiku ame ga futte kimashita.** Unfortunately, it started to rain.

**ainoko** *(n.)* hybrid; Eurasian.

**Ainu** Ainus (a minority tribe of northern Japan).

**airashii** charming; amiable; sweet.

**AIRON** iron (for pressing); **airon o kakeru** to iron.

**aisatsu** greeting, salutation; **aisatsu suru** to greet, salute.

**aiso** sociability, cordiality; **aiso no yoi** sociable, cordial; **aiso no nai hito** cold, blunt person; **oaiso o iu** to flatter; **-ni aiso ga tsukiru** to be disgusted with. **Aiso yoku hanashimashita.** He spoke very pleasantly.

**aisuhokkee** ice hockey.

**aisukuriimu** ice cream.

**aita** empty, vacant; opened; **te ga aita toki** when he is free.

**aitagai ni** with each other.

**AITE** companion; partner; adversary; **-no aite ni naru** to keep company with; to become a partner of; **-o aite ni shinai** to pay no attention to; **-o aite ni suru** to challenge; to deal with.

**aitsu** that fellow; that rascal (derogatory).

**aitsuide** one after another; successively.

**aizu** signal; **aizu suru** to signal.

**AJI** taste, flavor; relish; **aji no aru** tasty; **aji no nai** tasteless; **-no aji ga suru** it tastes like; **aji ga kawaru** to become stale, turn sour; **aji o tsukeru** to flavor, season.

**aji** bluefin tuna.

**AJIA** Asia; **Ajia no** *(adj.)* Asian, Asiatic; **Ajiajin** *(n.)* Asian, Asiatic.

**ajikenai** irksome, wearisome; lonely; **ajikenaku kurasu** to lead a miserable life.

**ajina** dainty; clever; smart; **ajina koto o suru** to act cleverly; **ajina koto o iu** to say something clever.

**ajisai** hydrangea.

**ajitsukenori** seasoned seaweed (a popular food item).

**ajiwau** to taste; to experience; to enjoy; to appreciate.

**AKA** *(n.)* red, crimson, scarlet; communism; communist; **aka no tanin** utter stranger.

**aka** dirt, filth; **aka darake** dirty, filthy; **-ni aka ga tsuku** to become dirty; **aka o nagasu** to wash off dirt; to wash (oneself).

**AKABOO** redcap, porter (for luggage).

**AKACHAN** = **akago** baby, infant.

**akagire** chap, crack (in the skin); **akagire ga kireru** to become chapped.

**akago** See **akachan.**

**akahaji** disgrace; open shame; **akahaji o kakasareru** to be put to shame.

**AKAI** red, ruddy, flushed; **akai kao o suru** to blush.

**akaji** red figures, deficit; **akaji o dasu** to go into the red; to have a deficit.

**akajimita** soiled, dirty.

**akaku** ruddily; redly; **akaku naru** to redden; to flush; to glow.

**akami** redness; tinge of red.

**akami** lean meat.

**Akamon** Red Gate of Tokyo University; synonym for Tokyo University.

**akanboo** baby, infant. (See also **akachan.**)

**akanuke** polish, gloss; refinement; **akanuke no shita hito** polished person; **akanuke no shinai hito** unpolished, uncouth person.

**akaramu** to turn red; to glow; to ripen (fruit).

**akarasama na** plain, clear; frank, candid; **akarasama ni** plainly; frankly; without reserve; **akarasama ni ieba** to be frank; to tell the truth in plain terms.

**akari** light, lamp; **akari o tsukeru** to light a lamp.

**AKARUI** bright; light; knowing well; versed in; **akaruku naru** to grow light; **akarui heya** well-lighted room; **hooritsu ni akarui** to be familiar with the laws; **akarui uchi ni** while it is light; before it gets dark.

**akarumi** light place; light; **akarumi e dasu** to bring a thing to light; to expose (something).

**akasu** to spend the whole night; to sit up all night; to reveal the truth, to confess; to speak one's mind.

**akasu** to weary, tire; **kane ni akashite** regardless of the expense; regardless of the cost.

**akatsuchi** red earth (clay).

**akatsuki** = **akegata** dawn, daybreak; **akatsuki chikaku** toward daybreak; **-no akatsuki ni wa** when; in the event of; in case of.

**akazatoo** brown sugar.

**akegata** See **akatsuki.**

**akehanasu** to throw open (a window).

**akekure** morning and evening; day and night; all the time.

**AKERU** to open; to turn over (pages); to make room (for); to evacuate (a house, premises); to empty (a box); to expire; **ie o akeru** to stay out; **ana o akeru** to make a hole; **mizu o akeru** to pour out water. **Yo ga akeru.** The day is breaking.

**AKI** room; space; vacancy; **aki o fusagu** to fill a gap.

**AKI** autumn, fall; **akibare** a clear autumn day.

**aki-** prefix denoting: vacant, unoccupied; spare; **akibin** empty bottle; **akichi** vacant lot; **akidaru** empty barrel; **akima** vacant room.

**akimekura** illiterate (person).

**akinai** trade, business; **akinai suru** to do business; **akinai o shite iru** to be in business; to be engaged in a trade; **akinai joozu** good at trade; **akinai beta** poor at trade.

**akinau** to deal in, trade in.

**AKIRAKA NA** bright; clear; **akiraka ni suru** to make clear; to account for; **akiraka ni** brightly; clearly; undoubtedly; no doubt. **Akiraka desu.** It is clear.

**akirame** resignation; relinquishment; **akirameru** to give up; to resign oneself to; to submit to one's fate; to relinquish.

**akireru** to be amazed at; to be dumbfounded; be disgusted with; **akirete** with astonishment; in amazement; **akirete mono ga ienai** to be dumbfounded.

**akiru** to get tired of, be sick of; to have enough of; **akiru hodo taberu** to eat one's fill; **-ni akiyasui** to be soon tired of; **akiru hodo asobu** to play to one's heart's content.

**akisu** sneak thief.

**AKIYA** vacant house; unoccupied house; house for rent.

**akkan** rascal, rogue.

**akka suru** to go from bad to worse.

**akke** *(n.)* being dumfounded when an event has happened; **akke nai** too soon; too brief; too sudden; **akke ni torareru** to be taken aback; to be amazed. **Tsukihi ga akke naku tatte shimatta.** The days passed all too quickly. **Sore de wa amari akke nai.** That's too abrupt.

**akkoo** abuse, insulting remarks; **akkoo suru** to abuse, insult.

**akogare** longing, yearning; desire.

**akogareru** to long for, yearn for, yearn after.

**aku** evil, vice; wrong; wickedness; **aku ni mukuiru ni zen o motte suru** to return good for evil.

**AKU** to open; to be opened; to become empty, become vacant; **te ga aku** to be free, be disengaged. **Maku ga aku.** The curtain rises.

**akubi** yawn; **ooakubi** great yawn; **akubi suru** to yawn.

**akudoi** tedious; heavy (color or food); glaring.

**akufuu** evil practices; evil manners; evil habit.

**akuheki** bad habit; vice.

**akuhitsu** illegible handwriting; poor penmanship.

**akui** malice, ill will; malicious intent; **akui de** from malice; purposely; **akui no aru hito** malicious, evil-minded person.

**akuji** evil thing; evil deed; criminal action.

**AKUKANJOO** ill feeling; ill will.

**akumade** to the utmost; to the best of one's ability; persistently; **akumade mo** to the last; stubbornly; to the end; **akumade yaru** to do one's utmost.

**akunin** bad person, villain.

**akuratsu na** unscrupulous; sharp; crafty; wicked.

**akurei** bad precedent; bad example; **akurei o tsukuru** to set a bad precedent.

**AKURU** next, following (time); **akuru asa** the following morning; **akuru toshi** the following year.

**akuseku** diligently, industriously; busily; restlessly; **akuseku suru** to busy oneself; worry about; **-ni akuseku to suru** to be busy with; **akuseku to kasegu** to work hard (for a living).

**akusento** accent, stress; pitch (of the voice).

**AKUSHU** handshake; **akushu suru** to shake hands.

**akushuu** bad habit; evil practices; **akushuu ga tsuku** to develop a bad habit; **akushuu o dassuru** to get rid of a bad habit.

**akutoo** villain, scoundrel.

**akuun** ill luck; evil fate.

**akuyoo** misuse; improper use; abuse; **akuyoo suru** to misuse; abuse.

**akuyuu** bad friend; bad companion; **akuyuu to majiwaru** to keep bad company.

**ama** diving woman (professional pearl-diver).

**AMA-** prefix denoting: rain; of rain, for rain; **amadare** raindrops; **amado** rain door; **amagasa** umbrella; **amagoi** prayers for rain; **amagu** rain gear; **amagumo** rain cloud; **amamizu** rain water; **amagu o yooi shite deru** to go out prepared for rain; **amagu no yooi o suru** to provide oneself with rain gear.

**amachua** amateur.

**amaeru, amattareru** to behave like a spoiled child; to coax; to be coquettish; to take advantage of; **amaeru yoo ni** coaxingly. **Okotoba ni amaemashoo.** I'll take advantage of your kind offer.

**amaguri** roast chestnuts.

**AMAI** sweet, sugary; not salted enough; indulgent; not strict; **amaku suru** to sweeten; **amai mono** sweets, candy; **amai kotoba** sweet (soft) words; **amaku miru** to have little regard for a person. **Kono sake wa ama-jio da.** This salmon is not salted enough.

**amajio** slightly salted.

**amakuchi** fondness for sweet things; sweet tooth; honeyed words. **Kare wa amakuchi da.** He has a sweet tooth.

**amami** sweet flavor; sweetness; **amami no aru** sweetish; **amami o tsukeru** to sweeten. **Amami ga tarinai.** It is not sweet enough.

**amamori** leak in the roof.

**amemoyoo** signs of rain; **amamoyoo no sora** a threatening sky. **Amamoyoo desu.** It looks like rain.

**AMANEKU** widely, universally; far and wide; **amaneku aekai ni shirarete iru** to be known all over the world; **amaneku zenkoku o jun'yuu suru** to travel all over the country.

**AMANJIRU, amanzuru** to be content with, be satisfied with; to put up with; **amanjite** contentedly; willingly; **amanjite seisai o ukeru** to submit willingly to punishment. **Kare wa kore ni amanjite wa inai.** He is not content with this.

**Amanogawa** Milky Way; Galaxy.

**amanzuru** See **amanjiru.**

**AMARI** See **ANMARI**

**AMARI** remainder, rest; surplus, excess; remnants.

**AMARU** to remain, be left over; to be too much; to be in excess; to be beyond one's power; **mini amaru kooei** an undeserved honor; **chikara ni amaru** beyond one's power.

**amasu** to leave over; to save; **kane o amasazu tsukau** to spend all one's money. **Hitotsu mo amasanakatta.** I didn't leave even one.

**amata** (a great) many; many a; a number of; numerous.

**amatsusae** besides; moreover; what is more; into the bargain; to make matters worse.

**amattareru** See **amaeru.**

**amattarui** sweetish; sugary; **amattarui kotoba** honeyed words; **amattarui shibai** sentimental play (drama).

**amayadori suru** to take shelter from the rain.

**amayakasu** to pet; to indulge (a child) too much; to spoil.

**amayoke** shelter from the rain; protection against rain.

**amazake** sweet drink made from fermented rice.

**amazarashi** exposure to rain.

**AME** rain; **ame no** rainy; wet; **ame tsuzuki** spell of rainy weather; **ame ni naru** to change to rain; to begin to rain; **ame ni au** to be caught in the rain. **Ame ga furisoo desu.** It looks like rain.

**AME** candy; wheat gluten.

**AMEFURI** rain; rainy weather; rainy day; **amefuri ni soto o aruku** to walk in the rain.

**ameiro no** light brown.

**AMERIKA** America; **Amerika no** (adj.) American; **AMERIKAJIN** (n.) American; **Amerika Gasshuukoku** United States of America.

**ami** net; fishing net; **ami no me** meshes (of a net).

**amibari, amiboo** knitting needles.

**amidana** rack (in a train or bus).

**amimono** (n.) knitting; crocheting; **amimono o suru** to knit.

**aminome** mesh.

**amu** to knit; to braid; **kutsushita o amu** to knit socks.

**an** proposal; bill; draft; plan; opinion; idea; **an o dasu** to make a proposal; **an o tateru** to make a plan; **an o tsukuru** to make a draft; **an ni sooi shite** contrary to expectation; **an no gotoku** as was expected.

**an** bean paste, bean jam.

**ANA** hole; aperture; den, cave; pit; loss; shortage; fault; **ana o akeru** to make a hole, perforate; **zaisan ni ana o akeru** to cut into one's assets; **ana o fusagu** to fill up a hole; stop a gap.

**anadori** contempt; disdain; **anadoru** to despise; to slight; to make light of; to look down upon; **anadori o ukeru** to be despised; to be scorned; **anadorigatai** formidable. **Shooteki o anadoru na.** Don't despise a weak enemy.

**anagachi** necessarily, of necessity; always (used with a negative). **Sore wa anagachi muri de wa nai.** It's not altogether unreasonable.

**anago** sea eel.

**an'anri ni** tacitly; by tacit agreement; secretly; **an'anri ni shoodaku suru** to give tacit consent. **An'anri ni itchi shita.** It was tacitly agreed.

**ANATA** you, sweetheart.

**ANATAGATA** you (pl. formal).

**ANATATACHI** you (pl.).

**anaunsaa** announcer.

**anbai** seasoning; taste; state of health; condition; **anbai suru** to season; to arrange; **yoi anbai ni** fortunately.

**anbaransu** unbalance; **eiyoo no anbaransu** unbalance of diet.

**anchaku** safe arrival; **anchaku suru** to arrive safely.

**anchoku na** cheap, low-priced, inexpensive; **anchoku ni** cheaply, inexpensively.

**anchuu mosaku suru** to grope in the dark.

**ANE** older sister.

**anemuko** husband of an older sister.

**ANGAI NA** unexpected; unforeseen; surprising; **angai ni** unexpectedly; **angai muzukashii** more difficult than imagined.

**ANI** older brother.

**aniyome** elder brother's wife.

**anji** hint; suggestion; **anji suru** to hint; to suggest; **anji o tsutaeru** to give a hint; **anji ni tonda** suggestive; full of suggestions.

**ANJIRU** to be anxious, be concerned; to worry.

**anka** cheapness; low price; **anka na** cheap; inexpensive; **anka ni** cheaply; at a low price; **anka na seikatsu** cheap living; **anka na kairaku** cheap pleasure.

**ankeeto** questionnaire.

**anki suru** to learn by heart, memorize.

**anma** masseur; massage; **anma suru** to massage.

**ANMARI, AMARI** too much; excessively; too hard; cruel; unreasonable. **Sore wa anmari desu.** That's too hard. That's too cruel. **Anmari omoshiroku nai.** It's not too interesting.

**ANMIN** quiet sleep; sound sleep; **anmin suru** to sleep well; **anmin o boogai suru** to disturb someone else's sleep.

**anmoku** tacit consent, tacit understanding. **anmoku no uchi ni** by tacit consent.

**ANNA** that sort of; like that; such; **anna ni** like that; in that way; **anna utsukushii musume** such a pretty girl; a girl as pretty as that; **anna hito** a person like that; that sort of person.

**ANNAI** guidance; conduct; invitation; **annai suru** to usher, guide; to invite; **annaijoo** letter or card of invitation; **annaiki** guidebook; **annaisha** guide; usher; pilot; **annaisho** guidebook, handbook; **annai nashi ni** unannounced; without knowing; without a guide; **annai o kou** to ask to see. **Annai nashi ni haitte kita.** She entered the room without knocking.

**annei** public peace; public welfare.

**an ni** by hints; tacitly; in secret; implicitly; **an ni shiraseru** to hint; suggest; insinuate.

**ANO** that; those; **ano yoo na** like that; of that sort; that sort of; **ano kata** he; she; that person. **Ano ne.** You see! I say, Listen!

**anoo** well; I say; look here.

**ano yo** other world; next world; **ano yo de** in the world to come.

**anpan** bean-jam bun; bun.

**ANPI** safety; welfare; health; **anpi o tazuneru** to inquire after (someone's) health.

**anpojooyaku** the (Japan-U.S.) Security Pact.

**ANRAKU** comfort, ease; **anraku na** comfortable, easy; happy; **anraku isu** easy chair; **anraku na seikatsu o suru** to lead a life of ease; **anraku ni kurasu** to live comfortably.

**ANSEI** quietness, rest; **ansei ni** quietly; in quiet; **ansei o tamotsu** to keep quiet; to lie quietly.

**ANSHIN** peace of mind, freedom from anxiety; confidence; **anshin suru** to feel at ease; to feel relieved; **anshin saseru** to set (someone) at ease; **anshin no dekiru hito** reliable person; **anshin no dekinai hito** unreliable person; **anshin shite** with confidence; with peace of mind.

**anshitsu** dark room.

**anshoo** recitation; **anshoo suru** say by rote.

**anshutsu** invention; contrivance; **anshutsu suru** to think out; to contrive, devise; to invent.

**ansoku** rest, respose **ansoku suru** to rest; to take a rest.

**ansokujitsu** Sunday, Sabbath.

**anta** (*colloq.*) you.

**antei** stability; equilibrium; **antei suru** to be stabilized; to be settled; **antei o tamotsu** to keep one's balance; **antei o ushinau** to lose one's balance.

**antena** antenna.

**ANZEN** safety, security; **anzen na** safe; secure; **anzen ni** safely; securely; **anzen chitai** safety zone; **anzen kamisori** safety razor.

**ANZU** apricot.

**anzuru** to be anxious about, worry about. **Watakushi no koto o anjinaide kudasai.** Don't worry about me.

**AO** blue; green; **aoao shita** verdant; freshly green; **aoba** green leaves, foliage.

**aodatami** new or freshly renovated mat.

**aogu** to fan; to raise one's eyes; to ask for; to depend upon; **hojo o aogu** to ask for aid. **Sora o aoida.** He looked up at the sky.

**AOI** blue; green; pale; unripe; inexperienced; **aoku naru** to become blue (pale); **aoku someru** to dye (something) blue. **Aoi kao o shite iru.** He looks pale. **Sora ga aoku harete iru.** The sky is clear.

**aoi** hollyhock.

**aoiki** gasp; **aoiki o tsuku** to gasp; to heave a deep sigh; **aoiki toiki de** gaspingly; with greatest effort. **Aoiki toiki desu.** I am in great distress.

**aojashin** blueprint.

**aojiroi** pale, pallid; sickly.

**aomi** blueness; blue tint; greenness; **aomi gakatta** bluish; greenish.

**aomono** vegetables; **aomono ichiba** vegetable market; **aomonoya** greengrocer; vegetable seller.

**aomuki ni** on one's back. **aomuki ni taoreru** to fall on one's back; **aomuku** to look up, turn one's face up.

**aonisai** greenhorn; raw youth; stripling.

**aonori** seaweed processed for food.

**aori** flapping; bump; **aori o kurau** to feel the influence of; to be hit by; **aoru** to fan; to flap; to stir up, incite; **kaze ni aorarete iru** to flap in the wind. **Kaze ga kaen o aotta.** The strong wind fanned the flames.

**aotenjoo** (azure) heaven; vault of heaven; open sky.

**aounabara** blue expanse of water; ocean.

**aozameru** to turn pale. **Aozameta kao o shite iru.** His face is white as a sheet.

**aozora** blue sky.

**APAATO** apartment house.

**appaku** pressure; stress; oppression; **appaku suru** to oppress; bear down upon.

**appare** (*n.*) being splendid; bravo!; well done! **appare na** splendid! admirable; **appare na hataraki** splendid achievement; **appare na**

**jinbutsu** person of fine (admirable) character.

**ara** ah! oh! good gracious! oh, my! (used by women).

**ara** defect, fault, blemish; bony parts (of fish); **ara o sagasu** to look for defects (in others); find fault with others.

**ara-** prefix denoting: coarse; rough, harsh; **arashigoto** a rough work.

**Arabia** Arabia; **Arabia no** (adj.) Arabic; Arabian; **Arabiago** Arabic language; **Arabiajin** (n.) Arab; Arabian; **Arabia suuji** Arabic numerals.

**aradateru** to excite; to agitate; to exasperate; to inflame; to complicate; **koto o aradateru** to complicate matters; to aggravate the matter.

**aragyoo** asceticism.

**ARAI** rough; coarse; rude; wild; violent; **arai shima** a rough pattern; **araku** harshly; roughly. **Umi ga arai.** The sea is rough.

**arai** wash; washing; raw fish slices; **araigami** newly washed and untied hair; **araitate** just washed; **araitate no** newly washed; **arai ga kiku** to wash well; to be washable; **arai ga kikanai** not washable.

**ARAKAJIME** previously; in anticipation; **arakajime tsuuchi suru** to inform beforehand; **arakajime yooi suru** to prepare beforehand.

**ARAKATA** for the most part; mostly; most of. **Shigoto wa arakata dekiagari mashita.** The work is nearly completed.

**arakezuri no** roughly planned; rough-hewn.

**arakure otoko** (n.) rough; rowdy.

**aramashi** roughly; nearly, almost; practically; all but; briefly.

**aramonoya** kitchenware dealer.

**arankagiri** as much as possible; **arankagiri ni** every; all; utmost; **arankagiri no chikara o dashite** with the utmost exertion; **arankagiri no koe de** at the top of one's voice; as loudly as possible.

**arappoi** rough; rough-mannered; violent.

**arare** hail; hailstone; salty rice cracker (seasoned with soy sauce). **Arare ga futte iru.** It is hailing.

**araryooji** drastic treatment, drastic remedy; drastic measures.

**arasagashi** (n.) fault-finding; **arasagashi o suru** to find fault (with).

**ARASHI** storm; **arashi no** stormy.

**arashigoto** rough work; rough labor.

**ARASOI** quarrel; contention; **arasoi o okosu** to start a dispute; **uchiwa no arasoi** family quarrel; internal troubles.

**ARASOU** to quarrel; to dispute; to struggle, compete, vie; **saki o arasou** to scramble

for a seat; **arasou koto no dekinai** indisputable.

**ARASU** to ruin, to devastate.

**arasuji** outline, brief summary.

**ARATAMARU** to be changed, be altered; to be improved, be reformed; to take a turn for the worse (in illness); to stand on ceremony. **Soo aratamaranaide kudasai.** Don't stand on ceremony.

**aratameru** to renew; to renovate, alter, change, revise; to improve; to examine.

**aratamete** anew; another time; **aratamete tazuneru** to ask again. **Aratamete mairimasu.** I'll come another time. I'll come again.

**arata na** new, fresh, novel; **arata na sumai** a new house; **arata ni hajimeru** to begin anew.

**arate** fresh force; new hand.

**ARAU** to wash; to purify; to cleanse; **ashi o arau** to wash one's hands of a matter; to quit.

**araumi** rough sea, stormy sea.

**arawareru** to come out; to make an appearance, turn up, show oneself. **Kao ni arawarete iru.** It is written on your face.

**ARAWASU** to show, display; to bring to light, lay bare; to write (a book, novel, etc.); to publish; to make known; **udemae o arawasu** to show ability; **tookaku o arawasu** to stand head and shoulders above others; **ikari o kao ni arawasu** to show anger (in one's face); **na o arawasu** to win fame; to distinguish oneself.

**ARAYURU** all; every possible; all sorts of; **arayuru shurui no hito** all sorts of people; **arayuru shudan o kokoromiru** to try every known method.

**ARE** that; it; roughness, coarseness; **ARE!** listen! look! **are hodo** like that; that (so) much; that degree; **are hodo itta noni** in spite of all that I have said; **are hodo kane ga atte mo** with all his riches; **are ka kore ka** this or that; **are ya kore ya** this and that; with one thing or another; **are ya kore ya de ki o momu** to worry oneself with one thing or another. **Are! Nan daroo?** Listen! What can that be?

**arebiyori** stormy weather.

**arechi** wasteland; uncultivated land.

**arehateru** to be dilapidated; to be utterly ruined; **arehateta** dilapidated; ruined.

**arekkiri** since then; any more; all; last. **Arekkiri otosata ga arimasen.** I haven't heard from him since then. **Arekkiri yoshimashita.** After that I left off completely.

**aremawaru** to rush about furiously.

**aremoyoo** threatening sky; signs of approaching storm.

**areno** wildness; wilds; wild tract of land.

**areru** to fall into decay; to lie waste; to rush about furiously; to be rough. **Umi wa arete ita.** The sea was rough.

**ari** ant; **arizuka** an anthill.

**ariamaru** *(pronoun)* ample; abundant; **ariamaru hodo kane ga aru** to have money to spare.

**ariari to** vividly; distinctly; plainly.

**ariawase** potluck; **ariawase no** ready; on hand; **mise no ariawase no shinamono** articles in stock; **ariawase no mono o taberu** to take potluck; to eat what is available.

**aribai** alibi.

**arifureta** common; ordinary.

**arigachi** frequent occurrence; **arigachi no** common; frequent. **Konna koto wa arigachi desu.** Such things are apt to happen.

**arigane** cash on hand.

**arigatagaru** to be thankful, feel grateful; **arigata meiwaku** unappreciated favor; misplaced kindness; **arigata namida** tears of gratitude. **Ano hito wa watashi no okurimono o arigatagarimashita.** She was thankful for my gift.

**ARIGATAI** thankful; **arigatai koto ni wa** fortunately; **arigataku** with thanks.

**arigatami** gratefulness, sense of gratitude.

**ARIGATOO** many thanks; I am much obliged to you. **Arigatoo gozaimasu.** Thank you.

**arika** whereabouts; place where a thing is.

**arikitari no** customary; conventional; **arikitari no hoohoo** the customary method.

**arisama** circumstances; state; condition. **Soo iu arisama desu.** That's the situation.

**arisoo na** seemingly possible; **arisoo mo nai** unlikely; improbable. **Arisoo na koto desu.** It's likely to happen.

**aritei** as it is; frankly *(colloq.);* **aritei ni iu** to speak the truth; state frankly.

**aritsuku** to come by, come upon; to find; to get, obtain; **shigoto ni aritsuku** to get work.

**arittake** all that there is; all that one has; **arittake no chikara o dasu** to put forth all one's efforts.

**ariubekarazaru** impossible; improbable; **ariubeki** possible; probable. **Sore wa ariubekarazaru koto desu.** That's impossible. That could never happen.

**ARU** certain; some; a; an; **aru tokoro de** at a certain place; **aru hi** one day; once; **aru hito** a certain person; a person; somebody; **aru toki** on a certain occasion; once upon a time.

**ARU** to be at; to exist, live; to be situated; to lie; to have; to take place; to experience; to find; to get. **Hon ga tsukue no ue ni arimasu.** The book is on the desk. **Oomori wa Tookyoo to Yokohama no aida ni aru.** Omori lies between Tokyo and Yokohama. **Tookyoo ni itta koto ga arimasu ka?** Have you ever been to Tokyo? **Kono hon wa doko ni arimashita ka?** Where did you find this book? **Taihen na koto ga atta no desu.** A dreadful thing happened.

**ARUBAITO** side job; **ARUBAITO SURU** to do a side job.

**ARUBAMU** album.

**arufabetto** alphabet.

**ARUIWA** or else; perhaps; probably; maybe. **Aruiwa soo ka mo shirenai.** It may be so. It is not impossible.

**aruji** master; host; head of the family.

**arukaseru** to make walk, let walk (said of a child, horse, etc.)

**arukikata** one's manner of walking.

**arukimawaru** to walk about; to wander about; to go around; to gad about.

**arukooru** alcohol.

**ARUKU** to walk, go on foot. **Aruku no wa karada ni taihen ii desu.** Walking is very good for your health.

**arumajiki** improper; unbecoming; improbable.

**arumi, aruminyuumu** aluminum.

**aruto** alto.

**ASA** morning; in the morning; **asa hayaku** early in the morning; **asa no aida** all morning; **asa kara ban made** from morning till evening; **asaban** every morning and evening.

**asa** hemp; flax, linen; **asaito** hemp yarn; **asanawa** hempen cord.

**asa-** prefix denoting: light; shallow; **asamidori** light green.

**asagao** morning glory.

**asagi** *(n.)* light blue.

**ASAGOHAN** breakfast. **Asagohan wa hachiji desu.** Breakfast is at eight.

**asaguroi** dark; dark-skinned; brown.

**asahaka na** shallow (of mind); superficial; half-witted.

**asahi** morning sun; rising sun.

**ASAI** shallow; superficial; short, brief; **asai kawa** shallow river; **asai kangae** shallow thought; **hi ga asai . . .** it is a short time (since).

**asakusa nori** dried seaweed (food).

**asamashii** mean, miserable; wretched; **asamashii yononaka** the wretched world; **asamashii kokoro no otoko a** mean-spirited man.

**asamidori** *(n.)* light green.

**asanagi** morning calm.

**asane o suru** to lie in bed late; to sleep late; **asaneboo** late riser, sleepyhead; **asaneboo o suru** to oversleep; to get up late.

**asaru** to fish for; to search for; to hunt for; **iro o asaru** to philander.

**asase** shoal; shallows; **asase ni noriageru** to run aground.

**asatsuyu** morning dew.

**ASATTE** day after tomorrow. **Asatte ome ni kakarimasu.** I will see you the day after tomorrow.

**asayake** morning glow; sky at dawn.

**ASE** sweat; perspiration; **asebamu** to become sweaty; to be wet with sweat; **asekaki** one who perspires profusely; **ase ga deru** to perspire; **ase o kaku** to perspire; to become sweaty; **asemidoro ni natte** in a sweat; soaked with sweat; **asemizu o nagashite hataraku** to sweat with hard work; work by the sweat of one's brow.

**asemo** prickly heat.

**aseru** to hurry; to get impatient; to be hasty.

**aseru** to fade, to discolor. **Iro ga aseru.** The color has faded.

**ASHI** foot; leg; paw; step; pace; **ashi no koo** instep; **ashi no ura** sole; **ashiato** footprint; **ashi ni makasete iku** to go without knowing where; **aşhi ga tsuku** to be traced; leave a clue.

**ashi** reed; rush.

**ashiba** scaffolding; foothold.

**ashibumi** step; **ashibumi suru** to step; stamp one's feet.

**ashibyooshi** keeping time with the feet.

**ashidamari** stand; footing; **ashidamari o eru** to get a footing.

**ashidematoi** encumbrance, burden, nuisance; **ashidematoi ni naru** to become a nuisance; to get in the way.

**ashidome** confinement; **ashidome o suru** to keep (someone) indoors.

**ashidori** gait; manner of walking; tread.

**ashikake** foothold; pedal. **Kite kara ashikake gonen ni naru.** It is five [calendar] years since I came here.

**ashikarazu.** Please don't take it amiss.

**ASHIKUBI** ankle.

**ashimoto** place where one stands; **ashimoto ni** at (near) one's feet; **ashimoto no akarui uchi ni** before it gets dark; before getting caught; **ashimoto o miru** to take advantage of (someone else's) weakness.

**ashinami** pace; **ashinami o soroete** with measured steps; keeping pace with; **ashinami o soroete aruku** to walk in step.

**ashioto** footfall, sound of a footstep.

**ashirai** treatment; reception.

**ashirau** to treat, entertain; to receive; to handle; to deal with; to harmonize; to add.

**ashi shigeku** often, frequently (refers to visits); **ashi shigeku kayou** to visit frequently.

**ASHITA, ASU** tomorrow. **Ashita mata.** See you again tomorrow.

**asobaseru** to leave (something) idle; **kane o asobasete oku** to let money lie idle.

**ASOBI** play; sport; amusement; pleasure; recreation; sensual pleasure; dissipation; **asobi ni iku** to go out to play; to seek recreation; **asobi gatera** for amusement; half in play.

**ASOBU** to play; to be idle; to go on a spree; to amuse.

**ASOKO** that place; there; **asoko ni** over there, yonder.

**assaku** pressure; compression; **assaku suru** to press.

**ASSARI** simply; lightly; moderately; briefly; **assari shita** simple; light; plain; **assari katazukeru** to make short work of.

**assen** mediation; **assen suru** to help, to mediate; arbitrate; **assensha** mediator, arbitrator.

**ASU** See **ASHITA.**

**asufaruto** asphalt. **asufaruto no michi** asphalt road.

**asupirin** aspirin.

**ataeru** to give; to let have; to present, award; **shigoto o ataeru** to give work; **-ni songai o ataeru** to inflict damage on; **ataerareta shigoto** work assigned.

**atafuta** hurriedly; helter-skelter.

**atai** price; value; **atai suru** to be worth; to cost; to deserve.

**ATAKAMO** just as if, so to speak. **Atakamo Nihonjin no yooni.** Just as if she were Japanese.

**ATAMA** head; top; brains; **atama o sageru** to bow respectfully; **atama ga yoi** a clear head; **atama ga warui** stupid; **atama gonashi ni** unsparingly; cruelly; **atama kara ashi no saki made** from head to foot; **atamakabu** leader; leading member.

**atamakazu** number of persons.

**atamawari** equal division; **atamawari ni suru** to divide equally, allot equal shares.

**ATARASHII** new, fresh, novel; recent, latest; **atarashii sakana** fresh fish; **atarashiku** newly; anew; afresh; **atarashiku suru** to renovate; freshen; **atarashiku hajimeru** to begin anew.

**atari** neighborhood; vicinity; near; **-no atari ni** in the neighborhood of; near; about; **atari kamawazu** regardless of the people present.

**atari** success; hit; **atari doshi** fruitful (successful) year; **atari fuda** price-number ticket; **atari hazure** hit or miss; success or failure; **atari o toru** to make a hit.

**ATARIMAE NO** right, proper, reasonable; deserving; natural; usual; **atarimae no koto** a matter of course. **Okoru no wa atarimae desu.** She has good reason to get angry.

**atarisawari** consequence; **atarisawari no nai** neutral, noncommittal; **atarisawari no nai koto o iu** to talk so as not to hurt someone's feelings.

**ataru** to strike; to come true; to be exposed; to disagree with; to warm oneself; to succeed; to try; **soozoo ga ataru** to guess right; **ataru bekarazaru** irresistible; overwhelming; overpowering. **Keikaku ga atatta.** The plan succeeded. **Tonikaku atatte kudakero da.** Try anyhow.

**ATATAKAI** warm; genial; mild; **atatakai hito** warmhearted, genial person; **atatakai fuyu** warm winter; **atatakaku naru** to become warm; **atatakami** mildness; warmth; geniality; **atatakami no aru** warm, warmhearted.

**atatakasoo ni** snugly.

**atatamaru** to get warm; to warm oneself; **Yatto kore de atatamarimashita.** Now I'm warm.

**atatameru** to warm up, heat; **kyuukoo o atatameru** to renew an old friendship; **te o atatameru** to warm one's hands (over a brazier).

**ate** aim, object; **ate ni naranai** unreliable; **ate nashi ni** aimlessly; at random; **atedo naku** aimlessly, without an aim, at random; **ate ni suru** to depend on; **ate ga nai** to find no clue.

**-ate** addressed to; **watashiate no tegami** letter addressed to me.

**ategai** appointment; allotment; **ategaibuchi** rations; stipend (*colloq.*).

**ategau** to apportion; to allow; to give rations; to supply.

**atehamaru** to apply to; to hold good for; to conform to; **atehameru** to apply; to fit; to conform.

**atekkosuri, atekosuri** sly hint; insinuating remark.

**atekomi** anticipation; expectation.

**atekomu** to expect; to hope; **atekonde** in expectation of.

**atekosuru** to make an insinuating remark; to satirize.

**atena** address (place); **atena no hito** addressee; **atena o kaku** to address a letter.

**ateru** to hit; to touch; to guess; to expose to; to address to; **mato ni ateru** to hit the mark. **Ano hito ni atete tegami dashimashita.** I sent a letter to her attention. **Hi ni atenaide kudasai.** Please do not expose it to the sun. **aterareru** to be hit; to be affected by; to disagree with. **Tabeta sakana ni ateraremashita.** The fish that I ate didn't agree with me.

**atezuiryoo** conjecture, random guess; **atezuiryoo o suru** to hazard a guess.

**atezuppoo** guess; guesswork; **atezuppoo ni** at random; **atezuppoo o iu** to hazard a guess.

**ATO** back, rear; results; **ato ni** behind; **ato de** later; **ato ni nokoru** to stay behind; **ato o ou** to chase after. **Ato ga warui daroo.** The results won't be good.

**atogama** successor; **atogama ni suwaru** to succeed (someone).

**atokara atokara** one after another, in rapid succession.

**atokata** trace, vestige; proof, evidence; **atokata mo nai** unfounded, groundless.

**atokatazuke** clearing up; **atokatazuke o suru** to put things in order after a work is completed.

**atomawashi** postponement, deferment; **atomawashi ni suru** to defer, postpone.

**atomodori** relapse; setback; **atomodori suru** to go back; to degenerate.

**atooshi o suru** to push from behind; to back up; to support; to abet.

**atosaki** fore and aft; first and last; both ends; **atosaki ni naru** to be mixed up; to be in the wrong order; **atosaki no kangae naku** regardless of the consequences; thoughtlessly.

**atoshimatsu** settlement (of an affair); **atoshimatsu o suru** to put in order.

**atotori** inheritor; successor.

**atsugami** pasteboard, cardboard.

**atsugaru** to be very sensitive to the heat. **Watashi wa atsugari desu.** I feel the heat.

**atsugeshoo** heavy makeup; **atsugeshoo shita** thickly made up; heavily powdered.

**atsugi** many layers of clothing; **atsugi suru** to be warmly dressed.

**ATSUI** very warm; hot; **atsuku naru** to become hotter; **atsuku suru** to warm; heat; **onna ni atsuku naru** to run madly after a woman.

**ATSUI** thick; heavy; **atsui kimono** heavy clothes; **atsui hon** bulky book.

**atsukai** management; handling, treatment; reception. **Shinsetsu na atsukai o ukemashita.** I received kind treatment.

**atsukamashii** impudent, brazen, shameless; **atsukamashiku suru** to act shamelessly; **atsukamashisa** impudence, shamelessness.

**atsukau** to handle, manage; to transact; **jimu o atsukau** to transact business; **kazoku to shite atsukau** to treat as a member of the family.

**atsukurushii** close; sultry; sweltering.

**ATSUMARI** meeting, assembly; crowd, group.

**atsumaru** to meet, assemble. **Kuji ni atsumarimashoo.** Let's meet at nine. **Atsumare!** Line up!

**atsumeru** to gather, collect; to call together; **hitai o atsumeru** to put two heads together; to talk over something.

**atsurae** order (purchase); **atsurae no** custom made; **atsuraeru** to order from; to place an order; **atsurae muki no** just the thing; the very thing (person) for . . .

**atsureki** friction. **Atsureki ga shoojiru.** Friction arises.

**atsuryoku** pressure; stress; **atsuryoku o kuwaeru** to pressure.

**ATSUSA** heat, warmth; **atsusa atari** heat prostration; sunstroke; **atsusa ni ataru** to suffer from the (summer) heat.

**ATSUSA** thickness. **Atsusa wa ikura arimasu ka?** How thick is that?

**attooteki na** overwhelming; **attooteki daitasuu** overwhelming majority.

**AU** to meet; to see; to have an interview with, meet with; **hito ni au** to meet someone; **hidoi me ni au** to have a terrible time; **ame ni au** to be caught in the rain.

**au** to agree with; to fit in; to be in tune with; **pittari au** to fit perfectly. **Kono tabemono wa watakushi ni wa aimasen.** This food doesn't agree with me.

**auto** out; out of play (in baseball).

**awa** millet.

**awa** bubbles, foam, lather; **awa ga tatsu** to bubble, foam; to ferment; **awa o kuu** to be flustered.

**awabi** abalone.

**aware** pity; sadness; **aware na** pitiful, poor, sad, miserable; **awaremi** pity, compassion, mercy; **awaremu** to pity; **awaremubeki** poor, pitiable, miserable, wretched; **awareppoi** pitiful, poor, sad, miserable; **aware ni omou** to feel pity; **awaremi o kakeru** to treat with tenderness or compassion; **awaremi no fukai hito** person of great compassion.

**awase** lined lightweight garment.

**awaseme** joint; seam.

**awaseru** to put together, unite; **chikara o awaseru** to combine efforts; **hanashi no chooshi o awaseru** to chime in; **tokei o**
**awaseru** to set a watch by; **genbun to awaseru** to compare with the original.

**awatadashii** restless; busy; hurried.

**awatemono** giddy (flighty) person.

**AWATERU** to be confused; to lose one's head; to hurry.

**awaya** exclamation of alarm, agitation, or surprise; **awaya to miru ma ri** in an instant; in the twinkling of an eye.

**awayokuba** if things go well.

**aya** figure, design; twill; damask; figure of speech.

**ayabumu** to fear; to doubt; to hesitate; to have misgivings.

**ayadoru** to interweave; to embellish; to make designs.

**ayamachi** fault; mistake; blunder.

**ayamari** mistake, error.

**ayamaru** to err. **Sentaku o ayamarimashita.** He made a mistake in his choice.

**ayamaru** to apologize.

**ayame** iris.

**AYASHII** suspicious; uncertain; **ayashii ningen** suspicious (shady) person; **ayashii eigo** poor English.

**ayashimu** to suspect; to doubt; to wonder at.

**ayasu** to amuse; to humor; to caress (an infant).

**ayatsuri ningyoo** puppet, marionette.

**ayatsuru** to handle; to control; to pull the wires; **hito o ayatsuru** to play on a person's weakness.

**ayaui** dangerous; very near; **ayauku** barely; narrowly; on the point of; **ayauku nogareru** to have a narrow escape; **ayauku suru** to imperil, jeopardize, endanger.

**ayu** sweetfish (fresh-water game fish).

**aza** birthmark.

**azami** thistle.

**azamuku** to deceive; to cheat; to impose upon; **azamuki yasui** gullible; **hana o azamuku bijin** a beautiful woman.

**azawarai** derisive laughter; contempt; ridicule; **azawarau** to laugh at, ridicule; to sneer at.

**azayaka na** clear; splendid; vivid; **azayaka ni** clearly; splendidly.

**aze** footpaths between rice fields; low dikes separating rice fields.

**azukari** taking charge (custody).

**azukarimono** something left in one's charge.

**azukaru** to be trusted with; to keep. **Sore o oazukari itashimashoo.** I will keep it for you.

**azukaru** to participate, to share; **soodan ni azukaru** to be consulted.

**azukeru** to deposit; to leave in someone's charge; **azukenushi** depositor; **okane o ginkoo ni azukeru** to deposit money in a bank. **Tomodachi ni kodomo o azukete Nihon e ikimasu.** I'm leaving my child with a friend as I'm going to Japan.

**azuki** red bean.

**azusa** catalpa tree.

**baabekyuu** barbecue.

**baagen** bargain sale.

**BAAI** occasion; time; moment; case; circumstances; **-no baai ni wa** when; in case; in the event that; on the occasion of; **baai ni yotte wa** according to circumstances; **hitsuyoo no baai ni wa** in case of need.

**BAI** double; twice (as large, as many, as much); **bai ni suru** to make twice as large; to double; times; **-fold** (a counter); **ni bai** twice; two times; **ni bai ni suru** to double.

**baibai** *(n.)* buying and selling; **baibai suru** to trade in; **baibai keiyaku** bargain; contract of sale.

**baidoku** syphilis.

**baika** selling price.

**baikai** mediation; matchmatching; **baikai suru** to mediate; to convey; **baikaibutsu** medium; agent; **baikaisha** go-between.

**baikin** bacillus.

**baimei** self-advertisement; **baimeika** publicity seeker.

**baiorin** violin.

**baishaku** *(n.)* matchmaking; **baishaku suru** to arrange marriages; **baishakunin** go-between; matchmaker.

**baishoo** compensation, indemnify, reparation; **baishoo suru** to indemnify, make reparation for a loss; **baishookin** money for reparations, damages.

**baishuu** purchase; bribe; **baishuu suru** to bribe, buy off.

**BAITEN** stand, stall, booth; store.

**baiyaku** contract of sale. **Baiyakuzumi!** Sold!

**baji toofuu** utter indifference; **baji toofuu o kikinagasu** to turn a deaf ear to.

**BAKA** fool, blockhead, idiot, folly, nonsense, absurdity; **baka o iu** to talk nonsense; **baka o miru** to be fooled; **baka o suru** to make a fool of oneself; **baka ni suru** to make fun of; make a fool of; **baka na hito** foolish person; **baka ni** awfully.

**BAKABAKASHII** foolish, silly; **bakabakashii koto** foolish matter. **Baka yaroo** You fool! Idiot! *(vulgar).*

**BAKARI** about; some; just; only; almost; on the point of; **-bakari de naku** not

only . . . but. **Ima kita bakari desu.** I've just come. **Nakan bakari de atta.** She was ready to cry.

**bakashoojiki** stubborn honesty; simpleness. **Ano otoko wa bakashoojiki da.** That man is too honest.

**bakawarai** boisterous laughter; horse laugh.

**bakazu** experience; **bakazu o fumu** to gain experience; **bakazu o funda** experienced; veteran.

**bakemono** ghost, goblin.

**baken** pool ticket, pari-mutuel ticket; **bakenjoo** grandstand at a racetrack.

**bake no kawa** dissemblance; disguise; **bake no kawa ga arawareru** to reveal one's true colors.

**BAKETSU** bucket.

**bakkin** fine, penalty; **bakkin o kasu** to levy a fine.

**bakku** back; background; backer; **bakku suru** to back up (a vehicle); **bakku miraa** rearview mirror (in a car).

**bakuchi** gambling; **bakuchi o utsu** to gamble; **bakuchiba** gambling place; **bakuchiuchi** gambler.

**bakudai na** enormous, vast; immense, tremendous.

**bakudan** bomb; **bakudan tooka** *(n.)* bombing; **bakudan o tooka suru** to bomb.

**bakuhatsu** explosion, detonation; **bakuhatsu suru** to explode, blow up, burst.

**bakuon** explosive sound; roaring of an engine; buzzing.

**bakuro** exposure; disclosure; **bakuro suru** to expose; lay bare.

**bakushin** rush; dash; **bakushin suru** to rush; to dash forward.

**bakuzen to shita** vague, uncertain; ambiguous, indefinite. **Imi ga bakuzen to shite iru.** The meaning is vague.

**BAN** evening; night; **ban ni** in the evening; **Nichiyoo no ban ni** on Sunday evening.

**BAN-** prefix denoting: numerous; innumerable; all; every; **banji** everything.

**ban** watch, guard, lookout; number; order; turn; time; round; game; **ban o suru** to keep watch.

**BANANA** banana.

**banbutsu** all things (under the sun); creation; entire universe.

**bancha** coarse tea; green tea of poor quality; **bancha mo debana** everything in its season.

**banchi** lot number; address.

**bandai** all ages; eternity; **bandai ni** through all ages; forever; **bandai fueki no** immutable, eternal.

**bando** belt; band (music).

**bangai** *(n.)* extra; additional turn; **bangai no** *(adj.)* extra; additional.

**bangata** evening; nightfall; **bangata ni** in the evening; toward evening.

**BANGOO** number; **bangoo o utsu** to number.

**BANGUMI** program; list.

**banji** everything; all things. **Banji kootsugoo ni itte iru.** Everything is going well.

**bankara** Bohemianism; bohemian; **bankara no** unconventional; uncouth; rough and coarse.

**banken** watchdog.

**bankuruwase** surprise; expected result; **bankuruwase no** unexpected.

**-BANME** suffix denoting: ordinal number; **kado kara sanbanme no ie** the third house from the corner.

**bannen ni** in one's old age.

**bannin** watchman; caretaker.

**banpaa** bumper.

**banpei** sentry, sentinel, guard.

**BANSAN** supper; dinner; **bansankai** dinner party.

**banshaku** evening drink; **banshaku o yaru** to have a drink with supper.

**bansoo** accompaniment; **bansoo suru** to accompany; **bansoosha** accompanist.

**bansookoo** adhesive plaster; bandage strip.

**bantoo** head clerk.

**banzai** cheers; "long live"; **"banzai";** "viva"; **banzai o sanshoo suru** to give three cheers.

**banzuke** list; program, schedule; playbill.

**bara** rose; rosebush.

**barabara** *(n.)* being in pieces, drops; **barabara ni** in bits or pieces; **barabara ni suru** to break up.

**barakku** barracks; shack.

**baramaku** to scatter; **kane o baramaku** to spend money recklessly.

**baransu** balance; **baransu o toru** to keep in balance.

**barasu** to break into pieces; to lay bare (a secret); to dispose of; to kill.

**baree** ballet.

**barikan** hair clippers.

**bariki** horsepower; **bariki o kakeru** to get up steam; to make an effort.

**basha** carriage; coach.

**basho** space, place; seat; location; situation; room.

**bashogara** character (of a place); locality; neighborhood.

**bassui** extract; selection; **bassui suru** to extract; select.

**bassuru** to punish; to bring to justice.

**BASU** bus; **yuuran basu** sight-seeing bus; **basu de** by bus.

**basu** bath; **basu tsuki no heya** room with a bath.

**basu** bass (music).

**basue** outskirts, suburbs.

**basuketto booru** basketball.

**BATAA** butter; **batakusai** exotic, alien (lit: having the smell of butter). **Ano hito wa batakusai.** He acts like a Westerner.

**batabata** with a clatter (onomatopoetic); one after another; noisily; **batabata suru** to flap. **Kaze de to ga batabata suru.** The wind makes the doors rattle (clatter).

**batoo** abuse; denunciation; **batoo suru** to abuse; denounce.

**batsu** clique, faction; clan.

**batsu** punishment, penalty; **bassuru** to punish; **batsu o ukeru** to be punished.

**batsugun no** distinguished; conspicuous.

**batta** grasshopper.

**battaa** batter (in baseball); **battaajun** batting order.

**BATTARI** suddenly; unexpectedly; with a thud. **battari yukiau** to come across, fall in with (a person); **battari butsukaru** to run against, bump into; **battari taoreru** to fall down with a thud; **battari tomaru** to come to an abrupt stop.

**batteki** selection, promotion; **batteki suru** to select, to promote.

**batten** demerit; black mark.

**batto** bat.

**bazaa** bazaar.

**beddo** bed.

**Beekoku** See **Bei.**

**beeru** veil.

**beesubooru** baseball.

**Bei-** prefix denoting: U.S.A. **Beigun** American Army; **Beijin, Beikokujin** *(n.)* American; **beika** American currency; **beikan** American warship; **BEIKOKU = Beekoku** America (U.S.A.).

**bei-** prefix denoting: of rice, pertaining to rice; **beika** the price of rice.

**bekkoo** tortoise shell; **bekkoo no kushi** tortoise-shell comb; **bekkoo buchi** tortoise-shell rims; **bekkoo buchi no megane** tortoise-shell glasses; **bekko iro** amber color; **bekkoo zaiku** tortoise-shell work.

**bekkyo** separation; **bekkyo suru** to be separated.

**ben** valve.

**ben** eloquence; **ben ga tatsu** to speak fluently.

**ben** feces.

**ben** convenience; **-no ben o hakatte** for the convenience of. **Basu no ben ga aru.** Buses are available.

**benchi** bench.

**bengi** convenience; facilities; **bengi o ataeru** to provide facilities; to give aid to; **bengijoo** for the sake of convenience.

**bengo** defense; **bengo suru** to plead; to defend; **bengonin** counsel (for the defense); lawyer; **bengoshi** lawyer; public attorney.

**beni** rouge; lipstick; **kuchibeni o tsukeru** to put on lipstick.

**benimasu** red trout.

**benjo** privy; toilet *(vulgar)*; **benjo ni iku** to go to the toilet; to wash one's hands.

**benkai** explanation; apology; **benkai suru** to explain; to apologize.

**benkeijima** checks, plaid (pattern).

**benki** chamber pot; bedpan.

**BENKYOO** study; diligence; industry; selling at a small profit; **benkyoo suru** to study; to work hard; **benkyoo suru mise** a shop where prices are cheap; **benkyooka** studious person; hard worker.

**benpi** constipation.

**BENRI** convenience; facilities; handiness; **benri na** convenient; handy; useful; **benri ni** conveniently; **benri na tokoro ni sunde iru** to live in a convenient location.

**benshi** orator, speaker.

**benshoo** reparation, compensation.

**BENTOO** box lunch; **bentoo o taberu** to eat a box lunch; **bentoobako** lunchbox; **bentoodai** lunch money; cost of lunch.

**bentsuu** bowel movement.

**benzetsu** eloquence; tongue; **benzetsu sawayaka na** eloquent; fluent; **benzetsu sawayaka ni** eloquently, fluently. **Benzetsu ga takumi da.** He speaks fluently.

**beppuu** separate cover; **beppuu no tegami** a letter under separate cover.

**berabera** continually; volubly; **berabera shaberu** to chatter unceasingly; to talk volubly.

**beraboo** (slang) blockhead; fool; **beraboo ni** awfully; **beraboo ni samui** awfully cold. **Beraboo me!** Confound it, you fool you! *(vulgar).*

**beranda** veranda, porch.

**beru** bell; doorbell; **beru o narasu** to ring a bell.

**beso** wry face; **beso o kaku** to be ready to cry.

**BESUTO** best; **besuto o tsukusu** to do one's best.

**betabeta** all over; thickly; sticky (referring to paint or powder); **betabeta oshiroi o nuru** to powder one's face thickly.

**BETSU** difference; discrimination; **betsu no** different; another; **betsu no hito** another person; **betsu naku** without discrimination; alike; **danjo no betsu naku** regardless of sex.

**betsu atsurae** special order; **betsu atsurae no** made to order; **betsu atsurae no kutsu** custom-made shoes.

**BETSUBETSU NO** separate; **betsubetsu ni** separately; **betsubetsu ni naru** to become separate; to be separated; **betsubetsu ni suru** to keep separate.

**betsudan** special; specially; particularly; in particular.

**betsujitate** specially made or equipped.

**bi** beauty; prettiness; grace; **bijin** beautiful woman; beautiful girl; **bidan** beautiful story; fine anecdote.

**bideo** video.

**BIFUTEKI** beefsteak.

**biganjutsu** facial (beauty treatment); **biganjutsushi** beautician.

**biiru** beer; ale; **nama biiru** draught beer, **chozoo biiru** lager beer.

**bijinesuman** businessman.

**bijutsu** fine arts; **bijutsu gakkoo** art school; **bijutsu tenrankai** art exhibition; **bijutsuhin** object (work) of art; **bijutsuka** artist; **bijutsukan** art museum; **bijutsuteki** artistic; **bijutsuteki ni** artistically.

**bikko** lameness; lame person; **bikko no** lame; crippled; wrongly paired; unsymmetrical; **bikko o hiku** to limp. **Kono tsukue no ashi wa bikko da.** The legs of this table are uneven.

**BIKKURI SURU** to start (with surprise); to be surprised; **bikkuri saseru** to startle; **bikkuri gyoten** astonishment; amazement; **bikkuri gyoten suru** to be frightened out of one's wits. **Aa bikkuri shita!** How you startled me!

**bikoo** incognito; **bikoo suru** to go incognito; to go in disguise.

**bikubiku suru** to tremble with fear, be afraid; to feel nervous.

**biku to mo shinai** to remain unmoved (calm, composed); to be unflinching; to be unperturbed.

**bimyoo na** delicate; nice; fine; **hijoo ni bimyoo na ten** a very delicate point.

**BIN** opportunity, occasion; message; news; mail; **tsugi no bin de** by the next mail; **kookuu bin de** by airmail.

**bin** bottle, jar, decanter; **momo no binzume a** jar of peaches.

**BINBOO NA** poor, destitute; **binboonin** poor person; poor (people).

**biniiru** vinyl.

**binkan na** susceptible; sensitive.

**binkatsu na** quick; alert; prompt; **binkatsu na shochi o toru** to take prompt measures; **binkatsu ni hataraku** to work rapidly.

**BINSEN** letter paper; pad of letter paper.

**binshoo na** quick, sharp, smart, shrewd;

**binshoo ni** quickly, etc.; **koodoo ga binshoo da** is quick in action.

**binsoku na** quick, prompt; **binsoku ni** quickly, promptly; **binsoku ni haitatsu suru** to deliver promptly.

**binzume no** bottled; in a jar; **binzume no sake** bottled sake.

**biri** *(n.)* last; bottom (of the class).

**biriyaado** billiards.

**biroodo** velvet.

**BIRU, BIRUDINGU** building.

**biryoku** slight ability; humble effort; **biryoku o tsukusu** to do one's best.

**bishibishi** rigorously; severely.

**bishobisho** thoroughly drenched, soaked to the skin; drizzling.

**bishonure no** dripping, drenched; **bishonure ni naru** to get wet through.

**bishoo** smile; **bishoo suru** to smile; **bishoo shite** with a smile.

**bishoonen** handsome youth; Adonis.

**bisshori** thoroughly; (wet) to the skin; **bisshori ase o kaku** to be soaked with sweat.

**BISUKETTO** cookies; tea biscuits.

**bitamin** vitamin.

**biten, bitoku** virtue; good quality.

**biwa** loquat (plumlike fruit).

**biwa** Japanese musical instrument with four strings; **biwa o hiku** to play the biwa.

**biyoo** beauty; **biyooin** beauty shop.

**bochi** graveyard, cemetery.

**bodaiju** linden tree.

**bohyoo** gravestone; tomb.

**boikotto** boycott.

**boin** vowel (sound).

**bokashi** gradation; shading, shade (of color); **bokasu** to shade, soften, blend colors.

**boke** Japanese quince.

**bokeru** to be senile; to be in one's dotage; to be weak-minded; to fade; to grow faint. **Kon ga boketa.** The indigo has faded. **Ano hito wa atama ga bokete iru.** He is senile.

**boki** bookkeeping; **bokichoo** account book.

**bokkoo** sudden rise; **bokkoo suru** to rise suddenly (in power); to spring into existence; **koogyoo no bokkoo** the growth of industry.

**bokkooshoo** *(n.)* independent; -towa **bokkooshoo de aru** to have no relation to; to have no connection (between).

**bokkusu** box.

**bokoku** mother country, homeland; **bokokugo** mother tongue.

**bokoo** alma mater.

**BOKU I** (used in men's talk).

**bokuchiku** stock farming; **bokuchikuka** stock farmer; **bokujoo** stock farm; pasture.

**bokumetsu** destruction, extermination; **bokumetsu suru** to destroy; stamp out.

**bokushi** pastor, minister.

**bokushingu** boxing.

**bokutotsu** honesty, artlessness, simplicity; **bokutotsu na** artless; simple; plain-spoken.

**Bon** Feast of Lanterns; Buddhist All Souls' Day in July.

**bon, obon** tray.

**bonchi** basin; valley.

**bonjin** ordinary, mediocre person.

**bonnoo** passion; lust.

**bonsai** dwarf tree; miniature garden set in a pot.

**bonseki** miniature landscape (on a tray).

**bon'yari** stupid person, blockhead; absentmindedly; vacantly; distractedly; **bon'yari kangaekomu** to be lost in reverie; **bon'yari ichinichi o kurasu** to idle away a whole day; **bon'yarimono** dull-witted, absent-minded person; **bon'yari shita** dull-witted, stupid; absent-minded; vacant; dim. **Imi ga bon'yari shite iru.** The meaning is vague. **Kesa wa atama ga bon'yari shite iru.** My head is not clear this morning.

**BOO** staff, club, rod, stick; **boo de utsu** to strike with a stick; **shindai o boo ni furu** to squander one's fortune; **ichinichi o boo ni furu** to waste a whole day.

**boo-** prefix denoting: one; certain (one); **boosho** (a certain) place; **booshi** (a certain) person.

**boobaku taru** vast, boundless, limitless; vague; obscure; **boobaku taru umi** a vast expanse of sea. **Zento wa boobaku taru mono da.** The prospects are very dim.

**boobi** defense; defensive preparations.

**booboo taru** extensive; boundless, vast; **booboo to** shaggily; thickly; **booboo to hige o nobashita otoko** a man with a shaggy beard.

**boochoo** attendance; sitting in conference; **boochooken** admission ticket (for a visitor to the Diet, a conference, etc.); **boochooryoo** admission fee.

**boodoo** disturbance; riot, insurrection.

**BOOEKI** trade; commerce; **booeki suru** to trade, carry on commerce; **booekifuu** trade wind; **booekishoo** merchant trader (importer or exporter); **booeki shookai** trading firm.

**booenkyoo** telescope.

**boofuu** storm; stormy weather; typhoon; **boofuu keihoo** storm warning; **boofuu no** stormy; **boofuu no chuushin** storm center.

**boofuzai** antiseptic; preservative.

**boogai** disturbance; obstruction, hindrance, obstacle; **boogai suru** to disturb, etc.

**boogen** violent language; **boogen o haku** to use violent (abusive) language.

**boogyo** defense; **boogyo no** defensive; **boogyo suru** to defend; **boogyosen** line of defense.

**boohatei** breakwater.

**booka** (*n.*) fireproof; fire prevention; **booka no** (*adj.*) fireproof; fire-resisting; **booka setsubi** fire protection; **bookaheki** fireproof walls.

**bookan** (*n.*) bully; rough; rowdy.

**bookan sha** spectator; onlooker; **bookan suru** to remain a spectator.

**booken** adventure; risk, hazard; **booken suru** to venture, hazard, run a risk; **bookendan** tale of adventure; adventure; **bookenka** adventurer; **bookenteki** risky, hazardous; adventurous.

**bookoo** violence, violent conduct; outrage; **bookoo suru** to use violence; **bookoo o kuwaeru** to assault.

**bookoo** bladder.

**bookun** tyrant, despot.

**bookyo** violence; violent conduct.

**boomei** flight; **boomei suru** to flee, take flight, seek refuge; **boomeisha** refugee; fugitive; exile.

**boonasu** bonus.

**boonenkai** social gathering at the end of the year.

**boorei** ghost.

**boori** excessive profit; **boori o musaboru** to profiteer, make excessive profit; **boori torishimari rei** ordinance to control excessive profits.

**booru** bowl; ball.

**boorubako** pasteboard box, carton.

**boorugami** cardboard, pasteboard.

**booryoku** brute force, violence; **booryokudan** gang of roughs.

**boosatsu sareru** to be hard-pressed with business.

**booseki** spinning; **booseki gaisha** fabric (spinning) company; **booseki koojoo** fabric mill.

**BOOSHI** hat, cap; bonnet; **booshi o kaburu** to put on one's hat; **booshi o kabutte miru** to try on a hat; **booshi o nugu** to take off one's hat; **booshikake** hat rack, hat peg; **booshiya** hatter; milliner; hat store.

**booshi** prevention.

**booshokuzai** antiseptic; anticorrosive.

**boosui** waterproof; protection against floods; **boosuifuku** waterproof cloth.

**booto** mob; insurgents; rioters.

**booto** rowboat; **booto o kogu** to row a boat.

**bootoo** abnormal rise; boom. **Satoo ga bootoo shita.** The price of sugar has gone up enormously.

**booya** (diminutive) my boy; my darling (said of a male infant).

**boozu** (derogatory) monk.

**bora** gray mullet.

**boro** rags, tatters; hidden fault; **boro no** ragged, threadbare; **boro o kita** in rags; **boro o dasu** to betray a weakness; show one's true colors; **boroboro no** tattered, ragged; **boroboro ni naru** to crumble, fall to pieces; **borogimono** old (threadbare) clothes; rags.

**boru** to charge exorbitant prices; to profiteer.

**bosei** motherhood, maternity; **boseiai** maternal love.

**boseki** tombstone.

**boshuu** levy; recruiting; **boshuu suru** to collect; recruit; raise.

**bosshuu** confiscation, forfeiture; **bosshuu suru** to confiscate, forfeit, seize.

**bossuru** to sink; to disappear; to die.

**BOTAN** button, stud; knob; **botan o kakeru** to button; **botan o hazusu** to unbutton; **botan o osu** to push a button.

**botan** tree peony.

**botchan** boy (someone else's son); green youth, young master.

**botsuraku** ruin, downfall, **botsuraku suru** to be ruined.

**bottoo suru** to be absorbed in; to devote oneself to; to be engrossed with; **shigoto ni bottoo suru** to bury oneself in work.

**boya** small fire.

**bu** rate, percentage; part, portion, section, division; **buai** rate, commission, royalty; **buai o dasu** to give (someone) a percentage. **Rishi wa san bu desu.** The interest rate is 3 percent.

**bu** department; **keiribu** accountant's department.

**-bu** copy (a counter for newspapers, pamphlets, etc.).

**buaikyoo** surliness; curtness; bluntness; **buaikyoo na** surly; blunt; unobliging.

**buaisoo** inhospitableness; curtness, unsociability; **buaisoo na** unsociable, curt, inhospitable; **buaisoo na henji** a curt reply; **hito ni buaisoo o suru** to be surly.

**bubun** part, portion, section; **bubunhin** parts (of machines); **bubunteki ni** partially; locally.

**buchi** spots, specks; patches; **buchi no** spotted, speckled; **buchi neko** tabby cat.

**buchoo** chief (head) of a department.

**budoo** grape; grapevine; **budoo no fusa** a bunch of grapes; **budooen** vineyard;

**budooshu** wine; claret; **shiro buddooshu** white wine; **aka budooshu** red wine.

**buenryo** rudeness; boldness; **buenryo na** unreserved; rude; bold; **buenryo ni** without reserve, boldly.

**buji** peace; safety; good health; **buji na** safe, sound; peaceful; **buji ni** safely; peacefully.

**bujoku** insult, affront; disgrace; **bujoku suru** to insult, disgrace; **bujoku o ukeru** to be insulted.

**buka** (*n.*) subordinate; under-officer.

**bukakkoo** clumsiness, awkwardness (in appearance); **bukakkoo na** clumsy, awkward; **bukakkoo ni** clumsily, bunglingly.

**buki** arms, weapons.

**bukiyoo** lack of skill, clumsiness; **bukiyoo na** unskillful.

**bukka** prices; **bukka o toosei suru** to control prices; **bukka choosetsu** price control. **Bukka ga geraku suru.** Prices are falling. **Bukka ga tooki suru.** Prices are rising.

**bukkaku** Buddhist temple.

**bukkiraboo** abruptness; curtness; **bukkiraboo na** curt. **bukkiraboo na kotae o suru** to make a curt reply; **bukkiraboo ni kotowaru** to refuse curtly.

**Bukkyoo** Buddhism; **Bukkyooto** Buddhist.

**bukotsu** bluntness; roughness; rusticity; **bukotsu na** blunt; rustic; clumsy.

**bukubuku** bubbling; baggy; bulging; **bukubuku futoru** to become very fat; **bukubuku awadatsu** to bubble up.

**bumon** class; branch; department; **bumon ni wakeru** to classify.

**bun** portion, share; social position, lot in life; **bun ni yasunzuru** to be contented with one's lot. **Kore wa watakshi no bun desu.** This is my share.

**bun** sentence, writing, composition. **Kono bun o yakushite kudasai.** Please translate this sentence.

**bun-** prefix denoting: writing, literature; civil life; **bundan** literary circles; **bungaku** literature; **bungaku no** literary; **bungei** literature; **bungo** literary expression; written language; classical Japanese; **bungoo** great writer.

**buna** beech tree.

**bun'an** draft, sketch; **bun'an o tsukuru** to make a draft; draw up (a deed, etc.)

**bunan na** safe, secure; **bunan ni** safely; tolerably well.

**bunboogu** stationery; **bunbooguya** stationer, one who sells paper, etc.

**bunchoo** rice (paddy) bird.

**bundori** capture, seizure; spoil, plunder; **bundorihin** trophy, booty, spoils.

**bunjoo** division; distribution; **bunjoo suru** to divide, distribute; **bunjoochi** land for sale in lots.

**bunka** culture, civilization; **bunkateki na** cultural.

**bunkai** analysis; decomposition; **bunkai suru** to analyze; to resolve; to decompose; to break up; to pull to pieces.

**bunkan** civil official.

**bunke** branch of a family.

**bunken** literature; documents, records.

**bunko** handbox; bookcase; library; collection of works.

**bunkoojoo** branch factory.

**bunmei** civilization; **bunmei no** civilized; **bunmeikoku** civilized country.

**bunpai** division, distribution; **bunpai suru** to divide, share; **rieki no bunpai** a division of profits.

**bunpoo** grammar. **Bunpoo o machigaeta.** I made a mistake in grammar.

**bunpu** distribution (geographical).

**bunretsu** split, rupture; **bunretsu suru** to break up; split.

**bunri** separation; isolation; **bunri suru** to separate; to isolate.

**bunrui** classification, assortment.

**bunryoo** quantity.

**bunseki** analysis, assay.

**bunshi** writer.

**bunshi** numerator, molecule.

**bunshoo** composition, writing; **bunshooka** good (clear) writer.

**bunsuirei** watershed.

**buntan** allotment, share; **buntan suru** to share; **buntankin** share of expenses.

**buntsuu** correspondence; **buntsuu suru** to write to.

**buppin** article; goods, commodities.

**burabura** idly, aimlessly; leisurely; **burabura aruku** to walk leisurely, take a stroll; **burabura suru** to loaf, be idle; **burabura shite hi o okuru** to while away one's time.

**burakku risuto** black list.

**buraku** community; village.

**buranko** swing.

**burashi** brush; **burashi o kakeru** to brush up; to brush.

**buratsuku** to wander about, walk aimlessly; **machi o buratsuku** to window-shop.

**burausu** blouse.

**bureeki, bureiki** brake. **Bureiki ga kikanai.** The brake does not work.

**burei** breach of etiquette; incivility, rudeness; **burei na** rude, insolent; **burei na koto o iu** to speak insultingly; **burei na koto o suru** to behave impolitely; to act insultingly.

**buri** yellowtail, yellowfish.

**-buri** suffix denoting: way, manner; after (a time); **gonenburi de** after a lapse of five years; **hanashiburi** way of talking.

**burikaesu** to relapse, have a relapse.

**buriki** tin plate; **burikikan** tin can.

**buroochi** brooch.

**-buru** suffix denoting: to give oneself airs.

**buruburu suru** to shiver, shudder.

**burui** class, order, sort, group; **burui o wakeru** to sort, classify; **burui wake** classification; **burui wake o suru** to catalogue.

**burujoa** *(n.)* bourgeois.

**buryoku** military power, armed force.

**busahoo mono** ill-mannered person, boor.

**busata** long silence; **gobusata suru** to neglect to write (or visit) for a long time.

**bushi** warrior, samurai.

**busho** appointed post; place of duty.

**bushoo** laziness, sloth, indolence; **bushoo na** lazy; **bushoo mono** lazy person; lazy-bones.

**busoo** arms, armaments; **busoo suru** to arm; **busoo kaijo** disarmament.

**bussan** products; produce.

**busshi** goods, commodities, raw materials, resources; **busshi no yutaka na** rich in natural resources.

**busshitsu** matter, substance; **busshitsuteki** material, physical; worldly; **busshitsuteki ni** materially, physically.

**bussoo na** unsafe, dangerous; suspicious; **bussoo na yononaka** restless times (days).

**busui na** unfashionable; in poor taste; inelegant.

**BUTA** pig, swine; pork; **buta no abura** lard; **butagoya** pigsty; **BUTANIKU** pork.

**butai** stage (theater); footlights; scene; sphere; **butai ni tatsu** to go on the stage; **butaigeki** theatrical drama.

**butoo** dance; dancing; **butoo suru** to dance; **butookai** ball, dance (party).

**butsubutsu** rash; **kao ni butsubutsu ga dekiru** to get a rash on the face.

**butsubutsu** murmuring; grumbling; **butsubutsu iu** to grumble; to murmur.

**butsubutsu kookan** barter.

**Butsudan** (household) Buddhist altar.

**Butsudoo** Buddhist teachings.

**butsugi** discussion; public censure.

**butsukaru** to collide with; to clash; to knock (run) against; to fall on; **konnan ni butsukaru** to encounter difficulties. **Saijitsu ga Nichiyoobi ni butsukaru.** The national holiday falls on Sunday.

**butsukeru** to throw at; to knock against. **Atama o hashira ni butsuketa.** I knocked my head against a post.

**butsuri** natural laws, physical laws, physics; **butsuriteki** physical.

**butsurigaku** physics; **butsurigakusha** physicist.

**butsuyoku** worldly desires.

**Butsuzoo** Buddhist image.

**buttooshi ni** throughout; all through; without a break; **tooka kan buttooshi ni** for ten days running.

**buttsuke ni** directly; personally; outright.

**buyo** gnat; sandfly.

**buyoo** ballet; dance; **buyoogeki** dance drama.

**buyoojin** insecurity. **buyoojin na** insecure, unsafe.

**buyuuden** heroic story.

**buzama na** ungainly; uncouth; clumsy.

**BYOO** second (of time); **byoo o kizamu** to tick away the time.

**byoo** tack, rivet; **byoo de tomeru** to tack down.

**byoo** ancestral shrine, mausoleum.

**byoo-** prefix denoting: disease, illness; **byoodoku** virus; disease germs; **byoogen** cause of a disease; **byoogenkin** germs; **byoogo** convalescence; **byoogo no hito** a convalescent; **BYOOIN** hospital; **byooin ni hairu** to be hospitalized; **BYOOKI** illness; **byooki ni kakaru** to fall ill; **byooki no** sick, ill; **atama no byooki** mental illness; **BYOONIN** sick person; **byoosei** condition (of a disease); **byooshin no** weak, sickly, delicate, in poor health; **byooshitsu** sickroom; ward; **byooshoo** sickbed. **Byoosei ga aratamarimashita.** He took a turn for the worse.

**-byoo** suffix denoting: disease, illness; **haibyoo** (lung) tuberculosis; **ganbyoo** eye disease.

**byoobu** folding screen; **byoobu o tateru** to set up a screen.

**byoodoo** equality; **byoodoo no** equal; **byoodoo ni** equally; without discrimination; **byoodoo ni suru** to make equal; **byoodoo no kenri** an equal right.

**byoosha** depiction; description, representation; **byoosha suru** to sketch, describe.


# CH

**CHA, OCHA** tea; **ocha o ireru** to prepare tea; **ocha o irekaeru** to make fresh tea; **ocha o dasu** to serve (offer) a cup of tea; **ocha o tsugu** to pour tea; **cha no yu** tea ceremony; art of tea-making; **chabanashi** tea-talk, gossip, chat (over a bowl of tea); **chabashira** tea stalk floating erect in one's cup (foretelling something good, according to superstition); **chadansu** tea cabinet; **chadoogu** tea-things; tea set; **chagara** used tea leaves; **chagashi** cake, sweets (served with tea); **CHAKA** = **saka** tea and cake; light refreshment; **chamise** tea stall; refreshment house; **chaseki** place where the tea ceremony is held; **chasen** (bamboo) tea whisk; tea stirrer for powdered tea (used in the tea ceremony); **chashaku** tea ladle; tea scoop, **chataku** tea saucer. **CHAWAN** teacup; rice bowl; **CHAYA** teahouse; roadside snack bar. **Chabashira ga tatte imasu.** A tea stalk is floating erect in his cup.

**chabudai** low eating-table.

**CHAIRO** (*n.*) light brown; **chairo no** (*adj.*) light brown; brownish.

**chakasshoku** light-brown color.

**chakasu** to laugh, banter; to make fun of.

**-chaku** suffix denoting: a "counter" for a suit of clothes; **yoofuku itchaku** a suit of Western clothes.

**-chaku** arrival; **rokuji chaku** arriving at six o'clock.

**chakuchaku** (*adv.*) steadily; step by step; **chakuchaku shinkoo suru** to make steady progress.

**chakuganten** point aimed at; viewpoint.

**chakujitsu** sincerity; steadiness and honesty; **chakujitsu ni** honestly; faithfully.

**chakuriku** (*n.*) landing; **chakuriku suru** to land, alight; **chakurikuba, chakurikujoo** landing field; airstrip.

**chakushoku** (*n.*) coloring; **chakushoku suru** to color.

**chakushu** commencement, start; **chakushu suru** to commence, set about, start, begin.

**chame** playfulness, sportiness; playful fellow, urchin; **chame o hakki suru** to be jovial (jolly).

**chanoma** sitting room; living room; tearoom.

**chanpon** mixture; **chanpon ni** alternately.

**CHAN TO** (*adv.*) in good order, neatly; properly; thoroughly; fully, exactly, precisely, correctly; **chan to shita fukusoo** proper dress; **kimono o chan to kiru** to dress properly.

**CHASAJI** teaspoon.

**chazuke** rice steeped in hot tea (eaten as a simple meal or after rich food); **chazuke o kakikomu** to eat a hasty meal.

**CHI** blood; blood relation; **chi ga deru** to bleed; **chi o tomeru** to stop bleeding; **chi no meguri no yoi** quick-witted; sensible; **chi no meguri no warui** dull-witted; not sensible; **chi o waketa** related by blood; **chibashiru** to become bloodshot;

**chibashitta me** bloodshot eyes; **chidarake no** bloody.

**chi** intellect; **chiteki** intellectual.

**chibi** dwarf, pygmy.

**chibusa** breast.

**CHICHI** father; **chichikata no** paternal. **Chichikata no shinseki ga aru.** I have relatives on my father's side.

**chichi** milk.

**chichuu** ground, earth; **chichuu ni** in the ground; underground.

**Chichuukai** Mediterranean Sea.

**chie** wisdom, intelligence; sense; advice, counsel; **chie no aru** wise; **chie no nai** unwise; **chie o kasu** to advise; **chie o shiboru** to rack one's brains; **chie o tsukeru** to suggest.

**chifusu** typhoid fever, typhus.

**chigaeru** to change, alter; to make a mistake; to dislocate, put out of joint; **yakusoku o chigaeru** to break a promise.

**CHIGAI** difference, disparity; distinction; mistake, error; **CHIGAI NAKU** certainly, surely; without doubt; **-ni chigai nai** there is no mistake about it (that); . . . **undei no chigai ga aru** to be as different as heaven and earth. **Chigai ga aru.** There is a difference. **Kimi wa kare ni atta ni chigai nai.** You must have seen him.

**CHIGAU** to be different, differ (from); to be unlike; to disagree, not be in accordance with, to be wrong, be mistaken. **Ano hito wa chotto hito to chigau.** He is a little different from other people.

**chigireru** to be torn off; to come off. **Sode ga chigireta.** A sleeve was torn off.

**chigiru** to tear off, to pluck, to pick.

**chiguhagu no** odd, uneven, unequal.

**chiheisen** horizon; **chiheisen joo ni** above (on) the horizon.

**chihoo** locality; country (rural area); **chihoo no** local; provincial; **chihooshoku** local color.

**chii** rank, social status, position.

**chiiki** tract of land; area.

**chiimu** team.

**CHIISAI** small, trifling; **chiisaku naru** to dwindle; to cringe, shrink.

**CHIIZU** cheese.

**chijimaru** = **chijimu** to shrink. **Keorimono wa nettoo ni irereba chijimimasu.** Woolen fabric shrinks in hot water.

**chijimeru** to shorten, to reduce, to draw in; **kimono o chijimeru** to shorten a dress.

**chijimi** cotton crepe.

**chijimiagaru** to tremble with fear, to cringe.

**chijimu** See **chijimaru.**

**chijin** acquaintance; friend.

**chijirege** frizzled, wavy hair.

**chijireru** to be wavy; to become curly.

**chijoku** disgrace, dishonor, shame.

**CHIJOO** surface of the earth; earth; world; **chijoo no** earthly, terrestrial; on the earth; **chijoo ni** on the ground, on the earth.

**chika** subterranean, underground; **chika ni** under the ground; **chikadoo** underground passage.

**CHIKAGORO** recently, lately; nowadays, in these days, **chikagoro made** till recent times; until lately.

**CHIKAI** near; intimate; verging on; akin to; **chikai miyori** a near relation; **chikai uchi ni** before long; one of these days; **kanzen ni chikai.** It is nearly perfect. It is close to perfection.

**chikai** oath, vow; **chikai o tateru** to make a vow, swear an oath, give a pledge; **chikai o mamoru** to keep an oath; **chikai o yaburu** to break an oath (vow). See also **chikau.**

**CHIKAKU** nearby place; nearly; in the neighborhood of; shortly, in a short time; **shoogo chikaku ni kaeru** to go home close to noon. **Sugu kono chikaku ni sunde imasu.** I live near here.

**chikamichi** shortcut; **chikamichi o suru** to take a shortcut.

**CHIKARA** strength, might, power, force; spirit; vigor; efforts, exertions; ability, talent; authority; **chikara ga yowai** weak; **chikara ga tsuyoi** strong; **chikara no aru** strong, powerful; **chikara no nai** powerless, incapable; **chikara ga tsukiru** to get exhausted; **chikara ni oyobanai** to be beyond one's power; **chikara o otosu** to be discouraged; **chikara o tsukeru** to cheer up, encourage; **chikarazuku** to recover one's strength or health; to be cheered up.

**chikashii** close, intimate; familiar; **chikashii aida de** between friends.

**chikashitsu** basement, cellar.

**CHIKATETSU** subway.

**chikatte** upon my word, upon my honor.

**chikau** to swear, vow, pledge one's word.

**chikayoru** to draw near, approach.

**chikazukeru** to keep company with, to allow to come close to; to allow.

**chikazuki** acquaintance; **chikazuki ni naru** to get acquainted with.

**chikazukigatai** to be inaccessible, be difficult of access.

**chikazukiyasui** to be accessible.

**chikazuku** to draw near, approach; **chikazukanai yooni suru** to keep away from.

**chikei** topography; lay of the land.

**chiki** acquaintance; friend.

**chikki** luggage receipt, baggage check; **chikki suru** to check one's baggage.

**chikkyo** confinement in one's house; **chikkyo suru** to stay indoors.

**chikoku** (*n.*) being late; **chikoku suru** to be late.

**chikubi** teat; nipple.

**chikuchiku** prickle; tingle; sharp pain.

**chikudenchi** storage battery.

**chikushoo** birds and beasts; beast; brute (of a man); **Chikushoo!** Damn it! Hang it! (*vulgar*)*;* **Kon chikushoo me!** You brute! (*vulgar*).

**CHIKYUU** earth; **chikyuugi** globe.

**chimayou** to go mad, be crazed.

**chimei** place name.

**chimidoro ni natte** strenuously; desperately.

**chin** Japanese spaniel.

**-chin** suffix denoting: charge, price; **denshachin** train fare; **yachin** house rent.

**chinamu** to be associated with; to call (or name) after.

**chinba** lameness; odd pair.

**chinbotsu** sinking; floundering; shipwreck.

**chingin** wages; **chingin seikatsusha** wage-earner.

**chinka** sinking, submersion; subsidence; **chinka suru** to sink to the bottom; to be put out; to be brought under control; to be extinguished.

**chinkyaku** rare guest; welcome visitor.

**chinmi** dainty (thing); delicacy.

**chinmoku** silence, reticence; **chinmoku suru** to be silent; to hold one's tongue; **chinmoku saseru** to silence.

**chinomigo** suckling, infant.

**chinpu na** stale; old-fashioned commonplace; hackneyed.

**chinretsu** exhibition, display, arrangement; **chinretsu suru** to exhibit, display, show; **chinretsubako** showcase; **chinretsukan** museum; gallery; exhibition; **chinretsumado** show window; **chinretsushitsu** showroom. **Sore wa chinretsu shite aru.** It is on view.

**chin shigoto** piecework; **chin shigoto o suru** to do piecework.

**CHIPPU** tip; **chippu o harau** to tip (a waiter, etc.).

**chirabaru** to be scattered, be in disorder. **Hon ga chirabatte ita.** Books were scattered about.

**chirachira** flutteringly; flickeringly; gleamingly. **Yuki ga chirachira futte ita.** The snowflakes were falling lightly. **Ki no aida kara hikari ga chirachira shite ita.** The light gleamed through the trees.

**Hikari de me ga chirachira suru.** The light dazzles my eyes.

**chirahora** here and there. **Sakura ga chirahora sakidashita.** The cherry trees have started to bloom here and there.

**chirakasu** to scatter; to disarrange.

**chirari to** at a glance; by accident; **chirari to kikikomu** to hear by accident; **chirari to miru** to catch a glimpse of; glance at (a thing).

**chirashi** handbill, leaflet.

**chirasu** to scatter, disperse; **ki o chirasu** to distract (someone's) attention; to divert. (See also **chirabaru.**)

**chiri** geography; topography.

**chiri** dust; **chiriharai** duster; **chiritori** dustpan. **chiri hodo mo nai.** There isn't a bit.

**chiribameru** to inlay; to set; **shinju o chiribameta yubiwa** a ring set with pearls.

**CHIRIGAMI** toilet paper; facial tissue.

**chirijiri ni** in all directions; separately; **chirijiri ni naru** to disperse in all directions, scatter; **chirijiri ni natte iru** to be scattered about, be dispersed.

**chirimen** crepe; **chirimengami** crepe paper.

**chirin chirin** tingling; jingle-jangle; **chirin chirin naru** to ring.

**CHIRU** to fall; to disperse; to be scattered; to be distracted; **ki ga chiru** to be distracted (mentally). **Kumo ga chitte iru.** The clouds are dispersing.

**chiryoo** medical treatment; cure; **chiryoo suru** to treat; to cure; **chiryoo o ukeru** to receive treatment.

**chisei** geographical features; topography.

**chishiki** knowledge, information, learning; **chishikijin** learned person; intellectual.

**chissoku** suffocation; **chissoku suru** to suffocate.

**chisuji** blood; lineage; descent.

**chitsujo** order; **chitsujo no aru** orderly; **chitsujo no nai** disorderly; **chitsujo ga midarete iru** to be out of order; **chitsujo tadashii** to be in good order; **chitsujo tadashiku** in an orderly manner; systematically.

**CHITTOMO** (used with a negative) not at all; not a bit. **Gohan ga chittomo oishikunai.** I don't have any appetite at all. **Chitto mo kamawanai.** He doesn't care a bit.

**chizu** map; topographical chart; atlas.

**chochiku** savings; **chochiku suru** to save up, store, lay by; **chochiku ginkoo** savings bank; **chochikushin no aru** thrifty; **chochikushin no nai** extravagant, prodigal.

**chokin** savings; **chokin suru** to save money.

**chokkaku** right angle; **chokkaku ni** at right angles.

**chokkei** diameter.

**chokkoo** nonstop trip; direct voyage; **chokkoo suru** to go direct to.

**chokkyuu** straight ball; line drive.

**choko** sake cup.

**chokochoko** at a trot; with short, mincing steps; **chokochoko komata ni aruku** to walk with short steps; to mince along.

**CHOKOREETO** chocolate.

**chokuchoku** now and then. **Chokuchoku hanashi ni kuru.** He comes to see us now and then.

**chokumen suru** to face, confront.

**chokuritsu suru** to stand up.

**chokusen** straight line.

**chokusetsu** directly; **chokusetsu no** direct; immediate; personal; **chokusetsu ni** directly; personally.

**chokutsuu** direct communication; through traffic; **chokutsuu ressha** through train.

**chokuyaku** literal translation.

**chomei na** well-known, famous, noted.

**CHOO-** prefix denoting: town; street; **choonai de** in the town.

**choo** intestines, bowels.

**-choo** suffix denoting: government office; **Kikakuchoo** Planning Board.

**-choo** suffix denoting: chief, director; **shachoo** company president.

**chooba** counter for Japanese-style establishment (hotel, etc.).

**choobatsu** discipline; punishment.

**choobo** account book; register; **choobo o tsukeru** to keep accounts.

**choochin** paper lantern; **-no choochin o motsu** to sing someone's praises; boast; **choochin ni tsurigane** an ill-assorted couple (in a marriage); an ill-matched pair.

**CHOOCHOO** butterfly; **Choochoo san** Madame Butterfly.

**choodai suru** (*humble*) to receive; to drink; to eat. **Koohii no kawari ni ocha o choodai itashimashoo.** I will take tea instead of coffee.

**CHOODO** just; right; exactly; **choodo goji ni** exactly at five o'clock; **choodo yoi toki ni** just at the right time; **choodo mannaka ni** right in the middle.

**chooetsu** superiority, excellence; **chooetsu suru** to surpass; to be superior to.

**choogoo** (*n.*) compounding, mixing, preparation; **choogoo suru** to mix, concoct, prepare; **choogoozai** compound, mixture.

**choohatsu suru** to requisition.

**choohonnin** ringleader; leader.

**choohoogaru** to find a thing useful.

**choohoo na** convenient; handy, useful; **choohoo na hito** handy man. **Kuchi wa choohoo na mono da.** The mouth is a convenient thing (You can say what you please).

**choohookei** rectangle; **choohookei no** rectangular, oblong.

**chooji** words of condolence; funeral address, eulogy.

**choojin** superman; **choojinteki** superhuman.

**choojo** oldest daughter.

**CHOOJOO** top, summit; **choojoo kaigi** summit conference.

**chooka** excess; **chooka suru** to exceed.

**chookan** morning edition (of a newspaper).

**chookeshi** cancellation; writing off; **chookeshi ni suru** to square accounts. **Kore de chookeshi da.** Now we're quits.

**chookoku** engraving; sculpture; **chookokuka** engraver; sculptor.

**chookoo** sign(s); symptom; **jidai no chookoo** a sign of the times.

**chookoo** attendance at a lecture; **chookooryoo** admission fee.

**chookyori** long distance; **chookyori denwa** long-distance telephone; **chookyori hikoo** long-distance flight.

**-CHOOME** suffix denoting: street (employed when an ordinal number is used to name a thoroughfare or section of town). **Itchoome** First Street; **Nichoome** Second Street.

**choomei** long life; longevity; **choomei no** long-lived.

**choomen** notebook.

**choomi** seasoning, flavor; **choomiryoo** seasoning, condiments, spices.

**choomusubi** rosette; bow.

**choonan** oldest son.

**chooryoku** (power of) hearing.

**chooryuu** tidal current, tide; tendency, trend.

**choosa** examination, investigation, inquiry; **choosa suru** to investigate, examine.

**choosei** regulation; adjustment; preparation, drafting, drawing up; **choosei suru** to regulate; to put in order; to prepare, draft, draw up.

**CHOOSEN** Korea; **Choosenjin** Korean people; **Choosengo** Korean language. (See also **Kankoku**.)

**choosen** challenge; defiance; **choosen suru** to challenge; **choosen ni oozuru** to accept a challenge; **choosenteki** challenging, aggressive; defiant.

**choosetsu** regulation, control; adjustment; **choosetsu suru** to regulate, control; **bukka o choosetsu suru** to regulate prices.

**chooshi** tune; pitch; key; rate of stroke; **chooshi ga atte iru** to be in tune; **chooshi ga atte inai** out of tune; **chooshi no yoi** harmonious; melodious.

**chooshinki** stethoscope.

**choosho** strong point; one's forte; merit.

**chooshu suru** to hear; to listen in.

**chooshuu** audience; (people in) attendance. **Chooshuu ga ooi.** There is a large audience.

**chooshuu** collection; levy, assessment; **chooshuu suru** to collect; levy; **zei o chooshuu suru** to collect taxes.

**chooteisha** arbitrator, mediator.

**chooten** highest point, apex, zenith.

**chooto** long distance; long journey. **Chooto no ryokoo ni tsuita.** He started on a long journey.

**chootsugai** hinge.

**choowa** harmony, accord, agreement; **choowa suru** to harmonize; to agree with; **iro no choowa** harmony of colors.

**choozen to** aloof; above the world.

**choozoo** sculpture; statue.

**chorochoro** trickling (of a brook).

**chosaku** literary work; **chosakuken** copyright; **chosakusha, chosha** writer, author.

**chosho** work (literary); production; publication.

**chosuichi** reservoir.

**CHOTTO** just for a moment; a few minutes; a little; a bit; **chotto no ma ni** in a moment; in no time. **Chotto matte kudasai.** Just a moment, please. Wait a bit, please. **Chotto dekinai.** It's no easy thing. **Chotto shita koto de kenka shita.** They quarreled over a trifle. **Chotto shita ie ga aru.** There's a nice-looking house.

**chozoomai** stored rice.

**chuu** comment; annotation; footnote.

**chuubu** central part; center; **Chuubu chihoo** Central Japan.

**chuucho** hesitation; indecision; **chuucho suru** to hesitate; waver; **chuucho shite** hesitatingly.

**chuudan** interruption; break; **chuudan suru** to cut in two, break in the middle.

**chuudoku** *(n.)* poisoning; ptomaine; **chuudoku suru** to be poisoned; **chuudokusei no** poisonous, toxic.

**chuugaeri** somersault.

**chuugakkoo** junior high school.

**chuugata** medium size; **chuugata no** medium-sized; medium.

**chuugen** midyear present.

**CHUUGOKU** China; **Chuugokujin** Chinese people; **Chuugokugo** Chinese language.

**chuui** attention, care; warning, caution; advice; hint; **chuui suru** to pay attention to; to attend to; to warn, etc.; **chuui shite** with care; **hito no chuui o hiku** to attract someone's attention; **chuui o ukeru** to be warned; **chuui o unagasu** to call attention to; **chuuibukai** cautious, careful; attentive; **chuui jinbutsu** marked person; suspicious character; **chuui ryoku** attentiveness; **chuuisubeki** noteworthy, worthy of notice.

**chuujitsu** faithfulness; honesty; **chuujitsu na** faithful; honest; **chuujitsu ni** faithfully; honestly.

**chuujun** middle ten days of a month; **Gogatsu no chuujun ni** about (in) the middle of May.

**CHUUKA** China; **chuuka ryoori** Chinese food; **Chuuka Minkoku** Chinese Republic (Nationalist China); **Chuuka Jinmin Kyoowa koku** People's Republic of China (Communist China).

**chuukan** the middle; midway; **chuukan no** middle, intermediate; **-no chuukan ni** halfway between.

**chuuken** main body; backbone; center field (in baseball).

**chuukoku** advice, counsel; warning; **chuukoku suru** to advise; to warn; **chuukoku o ireru** to follow advice; **chuukoku ni somuku** to act against advice.

**chuumoku** notice, observation; attention; **chuumoku suru** to pay attention to; to watch, keep an eye on.

**CHUUMON** order; command(s); request; **chuumon suru** to order; **chuumon o toru** to take an order.

**chuumon tori** traveling salesman; canvasser.

**chuunen** middle age; **chuunen no** middle-aged.

**chuuniku chuuzei** medium build.

**chuunyuu** injection, pouring into; cramming; **chuunyuu suru** to pour into.

**chuuoo** center, middle; **chuuoo shijoo** central market.

**chuuritsu** neutrality; **chuuritsu chitai** neutral zone.

**chuuryuu** midstream; middle class; **chuuryuu kaikyuu** middle class.

**chuusai** mediation, arbitration; **chuusai nin** mediator, peacemaker; **chuusai suru** to mediate, arbitrate.

**chuusan** moderate means (wealth); **chuusan kaikyuu** middle class.

**chuusei** neuter gender.

**chuusei** Middle Ages; **chuusei no** medieval.

**chuusen** lottery, drawing; **chuusen suru** to draw lots; **chuusen de sadameru** to decide by lots; **chuusenken** lottery ticket.

**chuushi** suspension, stoppage; steady gaze; close observation; **chuushi suru** to stop, suspend, discontinue; to gaze steadily at; to watch closely; **jigyoo no chuushi** work stoppage; **shiai o chuushi suru** to call off a game.

**chuushin** center, core, heart; balance; **chuushin o toru** to balance; **machi no chuushin ni** in the center of the city; **chuushin jinbutsu** central figure; leader.

**chuushoo** defamation, slander.

**CHUUTO** midway, halfway; in the middle; unfinished; **chuuto de yameru** to stop in the middle of; to drop out of; **chuuto hanpa** (*n.*) halfway; **chuuto hanpa no** (*adj.*) unfinished; **chuuto hanpa ni** (*adv.*) halfway; **chuuto hanpa na koto o suru** to do things by halves.

**chuutongun** army of occupation.

**chuutoo** medium quality; **chuutoo no** middle grade; medium; **chuutoo no shinamono** goods of medium quality.

**chuuya** day and night; **chuuya yasumazu hataraku** to work day and night without rest.

**chuuyoo** moderation; **chuuyoo o mamoru** to take the middle course; **chuuyoo o eta** moderate; **chuuyoo o enai** immoderate; one-sided.

**chuuzai** residence; **chuuzai no** (*adj.*) resident; **chuuzai suru** to reside.

**chuuzaisho** police station.

**chuuzetsu** interruption; suspension; **chuuzetsu suru** to be interrupted; to be suspended; discontinued. **Shigoto wa chuuzetsu shita.** The work has been held up. **Chuuzetsu shite iru.** It is in abeyance.

**DA** plain present of **desu**, it is. **Kore wa nan da?** What is this? **Fude da.** It is a writing brush. **Are wa dare da?** Who is he? **Boku wa iku no wa iya da.** I don't want to go.

**DAASU** dozen; **ichi daasu** one dozen; **daasu de uru** to sell by the dozen.

**dabi** cremation.

**dabokushoo** bruise.

**dabora** (*colloq.*) big talk; **dabora o fuku** to boast.

**dabudabu** loose; baggy; **dabudabu no zubon** baggy trousers.

**dachin** reward; tip; small consideration; **dachin ni** in payment for. **Kore wa otsukai no dachin da.** This is your reward for doing the errand.

**dadakko** spoiled child; cross, fretful child.

**daden** (*n.*) telegraphing; **daden suru** to telegraph, to wire.

**daeki** saliva, spittle.

**DAGA** but; for all that; all the same; at the same time; on the other hand.

**dagashi** coarse (cheap) confectionery (candy).

**dageki** blow; hit; shock; hitting, batting (in baseball); **dageki o kuwaeru** to deal a blow; **dageki o ukeru** to receive a blow.

**daha** *(n.)* overthrow; **daha suru** to break down; to overthrow; to frustrate.

**DAI** time, period, age, generation; reign, dynasty; (one's) lifetime; pedestal, block; stand; rest; table; bench.

**DAI** title, heading, theme, subject, topic; question, problem; **dai o tsukeru** entitle.

**dai** pedestal, block, stand, rest, table.

**dai-** prefix which makes an ordinal from a cardinal number; **daiichi** the first; **daini** the second.

**dai-** prefix denoting: big, large, great; grand, high; colossal; **daitokai** a big city; **daibubun** greater part, for the most part.

**-dai** money given in exchange; cost, price; **gasudai** gas bill.

**-dai** counter for vehicles (machines); **kuruma ichidai** one car.

**DAIBU, DAIBUN** greatly, considerably, remarkably, rather, much, many. **Daibu atsui.** It is pretty hot. **Kesa wa daibu yoi.** I am much better this morning. **Daibu son o shita.** He suffered a big loss. **Daibu kane ga kakaru.** It takes a lot of money.

**daichi** earth; ground.

**daichoo** large intestines; colon.

**daidai** bitter orange.

**daidai** successive generations; from generation to generation; **daidai no** successive; hereditary.

**daidaiteki** big, grand; splendid; wholesale; **daidaiteki ni** on a large (grand) scale; splendidly; **daidaiteki ni kookoku suru** to advertise extensively.

**DAIDOKORO** kitchen; **daidokoro doogu** kitchen utensils.

**daidoo enzetsu** soap-box oration; street speaker.

**daidoo shooi** general similarity; **daidoo shooi de aru** to be nearly the same. **Yoo suru ni daidoo shooi de aru.** In short, there is no choice between them.

**DAIGAKU** university, college; **daigakusei** college student.

**daigakuin** graduate school.

**daigishi** member of the House of Representatives.

**daihon** text of a play; libretto.

**daihyoo** representation; type; **daihyoo suru** to represent; **daihyoosha** *(n.)* representative,

deputy; delegate; **daihyooteki** *(adj.)* representative, typical.

**DAIICHI NI** in the first place, first of all, firstly; **daiichi no** first, foremost, primary.

**DAIJI** great enterprise; great thing; serious affair; emergency; **daiji na** important; serious; precious; **daiji na yooji** an important matter; **daiji ni suru** to take care of; **daiji o toru** to be cautious; **Kimi wa daiji o torisugiru.** You are overcautious. **Odaiji ni.** Take care of yourself.

**DAIJOOBU** safe, secure, certain; strong; certainly, undoubtedly, without fail; I am sure; I assure you. **Sono hako wa daijoobu desu ka?** Is that box safe? **Moo daijoobu desu.** I am quite out of danger now. **Daijoobu naorimasu.** You will surely get well.

**daika, daikin** price, charge; purchase money; **daikin hikikae** cash on delivery; C.O.D.; **daikin hikikae yuubin** C.O.D. **Daika wa ikura desu ka?** What is the price?

**daikin** See daika.

**daikirai** hateful, loathsome; abominable, detestable; **daikirai da** to hate, loathe, have an antipathy to, have a strong aversion to. **Watakushi wa hebi ga daikirai desu.** I loathe snakes.

**daikon** white radish; **daikon oroshi** radish grater; grated radish.

**daiku** carpenter; carpentry.

**daimeishi** pronoun.

**daimoku** title (of a book); heading.

**dainamaito** dynamite.

**dainashi** spoiled, ruined; dirty; **dainashi ni suru** to spoil, ruin; to soil; **dainashi ni naru** to become spoiled, ruined. **Kimono ga dainashi ni natta.** The garment is ruined. **Booshi o dainashi ni shita.** You've ruined your hat.

**dairi** deputation; agency; **dairi o suru** to act for, take the place of; **dairi no** acting; deputy; **dairinin** proxy; representative, agent; **dairiten** agency.

**dairiseki** marble.

**DAIROKU** sixth; **dairokujuu** sixtieth; **dairokkan** sixth sense.

**DAISAN** third; **DAISANJUU** thirtieth; **DAISANSHA** third person; bystander; **daisansha no tachiba kara kangaeru** to put yourself in a third person's position.

**daisharin** big wheel, giant swing.

**DAISHI** fourth.

**daishi** pasteboard, board-mounting; **shashin o daishi ni haru** to mount a photograph.

**DAISHICHI** seventh. **DAISHICHIJUU** the seventieth.

**daishin** doctor's assistant.

**daishonin** scribe, notary.

**daishoo** compensation, recompense; **-no daishoo to shite** in compensation for; in recompense for.

**daisoreta** audacious, bold, insolent; atrocious; **daisoreta mane o suru** to behave atrociously.

**daisuki** *(adj.)* favorite, pet; **daisuki de aru** to have a great liking (for), be extremely fond of; **watakushi no daisuki na hon** my favorite book.

**daisuu, daisuugaku** algebra.

**DAITAI** main points, gist; outline, mainly; on the whole; **daitai ni oite** on the whole, in general; taking all things together; **daitai no mitsumori** rough estimate; **jiken no daitai o hanasu** to give an outline of the case.

**daitan** bravery; boldness, audacity; **daitan na** brave, fearless; bold, daring; **daitan ni** fearlessly; boldly, audaciously.

**daitooryoo** president (of a republic).

**daiyamondo** diamond.

**daiyaru** dial.

**daiyoo** substitution; **daiyoo suru** to substitute for, use in place of; to serve as, serve the purpose of; **-no daiyoo ni naru** to be used as a substitute; to serve the purpose of; **daiyoobutsu** substitute.

**daizai** subject matter, theme.

**daizainin** great (criminal) offender.

**DAIZU** soya bean.

**dajare** poor joke; cheap jest; **dajare o iu** to crack a joke.

**DAKARA** accordingly, therefore, so; and so. **Dakara sonna koto o shite wa ikenai.** That's why you must not do such a thing.

**DAKE** only; alone; by; as much (many) as; as . . . as; worth; **ni inchi dake nagai** to be two inches too long; **dekiru dake hayaku** as fast (soon) as one can. **Onegai wa sore dake.** That's all I ask. **Boku hitori dake de atta.** I was all by myself.

**DAKEDO, DAKEDOMO, DAKEREDOMO** See **DAGA.**

**dakiageru** to lift up in one's arms.

**dakiau** to embrace (each other).

**dakikomu** to bring over to one's side, win over; to buy off; to entice.

**dakishimeru** to embrace closely, hug.

**dakitomeru** to stop by throwing one's arms round another; to hold (a person) back.

**dakitsuku** to fly into (someone's) arms; to cling, to embrace affectionately.

**dakiyoseru** to draw (someone) close to one's breast.

**daku** to embrace, to hug; to hatch (eggs).

**dakudaku** in stream; **dakudaku deru** to gush out, spout forth.

**dakuon** voiced consonant (such as **b, d, g,** or **z**).

**dakuryuu, dakusui** muddy stream or river; turbid water.

**dakyoo** compromise; agreement; **dakyoo suru** to compromise; to come to an agreement.

**DAMARU** to be silent. **Damatte kudasai.** Please stop talking.

**damasu** to deceive, cheat, defraud; to impose upon; to bewitch; to soothe, humor (a crying child).

**damatte** silently, in silence; without telling; without leave; **damatte kiite iru** to be listening in silence; **damatte hito no mono o tsukau** to use someone else's things without permission.

**DAME NA** fruitless; hopeless; futile; **dame de aru** to be useless; to be hopeless; to be futile; to be all over (with someone); **dame ni naru** to fail; **dame ni suru** to render useless; spoil.

**damu** dam.

**dan** platform, rostrum, dais; steps, stairs; flight of stairs; grade, class; act; scene; **saidan** altar.

**dan** talk, conversation; **ryokoodan** account of one's travels.

**-dan** suffix denoting: group, body, party, team; **ichidan o nashite** in a group; **jitsugyoodan** party of businessmen.

**dan'an** decision; conclusion; **dan'an o kudasu** to make a decision.

**dan'atsu** suppression; oppression.

**danboo** heating; **danboo soochi** heating apparatus.

**danchi** housing-development apartment.

**danchigai de aru** to be no match for; to outclass.

**danchoo** leader of a party.

**DANDAN** gradually, little by little; by and by. **Dandan kuraku natte kimashita.** By and by it became dark.

**dandori** plan, program, design.

**dangai** precipice, cliff.

**dangan** bullet, shot; shell.

**dangen** assertion; affirmation; **dangen suru** to assert, to declare.

**dango** dumpling.

**dangoku** warm country; warm climate.

**dangoo** consultation, conference; **dangoo suru** to consult, confer with.

**DANJITE** absolutely; decidedly; on my word; never; by no means. **Danjite ikenai!** Positively no!

**danjo** man and woman; both sexes; **danjo kyoogaku** coeducation.

**dankai** steps, grade, gradation.

**dankoo** resolute action; **dankoo suru** to take decisive steps, act resolutely.

**danko taru** decisive, resolute, determined, positive; **danko to shite** decisively, positively.

**danmari** dumb show; silence; reticence; man of few words.

**danna** *(colloq.)* master; husband; sir; gentleman; **dannasama** master (of the house).

**dannen suru** to abandon (an idea, hope, desire).

**danpan** negotiation; parley. **Danpan ga haretsu suru.** There is a breakdown in the negotiations.

**danpatsu** bobbed hair.

**danpen** fragment, piece; odds and ends; **danpenteki** fragmentary.

**danran** circle; harmony; **danran suru** to sit (around) together.

**danro** heating stove; fireplace.

**danryoku** elasticity; **danryoku aru** elastic, springy.

**dansaa** dancer; taxi dancer.

**DANSEI** male; man; masculinity; **danseiteki** masculine, manly.

**dansen** disconnection (of a wire). **Dansen suru.** A wire breaks.

**DANSHI** boy; man; **danshirashii** manly; **danshirashikunai** unmanly. **Danshi.** Men's Room.

**dansu** dance, dancing (occidental style).

**dantai** party, body; group.

**dantei** decision; conclusion; **dantei suru** to decide; to conclude.

**danwa** conversation, talk; **danwa suru** to talk, chat; **danwatai** colloquial, conversational style.

**danzetsu** disconnection, rupture; **danzetsu suru** to be cut off; to become extinct, be disconnected.

**danzoku** intermission; **danzokuteki no** intermittent; **danzokuteki ni** intermittently, on and off.

**daradara** in drops; lazily; sluggishly; leisurely; sloppily; **daradara suru** to work sloppily; **ase ga daradara nagareru** to sweat profusely; **daradara zaka** a gentle slope.

**-darake** suffix denoting: full of; covered with; **asedarake no** covered with sweat.

**darakeru** to feel dull, languid.

**daraku** depravity, corruption.

**darari to** loosely; languidly.

**darashi nai** loose; careless; untidy; **darashi nai fuu o suru** to dress sloppily.

**DARE** who; **dare no** whose; **dare de mo** anyone, anybody; whoever; **dare de mo mina** everyone, everybody; **dare ka** someone, somebody; anyone, anybody. **Dare ga shimashita ka?** Who did it? **Kore wa dare no desu ka?** Whose is this? **Dare ni agemashoo ka?** Who should I give it to? **Dare ka anata o yonde iru.** Someone is calling you.

**dareru** to grow listless; to get bored; to relax; to be dull. **Hanashi ga dareta.** The conversation lagged.

**-DAROO** I speculate, I guess. **Ashita ame ga furudaroo.** I guess it will rain tomorrow.

**DARUI** to be dull; to feel languid; to feel heavy; **Ashi ga darui desu.** My legs feel heavy.

**daruma** Dharma; toy image of Dharma.

**daryoku** See dasei.

**dasan** calculation; **dasan suru** to calculate, count; **dasanteki** calculating, mercenary.

**dasei, daryoku** inertia; **ima made no dasei** by force of habit.

**dashimono** program; repertoire.

**dashin suru** to tap, sound.

**DASHINUKE** suddenness, abruptness; **dashinuke ni** suddenly; abruptly; unexpectedly; without warning; **dashinuke o kurau** to be taken by surprise.

**dashinuku** to forestall; to get ahead of.

**dashishiburu** to begrudge.

**dassen** derailment, digression; **dassen suru** to digress; to deviate.

**dasshimen** absorbent cotton.

**dassoo** desertion; flight; escape; **dassoo suru** to desert, run away; **dassoosha** fugitive, runaway.

**dassuru** to get out; to escape from; to omit, leave out; to get rid of; **akushuu o dassuru** to get rid of a bad habit.

**DASU** to put forth; to take out; to produce; to turn on; to turn away; to lay bare; to serve (a meal, tea, etc.); **tegami o dasu** to mail a letter; **shigoto ni te o dasu** to throw oneself into the job.

**datai** abortion.

**datchoo** hernia, rupture.

**DATTA -ta** form (past) of **da.**

**datte** *(colloq.)* but, still; because; for. **Naze gakkoo e ikanai no desu ka? Datte atama ga itai n desu mono.** Why don't you go to school? Because I have a headache.

**DE** in; at; start; in the matter of; **mikka de** in three days; **jikan de** by the hour; **Tookyoo de wa ichiban ii mise desu.** In Tokyo, it's the best store. **Amerika de kaimashita.** I bought it in America. **Mizu de arau.** I wash it in water.

**de** flow; going out; rise; birth; origin; outset, start; turnout. **Kyoo wa hito no de ga ii.** There's a large turnout today.

**de aru** See **desu.**

**dearuku** to go out; to gad about.

**DEAU** to meet, come across; to happen to meet.

**debaboocho** big kitchen knife.

**debudebu no** fat, plump.

**debushoo** one who prefers to stay at home.

**dedokoro** source; origin.

**degarashi** tea leaves; coffee grounds.

**DEGUCHI** exit.

**deiri** entrance and exit; **deiri suru** to go in and out; to frequent, visit regularly; **deiriguchi** entrance, doorway.

**deisui** intoxication; **deisui suru** to be dead drunk; **deisuisha** drunkard.

**DEKAKERU** to go out; to start, set out; **degake ni** on the point of going, on one's way; **ryokoo ni dekakeru** to start on a trip. **Degake ni denwa ga kakatta.** Just as I was on the point of going out, I received a phone call.

**dekasegi** emigration; working in another country; **dekasegi suru** to work away from home; **dekaseginin** worker away from home.

**dekata** attitude, move.

**deki** workmanship; make; tailoring; cut; result, effect; crop, yield; **deki no yoi** of fine workmanship; **deki no warui** of poor workmanship; **deki fudeki** success and failure. **Deki fudeki ga arimasu.** It is not always successful.

**dekiagaru** to be finished, be completed, be ready.

**dekiai no** ready made.

**dekibae** effect, result; manner of execution. **Rippa na dekibae deshita.** It was a fine performance.

**dekigokoro** sudden impulse; passing fancy; **dekigokoro de** on the spur of the moment.

**dekigoto** event, incident; **hibi no dekigoto** daily occurrence; everyday event; **saikin no dekigoto** recent event.

**dekimono** boil; sore; tumor; ulcer.

**DEKINAI** cannot do; poor. **Nihongo ga yoku dekinai.** I can't speak Japanese well.

**DEKIRU** can, may; to be able; to be possible, to be capable of; be done; be completed; **dekiru koto nara** if possible [it is a thing that I can do]. **Shokuji ga dekita.** Dinner is ready.

**DEKIRU DAKE** to the best of one's ability; as . . . as possible; **dekiru dake hayaku** as soon as possible; as early as possible; **dekiru dake no koto o suru** to do what one can, to do everything one can.

**dekishi** drowning; **dekishi suru** to drown; **dekishisha** a drowned person.

**dekisokonai** failure; **dekisokonai no** defective; bungled; half-baked; clumsy; deformed.

**dekisokonau** to fail; to be a failure; to be badly done, be botched, be bungled. **Shigoto wa dekisokonatta.** The job was bungled.

**dekitate** brand-new; just made; fresh.

**dekki** deck.

**dekoboko** unevenness; **dekoboko no** uneven, bumpy; rough; jagged.

**demado** bay window.

**demae** catering. **Demae o suru.** They do catering.

**deme** protruding eyes; **deme no** goggle-eyed.

**demise** branch (store); **demise o dasu** to open a branch.

**DEMO** even, though; even if; as well, also; but, still. **Watakushi demo dekimasu.** Even I can do it. **Donna pen demo ii desu.** Any pen will do.

**demodori** divorced woman.

**demukae** meeting; reception; **demukae o ukeru** to be met (by someone).

**DEMUKAERU** to go to meet (on arrival).

**denaosu** to come again; to go again; to call again.

**den'atsu** voltage.

**denbun** telegram, telegraphic message.

**denchi** electric cell; battery.

**denchuu** telegraph or telephone pole; electric-light pole.

**dendoo** missionary work; **dendooshi** evangelist, missionary.

**den'en** country, farms; rural districts; **den'en no** rural, countrified.

**denka** electrification; **denka suru** to put in electricity; to operate by electricity.

**DENKI** electricity; **denki no** electric(al); **denkidokei** electric clock; **denkijikake no** operated by electricity.

**denki** biography.

**DENKYUU** electric bulb.

**denpoo** telegram; cable; **denpoo de** by wire, by cable; **denpoo o utsu** to send a telegram (wire, cable); **denpooryoo** telegraph fee. (See also **denshin.**)

**denryuu** electric current.

**densen** infection, contagion; **densen suru** to be infectious; to be infected with; **densenbyoo** infectious, contagious disease; epidemic.

**densetsu** tradition; legend; **densetsuteki** traditional, legendary.

**DENSHA** streetcar, train; **densha de iku** to go by streetcar; **densha ni noru** to take a streetcar; **denshachin** streetcar fare; **denshadoori** street with a trolley line.

**denshi renji** microwave oven.

**denshin** telegram; **denshin bashira** telegraph pole; **denshinkyoku** telegraph office. (See also **denpoo**.)

**denshin gawase** wire transfer.

**DENTOO** electric light; **dentoo o tsukeru** to turn on the lights; **dentoo o kesu** to turn off the lights.

**dentoo** tradition; convention; **dentooteki** conventional; traditional.

**DENWA** telephone; **denwa choo** telephone directory; **denwa de** by telephone; **denwa shitsu** telephone booth; **kooshuu denwa** public telephone; **denwa o kakeru** to call, make a phone call; **denwa o kiru** to hang up; **denwa o hiku** to have a phone installed.

**DEPAATO** department store.

**DERU** to come out; to appear; to rise; to be up; to go out; to attend; to flow out; to break out; **soto e deru** to go out (outside); **uchi o deru** to leave the house; **shiki ni deru** to attend a ceremony. **Mizu ga deru.** There is a flood.

**desakari** height of the season.

**desaki** place to which someone has gone. **Desaki ga wakaranai.** I don't know where he has gone.

**deshabaru** to meddle, interfere.

**deshi** pupil, disciple, apprentice.

**deshita** See **desu.**

**deshoo** See **desu.**

**desorou** to come out fully; to be all out.

**DESU, de aru, da** be; it is; equals. **Watakushi wa gakusei desu.** I am a student. **Amerikasei deshita.** It was an American make (product). **Eikokujin deshoo.** Probably he is British.

**desugiru** to protrude (stick out) too much; to be too far out; to be too strong.

**DESUKARA, DAKARA** that is why; therefore. **Desukara minna ni sukaremasu.** That is why she is liked by everyone.

**detarame** irresponsible remark; nonsense; **detarame o iu** to speak nonsense.

**DEWA** then, in that case, if so. **Dewa sayoonara.** Good-bye now. **Dewa mata.** I'll be seeing you. **Dewa soo shite kudasai.** If that is the case, please do so.

**DEZAATO** dessert.

**dezain** design.

**do** degree, measure, extent; times; **ichi ni do** once or twice; **do o sugosu** to go to extremes.

**DOA** door (Western style).

**dobin** earthen teapot.

**doboku** public works; engineering; **doboku gishi** civil engineer.

**dobu** ditch.

**dobunezumi** water rat.

**doburoku** raw (unrefined) sake.

**DOCHIRA** which way; which (of the two); where; what place; **dochira e?** where? **dochira demo** whichever; either; both.

**dodai** foundation, basis.

**dogimagi** in confusion; **dogimagi suru** to act confused, act flustered.

**dohyoo** sandbag; Japanese wrestling ring, arena. **dohyoo giwa de** at the last possible moment; at the eleventh hour.

**DOITSU** Germany; **Doitsu no** (*adj.*) German; **Doitsujin** (*n.*) German; **Doitsugo** German language.

**dojoo** earth, soil.

**dokadoka** in rapid succession; in crowds; **dokadoka haitte kuru** to come in crowds, to rush in.

**dokan to** See **dokkari.**

**dokata** laborer; coolie.

**dokeru** to remove; to get out of the way.

**doki** earthenware.

**doki** anger, resentment; **doki o obite** in anger.

**dokidoki suru** to throb violently. **Mune ga dokidoki shimasu.** My heart is beating rapidly.

**dokitto suru** to be startled, get a shock.

**dokkari to** = **dokan to** heavily; with a thud.

**dokku** dock; **dokku ni hairu** to dock (as a ship).

**DOKO** where, what place; **doko e itte mo** wherever you go; **doko ka** somewhere; **doko kara** from where; **doko made** how far; **doko mo** everywhere.

**dokoro ka** far from; to say nothing of; anything but. **Hikooki dokoro ka kuruma mo motte imasen.** He doesn't even own a car, let alone an airplane.

**doku** poison; harm; **doku no aru** poisonous; **doku ni naru** to be bad for; **doku suru** to harm; to poison. **Oki no doku sama.** I'm sorry for you.

**doku** to get out of the way; to move aside. **Doite kure.** Clear the way! Get out of my way! (rough).

**dokudan** arbitrary decision; **dokudanteki** dogmatic, arbitrary.

**dokudokushii** malicious, spiteful; poisonous-looking; **dokudokushii koto o iu** to say malicious things.

**dokuen** solo performance, recital.

**dokugaku** studying by oneself, without a teacher.

**dokuja** poisonous snake.

**dokuji no** original; personal; individual; **dokujisei** originality; **dokuji no kangae** personal opinion.

**dokukeshi** antidote.

**DOKURITSU** independence; self-support; **dokuritsu suru** to be independent, stand on one's own feet; **dokuritsu no** independent; **dokuritsu de** independently; **dokuritsukoku** independent state; **dokuritsushin** independent spirit. **Dokuritsu Kinenbi** Independence Day (Fourth of July).

**dokuryoku de** on one's own, by oneself, singlehanded; **dokuryoku de yaru** to do something on one's own.

**dokusai** dictatorship; **dokusai seiji** dictatorship; **dekusaisha** dictator.

**dokusatsu suru** to poison.

**dokusen** monopoly; **dokusen jigyoo** monopolistic enterprise, monopoly; **dokusenteki** monopolistic, exclusive.

**dokusha** reader; subscriber; reading public; **dokushoka** book-lover; great reader.

**dokusho** reading.

**dokusho suru** to read (books).

**dokushoo** vocal solo.

**dokushuu, dokugaku** studying without a teacher; **dokushuusho** book for self-teaching; "do-it-yourself" book.

**dokusoo** originality; **dokusooteki na** original; creative; **dokusoo no sai** creative ability; talent.

**dokuyaku** poison.

**dokyoo** spirit; courage; **dokyoo no aru** daring, courageous; **dokyoo no nai** timid, cowardly.

**doma** earthen floor.

**donabe** earthen pot.

**donaru** to shout, thunder at.

**DONATA** who *(respect)*, **donata de mo** anybody. **Donata desu ka?** Who are you? **Donata ka ome ni kakaritai soo desu.** Someone wishes to see you.

**donburi** deep bowl, **donburi meshi** boiled rice served in a deep bowl; **oyako donburi** chicken, eggs, and rice in a deep bowl.

**dondon** rub-a-rub, rat-a-rat; **dondon susumu** to advance rapidly; **dondon mookeru** to make money rapidly.

**DONNA** what; what sort of, kind of; **donna ni** how much; however. **Donna hon desu ka?** What kind of a book is it?

**DONO** which; what; **dono kurai** to what degree?; how long?; how far?; **dono hito** which person?

**donzoko** rock bottom; **donzoko seikatsu** poverty-stricken life.

**DOO** how; what; **doo atte mo** in any case. **Doo itashimashite.** Don't mention it! Not at all! **Sore wa doo ni mo narimasen.** It can't be helped.

**doo** copper.

**doo** torso.

**doo** temple, shrine, hall; **doo ni iru** to attain proficiency, to become an expert.

**doo** (can also be prefix) the same; the said (aforementioned); corresponding; equal; **doo banchi** the same street number; **doodan** same, ditto; **dooyoo** the same, ditto; **doo mikka** the third day of the same month.

**DOOBUTSU** animal; living creature; **doobutsuen** zoo; **doobutsugaku** zoology.

**DOO DE MO** in any way; **doo de mo koo de mo** by any means, at any cost; **doo de mo ii koto** a trivial matter. **Doo de mo ii desu.** It doesn't matter one way or the other.

**doodoo suru** to go with, accompany.

**doofuu** enclosure(s); **doofuu no tegami** the enclosed letter.

**doogi** morality, morals, principles, ethics.

**doogi** motion made during a meeting.

**DOOGU** tools, implements, utensils; sets; property; household goods; **doogubako** toolbox; **dooguya** secondhand dealer; curio shop; furniture shop.

**doohai** equal colleague.

**doohan suru** to accompany.

**dooi** consent, approval, agreement; **dooi suru** to consent to, approve.

**DOO ITASHIMASHITE!** Don't mention it. Not at all. The pleasure is mine.

**dooitsu** equality; **dooitsu no** same; identical, equal.

**dooji** same time; **dooji no** simultaneous, concurrent; **dooji ni** at the same time; **doojidai** same age; **doojidai no** contemporary; **doojitsu** same (very) day.

**doojoo** exercise hall (for Judo, fencing, etc.); arena; Buddhist seminary.

**doojoo** sympathy, compassion; **doojoo aru** sympathetic, warmhearted; **doojoo no nai** unsympathetic.

**DOOKA, DOOZO** please; somehow or other; **DOOKA KOOKA** somehow or other; some way or other; barely; with difficulty; **dooka shite** somehow, in one way or another.

**dooka** assimilation.

**dooka** copper coin.

**dookaku** same rank, status, etc.

**dookan** same sentiment, same feeling; same opinion; **dookan de aru** to be of the same opinion; to feel the same way.

**dooke** *(n.)* clowning; **dooke shibai** farce; **dooke yakusha** clown; **dooketa** comic, foolish; **dookeru** to clown.

**dookei** aspiration, longing; worship.

**dooki** motive, incentive.

**dooki** palpitation; **dooki ga suru** to throb, to palpitate.

**dooki** same period; same class; **dooki no** of the same year; **dookisei, dookyuusei** classmate.

**dookokujin** fellow countryman.

**dookoo** pupil of the eye.

**dookoo suru** to go together; **dookoosha** traveling companion.

**doomei** alliance; league; **doomei koku** ally.

**DOOMO** very; much; rather; quite. **Doomo arigatoo gozaimasu.** I'm much obliged.

**doonen** same year; same age; **doonen de aru** to be the same age.

**DOO NI KA** somehow or other; **doo ni ka suru** to manage somehow, try one's best.

**DOORO** road.

**dooryoku** motor power; power.

**DOOSE** anyway; after all, at best; of course; at all. **Doose yaranakereba naranai desu.** I must do it anyway.

**dooseiai** homosexuality.

**DOO SHITE** why; how; **DOO SHITE MO** in any case; by any means; whatever may happen. **Doo shite sore o gozonji desu ka?** How do you know that? **Doo shite mo ikanakereba narimasen.** Whatever may happen (in any case, no matter what happens), I have to go.

**dootoo** equality; parity; **dootoo no** equal, equivalent; **dootoo ni** equally; **dootoo ni suru** to make equal, equalize.

**DOOZO** please; if you please. **Doozo moo ichido itte kudasai.** Please say it again.

**doozoo** bronze statue.

**dora** gong.

**dorama** drama.

**doramu** drum (musical); **doramu kan** drum (for storage).

**DORE** which one? **Dore ga ichiban ii desu ka?** Which is the best?

**doro** mud; **doro darake no** muddy; **doromizu** muddy water.

**doroboo** thief.

**DORU** dollar; **doru sooba** exchange rate of the dollar.

**doryoku** effort, exertion; **doryoku suru** to exert oneself; to endeavor.

**dosakusa** confusion; tumult; trouble.

**doshidoshi** in large numbers; rapidly; in rapid succession.

**DOSSARI** in great quantity or numbers. **Tegami ga dossari kita.** Many letters came.

**DOTTO** all of a sudden; suddenly; with a rush.

**DOYOOBI** Saturday.

**dozoo** storehouse with earthen walls.

**E** particle denoting: to, toward, in the direction of; **Kyooto e ikimasu.** I'm going to Kyoto.

**E** picture, painting; drawing, illustration, sketch; **e o kaku** to make (draw, paint) a picture; **e no yoo na** like a picture; picturesque.

**e** handle, crank, haft, shaft.

**ebi** lobster; shrimp; prawn.

**ebicha** maroon; brownish red.

**eda** branch, bough; twig; **edaburi** spread of branches; **edaha** branches; ramifications; digressions; **hanashi ga edaha ni hairu** to digress; **edaha no giron** side issue; digression.

**EE, HAI** yes. **Ee, soo desu.** Yes, that is so. Correct.

**eeteru** ether.

**ee** to let me see; well (used when stalling for time). **Ee to, sore wa nan deshita ka?** Let me see, what was it?

**egao** smiling face; smile; **egao ni naru** to smile; **egao de** with a smile.

**egatai** hard to get; not easily obtainable; **mata to egatai kikai** a rare opportunity.

**EHAGAKI** picture postcard.

**ehon** picture book for children; illustrated book.

**Ei-** prefix denoting: Anglo-, English, British; **Eitaishi kan** British Embassy; **Eibungaku** English Literature.

**Ei-Bei** England and America; **Ei-Bei no** Anglo-American; **Ei-Beijin** the English and the Americans.

**eibin na** keen, sharp, smart, clever, quick-witted; **eibin na kansatsu** keen observation; **eibin na mimi** sharp ears.

**EIBUN** English; English sentence; English composition; English-language text; **Eibun wayaku** translation from English into Japanese.

**eien** eternity; permanence; **eien no** eternal; permanent; everlasting; **eien ni** forever, perpetually.

**EIGA** movie; motion pictures; **eigagaisha** film-producing company; **eigakai no meiyuu** movie star; **EIGAKAN** movie theater.

**EIGO** English language; English; **Eigo no** *(adj.)* English; written in English; **Eigo ga dekiru, Eigo de hanasu** to speak in

English; **Eigo ga wakaru** to understand English.

**EIGYOO** business, trade; trading; **eigyoo suru** to engage in business; trade in; **eigyoohi** business expenses; **eigyoo jikan** business (office) hours; **eigyoozei** business tax.

**eijuu** permanent residence; **eijuu no** settled; resident; **eijuu suru** to reside permanently.

**Eika** English currency; sterling; British-made goods.

**eikan** crown of glory; laurels.

**eiki** high spirits; vigor; energy. **eiki o sogu** to dampen one's enthusiasm.

**EIKOKU** England, Great Britain; **Eikoku no** (*adj.*) English; **Eikokujin** English person (See also **Eigo.**)

**EIKYOO** influence; effect; **eikyoo suru** to influence; to affect; **eikyoo o ukeru** to be influenced, be affected.

**eikyuu** permanence; eternity; **eikyuuteki** permanent; perpetual, eternal; **eikyuu ni** permanently, forever.

**eimin** death (human only); **eimin suru** to die.

**eiri** gain, profit; **eiriteki no** money-making; commercial; **eiri jigyoo** commercial undertaking; **eiri gaisha** commercial concern.

**eiri na** sharp, keen; sharp-edged.

**Eiryoo** British dominion.

**eisei** hygiene, sanitation; health; **eisei ni yoi** healthful; wholesome; **eisei ni warui** bad for the health; **eiseitekina** hygienic; sanitary.

**eisei** satellite; **eiseikoku** satellite nation; **jinkoo eisei** man-made satellite; **eisei chuukei** satellite telecast.

**eishaki** film projector.

**eishashitsu** projection room.

**eiten** transfer on promotion.

**EI-WA JISHO** English-Japanese dictionary.

**Eiyaku** English translation.

**eiyo** honor; glory.

**eiyoo** nutrition; nourishment; **eiyoo aru** nutritious, nourishing; **eiyoo furyoo** malnutrition; **eiyoobutsu** nutritious food.

**eizoku** permanence; continuation; **eizokuteki** lasting, permanent; **eizoku suru** to last long, remain permanently.

**eizuru** to be reflected (as in a mirror in water); to impress.

**EKI** use; good; benefit; advantage, profit; **eki no aru** beneficial, profitable; **eki no nai** useless; unprofitable; **eki suru** to benefit, do good to.

**EKI** = **teishajoo** railway station; **ekichoo** stationmaster; **ekiin** porter; station employee; **Tokyooeki** Tokyo Station.

**eki** sap, liquid, fluid.

**ekibyoo** epidemic, pestilence, plague.

**ekiri** dysentery; children's summer diarrhea.

**ekisu** extract, essence.

**ekitai** liquid, fluid.

**ekkususen** X rays.

**ekohiiki** partiality, favoritism; **ekohiiki no** partial, unfair; **ekohiiki no nai** impartial, fair; **ekohiiki suru** to show partiality to; be partial to.

**ekoji na** stubborn, perverse, obstinate; **ekoji ni natte** in spite; out of spite.

**ekubo** dimple.

**emono** game, a catch; trophy; prize, spoils.

**EN** yen (Japanese money); **hyaku en** 100 yen **hyaku en satsu** 100-yen note.

**en** circle.

**en** affinity; fate; blood relation, blood connection; **en o musubu** to marry.

**en** feast, dinner party; **en o haru** to give a dinner party.

**enban** disk, discus.

**enbifuku** (male) evening dress.

**enboo** vista; distant view.

**enchaku** delayed arrival; **enchaku suru** to arrive late; to be delayed.

**enchoo** continuation, extension; **enchoo suru** to extend, prolong, lengthen.

**endan** proposal (of marriage).

**endan** rostrum, platform.

**endoo** route; road; **endoo ni** en route; along the road.

**en'en** in a blaze; **en'en taru** blazing, flaming; **en'en to shite** in (fierce) flames.

**enerugii** energy.

**engan** coast; **engan no** on the shore along the coast.

**ENGAWA** veranda, porch.

**engei** dramatic performance; entertainment, **engeisha** performer, artist; **engeijoo** variety theater; an entertainment hall; **engeikai** variety show; **engei mokuroku** program; repertoire.

**engeki** play; theatrical performance.

**engi** luck; omen; history; legend; **engi no yoi** lucky, auspicious; **engi no warui** unlucky, ominous, ill-omened.

**engi** playacting, performance.

**engo** support; backing.

**engumi** marriage; alliance; adoption (of a son); **engumi suru** to marry; to adopt.

**enja** relative, kinsman.

**enjo** assistance; help, aid; **enjo suru** to assist, help; to support.

**enjuku** maturity; mellowness; perfection; **enjuku suru** to grow ripe, mature; to mellow; **enjuku shita** mature; mellow; perfect.

**enka** exchange rate, value of the yen.

**enkai** social gathering; feast, banquet; dinner party; **enkai o hiraku** to give a dinner party.

**enkai** coast, sea (near land); **enkai gyogyoo** inshore fishery.

**enkei** distant view; perspective; circle; **enkei no** round, circular.

**enki** postponement; adjournment; **enki suru** to postpone, put off.

**enkin** distance; far and near; **enkin kara** from far and near.

**enko** connection; relation; affinity.

**enkyori** far distance, great distance; **enkyori de** at a great distance.

**enmachoo** black list; teacher's record book.

**enman** perfection; harmony; **enman na** perfect; harmonious; peaceful; **enman ni** harmoniously, smoothly; peacefully; **enman na katei** happy home; **enman ni koto o osameru** to settle the matter smoothly.

**ennetsu** burning (scorching) heat; heat of the sun.

**ennichi** fete day (of a local deity); fair; festival.

**en no shita** ground or space under the veranda or floor in a Japanese house; **en no shita no chikaramochi o suru** to be engaged in a thankless task; to labor in the background.

**enogu** paints, oils; colors, pigments; **enoguzara** dish for blending colors.

**ENPITSU** pencil; **iro-enpitsu** colored pencils; **enpitsu kezuri** pencil sharpener.

**enpoo** great distance; distant place.

**enrai no kyaku** visitor (guest) from a distant place.

**enro** long way; great distance; long journey. **Enro go-sokuroo o wazurawashimashite sumimasen.** I thank you for coming all the way.

**ENRYO** reserve; modesty; respect; **enryo suru** to be reserved; to refrain from; to withhold; **enryo naku** without reserve, freely; **enryo bukai** modest; shy; **-ni enryo shite** out of respect for (someone); **enryo eshaku mo naku** without the least reserve.

**ensaki** edge of a veranda.

**ensei, enseikan** pessimism; **enseiteki** pessimistic; **enseika** pessimist.

**enshoo** inflammation; spread of a fire; **enshoo suru** to catch fire.

**enshutsu** performance (of a play, an opera, a film); **enshutsu suru** to play, perform, to execute.

**ensoku** excursion (on foot), hike; picnic; **ensoku ni iku** to go on a hike; to take a long walk.

**ensoo** musical performance; recital; **ensoosha** performer, player; **ensookai** concert, recital.

**entaku** round table.

**enten** blazing (burning) sun; heat of the day.

**ENTOTSU** chimney; chimney stack; funnel.

**en'yoo gyogyoo** deep-sea fishing.

**en'yoo kookai** ocean voyage.

**en'yuukai** garden party.

**enzetsu** speech, address; **enzetsu suru** to make a speech; **enzetsukai** speech meeting.

**enzuku** to get married.

**episoodo** episode.

**ERABU** to choose, select, elect, single out; to sort; **hon o erabu** to select a book. **Ii no dake o erabimashoo.** Let's choose only a good one.

**ERAI** great; extraordinary; worthy; eminent; wonderful; serious; heavy. **Erai koto ni natta.** It looks bad.

**EREBEETAA** elevator.

**ERI** neck; neckband; collar; **erikubi** nape of the neck; **erimaki** muffler, scarf; **eri o tadasu** to adjust one's dress; to sit up straight.

**eru** to gain; to get.

**eshaku** greeting, salutation; **eshaku suru** to greet; to bow slightly.

**esukareetaa** escalator.

**etai** form, shape; nature; **etai no shirenu** unfamiliar, strange; nondescript; **etai no shirenu hito** a perfect stranger.

**ete** skill; specialty, one's forte; **ete ni ho o ageru** to sail before the wind; to give scope to one's skill; **-ga ete da** to be a good hand at; **-wa ete de nai** to be a poor hand at.

**etoku** understanding, comprehension; **etoku suru** to understand, grasp; **etoku shiyoi** easy to understand; **etoku shinikui** difficult to understand.

# F

**FAAMASHII** pharmacy.

**faindaa** finder.

**fan** fan, enthusiast; **eiga fan** movie fan.

**fassho** fascist.

**fauru** foul ball (in baseball).

**feruto** See **fueruto.**

**fiito** = **fuiito** feet (a measure).

**Firipin** Philippine Islands; **Firipinjin** Filipino.

**firumu** = **fuirumu** film.

**firutaa** filter.

**fooku** fork.

**-fu** suffix denoting: urban prefecture (used only with Kyoto and Osaka); **Kyooto fu** Kyoto prefecture.

**fuan** insecurity; anxiety; **fuan na** unsafe; insecure; anxious.

**fuan ni omou** to feel insecure (uncertain, anxious) about. **Fuan de atta.** I felt uneasy.

**fuannai** unfamiliarity; ignorance; **fuannai na** unfamiliar; ignorant; **fuannai na tochi** strange place; **tochi ni fuannai na hito** stranger, person who is not familiar with a place. **Watakushi wa koko wa fuannai desu.** I am pretty much of a stranger here.

**fuantei** instability; **fuantei na** unstable; unsteady; insecure.

**FUBEN** inconvenience; **fuben na** inconvenient; **fuben o shoozuru** to cause inconvenience; **fuben o shinobu** to put up with inconvenience; **fuben o kanzuru** to be put to inconvenience.

**fubi** deficiency; defect, imperfection; **fubi no** defective; incomplete; imperfect; **fubi no ten** defects; imperfections.

**fubin na** pitiful; poor; **fubin ni omou** to pity, take pity on.

**FUBO** parents.

**fubuki** snowstorm, blizzard.

**fuchakuriku hikoo** non-stop flight.

**fuchaku suru** to stick to; to attach.

**fuchi** edge, brink, rim; margin, border; **fuchi o toru** to hem; to fringe; etc.; **fuchi o tsukeru** to frame, border.

**fuchi** deep pool, deep water; abyss.

**fuchin** ups and downs; rise and fall; **isshoo no fuchin ni kansuru daiji** a matter affecting one's whole life.

**fuchoo** disagreement; rupture; failure; **fuchoo ni owaru** to end in failure.

**fuchoowa** discord; incongruity; **fuchoowa na** unharmonious, discordant; **fuchoowa de aru** to clash.

**FUCHUUI** carelessness; inattention; **fuchuui na** careless; inattentive; **fuchuui ni** carelessly.

**fuchuujitsu** unfaithfulness, disloyalty; **fuchuujitsu na** unfaithful, disloyal.

**FUDA** card; label, tag; placard; **fuda o tsukeru** to attach a card (or label); to tag.

**FUDAN** usually, ordinarily; habitually; **fudan no** usual; habitual; common; **fudan no toori** as usual.

**fudangi** everyday clothes.

**fude** writing brush.

**fudeki** failure; poor work; **fudeki na** badly made (done); clumsy. **Kono hako wa fudeki desu.** This box is badly made. **Ine ga fudeki desu.** The rice crop is poor.

**fudoo** difference, diversity, dissimilarity; inequality; **fudoo de aru** to be unequal; to differ; to be irregular.

**fudooi** disagreement, difference of opinion.

**fudoosan** immovable property; real estate.

**fudootoku** immorality; **fudootoku na** immoral, unprincipled.

**fue** flute, whistle.

**fueisei na** unsanitary; unhealthy.

**FUERU** to increase (in number or quantity), multiply. **Mizu ga fuete kita.** The river is rising. **Okane ga fueta.** His income has increased.

**fueruto = feruto** felt.

**fuete** weak point; unskillfulness; **fuete na** unskillful, inexpert. **Sono hoo wa fuete desu.** I'm a poor hand at it. It's not in my line.

**fufuku** dissatisfaction, discontent; disapproval; objection; **fufuku ga aru** to be dissatisfied, etc.; **fufuku o iu** to express dissatisfaction.

**fugai nai** unmanly, effeminate; poor-spirited; cowardly.

**fugi** immorality; injustice; adultery; **fugi no** immoral; improper.

**fugiri** ingratitude; dishonesty; **fugiri no** unjust; dishonest; ungrateful; **fugiri ga aru** to owe a debt.

**fugoo** millionaire.

**fugoo** mark, sign, symbol, cipher.

**fugookaku** failure; elimination; rejection; **figookaku to naru** to fail.

**fugoori** absurdity; **fugoori na** absurd; irrational, illogical.

**fugu** deformity; **fugu no** deformed, disfigured, crippled; **fugu ni naru** to become disfigured.

**fuguu** misfortune, adversity; **fuguu no** unfortunate.

**fugyooseki** loose conduct; dissipation.

**fuhai** decomposition; decay; **fuhai suru** to rot; to be corrupted.

**fuhei** discontent; dissatisfaction; **fuhei o iu** to grumble, complain; **fuhei de aru** to be discontented; **fuhei o motte iru** to have a complaint; **fuheika** grumbler, malcontent.

**fuheikin** inequality, disproportion; **fuheikin no** unequal; disproportionate.

**fuhen** unchangeability; **fuhen no** unchangeable, constant; invariable.

**fuhinkoo** immoral conduct; dissipation; **fuhinkoo na** loose, immoral.

**fuhitsuyoo na** needless, unnecessary.

**fuhon'i** unwillingness, reluctance; **fuhon'i no** unwilling, reluctant; **fuhon'i nagara** against one's will.

**fuhoo na** unlawful, violent; illegal.

**fui** unexpectedness; suddenness; **fui no** unexpected; sudden; unlooked for; **fui o utsu** to take by surprise; **fui o kurau** to be taken by surprise.

**fuichoo** announcement; advertisement; recommendation; **fuichoo suru** to announce; to advertise; to make known.

**fuiito** See **fiito.**

**fuirumu** See **firumu.**

**fuiuchi** unexpected blow, surprise attack.

**fujichaku, fujichakuriku** forced landing, emergency landing.

**FUJIN** woman; lady; **fujinrashii** womanly; ladylike.

**fuji no** incurable; fatal.

**fujitsu** insincerity; faithlessness; lack of feeling; **fujitsu no** faithless; insincere; unfeeling.

**fujiyuu** inconvenience; want; discomfort; **fujiyuu na** uncomfortable; inconvenient; **fujiyuu o suru** to be short (wanting).

**fujo** assistance, aid; support; **fujo suru** to assist, aid.

**fujoori** unreasonableness, irrationality; **fujoori na** unreasonable, irrational.

**fujun** impurity; **fujun no** impure.

**fujun** unseasonability, irregularity; **fujun na** unseasonable, irregular.

**fujuubun** insufficiency; **fujuubun na** insufficient; incomplete.

**fuka** addition, supplement; **fuka suru** to add, supplement.

**fukagen** slight illness, indisposition; unsavoriness; **fukagen na** unsavory; indisposed, unwell.

**FUKAI** deep, profound; thick, dense; **fukai kangae** deep thought; **fukai kiri** dense fog; **fukai naka ni naru** to form a close relationship.

**fukai** unpleasantness. See **fuyukai.**

**fukairi** (n.) going too far; addiction; **fukairi suru** to go deeply into; to be taken up too much with.

**fukakai** mystery; **fukakai na** mysterious; insoluble; **fukakai na koto** mystery, mysterious affair.

**fukakooryoku** act of God; **fukakooryoku no** unavoidable; inevitable; irresistible.

**fukaku** negligence, fault; **fukaku o toru** to be beaten. **Sore wa watakushi no fukaku deshita.** It was my fault.

**fukakujitsu** uncertainty; unreliability; **fukakujitsu no** uncertain; unreliable.

**fukami** depth; deep place; **fukami no aru** deep, profound; **fukami ni hairu** to get beyond one's depth.

**fukanoo** impossibility; **fukanoo na** impossible; impractical. **Hotondo fukanoo de aru.** It is almost impossible.

**fukanzen** imperfection; incompleteness; **fukanzen na** defective; incomplete.

**fukkappatsu** inactivity; stagnation; dullness; **fukkappatsu na** dull; inactive; stagnant.

**fukasa** depth. **Fukasa ga go fiito desu.** It is five feet deep.

**fukeiki** depression; dullness; hard times; **fukeiki na** dull; depressed, gloomy, dismal.

**fukeizai na** uneconomical; wasteful.

**fukenkoo** unhealthiness; poor health; **fukenkoo na** unhealthy, unwholesome.

**fukenshiki** lack of proper judgment; **fukenshiki na** disgraceful, shameful.

**fukenzen na** morbid, unwholesome.

**FUKERU** to grow old, age; to grow late, advance; **yo ga fukeru made hataraku** to work late into the night. **Yo wa dandan fuketa.** The night wore away. It grew late.

**fuketsu** dirtiness; **fuketsu na** dirty, filthy; **fuketsubutsu** dirt, filth.

**fuki** appendix; **fuki suru** to add.

**fukiageru** to blow up; to spout; to throw up.

**fukichirasu** to scatter about; to blow away.

**fukidasu** to spout, gush out; to burst out laughing.

**fukidemono** (body) rash.

**fukikakeru** to pick (a quarrel); to breathe on. **Kimi wa boku ni kenka o fukikakeru no ka?** Do you want to pick a fight with me?

**fukikesu** to blow out a light.

**fukikomu** to blow into (a house, room, etc.); to inspire; to instill in one's mind; to record (make a sound recording); to polish, rub bright.

**fukimakuru** to blow about; to sweep along.

**FUKIN** a napkin; dish towel, dishcloth.

**fukin** neighborhood; **fukin ni** in the neighborhood; **fukin no** neighboring, adjacent.

**fukinshin na** indiscreet; immodest.

**fukiorosu** to blow down.

**fukiritsu** lack of discipline; irregularity; **fukiritsu na** disorderly; undisciplined; irregular.

**fukisoku** irregularity; **fukisoku na** unsystematic; irregular.

**fukisooji** wiping; cleaning; **fukisooji o suru** to mop.

**fukisusamu** to blow furiously.

**fukitoru** to wipe away; to wipe out.

**fukitsu** ill omen; ill luck; **fukitsu na** unlucky, ill-omened; ominous.

**fukitsukeru** to blow against; to beat against. **Ame ga mado ni fukitsukeru.** The rain beats against the window.

**fukiyoseru** to drift; to blow together.

**fukkatsu** revival; **fukkatsu suru** to revive.

**Fukkatsusai, Fukkatsusetsu** Easter.

**fukkoo** revival, renaissance; restoration; **fukkoo suru** to revive, be restored.

**fukkyuu** restoration; **fukkyuu suru** to restore to the original state; to be restored to normalcy.

**fukokoroe** indiscretion; misconduct; **fukokoroe na** unwise, indiscreet; **fukokoroe na koto o suru** to behave badly; to act indiscreetly.

**fukoku** decree, proclamation; notification; **fukoku suru** to notify; to decree, proclaim.

**FUKOO** misery; unhappiness; disaster; mishap; disobedience to parents; **fukoo na** unhappy, unfortunate; miserable; undutiful, unfilial; **fukoo ni mo** unfortunately; **fukoo ni au** to have a misfortune.

**fukoohei** unfairness, partiality; **fukoohei na** unfair, partial, unjust; **fukoohei ni** unjustly, unfairly.

**FUKU** to wipe; to dry; to mop, to rub off; **tenugui de te o fuku** to wipe the hands with a towel.

**fuku** to blow; to breathe; to whistle. **Hidoku fuite iru.** It's blowing hard. **me o fuku** to send out a new shoot; **fue o fuku** to play a flute; **hora o fuku** (colloq.) to boast.

**fuku-** prefix denoting: assistant, vice-; **fukugichoo** vice-chairman; **Fukudaitooryoo** Vice-President (of the U.S.A.).

**fuku-** sub, double, composite; **fukuri** compound interest.

**-fuku** suffix denoting: clothes, dress; garment; **yoofuku** European clothes; **fujinfuku** women's clothes.

**fukuan** plan, idea; scheme. **Watakushi ni fukuan ga arimasu.** I have a good plan.

**fukubiki** lottery; distribution of prizes.

**fukubukushii** happy-looking; radiant.

**fukugyoo** subsidiary business; side job.

**fukumuu** to have (hold) in the mouth; to bear in mind; to include; to imply. **Doozo kono koto o ofukumioki kudasai.** Please keep this in mind.

**fukurahagi** calf (of the leg).

**fukuramasu** to swell, expand, puff out.

**fukurami** bulge, swelling.

**fukureru** to swell, puff out; to be sulky; to become sore.

**fukurettsura** (colloq.) sulky, sullen look.

**FUKURO** bag, sack, pouch.

**fukurodataki** sound thrashing, drubbing.

**fukuryooji** vice-consul.

**fukusanbutsu** by-product.

**fukusayoo** ill effect; secondary reaction; harmful side effects; **fukusayoo no nai** harmless.

**fukusei** reproduction; duplication.

**fukusha** copying; **fukusha suru** to copy, reproduce; **fukushaki** duplicator.

**fukushachoo** vice-president (of a company).

**fukushi** adverb.

**fukushi** welfare.

**fukushin** devotion; confidence; **fukushin no** devoted; confidential; faithful; **fukushin no tomo** devoted friend.

**fukushoku** reappointment; **fukushoku suru** to resume office.

**fukushuu** review; **fukushuu suru** to review, go over.

**fukushuu** revenge, vengeance; **fukushuu suru** to be revenged.

**fukusuu** (n.) plural (number); **fukusuu no** (adj.) plural.

**fukutsu no** inflexible; indomitable.

**fukutsuu** stomachache; bellyache.

**fukuyoo suru** to take a dose of medicine.

**fukuzatsu na** complex, complicated, intricate; **fukuzatsu ni suru** to complicate.

**fukuzoo** reserve; **fukuzoo naku** without reserve, frankly; **fukuzoo no nai** frank, candid, unreserved; **fukuzoo naku ieba** to be frank with you; **fukuzoo naku iken o noberu** to express one's views freely, without reserve.

**fukyoo** business depression, slump, inactivity, slackness, displeasure; ill-humor, disfavor, **fukyoo no** inactive; depressed, weak; in a slump.

**fukyuu** diffusion, propagation, spread; **fukyuu suru** to diffuse, propagate, spread.

**fukyuu** immortality, eternity; **fukyuu no** eternal, immortal, undying.

**fuman, fumanzoku** discontent, dissatisfaction; **fuman na** discontented, dissatisfied; **fuman ni omou** to be displeased with, dissatisfied with.

**fumei** obscurity, uncertainty; ignorance; **fumei no** obscure, indistinct, vague; **fumeiryoo** not clear, indistinct. **Yukisaki wa fumei da.** His destination is unknown.

**fumeiyo** disgrace, dishonor; discredit; **fumeiyo na** disgraceful, dishonorable.

**fumetsu** immortality; indestructibility.

**fumidai** step; footstool.

**fumidan** step; steps, stairs.

**fumidasu** to step forward.

**fumihazusu** to miss (lose) one's footing.

**fumikatameru** to tread; to stamp down.

**fumikiri** railway crossing; grade crossing.

**fumikoeru** to step over (a thing).

**fumikomu** to step into; to make a raid; to rush in; to trespass; to force an entrance.

**fumikudaku** to trample.

**fumimochi** dissipation; immoral conduct.

**fuminarasu** to stamp (one's feet) noisily; to tread; to level by treading.

**fumin fukyuu** without sleep or rest.
**fuminijiru** to trample, crush with the feet.
**fuminshoo** insomnia, sleeplessness.
**fumitaosu** to kick down; to evade payment; to bargain.
**fumitodomaru** to stand one's ground, remain.
**fumitsukeru** to trample; to treat with contempt; **hito o fumitsuke ni shita koto o iu** to make an insulting remark.
**fumoto** foot of a hill or mountain.
**fumu** to step; to tread on; to go through; to value at; **jitchi o fumu** to experience; **tetsuzuki o fumu** to go through the formalities; **shinamono no ne o fumu** to put a price on something.
**fumuki** unfit for, unsuitable for.
**FUN, pun** minute; **ippun** one minute; **gofun kan** for five minutes.
**funaashi** speed, draft, headway (of a ship); **funaashi no hayai fune** fast boat.
**funaasobi** boat excursion; **funaasobi ni yuku** to go boating.
**funachin** passage fare; shipping freight; freightage.
**funade** ship departure; sailing; **funade suru** to set sail.
**funani shooken** bill of lading.
**funanori** sailor, seaman.
**funare** unfamiliarity; inexperience; **funare na** unfamiliar; inexperienced; **roodoo ni funare de aru** to be unaccustomed to labor.
**funayoi** seasickness.
**funbaru** to stretch one's legs; to straddle; to make an effort; to persevere; **saigo made funbaru** to hold fast to the end.
**funbetsu** discretion, good sense; discernment; **funbetsu no aru** discreet, prudent; thoughtful; **funbetsu no nai** indiscreet etc.; **funbetsu zakari no hito** mature person.
**fundan** ni in plenty, fully. **Tabemono ga fundan ni aru.** There is plenty to eat.
**FUNE** ship, boat, vessel; **fune ni noru** to board a ship; to go to sea; **fune ni you** to get seasick.
**funesshin** indifference; **funesshin na** halfhearted, indifferent, lukewarm.
**fungai** resentment, indignation; **fungai shite** indignantly; **fungai suru** to be indignant, resent.
**funiai** unbecoming (to), unsuitable; ill-matched; **funiai no fuufu** ill-matched couple.
**fun'iki** atmosphere.
**funinjoo na** unfeeling, coldhearted.
**funka** eruption, volcanic activity; **funkazan** volcano.

**funki suru** to be stirred up, be inspired by; to rouse oneself to action.
**funmatsu** powder; **funmatsu ni suru** to pulverize.
**funoo** impossibility; incompetency; impotency; **funoo no** impossible.
**funpatsu** exertion, endeavor(s); **funpatsu suru** to exert oneself; to rouse; to make a great effort.
**funsai suru** to shatter (smash) to pieces.
**funshitsu** loss; **funshitsu suru** to lose; to miss; to be missing; **funshitu butsu** lost article.
**funshutsu** spout, gush, jet; **funshutsu suru** to gush out.
**funsoo** trouble; dispute; difficulties.
**funsoo** disguise; **funsoo suru** = **funsuru** to disguise, to impersonate.
**funsui** fountain; jet.
**funsuru** See **funsoo suru.**
**funtoo** hard struggle, desperate fight; **funtoo suru** to struggle, fight desperately.
**funzen** resolutely; plucking up one's courage; indignantly; in a fit of anger.
**fuon** unrest; **fuon na** threatening; disquieting; improper; riotous; **fuon na nyuusu** unsettling news. **Keisei ga fuon de aru.** The situation is quite disturbing.
**fuontoo** impropriety, inappropriateness; **fuontoo no, fuontoo na** improper, inappropriate; unjust.
**furachi** outrageousness; insolence; misconduct; **furachi na** outrageous, insolent; vicious; **furachi na koto o suru** to misconduct oneself; to act viciously.
**furafura to** dizzy, unsteady; **furafura suru** to feel dizzy; to reel, stagger. **Atama ga furafura suru.** My head is swimming.
**furai** fry **sakana no furai** fried fish; **furaipan** frying pan.
**furanneru** flannel.
**FURANSU** France; **Furansugo** French language; **Furansujin** French person.
**furareru** to be jilted.
**furasshu** flashlight.
**furekomi** announcement, proclamation.
**furekomu** to announce; to represent oneself as.
**furemawasu** to broadcast, to spread news.
**fureru** to touch; to strike against; to refer to; to conflict with; **hooritsu ni fureru** to be contrary to the law; **mondai ni fureru** to refer to the question.
**furi** disadvantage, drawback; **furi na** disadvantageous, unfavorable; unprofitable.
**furi** appearance; air; pretension; **shiranai furi o suru** to pretend ignorance.

**furi-** prefix denoting: to shake; to brandish, wave, flourish.

**furidashi** drawing; start, starting point; issue.

**furidasu** to begin to fall (as rain or snow). **Ame ga furidashita.** It began to rain.

**furieki** disadvantage; handicap.

**furigana** Kana (Japanese syllabic sign) attached to *Kanji* to show the pronunciation.

**furihanasu** to shake free from; to break away.

**furiharau** to shake from.

**furikae** change; transfer.

**furikaeru, furimuku** to turn around; to look back over one's shoulder.

**furikakaru** to fall on; to befall, happen.

**furikakeru** to sprinkle over.

**furikazasu** to hold aloft; to brandish.

**furikiru** break away from.

**furiko** pendulum.

**furimawasu** to brandish, flourish.

**furimuku** See **furikaeru.**

**furiotosu** to shake off.

**furishikiru** to rain or snow incessantly.

**furisuteru** to leave, abandon, to shake off.

**furitateru** to shake; to toss; to raise one's voice.

**furitsuke** dance composition; choreography.

**furitsuzuku** to rain or snow continuously.

**FURO** bath, hot bath; **furo ni hairu** to take a bath; **furoba** bathroom; **furoya** bathhouse.

**furoku** supplement, appendix.

**furoonin** wanderer; tramp.

**FUROSHIKI** wrapping cloth (square piece of cotton or silk used to wrap and carry something); **furoshiki de tsutsumu** to wrap in a wrapping cloth.

**FURU** to fall, to come down (rain, etc.). **Hidoku ame ga futte iru.** Rain is falling heavily. **Yuki ga futta.** There was a snowfall.

**furu** to shake; to wave, wag; **kubi o tate ni furu** to nod, assent to.

**furu-** prefix denoting: old; **furuhon** old book; **furuhonya** secondhand book store; **furubiru** to be worn out; to be aged; **furubita** old, worn-out; **furumono** secondhand goods; **furudoogu** old furniture; secondhand household utensils; **furudooguya** secondhand dealer; curio shop; **furugi** old clothes; secondhand clothes; **furugi ya** secondhand-clothes dealer.

**furue** *(n.)* shaking, trembling, shivering; **furueagaru** to tremble with fear; **furuegoe** trembling voice; timid voice.

**furueru** to shake, shudder, tremble.

**furui** sieve; **furui ni kakeru** to sift (out) sieve.

**furui** old (used when speaking of things); ancient; antique.

**furuiokosu** to stir up, rouse, awaken; **yuuki o furuiokosu** to summon up courage.

**furuitatsu** to stir up; to be roused to action.

**furukizu** old wound; scar; former misdeed.

**furukusai** stale; old-fashioned; hackneyed.

**furumai** behavior, conduct, action.

**furumau** to behave, act; to treat, behave toward (a person).

**furutte** energetically; voluntarily; willingly. **Furutte goshusseki kudasai.** Please make every effort to attend.

**furuuto** flute (Western style).

**furyo no** unexpected, accidental; **furyo no dekigoto** accident; unforeseen event, an emergency.

**furyoo no** bad; poor; unsatisfactory; deliquent; **furyoo shoonen** bad boy(s); **furyoohin** inferior goods.

**furyooken** indiscretion; rash act; **furyooken na** rash; ill-advised.

**fusa** tassel; tuft; fringe; bunch; cluster.

**fusagaru** to get blocked; to become choked; to be occupied, engaged; to be filled. **Kono michi wa saki ga fusagatte iru.** This road is blocked. **Sono ie wa fusagatte iru.** That house is occupied. **Kono seki wa fusagatte iru.** This seat is taken. **Ima te ga fusagatte imasu.** I am tied up just now. I am busy now.

**fusagikomu** to be in low spirits; to mope.

**fusagu** to close, shut up; to stand in the way; to be dejected, depressed; **basho o fusagu** to take up room; **jikan o fusagu** to fill up the time; **michi o fusagu** to stand in the way.

**fusai** debt; loan.

**fusansei** disapproval; dissent; **fusansei de aru** to dissent; disapprove; **fusansei o tonaeru** to raise objections to; to express disapproval. **Kimi wa sansei ka fusansei ka?** Are you for or against it?

**FUSAWASHII** suitable, becoming.

**fusegu** to defend, protect, guard against; to prevent; to resist.

**fusei** dishonesty; injustice; unlawfulness; **fusei na** dishonest; wrong; corrupt; unlawful; **fuseihin** sham (fraudulent article).

**fuseijitsu** insincerity, dishonesty; **fuseijitsu na** dishonest; false.

**fuseikaku** uncertainty; inaccuracy.

**fuseikoo** failure; fiasco; miscarriage; **fuseikoo no** unsuccessful, abortive.

**fuseiseki** poor (unsatisfactory) result; bad record; poor performance; failure; **fuseiseki de aru** to be unsuccessful, be a failure; **fuseiseki ni owaru** to end in failure.

**fusen** tag, label; slip.

**fuseru** to put upside down; to turn over; to be down; to take cover.

**fusessei** neglect of health.

**fushi** joint; knuckle; knot; **fushi ana** knothole.

**fushiawase** unhappiness; misfortune, **fushiawase na** unhappy; unfortunate; unlucky; **fushiawase ni mo** unfortunately.

**fushidara** untidiness; looseness, laxity; **fushidara na** untidy; sloppy; irregular; loose; dissipated.

**FUSHIGI** wonder, miracle; **fushigi na** wonderful; marvelous; mysterious; miraculous; strange; **fushigi ni** wonderfully, miraculously.

**fushimatsu** mismanagement; carelessness; misconduct; prodigality; **fushimatsu na** lax; wasteful; irregular.

**fushin** doubt, suspicion; question; **fushin no** doubtful, suspicious, questionable; **fushin ni omou** to wonder; to think strange.

**fushinjin** unbelief; impiety; **fushinjin na** unbelieving, irreligious.

**fushinjitsu** insincerity; faithlessness; **fushinjitsu na** faithless, insincere.

**fushinkoo** unbelief; **fushinkoo no** unbelieving; freethinking.

**fushinsetsu** unkindness; **fushinsetsu na** unkind; unobliging.

**fushin'yoo** distrust, lack of confidence.

**fushizen na** unnatural, artificial; affected.

**fushoo** injury, wound; **fushoo suru** to be injured, get hurt; **fushoo sha** injured person.

**fushoo bushoo ni** reluctantly, unwillingly.

**fushoochi** dissent; disapproval; **fushoochi o iu** to dissent; to disapprove.

**fushoojiki** dishonesty; **fushoojiki na** dishonest.

**fushooka** indigestion.

**fushubi** failure; fiasco; displeasure; **fushubi ni naru** to fall into disfavor; **fushubi ni owaru** to end in failure.

**fusoku** shortage, deficiency; dissatisfaction; **fushoku suru** to want, lack, be short; **fusoku o iu** to grumble, complain; **fusoku gaku** shortage, deficit.

**fusoooo na** unsuitable, unfitting, unbecoming; undue; **mibun fusoooo na seikatsu o suru** to live above one's means.

**FUSUMA** sliding screen door covered with paper.

**FUTA** lid, cover; **futatsuki no** covered; **futa o suru, futa o shimeru** to cover, put on a lid; **futa o toru** to lift the lid.

**futae** double, twofold.

**futago** twins.

**futaoya** one's parents.

**FUTARI** couple, two persons.

**futashika** uncertainty; **futashika na** uncertain; doubtful.

**FUTATABI** again.

**FUTATSU** two; **futatsu henji de** ready enough; most willingly; **futatsu to nai** matchless, unique; **futatsu tomo** both; **futatsu ni wakeru** to divide in two.

**futei na** uncertain, indefinite; inconstant.

**futeisai na** unseemly, indecent; unsightly; clumsy.

**futeki** bold, daring, fearless.

**futekinin** unfitness, incompetency; **futekinin de aru** to be unfit (for a task), be unsuitable for, be unqualified for; **futekininsha** a misfit.

**futettei** imperfect; inconsistent; unconvincing; not thoroughgoing.

**FUTO** suddenly; by chance, by accident; **futo omoidasu** to remember in a flash.

**futodoki na** insolent, rude.

**FUTOI** big; thick; deep; sonorous.

**futokoro** bosom; purse; pocket; **futokoro ga sabishii** to be short (of money); **futokoro ni suru** to put in one's pocket.

**futokusaku** poor plan; unwise course; disadvantage; **futokusaku na** unwise, inadvisable, inexpedient.

**futomomo** thigh.

**FUTON** mattress; quilt; cushion; bedding, **futon o shiku** to make a bed.

**futoo** injustice; **futoo na** unjust, unfair; unreasonable; **futoo ritoku** unreasonable profits.

**futoppara** generosity; broad-mindedness; **futoppara no** generous; broad-minded.

**futoraseru** to fatten; **FUTORU** to grow fat; **shindai ga futoru** to prosper.

**futosa** thickness; bulk.

**FUTOTTA** fat; plump; **futotta hito** fat person.

**futsugoo** inconvenience; misconduct; **futsugoo na** wrong; improper, objectionable; inconvenient; **futsugoo na koto o suru** to behave wrongly.

**FUTSUKA** two days; second day (of the month); **Sangatsu futsuka** March 2.

**futsukayoi** hangover; **futsukayoi o suru** to have a hangover.

**futsuriai** incongruity; imbalance, disproportion; **futsuriai no** disproportionate; ill-matched.

**FUTSUU** usually, normally.

**futsuu ni naru** to be suspended, cut off, interrupted.

**futtei** scarcity, shortage; **futtei de aru** to be scarce; **futtei suru** to run short.

**futtemo tettemo** rain or shine; no matter what the weather.

**futtoo** boiling; bubbling; agitation; **futtoo suru** to boil up; to bubble; **futtoo ten**

boiling point. **Giron ga futtoo shita.** The discussion became heated.

**futtsuri** utterly, entirely. **Ito ga futtsuri kireta.** The string snapped.

**fuu** appearance; customs; manners; way; seal; closing.

**fuu** seal; **fuu o suru** to seal, to fasten.

**fuubun** rumor.

**fuubutsu** scenery; nature; landscape.

**fuuchoo** trend of the times; fashion, tendency.

**FUUFU** husband and wife; married couple; **fuufu ni naru** to marry; **fuufu wakare** divorce; **fuufunaka** married life.

**fuuga** elegance; refinement; **fuuga na** elegant; refined.

**fuugetsu** scenery; (beauties of) nature.

**fuugi** manners; customs; **fuugi no yoi** well-mannered; well-bred; **fuugi no warui** ill-mannered; ill-bred.

**fuuha** wind and waves; storm; heavy sea; discord; trouble.

**fuuhyoo** current rumor; report.

**FUUKEI** landscape; scenery; **fuukeiga** landscape; seascape (painting); **fuukeigaka** landscape painter.

**fuukiri** release; **fuukiri suru** to break a seal; to release (a film, etc.).

**fuumi** flavor; taste; **fuumi no yoi** tasty, delicious.

**fuun** misfortune; ill luck; **fuun na** unfortunate, unlucky.

**fuurin** wind bell (tiny bell that tinkles in the wind).

**fuuryuu** elegance; taste; **fuuryuu na** elegant.

**fuusa** blockade.

**fuusen** balloon.

**fuusetsu** snowstorm, blizzard.

**FUUSHUU** manners; custom, usage, practice.

**fuusoku** wind velocity.

**fuutei** appearance; looks; dress.

**FUUTOO** envelope. **Fuutoo ni irete kudasai.** Please put it in an envelope.

**fuuu** wind and rain; rainstorm; **fuuu ni sarasareta** weather-beaten; **fuuu ni sarasu** to expose to the weather; **fuuu o okashite iku** go in spite of the storm.

**fuuzoku** customs; manners; public morals.

**fuwa** discord; strife; **fuwa de aru** to be on bad terms; **fuwa ni naru** to become estranged.

**fuwafuwa** light; thin; soft; spongy; lightly; softly.

**fuwari** lightly; softly; buoyantly.

**fuyakasu** to steep, soak.

**fuyakeru** to swell up; to get soaked; to be saturated.

**fuyasu** to increase; to add to; to raise.

**fuyoo ni naru** to be out of use; to fall into disuse.

**fuyooi na** unprepared, careless; thoughtless.

**fuyoojoo** neglect of health; intemperance; **fuyoojoo na** careless of one's health.

**FUYU** winter; **fuyu no** wintry; winter, **fuyufuku, fuyu mo no** winter clothes; **fuyuyasumi** winter vacation.

**fuyukai, fukai** unpleasantness; discomfort; **fuyukai na** unpleasant; uncomfortable; **fuyukai ni** unpleasantly, uncomfortably.

**fuyukitodoki** carelessness; neglect; **fuyukitodoki na** careless, negligent.

**fuzai** absence; **fuzai de aru** to be absent.

**fuzoku** attached to; belonging to; **fuzoku suru** to be attached to; to belong to; **fuzokuhin** accessories.

# G

**GA** particle marking an emphatic subject; but; and yet; however; although. **Sumisu san ni denwa o kakemashita ga rusu deshita.** I phoned Mr. Smith, but he was not in.

**ga** self, ego; self-will, selfishness; **ga o oru** to give in, to yield; **ga o toosu** to have one's way; **ga no tsuyoi** self-willed, obstinate.

**gaarusukauto** girl scout.

**gaaze** cheesecloth; surgical gauze.

**gaba to** all of a sudden; **gaba to okiagaru** to spring out of bed; to spring to one's feet.

**gabugabu** used only with **nomu** to take long draughts; to swill.

**gaburi to** used only with **nomu, kuitsuku; gaburi to nomu** to drain at one gulp; to gulp down; **gaburi to kuitsuku** to bite (snap) at.

**gachagacha** clattering, rattling; **gachagacha saseru** to clatter, rattle.

**-GACHI** suffix denoting: apt to, prone to; prevailing; of frequent occurrence; **okotarigachi no** prone to neglect; **byookigachi** prone to illness; ill most of the time; **kumorigachi no** cloudy; gloomy.

**gahaku** great painter.

**gai** injury, harm, damage; **gai suru** to injure, harm, hurt; **gai ni naru** to be injurious or harmful.

**gaibu** outside, exterior; **gaibu no** external, outer; **gaibu no hito** outsiders.

**gaibun** reputation; honor.

**gaichuu** harmful insect; blight; vermin.

**GAIDO** tourist guide.

**gaihaku suru** to stay out, stay away from home (at night).

**gaijin** foreigner.

**gaikai** outside world.

**gaikan** external appearance; outside view; general view; outline.

**gaikei** external form.

gaiken outward appearance.

GAIKOKU foreign country; gaikoku no foreign; exotic; alien; gaikoku e iku to go abroad; gaikoku sei foreign (product); gaikoku booeki foreign trade; gaikoku kawase foreign exchange (rate); gaikoku shijoo foreign market; gaikokusen foreign ships; GAIKOKUGO foreign language; GAIKOKUJIN foreigner; gaikokujin machi section where many foreigners live.

gaikoo diplomacy; gaikooka, gaikookan diplomat; gaikooteki diplomatic; gaikoodan diplomatic corps.

gaikooin canvasser.

gaikotsu skeleton; bones.

gaimen (n.) outside; surface; gaimen no exterior, external; outside.

gaimu foreign affairs.

gainen concept, general idea; conception.

gairai foreign; exotic; imported.

GAISHITE in general; generally speaking; on the whole.

gaishutsu suru to go out; gaishutsugi street dress.

gaitoo street lamp.

gaitoo street; gaitoo enzetsu soapbox oratory; gaitoo ni tatsu to go out (in the street).

gaitoo suru to fall under, to correspond to.

gaiyuu suru to travel abroad.

gaka painter; artist.

gake cliff, precipice; gakekuzure landslide.

-gake suffix denoting: being on the way to; toorigake ni in passing; negake ni just before going to bed.

gakka lesson; course of study, subject.

GAKKARI SURU to be disappointed; to lose heart; to be tired out, be exhausted. Kabuki ni ikenakute gakkari shita. I was disappointed because I could not get to the Kabuki theater.

gakki musical instrument.

gakki school term, semester.

GAKKOO school; college; gakkoo e yuku to go to school; gakkoo tomodachi schoolmate.

gakkyoku musical piece.

gakkyuu class, grade.

gaku prefix or suffix denoting: learning, studies; science.

gaku amount, sum, denomination.

gaku framed picture; gaku buchi picture frame.

gakuha school; academic group.

gakui academic degree.

gakumen face value; par; gakumen ika ni sagaru to fall below par.

gakumon learning; study; gakumon suru to study.

GAKUSEI student; schoolboy (-girl); gakusei jidai schooldays.

gakusetsu theory; doctrine.

gakusha learned man; scholar.

gakushiki scholarship; learning.

gakushuu study; gakushuu suru to study.

gakutai (musical) band.

gakuto students; scholars.

gakuya dressing room; gakuya guchi stage door.

gakuyuu fellow student; classmate.

gakuzen in amazement; amazed; aghast; gakuzen to suru to strike with horror; to shock.

GAMAN patience, endurance; pardon; gaman zuyoi patient; having great endurance; gaman suru to bear, endure. Kare ni wa gaman ga dekinai. I'm out of patience with him.

gan invocation, prayer.

gan cancer.

gan- prefix denoting: pertaining to the eye; ganbyoo eye disease; sore eyes.

ganbaru to persist in; to stand firm, refuse to give in.

ganboo desire, wish.

ganchuu ni in one's eyes; ganchuu ni nai beneath one's notice; ganchuu ni okanai to take no notice of; to ignore; to think nothing of.

gangan dingdong; clang; gangan naru to clang, ring noisily. Mimi ga gangan suru. My ears are ringing. Atama ga gangan suru. My head aches.

GANJITSU New Year's Day.

ganjoo na solid; robust; strongly built.

ganko stubbornness, obstinacy; ganko na stubborn, obstinate.

gankyoo stubbornness; persistence; gankyoo na obstinate, stubborn; persistent; gankyoo ni stubbornly, obstinately.

ganpeki quay, wharf, pier.

ganrai originally; from the first; by nature.

ganseki rock; crag; stones.

ganshiki discernment, insight; critical eye.

gansho written application.

ganso originator, founder, father of.

GANTAN New Year's Day; morning of New Year's Day.

gan'yaku pill; pellet.

ganze nai innocent, artless; helpless.

ganzoo forgery.

gappei union; combination; amalgamation; gappei suru to amalgamate; incorporate.

GARA pattern, design; build; nature (character); iegara the family standing.

garagara clattering; rattling; rattle (toy).

garakuta rubbish; worn-out articles.

**garandoo** empty, vacant; hollow.

**garan to suru** to appear empty; to seem deserted.

**garari to** completely; with a clatter; suddenly **garari to kawaru** to change completely.

**GARASU** *(n.)* glass; **garasu no** *(adj.)* glass; glazed; **garasu ita** (glass) pane; plate glass; **garasu kooba** glass factory.

**GAREEJI** garage.

**garigari** noisily, with noise; **garigari kajiru** to munch; **garigari hikkaku** to scrape; to scratch.

**garon** gallon.

**-garu** suffix denoting: to wish, want; to be inclined to; **mitagaru** to want to see; **ikitagaru** to want to go; **ureshigaru** to feel glad.

**garyoo** generosity; tolerance; **garyoo no aru** tolerant; generous; broad-minded; **garyoo no nai** intolerant; ungenerous.

**garyuu de** in one's own way.

**gasagasa suru** to rustle; **gasagasa no** rough; loose.

**gasatsu na** rude, rough, unmannerly; **gasatsu na otoko** unmannerly (rude) man.

**gashi suru** to starve to death.

**gashitsu** studio.

**GASORIN** gasoline; **gasorin sutando** gas station.

**gassaku** collaboration; **gassaku suru** to collaborate, work jointly; **gassakusha** a collaborator.

**gasshiri to** tightly; closely; **gasshiri shita** massive; well built; sturdy; **gasshiri shite iru** to be massive, etc.

**gasshoo** chorus; **gasshoo suru** to sing together; **gasshootai** chorus; choir.

**gasshuku** lodging together; **gasshuku suru** to lodge together.

**gasshukusho** training camp.

**Gasshuukoku** United States.

**gassoo** playing music together; **nibu gassoo** duet.

**gassuru** to add (join) together; to unite.

**GASU** gas; **gasu o tsukeru** to light the gas; **gasu o tomeru** to turn off the gas; **gasu sutoobu** gas heater; **gasugaisha** gas company.

**gatagata** rattling (clattering) sound; **gatagata furueru** to shake, shiver, tremble; **gatagata iu** to rattle, to shake.

**-gatai** suffix denoting: cannot; hard, difficult; impossible; **egatai** hard to get; unobtainable; **shinjigatai** difficult to believe; incredible.

**gatapishi** noisily; roughly; with a bang.

**gaten** comprehension, understanding; consent, agreement; **gaten suru** to understand, grasp the meaning; to be convinced of; to agree, consent; **gaten no ikanai** puzzling; doubtful.

**-GATSU** counter denoting: month of; **Ichigatsu** January.

**gatsugatsu** greedily; ravenously; **gatsugatsu taberu** to eat greedily.

**-gawa** suffix denoting: side; **soto gawa** outside; **uchi gawa** inside; **minami gawa** south side.

**gayagaya** noisily; **gayagaya sawagu** to make noise, clamor.

**gebita** vulgar; low; mean.

**geemu** game; **geemu o yaru** to play a game.

**gehin** meanness; vulgarity; **gehin na** mean; vulgar; low.

**gei** arts; accomplishments; feats; tricks; performance; **gei no aru hito** accomplished person.

**geijutsu** art; fine arts; **geijutsuteki** artistic; **geijutsuka** artist.

**geinin** professional entertainer.

**geisha** geisha (girl).

**GEJUN** latter part of a month; last ten days of a month.

**geka** surgery; **gekai** surgeon.

**gekai** this world; earth.

**geki** play, drama; **gekiteki** dramatic; **gekidan** theatrical world; dramatic company; **gekihyoo** theatrical criticism; **gekihyooka** theater critic; **GEKIJOO** theater, playhouse; **gekisakka** dramatist; playwright. (See also **gikyoku**.)

**gekiha suru** to defeat, rout.

**gekirei** encouragement; **gekirei suru** to encourage.

**gekiron** heated discussion; **gekiron suru** to argue hotly.

**gekiryuu** rapid stream; swift current.

**gekishin** severe earthquake. **Sakuban gekishin ga atta.** There was a severe earthquake last night.

**gekiyaku** powerful medicine; violent poison.

**gekizoo** sudden increase.

**gekkan** monthly publication; **gekkan zasshi** monthly magazine.

**gekkei** menstruation.

**gekken** fencing (Japanese style).

**GEKKOO** moonlight; moonbeams.

**GEKKYUU** monthly salary; **gekkyuu bi** payday; **gekkyuu bukuro** pay envelope; **gekkyuu tori** a salaried man.

**gen** words; speech; **gen o sayuu ni takushite** on one pretext or another.

**gen-** prefix denoting: original; primary; fundamental; **genbun** original text; **genga** original picture.

**genan** manservant.

**genba** the actual place, scene; **genba de** on the spot.

**genbaku** atomic bomb.

**genbatsu** severe punishment.

**GENDAI** present time; modern times; **gendaiteki na** modern; **gendaika suru** to modernize.

**gengai** unexpressed; between the lines; **gengai no imi o toru** to read between the lines.

**gengakki** stringed instrument.

**gengaku** reduction, discount; **gengaku suru** to reduce, cut down, curtail.

**GENGO** language, speech; words; **gengo ni zessuru** to be unspeakable; to be beyond description.

**gen'in** cause; origin; **-ni gen'in suru** to be due to, attributable to; **gen'in fumei** unaccountable; unknown.

**genjitsu** reality, actuality; **genjitsu no** real, actual; **genjitsu bakuro** disillusionment; **genjitsu shugi** realism.

**genjoo** status quo, existing state of things; **genjoo iji** maintenance of the status quo.

**genjuu** severity, strictness; **genjuu na** severe, strict; **genjuu ni** severely.

**genkai** limit, boundary.

**genkaku** strictness; sternness; **genkaku na** strict; rigorous; stern; **genkaku ni** rigorously.

**GENKAN, genkanguchi** entrance hall.

**GENKI** spirits; courage; vigor; energy; **genki no yoi** cheerful; healthy; **genki yoku** in high spirits; cheerfully; **genki no nai** in poor (low) spirits; **genki o dasu** to brace up; **genki o tsukeru** to encourage; to cheer up; **genki na** healthy, spirited.

**GENKIN** cash; **genkin de kau** to buy for cash; **genkin barai** cash payment; **genkin gakari** cashier; **genkin torihiki** cash transaction.

**genkin** strict prohibition, ban; **genkin suru** to ban.

**genko** fist; **genko o katameru** to clench a fist.

**genkoku** plaintiff; accuser.

**genkoo** words and deeds; **genkooroku** memoirs; **genkoo itchi suru** to live up to one's words.

**genkoo** manuscript; draft; **genkoo yooshi** copy paper; writing pad.

**genkoohan** flagrant offense. **Genkoohan de kare wa taihosareta.** He was caught red-handed.

**genmai** unpolished rice, unhulled rice (eaten for high nutritive value).

**genmei** declaration, statement; announcement; **genmei suru** to make a statement.

**genmetsu** disillusionment.

**genmitsu** strictness; precision; **genmitsu na** strict; precise; exact; **genmitsu ni** strictly;

closely; **genmitsu ni ieba** strictly speaking.

**gen ni** actually; before one's eyes. **Watakushi wa gen ni sore o mita no desu.** I saw it with my own eyes.

**genpin** goods; thing.

**genri** See **gensoku.**

**genryoo** raw materials.

**gensanchi** country of origin; habitat; home.

**genshi** atom; beginning; origin; **genshi no** atomic; **genshi bakudan** atomic bomb; **genshiro** nuclear reactor; **genshiryoku** nuclear energy.

**gensho** original (work); **Eigo no gensho de yomu** to read in the original English.

**genshoku** primary color(s).

**genshoo** decrease; **genshoo suru** to decrease, diminish.

**genshoo** phenomenon.

**genshu** strict observance; **genshu suru** to observe strictly; **jikan o genshuu suru** to be punctual.

**genshuku** gravity, solemnity; **genshuku na** solemn; grave.

**genshutsu** appearance; disclosure; **genshutsu suru** to appear; to be disclosed.

**genso** element (chem.).

**gensoku, genri** principle; fundamental law; **gensoku to shite** as a general rule.

**genson** no existing, in existence.

**gentoo** lantern slide.

**GENZAI** (*n., adv.*) present time; at present; actually; at the present moment.

**genzei** tax reduction.

**genzoo** (*n.*) developing; **genzoo suru** to develop (photography).

**geppoo** monthly salary.

**geppu** monthly installment; **geppu de** by monthly payments.

**geragera warau** to cackle; to give a horselaugh.

**geraku** fall; decline; depreciation; **geraku suru** to fall; decline; depreciate.

**geri** diarrhea.

**gesha suru** to dismount.

**GESHUKU** (*n.*) lodging; boarding; lodging house; **geshuku suru** to lodge; to board; **geshukunin** lodger; **geshukuya** lodging house; **geshukuryoo** lodging charge (rate).

**geshunin** murderer; criminal.

**gessha** monthly fee; tuition fee.

**gesui** sewer; drain; sewage.

**geta** wooden clogs; **geta o haku** to put on clogs; **geta o nugu** to take off clogs; **getaya** clog shop.

**getsugaku** monthly sum (amount).

**getsumatsu** end of a month; **getsumatsu kanjoo** end-of-the month payment.

**GETSUYOOBI** Monday.

**gezai** laxative.

**gichoo** chairperson.

**gidai** subject for discussion.

**gidayuu** ballad drama.

**gihitsu** forgery (handwriting or picture).

**giin** member of assembly or Diet.

**giji** proceedings.

**gijoo** assembly hall; chamber; conference site.

**GIJUTSU** art; useful art; technique; skill; **sentan gijutsu** advanced technology; **gijutsujoo no** technical.

**gikai** Diet; assembly.

**gikan** chief engineer; technical offical.

**gikei** older brother-in-law.

**giketsu** decision, resolution.

**gikochinai** stiff-mannered; awkward.

**gikoo** artistic excellence; technical skill.

**gikyoku** drama; **gikyoku sakusha** dramatist, playwright. (See also **geki**.)

**gikyoodai** brother-in-law; sister-in-law.

**gimei** assumed name, false name.

**GIMON** question; doubt; **gimonfu** question mark.

**gimu** duty; obligation; **gimu o hatasu** to perform one's duty.

**GIN** silver, **gin no** silvered; silver; **gin iro no** silvery; **gingami** silver paper; tin foil; **ginka** silver coin; **ginkonshiki** silver wedding anniversary; **genmekki no** *(adj.)* silver-plated; **ginpai** silver medal; silver cup.

**GINKOO** bank; **ginkooka** banker; **ginkoo'in** bank employee; **ginkoo yokin** bank deposit; **ginkoo yokin kooza** bank account; **ginkoo yokin zandaka** bank balance; **ginkoo kawase tegata** bank exchange; **ginkoo kanjoo hookoku sho** bank statement.

**ginmi** examination, trial.

**ginnan** fruit of the gingko; gingko nut.

**ginoo** ability, capacity; skill; **ginoo no aru** able; skillful; talented.

**giragira** glittering; dazzling; **giragira suru** to glitter, to dazzle; to glare.

**giri** obligation; duty; honor; courtesy; **giri no** adoptive; step-; -in-law; **giri no kyoodai** brother-in-law, sister-in-law; **giri o kaku** to fail to do one's duty; **girigatai** having a high sense of duty.

**Girisha** Greece; **Girishajin** *(n.)* Greek; **Girishago** Greek language.

**giron** argument; discussion; debate; dispute; **giron suru** to argue, etc.; **gironzuki na** argumentative.

**giryoo** ability; talent, skill; **giryoo no aru** talented.

**gisei** sacrifice; victim; scapegoat.

**gishi** engineer; technical expert; **gishi choo** chief engineer.

**gishiki** ceremony, rite; **gishiki no** *(adj.)* ritual.

**gishu** artificial arm.

**gisoku** artificial leg.

**gisshiri** closely; compactly; **gisshiri tsumekomu** to pack, jam, cram.

**gitaa** guitar.

**gitei** younger brother-in-law.

**gizagiza** notches.

**gizen** hypocrisy; **gizensha** hypocrite; **gizenteki** hypocritical.

**gizoo** forgery. (See also **gihitsu**.)

**GO** word, term; language; **Eigo** (an) English word; English language; **go o tsuyomete iu** to speak emphatically; **gobi** ending (of a word); end (of a sentence); **gobi henka** inflection.

**GO** five; **DAIGO** fifth; **GOJUU** fifty; **GOJI** five o'clock; **gojuu no too** five-story pagoda.

**go** game resembling checkers; **go o utsu** to play "go"; **goban** "go" board; checkerboard; **goban gata no** checkered; **goishi** pieces used in playing "go."

**-go** suffix denoting: after; **sonogo** after that; since then; **sensoogo** postwar.

**gobugari** short haircut, crew cut.

**gobugobu** equally well matched; equal; **gobugobu ni naru** to end in a draw (tie); **gobugobu no tachiba de** on equal terms.

**GOBUSATA SURU** to neglect to write or call. **Gobusata itashimashita.** I am sorry I didn't write you. I am sorry I didn't call you earlier.

**gochagocha no** mixed up, confused; **gochagocha suru** to mix up, jumble; **gochagocha ni naru** to be confused.

**GOCHISOO** treat; feast. **Kyoo wa watashi ga gochisoo shimashoo.** Let me treat you to dinner today. Be my guest at dinner today. **Gochisoosama.** Thanks for the fine dinner.

**gochoo** tone of voice; accent.

**goei** guard; escort; **goei suru** to guard; to escort.

**gofuku** kimono fabric; **gofukuya** fabric dealer.

**gogaku** study of languages, linguistics.

**GOGATSU** May.

**GOGO** afternoon; **gogo niji** two p.m.

**GOHAN** boiled rice; meal; **gohan o taberu** to eat a meal; **gohan o taku** to cook rice.

**gohoo** false report.

**gojitsu** some other day; in the future.

**gojuunensai** semi-centennial; jubilee.

**gojuuon** Japanese syllabary.

**gokai** misunderstanding; **gokai suru** to misunderstand; to take amiss.

**goke** widow; widowhood.

**goki** tone; manner of speaking; **goki surudoku** sharply, in a sharp tone; **goki o tsuyomete hanasu** to speak emphatically.

**gokoo** halo; glory.

**GOKU** very; extremely; **goku mezurashii** extremely rare; **goku chiisai** very small.

**gokui** secret; secret principles.

**gokuin** stamp; hallmark.

**gokujoo** *(n.)* first-rate; best quality; **gokujoo no** *(adj.)* best; first-rate; first-class.

**gokuraku** paradise; Eden.

**goma** sesame seed; **goma o suru** to grind sesame seed; to flatter; to fawn upon; **gomaabura** sesame oil.

**gomakashi** trickery; hocus-pocus; deception; **gomakashi no** fraudulent; sham; **gomakasu** to deceive; to cheat; to cover up; to tamper with.

**GOMEN** pardon, permission; **GOMEN NASAI.** Pardon me. Excuse me. **Chotto gomen kudasai.** Excuse me a minute.

**GOMI** rubbish, refuse; dirt; **gomitori** dustpan; **gomibako** garbage (rubbish) can.

**GOMU** gum; rubber; **gomubando** rubber band; **gomuhimo** elastic tape; **gomumari** rubber ball; **gomunori** mucilage; **gomuwa** rubber tire.

**gongo doodan** unspeakable; outrageous; absurd.

**goo** district. **Goo ni itte wa goo ni shitagae.** When in Rome, do as the Romans do.

**goo** fate; **goo no fukai** sinful; **goo o niyasu** to be greatly aggravated.

**-goo** number; issue; **dai san goo** issue no. 3; **sono zasshi no Gogatsugoo** the May issue of the magazine.

**goodatsu** seizure; extortion; plunder; **goodatsu suru** to plunder.

**goodoo** combination; union; **goodoo suru** to amalgamate; to incorporate; **goodoo no** united; incorporated.

**googai** "extra"; special issue of a newspaper.

**gooi** agreement; mutual understanding; **gooi de** by mutual agreement.

**goojoo** obstinacy, stubbornness; **goojoo na** stubborn, obstinate; **goojoo o haru** to be obstinate.

**gookaban** deluxe edition.

**gookaku** eligibility; success; **gookaku suru** to be eligible for; to pass; to be successful in.

**gookan** rape; assault.

**gookasen** luxury liner.

**GOOKEI** sum, total, total amount; **gookei suru** to sum up; **gookei . . . ni naru** to amount to . . . in all; to add up to.

**gooketsu** hero; great man.

**gookin** metallic compound; alloy.

**gooman** haughtiness, arrogance; **gooman na** haughty, arrogant.

**goomon** torture; **goomon ni kakeru** to torture.

**goorei** command, order; **goorei suru** to give a command or order.

**gooriki** great strength; mountain guide.

**gooru** goal.

**goosha** luxury; magnificence; **goosha na** luxurious; magnificent; **goosha o kiwameru** to live in magnificent style.

**gootan** fearlessness; boldness; **gootan na** fearless; daring; bold.

**gootoo** burglar, thief.

**goou** heavy rain.

**gooyoku** avarice, greed.

**gooyuu** extravagant pleasures; spree; **gooyuu suru** to go on a spree.

**goozen** haughtily, arrogantly; proudly.

**goraku** pleasure; pastime; amusement; recreation; **gorakuyoo no** for amusement; **gorakushitsu** recreation room.

**goran** *(n.)* seeing, viewing (used only in reference to the second or third person); **goran ni ireru** to present something for inspection. **Goran kudasai.** Please take a look. **Goran no toori.** As you see. **Chotto kore o goran nasai.** Just look at this. **Maa kangaete goran nasai.** Think it over, anyway.

**gorira** gorilla.

**-GORO** suffix denoting: about (in point of time); around; toward; **nijigoro** about two o'clock; **yoakegoro** toward dawn.

**goro** sound; **goro ga ii** euphonic.

**goro** grounder (in baseball).

**gorogoro** rumbling; rolling; gurgling; lying idle; **gorogoro korobu** to roll about; **me ga gorogoro suru** to have a sore (an irritated) eye. **Kare wa mainichi gorogoro shite iru.** He idles away his time every day. **Neko ga nodo o gorogoro narasu.** The cat purrs.

**gorufu** golf; **gorufu o suru** to play golf; **gorufujoo** gold links.

**gosai** second wife; **gosai o mukaeru** (for a man) to marry again.

**gosan** miscalculation; **gosan suru** to miscalculate.

**goshin suru** to diagnose wrongly.

**Gosho** Imperial Palace.

**goshoo daiji ni** with the greatest possible care; most carefully; **goshoo daijin ni suru** to take care of; **goshoo daiji ni tsutomeru** to serve most faithfully.

**gosoo** escort; convoy; **gosoo suru** to escort, to accompany.

**gotagota** trouble; difficulties; confusion; disorder; **gotagota suru** to be in confusion; to be disordered. **Gotagota ga okorikakete iru.** Trouble is brewing.

**gotamaze** jumble; muddle.

**gotatsuku** to quarrel; to be agitated; to be in disorder.

**gotcha** in confusion.

**-GOTO NI** every; every time; at intervals of; **ni mairu goto ni** every two miles; **hi goto ni** every day; **mikka goto ni** every three days.

**gotsugotsu** rough; rugged; harsh; stiff; **gotsugotsu iu** to speak harshly; **gotsugotsu shite iru** to be stiff, rough.

**goza** mat; matting; **goza o shiku** to spread a mat (on the floor).

**GOZAIMASU** there is, there are *(humble)*.

**GOZEN** forenoon; **gozen ni** in the morning.

**guai** condition; fitness; manner; working order; **guai ga warui** to feel indisposed, be unwell; to be out of order. **Kono hikidashi wa guai ga warui.** This drawer does not work smoothly. **Banji guai yoku itta.** Everything went very well.

**guchi** idle complaints; **guchi o kobosu** to grumble; complain; **guchippoi** grumbling; complaining.

**-gumi** company, firm; gang; **Fujita gumi** Fujita Company.

**gun** district; county.

**gun** crowd; **gun o nasu** to crowd; to flock; **gun o nuku** to be far above the crowd (to distinguish oneself); **gunshuu** crowd of people, multitude.

**gun** *(n.)* military; **gunbi** arms; **gunbi shukushoo** disarmament; **guntai** armed forces.

**guntoo** archipelago, group of islands.

**gunyagunya** flabby; limp.

**guragura suru** to be shaky; to totter, waver.

**-GURAI** = **kurai** suffix denoting: about; almost; some; something like; or so. **Ano hito wa sanjuu-gurai deshoo.** She must be about 30 years old.

**guramu** gram.

**guratsuku** to totter; to be shaky.

**guretsu na** stupid; ridiculous; absurd; silly.

**guron** foolish argument; absurd opinion.

**guru** conspiracy, collusion; accomplice, conspirator; **guru ni naru** to conspire with, plot together; **-to guru ni natte** in collusion with (someone).

**GURUGURU** round and round; **guruguru mawaru** to whirl; spin round and round.

**gururi** circumference; surroundings; **gururi to** round.

**-gurushii** suffix denoting: to be unpleasant to; repulsive to; **negurushii** to be sleepless; to sleep badly.

**guruupu** group.

**gutto** considerably; firmly; with great strength; **gutto nomu** to gulp down; **gutto fueru** to increase markedly.

**guusuu** even number; **guusuu no** even-numbered.

**GUUZEN** by chance; accidentally; **guuzen no** accidental; unexpected; casual; **guuzen no dekigoto** an accident; **guuzen desu** to come across, meet by chance.

**guuzoo** image, idol, statue.

**guzu** imbecile; weak-minded person.

**guzuguzu** lazily; idly; tardily; **guzuguzu suru** to hesitate; to loiter; **guzuguzu iu** to complain; to murmur.

**guzuru** to be peevish; to be fretful.

**gyakkoo** retrogression; **gyakkoo suru** to move back; to run counter to; to retrogress.

**gyaku** opposite, contrary, reverse, **gyaku ni** contrarily, conversely; **gyaku ni suru** to reverse; to invert; **gyaku ni mawasu** to turn (something) the other way; **gyakumodori** retrogression; reversal; **gyakumodori suru** to go (turn) backward; to have a relapse; to lapse into; **gyakuten** sudden change; reversal; **gyakuten suru** to retrogress.

**gyakusatsu** slaughter; massacre.

**gyakutai** ill-treatment; **gyakutai suru** to ill-treat.

**gyangu** gang.

**gyogyoo** fishery; fishing industry.

**gyokuro** sweet green tea (the best and most expensive type).

**gyoo** line; verse.

**gyoogi** behavior; manners; **gyoogi no yoi** well behaved; well mannered; **gyoogi no warui** poorly behaved; **gyoogi sahoo** etiquette.

**gyooja** devotee; pilgrim; ascetic.

**gyooji** observances; functions; proceedings.

**gyooji** referee (of Japanese wrestling, sumoo).

**gyoojoo** behavior, conduct.

**gyooketsu** coagulation, congealing.

**gyoomu** business; affairs; duties.

**gyooretsu** procession, parade; **gyooretsu o nashite** in procession.

**gyoosei** administration; **gyooseikan** administrator.

**gyooshoo** peddling; peddler.

**gyooten suru** to be surprised, amazed, astounded.

**gyoozui** *(n.)* taking a shower (Japanese style: pouring water over the body from a small tub); bathing; **gyoozui suru** to take a Japanese-style shower.

**gyosen** fishing boat.

**gyoson** fishing village.

**gyotto suru** to be startled, alarmed.

**gyuuba** oxen and horses; horses and cattle.

**GYUUNIKU** beef; **gyuunikuya** butcher shop.

**GYUUNYUU** cow's milk; **gyuunyuu ya** milkman; **gyuunyuu bin** milk bottle.

**gyuutto** hard; violently; firmly; **gyuutto osu** to push violently (with force); **gyuutto hiku** to pull with a jerk.

# H

**HA** tooth; cog; **ha no aru** toothed; cogged; **ha no nai** toothless; blunt; **ha no tsuita** sharp-edged; **ha ga uku** to set the teeth on edge; **ha o migaku** to brush the teeth; **ha ga itamu** to have a toothache.

**ha** leaf (of a plant).

**haamonika** harmonica.

**haapu** harp.

**haato** heart (in a card game).

**HABA** width, breadth; **haba ga kiku** to have great influence over; **haba o kikasu** to exert great influence; **haba go inchi aru** five inches wide.

**habakiki** influential person.

**habataki suru** to flutter, flap wings.

**habikoru** to spread; to grow thick; to become powerful.

**habuku** to curtail; to save; to leave out; **jikan o habuku** to save time; **hiyoo o habuku** to cut expenses.

**HABURASHI** toothbrush.

**haburi** influence; power; **haburi ga yoi** to be influential.

**habutae** glossy silk.

**HACHI** eight; **dai hachi** eighth.

**HACHI** bowl, basin; pot.

**hachi** bee; **hachi no su** beehive; **hachimitsu** honey.

**hachiawase suru** to be brought face to face (bump heads together).

**HACHIGATSU** August.

**HACHIJUU** eighty; **dai hachijuu** eightieth.

**hachimaki** headband; hand towel tied around the head.

**hachiue** potted plant.

**hada** skin; body; disposition; character; **shiroi hada** fair skin; **hada ga au** to get on well (with).

**HADAGI** underwear.

**hadaka** nakedness, nudity; **hadaka no** naked, nude, bare; **hadaka ni naru** to strip off one's clothes.

**hadashi** bare feet; **hadashi de aruku** to walk barefoot; **kurooto hadashi da** to put even a professional to shame.

**hadazawari** touch. **Biroodo wa hadazawari ga yoi.** Velvet feels soft [is agreeable to touch].

**HADE** gaiety; flashiness; display; **hade na** gay; bright; flashy; **hade na iro** bright (gay) color; **hade zuki de aru** to be fond of display.

**HAE** fly.

**haegiwa** hairline.

**haeru** to grow; to sprout; to spring up. **Hana no me ga haeta.** The flower seeds sprouted.

**haetataki** flyswatter.

**haetori** flytrap.

**HAGAKI** postcard; **hagaki o dasu** to drop (send) a card.

**hagami suru** to gnash one's teeth.

**hagane** steel.

**hagasu** to strip; to tear off.

**hagayui** to feel impatient; to feel irritated. **Kare no guzuguzu shite iru no ga hagayukatta.** I was irritated by his dawdling.

**hage** bald spot; bald head; **hageatama** bald head.

**hagemasu** to encourage; to cheer up; to stimulate.

**hagemi** stimulation; encouragement; diligence; **hagemi ga tsuku** to be stimulated; to be encouraged; **hagemi o tsukeru** to stimulate; to encourage.

**HAGEMU** to endeavor; to exert onself; to be diligent.

**hageru** to grow bald; to come off; to fade; **iro no hageta** discolored; faded.

**hageshii** violent, severe, intense; furious; **hageshiku** violently; **hageshii seishitsu** violent nature (referring to a person); **hageshii atsusa** intensely hot weather.

**hagishiri suru** to grit one's teeth.

**hagitoru** to strip off; to deprive; to tear off.

**hagu** to strip; to strip off clothes; **ki no kawa o hagu** to strip the bark off a tree.

**haguki** gums (of the mouth).

**hagureru** to stray; to be separated from (one's companions).

**haguruma** cog, gear (of a wheel); toothed wheel.

**HAHA, HAHAOYA** mother, motherhood; **haha rashii** motherly; maternal; **Haha no hi** Mother's Day; **hahakata** maternal (side); **hahakata no shinseki** maternal relative.

**HAI** yes; yes, sir.

**hai** lungs; **haibyoo** consumption; **haigan** lung cancer; **haien** pneumonia.

**hai** ashes; cinder; **hai ni naru** to be reduced to ashes; lungs.

**haiagaru** to creep (crawl) up; to climb up.

**haichi** arrangement; **haichi suru** to dispose; to arrange; to station.

**haidasu** to crawl out, creep out.

**haigamai** rice with embryo buds.

**haigo** rear; back (of a person); **-no haigo ni** at the rear of; behind. **Kare no haigo ni shisanka ga hikaete iru.** He has a wealthy supporter behind him.

**haigoo** harmony; combination; arrangement; **haigoo suru** to harmonize; to combine; to match. **Iro no haigoo ga warui.** These colors do not match.

**haigyoo** to close up shop; to give up one's practice; to quit business.

**haihiiru** high heel.

**haiiro** ash-gray (color).

**haikan** discontinuance of publication; **haikan suru** to discontinue publication.

**haikara na** stylish; foppish; fashionable. **Haikara na yoofuku o kite imashita.** He was wearing a high-styled suit.

**haikei** background; background scenery.

**haikei** Dear Sir or Madam (as used in a formal letter).

**HAIKEN** looking at; inspection *(humble);* **haiken suru** to see; to look at. **Chotto haiken.** Please let me see it. **Haiken shimashita.** I saw it.

**haikingu** hiking.

**haikomu** to crawl (creep) in.

**haiku** seventeen-syllable poem.

**haikyuu** distribution; supply; **haikyuu suru** to distribute; supply.

**hainichi** anti-Japanese.

**hairetsu** arrangement; distribution; **hairetsu suru** to arrange in order.

**hairikomu** to get in; to force one's way in.

**HAIRU** to enter; to go in; to break into; to join; to hold; to accommodate; **kurabu ni hairu** to join a club; **oyu ni hairu** to take a bath. **O hairi.** Come in! Walk in! **Hi ga nishi ni hairu.** The sun sets in the west.

**haiseki** expulsion; exclusion; **haiseki suru** to exclude; to ostracize.

**HAISHA** dentist.

**haishaku suru** to borrow *(humble).* **Haishaku itashimasu.** I'll borrow it.

**haishi** abolition; **haishi suru** to abolish, discontinue.

**haishutsu suru** to discharge; to exhaust; **haishutsuguchi** outlet; issue; **haishutsukan** exhaust pipe.

**haisui** drainage; sewerage; supply of water; **haisui suru** to drain; to pump out.

**HAITATSU** delivery; distribution; **haitatsu suru** to deliver; to distribute; **haitatsu ryoo** delivery charge; **haitatsunin** distributor; carrier; **haitatsusaki** receiver; destination (of a delivery).

**haitoo** allotment; dividend; **haitoo suru** to pay a dividend; to allot to; **haitookin** dividend.

**haiyuu** actor; actress.

**haizara** ashtray.

**haji** shame; disgrace; dishonor; **haji o kaku** to be put to shame; **haji o kakaseru** to put to shame; **haji shirazu** without a sense of shame; shameless.

**hajikeru** to split open; to pop.

**hajiku** to flip; to snap; to repeal; to repel; **yubi o hajiku** to snap one's fingers.

**HAJIMARU** to begin, commence; to be opened; to originate from.

**HAJIME** commencement, beginning; outset; origin; **hajime no** first; original; initial; **hajime kara owari made** from beginning to end; **hajime wa** at first.

**HAJIMERU** to begin; commence; to open; **shoobai o hajimeru** to open a business; **benkyoo o hajimeru** to begin studying.

**HAJIMETE** first; for the first time; for once. **Hajimete ome ni kakarimasu.** How do you do. Glad to meet you [I meet you for the first time]. **Hajimete ikimashita.** I went there for the first time.

**hajiru** to be ashamed of.

**haka** grave, tomb; **hakaba** graveyard, cemetery.

**hakadoru** to progress rapidly; to make good progress.

**hakai** destruction; demolition; **hakai suru** to destroy, demolish, wreck; **hakaiteki** destructive; **hakairyoku** destructive power.

**hakaku no** exceptional; unprecedented; special.

**hakama** loose Japanese trousers; pleated skirt.

**hakanai** transient, passing; uncertain; vain; hopeless; **hakanai saigo o togeru** to meet with an untimely death; **hakanai nozomi** vain hope.

**hakarai** management; arrangement; disposal; **Kono hen wa anata no ohakarai ni omakaseshimasu.** I'll leave the matter to your discretion.

**hakarau** to manage; to arrange; to take measures; **Sore ni tsuite wa anata ga yoi yoo ni hakaratte ii desu.** You can do about it as you think best.

**HAKARAZU MO** unexpectedly; by chance.

**hakari** balance, scales; **hakari ni kakeru** to weigh on a scale.

**hakarigoto** stratagem, ruse; artifice; plan, scheme; **hakarigoto ni ochiru** to fall for a trick; **hakarigoto o megurasu** to devise a stratagem; to form plans.

**HAKARU** to measure; to weigh; to survey; to sound; to judge (a person's mind); **mekata o hakaru** to check a weight; **nagasa o hakaru** to measure a length. **Ano hito no kimochi o hakaru koto wa muzukashii.** It is hard to understand his mind.

**hakase** See **hakushi.**

**hake** drainage; flow; sale; demand; **hake ga yoi** to flow freely; to sell well.

**hake** brush.

**haken** dispatch; **haken suru** to dispatch, send; **hakengun** expeditionary force.

**hakeru** to drain off; to sell.

**haki** breach; annulment; **haki suru** to break and throw away; to annul.

**hakichigaeru** to wear someone else's shoes by mistake; to mistake; to misunderstand.

**hakidame** rubbish heap.

**hakidasu** to spit out; to emit; to breathe out.

**hakidasu** to sweep out.

**hakike** nausea; **hakike o moyoosu** to feel sick; to be nauseous.

**HAKIMONO** footgear; clogs.

**hakiyoseru** to sweep up, gather up with a broom.

**hakka** peppermint; mint.

**hakka** firing; ignition; **hakka suru** to catch fire, ignite.

**hakken** discovery; **hakken suru** to discover; **hakkensha** discover.

**hakkin** platinum.

**HAKKIRI** clearly; distinctly; positively; definitely; exactly; **hakkiri shita** clear, distinct, positive; **hakkiri shita koe** clear voice; **hakkiri shita henji** definite answer. **Hakkiri zonjimasen.** I don't know exactly.

**hakkoo** publication; issue; **hakkoo suru** to publish; to issue.

**hakkoo** fermentation; **hakkoo suru** to ferment.

**hakkotsu** skeleton; bleached bones.

**hakkutsu** excavation; **hakkutsu suru** to excavate.

**hakkyuu** low (small) salary.

**HAKO** box; case; chest. **Hako ni irete kudasai.** Please put it in the box.

**hakobi** progress; arrangement; **ashi no hakobi** walking pace.

**HAKOBU** to carry, convey, transport; to go on; to progress; **nimotsu o hakobu** to carry the baggage; **shibashiba ashi o hakobu** to make frequent calls. **Subete umaku hakobimashita.** Everything went all right. Everything turned out all right.

**hakoniwa** miniature garden.

**hakozume** packed in a box; boxed; **hakozume ni suru** to pack in a box.

**HAKU** to put on (from waist down; clogs, sandals, shoes, socks, pants, skirts, etc.); **kutsu o haku** to put on shoes.

**haku** to sweep; **heya o haku** to sweep the room.

**hakubutsukan** museum.

**hakuchi** idiot; imbecile.

**hakuchoo** swan.

**hakuchuu** broad daylight.

**hakugai** persecution; **hakugai suru** to persecute.

**hakugaku** erudition, learning; **hakugaku no** erudite; learned.

**hakuhatsu** white hair; gray hair; **hakuhatsu no roojin** white-haired old person.

**hakujaku** feebleness, weakness; **hakujaku na** feeble, weak; fragile; **seishin hakujaku jidoo** mentally handicapped child.

**hakujin** white person; white race (Occidental).

**hakujoo** confession; **hakujoo suru** to confess, make a clean breast of.

**hakujoo** coldheartedness; **hakujoo na** unfeeling, heartless. **Ano hito wa hakujoo na hito desu.** She is a coldhearted woman.

**hakumai** hulled (cleaned) rice.

**hakumei** misfortune; sad fate; **hakumei na** unfortunate; ill-fated.

**hakurai** imported; **hakuraihin** imported merchandise. **Hakuraihin wa takai kara kaemasen.** I can't buy imported goods because they are expensive.

**hakurankai** exposition; fair; **hakurankaijoo** fair grounds.

**hakushi, hakase** doctor; doctorate degree, Ph.D.; **hakushigoo** doctorate degree; **Yamada Hakushi** Dr. Yamada.

**hakushi** blank sheet of paper; white paper; clean slate.

**hakushiki** wide knowledge, erudition.

**hakushu** applause; **hakushu suru** to clap hands, applaud; to cheer; **hakushu kassai** applause and cheers.

**hakyuu** propagation, spread; **hakyuu suru** to extend, spread, propagate; to influence; to effect; **zenkoku ni hakyuu suru** to extend over the whole country.

**hama** seashore, beach; **hama zutai ni** along the beach; **hamabe** seashore; beach.

**hamaguri** clam.

**hamaki** cigar.

**hamarikomu** to fall (sink) into; to become infatuated with; to be addicted to; **onna ni hamarikomu** to be infatuated with a woman.

**hamaru** to be fixed; to fit; to fall into.

**hameru** to put in, insert; to fix in; to set; to have (wear) on (one's finger or hand).

**hametsu** ruin, destruction; **hametsu suru** to be ruined, destroyed.

**hamidasu** to protrude, stick out.

**HAMIGAKI** toothpaste.

**hamon suru** to excommunicate; to expel.

**hamono** edged tool; cutlery.

**HAMU** ham; **hamu sarada** ham salad.

**HAN** stamp; personal seal (used in place of a signature); **han o osu** to stamp; to seal; **han de oshita yoo na** stereotyped, cut-and-dried.

**HAN-** prefix denoting: half; **hantoshi** half a year; **hantsuki** half a month.

**han** edition; **han o kasaneru** to go through many editions; **shohan** first edition.

**han-** prefix denoting: opposition; **hankyoo** anti-communism.

**HANA** flower, blossom; essence, spirit; belle; **hana no** floral; **hana o kiru** to cut flowers; **hana o ikeru** to arrange flowers; **hanabasami** flower scissors; pruning shears; **hanaike** flower vase; **hanataba** bunch of flowers, bouquet; **hanawa** wreath, garland; **hanaya** florist, flower shop; **hanayaka na** flowery; showy; gay. **Wakai uchi ga hana.** Youth is the springtime of life. **Giron ni hana ga saite kita.** The discussion is becoming heated.

**HANA** nose, nasal mucus; **hana o susuru** to sniff; **hana o kamu** to blow one's nose; **hana o tarasu** to have a runny nose; **hana ga kiku** to have a good sense of smell; **hana ni kakeru** to be vain; **hana o akasu** to take the conceit out of someone; **hana o takaku suru** to be proud; **hanasaki ni** under one's very nose; **hanagoe** nasal sound; twang; **hanaiki** *(n.)* breathing through the nose; snoring; **hanaiki ga arai** to be arrogant; to swagger; **hito no hanaiki o ukagau** to curry favor with someone; **hanaji** nosebleed; **hanaji o dasu** to have a nosebleed; **hanakaze** head cold. **Hanakaze o hiita.** I have a cold in the head. **hanabashira, hanappashira, hanasuji** bridge of the nose. **Hanabashira ga tsuyoi desu.** He is haughty.

**hanabanashii** brilliant; splendid; glorious; **hanabanashiku** brilliantly; splendidly.

**hanabi** fireworks display; **hanabi o ageru** to set off fireworks.

**hanagata** floral pattern; star; **eiga no hanagata yakusha** screen star; **hanagata senshu** star player.

**hanagumori** springtime cloudy weather.

**hanahadashii** excessive, extreme, exceeding.

**hanami** *(n.)* flower-viewing; **hanami ni iku** to visit places well known for their flower displays (such as cherry blossoms).

**hanamuko** bridegroom.

**hanao** clog thong; straps.

**hanare** detached room; **hanareya** detached house; **hanarezashiki** detached guest room.

**hanarebanare** separation; **hanarebanare ni** separately, apart from each other; **hanarebanare ni naru** to become separated.

**HANARERU** to separate; part from; to come off; **hanareta** separated, detached, isolated, distant, far off; **hanareta tokoro kara miru** to watch from a distance; **hanareta tochi** distant place; **hanarete iru** be distant, live apart from. **Ima shoku o hanarete iru.** He is now out of work.

**HANASHI** talk, conversation, chat; gossip, story; **hanashi joozu** good speaker; **hanashibeta** poor speaker; **hanashi aite** companion to talk with; **hanashi o suru** to talk, chat; **hanashiburi** way (manner) of speaking; **hanashichuu** busy signal (telephone); **hanashiai** conference, consultation; **hanashiau** to talk with, consult with; **hanashigoe** voices (in conversation); **hanashi no tane** topic for conversation; **hanashi ga tsuku** to arrive at an understanding; **hanashi o soraseru** to change the subject; **hanashika** professional storyteller; **hanashikomu** to chat for hours; **hanashizuki na** talkative.

**HANASU** to speak, talk, converse; to tell, state. **Eigo de hanashite kudasai.** Please speak English. **Anata ni hanashitai koto ga aru.** I have something I'd like to tell you.

**hanasu** to separate, to part, to set free; **te o hanasu** to loosen one's hold, to let go of someone's hand.

**hanauta** humming; **hanauta o utau** to hum a song or tune.

**hanayome** bride.

**hanazakari** full bloom.

**hanazono** flower garden.

**hanbai** sale; **hanbai suru** to sell, deal in; **hanbainin** dealer, **hanbaigakari** salesman, saleswoman; **hanbaiten** distributor.

**HANBUN** half; **hanbun ni suru** to divide into halves.

**handan** judgment, interpretation.

**handobaggu** handbag.

**handon** half-holiday.

**handoo** reaction; **handoo suru** to react upon; **handooteki** reactionary.

**handoru** handle; steering wheel.

**hane** feather; plumage; wing; shuttlecock; **hane buton** feather quilt.

**hane** *(n.)* splashes of mud, close; **hane ga agatte iru** to be splashed with mud; **Shibai no hane wa juuji desu.** The theater closes at ten.

**hanekaeru** to rebound, spring back.

**hanemawaru** to bounce about, leap about; to romp.

**han'enkei** semicircle; **han'enkei no** semicircular.

**haneru** to leap, spring, bound; to splash, splatter. **Sooba ga haneta.** Prices jumped. **Abura ga hanete yakedo o shita.** The cooking oil splashed and I got burnt.

**haneru** to reject, to throw out, to exclude.

**hanetsukeru** to refuse; to reject; to repel.

**hangaku** half (amount); half the sum (price, fare, etc.); **hangaku de** at half-price, half-fare. **Kodomo no jooshachin wa hangaku desu.** Children can travel for half-price. **Kodomo no nyuujoo ryoo wa hangaku desu.** Children are admitted for half-price.

**hangen** reduction by half; **hangen suru** to reduce by half.

**han'i** scope, sphere; limit, bounds.

**hanikamu** to be shy, bashful.

**hanji** judge.

**HANJIKAN** half an hour.

**hanjoo** good business; prosperity; **hanjoo suru** to prosper, flourish, do a good business.

**hanjuku** half-cooked; soft-boiled; half-ripe; **hanjuku no tamago** soft-boiled egg.

**HANKACHI** handkerchief.

**hankan** antipathy, ill-feeling; **hankan o idaku** to provoke ill-feeling.

**hankechi** See **HANKACHI.**

**hankei** radius.

**hanko** seal.

**hankoo** resistance, opposition; defiance; **hankooteki** defiant, rebellious.

**hankyoo** echo; response; anti-communism; **hankyoo suru** to echo, resound.

**hankyuu** half-holiday.

**hanmen** profile, silhouette; one side; **hanmen no shinri** half truth; **kao no hanmen** one side of the face; **hanmenzoo** profile.

**hanmoku** hostility, antagonism.

**hanmon** anguish; agony; mortification; **hanmon suru** to be in agony; to feel anguish; to be mortified.

**hanne** half the price; **hanne de uru** to sell at half the price.

**hannichi** half a day.

**hannin** offender, criminal.

**hannoo** reaction, response; **hannoo suru** to react, respond; to act upon.

**hanpa** odds; odds and ends; fragments; **hanpa no** odd; half-done; incomplete; **hanpa mono** a broken set. **Ano hito wa hanpa na shigoto shika dekimasen.** He never finishes his tasks.

**hanran** rebellion, revolt.

**hantai** opposition; contradiction; **hantai suru** to oppose; to object to; **hantai no** opposite; opposed; **hantai ni** on the contrary; in the opposite direction; **hantai undoo** opposition movement, counter movement; **hantaisha** opponent; objector; **hantaitoo** opposition party.

**hantei** judgment, decision.

**hanten** spot; speck; dot.

**hantoo** peninsula.

**hantoshi** half a year.

**hantsuki** half a month.

**han'yake** partly burned; half-roasted, half-baked.

**hanzai** crime, offense; **hanzai nin** criminal, culprit; **hanzai kooi** criminal act.

**hanzatsu** complication; **hanzatsu na** complex, complicated.

**hanzen to** clearly, distinctly; definitely; **hanzen to shita** clear, distinct; definite. **Sono hanashi o kiite hanzen to simashita.** Now that I've heard that explanation, the whole story has become clear.

**haori** Japanese coat.

**happoo** all directions; all sides; **happoo ni** in all directions; on all sides; all around; **happoo bijin** everybody's friend.

**happun suru** to be roused to action.

**happyoo** announcement; publication; **happyoo suru** to announce; to publish; to make known.

**hara** field; plain; moor; prairie; wild region.

**hara** (colloq.) belly, bowels; abdomen; stomach; **hara no ookii** magnanimous; **hara no suwatta** resolute, firm; **hara ga tatsu** to be offended; **hara o kakaete warau** to split with laughter; **harabai ni naru** to lie on one's stomach; **haramaki** belt.

**harachigai** half brother, half sister.

**harahara suru** to feel uneasy; to be in suspense. **Namida o harahara to nagashita.** The tears fell in big drops. **Mite ite mo harahara shita.** I felt nervous just looking at it.

**harai** payment; account **haraikomi** payment; installment payment; **haraikomu** to pay in, pay up; **haraimodoshi** repayment; refund; **haraimodosu** to pay back, repay.

**haraisage** government surplus sale.

**harasu** to clear away; to divert; **urami o harasu** to pay off old scores.

**HARAU** to pay (a bill, etc.); to brush off, to clear away; **shakkin o harau** to pay off a debt. **Namida o haratte shigoto o tsuzuketa.** She brushed away her tears and resumed her task.

**harawata** (colloq.) intestines; bowels; heart; character; **harawata o tatsu** to break (someone's) heart.

**hare** *(n.)* swelling; **hareru** to swell, **haremono** swelling, boil.

**hare** fine (fair) weather; **hare no kimono** holiday (Sunday) clothes; **haregi** holiday clothes.

**HARERU** to clear up (weather); to clear away; to be dispelled; **kengi ga hareru** to be cleared of a charge. **Sora ga hareta.** The sky has cleared.

**haretsu** explosion; eruption; **haretsu suru** to explode, burst, blow up; to be broken off.

**HARI** needle; pin; hand (of a watch); fishhook; sting (of a bee); **hari no me** eye of a needle; **haribako** needlecase; workbox; **harisashi** pincushion; **harishigoto** needlework; **harishigoto o suru** to sew.

**haridasu** to post (on a bulletin board); **keiji o haridasu** to post a notice.

**harifuda** bill; poster; **harifuda o suru** to put up a poster.

**harigami** label; poster.

**harigane** wire.

**haritsukeru** to stick on, paste on; to paste over.

**HARU** spring (season). **Haru ni Amerika e kaerimasu.** I am returning to the United States in the spring.

**haru** to stick; **kitte o haru** to paste on a stamp.

**hasamaru** to get in between; to lie between. **Niku ga ha no aida ni hasamarimashita.** A piece of meat got stuck between his teeth.

**HASAMI** scissors, shears; **niwaki ni hasami o ireru** to prune bushes.

**hasamu** to place; to hold between; to pinch; to pick up; **hibashi de mono o hasamu** to pick up something with tongs.

**HASHI** pair of chopsticks; **hashi o tsukeru** to start eating.

**HASHI** bridge; **hashi o wataru** to cross a bridge.

**hashi** edge, border; end; **hashi kara hashi made** from end to end; **dooro no hashi no hoo o tooru** to keep to the side of the road.

**hashigo** ladder; flight of stairs; **hashigodan** staircase.

**hashika** measles.

**hashikkoi** smart, shrewd, sharp.

**HASHIRA** pillar, post, column; pole; prop; **hashira dokei** wall clock; **daikoku hashira** main pillar; main support (a person).

**hashiri** *(n.)* running; movement; first (of something); **hashiri mawaru** to run about; **cha no hashiri** the first supply of tea; **hashirigaki suru** to write hurriedly; to scribble; **hashiriyomi o suru** to read hurriedly; to skim; **hashirizukai** running

an errand. **Kono to no hashiri ga yoi.** This sliding door moves easily.

**HASHIRU** to run; to sail; to move fast. **Kare wa ya no yoo ni hashitte itta.** He was off like a shot.

**hashita** fraction; fragment; odds and ends.

**hashutsufu** daily houseworker (female).

**hashutsusho** branch station; police box.

**hassha** starting (of a train, bus, etc.); **hassha suru** to start; to depart.

**hasshin suru** to dispatch a message; to send a letter.

**hassoo suru** to send off; to forward (a letter or package).

**hassuru** to emit; to radiate; to fire; to discharge (a gun); to issue.

**hata** flag, banner, standard; **hatazao** flagstaff.

**hata** side; neighborhood; **hata de** nearby; beside; **hata no mono** bystanders; outsiders.

**HATACHI** twenty years old (said of a person). **Watakushi wa hatachi desu.** I am twenty years old.

**hatairo** outlook, circumstances; **hatairo o miru** to see how things go.

**hatake** field; kitchen garden; farm.

**hataki** duster (made of pieces of cloth attached to a stick).

**hataku** to dust; to beat; to slap; to empty; to use up; **saifu no soko o hataku** to spend every penny one has.

**hataori** weaver, weaving; **hataori kikai** power loom; **hataori kooba** mill.

**HATARAKI** action; motion; work, labor; ability; talent; merits; **hataraki no aru hito** an able person; **hataraki mono** a hard worker.

**HATARAKU** to work, toil, labor; to commit; to do. **Ichinichi juu soto de hatarakimashita.** I worked outside all day long.

**HATASHITE** sure enough; just as I expected.

**hatasu** to accomplish, achieve; to fulfill; **yakusoku o hatasu** to fulfill one's promise; **mokuteki o hatasu** to achieve one's purpose; **gimu o hatasu** to do one's duty.

**hata to** suddenly; completely.

**HATE** end, termination; consequence, result; limit; **hate wa** finally; in the end; **hate ga nai** limitless, endless.

**hatenkoo** record-breaking; unprecedented; unheard of.

**hateshi** end; limits; **hateshi nai** endless, boundless; **hateshi nai giron** an endless argument.

**hato** dove, pigeon.

**hatoba** wharf, dock, pier.

**hatsu** first, beginning; **hatsu no** first; initial; new.

**hatsuan** suggestion, proposal; **hatsuan suru** to suggest, propose.

**hatsubai** for sale; **hatsubai suru** to offer for sale, put on sale.

**hatsubutai** debut; first public performance.

**hatsubyoo suru** to fall ill.

**hatsudooki** engine; motor.

**hatsufuyu** early winter.

**hatsugen** speech; **hatsugen suru** to open one's mouth; to speak (at a conference); **hatsugensha** speaker.

**hatsugi** proposal, motion.

**hatsui** suggestion; instance; proposal; original idea; **jibun no hatsui de** on one's own initiative.

**HATSUKA** the twentieth (of the month); (for) twenty days.

**hatsukookai** maiden voyage.

**hatsumei** invention; **hatsumeisha** inventor.

**hatsumimi** news (to a person). **Kore wa hatsumimi da.** This is news to me.

**hatsunetsu suru** to have a fever.

**HATSUON** pronunciation; **hatsuon suru** to pronounce. **Ano hito no Nihongo no hatsuon wa taihen ii desu.** His pronunciation of Japanese words is very good.

**hatsuratsu to shita** lively; keen; animated.

**hattatsu** development, progress, growth; **hattatsu suru** to develop, make progress, grow.

**hatten** development, expansion, growth; **hatten suru** to develop, expand, extend.

**hau** to crawl, creep.

**haya-** prefix denoting: quick; fast; swift; early; **hayaashi** quick steps; trot; **hayagaten** hasty conclusion; **hayagaten suru** to jump to a conclusion; **hayagawari** quick change (of costume); **hayagawari suru** to make a quick change.

**HAYAI** quick, fast, rapid, swift; early; **hayaku** quickly, promptly, early, etc.; **ki no hayai** excitable (person).

**hayaku** breach of contract; **hayaku suru** to break a contract.

**hayakuchi** rapid speech; **hayakuchi de hanasu** to jabber; to speak rapidly; **hayakuchi no** glib-tongued; **hayakuchi kotoba** tongue twister.

**hayamaru** to be overhasty, be rash; to act hastily; **hayamatta** rash; hasty; **hayamatta koto o suru** to act rashly. **Sonna ni hayamatte wa ikemasen.** Don't be so hasty. **Nan to iu hayamatta koto o shite kureta.** What a rash thing you've done!

**hayame ni** somewhat early, before time; **uchi o hayame ni deru** to leave home a little early.

**hayameru** to quicken, hasten, accelerate; **ashi o hayameru** to quicken one's steps.

**hayane o suru** to go to bed early; **hayane hayaoki** early to bed and early to rise.

**hayanomikomi o suru** to jump to a conclusion.

**hayaoki suru** to get up early.

**hayari** fashion, mode, vogue; **hayari no** fashionable, popular; **hayari no shingata** new style.

**hayariuta** popular song.

**HAYARU** to be in fashion; to prevail; to rage; to prosper; to be hasty; to be impetuous; **hayaranaku naru** to go out of fashion; to lose popularity. **Ano mise wa yoku hayatte iru.** That store is doing a good business.

**hayasa** quickness, swiftness, rapidity, speed, velocity.

**HAYASHI** forest, wood, grove.

**hayasu** to cut into small fragments; to slice up; to hash; to grow; to let grow; **hige o hayasu** to grow a beard; to grow a mustache.

**hayawakari** quick understanding; **hayawakari no suru** to be quick of understanding; to be intelligent; to be easy to understand.

**hayawaza** clever trick; sleight of hand.

**HAZU** ought to; is to be; **-hazu wa nai** cannot be; must not be; there is no reason to believe that . . . **Kare wa kesa shuppatsu suru hazu deshita.** He was to start this morning. **Ano hito wa kyoo kuru hazu desu.** He is expected here today. **Ano hito ga kyoo kuru hazu wa nai.** There is no reason to believe that he would come here today.

**hazukashigaru** to be shy, be bashful.

**Hazukashii** to be ashamed; to be shameful; to be dishonorable; to be bashful. **Ohazukashii koto desu ga . . .** To my shame I must confess that . . .

**hazukashime** shame, disgrace; insult; **hito kara hazukashime o ukeru** to be humiliated by someone; **hazukashimeru** to put to shame; to outrage.

**hazumi** momentum, impetus; **hazumi o tsukeru** to give impetus to; **hazumi ga tsuku** to be encouraged; to be stimulated; **toki no hazumi de** on the spur of the moment.

**hazumu** to bounce; to rebound; to get lively; to treat oneself to; **iki ga hazumu** to be out of breath; to pant.

**hazure** end, edge; outskirts; miss; disappointment; failure (of crops); poor harvest; **machi no hazure** the end of a street.

**hazureru** to be disconnected, to be dislocated; to come off; to be out of joint; to fail; to miss; **ate ga hazureru** to be disappointed in one's expectations.

**hazusu** to remove; to unfasten; to lose; to avoid; **megane o hazusu** to take off one's glasses; **kikai o hazusu** to lose an opportunity; **seki o hazusu** to slip out of the room; to leave the table.

**hebi** snake, serpent.

**hedatari** distance; difference; gap.

**hedataru** to be distant; to become estranged.

**hedate** distinction; discrimination; reserve; estrangement; barrier; **hedate no aru** distant; discriminating; **hedate no nai** candid; openhearted; **hedate naku hanasu** to speak without reserve.

**hedateru** to part from; separate by; to intervene, come between; to alienate; **hedatete** apart; at a distance; at intervals of; **juunen o hedatete** after an interval of ten years.

**heddofoon** headphones.

**heddoraito** headlight.

**hei** wall; fence; **hei o megurasu** to surround with a wall.

**heian** peace, tranquility; **heian ni** peacefully, in peace.

**heibon** commonness; mediocrity; **heibon na** commonplace, mediocre; tame; uneventful; **heibon na tsuki** an uneventful month.

**heigai** evils; evil influence, evil effect.

**heihei bonbon** commonplace, mediocre.

**Heika** His (Her) Majesty.

**heikai** closing, adjournment; **heikai suru** to adjourn.

**heiki** coolness, calmness, composure; **heiki na** cool, calm, composed; indifferent; unconcerned; **heiki de** calmly; with composure. **Heiki na kao o shite imashita.** He looked unconcerned.

**heikin** average; balance; equilibrium; **heikin shite** on the average.

**heikoo suru** to be defeated; to be silenced; to be annoyed; to be embarrassed.

**heion** tranquility; peace and quiet; **heion no, heion na** quiet; tranquil; **heion ni naru** to become quiet.

**Heisei** present era (counted from ascent of present emperor to throne in 1989); **Heisei 4 nen** the year 1992.

**heisei** composure; **kokoro no heisei o tamotsu** to keep one's presence of mind.

**heitai** soldier.

**heiten** (*n.*) closing of a shop or business; **heiten suru** to close up shop.

**HEIWA** peace; **heiwa no, heiwa na** peaceful, peaceable; **heiwa ni** peacefully; **heiwaronsha** pacifist.

**heiya** plain; moor; prairie.

**heizei** at ordinary times; usually. **Heizei wa yoru uchi ni imasu.** I am usually at home at night.

**heizen to shite** calmly, composedly.

**hekieki suru** to shrink from; to flinch; to be nonplussed.

**hekomasu** to hollow, to depress; to defeat; to silence.

**hekomu** to become hollow; to become depressed; to be humiliated; to give in, yield.

**hekotareru** to be discouraged; to be exhausted.

**hen** neighborhood; region; side; **kono hen ni** in this neighborhood.

**-hen** chapter; book, volume.

**henden** telegram (in reply); **henden suru** to reply by telegram.

**hendoo** change, alteration; fluctuations; **hendoo suru** to change; to fluctuate.

**HENJI, hentoo** reply, answer; **henji suru** to reply, answer; **tegami no henji o dasu** to answer a letter.

**henjin** eccentric person, odd fish.

**henka** change, variation; **henka suru** to change, alter.

**henken** prejudice; prejudiced view.

**henkin** repayment; refund; **henkin suru** to pay back, repay.

**henkoo** alteration, making changes.

**henkutsu** eccentricity; obstinacy; narrow-mindedness; **henkutsu na** eccentric; narrow-minded; cranky; obstinate. **Ano hito wa henkutsu na hito desu.** He is an eccentric person.

**henmei** alias; assumed name.

**HEN NA** odd, strange, queer; **hen na me ni au** to have an odd experience; **hen na kokochi ga suru** to have a strange sensation; **hen ni omou** to think (something) to be strange.

**hennyuu** admission; assignment.

**henrei** return (of a present or call); **-no henrei ni** in return for.

**hensai** repayment; **hensai suru** to repay.

**hensan** compilation; editing.

**hensei** organization; formation.

**hensen** change; vicissitudes; **hensen suru** to change, undergo a change.

**henshi** unnatural death.

**henshin** change of mind; unfaithfulness; **henshin suru** to change one's mind.

**henshoku** partiality (weakness) for a particular kind of food.

**hensoo** disguise.

**hentai** abnormality.

**hentoo** See **HENJI.**

**hentoosen** tonsils; **hentoosen en** tonsillitis.

**herasu** to decrease, lessen, reduce.

**heri** border, edge, brim, brink; **heri o toru** to hem, border.

**herikoputaa** helicopter.

**herikudaru** to be modest; to humble oneself; **herikudatte** modestly, humbly.

**herikutsu o iu** to quibble; to argue for the sake of arguing.

**HERU** to decrease, lessen; to be reduced. **Ame de hitode ga hetta.** Because of the rain, the crowds have thinned out.

**heru** to pass; to elapse; to pass through; to go by way of.

**herumetto** helmet.

**hesokurigane** secret savings; pin money.

**HETA** unskillfulness, awkwardness; **heta na** unskillful, awkward, clumsy. **Watakushi wa Nihongo ga heta desu.** My Japanese is poor.

**heta** calyx.

**hete** after; through; by way of; **ichinen o hete** after a year; **yuujin no te o hete** through a friend; **Rondon o hete** by way of London.

**hetoheto ni naru** to be reduced to a pulp; to be tired out; to be exhausted.

**hetsurai** flattery; **hetsurai mono** flatterer; **hetsurau** to flatter; to fawn on.

**hetto** beef fat.

**HEYA** room, chamber.

**HI** sun; day; time; date; **hi no de** sunrise; **hi no iri** sunset; **aru hi** one day; **hiatari** exposure to sun; **hiatari ga yoi** to be sunny, have plenty of sunshine; **hiatari ga warui** to be dark and gloomy; **hi ni yakeru** to be sunburnt; **hi ni sarasu** to expose to the sun; **hi no me o miru** to see the light of day; **hi no me o minai** to lack sun. **Hi ga nagaku natte kita.** The days are getting longer. **Hi wa rokuji ni deta.** The sun rose at six.

**HI** fire, flame; spark; light; **hi ga tsuku** to catch fire; **hi ni ataru** to warm oneself by a fire; **hi no ko** flying sparks; **hi no te** flames; blaze; **hi no te ga agaru** to burst into flames; **hi no yoo na** fiery, blazing.

**hi** error, fault; **hi o narasu** to attack, to declaim against; **hi no uchidokoro ga nai** impeccable, unimpeachable.

**hi** tombstone, monument.

**hi-** prefix denoting: un-; anti-; non-; **hikinzoku** non-metal.

**hiagaru** to dry up; to be parched; to starve to death.

**hiai** sadness; sorrow.

**hibachi** brazier; charcoal brazier; **hibachi ni ataru** to warm oneself at a brazier.

**hiban** off duty; **hiban de aru** to be off duty.

**hibana** sparks; **hibana o tobasu** to shoot out sparks. (See also **kasai.**)

**hibi** crack; fissure; flaw; **hibi ga iru** to be cracked; to have a flaw; **hibi ga kireru** to be chapped.

**hibiki** sound; echo; reverberation; **hibiki wataru** to resound, reverberate.

**hibiku** to sound; to echo; to affect; to influence; **myoo ni hibiku** to sound strange.

**hibon na, hibon no** out of the ordinary, extraordinary; uncommon.

**hiboshi** drying in the sun.

**hibukure** blister caused by a burn.

**hibunmei** uncivilized; uncultured.

**hida** fold; tuck; plait; **hida o toru** to tuck; to fold; crease.

**hidachi** growth; recovery; convalescence.

**HIDARI** left; **hidari no** left; left side; **hidari ni** to the left; on the left; **hidari kiki** left-handedness; left-handed person; winelover, a heavy drinker; **hidari kiki no** left-handed.

**hidarimae** adversity; downward course. **Shinshoo ga hidarimae ni naru.** His luck is failing. Luck is deserting him.

**hiden** secret; trade secret.

**hideri** drought, dry weather.

**HIDOI** severe; excessive; intense; violent; awful; terrible; **hidoi me ni au** to have a bad time of it.

**hidoku** severely; intensely; violently; hard.

**hidori o kimeru** to fix a date, fix on a day; to name a day.

**hieru** to grow cold, get chilly.

**HIFU** skin.

**higaeri** return trip made in one day; **higaeri suru, higaeri ni suru** to go and return in one day.

**higai** damage, injury; **higaisha** sufferer; victim.

**higami** jaundice; warp.

**higamu** to be jealous; to be prejudiced.

**higan** other shore (side); goal.

**HIGASHI** east. **Taiyoo wa higashi kara deru.** The sun rises in the east.

**higashi** confectionery.

**hige** mustache; beard; whiskers; **hige o hayasu** to grow a mustache (or beard); **hige moja no** heavily bearded.

**higeki** tragedy, tragic event.

**HIGORO** always; for a long time; **higoro no** usual; long-cherished. **Kare wa higoro kara kinben da.** He has always been industrious. **Higoro no negai ga kanatta.** My long-cherished dream has been fulfilled.

**higoto ni** everyday; day by day.

**HIGURE** twilight; nightfall; **higure ni** toward evening; at dusk.

**hihan** comment; criticism; **hihan suru** to criticize; to censure.

**hihoo** sad news.

**hihyoo** critique; comment; **hihyoo suru** to criticize, comment, review; **hihyooteki** critical; **hihyooka** critic, reviewer.

**hiiki** favor; patronage; partiality; **hiiki o suru** to favor, be partial to; **hiiki no** favorite; **hiikikyaku** patron.

**HIJI** elbow; **hijikake isu** armchair.

**hijideppoo** rebuff; cold shoulder; **hijideppoo o kuwaseru** to give (someone) the cold shoulder.

**hijoo** extraordinary occasion; emergency; **hijoo na** extraordinary; uncommon; **HIJOO NI** extraordinarily; exceedingly; **hijoo no sai ni wa** in case of emergency; **hijooguchi** emergency exit; **hijooji** emergency, crisis; **hijooshudan** exceptional measures.

**hijooshiki** lack of common sense; **hijooshiki na** eccentric; nonsensical. **Hijooshiki na hito desu.** He lacks common sense.

**hikae** note, memorandum; duplicate.

**hikaeme** moderation; modesty; temperance; **hikaeme ni** moderately; with reserve; **hikaeme ni suru** to be moderate; **banji hikaeme ni suru** to do all things with moderation.

**hikaeru** to jot down, note down; to wait; to be moderate; to stop.

**hikage** shade; shadow; shady spot.

**hikaku** comparison; **hikaku suru** to compare; **hikakuteki** comparatively.

**hikan** pessimism; **hikan suru** to be pessimistic; **hikan ronsha** pessimist.

**hikarabiru** to dry up, shrivel, wither.

**hikaraseru** to brighten; to polish; to cause to shine; to glimmer.

**HIKARI** light, brightness, brilliancy; glimmer, twinkle, luster, gloss; **hikari tsuushin** fiber-optic communication.

**hikaru** to shine; to be bright, sparkle; etc.

**hikazu** number of days; **hikazu ga kakaru** to take many days.

**hike** weak point; **hike o toru** to be defeated, be inferior to.

**hikeru** to be closed; to close; to lose courage; to feel small. **Yakusho ga goji ni hikeru.** The office closes at five. **Watakushi wa sore o kangaeru to ki ga hikeru.** I feel small when I think of it; **hikedoki** closing hour.

**hiketsu** secret; **seikoo no hiketsu** secret of success.

**-HIKI** counter head denoting (for fish or four-legged animals); **ippiki no ushi** one head of cattle; **nihiki no ushi** two head of cattle.

**hiki** joy and sorrow; **hiki komogomo** a mixed feeling of joy and sorrow.

**hiki** (*n.*) pulling; help, backing; influence. **Ano hito wa yoi hiki ga aru.** He has good connections.

**hiki-** prefix denoting: pulling; drawing; **hikishio** ebb tide; low tide.

**hikiage** pulling up; evacuation; withdrawal.

**hikiageru** to pull up, draw up; to evacuate; to withdraw.

**hikiai** witness; instance; example; **hikiai ni dasu** to use as an example.

**hikiau** to pay (off) well; to make a good return. **Sono shigoto wa hikiawanai.** The work does not pay.

**hikiawase** introduction; bringing together; comparison; **hikiawaseru** to introduce; to compare with; to check up.

**hikicha** powdered tea.

**hikichigiru** to pull off; to tear off.

**hikidashi** drawer; **hikidashi o akeru** to open a drawer.

**hikidasu** to draw out; to pull out; **yokin o hikidasu** to draw money from a bank.

**hikifune** towboat; tugboat.

**hikigeki** tragicomedy.

**hikiharau** to vacate; to remove; **ie o hikiharau** to move from a house.

**hikiireru** to draw into; to pull into; to win over; **mikata ni hikiireru** to win a person (over) to one's side.

**hikiiru** to lead; to head; to control; to manage.

**hikikae** exchange; conversion; **-to hikikae ni** in exchange for.

**hikikaeru** to exchange; to convert; **sore ni hikikaete** on the contrary; on the other hand.

**hikikaesu** to come back; to turn back; to return.

**hikikomisen** railway siding, service wire.

**hikikomoru** to shut oneself in; to be confined.

**hikikomu** to retire.

**hikimodosu** to bring back; to revert to; to restore.

**HIKINIKU** chopped meat; **hikinikuki** meat grinder.

**hikin na** familiar; common; popular; **hikin na rei** familiar example.

**hikinobasu** to stretch; to draw out; to enlarge (a photo); to postpone; to put off.

**hikinobashi shashin** enlarged photograph.

**hikiokosu** to raise up; to lift up; to cause; to give rise to; to awaken.

**hikiorosu** to pull down.

**hikisagaru** to withdraw; to retire.

**hikisaku** to tear up, tear to pieces.

**hikishimaru** to tighten; to tie harder; to brace; to be tightened up; to grow tight; to be braced up; **hikishimatta** firm; tight; tense;

**fukuro no himo o hikishimeru** to draw the strings of a bag together.

**hikitaosu** to pull down.

**hikitate** favor; patronage.

**hikitateru** to favor; to patronize; to set off (beauty); to set off to advantage; **ki o hikitateru** to encourage.

**hikitatsu** to look well (better); to improve; to become active; **ki ga hikitatsu** to cheer up; to be inspired with hope.

**hikite** catch; knob.

**hikitomeru** to detain; to stop.

**hikitoru** to withdraw; to take back; to take over.

**hikitsugu** to succeed in; to take over.

**hikitsuke** convulsion.

**hikitsukeru** to draw toward me; to attract.

**HIKITSUZUITE** continually; successively; **gonen hikitsuzuite** for five years running.

**hikitsuzuki** continuation; succession; sequel.

**hikitsuzuku** to continue; to last.

**hikiuke** undertaking. **Ano ginkoo wa kono tegata no hikiuke o kobanda.** That bank didn't honor this check.

**hikiukeru** to undertake; to accept; to take over; to assume; to shoulder the responsibility for.

**hikiwake** draw, tie; **hikiwake ni naru** to end in a draw.

**hikiwakeru** to part; to pull apart; to separate.

**hikiwatashi** delivery; transfer; surrender. **Shoohin no hikiwatashi wa yokka ni sunda.** The delivery of merchandise was completed on the fourth.

**hikiwatasu** to deliver; to hand over; to surrender.

**hikiyoseru** to draw near; to bring close; to pull near.

**hikizan** subtraction.

**hikizuru** to drag, pull along; **ashi o hikizutte aruku** to drag one's feet; **hikizuridasu** to pull out, drag out; **hikizurikomu** to drag in; to bring in.

**hikkaburu** to pull (draw) over one's head.

**hikkakaru** to be caught (on a nail, tree, etc.); to be hooked; to be entangled; to be cheated.

**hikkakeru** to hook; to hang on; to cheat; to seduce; to evade payment; **ippai hikkakeru** to have drink.

**hikkaku** to scratch; to claw.

**hikki** transcript; **hikki suru** to write down; to copy; to take notes; **hikkisha** stenographer; **hikkichoo** notebook; **hikkishiken** written examination.

**hikkomeru** to pull (draw) in; to draw back; to move back.

**hikkomu** to retire, withdraw; to disappear; **hikkomigachi no, hikkomijian no** retiring

(in disposition); **inaka e hikkomu** to retire to the country. **Ie wa dooro kara hikkonde iru.** The house stands back from the road.

**hikkonda** secluded; sunken; hollow; **hikkonda basho** secluded place.

**HIKKOSU** to move (into another house); **hikkoshi no torrakku** moving van. **Tookyoo e hikkoshimasu.** I am going to move to Tokyo.

**hikkurikaeru** to tumble down; to be upset; to tip over; to be overturned.

**hikkurikaeshi** topsy-turvy; upside down; wrong side up; inside out. **Uchi no naka wa hikkurikaeshi ni natte imasu.** The house is upside down.

**hikkurikaesu** to overturn, upset; to topple over; to knock down.

**hikkurumeru** to bundle (together); to include.

**hikoku** defendant; prisoner.

**HIKOO** flight; aviation; **hikoo suru** to fly; **HIKOOJOO** airport; **HIKOOKI** airplane; **hikoosen** blimp; dirigible.

**hikooshiki no** informal, not official; **hikooshiki ni** unofficially; informally.

**HIKU** to draw; to attract; to lead; to install; to quote; to consult; to subtract; **kuji o hiku** to draw lots; **sode o hiku** to pull (someone) by the sleeve; **kuruma o hiku** to draw a cart; **chuui o hiku** to attract attention; **doojoo o hiku** to win sympathy; **kaze o hiku** to catch a cold; **denwa o hiku** to install a telephone; **jisho o hiku** to refer to a dictionary; **nedan o hiku** to cut the price; **chisuji o hiku** to descend from.

**hiku** to play (an instrument); **piano a hiku** to play the piano.

**hiku** to resign, to retire; recede, ebb. **Hare ga hikimashita.** The swelling has gone down. **Netsu ga hikimashita.** The fever has dropped.

**HIKUI** low; humble; short; flat; **hikui hana** a flat nose; **hikui koe** a low voice. **Sei ga hikui.** She is short (in stature).

**hikutsu** meanness; servility; **hikutsu na** servile; mean.

**hikyoo** cowardice; **hikyoo na** cowardly; **hikyoo mono** coward.

**HIMA** leisure; (spare) time; dismissal; leave; interval; recess; **hima de aru** to be free, be at leisure; **hima ga iru** to require (more) time; **hima ga nai** to have no time; **hima o dasu** to dismiss (a servant); **hima o toru** to resign; **himadoru** to take (much) time; to delay; **himajin** leisured or unemployed person. **Shoobai ga hima de aru.** Business is slack.

**himashi ni** more and more each day; **himashi**

ni byooki ga yoku naru to get better day by day.

**himei** cry of distress; shriek; **himei o ageru** to utter a groan.

**himitsu** secret; secrecy; **himitsu no** secret, confidential, private; **himitsu ni** secretly, privately; **himitsu ni suru** to keep secret; **himitsu o abaku** to divulge a secret.

**HIMO** string, cord; braid; tape; ribbon; thong; **himo o musubu** to tie a string. **himo de musubu** to tie (something) with string.

**himojii** to be starved. **Taihen himojii omoi o shimashita.** I was very hungry.

**himono** dried fish.

**hin** poverty; **hin suru** to be poor.

**hin** elegance; grace; refinement; **hin ga tsuku** to be refined; **hin no yoi** refined; elegant; **hin no warui** vulgar; uncouth; coarse; **hin o sageru** to disgrace oneself.

**hinaka** broad daylight; daytime.

**hinan** blame, censure, reproach; **hinan suru** to blame.

**hinan** refuge, shelter; **hinan suru** to take shelter; **hinansha** refugee; **hinansho** refugee shelter.

**hinata** sunny place; sunshine; **hinata ni hosu** to dry in the sun; **hinata bokko o suru** to take a sunbath.

**hinekureru** to become crooked; **hinekureta** distorted, crooked; perverse; **hinekureta onna** perverse woman; **hinekureta kangae** distorted view.

**hinekuru** to twirl; to finger; to toy with.

**hineru** to twirl; to turn on (or off); **gasu o hineru** to turn on the gas (in a stove).

**hiniku** sarcasm; caustic remark; **hiniku na** sarcastic; cynical, ironic; **hiniku o iu** to speak sarcastically or ironically.

**hinin** birth control, contraception.

**hinjaku** meagerness; poverty; **hinjaku na** meager; shelter.

**hinketsu** anemia.

**hinkoo** behavior, conduct; **hinkoo no yoi** well-behaved.

**hinminkutsu** slums.

**hinobe** postponement; extension of time; reprieve; **hinobe suru** to postpone, etc.

**hinoki butai** (theater) stage (of cypress); (= first-class stage).

**hi no kuruma** extreme poverty; **hi no kuruma de aru** to be in great financial difficulty.

**hi no maru** national flag of Japan; disk of the sun; red circle.

**hinpan** frequency, **hinpan na** frequent; incessant; **hinpan ni, hinpan to** frequently, incessantly.

**hinshi** dying; **hinshi no jootai ni aru** to be on the verge of death.

**hinshitsu** quality.

**hinsoo** poor appearance; **hinsoo na nari o shite iru** to be poorly dressed.

**hippaku** pressure (for money); tightness (of money). **Ano hito wa shikin ni hippaku shite iru.** She is pressed for funds.

**hipparidako de aru** to be sought for eagerly; to be in great demand.

**HIPPARU** to pull, draw, drag, tug; to stretch; to entice; to solicit; **mikata ni hipparu** to win over to our side.

**hira-** prefix denoting: flat, level; plain, simple; common; **hiraya** one-story house; **hirachi** level land, flat ground.

**HIRAGANA** one of the two sets of Japanese syllabary called **kana.**

**hirashira** fluttering; flapping. **Ki no ha ga hirashira to chitta.** The leaves fluttered down.

**hiraishin** lightning rod.

**hirakeru** to become civilized; to become modernized; to be cultivated; to develop; to grow; **hiraketa** modernized; up-to-date; civilized; **hiraketa hito** person of the world.

**hiraki** opening; closet; difference; distance; gap.

**HIRAKU** to open; to lift (a lid); to unfold; to commence; to set up; to cultivate; to bloom; **tenrankai o hiraku** to open an exhibit. **Hana ga hiraite iru.** The flower is blooming.

**hiramekasu** to flash; to brandish.

**hirameki** flash; flashing; gleam.

**hirameku** to flash; to gleam; to wave.

**hira ni** humbly; earnestly; intently. **Hira ni goyoosha o kou.** I sincerely hope you will pardon me (used in letters).

**hirari to** nimbly; lightly.

**hiratai, hirattai** flat, level; simple, plain; **hirataku** flatly; evenly; easily; simply, plainly; **hirataku suru** to flatten; **hirataku ieba** to speak plainly.

**hirate** palm of the hand; open hand; **hirate de utsu** to slap.

**hiraya** one-story house.

**hire** fin.

**hireniku** steak; filet mignon.

**hiretsu** meanness; baseness.

**hirihiri suru** to be pungent; to have a burning taste; to smart.

**hiroba** open space; square (of a town).

**hirobiro to shita** spacious; roomy; open; extensive.

**hirogari** extension; expansion; spread.

**hirogaru** to extend; to expand; to spread.

**HIROGERU** to spread; to extend; to widen; to open; to unfold; to unroll. **Michi o hirogemashita.** They widened the road.

Mise o hirogeru tsumori desu. I intend to expand (enlarge) the store.

**HIROI** wide, broad; extensive; roomy; **hiroi heya** spacious (big) room.

**hiroiageru** to pick up.

**hiroiatsumeru** to gather, collect; to select.

**hiroimono** piece of good luck; find; **hiroimono o suru** to find (pick up) (something); to make a rare find.

**hiroiyomi o suru** to read here and there; to skim; to skip over (details); to pick up the chief points.

**hiroku** widely, extensively; generally; universally; **hiroku suru** to widen; to enlarge.

**hiroma** spacious room; hall.

**hiromaru** to circulate; to be circulated; to be diffused.

**hirome** announcement; debut.

**hiromeru** to spread, propagate.

**hiroo** fatigue; exhaustion; **hiroo suru** to get weary, to be exhausted.

**hiroo** announcement; introduction; **hiroo suru** to announce; to introduce.

**hirosa** width, breadth; area; dimension. **Kono kooen no hirosa wa dore hodo arimasu ka?** How large is this park?

**HIROU** to pick up; to find; to gather. **Michi de sen en satsu o hirotta.** I found a thousand-yen bill on the road.

**HIRU** daytime; noon, midday; **hiru hinaka in** broad daylight.

**HIRUGOHAN** lunch, midday meal; **hirugohan o taberu** to have lunch.

**hirugaeru** to wave; to fly; to float; to flap; **hirugaesu** to wave; to fly; to change.

**hiruhan** See **hirugohan.**

**HIRUMA** daytime; **hiruma ni** in the daytime.

**hirumae** forenoon; **hirumae ni** in the morning.

**hirumu** to flinch; to shrink.

**hirune** midday nap; siesta; **hirune o suru** to take a nap.

**hirusugi** shortly after noon.

**HIRUYASUMI** midday recess; lunch hour.

**hiryoo** manure; fertilizer.

**hisan** misery; distress; **hisan na** tragic; miserable, wretched.

**hisashi** visor (of a cap); eaves; canopy.

**HISASHIBURI DE** after a long time; for the first time in many days (weeks, years, etc.); **hisashiburi de au** to see after a long interval. **Hisashiburi desu nee!** It's a long time since I last saw you.

**hisashii** long; long continued; of long standing; **hisashii aida** for a long time.

**HISASHIKU** for a long time. **Kare ni wa hisashiku awanai.** I haven't seen him for a long time.

**hisenron** pacifism; **hisenronsha** pacifist.

**hishaku** ladle, dipper.

**hishihishi to** firmly; tightly; densely; deeply.

**hishimeku** to clamor, make a noise.

**hishochi** summer resort.

**hisohiso** in whispers; secretly; **hisohiso banashi** whispered conversation.

**hisomeru** to raise or knit (one's brows); **mayu o hisometa** with a frown.

**hisoo na** touching, pathetic.

**hisshi** desperation; **hisshi no** desperate; **hisshi ni** desperately; **hisshi to natte** in desperation; **hisshi no doryoku o suru** to make desperate efforts.

**hisuterii** hysteria, hysterics; **hisuterii o okosu** to go into hysterics.

**HITAI** forehead; brow.

**hitasu** to steep; to dip; to soak.

**HITO** person; people; others; nature; disposition; **hito no yoi** good-natured; **hito no warui** ill-natured; **hito no ooi jikoku** rush hour.

**hito-** prefix denoting: one; **hitoban** one night (evening); all night; whole night; **hitohako** one box.

**HITOBITO** people.

**hitochigai** mistaken identity.

**hitodanomi o suru** to depend on someone else.

**hitode** helping hand; help; **hitode ga tarinai** short of hands; short of help; **hitode o kariru** to ask for help; **hitode ni wataru** to change hands.

**hitode, hitogomi** crowd; throng. **Taihen na hitode de atta.** There was a large crowd.

**hitodenashi** inhuman wretch; ungrateful person.

**hitodoori** pedestrian traffic; **hitodoori no ooi machi** a busy street. **Koko wa hitodoori ga ooi.** It is very crowded here.

**hitoemono** summer clothes.

**hitofude** line; stroke; **hitofude de** with one stroke of the brush.

**hitogara** personal character; personal appearance.

**hitogoe** voice.

**hitogomi** (See also **hitode.**) **hitogomi no naka o oshiwakete iku** to push through a crowd of people.

**hitogoroshi** murder; murderer.

**hitogoto** other people's affairs. **Hitogoto to wa omoenai.** I feel as if it were my own concern.

**hitohada nugu** to lend a helping hand; to give every assistance possible.

**hitoiki** one breath; **hitoiki tsuite** after a pause; **hitoiki de** in one breath; at a stretch.

**hitokata naranu** unusual, uncommon; great, immense.

**hitokata narazu** not a little; extremely; immensely.

**HITOKIWA** especially, particularly; conspicuously; in a high degree; still more.

**hitokoto** single word; **hitokoto mo iwanai** to be silent; not to say a single word.

**hitokuchi** mouthful; bite; morsel; **hitokuchi ni taberu** to eat in one bite.

**hitokuse** peculiarity; uncommon trait.

**hitomae de** in public.

**hitomaku** act; scene; **hitomaku mono** one-act play.

**hitomane** imitation; mimicry.

**hitomatome ni** in a lump; in a bunch; **hitomatome ni suru** to put together.

**hitomawari** turn; round; **hitomawari suru** to go on one's rounds; **kooen o hitomawari sanpo suru** to take a walk through the park.

**HITOMAZU** for the present; for the time being; for a while; anyhow.

**hitome** notice; attention; **hitome o shinobu** to avoid the public eye; **hitome o shinonde** in secret; secretly; **hitome o hiku** to attract attention.

**hitome** look; glance; **hitome de** at a glance; **hitome miru** to glance at.

**hitomishiri suru** to be afraid of strangers; to be bashful.

**hitomukashi** age; decade.

**hitonaka** crowd of people; **hitonaka de** in the presence of others.

**hitonami no** average; common; ordinary; **hitonami ni** like other people; **hitonami hazureta** uncommon; eccentric.

**hitonemuri** nap; short sleep.

**hitonigiri** handful; **hitonigiri no kome** handful of rice.

**hitoomoi ni** without further hesitation; instantly; at once; without further ado.

**HITORI** (single) person; **hitori de** alone; unaided; **hitorimono** bachelor. **Hitori de shimashita.** I did it myself.

**hitori bitori, hitori hitori** one by one; one after another (person). **Hitori bitori de kangae ga chigau.** Each person has his or her own opinion.

**hitoride ni** spontaneously.

**hitorigaten** one's own judgment; hasty conclusion.

**hitorigoto** soliloquy; **hitorigoto o iu** to talk to oneself.

**hitorigurashi** living alone; bachelorhood.

**hitori hitori** (See **hitori bitori**.) one by one; one at a time. **Hitori hitori no kangae o itte kudasai.** Will each of you express your opinion?

**hitorikko** only child.

**hitorimusuko** only son.

**hitorimusume** only daughter.

**hitori nokorazu** everyone.

**hitoritabi** (n.) traveling alone.

**hitoriyogari** self-satisfaction; self-complacency; **hitoriyogari no** self-satisfied.

**hitosarai** abduction, kidnapping; kidnapper.

**HITOSASHIYUBI** forefinger.

**hitosawagase** scare; false alarm.

**hitoshii** equal to, equivalent to.

**hitosoroi** set; suit; **hitosoroi no chadoogu** tea set; **fuyugi hitosoroi** winter suit.

**hitosuji** line; **hitosuji michi** straight road; **hitosuji ni** straight, in a straight line; intently.

**HITOTONARI** personality; character.

**hitotoori** in a general way; **hitotoori no** general; common; **hitotoori naranu** unusual, uncommon; **hitotoori hanashite kikaseru** to give a short account.

**HITOTSU** one; same; identical; **hitotsu no** one; single; **hitotsu ni suru** to unite, join, combine; **hitotsu bitotsu** one by one; separately; **hitotsu oki ni** alternately.

**hitotsubu** grain; **hitotsubu no kome** grain of rice.

**hitotsukami** handful; fistful.

**hitouchi** blow; stroke; **hitouchi ni** at one blow.

**hitozuki** attractiveness; amiability; **hitozuki no suru** attractive; pleasing; amiable; charming; **hitozuki no shinai** unprepossessing; unattractive.

**hitozute** hearsay; **hitozute ni** secondhand; by hearsay. **Hitozute ni kiite shitte imasu.** I know it through hearsay. **Sore wa hitozute ni kiita no desu.** It came to me secondhand.

**HITSUYOO** necessity; need; **HITSUYOO NA** necessary; requisite, required; **hitsuyoo no sai wa** in case of need. **Ano hon ga zehi hitsuyoo desu.** I must have that book.

**hittakuru** to snatch, take by force.

**hiwari** daily rate; schedule; program; **hiwari de harau** to pay by the day; **hiwari o kimeru** to fix the dates.

**hiyaase o kaku** to be in a cold sweat.

**hiyahiya suru** to be chilly; to be in great fear.

**hiyakashi** banter; jeering; ridicule; (mere) inspection.

**hiyakasu** to make fun of; just to look at. **Chotto hiyakashi ni iku dake desu.** I'll just go and look at the things. **Ano hito wa anata o hiyakashite iru no da.** She is making fun of you.

**hiyari to suru** to feel chilled; to be startled, be alarmed at.

**hiyasu** to cool; to refrigerate; **hiyashite oku** to keep (something) cool.

**hiyayaka** coldness; coldheartedness, **hiyayaka ni** coldheartedly; coolly; **hiyayaka na hito** coldhearted person; **hiyayaka na kaze** chilly wind.

**hiyoke** screen (against sun); awning; **hiyoke o suru** to screen from the sun.

**HIYOO** cost, expense, expenditure; **hiyoo ga kakaru** to be expensive. **Dore hodo hiyoo ga kakarimashita ka?** How much did it cost you?

**HIYORI** weather; fine weather; condition; state of affairs; **hiyori o miru** to watch which way the wind blows; to sit on the fence. **Hiyori ga kawatta.** The weather has changed.

**HIZA** knee; lap; **hiza o tsuku** to kneel; **hizagashira** kneecap; **hizakake** lap robe (rug); **hizamazuku** to kneel; to fall on one's knees.

**hizoo** treasure, valuable possession; **hizoo no** treasured, valued; dearest; **hizoo suru** to treasure, cherish, keep with great care; **hizoohin** valued possession.

**hizuke** date.

**hobashira** mast.

**HOBO** almost, nearly; about.

**HOBO** kindergarten teacher.

**hochoo** pace, step; **hochoo o soroeru** to keep pace with.

**HODO** degree; limit; moderation; some; about; the more . . . the more; as; **hodo yoku** moderately; properly; modestly; **kore hodo** this much; so much; **sore hodo** that much. **Joodan ni mo hodo ga aru.** There is a limit even to a joke. **Hayakereba hayai hodo yoi desu.** The sooner the better.

**hodoai** moderation; golden mean.

**hodokeru** to come loose; to get untied.

**hodokoshi** alms, charity.

**hodokosu** to give; to give alms; to practice; to try; **arayuru shudan o hodokosu** to try every means.

**HODOKU** to untie, unfasten; to loosen; to disentangle; **nimotsu o hodoku** to unpack (luggage); **himo o hodoku** to untie a knot.

**HODONAKU** shortly; before long; by and by.

**hodoo** footpath; sidewalk; pavement; paved road.

**hoeru** to bark; to howl; to roar. **Ano inu wa yoku hoeru.** That dog is noisy.

**hogaraka** melodiousness; cheerfulness; **hogaraka na** sonorous; cheerful, bright; **hogaraka na koe** in a clear voice; **hogaraka ni** cheerfully.

**hogo** protection; **hogo suru** to protect; **hogosha** protector, guardian.

**hogu, hogo** wastepaper; **hogu ni suru** to annul, invalidate.

**hogusu** to unfasten, untie; to disentangle; to unravel.

**hojiru, hojikuru** to pick; to dig; to ferret out.

**hojo** assistance, aid, subsidy; **hojo no** subsidiary, auxiliary; **hojo suru** to aid, subsidize; **hojo o ukeru** to be subsidized; **hojokin** subsidy, grant-in-aid.

**hojuu suru** to supplement; to replenish.

**HOKA** others; rest; besides; another phase; **hoka ni** besides; **hoka no** another; the other; **-no hoka wa** except; **hoka no tokoro** another place; elsewhere; **hoka no hitotachi** other people.

**hokan suru** to take custody of; to take in charge; **hokannin** custodian.

**hoken** insurance; **hoken o kakeru** to insure (against accidents); **seimei hoken** life insurance; **kasai hoken** fire insurance.

**hoketsu** substitute, filling a vacancy; **hoketsu senshu** substitute player.

**hokki** promotion; proposal, suggestion.

**hokku** hook.

**HOKORI** dust; **hokori darake** dusty; **hokori ga tatsu** to be dusty; **hokori o harau** to dust.

**hokori** pride. **Kodomo o hokori ni shite imasu.** She takes pride in her children.

**hokorobi** rip; run (ravel).

**hokorobiru** to get ripped; to be torn open; to unravel, run.

**hokoru** to boast of; to be proud.

**hokuro** mole (body).

**hokyuu** supply; replenishment; **hokyuu suru** to supply; to make up the lack.

**HOMERU** to praise, commend; to admire. **Mina anata o homete imasu.** Everybody speaks well of you.

**HON** book, volume; **hon'ya** bookstore; bookdealer; **honbako** bookcase; **hondana** bookshelf.

**HON-** prefix denoting: original; natural; proper; main; head; chief; true; real; regular; genuine; this; present; our; **honbun** body (of a letter); text; **hondo** mainland; **honkan** main building; **honke** head (main) family; originator; original manufacturer; head house.

**-hon** counter denoting: things which have length, such as pencils, sticks, and poles; **enpitsu nihon** two pencils.

**honba** home; best place for.

**honbu** home office; headquarters.

**honburi** downpour. **Ame ga iyoiyo honburi ni narimashita.** The rain was coming down in earnest.

**hone** bone; frame (of a sliding door); spirit; **hone to kawa bakari** (only) skin and bones; **hone o oru** to take the trouble to; **hone ga oreru** to be troublesome; to require great effort; **hone no aru otoko** man of courage; **honedarake na** bony; full of bones; **honegumi** build; physique; framework.

**honeori** exertion; labor; foil; **honeorizon** (n.) working for nothing. **Honeorizon no kutabire mooke.** It was so much useless labor.

**honeoshimi** laziness; **honeoshimi suru** to spare oneself.

**honki** seriousness, earnestness; **honki no** serious, earnest; **honki de** seriously, in earnest. **Anata wa honki desu ka?** Are you serious?

**honkyoku** head (main) office.

**honmono** real thing; genuine article; original article; **honmono no** real, genuine.

**honnin** person in question.

**HONNO** mere; just; little; few; **honno sukoshi** just a little. **Mada honno kodomo desu.** He is a mere child.

**honnoo** instinct.

**honomekasu** to allude, hint, suggest.

**honoo** flame.

**honpoo** principal salary.

**honsai** (legal) wife.

**honseki** permanent residence.

**honshiki** regular (orthodox) way; **honshiki no** regular; formal; orthodox.

**honshoku** one's regular occupation; **honshoku no** professional.

**honsoo suru** to run about (in pursuit of something); to busy oneself about.

**hontate** bookstand; bookrest.

**HONTOO** truth; reality; fact; **hontoo no** true, real, genuine; regular; **hontoo ni** truly, really; **hontoo ni suru** to accept as fact; to take seriously.

**hon'yaku** translation; **hon'yaku suru** to translate; **hon'yakusha** translator.

**HOO** direction; quarter; side; **migi no hoo ni** on the right side. **Kono hoo ga ii desu.** This is better. **Iku hoo ga ii desu.** It's better to go.

**HOO** cheek; **hoobone** cheekbone; **hoobeni** rouge; **hoohige** whiskers.

**hoo** law.

**hoobaru** to stuff one's mouth; to eat in one mouthful.

**hoobi** prize; reward; **hoobi o morau** to win a prize.

**hooboo** everywhere, in all directions. **Hooboo anata o sagashimashita.** I looked all over for you.

**hoochiku** dismissal; banishment; **hoochiku suru** to expel, dismiss; to banish; to turn out.

**HOOCHOO** kitchen knife.

**-hoodai** suffix denoting: as one pleases; to one's heart's content; **iitaihoodai o iu** to talk as one likes; **shitaihoodai o suru** to act as one pleases.

**hoodoo** information; report.

**hoofu** abundance; **hoofu na** rich; abundant.

**hoofu** ambition, aspiration.

**hoogai na** exorbitant; **hoogai no takane** exorbitant price.

**hoogaku** direction; bearing; **hoogaku ga wakaranaku naru** to lose one's bearings; be unable to find one's way.

**hoogen** dialect; provincialism.

**hoohoo no tei de** precipitately, hurriedly; sneakingly; **hoohoo no tei de nigedasu** to beat a hasty retreat.

**hooka** arson.

**HOOKI** broom; **hooki no e** broomstick.

**hookoku** report; information, direction, course; **hookoku suru** to report; to inform.

**hookoo** public duty; service; apprenticeship; **hookoonin** servant; domestic; **hookooguchi** domestic position; **hookoo suru** to enter (domestic) service.

**hookyuu** salary; **hookyuubi** payday; **hookyuu seikatsusha** salaried person.

**hooman** laxity, looseness; **hooman na** lax, loose; reckless; wild.

**hoomen** release; acquittal; **hoomen suru** to release, liberate, release from custody; to acquit.

**hoomen** direction; quarter, district; **Shizuoka hoomen** the Shizuoka district.

**HOOMON** call; visit; **hoomon suru** to call on, visit; **hoomon kyaku** visitor; **hoomon o ukeru** to receive a visit.

**hoomotsu** treasure; heirloom.

**hoomuran** home run (in baseball).

**hoomushikku** homesick.

**hooriageru** to furl up; to throw up.

**hooridasu** to throw away, cast away, cast out.

**hoorikomu** to throw in, into.

**hooritsu** law. **Sore wa hooritsu ihan da.** It's against the law.

**hooritsukeru** to throw at, against.

**hooroku** baking pan; earthen pan used for parching tea, etc., at high temperatures.

**hooru** to throw, fling.

**hooshin** course, aim; plan; principle; policy; **hooshin o sadameru** to shape one's course; to decide on a policy.

**hoosoo** = **shutoo** vaccination.

**hoosoo** (radio) broadcasting; **hoosookyoku** broadcasting station.

**hoosu** hose.

**hootai** bandage.

**hora** boast; brag; tall (big) talk; **hora o fuku** to blow one's own horn; to boast; **horafuki** braggart.

**horaana** cave, cavern; natural cavity.

**horebore suru** to be charmed; to be fascinated.

**horeru** (colloq.) to fall in love; to be enamored of.

**horidasu** to dig out; to unearth, excavate.

**horikaesu** to dig (turn over the soil).

**horu** to dig; to excavate; to burrow; to scoop out; to sink (a well).

**HOSHI** star. **Sora ni hoshi ga kagayaite iru.** Stars are glittering in the sky. **Kotoshi wa hoshimawari ga yoi.** I am lucky this year.

**hoshigaru** to wish for; to long for; to crave; to covet.

**HOSHII** to be desirous of having (something); to want. **Ano hon ga hoshii.** I want that book.

**hoshimono** laundered clothes.

**hoshoo** guarantee; **hoshoonin** guarantor; certifier.

**hosobiki** cord, rope.

**HOSOI** slender; fine; narrow; thin; **hosome ni** slightly; narrowly; **hosome ni kiru** to cut fine; **hosomichi** narrow path; lane; **hosonagai** long and slender; lanky.

**hosu** to dry (in the air); to sun; to empty a liquid; to draw off; to pump dry; **sakazuki o hosu** to drink up.

**hoteru** to feel hot; to burn. **Kao ga hoteru.** My face burns.

**HOTERU** hotel.

**hotoke** Buddha; deceased (person); departed soul.

**HOTONDO** almost, very nearly, all but; approximately; hardly, scarcely. **Ano biru wa hotondo kanseishite iru.** That building is near completion.

**hotsureru** to become loose; to be frayed.

**hotto suru** to sigh with relief; **hotto iki o tsuku** to heave a deep sigh.

**hoyoo** preservation of health; recreation; relaxation; **hoyoo suru** to take care of oneself; to recuperate; to relax.

**HYAKU** (n.) hundred; **hyaku mo shoochishite iru** to know too well; to be well aware of.

**hyakushoo** peasant, farmer.

**hyoo** table, chart; **jikanhyoo** timetable.

**hyooban** reputation; fame; popularity; report; rumor; **hyooban no** famed; notorious; **hyooban no yoi** popular; of good reputation; **hyooban no warui** unpopular; **hyooban ni naru** to be much talked about.

**hyoomen** (n.) surface; outside; **hyoomen no** (adj.) outside, external.

**hyoosatsu** doorplate; name plate.

**HYOOSHI** binding; **kami hyooshi** paper cover, paper binding.

**hyooshi** time, rhythm; chance; **hyooshi o toru** to beat time.

**hyorohyoro** staggeringly; slimly; **hyorohyoro shita** staggering, reeling; slim; lanky.

**HYOTTO** by chance, by accident; **hyotto shitara** possibly, maybe.

**hyuuhyuu** whistling; whizzing. **Kaze ga hyuuhyuu fuku.** The wind whistles.

# I

**I** stomach.

**iawaseru** to happen to be present.

**ibaru** to be haughty; to brag; to give oneself airs.

**ibiki** snoring; **ibiki o kaku** to snore.

**iburu** to smolder, smoke. **Kono sumi wa iburu.** This charcoal smokes.

**ibusu** to smoke; to fumigate.

**ICHI** one; **ICHIBAN** first; number one; game, round; **ichiban ato de** last of all; at the very end; **ichiban saki no** first, foremost; **ichiban osoi** slowest.

**ichi** position; situation; location.

**ICHIBA** marketplace, market; **aomono ichiba** vegetable market; **uo ichiba** fish market.

**ichibu** part, portion; some part; **ichibu shijuu** the whole, all the details; from beginning to end.

**ichidaiji** serious affair.

**ICHIDO** once, one time.

**ICHIDOO** all; all (the persons) present; **kanai ichidoo** all the members of the family.

**ICHIGATSU** January.

**ICHIICHI** in every single case; in detail. **Ichiichi monku o iwanaide kudasai.** Please don't complain all the time.

**ICHIJI** one o'clock; for the present; for a while; **ichijiteki no** temporary.

**ICHIMAI** one (sheet, leaf, card).

**ICHIMEN** entire area, whole surface; one side; other hand; first page (of a newspaper); **ichimenkiji** front-page news; **-no ichimen ni wa . . .** on the other hand . . . **Ichimen ni hana ga saite iru.** Everything is in bloom.

**ichimoku** glance, look; **ichimoku ryoozen to** be clear at a glance; **ichimokusan ni** at full speed.

**ICHINEN** one year; **ichinen juu** all year round.

**ICHINICHI** one day; whole day through; all day; **ichinichi oki ni** every other day.

**ICHIOO** once; for the time being; in the first place; first; in outline. **Ichioo soo shite okimashoo.** We will leave it that way, at least for the time being.

**ICHIRYOOJITSU** day or two; **ichiryoojitsu chuu ni** in a day or two.

**ichiryuu** first class; **ichiryuu no** first rate.

**ichiyaku** at a single bound.

**iden** heredity.

**ido** well (for water); **idobata** side of a well. **idobata kaigi** gossiping.

**IDOKORO** address; residence; whereabouts.

**IE** house; dwelling; cottage; home; family; **ie o tateru** to build a house; **ie ni kaeru** to go home.

**iegara** birth, lineage.

**igai na** unexpected; unlooked for; **igai ni** unexpectedly.

**igen** dignity; prestige; **igen aru fuusai** dignified appearance.

**IGIRISU = Eikoku** the United Kingdom; **Igirisu no** *(adj.)* British.

**igokochi** comfortableness; **igokochi ga yoi** snug; comfortable; **igokochi ga warui** uncomfortable.

**ihan** violation; infringement; **ihan suru** to act against; to infringe upon.

**II = yoi** good; pretty; likable; **ii hito** nice person. **Ii kimi da.** It serves you right.

**iiarasou** to dispute, quarrel.

**iiateru** to guess correctly.

**IIE** no. **Ie, moo kekko desu.** No, thank you. (I've had enough.)

**iifurasu** to spread a story, circulate a tale.

**iiharu** to insist on; to persist in; to assert positively.

**iihiraki** vindication.

**iikaeru** to express in another word; **iikaereba** that is to say.

**iikaneru** to hesitate to say; to be unable to speak out.

**iikata** way of speaking; expression.

**iikiru** to speak positively; to assert.

**iimorasu** to neglect to tell; to forget to tell.

**iin** committee; committee member.

**iinazuke** fiancé; fiancée.

**iine de** at the price asked.

**iinuke** excuse; evasive answer.

**iisokonai** slip of the tongue; misstatement.

**iisugi** exaggeration.

**iisugiru** to say too much; to exaggerate.

**iitsuke** order, command; instruction.

**iitsukeru** to order, command; to bid.

**iitsutae** tradition; legend; hearsay.

**IIWAKE** apology; excuse; pretext; **iiwake o suru** to make an excuse; **iiwake ga tatanai** to be inexcusable.

**iiwatasu** to tell; to pass judgment; to sentence.

**iji** temper; disposition; **iji o haru** to be obstinate, be stubborn; **soko iji ga aru** strong-willed.

**ijikeru** to cower.

**ijikitanai** greedy.

**ijimeru** to tease; to treat badly; to torment.

**ijiparu** to persist in; to be obstinate.

**ijirashii** pitiable; pathetic; touching.

**ijiru** to finger; to play with.

**IJIWARU** ill-natured person; **ijiwaru na** nasty, mean.

**ijiwarui** ill-natured, ill-tempered; **ijiwaruku** spitefully.

**IJOO** more than; above-mentioned; above; upward of, beyond; since, now that; **yottsu ijoo** more than four.

**ijoo** something unusual; abnormal symptoms; deformity; **ijoo na** unusual, abnormal. **Betsu ni ijoo wa arimasen.** There is nothing unusual.

**ijuu suru** to move to; to migrate.

**IKA** *(n.)* following; less than, under. **Juunisai ika wa tada desu.** There is no charge for children under twelve. **Sore wa gosen en ika desu.** It costs less than 5000 yen.

**IKAGA** how; what *(pol.)*. **Kyoo wa okagen wa ikaga desu ka?** How do you feel today? **Goiken wa ikaga desu ka?** What is your opinion?

**ikagawashii** questionable, doubtful.

**ikahodo** how much; how many.

**ikameshii** solemn, grave; stern; authoritative.

**IKANIMO** very; truly; indeed.

**ikasu** to make good use of; to spare one's life; to keep alive; **kane o ikashite tsukau** to make good use of money.

**ike** pond.

**ikedoru** to capture.

**iken** opinion; view; **iken o noberu** to give an opinion; **iken suru** to admonish; to give advice.

**IKENAI** be of no use; will not do. **Kore wa ikenai.** This will not do. **Ame ga furu to ikenai kara.** Lest it rain. **Ikanakereba ikenai.** I must go. [It won't do if I don't go.]

**ikeru** to arrange flowers.

**iki** breath; spirit; **iki ga kireru** to be out of breath; **iki o tsuku** to breathe; to heave a sigh of relief; **iki yoo yoo to** triumphantly.

**iki** smartness, stylishness; **iki na** smart, stylish, fashionable.

**ikidooru** to be angry, be enraged; to be indignant.

**ikigomi** eagerness; ardor, zeal.

**ikigomu** to set one's heart on.

**ikigurushii** suffocating, stifling, choking.

**iki iki shita** lively; active; spirited; vivid; fresh; **iki iki shita sakana** fresh-looking fish.

**ikimono** living thing, creature; animal.

**IKINARI** suddenly; all at once.

**ikinokoru** to survive, to outlive.

**ikioi** power, force, energy; **ikioi no nai** spiritless, lifeless; **ikioi no yoi** lively; vigorous; **ikioi yoku** vigorously.

**IKIRU** to live.

**ikiutsushi** exact copy; **ikiutsushi no** lifelike, true to life.

**ikka** whole family.

**IKKAI** first floor; one floor, one story; **ikkai date no uchi** one-story house. **Kutsu wa ikkai de utte imasu.** Shoes are sold on the first floor.

**ikken** affair; matter.

**ikkoku** moment; second; **ikkoku mo hayaku** as soon as possible.

**ikkoo** party (of tourists); suite.

**ikoo** intention; **ikoo o saguru** to sound; to speak one's mind.

**IKU** = **yuku** to go; **machi e iku** to go to town. **Hayaku itte kudasai.** Please go quickly.

**IKU-** prefix denoting: now many; **IKUDO** how often; how many times; **ikudo to naku** countless times; **ikue** manyfold; **ikue ni mo** many times over; repeatedly; earnestly; on bended knee; **ikunichi** how many days; **IKURA** how many; how much; **ikura ka** somewhat; to some extent; **ikura demo** as many (much) as one pleases; any amount; **IKUTSU** how many; how old. **Ikura desu ka?** How much? **Kyoo wa ikura ka kibun ga yoi.** I feel a little better today. **Nihongo ga ikura ka hanasemasu.** I can speak Japanese to some extent. **Ikutsu desu ka?** How old are you? **Ikutsu arimasu ka?** How many are there?

**IKUBUN** partly; somewhat. **Anata mo ikubun ka sekinin ga aru.** You, too, are responsible for it.

**iku dooon ni** unanimously.

**ikuji** spirit; backbone; **ikuji no nai** spiritless; weak.

**IMA** now; **ima motte** as yet. **Ima ni kimasu.** She will soon come.

**imada** yet (used only with a negative verb). **Imada ni konai.** It hasn't come yet.

**IMADOKI** now; nowadays; these days.

**IMAGORO** about this time. **Imagoro nani o shite iru daroo.** What would she be doing at this time?

**imaimashii** provoking; mortifying; disgusting.

**imani** very soon; before long; by and by. **Imani kuru deshoo.** He will probably come very soon.

**imasara** now; at this time (in a negative sense). **Imasara sonna koto mo iemasen.** How can you say such a thing now!

**imashime** instruction; warning, admonition, rebuke, reprimand; **imashimeru** to instruct; to caution, admonish; to warn against; to reprimand, rebuke.

**IMASU** (form of **iru**) there is.

**imawashii** offensive; abominable.

**IMI** meaning, sense, significance; **imi arige na** significant, meaningful; **imi shinchoo** profound meaning. **Sore wa doo iu imi desu ka?** What do you mean by that?

**IMOOTO** younger sister.

**-in** suffix denoting: one who; member of; **jimuin** clerk; **kaishain** businessman.

**inagara** without any effort; without stirring.

**INAI** within; less than; not exceeding. **Gofun inai ni ome ni kakarimasu.** I will see you within five minutes.

**inaka** countryside, country; **inaka no** rural, rustic. **Inaka ni sunde imasu.** I live in the country.

**inbai** prostitution; **imbaifu** prostitute.

**inchi** inch.

**inchiki na** fraudulent; sham; feigned.

**Indo** India; **Indoyoo** Indian Ocean; **Indojin** Indian; Hindu.

**ine** rice plant.

**inemuri** nap; **inemuri suru** to nap; to doze.

**infure** inflation.

**infuruenza** influenza.

**inga** cause and effect; misfortune; **inga na** unlucky; **inga to akirameru** to resign oneself to fate.

**ingin** politeness, courtesy; **ingin na** polite, courteous.

**ingoo na** stubborn; merciless.

**inki** gloominess; melancholy; **inki na** cheerless, gloomy, dismal.

**INKU** = **INKI** ink.

**innen** affinity; relation; fate; objection.

**INOCHI** life; **inochi biroi o suru** to have a narrow escape.

**inokoru** to remain behind; stay behind.

**inoru** to pray; **seikoo o inoru** to wish someone every success.

**insatsu** (n.) printing; **insatsubutsu** printed matter; **insatsujo** printing house; press.

**inseki** relative by marriage.

**inshoo** impression; **inshoo o ataeru** to impress; to make an impression.

**insotsu suru** to lead, conduct, command.

**intai** retirement; **intai suru** to retire; to resign.

**interi** intelligentsia; intellectuals.

**INU** dog; **inugoya** kennel.

**in'utsu** gloom, gloominess; **in'utsu na** gloomy.

**inwai** obscenity; indecency; **inwai na** obscene, lewd, indecent.

**inzei** royalty (on a literary work).

**ioo** sulphur.

**ippa** religious sect; school; party; faction.

**IPPAI** cupful, bowlful; full of. **Mizu o ippai kudasai.** May I have a glass of water?

**ippaku** night's lodging; **ippaku suru** to put up for the night.

**IPPAN** generality; outline; **ippan no** general; common; **ippan ni** generally.

**ippen** once.

**ippen suru** to change completely, to undergo a complete change.

**ippon chooshi** monotone; **ippon chooshi no** monotonous; simpleminded.

**ippondachi** independence; **ippondachi de** independently.

**ippoo** one side; one party; **ippoo ni oite wa** on the one hand.

**ippuu kawatta** curious; funny; queer.

**iradatsu** to be irritated; to be excited.

**IRAI** since; since then.

**irai** dependence; reliance; request; **irai suru** to rely on; to request; **irai ni oozuru** to comply with a request.

**ira ira suru** to be irritated; to be fretful.

**IRASSHARU** to come, go, be at *(respect)*. **Yamada-san wa Tookyoo ni irasshaimasu.** Mr. Yamada is in Tokyo. **Tanaka-san wa Kyooto e irasshaimashita.** Ms. Tanaka went to Kyoto.

**ireba** artificial tooth.

**irechigaeru** to misplace, put in the wrong place.

**irechigau** to come just as someone else leaves; to leave just as someone else comes in. **Yamada-san wa Tanaka-san to irechigai ni dete itta.** Mr. Yamada had just gone out when Ms. Tanaka came in.

**irekaeru** to replace; to change; to make (tea, coffee) afresh.

**irekawaru** to change places; **sekio irekawaru** to change seats with someone else; **irekawari tachikawari** in rapid succession, one after another.

**iremono** receptacle; vessel; case.

**IRERU** to put in; to let in; to hold; to comply with; to listen to; **hito no setsu o ireru** to take advice; **ocha o ireru** to make tea.

**irezumi** tattoo.

**iri** attendance, audience; contents; **ooiri** full house.

**iribitaru** to be a constant guest; to stay all the time.

**irie** inlet; creek.

**IRIGUCHI** entrance; door.

**irihi** twilight, sunset.

**irikomu** to enter; to force an entrance.

**irikumu** to be complicated.

**irimidareru** to be mixed up; to be in confusion.

**iritsukeru** to parch; to sizzle.

**IRO** color, tint, hue; lover *(colloq.); iro age (n.)* redying; restoring a color; **iro otoko** lover; **iro onna** mistress; **iroke** coloring; shade; tone; sexual passion; tender passion; **irozuri** color print; **iroke no aru** seductive; amorous; **iroke no nai** unromantic; innocent; **kaoiro** complexion (facial); **iro age suru** to redye; **iro o nasu** to turn red with anger; **irodoru** to color; to paint.

**iroha** 47-syllable poem containing all of the 47 syllables in the traditional table of Japanese syllabaries. **Iroha mo shiranai.** He doesn't know even the simplest things (not even the ABC's).

**IROIRO NA** various; many; diverse; (all) kinds of. **Iroiro shitsumon sareta.** I was asked several questions.

**iromeku** to be alive; to be stirred; to show signs of uneasiness; to become animated.

**irori** hearth; fireplace.

**irotsuya** gloss; luster; complexion; **irotsuya no yoi** ruddy; healthy.

**irozuku** to color; to be tinged; to turn red (as foliage).

**IRU** to require, want, need. **Watakushi wa kore ga irimasu.** I need this. **Soko e hairu ni wa okane ga irimasu.** You have to pay [money] to enter. **Sore wa iranai deshoo.** It would not be necessary.

**IRU** to be at, exist *(animate objects);* to be present; to live; to stay. Following a *-te* form verb, it makes a progressive or stative form (describing a state resulting from an action that has taken place). **Sono hito wa heya ni imasu.** He is in the room. **Ame ga futte imasu.** It is raining. **Yamada-san wa kite imasu.** Yamada is here (as a result of having come). **Tookyoo ni imasu.** He is in Tokyo. **Kyooto ni mikka imashita.** I was in Kyoto for three days. **Nihongo o benkyoo shite imasu.** I'm studying Japanese. **Tegami ga kite imasu.** There is [has come and is here] a letter for you.

**iru** to toast; to parch.

**irui** clothes, garments.

**iryoo** medical treatment.

**iryuuhin** lost article; (thing) left behind.

**isagiyoi** clean; pure; upright; brave; manly.

**isai** particulars, details.

**isakai** quarrel.

**isamashii** courageous, brave.

**isame** admonition; advice, counsel.

**isamu** to be encouraged; to be in high spirits; to take heart.

**isan** legacy, inheritance; **isan soozokunin** heir, heiress.

**isasaka** little; bit, slightly; rather. **Isasaka odorokimashita.** I was a bit surprised.

**iseebi** lobster.

**isei** other (opposite) sex. **Ano hito wa isei no aida ni koosai ga hiroi desu.** He has a large acquaintance among the opposite sex.

**isei** power, influence.

**iseisha** statesman.

**iseki** ruins, remains, relics.

**isetsu** different view(s); conflicting opinion.

**ISHA** doctor, physician; M.D. **isha ni kakaru** to go to a doctor; **isha ni mite morau** to consult a doctor. **Isha ni kakaru to nakanaka kane ga irimasu.** Medical expenses are very high.

**isha** comfort, consolation; **isharyoo** consolation money.

**ishi** stone; rock; **ishi dooroo** stone lantern (in front of a shrine); **ishidan** stone steps; **ishigaki** stone wall; **ishiya** stonecutter.

**ishi** will, intention; **ishi ga tsuyoi** to have a strong will; **ishi ga sotsuu suru** to come to an understanding.

**ishiki** consciousness; **ishikiteki ni** consciously; **ishiki suru** to be conscious of.

**ishin** restoration; renovation.

**ishin denshin** tacit understanding; telepathy.

**ishiwata** asbestos.

**ishizue** foundation; basis; groundwork.

**isho** will, testament.

**ishoku** food and clothing; means of support; **ishokujuu** food, clothes, and shelter.

**ishoku** commission; request; charge.

**ishoo** design; idea.

**ishoo** clothes, dress, garments.

**isobe** beach, shore.

**isogaseru** to hurry up, urge on.

**ISOGASHII** busy, occupied, engaged. **Shiken de taihen isogashii desu.** I am very busy with my exams.

**ISOGI** hurry, haste; **isogi no** hasty; urgent, pressing.

**ISOGU** to hurry, hasten; to be in a hurry. **Isogu hitsuyoo wa arimasen.** There is no rush.

**isoiso to** cheerfully; lightheartedly.

**isooroo** hanger-on.

**issai** all; altogether, every; wholly.

**issakuban** evening before last.

**issakujitsu** day before yesterday.

**issakunen** year before last.

**issakuya** night before last.

**issei ni** simultaneously; all at once.

**issha senri** rush; **issha senri ni** in a rush; in a hurry; at full speed.

**isshiki** complete set (of).

**isshinfuran** whole mind; single heart; **isshinfuran ni** wholeheartedly; intently; with undivided attention.

**ISSHO** together; at the same time; all at once; **ISSHO NI** together with; simultaneously. **Issho ni ikimashoo.** Let's go together.

**isshoo** laugh; smile; **isshoo shite** with a laugh; with a smile; **isshoo ni fusu** to dismiss with a laugh; to laugh one's troubles away.

**isshoo** lifetime, all through one's life; **isshoo ho nozomi** life-long desire.

**ISSHOOKENMEI** as hard as one can; with all one's might (efforts); with one's whole heart. **Isshookenmei benkyoo shite imasu.** He is studying hard.

**isshu** kind, type, variety.

**isshuu** one round, lap; **isshuu suru** to go round; to make a tour; **sekai isshuu ryokoo** round-the-world trip.

**ISSHUUKAN** one week.

**isso** rather; sooner; preferably.

**issoku** pair (of shoes or other footgear).

**ISSOO** much more; all the more.

**ISSUN** one *sun* (Japanese unit of length, one tenth of a *shaku*); **issun saki mo mienai** pitch dark.

**issuru** to miss; to lose; **kooki o issuru** to miss a good opportunity.

**ISU** chair; sofa; couch; **isu ni kakeru** to take a seat.

**Isuraeru** Israel.

**isuwaru** to remain in the same position (in office); to remain in power.

**ita** board; plank; plate; sheet; **itabei** wooden wall; board fence.

**itabasami** fix; predicament; **itabasami ni naru** to be in a fix.

**itachi** weasel.

**ITADAKU** to receive; to be presented with; to be given; to accept with gratitude *(humble)*. **Juubun itadakimashita.** I've had enough, thank you.

**itade** hard blow; severe wound.

**itagane** sheet metal.

**itagarasu** plate glass.

**ITAI** painful; sore. **Atama ga itai desu.** I have a headache. **Onaka ga itai desu.** I have a stomachache.

**itaitashii** pathetic, sad, pitiful.

**itamashii** miserable; touching, sad, pathetic.

**itameru** to hurt, injure; to worry; **kokoro o itameru** to be worried about (something).

**itami** pain, ache; sore, bruise.

**itami iru** to be greatly obliged; to feel grateful. **Doomo itamiirimasu.** I'm much obliged to you.

**itamu** to ache, feel a pain.

**ITARII = ITARIYA** Italy.

**itaru** to arrive, reach; to result in; to come to; **itaru tokoro** everywhere; throughout; **haru kara aki ni itaru made** from spring to autumn.

**itasa** pain.

**itashikata nai** it can't be helped; **itashikata naku** necessarily; of necessity.

**ITASU** to do, make *(humble)*. **Soo itashimashoo.** Let's do so. **Doo itashimashite.** Don't mention it.

**itatte** exceedingly, extremely, very.

**itawaru** to pity, sympathize with, console.

**itazura** mischief; prank; **itazura hanbun** for fun; **itazura na** naughty; mischievous; **itazura ni** needlessly; to no purpose.

**itchaku** first (in a race); one suit of clothes.

**itchi** agreement; harmony; **itchi suru** to agree with; harmonize.

**itchokusen** straight line; **itchokusen ni** in a straight line.

**itchoo** once; one day *(literary usage);* **itchoo isseki ni** in a single day; in a short space of time.

**iten** transfer, removal; **iten suru** to transfer; to move. **Inaka kara machi e iten shimashita.** We moved from the country to the city.

**ITO** thread; yarn; twine; string; **momen ito** cotton thread; **kinu ito** silk thread.

**itoguchi** clue; beginning; **itoguchi o hiraku** to make a start.

**itoguruma** spinning wheel.

**ITOKO** cousin.

**itoma** leisure; time to spare; leave of absence; **yasumu itoma mo nai** to have no time to rest.

**itomaki** spool, bobbin, reel.

**itonamu** to carry on; to conduct (business); to run, operate; **seikei o itonamu** to earn a living.

**itoosu** to shoot through; to pierce.

**ITSU** when; at what time; how soon; **itsu demo** at any time; at a moment's notice; **itsu kara** how long; since when; **itsu made** how long; till when; **itsu ka** some day; **itsu mo** always.

**itsukushimi** love; affection; compassion *(literary usage);* **itsukushimu** to love; to treat with tenderness.

**itsu ni** solely, entirely.

**ITSUTSU** five.

**itsuu** one letter.

**itsuwa** anecdote.

**itsuwari** lie; **itsuwari no** false, untrue.

**itsuwaru** to lie, tell a lie.

**ittai zentai** on earth; in the world. **Ittai zentai dare daroo.** I wonder who in the world it can be.

**ittan** part; outline; one end.

**ittan** once, if. **Ittan kankyuu areba . . .** Should an emergency arise . . .

**itte hanbai** sole agency; monopoly; **itte hanbainin** sole agent; sole distributor.

**ittei no** fixed, immovable, set; definite; regular.

**itten** point; dot; spot.

**ittenbari** persistency; **ittenbari de** sticking to; solely by.

**ITTOO** first class; **ittoo ni noru** to travel first class; **ittoo no kippu** first-class ticket; **nitoo sha** second-class car. **Ittoo ii mono desu.** It is the best.

**IU = YUU** to say, speak, tell, relate, mention; **ookiku iu** to exaggerate; **iu made mo naku** of course, naturally. **Iu made mo nai.** It goes without saying.

**iwa** rock; **iwa no ooi** rocky.

**iwaba** in a word; so to speak.

**iwai** celebration; feast; festival.

**iwaku** reason; **iwaku ga atte** for certain reasons; **iwaku o tsukeru** to find fault with.

**iware** reason, cause; origin; **iware mo naku** without any cause; **iware no nai** unreasonable; unwarranted.

**iwashi** sardine.

**iwau** to congratulate; to celebrate.

**IWAYURU** so-called; what you call. **Kare wa iwayuru jiyuu shugisha desu.** He is a so-called liberal.

**IYA, IIE** no.

**iyafoon** earphone.

**iyagaru** to dislike, to hate.

**iya iya** reluctantly; **iya iya nagara** unwillingly; with reluctance.

**iyaku** medicine; physic.

**iyami** offensiveness, bad taste, sarcasm; **iyami no aru** offensive, disagreeable.

**iya na** disagreeable, unpleasant; **iya na kao o suru** to frown.

**iyashii** low; humble; vulgar.

**iyashikumo** at all; in the least.

**iyashimu** to despise, to look down on, to scorn.

**iyoiyo** still more; all the more; certainly; positively; no doubt.

**iza** come now; now then; **iza to nareba** at the last moment; when the time comes; at a pinch. **Iza saraba.** Farewell *(archaic).*

**izakaya** tavern, saloon, bar.

**izen** ago; before; prior to; formerly. **Tooka izen ni kite kudasai.** Please come before the tenth.

**izen** as before; as it was.

**izon** objection; **izon nai** to have no objection; **izon ga aru** to have an objection.

**izumi** spring; fountain.

**IZURE** which; someday; sometime; sooner or later; **izure mo** any; all; either; every; both; **izure ni shite mo** in either case; **izure sono uchi ni** one of these days.

# J

**JA, JAA** well; then; in that case. **Ja, sayonara.** Well, so long.

**jaanarisuto** journalist.

**JAGAIMO** potato.

**jaguchi** faucet, tap; spout.

**jaken** meanness, unkindness; **jaken na** cruel, unkind.

**jaketto** sweater.

**jakkan** some; little; number of.

**-jaku** suffix denoting: little less than, little short of. **Yokohama made wa nijuu mairujaku desu.** It is a little less than twenty miles to Yokohama.

**JAMA** obstruction, obstacle, hindrance; **jama suru** to obstruct, hinder; **jama ni naru** to stand (be) in the way; **jama o nozoku** to remove an obstacle. **Ojama shimashita.** Excuse me for disturbing you. **Ojama de wa arimasen ka.** I hope I'm not disturbing you.

**jamu** jam, jelly.

**janen** vicious mind; evil thought.

**jan jan** jingle jingle; dingdong; profusely; a lot (slang).

**janken** Japanese equivalent of toss-up. **Janken de kimemashoo.** Let's toss for it.

**jaratsuku** to flirt with.

**jareru** to be playful.

**jari** gravel; pebbles.

**jasui** distrust; groundless suspicion; **jasui suru** to distrust; suspect without reason. **jasui bukai** suspicious, distrustful.

**jazu** jazz.

**JI** character, letter, ideograph; **ji o kaku** to write. **ji o oboeru** to learn how to read and write (characters); **kanji** Chinese characters (used in Japanese writing system).

**ji** piles, hemorrhoids.

**ji** ground, earth, soil; **jimoto** local.

**ji-** prefix denoting: next; second; vice-; **jikai** next session.

**-JI** counter denoting: o'clock; hour; time; **ichiji** one o'clock. **Ichiji wa soo omoimashita.** Once I thought that way but now I have a different opinion.

**jiban** base, foundation.

**jibara o kiru** to pay out of one's own pocket.

**JIBIKI** dictionary; lexicon; **jibiki o hiku** to look something up in the dictionary; to use a dictionary.

**jiboojiki** desperation; despair; **jiboojiki ni naru** to become desperate.

**JIBUN** oneself; **jibun no** my/his/her/their own, your own, mine/yours/his/hers/theirs; personal; **jibun hitori de** by oneself; **jibun to shite wa** for my part.

**jibyoo** chronic disease.

**jichi** self-government.

**jichoo** self-respect; self-love; caution; **jichooshin** self-respect. **Jichoo shite kudasai.** Take good care of yourself.

**jidai** time, period, epoch, era; **jidai sakugo** anachronism; **jidaimono** old-fashioned article (furniture, etc.); historical drama; **jidaiokure** one who is old-fashioned; **jidaiokure no** old-fashioned, antiquated.

**jidan** private settlement; compromise.

**jidaraku** sloppiness, untidiness; **jidaraku na** sloppy, untidy.

**jiden** autobiography.

**jidoo** child; boys and girls; **jidoo no** juvenile.

**jidoo** automatic action; **jidoo no** automatic; **jidoo hanbaiki** slot machine; **jidoo tobira** automatic door.

**JIDOOSHA** automobile, car; **jidoosha ni noru** to ride in a car.

**jiei** self-defense.

**jifushin** pride; self-confidence.

**jigane** metal, ore; true character.

**jigoku** hell.

**jigyoo** enterprise, undertaking; achievement; deed; work; **jigyookai** the business (industrial) world.

**jihaku** confession; **jihaku suru** to confess.

**jihatsuteki** voluntary; spontaneous; **jihatsuteki ni** voluntarily.

**jihen** emergency; disaster; incident.

**jihi** mercy; benevolence; pity; **jihi bukai** benevolent; charitable.

**jihitsu** handwriting; autograph.

**jihoo** time signal; current news.

**jii** intention to resign.

**jiin** Buddhist temple.

**jiji** current events.

**jijii** (colloq.) grandfather; old man (derogatory).

**jijitsu** fact; truth; **jijitsujoo** practically, virtually; in reality, actually.

**jijitsu** time; date.

**jijoo** circumstances; reasons; state of affairs; **koo iu jijoo da kara** under these circumstances.

**jika** current price.

**jikaku** self-consciousness; **jikaku suru** to be conscious, aware of; to realize.

**JIKAN** time; hour; **jikan ni ma ni au** to be on time; **jikan ni ma ni awanai** to be late. **Mada daibu jikan ga aru.** There is still plenty of time.

**jikanhyoo** timetable; schedule.

**jikani** personally; at firsthand; directly.

**jikatsu suru** to support oneself.

**jiken** affair; matter; scandal.

**jiketsu** self-determination; resignation; suicide.

**JIKI** time; period; season.

**jiki-** prefix denoting: direct; **jikideshi** one's immediate apprentice.

**JIKI NI** immediately; at once; presently.

**jikken** experiment; test.

**jikkoo** practice; action; execution; **jikkoo suru** to carry out; to put into practice; **jikkoo shigatai** impractical; difficult to put into practice.

**jiko** self; ego; **jiko chuushin no** egocentric.

**jiko** accident, incident; **kootsuu jiko** traffic accident.

**jikoku** time; hour; **jikokuhyoo** transportation schedule.

**JIKOO** season; weather; current fashion; latest style, vogue; **jikoo hazure no** unseasonable.

**jiku** phraseology; expressions; wording.

**jiku** axis; axle; pivot; shaft; stem; stalk.

**jikyoku** situation, state of affairs; political situation.

**jikyuu** self-support; independence.

**jiman** pride, boast; **jiman suru** to boast; to be conceited.

**jime jime shita** damp; wet; moist; humid.

**jimen** ground; surface of the earth; plot of land.

**jimi na** simple; modest; unpretentious; **jimi na hito** unpretentious person; quiet person.

**jimu** business; duties; **jimuin** clerk; office worker; **jimusho** office; **jimuchoo** chief clerk; head official; purser (of a ship).

**-JIN** suffix denoting: people; **Nihonjin** Japanese; **Amerikajin** American.

**jinan** second son.

**jinboo** popularity; **jinboo aru hito** idol (of the people).

**jinbutsu** person; personality; portrait.

**jinchooge** sweet-smelling daphne (common garden plant in Japan).

**jindai na** extraordinary; enormous, huge,

great. **Songai wa jindai na mono deshita.** The damage was very great.

**jindoo** sidewalk, pavement; **jindoo o aruku** to walk on the pavement.

**jindoo** humanity; morality.

**jinguu** Shinto shrine (a national monument).

**jinja** Shinto shrine.

**jinji fusei** unconsciousness; **jinji fusei ni naru** to faint; **jinji fusei no** unconscious.

**jinjoo** commonness; **jinjoo no** common, ordinary; **jinjoo ni** commonly.

**jinkaku** personality, character.

**jinken** artificial silk; rayon.

**jinken juurin** infringement of personal rights.

**JINKOO** population, **jinkoo chuumitsu na** thickly populated.

**jinkoo** artificiality; **jinkoo no** artificial; **jinkoo kokyuu** artificial respiration.

**jinmei** the name of a person; **jinmeibo** list of names of persons; directory; **jinmeijisho** biographical dictionary.

**jinmin** people; public.

**jinmon** inquiry; examination.

**jinrin** moral law; human relations.

**jinrui** human race.

**jinryoku** human power, human strength; effort, endeavor; help; **jinryoku suru** to make an effort; to work on someone's behalf.

**jinsei** human existence; life.

**jinshu** (human) race; **jinshuteki henken** racial prejudice.

**jinsoku** swiftness, rapidity; **jinsoku na** swift, rapid, quick.

**jintai** human body.

**jinushi** landlord.

**jinzoo** artificial, synthetic; **jinzoo gomu** synthetic rubber.

**jinzoo** kidney.

**jippa hitokarage ni** in a wholesale way; sweepingly.

**jippi** actual expenses; cost of production; **jippi de** at cost.

**jippu** one's natural father.

**jirasu** to provoke, irritate; to tease.

**jirei** government order; written order; manner of speaking.

**jirenma** dilemma.

**jireru** to be irritated; to fret and fume; to become impatient.

**jirettai** irritating, provoking; irritated.

**JIRIJIRI** slowly; gradually, little by little. **Jirijiri tsume yorimashita** He edged up to me.

**jiriki de** by oneself.

**jiritsu** independence; self-support; **jiritsu suru** to stand on one's own feet.

**jiro jiro miru** to stare at.

**jiron** personal opinion; pet theory.

**jirori to** with a glance; **jirori to miru** to glance at.

**jiryoku** magnetism.

**jisan** (n.) bringing; carrying; **jisan suru** to bring; to carry along.

**jisatsu** suicide (the act); **jisatsusha** suicide (person).

**jisei** times; mood of the times; **jisei ni okureru** to fall behind the times.

**jisei** self-control; **jisei suru** to control oneself.

**jisetsu** season; times; age; **jisetsu hazure no** out of season; **jisetsu toorai** the time has come.

**jishaku** magnet; compass.

**JISHIN** earthquake. **Nihon wa jishin ga ooi.** Earthquakes occur frequently in Japan.

**JISHO** dictionary.

**jisho** land, plot of ground, estate.

**jishoku** resignation.

**jison** self-respect; pride; **jison shin o kizutsukeru** to hurt one's pride.

**jishoo** self-styled, would-be; **jishoo shijin.** A would-be poet.

**jissai** truth; reality; **jissai wa** in reality; in fact; **jissai no** actual; practical.

**jisshi** enforcement; **jisshi suru** to put into effect; to enforce.

**jisshi** one's natural child.

**jisshin hoo** decimal system.

**jisshitsu** substance, essence.

**jisuberi** landslide.

**jisui suru** to cook one's meals.

**jisuru** to decline; to refuse; to resign.

**jitai** situation; state of affairs.

**jitaku** house, residence; **jitaku e kaeru** to go home.

**jiten, jisho** dictionary.

**JITENSHA** bicycle; **jitensha ni noru** to ride a bicycle.

**JITSU** truth; reality; **JITSU NI** really; truly; very, exceedingly; in fact; surely; exceedingly; **jitsu no** true; real; **jitsu wa** in reality; to tell the truth.

**jitsubo** one's natural mother.

**jitsubutsu** real thing; actual object; **jitsubutsu dai no** life-size.

**jitsugen** realization; **jitsugen suru** to realize; to materialize.

**jitsugyoo** business, industry; **jitsugyoo no** commercial, industrial; **jitsugyookai** business world.

**jitsujoo** actual condition; true state of affairs. **Jitsujoo wa koo desu.** The fact is this.

**jitsuyoo** utility; practical use; **jitsuyoo ni tekisuru** to be of practical use. **jitsuyoo muki no** serviceable; practical; **jitsuyoohin** necessity; article having practical use.

**jitsuzuki** adjoining land.

**jitto** fixedly; firmly; steadily; **jitto mitsumeru** to stare at, look fixedly at; **jitto shite iru** to keep still.

**jiyoo** nourishment; **jiyoo butsu** nourishing food; **jiyoo aru** nourishing, nutritious.

**jiyuu** liberty, freedom; **jiyuu booeki** free trade; **jiyuu kyoosoo** open (free) competition; **jiyuu na** free; **jiyuu ni suru** to do as one pleases. **Gojiyuu ni.** Help yourself.

**jizen** philanthropic work; **jizen ka** philanthropist; **jizen jigyoo** philanthropic work.

**jobun** preface, foreword, introduction.

**jochoo** promotion; advancement; **jochoo suru** to promote, foster, encourage.

**jodooshi** auxiliary verb; inflected particle, i.e., *-(r)areru* (passive) and *-(s)aseru* (causative).

**jogai** exception; **jogai suru** to make an exception of; to exclude; to exempt from.

**jogen** advice, counsel; suggestion, hint; **jogen suru** to give advice; to suggest.

**joi** female doctor.

**jojo ni** slowly; gradually.

**jojooshi** lyrical poem, ballad.

**jojutsu** description; **jojutsu no** descriptive; **jojutsu suru** to describe; to narrate; **jojutsubun** description.

**jokoo** slow pace; **jokoo suru** to go slowly. **jokoo.** Go slow. Drive slowly.

**joo** feeling, emotion, sentiment; affection, love; sympathy; **joo ga fukai** affectionate; warmhearted; **joo ga nai** cold, heartless; **joo ni moroi** emotional, sentimental.

**joo** lock; **joo o kakeru** to lock; **joo o hazusu** to unlock.

**-joo** article; **Dai Kyuujoo** Article IX.

**-joo** floor mat (Japanese rooms are measured by the number of **joo** mats they contain); **juujoo no ma** 10-mat room.

**-joo** suffix denoting: letter; **shookaijoo** letter of introduction; **annaijoo** (letter of) invitation; **shookanjoo** warrant.

**jooai** affection, love; **jooai no fukai** loving, affectionate.

**jooba** horseback riding.

**JOOBU** good health; soundness of body; **joobu na** durable; robust, strong; **joobu soo na** strong-looking, healthy-looking; **joobu ni naru** to grow strong.

**joobu** top, upper part, upper surface.

**joocho** mood; atmosphere.

**joodan** joke, prank; fun; **joodan o iu** to joke; **joodan ni suru** to take as a joke.

**joodeki** good performance; success; good work; **joodeki no** well-done; excellent. **Joodeki!** Well done! Bravo!

**jooen suru** to put on, perform (a play); to put on the stage.

**jooge** top and bottom, upper and lower.

**joogi** ruler; square; standard; norm.

**joogo** drinker, sake-lover.

**joogo** funnel.

**joohatsu** evaporation; **joohatsu suru** to evaporate.

**joohin** elegance; refinement; **joohin na** refined; elegant; graceful.

**jooho** concession, compromise.

**joohoo** report; information.

**joojiru** = **joozuru** to multiply; to take advantage of.

**joojitsu** personal feelings (considerations).

**jooju** accomplishment, achievement; **jooju suru** to achieve, realize, accomplish.

**JOOJUN** first ten days of the month; **Ichigatsu joojun** early in January.

**jooken** condition; term; **jooken zuki** conditional; qualified.

**jooki** regular (normal) course; **jooki o issuru** to deviate, depart from the normal course.

**jooki** steam, vapor; **jooki kikan** steam engine.

**jookigen** good humor; **jookigen de** in a good humor.

**jookyaku** passenger.

**jookyoo** state of affairs; conditions.

**joomae** lock.

**joomuin** crew.

**joomu torishimari** managing director.

**joomyaku** vein.

**joonetsu** passion.

**joooo** queen.

**jooriku suru** to disembark, go ashore; **jooriku chiten** point of embarkation.

**jooro** watering can.

**jooruri** Japanese ballad-drama.

**jooryokuju** evergreen (tree or shrub).

**joosei** state of affairs; **genka no joosei de wa** under the present circumstances.

**joosha** (n.) taking a train, bus, etc.; **joosha suru** to take a train; to board a train; **jooshachin** carfare, train fare; **jooshaken** ticket (for a train, streetcar, or bus).

**jooshiki** common sense; **jooshiki o kaku** to lack common sense; **jooshikiteki na** sensible; practical.

**jooshubi** success; happy result; **jooshubi no** successful. **Jooshubi da.** It's all right.

**joosoo** upper layer; upper stories (of a building); (top) social class.

**jootai** condition, state; circumstances; **mokka no jootai de wa** as matters now stand.

**jootatsu suru** to improve; advance; progress.

**jootenki** fine (splendid) weather.

**JOOTOO** (n.) best; first class; **jootoo hin** first-class article; **jootoo no** (adj.) best, superior.

**jootoogo** hackneyed expression, trite saying.

**jooyaku** treaty, pact, agreement.

**jooyoku** lust.

**jooyoo kanji** ideographic characters included in the Japanese Government's 1945 list of basic symbols for writing.

**joozai** tablet (medicinal).

**JOOZU** skill, dexterity, proficiency; **JOOZU NA** skillful, expert, proficient. **Joozu desu.** He is skillful. **Ano hito wa hanashi ga joozu desu.** He/she is a good speaker.

**joozuru** See **joojiru.**

**joryoku** aid, assistance; **joryoku suru** to aid, help.

**joryuu sakka** female author.

**josainai** shrewd, clever, smart.

**josanpu** midwife.

**josei** womanhood, femininity; **joseiteki** feminine.

**josei** aid, assistance; **josei suru** to aid, to assist (financially); to subsidize; **joseikin** subsidy.

**joshi** particle (grammar) e.g., **wa, ga, o,** etc. (used in postposition).

**joshi** woman; girl; daughter; female.

**JOYA** New Year's Eve.

**joyaku** assistant official.

**joyuu** actress.

**jugaku** = **jukyoo** Confucianism.

**JUGYOO** teaching, instruction; **jugyoo o suru** to teach; **jugyoo o ukeru** to take lessons.

**jukkoo** reflection; careful consideration; **jukkoo suru** to consider carefully; to reflect; to deliberate. **Sono mondai wa jukkoo chuu desu.** That matter is receiving careful consideration.

**jukuchi suru** to have full knowledge of; to be familiar with. **Watakushi wa sono koto o jukuchi shite imasu.** I'm fully aware of that.

**jukuren** skill, dexterity; **jukuren suru** to become skilled; **jukuren o kaku** to lack skill.

**jukusui suru** to sleep soundly.

**juku suru** to ripen, mature, become ripe.

**jukyoo** See **jugaku.**

**jumoku** trees. **Sono kooen ni wa jumoku ga ooi desu.** There are many trees in that park.

**jumyoo** life; life span.

**jun** pureness, purity; **jun na** pure; genuine; innocent; **junkin** pure gold.

**jun, junban** regular order; turn; **jun ni, junban ni** in regular order; in turn; **jun ni naraberu** to arrange in order. **Junban o matte kudasai.** Please wait your turn.

**junbi** preparation, arrangements; **junbi suru** to prepare, arrange; to get ready for; **junbi ga dekite iru** to be prepared.

**junchoo** favorable, satisfactory condition; **junchoo ni** smoothly; favorably, without a hitch; **junchoo ni iku** to go well; **junchoo ni mukau** to improve.

**jun'eki** net profit. **jun'eki o eru** to earn a net profit, to clear.

**junjo** order, sequence; **junjo tadashiku** in good order.

**junkan suru** to circulate; recur.

**junkesshoo** semifinals.

**junketsu** purity; cleanliness; **junketsu na** pure, chaste; clean.

**junrei** pilgrim; pilgrimage.

**junsa** policeman; **junsa hashutsujo** police box; **junsa buchoo** police sergeant. **Keisatsusho de junsa ni hanashimashita.** I told it to a policeman at the police station.

**junshi** inspection tour; **junshi suru** to make the rounds.

**junshin** pureness; genuineness; **junshin na** pure; unsophisticated.

**junsui** purity, genuineness. **Kore wa junsui no Nihon no kinu desu.** This is genuine Japanese silk.

**juntoo** natural; regular; appropriate; normal. **Juntoo ni ikeba tooka ni dekimasu.** If all goes well, it will be done on the tenth.

**jushin suru** to receive a letter or message.

**jutai suru** to conceive, become pregnant.

**jutsu** art; technique; means; way; trick.

**JUU** ten, tenth; **juu ga juu made** in every case.

**-JUU** suffix denoting: all through the course of; during; all over; throughout. **Tookyoojuu** throughout Tokyo. **Uchijuu de dekakemasu.** The entire family goes out together.

**juubako** pile (nest) of lacquered boxes used as picnic boxes or as containers for foods at festivals.

**juuban** undergarment worn with Japanese clothing.

**JUUBUN** plenty; enough; **juubun na** full; sufficient; enough; **juubun ni taberu** to eat enough.

**juubyoo** serious illness.

**juudai** importance; seriousness; **juudai na** important; **juudaishi suru** to take seriously.

**JUUGATSU** October.

**JUUGO** fifteen; **juugoya no tsuki** harvest moon.

**JUUHACHI** eighteen; **juuhachiban** one's forte; hobby; favorite trick.

**JUUICHI** eleven.

**JUUICHIGATSU** November.

**juuji** *(n.)* cross; **juuji ni** crosswise; **juuji no** cross-shaped; **juujigun** crusade.

**juujika** (See also **juuji.**) **juujika zoo** crucifix.

**juuji suru** to engage in, practice, pursue.

**juujitsu** perfection; enrichment; fullness.

**juujun** gentleness; obedience; **juujun na** gentle, meek; obedient.

**juuketsu** congestion (medical). **Me ga juuketsu shite imasu.** His eyes are bloodshot.

**JUUKU** nineteen; **dai juuku** nineteenth.

**juukyo** dwelling, residence; **juukyonin** resident.

**juuman suru** to be filled with; to be replete with.

**juumin** residents, inhabitants.

**juumonji** cross; **juumonji ni** crosswise. (See also **juuji.**)

**juunen** decade.

**JUUNI** twelve, dozen; **juunibun ni** more than enough.

**JUUNIGATSU** December.

**juunin** ten persons; **juunin nami no** ordinary, average, normal; mediocre.

**juurai** heretofore; so far; up to now; **juurai no** old, traditional; **juurai no toori** as in the past.

**JUUROKU** sixteen.

**juurui** beast, animals.

**juuryoo** weight; **juuryoo busoku** short weight.

**juuryoo** hunting (with a gun); **juuryooka** sportsman.

**JUUSAN** thirteen.

**JUUSHI** fourteen.

**JUUSHICHI** seventeen.

**juushimatsu** lovebird.

**juushoku** high office; responsible position.

**JUUSHO** dwelling, residence; address; **juusho seimei** name and address. **Gojuusho wa dochira desu ka?** What's your address?

**juushoo** serious wound, injury.

**juusoo** bicarbonate of soda.

**JUUSU** juice; **orenji juusu** orange juice.

**juutai** critical stage; serious condition.

**juutaku** house, residence; **juutakuchi** residential section.

**juuyaku** director; board of directors.

**juuyoo** importance; **juuyoo na** important; **juuyoo de nai** unimportant.

**juuzai** felony; capital offense.

**juuzei** heavy taxation; heavy tax.

**juwaki** telephone receiver.

**juyo suru** to award (a prize); to confer (a degree).

**juyoo** demand; **juyoo ga aru** to be in demand; **juyoo o mitasu** to meet the demand.

**juzu** rosary (mainly Buddhist).


# K

**kabu** turnip.

**kabu** stock, share; **kabunushi** shareholder.

**kabuki** classic Japanese play.

**kabun** superfluous; **kabun no** excessive; undue.

**kabureru** to be poisoned; to be influenced.

**KABURU** to put on or over one's head; to be covered with; to take upon oneself; **booshi o kaburu** to put on a hat.

**kabusaru** to get covered; to overlap.

**kabuseru** to cover with; to put a thing on.

**kabuto** helmet; **kabuto o nugu** to admit defeat; to throw in the sponge; **kabuto mushi** beetle.

**kachi** victory, conquest; success.

**kachi** value, worth, merit; **kachi ga aru** valuable.

**kachiau** to clash with; to knock against; to collide with.

**kachiki na** unyielding; strong-minded; resolute.

**kachiku** domestic animals; livestock.

**kadai** *(n.)* being too big; **kadai no** too big; exaggerated; too much; too heavy.

**kadai** subject; theme.

**kadan** garden; flower bed.

**KADO** corner; turn; angle; edge; **kado no mise** corner store. **Soo iu to kado ga tatsu.** That sounds harsh.

**kado** excess, immoderateness.

**kado** charge; suspicion; grounded; **-no kado de** on the grounds of, on account of, for the reason that.

**kadode** departure; **kadode suru** to set out; to leave home.

**kaede** maple tree.

**kaerigake ni** on the way back; upon one's return.

**kaeri michi** return road; way home.

**kaerimiru** to look back; to reflect upon; to think of.

**KAERU** to return, come back; to go back. **Okaeri nasai.** Welcome back!

**KAERU** to change, alter; to exchange; to replace; to convert; **setsu o kaeru** to change one's opinion; **michi o kaeru** to take another road; **kane o kaeru** to change money.

**kaeru** to be hatched.

**kaeru** frog.

**KAESU** to give back, restore, return; to pay back; **okane o kaesu** to repay money.

**kaesu** to hatch (eggs).

**KAETTE** on the contrary; instead; on the other hand; all the more.

**kafun** pollen.

**kafusu** cuff(s).

**kafuu** family customs (tradition).

**kagaisha** assailant.

**kagaku** science; **kagaku no** scientific; **kagakusha** scientist.

**kagaku** chemistry; **kagakusha** chemist; **kagaku koogyoo** chemical industry.

**kagameru** to bend; to bow; **koshi o kagameru** to stoop, bend down.

**KAGAMI** mirror; **kagami o miru** to look in a mirror.

**kagamu** to bend, bow; to crouch.

**kagaribi** campfire; bonfire.

**kagayakasu** to light up; to make shine; to brighten.

**kagayaki** luster; brilliance; glitter.

**kagayaku** to shine, glitter, sparkle, glisten.

**kage** shadow; silhouette; image; reflection, shade; **kage ni naru** to be shaded; **kage ni** in the shade; **kage ga sasu** to cast a shadow.

**kageguchi** malicious gossip; **kageguchi o iu** to gossip maliciously.

**kagehinata** two-faced; faithless; **kagehinata no nai** faithful; conscientious.

**kageki** opera; operetta; **kageki dan** opera company; **kagekijoo** opera house.

**kageki** excessive; extreme; violent; radical; **kagekiha** radicals (political); **kageki shisoo** radical ideas; dangerous thoughts. **Kageki na undoo o shite wa ikemasen.** You must not engage in strenuous physical exercise.

**kagemusha** man who pulls strings or exerts influence behind the scenes.

**kagen** degree, proportion, extent.

**kageroo** fly living only one day; **kageroo no yoo na** short-lived, ephemeral.

**kageru** to become shady; to get dark; to darken.

**-KAGETSU** counter denoting: (one) month's duration; **ikkagetsu** one month; **nikagetsu** two months; **sankagetsu** three months.

**KAGI** key; **kagi ana** keyhole; **kagi de akeru** to unlock; **kagi o kakeru** to lock.

**kagi** hook.

**kagiri** limit, bounds; **kagiri no aru** limited, restricted. **Watakushi no shiru kagiri.** As far as I know.

**kagiru** to limit, restrict.

**kago** basket; cage; sedan chair; **kago ni noru** to ride in a sedan chair.

**kagoo suru** to combine.

**KAGU** furniture, furnishings; **kaguya** furniture store.

**kagu** to smell; to scent; to sniff; **kagitsukeru** to get wind of.

**kagura** sacred music and dancing in front of a shrine (Shinto).

**kahei** money; currency.

**kahi** right or wrong; good or bad; propriety. **Sono kahi wa toohyoo de kimemashoo.** Let's decide the matter by vote.

**kahoo** ancestral treasure; heirloom.

**kahoo** luck; good fortune; **kahoo na** lucky.

**kai** avail, effect, use; **kai ga nai** of no effect; **kai naku** without avail; **kai no nai** useless; fruitless.

**kai** meeting, assembly; association; society; (society) member; **kai hi** membership fee; subscription; admission fee.

**kai** time, cycle; **nikai** two times, twice.

**kai** oar, paddle; **kai de kogu** to row.

**kai** shellfish.

**-kai** suffix denoting: stairs; story (of a building); **ikkai** first floor; **nikai-date** two-story house.

**-kai** suffix denoting: sea, **Nihonkai** Japan Sea.

**kaiageru** to purchase, buy; to requisition.

**kaibatsu** above sea level.

**kaiboo** autopsy; dissection; analysis.

**kaibutsu** monster.

**kaichiku** rebuilding, reconstruction.

**kaichuu** pocket; **kaichuu mono** purse; **kaichuudokei** pocket watch.

**kaidaku** willing consent; **kaidaku suru** to give ready consent; to consent readily.

**KAIDAN** stairway, staircase; flight of steps. **Heya wa kaidan o agatte hidari no hoo desu.** My room is to the left of the stairway.

**kaidashi** marketing, shopping; daily needs.

**kaidasu** to drain off; to ladle; to scoop out.

**kaifuku** recovery; restoration; re-establishment; **kaifuku suru** to recover; restore.

**kaifuu suru** to open a letter; break a seal.

**kaiga** pictures; painting(s); **kaiga tenrankai** art exhibition.

**kaigai** (n.) abroad; foreign country; **kaigai kara** from abroad; **kaigai ni iku** to go abroad.

**kaigaishii** prompt; brisk; faithful; **kaigaishiku** promptly; briskly; willingly.

**kaigan** seashore, coast; **kaigansen** coastline.

**kaigi** council; conference; convention.

**kaigoo** meeting, assembly.

**kaigun** navy; **kaigun no** naval.

**kaigyoo suru** to open a shop; to open a business.

**kaihan** revised edition.

**kaihatsu suru** to develop; to exploit; to cultivate; to open up.

**kaihen** seashore, seaside, beach.

**kaihi suru** to avoid, shun, evade.

**kaihoo** liberation, release; **kaihoo suru** to set free.

**kaihoo** good news.

**kaihoo** opening; **kaihoo suru** to open to the public.

**kaihoo suru** to nurse (tend) a sick person.

**kaihyoo suru** to count votes.

**kaiin shiki** opening ceremony of the Diet (Japanese Parliament).

**kaijin** ashes; **kaijin ni kisuru** to be reduced to ashes.

**kaijo** cancellation; release, discharge; **kaijo suru** to cancel, rescind, etc.

**kaijoo** sea; **kaijoo no** marine, maritime.

**kaijoo** circular (letter); **kaijoo o mawasu** to send out a circular.

**kaijoo ni** upstairs; **kaijoo e iku** to go upstairs.

**kaikaburu** to pay too much; to overestimate; overrate.

**kaikaku** reformation; reorganization; **kaikaku suru** to reform; reorganize; innovate.

**kaikan** hall; assembly hall.

**kaikata** buyer.

**kaikatsu** cheerfulness; **kaikatsu na** cheerful, gay; jovial.

**kaikei** accounts; **kaikeibo** account book; **kaikei gakari** accountant; cashier; **kaikei hookoku** financial report.

**kaiken** interview, audience; **kaiken o mooshikomu** to ask for an interview; **kaiken suru** to interview.

**kaiketsu** settlement; solution; **kaiketsu suru** to settle; to solve; to fix up; **kaiketsu ga tsuku** to come to a settlement; to arrive at a solution.

**kaiko** retrospection; reflection; review; **kaiko suru** to look back; to reflect.

**kaiko** discharge; dismissal; **kaiko suru** to discharge, dismiss.

**kaiko** silkworm.

**kaikomu** to hold (carry) under one's arm.

**kaikon** development; clearing.

**kaikoojoo** open port.

**kaikyoo** strait; sound.

**kaikyuu** class; rank; order; grade.

**kaimen** surface of the sea.

**kaimetsu** destruction, ruin.

**kaimodosu** to buy back, repurchase.

**kaimoku** entirely, utterly, altogether (used with a negative). **Kaimoku wakarimasen.** I don't understand it at all.

**KAIMONO** shopping; marketing; purchase; **kaimono o suru** to buy, shop; **kaimono ni iku** to go shopping.

**kaimu** (n.) having nothing; having none at all;

nil. **Okane wa kaimu desu.** I have no money at all.

**kain** Lower House of the Diet.

**kainarasu** to tame, domesticate.

**kainushi** owner of an animal; keeper; master.

**kainushi** buyer; purchaser. **Watakushi no ie no kainushi ga mitsukarimashita.** We found a buyer for our house.

**kairi** nautical mile.

**kairiki** superhuman strength.

**kairo** sea route; **kairo o iku** to go by sea.

**kairo** circuit.

**kairoo** corridor; passageway; gallery.

**kairyoo** improvement; reform; **kairyoo suru** to reform; to improve.

**kairyuu** tide; tidal current; trend.

**kaisaku** adaptation.

**kaisan** dispersion; liquidation; breakup; **kaisan suru** to break up; to dissolve; to liquidate.

**kaisanbutsu** marine products.

**kaisangyoo** marine products industry (processing and selling fish, lobsters, shellfish, and edible seaweeds).

**kaisatsuguchi** ticket gate.

**kaisei** fine weather; clear sky.

**kaisetsu** explanation; interpretation; **kaisetsu suru** to explain; to interpret; to comment on.

**KAISHA** company; corporation; firm; **kaishain** employee of a business firm; businessperson. **Ano kaisha ni tsutomete imasu.** I am working for that firm.

**kaishaku** interpretation; construction; explanation.

**kaishimeru** to buy up; to corner (the market).

**kaishi suru** to begin.

**kaishoo** dissolution; extinction; cancellation.

**kaishuu** withdrawal; collection; **kaishuu suru** to withdraw; to call in.

**kaisoku** regulations, rules of an organization.

**kaisoo** shipping; forwarding; **kaisoo suru** to forward; to transport; **kaisoogyoosha** shipping agency.

**kaisoo** seaweed.

**kaisoo** recollection, reminiscence; **kaisoo suru** to recollect, to reminisce.

**kaisui** seawater; salt water; **kaisuiyokujoo** seaside resort; beach; **kaisuiyoku o suru** to go bathing in the sea.

**kaisuu** frequency; **kaisuu o kasaneru** to repeat many times.

**kaitai** dissection; dismemberment.

**kaite** buyer, purchaser.

**kaiten** revolution, rotation; **kaiten suru** to revolve, rotate; **kaitengi** gyroscope.

**kaitoo** solution; reply; answer; **kaitoo suru** to solve; to reply, answer.

**kaitoo** president (of an organization).

**kaitsumande** to make a long story short; in a word. **Kaitsumande ohanashi shimashoo.** I will tell you briefly.

**kaiungyoo** marine shipping. (See also **kaisoo**.)

**KAIWA** conversation.

**kaiwai** neighborhood; **kaiwai ni** in the neighborhood.

**kaizoku** pirate.

**KAJI** fire. **Watakushi wa kyonen kaji ni aimashita.** I experienced a fire last year.

**kajikamu** to be numb with cold; to be numbed.

**kajiritsuku** to hold on to; to clutch.

**kajiru** to gnaw; to nibble; to bite; to get a smattering of.

**kajitsu** fruit; berry; nut.

**kajoo** article, item; clause; **kajoo o ageru** to itemize.

**kajoo** excess, surplus.

**kajuu** overweight.

**kakae** embrace; employ.

**kakaeru** to hold under one's arms, to embrace; to employ, to hire.

**kakageru** to hold up; to raise, hoist.

**KAKAKU** price; value; **kakaku o tsukeru** to set a price; to fix the value of.

**KAKARI** charge(s); duty; **kakariin** official in charge.

**kakariai** implication; involvement; **kakariai ni naru** to be involved in.

**KAKARU** to hang; to stand; to rest (against); to set about; to be dependent on; to concern; to catch; to be caught; to begin, start; to take; to need; to cost; **byooki ni kakaru** to become ill; **isha ni kakaru** to consult a doctor. **Soko e iku no ni ichijikan kakarimasu.** It takes an hour to get there. **Ikura kakarimasu ka?** How much does it cost? **Kono uchi ni wa okane ga kakatte iru.** This house cost a lot of money.

**kakasazu** regularly, consistently; without missing; constantly.

**kakashi** scarecrow.

**KAKATO** heel.

**KAKAWARAZU** in spite of, despite; no matter (how, what); regardless of; **ame ni mo kakawarazu** in spite of the rain.

**kakawaru** to take part, participate in; to concern; to affect; to be at stake.

**kake** betting; **kakegoto** gambling; **kake o suru** to make a bet, wager.

**kakeai** negotiation; consultation; **kakeai o suru** to negotiate (with).

**kakeau** to negotiate; to bargain with.

**kakeashi** run; double time; gallop; **kakeashi de** on the double; at a run; **kakeashi ni naru** to break into a run; to gallop.

**kakebuton** quilt; bed-coverlet.

**kakedasu** to start running; to run out.

**kakegae** substitute; spare; **kakegae no nai** irreplaceable (most precious) thing.

**kakegoe** yell, shout; **kakegoe o kakeru** to yell, shout.

**kakehi** waterpipe, drainpipe.

**kakehiki** bargaining; tactics; tact, diplomacy; **kakehiki o suru** to bargain (with a person).

**kakei** lineage, genealogy.

**kakekin** installment; premium; **kakekin o suru** to pay in installments.

**kakekko** race; **kakekko o suru** to run a race.

**kakemochi** part-time job; working at two or more jobs at one time.

**kakemono** hanging picture-scroll.

**kakene** overcharge; high price; **kakene o iu** to overcharge.

**kakeochi** elopement.

**KAKERU** to sit, take a seat; to spend; to invest; to gallop; to run; to hang; to suspend; to cover; to spread on; to put on; to pour on; **isu ni kakeru** to sit on a chair; **kane o kakeru** to spend money; **koshi o kakeru** to sit down; **kugi ni kakeru** to hang (something) on a peg; **megane o kakeru** to wear glasses.

**kakeru** run, gallop.

**-kakeru** to begin to; **yomikakeru** to begin to read.

**kakeru** to be broken; to be cracked; to be short of.

**kaketsu** approval; adoption; passage; **kaketsu suru** to pass, be approved.

**kakezu** map, chart.

**kaki** oyster; **kaki furai** fried oysters.

**kakiarawasu** to put in writing.

**kakiatsumeru** to collect; to rake together; to gather up.

**kakiawaseru** to adjust, arrange.

**kakiire** entry; notes; insertion; **kakiireru** to insert; to write in.

**kakikae** rewriting; transfer; **kakikaeru** to rewrite; to transfer.

**kakimawasu** to stir (coffee, etc.); to beat; to rummage; to ransack.

**kakimidasu** to confuse, throw into confusion; to disturb.

**kakimono** written document; writing.

**kakimushiru** to tear; to scratch off.

**kakine** hedge.

**kakinokeru** to push aside.

**kakinuki** extract; abstract.

**kakioki** will; posthumous letter.

**kakiorosu** to write down.

**kakiotosu** to scrape off.

**kakisoeru** to add a postscript.

**kakitateru** to play up; to write up; to make a big story of.

**kakitome** = **kakitome yuubin** registered mail. **Kono tegami o kakitome ni shite kudasai.** Please register this letter.

**kakitomeru** to make notes of; to make a memo.

**kakitome yuubin** See **kakitome.**

**kakitoru** to dictate.

**kakitsuke** document; bill.

**kakiwakeru** to push (elbow) aside, to force oneself through.

**kakka** Your (His) Excellency.

**kakke** beriberi.

**kakki** animation; spirit; **kakki no aru** animated; **kakki no nai** lifeless; dull.

**kakko** parentheses, brackets.

**kakkoo** shape, form; appearance; style; **kakkoo na** suitable; moderate; **kakkoo no yoi** well-formed; stylish.

**kako** (n.) past; bygone days; previous existence; **kako ni oite** in the past.

**kakoi** enclosure; fence; **kakoi o suru** to enclose; to fence in.

**kakomi** siege.

**kakomu** to surround; to enclose; to close in on.

**kakotsuke** pretense, pretext.

**kakotsukeru** to make a pretense of; **kakotsukete** under the pretext (pretense) of.

**kakou** to keep; to store; to preserve.

**KAKU** to write; to draw; to paint; **tegami o kaku** to write a letter; **e o kaku** to draw (paint) a picture.

**kaku** to rake, to scratch; **yuki o kaku** to clear away snow.

**kaku** each, every.

**kaku** angle; **chokkaku** right angle.

**kaku** nucleus; **kaku sensoo** nuclear war.

**KAKUBETSU** especially, particularly. **kakubetsu no** particular, special.

**kakuchoo suru** to extend, expand, enlarge.

**kakudai suru** to magnify; **kakudai kyoo** magnifying glass.

**kakugen** maxim, saying.

**kakugetsu** every other month.

**kakugo** preparedness; resolution; resignation; **kakugo suru** to be prepared; to be resolved.

**kakuhoo** authentic news, definite report.

**kakuhoomen** in every direction; in all directions.

**kakujitsu** reliability; authenticity; certainty; **kakujitsu na** reliable; sure; authentic; **kakujitsu ni** certainly.

**kakujitsu** every other day.

**kakumau** to shelter; to protect.

**kakumei** revolution; **kakumeiteki** revolutionary.

**kakunin** confirmation; **kakunin suru** to confirm, affirm.

**kakunooko** airplane hangar.

**kakuran** disturbance.

**kakurega** hiding place; den.

**KAKURERU** to hide oneself; to take shelter; to disappear. **Tsuki ga kumo ni kakureta.** The moon disappeared in the cloud.

**kakuri** isolation; **kakurishitsu** isolation ward.

**kakuritsu suru** to establish; to fix; to settle.

**kakusaku** plan, scheme; project; **kakusaku suru** to plan, scheme.

**kakusei** disillusionment; **kakusei suru** to awake; be awakened; to be disillusioned.

**kakuseiki** loudspeaker.

**kakushidate** concealment; **kakushidate o suru** to conceal a fact.

**kakushiki** social status.

**kakushin** reform, renovation; **kakushin suru** to believe strongly, to be confident of.

**kakusho** every place; various places; **kakusho ni** everywhere; in several places.

**kakushoo** conclusive evidence; proof.

**KAKUSHU** every kind; **kakushu no** of every kind.

**KAKUSU** to hide, conceal.

**kakutei** decision; settlement; **kakutei suru** to decide; to settle.

**KAKUTERU** cocktail.

**kakutoku** acquisition; possession; **kakutoku suru** to acquire, obtain, secure.

**kakutoo suru** to give a definite answer.

**kakuu no** imaginary; fanciful.

**KAKUYASU NA** cheap; **kakuyasu ni** cheaply; at a moderate price.

**kakuzatoo** lump (cube) sugar.

**kakuzuke** classification, grading; **kakuzuke suru** to classify, grade.

**kakyoku** melody, tune.

**kakyuu no** petty; low-grade; low-class; inferior; subordinate.

**kakyuu no** pressing, urgent; imminent.

**kama** kettle; iron pot; kiln.

**kama** scythe.

**kamae** structure; appearance.

**kamaeru** to build, construct; to set up house; to take an attitude.

**KAMAU** to care, mind, be concerned about; to trouble oneself about; to give attention to; **kamawazu** regardless of. **Kamawanaide kudasai.** Please don't trouble yourself on my account. Don't bother me.

**kame** turtle.

**kame** jar; jug; vase; urn.

**kamei** family name; family honor.

**kamei** alliance, affiliation.

**kamen** mask; disguise.

**KAMERA** camera.

**KAMI** paper; **kami byooshi** paper cover; **kami kuzu** wastepaper; scraps of paper;

**kamibasami** paper clip; **kamiyasuri** sandpaper.

**kami** god, deity; **kami dana** family shrine (a shelf in a Japanese house for Shinto tablets).

**kami** hair; **kami o toku** to comb one's hair.

**KAMINARI** thunder. **Kaminari ga natte imasu.** It is thundering.

**KAMISORI** razor; **kamisori o ateru** to shave.

**kamite** upstage (in a theater).

**KAMOKU** course, subject, lesson.

**kamosu** to stir up, arouse.

**kamotsu** freight, cargo; merchandise; **kamotsusen** freighter (ship).

**KAMU** = **kami-** to chew; to bite; to gnaw. **Kande fukumeru yoo ni setsumei shimashita.** He explained it, taking great pains to make it clear.

**kamufuraaju** camouflage, disguise.

**kan** perception; feeling, sentiment, emotion; **kan kiwamaru** to be filled with emotion; to be deeply moved.

**kan** tin can; **kanzume** canned goods.

**kan** temper; irritability; **kan o okosu** to become impatient; **kan ga tsuyoi** to be hot-tempered; **kan o osaeru** to control one's temper.

**-kan** counter for volume; reel (motion picture); **dai ikkan** the first volume.

**-kan** suffix denoting: duration or space between; **isshuukan** one week; **Tookyoo Oosaka kan** between Tokyo and Osaka; **ikkagetsukan** during one month.

**kana** Japanese syllabary.

**kanaboo** crowbar; metal rod; horizontal bar.

**kanadarai** metal basin; washbowl.

**kanaeru** to grant; to comply with; **negai o kanaeru** to grant one's wishes; to answer one's prayers.

**kanagu** metal ornaments or fittings.

**KANAI** family; household; wife; **kanaijuu** the whole family.

**kanakirigoe** shrill, voice; **kanakirigoe o dasu** to scream.

**kanamono** hardware; ironware; **kanamonoya** hardware store or dealer.

**KANARAZU** certainly; no doubt, by all means; without fail; invariably. **Kanarazu kite kudasai.** Please be sure to come. Please come without fail.

**KANARI** fairly; pretty; considerably; **kanari no** considerable; **kanari yoi** fairly well.

**kanariya** canary.

**KANASHII** sad, sorrowful.

**kanashimi** sorrow, grief.

**kanashimu** to lament; to mourn; to regret.

**kanau** to suit; to be suitable; to conform to; to accomplish; to agree with. **Mokuteki ni kanau.** It answers the purpose.

# kanazuchi                                          kanoo

**kanazuchi** iron hammer.
**kanban** signboard, billboard.
**kanbashii** sweet; fragrant.
**kanbashitta** shrill, piercing; sharp.
**kanbatsu** drought.
**kanben na** handy; convenient; **kanben ni** simply; easily.
**kanben suru** to pardon, forgive. **Kanben shite kudasai.** Please excuse me.
**kanbi** completion; perfection.
**kanboo** cold; flu.
**kanbotsu suru** to sink, subside; to cave in.
**kanbu** staff; management.
**kanbutsuya** grocery specializing in dried vegetables and fruits.
**kanbyoo** = **kango** (n.) nursing; **kanbyoonin** nurse.
**kanchoo** spy.
**kanchoo** government office.
**kandai** generosity; leniency; tolerance; **kandai na** generous; lenient; tolerant.
**kandankei** thermometer.
**kandan nai** continual, incessant, endless; **kandan naku** continually.
**kandoo** emotion; impression; excitement; **kandoo suru** to be moved, be affected; to disown; **kandoo saseru** to move; to impress; to inspire; to appeal to.
**kandoo** disinheritance; **kandoo suru** to disinherit.
**KANE, OKANE** money; **kane ga nai** to have no money; **kaneire** money box; purse; **kanekashi** moneylender; **kanemochi** rich person; **kanezukai** manner of spending money; **kane banare no yoi** generous with money; **kane ga kakaru** to be costly; **kanekashi suru** to lend money; **ooganemochi** very rich man; **kanezukai no arai hito** a free spender.
**kane** bell; **kanetsukidoo** bell tower.
**kanegane** previously; beforehand.
**kanete** already; previously; lately; some time ago.
**kangae** thought, idea, opinion.
**kangaechigai** misunderstanding; mistake; mistaken ideal; **kangaechigai suru** to misunderstand.
**KANGAERU** to think, consider, deliberate, believe, be of the opinion; **kangae bukai** thoughtful; **kangaenaosu** to reconsider. **Sore wa kangaeru no mo iya desu.** I dislike the very thought of it.
**kangei** welcome; reception; **kangei suru** to welcome; **kangei o ukeru** to be received warmly.
**kangeki** (n.) theatergoing; **kangeki ni dekakeru** to go to the theater; **kangekikai** theater party.

**kangeki** emotion; excitement; inspiration. **Sono hanashi o kiite kangeki shimashita.** I was very much moved when I heard the story.
**kango** See **kanbyoo; kangofu** nurse.
**kani** crab.
**kan'i** simplicity; **kan'i na** simple; **kan'i ni** simply.
**kan'in** adultery.
**kanja** (n.) patient.
**KANJI** sense, feeling; **kanji no nibui** insensitive; **kanjiyasui** sensitive; sentimental.
**KANJI** Chinese character (ideograph) used in Japanese writing system.
**kanji** manager; staff secretary; executive committee.
**kanjin na** important; essential, vital.
**KANJIRU** = **KANZURU** to feel; **atsusa o kanjiru** to feel the heat; **konnan o kanjiru** to find difficulty.
**KANJOO** calculation, counting; **kanjoo ni ireru** to take into account; **kanjoogaki** check, bill. **Hayaku kanjoo shite kudasai.** Please count it quickly. **Kanjoo o machigaeta.** I miscalculated.
**kanjoo** feeling, sentiment, passion; **kanjooteki** emotional.
**kanjusei** susceptibility; receptivity.
**kanka** influence.
**kankaku** space, distance, interval.
**kankaku** sensation, sense.
**kankei** relation, connection; concern, interest; relationship; **-to kankei ga aru** to have a relation to, be connected with.
**KANKOKU** South Korea.
**kankoo** sight-seeing; **kankoo kyaku** sight-seer; **kankoo ni iku** to go sight-seeing; **kankoodan** tourist party.
**kankoo** publication; **kankoo suru** to publish; **teiki kankoobutsu** periodical.
**kankyoo** environment, surroundings.
**kankyuu** emergency.
**kankyuu suru** to be moved to tears.
**kanmei** deep impression; **kanmei suru** to impress deeply; to be deeply impressed; to be deeply moved.
**kanmei** terseness; **kanmei na** terse, concise, simple and brief.
**kanmuri** crown.
**kannen** idea, sense, concept, notion.
**kannin** patience; forgiveness.
**kannuki** bolt, bar (of a gate or door); **kannuki o kakeru** to bolt; **kannuki o hazusu** to unbolt.
**kanoo** suppuration; infection; **kanoo suru** to be infected.
**kanoo** possibility; **kanoo na** possible.

80

**kanpai** toast; **kanpai suru** to drink a toast.

**kanpan** deck; **jookanpan** upper deck; **chuukanpan** main deck.

**kanraku** fall; cave in; **kanraku suru** to fall; to sink; to collapse; to cave in.

**kanri** management, administration, control; **kanrisha** superintendent; manager.

**kanryaku** simplicity; brevity; **kanryaku na** simple; brief; **kanryaku ni** simply; briefly. **Kanryaku ni shite kudasai.** Please make it very brief.

**kanryoo** completion; conclusion.

**kansatsu** observation.

**kansen** infection; contagion.

**kansen** trunk line; main line.

**kansetsu** indirectness; **kansetsu no** roundabout, indirect; **kansetsu ni** at second hand, indirectly.

**kansetsu** joint; **kansetsu o kujiku** to dislocate.

**kansha** thanks, gratitude. **Kansha no kotoba mo arimasen.** I can't thank you enough.

**kansha** official residence.

**kanshaku** passion; temper; impatience; **kanshaku no tsuyoi** hot-tempered; irritable; **kanshaku o okosu** to lose one's temper.

**kanshi** watch, lookout, vigil; **kanshi suru** to watch, keep an eye on.

**kanshin** concern, interest; **kanshin o motsu** to be concerned about, be interested in.

**kanshin** admiration; **kanshin na** admirable, praiseworthy; **kanshin ni** admirably; **kanshin suru** to admire, to be impressed.

**kanshoku suru** to eat between meals.

**kanshoo** appreciation; **kanshoo suru** to appreciate; **kanshooteki** appreciative.

**kanshoo** sentimentality; **kanshoo shugi** sentimentalism; **kanshooteki** sentimental.

**kanshuu** spectators.

**kansoku** observation; survey; **kansokusho** observatory (weather, etc.).

**kansoo** impression(s); thoughts; **kansoo o noberu** to give one's impression.

**kansoo** aridity; **kansoo suru** to dry.

**kan suru** to be concerned with; to relate to, bear on; to be connected with: **-ni kan shite** in regard to.

**kanjoo** account.

**KANTAN** brevity; simplicity; **KANTAN NA** simple, brief; **kantan ni** briefly; in a few words; simply, easily. **Soko e wa kantan ni ikemasu.** You can go there very easily.

**kantan suru** to admire.

**kantei** judgment; expert opinion; appraisal.

**kantei** official residence.

**kantoku** supervision; control; superintendent; inspector; **kantoku suru** to supervise; control.

**kantsuu** penetration; **kantsuu suru** to penetrate, pierce.

**kan'yoo na** important; necessary.

**kanyuu** entry; joining; admission; **kanyuu suru** to join; to subscribe; to enter; **kanyuusha** member; subscriber.

**kanzei** customs (duty); **kanzei no kakaru** dutiable; **kanzei no kakaranai** duty free.

**KANZEN** perfection; completeness; **kanzen na** perfect; complete; integral; **kanzen ni** perfectly.

**kanzuku** to get wind of; to have an inkling of; to suspect.

**KANZURU** See **KANJIRU.**

**KAO** face; looks; complexion; **kao ga urete iru** to be well known.

**kaoru** to smell; to be fragrant.

**kappa** old-fashioned raincoat; oilskin; water spirit.

**kapparai** shoplifter; pilfering, thieving.

**kappatsu** activity; briskness; **kappatsu na** active, lively; brisk.

**kappu** cup (trophy). (See also **koppu.**)

**KARA** *(n.)* being empty; vacant *(adj.)* **kara no** empty; **kara ni suru** to empty. **Kara desu.** It is empty.

**KARA** from; out of; since; on; in; and so; because; as; for (following a sentence-ending form of a verb, the copula, or adjective); **kore kara nochi** from now on; **Tookyoo kara Oosaka made** from Tokyo to Osaka. **Byooki deshita kara ikimasen deshita.** I was sick so I didn't go.

**kara** husks, hulls, shells.

**KARADA** body; **karada no** physical; bodily; **karada no tame ni naru** to be good for one's health. **Karada ga warui.** She is sick. I am sick.

**karageru** to tie up, bind; to tuck in.

**KARAI** hot; acrid; salty; pungent. **Kono otsuyu wa karai desu.** This soup is too salty.

**karaibari** bluff; empty boast.

**karakau** to tease; to make fun of; to play a joke on.

**karakaze** dry wind.

**karamaru, karamu** to twine around; to coil; to be entangled.

**karari to** completely, fully, entirely. **Sora ga karari to haremashita.** The sky has cleared.

**kara sawagi** much ado about nothing; **kara sawagi suru** to make a big fuss about nothing.

**karasu** to let wither; to dry up. (See also **KARERU**.)

**karatto** carat.

**karazeki** dry (hacking) cough.

**KARE** he; **kare no** his; **kare ni** to him; **kare o** him; **karera** they.

**kare-** prefix denoting: dry; withered; hoarse; **karegoe** hoarse voice.

**karee** curry; **raisu karee** curried rice; **kareiko** curry powder.

**KAREKORE** this and that; one thing and another; some; about; **karekore ninen bakari** two years or so.

**karendaa** calendar.

**KARERU** to wither, dry up; to die; to get hoarse. **Koe ga karete kimashita.** My voice is hoarse. **Ido ga karemashita.** The well has dried up. **Ki ga karemashita.** The tree has died. (See also **karasu**.)

**KARI** (*n.*) loan; debt; borrowing.

**kari** hunting.

**kariatsumeru** to gather together, muster.

**karidasu** to hunt out; to round up.

**kariireru** to harvest, gather in.

**karikomi** (*n.*) cutting, pruning.

**karikomu** to cut, trim, prune.

**karikoshi** outstanding debt; overdraft.

**kari no** temporary; **kari ni** temporarily; tentatively.

**karinui** (*n.*) basting, sewing loosely; **karinui suru** to baste.

**kariru** to borrow; **karikata** debtor; **kariukenin** borrower. **Yamada-san ni okane o karimashita.** I borrowed some money from Mr. Yamada.

**KAROOJITE** with much difficulty; barely, hardly.

**karu** to reap; to cut; to trim; to hunt; to chase; **kusa o karu** to cut grass; **ine o karu** to harvest rice.

**karuhazumi** rashness; hastiness; **karuhazumi na** rash; hasty; thoughtless.

**KARUI** light, not heavy, slight, trifling; not serious; simple; insignificant; **karui shigoto** light work; **karui nimotsu** light baggage; **karuku** lightly; slightly; **karuku suru** to lighten, ease; **karuku utsu** to tap; to pat.

**karyoku** heating power.

**karyuu** downstream.

**KASA** umbrella; parasol.

**kasa** bulk, volume; size; quantity; **kasabatta** bulky.

**kasabuta** scab.

**kasai** fire, blaze; **kasai o okosu** to start a fire; **kasai hoochiki** fire alarm; **kasai hoken** fire insurance. (See also **hi**.)

**kasamu** to swell, increase in volume.

**kasanaru** to be piled up; to lie one on top of another.

**kasanegasane** repeatedly, again and again, over and over.

**kasaneru** to pile up, put one on top of the other; to repeat; **kasanete** in layers; one on the other; repeatedly.

**Kasei** Mars.

**kasei** (*n.*) keeping house; **kaseigaku** home economics.

**kasetsu** construction; **kasetsu suru** to construct, erect; to lay; **denwa o kasetsu suru** to have a telephone installed; **kasetsuchuu de aru** to be under construction.

**kasetsu** hypothesis.

**kasetsu no** temporary, provisional.

**kasetto** cassette.

**kasha** freight car.

**kashi** lending; **kashikata** creditor; **kashikin** loan.

**kashi, OKASHI** cake; confectionery; sweets; candy; **kashiya** confectionery store.

**kashigeru** to incline; **kubi o kashigeru** to tilt one's head.

**Kashi kandankei** Fahrenheit thermometer.

**kashikiri** charted (bus, etc.).

**KASHIKOI** wise, clever, intelligent.

**kashikomaru** to obey; to assent to; to sit straight. **Kashikomarimashita.** Yes, sir. I'll follow your instructions.

**KASHIMA** room to let; apartment; **kashiya** house for rent.

**kashimashii** noisy, boisterous.

**kashira** (*n.*) head, chief; ringleader; **kashira datta** (*adj.*) chief, leading, principal.

**kashu** singer.

**kassai** ovation.

**KASU** to lend; **kane o kasu** to lend money.

**kasu** refuse, dregs, scum; sediment.

**KASUKA NA** faint, dim, vague, indistinct; **kasuka ni** faintly, etc.; **kasuka ni kioku suru** to have a faint recollection.

**kasumi** haze; mist; **kasumi no kakatta** hazy; misty.

**kasumu** to grow hazy, grow dim.

**kasureru** to get hoarse.

**kasurikizu** scratch; bruise.

**kasuru** to graze, scrape, scratch.

**KATA** shoulder; **katakake** shawl; **kata o motsu** to take sides. **Kata ga koru.** I have a stiff neck.

**kata** form, shape; pattern, model, figure; design, mold.

**kata-** prefix denoting: single; **katahoo** one of a pair; **kataashi de tatsu** to stand on one leg.

**-kata** suffix denoting: person (*respect*); **kono kata** this person; **ano kata** that person.

**KATACHI** form, shape; figure; personal appearance; **mime katachi no ii**

handsome; shapely. **Sore wa donna katachi o shite imasu ka?** What kind of shape does it have?

**katachinba** odd; mismatched.

**katagata** by way of; at the same time; partly; combined with. **Sanpo katagata ikimashita.** I went there both to take a walk and [at the same time] pay a visit.

**katagawa** one side; **katagawa tsuuko** one-way street.

**katagi no** honest; honorable; decent.

**KATAI** hard; tough; stiff; upright; strong; firm; conscientious; **kataku** strongly; firmly; tightly; strictly; resolutely; stubbornly; **katakurushii** strict; stiff-mannered; formal; **kataku suru** to harden; stiffen. **Ano hito wa katai hito desu.** He is a conscientious person. **Kono niku wa taihen katai desu.** This meat is very tough.

**KATAKANA** one of the two sets of Japanese syllabary called **kana. Sore wa katakana de kaite kudasai.** Please write it in **katakana.**

**katamari** lump; clod; mass.

**katamaru** (intrans.) to coagulate; congeal; to group together.

**katameru** (trans.) to harden; to solidify; to stiffen; to consolidate.

**katami** memento, souvenir; **katami to suru** to keep as a memento.

**KATAMICHI** one way; one trip; **katamichi jooshaken** one-way ticket.

**katamukeru** to incline, bend, tilt.

**katamuki** trend; slant; slope; **-no katamuki ga aru** to be apt to, to be inclined to.

**katamuku** to incline, lean; to decline.

**katan ito** cotton thread.

**katana** sword.

**katappashi** *(colloq.)* one by one; one and all; wholesale.

**katasa** hardness; toughness; solidity.

**katasumi** corner; nook; **heya no katasumi ni** in a corner of the room.

**kataware** fragment, piece.

**katazukeru** to put in order; to clear; to put away; to dispose of; to settle.

**katazuku** to be put in order; to be settled; to come to an end.

**KATEI** home; family; household; **katei no** domestic; household; house.

**katei** assumption, supposition; **katei suru** to assume, to suppose.

**katoo** inferiority; **katoo no** low; coarse; vulgar.

**katsu** to conquer, be victorious, win.

**katsudoo, katsuyaku** activity; **katsudooteki** active; energetic; **katsudooka** active person; **katsudooryoku** vitality; energy.

**katsugu** to shoulder, carry; to carry on the shoulder.

**katsuyaku, katsudoo** activity; action; boom (rapid, expanding growth); **katsuyaku suru** to be active in; to play an active part.

**KATTE** one's own way; selfishness; condition; circumstances; **KATTE NA** selfish; willful; **temae katte ni** selfishly; **katte ni furumau** to have one's own way; **katte no yoi** handy, convenient.

**KAU** to buy, purchase; to incur; to provoke; **kenka o kau** to pick a quarrel. **Kono hon o hyakuen de kaimashita.** I bought this book for one hundred yen.

**KAU** to keep, raise (an animal or bird). **Watakushi wa inu o katte imasu.** I have a dog.

**KAWA** skin, hide; leather; bark; peel; etc.; **kawa o hagu** to peel off (skin or bark); **kawazuki no** unpeeled.

**KAWA** river, stream; **kawa o wataru** to cross a river.

**KAWAIGARU** to love; to pet, fondle, caress. **Kare wa muyami to neko o kawaigatta.** He made a great pet of a cat.

**KAWAII** dear; darling; loving; tiny; **kawaii akanboo** precious baby; **kawaii koe** sweet voice; **kawairashii** sweet; lovely; pretty; charming; amiable; pathetic. **Ano hito ni wa kawairashii akanboo ga arimasu.** She has a cute baby.

**KAWAISOO NA** poor, pitiful, pathetic. **Kawaisoo ha koto o shita.** That was a pity.

**KAWAKASU** to dry.

**KAWAKI** thirst.

**KAWAKU** to dry; to get dry; to feel thirsty; **nodo ga kawaku** to be thirsty. **Kuchi ga kawaita.** My mouth felt dry.

**kawara** tile; **kawarabuki no** tile-roofed.

**KAWARI** substitute, proxy; compensation; **kawari ni** on behalf of; in place of; **kawari o suru** to substitute, take someone's place. **Kawari ga nai.** Nothing is the matter.

**kawaru** to replace, **kawarugawaru** in turn, by turns.

**kawaru** to change; **yoku kawaru** changeable. **Ame ga yuki ni kawarmashita.** The rain changed into snow.

**KAWASE** money order; exchange; **kawase sooba** rate of exchange. **Kawase de gosenen okutta.** I sent a money order for 5,000 yen.

**KAYOOBI** Tuesday.

**kayou** to pass to and fro; to frequent; to go regularly; **gakkoo e kayou** to attend school.

**kayowai** weak; tender; delicate, fragile.

**kayui** itchy.

**KAZARU** to adorn, decorate, embellish; to display; **kikazaru** dress up.

**KAZE** wind; breeze; **kasuka na kaze** breath of air; light breeze. **Kaze ga fuite imasu.** The wind is blowing.

**KAZE** cold; **kaze o hiku** to catch a cold.

**kazei** taxation; **kazeihin** taxable item; **kazeiritsu** tax rate.

**KAZOERU** to count, calculate; to number; **hi o kazoeru** to count the days.

**KAZOKU** family; household.

**KAZU** number; **kazu kagiri nai** innumerable, countless; **kazu no ooi** many; numerous.

**KE** hair **ke darake no** hairy; **ke no nai** bald, hairless.

**-KE** suffix denoting: house, family; **Fujiwarake** the Fujiwaras.

**-KE** suffix denoting: temper, feeling; nature; **hinoke** signs of fire.

**kebakebashii** gaudy, showy.

**kechi** fault; stinginess; poor quality; **kechi na** stingy, miserly; **kechi o tsukeru** to find fault with.

**kechirasu** to kick about.

**kedakai** dignified; noble.

**kedamono** beast.

**KEGA** wound, injury; accident; **KEGA O SURU** to get hurt; **kega o saseru** to injure, hurt; **kega no koomyoo** lucky mistake; lucky hit.

**kegare** pollution, contamination; stain.

**kegareru** to be polluted.

**kegasu** to stain; to soil; to pollute; to disgrace.

**kegirai** prejudice; **kegirai suru** to be prejudiced against.

**keiba** horse race; **keibajoo** racetrack.

**keibetsu** contempt; slight; insult; **keibetsu suru** to despise; to sneer at.

**keiei** management; conduct.

**keifuku suru** to respect; to admire; to look up to.

**keiji** notice, notification; **keijiban** bulletin board.

**keika** progress; development; course; **jiken no keika** the course of an event.

**keikai** watch; guard; **keikai shingoo** warning signal; **keikai suru** to watch for; guard against.

**keikaku** plan, project, scheme; **keikaku suru** to plan, etc.

**KEIKEN** experience; **keiken aru** experienced; **keiken no nai** inexperienced; **keiken suru** to experience; **keikensha** experienced person.

**keiken na** pious, devout.

**keiki** condition, state; times; **kookeiki** business boom. **Keiki ga yoi desu.** Trade is brisk.

**keiko** exercise, practice, drill; study; **keiko suru** to practice; to take lessons.

**keikoku** warning; advice; **keikoku suru** to warn, admonish.

**keikoo** tendency, inclination; trend.

**keimusho** prison.

**keiniku** chicken (as food).

**keiran** (chicken) egg.

**keirei** salute, salutation.

**keiren** convulsions; spasm.

**keiryaku** stratagem, artifice.

**keisan** calculation, reckoning; estimation; **keisangakari** accountant; **keisanki** adding machine, calculator.

**KEISATSU** police station; **keisatsukan** police officer.

**keisha** slant, incline, slope.

**keishiki** forms; formality; **keishikiteki** formal; conventional; **keishikiteki ni** formally.

**keiteki** foghorn; police whistle; alarm whistle.

**keito** worsted; woolen yarn.

**keitoo** system; lineage; **keitoo o tateru** to systematize; **keitooteki** systematic.

**keitoo suru** to exhaust; to concentrate.

**keiyaku** contract; agreement; promise; **keiyaku suru** to make a contract; **keiyakusho** written contract.

**keizai** economy; finance; **keizaiteki** economical; **keizaijoo** financially.

**KEKKA** result, outcome, consequence, effect; **sono kekka** consequently.

**kekkan** blood vessel.

**KEKKIN** absence (from work); **kekkin suru** to be absent; **kekkinsha** absentee.

**kekkon** marriage; wedding; **KEKKON SURU** to marry; **kekkonshiki** marriage ceremony.

**kekkoo na** splendid; fine; good; beautiful; **kekkoo na niku** delicious meat.

**kekkoo suru** to take decisive action; to carry out (something) decisively.

**KEKKYOKU** eventually, finally, ultimately, in the end; **kekkyoku no** final, ultimate.

**kemono** beast, brute.

**kemui** smoky.

**KEMURI** smoke; fumes.

**KEN** prefecture; **kenchoo** prefectural office; **kenchiji** prefectural governor; **Chibaken** Chiba prefecture.

**ken** sword, saber.

**-ken** house (used as a counter). **Kado kara sangenme no ie desu.** It is the third house from the corner. (In *sangenme,* "g" takes the place of "k.")

**kenage na** brave, heroic; manly; **kenage ni** bravely; heroically; nobly.

**ken'aku na** dangerous; serious; stormy; rough; **ken'aku na sora** stormy (threatening) sky.

**kenasu** to abuse, slander.

**kenbikyoo** microscope.

**KENBUTSU** sight-seeing; **kenbutsunin** sight-seer; visitor; **kenbutsu suru** to see, look at; to pay a visit to; **kenbutsu ni iku** to go sight-seeing.

**kenchiku** construction, erection; building; architecture; **kenchiku yooshiki** architectural style; **kenchiku suru** to build.

**ken'etsu** censorship.

**kengaku** observation; inspection; **kengaku suru** to visit (a factory, etc.) for study.

**kengi** suspicion; **kengi o kakeru** to suspect; **kengi ga kakaru** to be under suspicion.

**kengo na** strong; stable; firm, solid; **kengo ni** firmly; strongly.

**kenka** quarrel, dispute, brawl; **kenka suru** to quarrel, fight; **kenka o shikakeru** to pick a fight.

**KENKOO** health; **kenkoo na** healthy.

**KENKYUU** research, study, investigation; **kenkyuu suru** to study; to do research; **kenkyuukai** learned society; society for scientific research; **kenkyuujo** laboratory; research institute.

**ken mo hororo no aisatsu** curt, blunt, or brusque reply; rebuff.

**kenpoo** constitution; constitutional law.

**kenpu** silk cloth.

**kenri** right, privilege; **kenri o shuchoo suru** to insist on one's rights.

**kenryoku** power, authority, influence; **kenryoku no aru** powerful, influential.

**kensa** inspection; investigation; **kensa suru** to inspect, examine.

**kensetsu** construction; establishment; building; **kensetsu suru** to construct; to found; to establish.

**kensoku** arrest, restraint; surveillance; **kensoku suru** to restrain, check.

**kenson** modesty, humility; **kenson na** modest, humble; **kenson suru** to be modest.

**kentoo** boxing; **kentoo suru** to box; **kentooka** boxer, fighter.

**kentoo** aim; anticipation; **kentoo o tsukeru** to anticipate; to take aim at; **kentoo ga hazureru** to miss one's aim.

**ken'yaku** economy; thrift; **ken'yaku suru** to economize; **ken'yaku no** economical, thrifty.

**keorimono** woolen fabric.

**keppaku** purity, innocence; **keppaku na** pure, innocent, spotless, clean.

**KEREDOMO** but, however, although, yet. **Kyoo wa hidoku atsui keredomo ikimashoo.** It is hot today, but let's go anyway.

**KERU** to kick.

**KESA** this morning. **Kesa wa ikaga desu ka?** How are you feeling this morning?

**keshikaran** outrageous; rude; insulting; insolent.

**KESHIKI** view, sight, scenery, landscape. **Taihen keshiki ga yoi.** The scenery is very good.

**keshitomeru** to put out (a fire).

**kessaku** masterpiece.

**kesseki** absence (from school or a meeting); **mukesseki** regular attendance.

**kesshin** resolution, determination; **kesshin suru** to be resolute, to make up one's mind.

**KESSHITE** never, by no means; not at all; not in the least. **Kesshite sonna koto wa itashimasen.** I wouldn't do it for anything. **Kesshite sawatte wa ikemasen.** Don't touch it under any circumstances.

**KESU** to put out, extinguish; to blow out; to switch off, to erase; to cancel; **sugata o kesu** to vanish, to disappear; **akari o kesu** to switch off the light; to put out the light.

**ketatamashii** noisy, loud; piercing; alarming; **ketatamashiku** frantically; noisily, loudly.

**ketsuron** conclusion; **ketsuron suru** to conclude; **ketsuron o shite** in conclusion.

**kettei** determination; decision; conclusion; **ketteiteki** decisive; conclusive; **kettei suru** to decide upon; to be decided.

**ketten** flaw, defect, blemish; **ketten no aru** defective, imperfect; **ketten no nai** flawless; perfect.

**kewashii** steep, precipitous.

**KEZURU** to shave; to sharpen; **enpitsu o kezuru** to sharpen a pencil; **namae o kezuru** to remove a name from a list. **Honemi o kezutte shigoto ni hagenda.** He worked hard without sparing himself.

**ki-** prefix denoting: air; vapor; atmosphere; **kiatsu** atmospheric pressure; **kion** temperature (of the air).

**kibarashi** diversion, pastime; **kibarashi o suru** to amuse oneself.

**kibaru** to exert oneself; to bear down.

**kibatsu na** original; extraordinary; novel; unusual.

**kibikibi shita** vivacious, full of life.

**kibin** smartness; **kibin na** smart, clever, quick-witted; **kibin ni** cleverly.

**kibishii** severe, strict, stern; **kibishiku** severely, strictly.

**kibone** care, worry; **kibone no oreru** to be troublesome.

**KIBOO** wish, desire, hope; **kiboo suru** to hope, wish, desire.

**KIBUN** feeling, frame of mind, mood; **kibun ga yoi** to feel better. **Kibun ga warui desu.** I feel sick.

**kichi** dangerous situation; **kichi o dassuru** to have a close shave; to have a narrow escape.

**kichigai** madness, insanity; insane person; **kichigai ni naru** to go mad.

**kichin to** precisely; neatly; **kichin to shita** orderly, tidy; **kichin to shite iru** to be in good order.

**kichoomen na** orderly; precise; **kichoomen na hito** one who works in an orderly manner.

**kidate** disposition, temper; **kidate no yoi** good-tempered.

**kidoru** to assume airs, be conceited; **kidotte** affectedly.

**kien** tall talk; **kien o ageru** to talk big; to boast.

**KIERU** to go out; to be put out, be extinguished; **sugata ga kieru** to disappear. **Hi ga kieta.** The fire has gone out.

**kifu** contribution, donation; subscription; **kifu suru** to contribute; to subscribe; **kifusha** contributor; subscriber.

**kigae** change of clothes.

**kigakari** anxiety, worry; misgivings.

**KIGARU NA** cheerful, lighthearted; pleasant, agreeable.

**KIGEN** state of health; temper; mood; **kigen no yoi** good-humored; cheerful; **kigen o sokonau** to offend.

**KIGEN** term, period, time; **kigen ga kuru** to come due; **kigen ga keikasuru** to be overdue.

**kigoo** sign, symbol, mark, emblem.

**kigurai** pride; **kigurai no takai** proud.

**kihon** foundation, basis; standard; **kihonteki** fundamental, basic.

**KIIROI** yellow; **kiiroi booshi** yellow cap; **kiiroi koe** shrill voice.

**kiji** description; account (in a newspaper or magazine).

**kiji** grain (of wood), color (of wood).

**kijitsu** appointed date; fixed date.

**KIKAI** machine; implement; apparatus; machinery; **kikaiteki** mechanical; **kikaigaku** mechanics.

**KIKAI** opportunity, chance; **kikai no arishidai** at the first chance; **kikai o toraeru** to seize the opportunity.

**kikiawaseru** to inquire, make inquiries.

**KIKIDASU** to hear; to find out; to get wind of.

**kikiireru** to comply with, assent to, consent to.

**kikiiru** to listen to.

**kikikajiri** smattering (of information).

**kikikajiru** to get a smattering of.

**kikikomu** to be informed of, get wind of.

**kikime** effect; efficacy; benefit; **kikime no aru** effective; **kikime no nai** ineffective.

**KIKIMORASU** to fail to hear; not to hear (catch) what is said.

**kikin** famine.

**kikinagasu** to pay no heed (to what is said).

**kikinaosu** to ask someone to repeat (something).

**kikinareru** to get used to hearing, be accustomed to hearing.

**kikinikui** difficult to hear.

**kikioboe** recollection (feeling) that one has heard (something) before.

**kikisokonai** mishearing; misunderstanding.

**kikitadasu** to ascertain, confirm.

**kikitagaru** to be inquisitive, be curious.

**kikitoru** to hear; to get wind of.

**kikitsutae** hearsay.

**kikitsutaeru** to hear from others, hear at second hand.

**KIKKARI** punctually; exactly, precisely.

**KIKOERU** to hear; to be able to hear; to be audible. **Watakushi wa mimi ga yoku kikoemasen.** I'm hard of hearing. **Uta ga kikoemasu.** I hear a song.

**KIKOO** climate, season; weather; **onwa na kikoo** mild climate.

**KIKU** to hear, listen to; to ask; to accept; **kiku tokoro ni yoreba . . .** I hear that . . . it is said that . . .

**kimae** generosity; **kimae no yoi** generous; openhanded; **kimae yoku kane o tsukau** to be generous with one's money.

**kimagure** caprice; **kimagure na** capricious, whimsical; **kimagure ni** capriciously.

**kimama** willfulness; waywardness; selfishness; **kimama na** selfish, etc.

**kimari** settlement; conclusion; rule; custom; **kimari o tsukeru** to settle, arrange.

**kimaru** to be settled, to come to an agreement, to be fixed. **Hanashi ga kimaru.** The matter is settled. **kimatta** regular, fixed, routine.

**KIMERU** to settle, decide; to arrange; to determine; **hi o kimeru** to set the day; **kimeta jikan ni** at the appointed time; **hara o kimeru** to make up one's mind.

**kimazui** disagreeable, unpleasant.

**kimetsukeru** to scold, reprimand.

**kimi** you (used colloq. by men).

**kimi** egg yolk.

**kimijika na** short-tempered, touchy.

**kimochi** feeling, sensation; **kimochi no yoi** pleasant; refreshing; **kimochi ga warui** to feel uncomfortable.

**KIMONO** Japanese clothing, garment; **kimono o kiru** to get dressed; **kimono o nugu** to get undressed; **kimono o kikaeru** to change one's clothes.

**kimuzukashii** hard to please; moody.

**KIN** gold; **kin'iro no** golden; **kinpatsu** blond hair.

**kinchoku** conscientiousness; **kinchoku na** conscientious; scrupulous; discreet; honest.

**kinchoo** tension, strain; **kinchoo suru** to strain; to become tense.

**kindai** modern times; **kindai shisoo** modern ideas; **kindaika suru** to modernize.

**kin'en** prohibition against smoking; **kin'ensha** nonsmoker.

**kinen** commemoration, remembrance; memory; **kinen suru** to commemorate; **kinen no tame ni** in memory of; **kinenhi** monument.

**kingan** nearsightedness; **kingankyoo** eyeglasses for a nearsighted person. (See also **kinshigan**.)

**KINJO** neighborhood; **kinjo no** neighboring; **kinjo no hito** neighbor.

**kinkan** kumquat.

**kinko** safe; cashbox.

**kinniku** muscles; **kinniku roodoo** physical labor; **kinniku no** muscular.

**kinomi kinomama de** in the clothes one is wearing; without changing clothes; **kinomi kinomama de neru** to go to sleep without changing into pajamas.

**KINOO** = **sakujitsu** yesterday; **kinoo no hiru** yesterday at noon. **Kinoo gakkoo o yasuminashita.** I was absent from school yesterday.

**kinshi** prohibition, ban, embargo; **kinshi suru** to prohibit, forbid; **kinshi o toku** to lift an embargo. **Kitsuen kinshi.** No smoking.

**kinshigan** = **kingan** nearsightedness; **kinshigan no** nearsighted.

**kinshu** abstinence, teetotalism; **kinshu suru** to abstain from drinking alcoholic beverages.

**KINU** silk; **kinu ito** silk thread; **kinu orimono** silk fabric; **kinu ura** silk lining.

**kinuke** (n.) being dejected; **kinuke no shita** dejected, spiritless; absentminded; **kinuke suru** to be dejected.

**KIN'YOOBI** Friday.

**kinzoku** metal; **kinzoku no** metallic; **kinzoku seihin** metal goods; hardware.

**kinzuru** to forbid, prohibit; to suppress.

**kioku** memory, recollection; **kioku suru** to remember, recollect; **kioku subeki** memorable, noteworthy; **kioku ryoku ga yoi** to have a good memory; **kioku ryoku ga warui** to have a poor memory.

**kippari to** explicitly, distinctly; definitely, decidedly; **kippari to kotowaru** to refuse flatly.

**KIPPU** ticket, pass; **kippu o kiru** to punch a ticket; **kippu uriba** ticket window.

**KIRAI** dislike, distaste, aversion; **kirai na** distasteful; abominable. **Kirai desu.** I dislike it. I don't like it.

**kirakira** brilliantly; glitteringly; **kirakira suru** to glitter, to dazzle.

**KIRAKU** easygoing, easy, carefree, happy-go-lucky; **kiraku na mono** easygoing person; **kiraku ni kurasu** to take things easy; to lead a relaxed life. **Doozo okiraku ni.** Make yourself comfortable!

**kirameku** to glitter, sparkle.

**kirasu** to run out of, be short of; **iki o kirasu** to be short of breath.

**kirau** to dislike, to hate, detest.

**-kire** counter for: piece, bit, scrap, fragment; slice. **Pan o hitokire kudasai.** Please give me a piece of bread.

**KIREI NA** beautiful, lovely, pretty; handsome, good-looking; clean; clear; **kirei na onna no hito** a beautiful (good-looking) woman; **kirei na mizu** clear water; **kirei ni suru** to clean; to tidy up; to put in order.

**kireme** gap, break; pause, intermission; **kireme o tsunagu** to close a gap.

**kiremono** cutlery, knives.

**kireru** to cut (well), to be sharp; to run out; to be worn out; to wear out. **Kimono ga kireta.** The clothes have worn out. **Naifu ga yoku kireru.** The knife cuts well. **Kigen ga kireta.** The term has expired.

**kiri** fog, mist; **kiribue** foghorn. **Kiri ga fukai.** It is foggy.

**kiri** end; limit; **kiri ga nai** unlimited.

**-kiri** suffix denoting: all (there is); only; sole; no more. **Korekkiri desu.** This is all I have.

**kiriageru** to stop; to close; to cut short; to wind up; **hanashi o kiriageru** to end a talk; cut a conversation short.

**kiridasu** to quarry; to cut down (timber) to break ice; **hanashi o kiridasu** to broach a subject; to break the ice (conversationally).

**kirihanasu** to cut off; to separate.

**kiriharau** to cut and clear away; prune.

**kirihiraku** to cut open; to clear (land).

**kirikabu** tree stump.

**kirikuchi** cut end; opening; slit; section.

**kirikuzusu** to cut down; to demolish.

**kirimi** fish slices, fillets.

**kirinukeru** to cut one's way through; to find the way out of (a difficulty); to struggle through.

**kirinuki** cutting, clipping, scrap; excerpt.

**kirinuku** to cut out, clip.

**kirisame** drizzle.

**KIRISUTO** Christ.

**KIRISUTOKYOO** Christianity;
**Kirisutokyoo Seinenkai** Y.M.C.A.,
**Kirisuto kyookai** Christian church.

**kiritsu** order, discipline; rule, regulations; *(n.)*
standing up; **kiritsu aru** orderly,
disciplined; **kiritsu o mamoru** to obey the
rules; **kiritsu suru** to stand up, get to one's
feet; **kiritsu o yaburu** to break the rules.

**kiritsumeru** to shorten, reduce, curtail; **hiyoo
o kiritsumeru** to cut down on expenses.

**-KIRO** counter denoting: kilometer; kilogram;
kiloliter; kilowatt.

**kiroku** annals; archives; minutes, record;
**kiroku suru** to record, write down, keep
records.

**KIRU** to cut; to chop; to carve; to break off
(relations); **yubi o kiru** to cut one's finger;
**denwa o kiru** to hang up (the telephone
receiver). **Kare to wa te o kitta.** I am
through with him.

**KIRU** to wear; to put on; **kimono o kiru** to
put on clothes, dress; **kite iru** to be
dressed in; to have on. **Nani o kite ikoo
ka?** What shall I wear (in going there)?

**kiryoku** energy, vigor; virility; **kiryoku ga nai**
to be languid, lacking in energy; **kiryoku
ga otoroeru** to lose one's vigor; to have
less energy.

**kiryoo** personal appearance, looks, features
(usually used when speaking of women);
**kiryoo no yoi** pretty, beautiful, handsome.

**KISEN** steamship, steamer; **kisen de** by ship;
**kisen de iku** to go by ship; **kisen gaisha**
steamship company.

**kiseru** to dress, clothe; to plate, gild, coat; to
impute; **tsumi o hito ni kiseru** to put the
blame on someone else.

**KISETSU** season; **kisetsu no** in season,
seasonal; **kisetsu hazure no** out of season;
**kisetsu fuu** monsoon season; **sakura no
kisetsu** cherry blossom season.

**KISHA** railroad train; **kisha ni noru** to get on
a train; **kisha de iku** to go by train; **kisha
o oriru** to get off a train; **kishachin** train
fare; **yogisha** night train.

**kisha** journalist; **tsuushin kisha**
correspondent; **kishaseki** press gallery.

**KISHI** shore, coast; bank; **mukoo gishi** other
side of the river.

**kishitsu** disposition, temperament; **yoi
kishitsu no hito** person of good
disposition.

**kishoku** mood, feeling; **kishoku ga yoi** to be
in a good mood; to feel well; **kishoku ga
warui** to be in a bad mood.

**kishoo** weather; weather conditions;
**kishoodai** weather bureau.

**kishu** horseman, jockey, rider.

**kishuku** lodging; room and board;
**kishukunin** a boarder; **kishuku suru** to
board at; **kishukusha** dormitory.

**KISOKU** rule, regulations; **kisoku tadashii**
regular; systematic; orderly; **kisoku
tadashiku** regularly, systematically;
**kisoku o mamoru** to observe the rules.

**KISSATEN** tearoom; coffee shop.

**kissui no** pure; genuine.

**kisuu** odd number.

**KITA** north; **kita no** northerly; northern.

**kitaeru** to forge; to drill, train; to discipline; to
harden.

**kitai** expectation, anticipation; **kitai suru** to
expect, hope for; to look forward to; to
count on; **kitai ni sou** to meet
expectations.

**kitaku suru** to go home; to come home.

**KITANAI** dirty; filthy; nasty; shabby;
**kitanaku suru** to soil, make dirty.

**kitchiri** punctually, sharp; exactly; **kitchiri
niji ni** at two o'clock sharp; at two on the
dot.

**kiteki** siren; steam whistle; **kiteki o narasu** to
blow a whistle; to sound a siren.

**kiten** ready wit; tact; **kiten no kiita** tactful;
quick-witted; **kiten o kikasu** to be on the
alert.

**kitoku** serious, critical. **Seimei kitoku desu.**
He/she is seriously ill.

**kitsuen** smoking; **kitsuen suru** to smoke;
**kitsuenshitsu** smoking room; **kitsuensha**
smoking car (on a train).

**kitsui** brave; strong; intense; severe.

**KITTE** postage stamp; **kitte o haru** to put a
stamp on (a letter). **Kono tegami ni wa
ikura no kitte o haru n desu ka?** How
much is the postage for this letter?

**KITTO** certainly, without fail; undoubtedly,
surely. **Kitto kite kudasai.** Please be sure
to come. **Kitto mairimasu.** Certainly I'll
come.

**kiwadatsu** to stand out, be conspicuous; to be
in contrast with.

**kiwadoi** critical; dangerous, risky; **kiwadoi
shoobu** a close game (match); **kiwadoi
tokoro de** in the nick of time; at the last
minute.

**kiwameru** to exhaust; to get to the bottom of;
to carry to an extreme; **shinsoo o
kiwameru** to get at the truth.

**kiwamete** extremely, exceedingly;
excessively.

**kiyoo na** clever, skillful; ingenious; **kiyoo na
hito** jack-of-all-trades; handy person.

**kiyowai** timid, shy.

**kiza na** offensive; conceited.

**kizetsu** *(n.)* fainting; **kizetsu suru** to faint.

**KIZU** wound, injury, bruise; flaw, defect; **kizuato** scar; **kizugusuri** ointment for a bruise or wound.

**kizukai** fear; anxiety.

**kizukare** worry; mental fatigue; **kizukare ga suru** to be worried.

**kizuku** to become aware of.

**kizutsukeru** to hurt, injure, wound.

**kizutsuku** to be wounded, hurt.

**kizuyoi** resolute; brave; **kizuyoku omou** to be reassured; to be confident.

**KO** child; infant, baby; cub of an animal.

**ko-** prefix denoting: little, small; **koburi** light rain; light fall of snow; **kozakana** small fish; **kojima** small island.

**-ko** suffix denoting: lake; **Biwako** Lake Biwa.

**kobiritsuku** to stick fast, cling.

**kobore** overflow; droppings; **koboredane** fallen seed.

**KOBORERU** to run over, overflow; to drop; to spill; to be scattered.

**kobosu** to spill; to drop; to pour out; **namida o kobosu** to shed tears; **mizu o kobosu** to spill water.

**kobu** bump, swelling, protuberance.

**KOCHIRA** this place, here; this one; **KOCHIRAGAWA** this side. **Doozo kochira e.** This way, please. **Tabakoya wa toori no kochiragawa desu.** The cigar store is on this side of the street.

**kodachi** grove, clump of trees.

**KODOMO** child; **kodomo rashii** childish; **kodomoppoi** childlike; childish. **Watakushi wa kodomo ga sannin arimasu.** I have three children. **Kodomoatsukai ni suru na.** Don't treat me like a child.

**KOE** voice; **koedaka ni** in a loud voice; **koe o kagiri ni** at the top of one's voice; **chiisai koe de** in a low voice; softly; **kogoe** low voice; whisper; **kogoe de** in a low voice; in a whisper.

**koeda** twig, sprig, small branch.

**koeru** to cross; go across; to pass; to go beyond; exceed.

**kogasu** to burn; to scorch, singe.

**kogatana** small knife; pocketknife.

**kogawase** postal money order.

**kogechairo** dark brown, umber.

**kogeru** to get scorched, to get burned.

**KOGITTE** (bank) check; **kogitte o kiru** to issue a check; **kogitte de shiharau** to pay by check.

**kogoeru** to be frozen; to be chilled to the bone, be numb with cold.

**kogoto** scolding; blame; **kogoto o iu** to scold; **kogoto o iwareru** to be scolded; to be blamed.

**kogu** to row; **kogiwataru** to row across.

**kohaku** amber.

**KOI** (n.) love; **koi suru** to love; to fall in love; **koibito** lover; **koishii** dear; beloved; **koishigaru** to yearn for.

**koi** evil intention; evil will; **koi no** intentional, deliberate; **koi ni** on purpose, intentionally. **Koi no koto de wa arimasen.** It isn't anything that was done intentionally.

**koi** dark, deep, thick, strong (as tea).

**koishi** pebble.

**koitsu** this man (vulgar). **Koitsu!** You rat!

**kojiakeru** to wrench open.

**kojiki** beggar.

**kojin** individual; private citizen; **kojinteki** personal, private individual; **kojinsei** individually.

**kojinmari to** cozily; **kojinmari to shita** snug, cozy.

**kojireru** to go wrong; to get complicated.

**kojitsuke** distortion; forced meaning; **kojitsuke no** distorted; farfetched.

**kojitsukeru** to distort, (twist) the meaning.

**kokage** shade of a tree.

**kokiorosu** to disparage; to abuse.

**kokitsukau** to work like a horse; to drive (someone) hard.

**kokka** state, country, nation; **kokka shugi** nationalism.

**kokkai** parliament, national assembly, Diet.

**kokkan** severe cold; intense cold.

**kokkei na** comical; **kokkei na hanashi** funny (comical) story.

**kokki** national flag.

**kokkoo** diplomatic relations.

**kokkyoo** frontier, border; boundaries.

**KOKO** this place; here; **koko ni** here, in this place; **koko kara** from here; **koko shibaraku** for the present; for some time to come. **Koko da, koko da.** Here we are. This is the place.

**kokoku** one's native land.

**KOKONOKA** ninth day of the month.

**KOKONOTSU** nine.

**KOKORO** heart; mind; spirit; **kokoro aru hito** thoughtful person; **kokoro yuku** made as one pleases; to one's heart's content; **kokoro ni kakaru** to be anxious; **kokoro ni ukabu** to occur to one; **kokoro ni tomeru** to bear in mind; **kokoro ga kawaru** to change one's mind; **kokoro yasuku naru** to become intimate; **kokoro no ookii** broadminded; **kokoro atari** clue; **kokoro atari ga nai** to have no idea of; **KOKORO BOSOI** helpless; uneasy; **kokoro bosoku omou** to feel helpless.

**kokoroe** understanding; knowledge; **kokoroe chigai** misbehavior, misapprehension.

**KOKOROERU** to know; to think; to consider.

**kokorogakari** care; anxiety; concern; **kokorogakari ni naru** feel uneasy; to be anxious.

**kokorogake** purpose, intention, aim; attention; **kokorogake no yoi** careful; conscientious.

**kokorogakeru** to keep in mind; to think about.

**kokorogamae** preparedness.

**kokorogawari** change of mind; caprice; **kokorogawari no suru** fickle; faithless; capricious.

**kokorogurushii** to be uneasy.

**kokoromi** trial; experiment; attempt; **kokoromi ni** tentatively.

**kokoromiru** to try, attempt, make an attempt.

**kokoromochi** feeling, sensation; mood; idea; shade; **ii kokoromochi ga suru** to feel comfortable; **kokoromochi yoku** willingly; **kokoromochi o waruku suru** to hurt (someone's) feelings; to displease.

**kokoromotonai** insecure; apprehensive.

**kokoronaki** thoughtless; heartless.

**kokorone** feelings; heart.

**kokoroyoi** pleasant, agreeable, nice; delightful.

**kokorozashi** will; intention; motive.

**kokorozasu** to intend; to aim at, aspire to.

**kokorozukai** worry, anxiety, concern.

**kokorozuke** tip, gratuity.

**kokorozuyoi** assuring.

**koku-** prefix denoting; pertaining to a country, nation, or state; **kokuboo** national defense; **kokufu** national wealth; **kokuhoo** law of the land; **kokugai** abroad; overseas; outside the country; **kokugo** national language; Japanese language; **KOKUMIN** nation; people; **kokumin keizai** national economy; **kokumin seikatsu** national life; **kokuseki** nationality, citizenship.

**kokuban** blackboard; **kokuban fuki** blackboard eraser.

**kokubyaku** black and white; right and wrong; **kokubyaku o tsukeru** to tell right from wrong; to discriminate between good and bad; **kokubyaku o arasou** argue the merits (of something).

**kokuhatsu** prosecution; indictment; accusation.

**Kokujin** black person; **Kokujinshu** black race.

**kokumotsu** cereals, grain, corn; **kokumotsugura** granary.

**kokunai** (*n.*) interior; **kokunai no** domestic; internal; home; **kokunai shoogyoo** domestic commerce.

**kokyuu** breath; breathing; **kokyuu suru** to breathe.

**KOMAKA NA, KOMAKAI** small, minute; fine, detailed; delicate, thrifty; **komaka na**

**koto** trifling matter; **komakaku chuui suru** to pay close attention.

**komaraseru** to annoy; to trouble; to muzzle.

**KOMARU** to be distressed; to be embarrassed; to be in trouble; to have a hard time, be hard up.

**KOME** rice; **kome o tsukuru** to grow (cultivate) rice.

**komiau** to be crowded; to be full; to swarm.

**KOMU** to be crowded; to be jammed; to be full up. **Kono kisha wa komu deshoo.** This train will probably be crowded.

**komichi** path, lane.

**komiiru** to be complicated; to get entangled.

**komogomo** alternately, by turns; reciprocally.

**komugi** wheat; corn; **komugiko** wheat flour.

**kon-** prefix denoting: present, current; **KONBAN** this evening; tonight; **KONGETSU** this month; **kongetsu tooka** on the tenth of this month; **KONNICHI** today; nowadays; the present time; **konnichi igo** from now on; from today on. **KONBAN WA.** Good evening. **KONNICHI WA!** Good afternoon! Good day!

**kona** flour; powder; **konagona ni kudaku** to break into pieces; pulverize.

**konasu** to grind, reduce to powder; to digest; to handle; **joozu ni konasu** to handle with skill.

**konboo** club, cudgel.

**KONDATE** menu.

**KONDO** now; this time; next time; new; **kondo no** this; next; coming; **kondo iku toki** the next time I go. **Kondo no densha de ikimashoo.** Let's take the next train. **Kondo wa yurushite agemasu.** I'll forgive you this time.

**kongaragaru** to get entangled, become involved; to get confused.

**kon'i** acquaintance; friendship; **kon'i na** intimate, familiar; **kon'i ni shite iru** to be on friendly terms.

**konimotsu** baggage, luggage.

**konki** energy; perseverance; patience; **konki no yoi** energetic.

**konmori** densely; thickly; **konmori shigetta** densely wooded.

**KONNA** such; this sort of; **konna fuu ni** in this manner; **konna toki ni** at a time like this.

**konnan** difficulty; difficulties; troubles; **konnan na** difficult; troublesome.

**KONO** this; these; **kono hen ni** in this neighborhood; **kono tsugi** next time; **kono mae** before this; the last time; **kono saki** hereafter; in the future; **kono yo** this world; this life; **kono yo no** worldly, mundane; **kono yoo na** such; of this sort.

**KONOAIDA** the other day; recently; not too long ago; **konoaida no ban** the other evening.

**KONOGORO** these days. **Konogoro wa ikaga desu ka?** How have you been lately?

**KONOKATA** since; **juunen konokata** these ten years; in the past ten years.

**konomi** liking, preference, choice.

**konomu** to like, be fond of; to prefer.

**KONPYUUTAA** computer. **dejitaru konpyuutaa** digital computer; **konpyuutaa gengo** computer language; **konpyuutaa puroguramu** computer program; **pasokon** personal computer.

**konran** commotion, confusion, disorder; **konran suru** to be confused, be in confusion.

**KONSHUU** this week. **Konshuu no Kin'yoobi ni kite kudasai.** Please come to see me this week on Friday.

**konton** chaos; **konton taru** chaotic.

**kon'yaku** (marriage) engagement, betrothal; **kon'yaku suru** to be engaged. **kon'yaku o haki suru** to break an engagement.

**konzatsu** disorder; complication; **konzatsu suru** to be in disorder, to be confused; to be complicated.

**KOO** this way. **Koo shite kudasai.** Please do it this way. **Koo natte wa shikata ga nai.** We can't do much when things go this way.

**kooan** design, plan; **kooan suru** to design, scheme, plan.

**KOOBA** = **KOOJOO** factory, mill. **Watakushi wa ano kooba de hataraite imasu.** I am working at that factory.

**koobashii** fragrant; savory; favorable.

**KOOCHA** Western black tea.

**koochoo** school principal.

**koochoo** high tide, climax.

**koodan** platform, pulpit, rostrum.

**koodoo** lecture hall, auditorium.

**koodoo** action, movement; conduct, behavior; **koodoo suru** to act, conduct oneself; to move.

**KOOEN** park, public garden.

**KOOEN** lecture, address; **kooen suru** to give a lecture; **kooensha** lecturer.

**kooen** support, aid, backing; **kooen suru** to back up, support; **kooensha** supporter.

**koofu** workman.

**koofuku** happiness; well-being; bliss; good fortune; **koofuku na** happy; fortunate; **koofuku ni kurasu** to live a happy life.

**koofun** stimulation; excitement; **koofun suru** to be stimulated; to be excited.

**KOOGAI** suburbs.

**KOOGAI** public hazard.

**koogen** plateau.

**koogi** lecture, discourse.

**koogyoo** industry; manufacturing; **koogyoochi** manufacturing district; **koogyooka** manufacturer; **koogyoo no** industrial.

**koohei** impartiality; fair play; **koohei na** fair, just, impartial.

**KOOHII** coffee.

**koohyoo** favorable criticism; **koohyoo de aru** to be popular, win popularity; to receive favorable criticism.

**kooi** kind intentions; kindness.

**KOO IU** such; this sort of; **koo iu fuu ni** in this way; **koo iu koto** such a thing as this.

**kooji** construction; works; **kooji chuu** under construction.

**kooji** alley, lane, narrow street.

**koojiru** to grow worse, change for the worse.

**koojitsu** excuse, pretext.

**KOOJOO** See **KOOBA.**

**kooka** effect, result; **kooka ga nai** not to take effect; to have no result or effect; **kooka ga aru** to be effective.

**kookai** voyage, crossing; **kookai suru** to sail; navigate.

**KOOKAN** exchange; **iken kookan** exchange of views; **kookan kakaku** exchange value; **kookandai** telephone switchboard; **kookanshu** telephone operator.

**kookan** favorable impression, good feeling.

**kookei** spectacle, sight; scene.

**kooken suru** to contribute, make a contribution toward; to be conducive to; to go far toward.

**kookishin** curiosity; **kookishin no tsuyoi** curious.

**KOOKOKU** advertisement; notice, announcement; **kookoku bira** poster, placard; **kookoku suru** to advertise; **sangyoo kookoku** classified advertisement.

**kookoo** so and so; such and such; **kookoo iu wake de** under such (these) circumstances.

**kookoo** filial piety, obedience to parents.

**kookotsu** rapture, ecstasy; **kookotsu to suru** to be in ecstasy; to be enraptured; to be enchanted.

**kookuubin** airmail.

**kookuuki** aircraft.

**kookyoo** (n.) public; society; **kookyoo no** public; common; **kookyooshin no aru** community-minded.

**kookyoo** prosperity, business boom.

**kookyoogaku** symphony; **kookyoogakudan** symphony orchestra.

**koonoo** effect, efficacy; virtue; **koonoo no nai** ineffective; **koonoo no aru** effective; useful; **koonoo ga aru** to be good for; to be effective, be useful.

**KOORI** ice; **koori no hatta** frozen, covered with ice; **koorizume no** refrigerated; iced.

**kooron** dispute; **kooron suru** to dispute, quarrel.

**kooroo** merits, meritorious deed; **kooroo aru** meritorious.

**kooru** to freeze.

**kooryoku** effect, efficacy; **kooryoku no aru** valid; effective.

**koosa** intersection, crossing; **koosa suru** to intersect, cross; **koosaten** intersection, crossroad.

**koosai** intercourse; association; society; company; fellowship; **koosaika** sociable person; good mixer.

**koosan** surrender, capitulation; **koosan suru** to surrender, submit; **koosan saseru** to make someone surrender.

**koosatsu** consideration; contemplation; **koosatsu suru** to consider; weight; to examine; to contemplate.

**kooseki** distinguished service.

**koosen** light; beam (ray) of light; **koosen o ireru** to let in the light.

**koosetsu** public; municipal **koosetsu shijoo** public market.

**kooshi** lecturer.

**kooshi** minister (diplomatic service); **kooshikan** legation.

**kooshiki** formula; formality; **kooshiki no** formal; state; official; **kooshiki de arawasu** to formulate.

**kooshoo** negotiation; **kooshoo chuu** under negotiation; **kooshoo suru** to negotiate; **nanra no kooshoo mo nai** to have nothing to do with.

**kooshuu** (n.) public; **kooshuu toire** restroom, public lavatory; **kooshuu yokujoo** public bath; **kooshuu no** public; common.

**koosoku** confinement; restraint; detention; **koosoku suru** to confine, detain; **koosoku o ukete inai** to be free from restraint.

**koosokudo** high speed; rapid transit.

**koosui** perfume, cologne, scent; **koosui o tsukeru** to use perfume.

**kootai** relief; substitution; **kootai ni** alternately; in turn; **kootai suru** to relieve; take turns.

**Kootaishi** Crown Prince.

**kootei** affirmation; **kootei suru** to affirm; to acknowledge; **kooteiteki** affirmative.

**kootei** fluctuation, high and low, unevenness, undulations; **kootei aru** fluctuating, undulating.

**kootoo** oral, verbal; **kootoo de** orally, verbally.

**kootoo gakkoo** senior high school.

**kootsugoo** favorable circumstances; **kootsugoo no** convenient; **kootsugoo na** favorable; fortunate; **kootsugoo ni** conveniently, etc.; **kootsugoo de aru** to suit one's convenience.

**KOOTSUU** communication; traffic; **kootsuu kikan** means of communication; **kootsuu o seiri suru** to control traffic; **kootsuu no ben o hakaru** to facilitate communications.

**kooun** good luck, stroke of luck; **kooun na** lucky, fortunate; **kooun ni mo** fortunately; luckily.

**kooza** (university) chair, professorship; university course.

**koozan** mine; **koozan gishi** mining engineer; **koozangyoo** mining industry.

**koozen** openly; in public; **koozen no** open; public; official.

**koozoo** construction; structure; formation.

**koozui** flood, inundation.

**KOPPU** glass (for drinking). **Koppu ni mizu o ippai kudasai.** May I have a glass of water? (See also **kappu.**)

**koraeru** to bear, endure; to control; to restrain; **itasa o koraeru** to endure the pain.

**KORE** this; these; **kore hodo** this much; so much, so many; **kore kagiri** this is all; once and for all.

**korigori suru, koriru** to take warning from; to learn by experience.

**korikatamaru** to coagulate; to be absorbed in, to be bigoted.

**koroai** suitable; adequate, handy; **koroai o hakatte** just in time.

**korobu** to fall to the ground.

**korogaru** to roll; to tumble; to fall; to lie down.

**korogasu** to roll; to tumble down.

**korosu** to kill, put to death; **iki o koroshite** with bated breath, breathlessly.

**koru** to be absorbed in; to be devoted to; to get stiff; **kenkyuu ni koru** to be absorbed in one's studies; **tabemono ni koru** to be fussy about eating.

**kosame** light rain, drizzle.

**kosei** individuality; personality; idiosyncrasy.

**KOSHI** hip(s); waist; loin; **koshi o sueru** to settle down; **koshikake** seat, stool, etc.

**KOSHIKAKERU** to sit on a chair.

**KOSHIRAERU** to make, manufacture; to prepare; to build; to raise; **hako o koshiraeru** to make a box; **kane o koshiraeru** to raise funds; to make a fortune.

**KOSHOO** pepper.

**koshoo** obstacle, hitch; defect; accident; protest, objection; mechanical trouble; **koshoo naku** without a hitch; without any trouble. **Koshoo ga nai.** Nothing is wrong. Nothing is the matter.

**kosokoso** stealthily, secretly, sneakingly; **kosokoso dete iku** to sneak out.

**kosu** to go over, go across; to outrun; to move; to pass; **yama o kosu** to go over the top; to pass the most difficult point.

**kosui** lake; **kosui no soba** lakeside.

**kosuru** to rub; to scrub; to scrape; **me o kosuru** to rub one's eyes.

**kotae** answer, reply, response; solution.

**KOTAERU** to answer, reply, respond; **-ni kotaete** in reply (answer) to; **soo da to kotaeru** to answer in the affirmative; **shitsumon ni kotaeru** to answer a question.

**kotaeru** to come home, to strike home, to have an effect on; to be a strain on. **Ano hito no kotoba wa mi ni kotaemashita.** Her words came home to me.

**kote** iron (for clothes); soldering iron; trowel; **kote o ateru** to iron clothes; to solder; to curl with tongs.

**KOTO** thing; matter; affair; account; event, occurrence; duty, task; **koto naku** without a hitch; uneventfully, peacefully. **Sore wa nan no koto desu ka?** What does it mean? What do you mean? **Sore wa koto to baai ni yoru.** That depends on the circumstances.

**KOTOBA** language; word; term; speech; expression; **kotoba o kakeru** to speak; to call to; **kotoba o kawasu** to exchange words with; **kotoba o nigosu** to give a vague answer; **kotoba takumi ni** persuasively, convincingly. **Kono kotoba no imi wa nan desu ka?** What is the meaning of this word?

**KOTOGOTOKU** wholly, entirely; completely; without exception, in every case. **Koko ni aru hon wa kotogotoku yomimashita.** I have read all the books here.

**KOTO NI** especially; above all; moreover.

**koto no hoka** remarkably, extremely, unusually.

**kotosara ni** intentionally, on purpose, purposely.

**KOTOSHI** this year; present year. **Kotoshi no natsu wa taihen atsui desu.** It is very hot this summer.

**kotowari** excuse; denial; refusal; warning; notice; **kotowari mo naku** without permission, without one's knowledge.

**KOTOWARU** to make excuses; to refuse, decline; to ask permission; **tei yoku kotowaru** to decline politely.

**kotowaza** saying, maxim, proverb.

**kotsukotsu to** untiringly; laboriously; **kotsukotsu to aruku** to plod; **kotsukotsu to shigoto o suru** to work untiringly.

**kowabaru** to stiffen; to get stiff.

**kowagaru** to fear, be afraid of; to be frightened; **kowagowa** timidly, fearfully. **Nani mo kowagaru koto wa nai.** You have nothing to be afraid of.

**kowai** fearful, frightful, terrible, horrible; **kowai kao** angry look; grim face; **kowai me ni au** to have a terrible experience.

**koware** breakage; fragment; **kowaremono** fragile thing.

**KOWARERU** to break; to be broken; to be ruined; **Mado ga kowarete imasu.** The window is broken. **kowareyasui** fragile.

**KOWASU** to break down; to destroy, demolish, smash, wreck; **ie o kowasu** to pull down a house; **karada o kowasu** to ruin one's health.

**koya** hut, shed, cabin; pen.

**koyashi** manure; fertilizer.

**koyomi** calendar; almanac.

**KOZUTSUMI** parcel; small package; **kozutsumi yuubin de** by parcel post.

**KU** pain; suffering; bitterness; **ku ni naru** become worried about; bother; to cause anxiety; **ku ni suru** take seriously; be concerned about, be worried about. **Ame wa sukoshi mo ku ni narimasen.** The rain doesn't bother me at all. **Sonna koto o ku ni suru na.** Don't trouble yourself about such a matter.

**KU = KYUU** nine; **daiku** ninth.

**kubaru** to distribute; to deal out; to dispose (of); **shinbun o kubaru** to deliver a newspaper.

**kubetsu** distinction; classification, division; **kubetsu suru** to distribute, to differentiate (between good and bad); **kubetsu o tsukeru** to make a distinction.

**KUBI** neck; head; **kubi ni suru** to dismiss; discharge; **kubi ni naru** to be dismissed; **kubi o nagaku shite matsu** to wait impatiently; **kubimaki** scarf, muffler; **kubiwa** (dog) collar.

**kubomi** cavity; hollow; dent.

**kubomu** to become hollow; to be depressed; to sink.

**KUBU DOORI** nearly; in all probability; ten to one. **Kubu doori dekimashita.** It is nearly done.

**kubun** division; **kubun suru** to divide, partition.

**KUCHI** mouth; door, aperture; hole; post; kind; share; **kuchi no tassha na** fluent; **kuchi no karui** talkative; **kuchi ga aku** to open; burst open; **kuchi o kiru** to break a seal; to open the mouth; **KUCHIBIRU** lips; **kuchibue** whistle; **kuchibue o fuku** to whistle.

**kuchidashi** meddling, interference; **kuchidashi suru** to meddle; to poke one's nose into someone else's business.

93

**kuchidome suru** to hush up (a matter); to stop (someone) from speaking.

**kuchigotae** retort; **kuchigotae suru** to answer back.

**kuchiurusai** See **kuchiyakamashii.**

**kuchiyakamashii = kuchiurusai** nagging; critical.

**KUDAMONO** fruit; **kudamonoya** fruit-seller. **Kudamono ga hoshii desu.** I want some fruit.

**KUDARANAI** stupid, foolish; absurd; useless, insignificant; **kudaranai koto o iu** to talk foolishly.

**kudari** *(n.)* going down, down; **kudarizaka** downgrade, downhill.

**KUDASAI** please give me. **Sore o kudasai.** Please give it to me.

**KUDASARU** to offer; to give (respect). **Kore o watakushi ni kudasaru no desu ka?** Is this for me? **Hitotsu kudasaru wake ni wa ikimasen ka?** Can't you spare me one of these?

**kudoi** tedious; long-winded.

**kudoku** to make love to; to attempt to seduce; to entreat; to solicit.

**kufuu** device; contrivance; plan; scheme; means; expedient; **kufuu suru** to scheme, etc.

**KUGATSU** September.

**kugi** nail; **kugi o utsu** to nail; **kugi o sasu** to remind someone of what he or she must do.

**kugiri** full stop; pause; period; **kugiri o tsukeru** to settle; to put an end to.

**kuguru** to pass through; **mon o kuguru** to go through a gate.

**kui** post; stake; pile.

**kuiki** limit; boundary; **kuiki no** inside the boundary.

**kuikomi** loss; deficit.

**kuikomu** to eat into; to encroach upon; to leave a deficit; to go into one's capital. **Sengetsu wa ichi man en kuikomimashita.** Last month there was a deficit of ten thousand yen.

**kuiru** to regret; be sorry for.

**kuitomeru** to check; hold in check; arrest.

**kuitsuku** to bite; to snap; to take the bait. **Inu ni ashi o kuitsukaremashita.** I was bitten by a dog.

**kuitsumeru** to have no means of subsistence.

**kujikeru** to be disheartened; to lose heart.

**kujiku** to sprain; wrench; break; crush; discourage; **ude o kujiku** to break an arm; **ashikubi o kujiku** to sprain an ankle.

**KUKKIRI** clearly; distinctly; plainly; strikingly.

**kukyoo** adversity; awkward situation; **kukyoo ni ochiiru** to be put in an awkward situation.

**kumen** contrivance; makeshift; **kumen suru** to devise; to contrive; to manage.

**KUMI** class; gang; band; company; team; crew; set, pack; **kumigashira** head of a group; boss; **kumiawaseru** to combine, join together; to match; **kumiai** association; guild; partnership; **kumiaiin** member (of an association); **kumiai keisan** joint account.

**kumidasu** to dip out; to bail out.

**kumitate** structure, framework; system, organization.

**KUMO** cloud(s); **kumo o tsuku yoo na** lofty; towering; **kumo o tsukamu yoo na** vague; visionary; **kumogire** break in the clouds; **kumo yuki o miru** to see how the wind blows; to wait for the results.

**kumori** cloudy, overcast; **kumori naki** clean; clear; cloudless; spotless; **kumoribi** cloudy day; **kumori garasu** frosted glass.

**KUMORU** to get cloudy. **Sora ga kumotte kimashita.** The sky is getting cloudy. **Kare wa kao ga kumorimashita.** His face became clouded.

**kumu** to unite; to associate with; to be in a partnership with; to braid; to fit together; to pair with; **hiza o kumu** to cross one's legs; **ude o kumu** to fold one's arms.

**-kun** suffix denoting: Mr. (same as **san** but usually used for and by men); **Yamada-kun** Mr. Yamada.

**KUNI** country, land, state, nation; province; territory; **kunimoto** native (home) province; **kuni namari** dialect. **Dono kuni kara irasshaimashita ka?** From which country have you come?

**kura** warehouse; storehouse; granary; **kurabarai** clearance sale.

**KURABERU** to compare; to contrast; to match; **ookisa o kuraberu** to compare the size.

**kuragari** darkness; dark place; **kuragari de** in the dark.

**KURAI** dark, dim, gloomy, obscure; **kuraku naru** to become dark. **Totemo kurai desu.** It's very dark.

**kurai** grade, rank; **kurai suru** to stand; to be situated, be located; to lie; **kurai ga tsuku** to gain in dignity.

**-kurai** See **-GURAI.**

**kurashi** living, livelihood; **kurashikata** one's manner of living; **kurashi o tateru** to make one's living.

**KURASU** to live; to make a living; **rippa ni kurasu** to live well.

**kurayami** dark, darkness; **kurayami de** in the dark.

**Kureguremo** repeatedly; earnestly.

**KURERU** to give; to grant. **Ano hito ga watakushi ni sore o kureta.** He/she gave it to me.

**kureru** to grow dark. **Hi ga kurete kimashita.** The day is growing dark.

**kureyon** crayon.

**kuriageru** to move up; advance; **kijitsu o kuriageru** to move up a date.

**kuriawase** arrangement.

**kuriawaseru, kuriawasu** to make time; to arrange the time.

**KURIKAESU** to repeat; reiterate. **Moo ichido kurikaeshite kudasai.** Please repeat it.

**kurikomu** to carry over; to carry into.

**kurikosu** to transfer; to carry forward; to bring over.

**kurireru** to transfer; to carry forward.

**KURISUMASU** Christmas.

**KURO** black; **kuro nuri no** black-lacquered; painted black; **kuro kumo** dark clouds.

**KUROI** black; tanned; dusky; **kuroi kami** black hair. **Ano hito wa iro ga kuroi.** He has a dark complexion.

**kuroo** hardship; suffering; care, concern; **kuroo shoo no** nervous; worrisome; **kuroo suru** to work hard.

**kurooto** expert; professional; specialist; connoisseur.

**KURU** to come; to come over; to arrive. **Haru ga kimashita.** Spring has come. **Otegami ga kimashita.** Here is a letter for you. **Ashita kuru deshoo.** It will probably come tomorrow.

**kurui** disorder, confusion; madness; **kurui ga kuru** to get out of order.

**KURUMA** car, vehicle, carriage, cart, wagon; wheel; **kuruma de iku** to go by car.

**kurumaru** to be wrapped up in; to tuck oneself into or wrap oneself in; **kurumu** to wrap up; to cover up; to coat, gild.

**KURUSHII** painful; hard; trying; distressing; **kurushii me ni au** to undergo great suffering; **kurushii tachiba ni iru** to be in an awkward position.

**kurushimeru** to torment, torture; to persecute; **kokoro o kurushimeru** to worry; **doobutsu o kurushimeru** to be cruel to (an) animal(s).

**kurushimi** pain, suffering; hardship; agony; torture.

**KURUSHIMU** to feel pain; to suffer from; to be worried; **hin ni kurushimu** to be poverty-stricken. **Nani o sonna ni kurushinde iru no desu ka?** What are

you suffering so much from? What makes you suffer so?

**kuruu** to go mad; to get out of order; to go wrong; to fluctuate. **Kono tokei wa doko ka kurutte iru.** There is something wrong with this watch.

**kusa** grass; herb; weed; **kusa o karu** to mow grass; **niwa no kusa o toru** to weed a garden.

**kusai** stinking, bad-smelling.

**kusami** stink, offensive odor.

**kusarasu** to corrupt; to cause to decay; to spoil.

**kusari** chain; tether.

**kusaru** to rot, decay; to turn sour; to corrode; **kusatta** rotten, sour. **ki ga kusaru** to feel low.

**kuse** habit, way; characteristic, peculiarity; **kuse ga tsuku** to get into a habit; **kuse o tsukeru** to form a habit; **kuse o naosu** to break a habit.

**kushakusha na** creased; wrinkled.

**kushami** sneezing; sneeze; **kushami ga deru** to sneeze.

**KUSHI** comb; **kushi** skewer, spit; **kushi de kami o toku** to comb hair.

**kushin** care; anxiety; struggle; **kushin suru** to take pains; to do one's best.

**kushoo** bitter smile; forced smile.

**kusuburu** to smoke, smolder; **uchi ni kusubutte iru** to remain indoors.

**KUSURI** medicine, drug; remedy; cure; physic; **kusuri o kau** to buy a medicine; **kusuri o nomu** to take a medicine; **kusuriya** pharmacist; druggist; drugstore.

**KUTABIRERU, TSUKARERU** to get tired; to be exhausted; **machikutabireru** to be tired of waiting.

**KUTSU** shoes; boots; **kutsu zure ga dekiru** to have one's feet hurt from wearing shoes; **kutsunugui** doormat; **kutsu himo** shoelace; **kutsuzumi** shoe polish; **KUTSUYA** shoe store; shoe-repair shop.

**kutsurogu** to be at ease; to relax; to make oneself comfortable; **kutsuroide hanasu** to have a heart-to-heart talk.

**KUTSUSHITA** socks; stockings; **kutsushitadome** garters.

**kuttsukeru** to join; to attach; to glue; to stick.

**KUUKI** air; atmosphere; **shinsen na kuuki** fresh air; **kuuku no ryuutsuu** the ventilation of air.

**kuusoo** fancy; vision; fantasy; **kuusooka** dreamer; **kuusooteki** visionary; imaginary; **kuusoo o egaku** to build castles in the sky.

**kuuzen no** unprecedented; unequaled; record-breaking. **Sore wa kuuzen no dekigoto desu.** That is an unprecedented event.

**kuwadate** plan, scheme; attempt, undertaking; **kuwadateru** to plan, scheme; to devise; to attempt, undertake.

**kuwaeru** to add (up); to give; to deliver; to offer; **bujoku o kuwaeru** to insult someone. **Ni ni ni o kuwaeru to yon desu.** Two and two are four.

**kuwaeru** to hold in the mouth; to bite; **yubi o kuwaete** looking wistfully [with finger in the mouth].

**KUWASHII** to be well versed; detailed; minute; particular; familiar with; **kuwashiku** minutely; to detail; at length; particularly; **kuwashiku noberu** to explain in detail; to give full particulars. **Kuwashii hanashi wa ato de hanashimashoo.** Later we shall talk about it in detail. **Ano hito wa rekishi ni kuwashii desu.** He is well versed in history.

**KUWAWARU** to join; to enter; to participate, take part in; **ikko ni kuwawaru** to join the party; **kyoogi ni kuwawaru** to take part in the game.

**kuyami** condolence; repentance; regret; **kuyamijoo** letter of condolence; **kuyami o noberu** to offer one's condolences.

**kuyamu** to regret; to repent of; to lament.

**kuyashii** regrettable; vexing.

**kuyashisa** regret.

**kuyokuyo suru** to worry about; to worry (oneself); to take to heart; to brood over.

**kuzu** waste, refuse, trash; **kuzukago** wastepaper basket; **kuzutetsu** scrap iron.

**kuzureru** to go to pieces, collapse, give away; to get out of shape.

**KUZUSU** to pull down; to break down; to destroy; to change. **Kono sen en satsu o kuzushite kudasai.** Please break this one-thousand-yen bill.

**KYAKU** visitor; guest; customer; patron; passenger; **kyakusha** passenger train; **kyakusen** passenger boat; **okyaku sama** personal guest; customer *(respect)*.

**kyakuhon** script, scenario; **kyakuhonka** playwright.

**kyakushoku** dramatization; adaptation; plot.

**kyohi suru** to deny, refuse; to reject.

**kyoka** permission; leave; admission; license; **kyoka suru** to permit, allow; to admit; to authorize.

**kyoku** office; department; bureau; **yuubinkyoku** post office.

**KYOKUTOO** Far East.

**KYONEN** = **sakunen** last year; **kyonen no Ichigatsu** January of last year.

**KYOO** today. **Kyoo wa nan'yoobi desu ka?** What day of the week is today?

**kyoo** interest; amusement; **kyoo o samasu** to spoil the fun; **kyoo o soeru** to add to the fun; **kyoo ga noru** to become interested.

**kyooboo** collusion, complicity; **kyooboo suru** to conspire; plot together; **kyooboosha** accomplice.

**kyoochoo** cooperation; **kyoochoo suru** to cooperate; to act harmoniously.

**KYOODAI** brothers and sisters. **Kyoodai wa nan nin in arimasu ka?** How many brothers and sisters do you have?

**kyoodan** teacher's platform; pulpit.

**kyoodoo** cooperation; collaboration; partnership; association; union; **kyoodoo doosa** united action; **kyoodoo kanri** joint control; **kyoodoo no** common, joint.

**kyoofu** fear, fright, dread; **kyoofu o kanjiru** to fear, etc.

**kyoogaku** coeducation.

**kyoogi** game, match; **kyoogijoo** arena; **kyoogikai** tournament, meet; **kyoogisha** contestant.

**kyoogi** conference; discussion; **kyoogi suru** to consult; to confer with.

**kyooguu** condition; situation; circumstance.

**kyoohaku** compulsion; threat, menace; **kyoohaku suru** to compel; to threaten, intimidate.

**kyoohan** complicity; **kyoohansha** accomplice.

**kyooi** astonishment, wonder; **kyooiteki** surprising; wonderful.

**kyooiku** education; training; **kyooiku suru** to educate; to train; to bring up.

**kyooin** schoolteacher.

**kyooju** teaching; instruction; professor; faculty; **kyoojuhoo** methods of teaching.

**kyookai** association.

**kyookai** church; religious association; **kyookaidoo** church building; cathedral.

**kyookai** border, boundary.

**kyoomei** resonance; sympathy; response; **kyoomei suru** to sympathize with; to echo; respond to.

**kyoomi** interest, appeal; **kyoomi no aru** interesting; attractive; **kyoomi no nai** dull, uninteresting; lacking in appeal.

**kyooshi** teacher, tutor; professor; master. (See also **KYOOIKU.**)

**kyooshitsu** schoolroom, classroom.

**kyooshuku** obligation; humiliation; **kyooshuku suru** to be much obliged, be grateful to, appreciate deeply; to be sorry for, regret. **Osokunatte kyooshuku desu.** I am sorry to be late.

**kyoosoo** competition, rivalry; footrace; sprint; **kyoosoo shiken** competitive examination; **kyoosoo suru** to compete, contest; to run a race; **kyoosoosha** rival, competitor.

**kyootaku kin** securities deposit.

**kyootei** agreement, pact; **kyootei suru** to agree; to agree upon; **kyootei nedan** stipulated price.

**kyootsuu no** common.

**kyootsuuten** common feature; thing in common.

**kyooyaku** agreement, pact.

**kyooyoo** extortion; exaction; **kyooyoo suru** to extort.

**kyooyoo no** for common use; **kyooyoo suru** to use something in common.

**kyooyuu** co-ownership; **kyooyuu suru** to hold jointly; **kyooyuusha** co-owner, joint owner; **kyooyuuzaisan** common property.

**kyoozai** teaching materials.

**kyori** distance; range; radius; **kyori ga aru** to be far, distant.

**kyozetsu** refusal; rejection; **kyozetsu suru** to refuse; reject.

**KYUU = KU** (see **KOKONOTSU**) nine.

**KYUU** urgency; emergency; **kyuu ni** suddenly; **kyuu ni sonaeru** to provide for an emergency; **kyuu o tsugeru** to be urgent; to become critical; **kyuu o yoosuru** urgent; **kyuuba** critical moment; **kyuuba no shochi** emergency measure.

**kyuu** class; grade (in a school); **ikkyuu** first grade; **nikyuu** second grade.

**kyuu-** prefix denoting: quick, sudden, abrupt; steep; **kyuubyoo** sudden illness; **kyuuhen** sudden change.

**kyuuchi** difficult situation; fix.

**kyuuen** rescue; help; **kyuuen suru** to relieve; rescue; to reinforce.

**kyuugyoo** vacation; suspension of operation; **kyuugyoo suru** to close; to take a holiday; to suspend one's business.

**kyuujo** relief, help **kyuujo suru** to rescue, save; to help; **kyuujoami** safety net; **kyuujosen** lifeboat.

**KYUUJUU** ninety.

**kyuuka** holidays, vacation; leave of absence.

**kyuukai** adjournment; **kyuukai suru** to adjourn.

**KYUUKOO** express (train); **kyuukoo suru** to rush; to dash; to go like an express; **kyuukooressha** express train. **tokubetsu kyuukooressha** special express train; **kyuukooryookin** express charges.

# M

**ma** space; room; apartment; time, interval, spare moments; **ma ga aru** to have time; **ma mo naku** before long, in a little while;

**magashi suru** to rent out a room; **ma ga waruku** unfortunately.

**ma** truth; **ma ni ukeru** to accept as truth, to believe what one hears.

**MAA** 1. Indeed! Dear me! **Maa dooshita no?** Dear me! What happened? 2. I should say, well. **Maa soo desu.** Well, it's something like that. 3. Just. **Maa matte kudasai.** Just wait, please.

**maaketingu** marketing.

**maatarashii** brand-new.

**mabara** sparsity; **mabara na** sparse, thin, scattered; **mabara ni** sparsely, thinly; here and there.

**mabataki** wink, blink; **mabataki suru** to wink, blink; **mabataki suru ma ni** in the twinkling of an eye.

**mabayui** dazzling, glaring.

**mabiku** to thin out; to eliminate.

**maboroshi** phantom; apparition; vision; illusion.

**mabusu** to cover with, sprinkle with.

**MABUTA** eyelid.

**MACHI** town, city; street; **machi hazure** outskirts of town; **machi e iku** to go to town.

**MACHIAISHITSU** waiting room.

**machiawaseru** to meet, rendezvous (with); to wait for.

**machibooke** waiting in vain; **machibooke o kuu** to wait for someone in vain; **machibooke o kuwasu** to keep someone waiting in vain.

**machidooshii** to be impatient; to be long in coming.

**MACHIGAERU = MACHIGAU** to mistake, err, make a mistake, blunder; **hatsuon o machigaeru** to pronounce incorrectly; **michi o machigaeru** to take the wrong road; **machigaete** by mistake, in error. **Futatsu machigaemashita.** I made two mistakes.

**MACHIGAI** mistake, error; fault; accident; **machigai naku** without fail; certainly; **machigai o shoozuru** to cause an accident.

**MACHIGAU, MACHIGAERU**

**machikamaeru** to await eagerly; to wait anxiously.

**machikaneru** to wait impatiently for. **Omachikane no nimotsu ga todokimashita.** The baggage that you have been waiting for so long has arrived.

**machimachi** diversity; variety; **machimachi no** diverse, various; divergent, conflicting.

**MADA** as yet; not yet (when used with a negative); still; so far. **Ano ko wa mada honno kodomo desu.** She (he) is still a mere child. **Mada futatsu arimasu.** We still have two.

**MADE** till, until, up to; to; as far as; **Tookyoo made** as far as Tokyo; **asa kara ban made** from morning till night.

**MADO** window; **mado garasu** windowpane; **mado o akeru** to open a window; **mado o shimeru** to close a window.

**MAE** time before; past; front; since; **mae no** previous, former; **mae ni** formerly, prior; **mae motte** beforehand; **mae kara** previously; from the front.

**maeba** front tooth.

**maebarai** prepayment; **maebarai no** prepaid; **maebarai suru** to pay in advance.

**maebure** announcement; preliminary notice.

**maekake** apron.

**maekoojoo** prologue; preamble.

**maeoki** preliminary statement, introduction.

**magari** crook, bend, turn.

**MAGARU** to bend, to yield; to turn; to wind; **magatta** bent, crooked, etc.; **magarikunetta michi** winding (rambling) road.

**MAGERU** to bend, curve. **Soko o magete onegai itashimasu.** Please say yes. [Please bring yourself to consent (against your will).]

**magirasu** to turn away, divert; **ki o magirasu** to divert (someone's) attention.

**magirawashii** confusing; ambiguous; misleading.

**magire** confusion; **magire no nai** evident, unmistakable; **magire mo naku** undoubtedly.

**magirekomu** to get mixed with; lost among; **gunshuu ni magirekomu** to get lost in the crowd; to be hidden in the crowd.

**magireru** to be mistaken for; to become confused.

**magiwa** verge, brink; **magiwa ni** on the verge of; **magiwa ni natte** at the last minute.

**MAGO** grandchild.

**magokoro** sincerity; devotion; **magokoro no aru** sincere.

**magomago suru** to be at a loss; to be bewildered.

**magureatari** lucky hit, lucky shot; fluke.

**MAGURO** tuna fish.

**mahi** paralysis; numbness; **mahi suru** to be paralyzed; **mahi shita** paralyzed.

**MAI-** prefix denoting: every, each; **maido** every time, each time; **maigetsu** every month; **mainen** every year; **maiasa** every morning; **maiban** every evening.

**-MAI** counter denoting: sheet; piece; page; leaf (a counter); **kami sanmai** three sheets of paper.

**majiwari** association; relations.

**majiwaru** to associate with; to mingle with. **Ano hito wa hito to majiwaru koto o kiraimasu.** She dislikes mingling with people.

**makaseru** to entrust (something to someone); to leave a person with some matter or business; **nariyuki ni makaseru** to let the matter take its course. **Banji kimi ni makasemasu.** I leave everything to you.

**makasu** to beat; to overpower; to beat down (a price), to bargain; **hyaku yen ni makasu** to beat down the price to 100 yen. **Kare o iimakasu koto ga dekinai.** I can't beat him in an argument.

**make** defeat, loss; lost game.

**makeru** to lose, be defeated; to concede, yield; to be outdone; to reduce (the price); **makezu otorazu** closely matched. **Makete kuremasen ka?** Can't you make it cheaper?

**makijaku** tape measure.

**makikomu** to roll up; to wrap up, enfold in.

**makitabako** cigarette; **makitabako ikko** pack of cigarettes; **makitabakoire** cigarette case.

**MAKKA NA** crimson, deep red; **makka na uso** outright lie; **makka ni naru** to turn red, blush deeply.

**makkura** pitch darkness; **makkura na** pitch dark.

**MAKKURO NA** deep black, ebony; **makkuro na kami no ke** jet-black hair.

**MAKOTO** truth; sincerity; honesty; faithfulness; **makoto no** genuine; real; sincere; **MAKOTO NI** truthfully; sincerely; really; greatly, exceedingly.

**MAKU** to wind, roll, coil, reel; **tokei no neji o maku** to wind up a clock.

**MAKU** to scatter, strew, sprinkle; to sow; **shibafu ni mizu o maku** to sprinkle the lawn with water.

**maku** curtain, hanging screen, drapery; act; **shomaku** opening act, first act; **maku o hikishiboru** to pull a curtain aside. **Maku ga aku.** The curtain rises.

**MAKURA** pillow, cushion; **makura o suru** to rest one's head on a pillow.

**makuru** to turn (roll, tuck) up; **ude o makuru** to roll up one's sleeves.

**makushitateru** to argue furiously.

**MAMA** as; as is; as it stands; intact; **sono mama** just as it is; **sono mama ni shite oku** to leave (something, or someone) as is. **Mama yo.** I don't care. Never mind.

**mame** beans; peas; soybeans; midget; tiny; **mame jidoosha** midget car.

**mame na** healthy, robust; brisk, active; faithful; **mame ni hataraku** to work briskly.

**mamireru** to be covered, stained with; **doro ni mamireru** to be covered with mud.

**MAMORU** to protect, defend, guard; to obey; **hoo o mamoru** to obey the laws; **yakusoku o mamoru** to keep a promise.

**MAMUKOO** just opposite; just in front of; **mamukoo no** just opposite; **mamukoo ni** right (just) in front of.

**MAN** ten thousand; myriad; **man ni hitotsu** one in ten thousand.

**manabu** to learn, study.

**manben naku** without exception; equally; uniformly.

**mane** imitation, mimicry; **maneru** to imitate; copy, mimic, simulate; **manete** in imitation of.

**maneki** invitation; beckoning.

**MANEKU** to invite; to call in; to bring upon oneself.

**maniawase** (n.) makeshift, expedient; **maniawase no** temporary.

**maniawaseru** to manage with, make do, serve the purpose.

**MAN'ICHI** by any chance; by any possibility; even though; **man'ichi no baai ni wa** if anything should happen; in case of emergency.

**MAN'IN** no vacancy; full house; crowded; **man'in fuda** "sold out" notice; "SRO" notice.

**manjoo** whole house, hall, assembly; **manjoo ittchi de** unanimously; with one accord.

**manki** expiration (of a contract); maturity; **manki ni naru** to fall due; to expire; to serve a full term.

**manmaru na, manmarui** perfectly round.

**MANNAKA** center, middle; heart; **mannaka ni** in the center; right in the middle.

**mannenhitsu** fountain pen.

**mansei no** chronic, confirmed.

**manukareru** to escape; to get rid of, be freed from; to be exempt; **ayauku manugareru** to have a narrow escape.

**manuke** (colloq.) stupid person, ass; half-wit; **manuke na** stupid, foolish.

**manzara** not wholly; not altogether. **Manzara baka de wa nai.** He is not a complete fool.

**manzen** at random, aimlessly; vaguely.

**MANZOKU** satisfaction, gratification; **manzoku na** satisfactory; complete; **manzoku ni** satisfactorily; **manzoku shite** contentedly; **manzoku suru** to be satisfied. **Manzoku shimashita.** I am satisfied.

**mappadaka** nakedness, nudity; **mappadaka no** stark naked.

**mappira** not by any means; not for anything. **Sonna koto wa mappira desu.** I wouldn't do it for anything.

**mapputatsu ni** right in two; **mapputatsu ni suru** to cut right in two.

**marason** marathon (race).

**MARE NA** rare, unusual, uncommon; **mare ni** rarely, seldom.

**mari** ball; **mari o tsuku** to play (with a) ball.

**maru** circle, ring.

**MARUI** circular, round, spherical. **marui kao (marugao)** round face; **MARUKU** round; in a circle; peacefully; smoothly; **me o maruku shite** wide-eyed; with the eyes wide open; **maruku osameru** to smooth over (a quarrel); to patch up.

**MARUDE** quite; thoroughly; almost like. **Marude natte inai.** It's quite hopeless. **Marude Nihonjin no yoo ni hanashimasu.** He speaks almost like a Japanese.

**marukiri** = **marukkiri** completely, entirely.

**marumeru** to make round.

**marumooke** clear profit; cleanup; **marumooke o suru** make a clear profit.

**MASAKA** by no means, on no account; surely not; you don't say; **masaka no toki ni** in time of need; in an emergency. **Masaka sonna koto wa arumai.** It's not at all likely.

**masa ni** just, exactly. **Masa ni sono toori desu.** It's exactly true.

**masaru** to surpass, excel.

**masashiku** certainly, no doubt. **Masashiku ano hito no yatta koto desu.** There is no question that he has done it.

**masatsu** rubbing, chafing, friction; **masatsu suru** to rub (against or with), chafe.

**maseta** precocious; **maseta kodomo** precocious child; **masete iru** to be precocious.

**mashi** increase; addition; extra; **mashi jikan** overtime; extra time; **ichi wari mashi** a 10 percent increase.

**-MASHITA** verb ending; past of **masu** (marks ordinary pol. verbs). **Kinoo gakkoo e ikimashita.** I went to school yesterday. **Tsukue no ue ni hon ga arimashita.** There was a book on the table.

**mashitani** right under, directly below; **mado no mashita ni** right beneath the window.

**mashite** much more; how much more. **Hawai ni itta koto mo nai no desu. Mashite Nihon ni wa ichido mo ikimasen.** I haven't been to Hawaii, let alone Japan.

**massaichuu** in the midst of; at the height of.

**massakari** height; prime; full bloom; **massakari de aru** to be at the height of; to be in full bloom.

**massakasama ni** headfirst; headlong; head over heels.

**massaki** (n.) foremost; head; **massaki no** first; foremost; **massaki ni** at the very beginning; first of all.

**massao na** deep blue; deadly pale; white as a sheet; **massao ni naru** to turn as white as a sheet.

**masshigura ni** impetuously; at full speed; full tilt.

**MASSHIRO NA** pure white; snow white; **masshiro na kimono** pure white clothes.

**MASSHOOMEN** direct, front; **masshoomen ni** directly in front of; directly opposite; full in the face; **masshoomen no tatemono** the building directly opposite.

**MASSUGU NA** straight; direct; upright; **massugu ni** directly; in a straight line.

**MASU** to increase; to swell; to raise; to rise. **Jinkoo ga kyonen yori niwari mashimashita.** The population increased by 20 percent over last year.

**MASUMASU** more and more; still more; increasingly. **Masumasu muzukashiku naru deshoo.** It will probably get increasingly difficult.

**MATA** and; besides; again; too; also; indirect; another; **MATA WA** or else; **mata aru toki wa** on another occasion; **matagiki** indirect information; hearsay; **mata tanomisuru** to ask something (of someone) indirectly (through someone else). **Watakushi mo mata motte iru.** I have it, too. So have I. **Mata dekakeru n desu ka?** Are you going out again?

**matagaru** to mount (a horse); to extend over, stretch over, span; **uma ni matagaru** to ride horseback; **sannen ni matagaru** extending over three years.

**matagu** to step over; to straddle.

**mataseru** to keep a person waiting.

**matataku** to wink, blink.

**MATCHI** match; matches; **matchibako** matchbox; **matchi o suru** to light a match; **matchibako no yoo na ie** tiny house (like a matchbox).

**mato** target, mark; point; **mato ga hazurete iru** to be wide of the mark; miss the point.

**matomari** conclusion; settlement; unity; coherence.

**matomaru** to be settled, decided; to come to a conclusion; to be completed.

**matomeru** to adjust, settle; to decide; to finish.

**matomo ni** right in front.

**MATSU** to wait; to await; to watch for, be on the lookout for; to expect; **mate!** wait!; hold on!; **nezu ni matsu** to sit up and wait for (someone).

**matsu** pine (tree); **matsukasa** pine cone; **matsubayashi** pine forest, grove.

**matsubazue** crutches.

**matsuri** festival; memorial services for one's ancestors.

**matsuru** to deify; to worship; to enshrine.

**MATTAKU** completely, entirely, totally; quite; perfectly; **mattaku no** entire, complete. **Mattaku soo desu!** You're quite right! **Makkaku fushigi desu!** How strange! **Mattaku wakarimasen.** I don't get it at all.

**mattoo suru** to accomplish; to fulfill; to complete.

**mau** to dance.

**maue** just above, right above; **atama no maue ni** directly overhead. **Ano hito no heya wa kono maue ni arimasu.** His room is right over this room.

**MAWARI** circumference; surroundings; neighborhood; **mawaridooi** roundabout; **mawarimichi** detour; roundabout road, roundabout way. **Ie no mawari wa hatake desu.** The farmland surrounds my house. **Mawari wa roku mairu arimasu.** The circumference is six miles.

**mawari awase** luck; chance.

**MAWARU** to turn (around); to go round; to come around, revolve, rotate; to spin. **Ichinen ni nido mawatte kimasu.** He comes around twice a year.

**MAWASU** to turn; to revolve, rotate; to roll; to whirl; to forward; to pass around; **kuruma o mawasu** to turn a wheel; to dispatch a car; **tsugi e mawasu** to pass on to the next.

**mayaku** drug, narcotic; **mayaku chuudoku** drug addiction.

**mayoi** delusion; superstition; illusion; infatuation.

**mayonaka** dead of night.

**mayou** to be puzzled; to waver, hesitate; to go astray; to lose one's way.

**mayowasu** to puzzle, bewilder; to mislead, misguide; to fascinate, captivate; to seduce.

**MAYU** eyebrows; **mayu o hisomeru** to frown; **mayuzumi** eyebrow pencil.

**mazamaza to** clearly, distinctly, vividly.

**mazarimono** mixture; compound.

**mazaru** to mingle.

**mazeru** to mix, adulterate.

**mazekaesu** to interrupt, butt in; to ridicule, sneer at.

**MAZU** first; in the first place; to begin with; about; almost; nearly; anyway; anyhow. **Mazu!** Well! **Mazu joodeki da.** It is fairly successful.

**MAZUI** tasteless, untasty, insipid; plain, homely; poor; awkward, clumsy; **mazusoo na** unappetizing. **Gohan ga mazui desu.** I don't enjoy eating.

**ME** eye; sight, look, glance; eyesight, vision; notice, observation; point of view; discrimination; insight; bud, sprout, shoot; **me no todoku kagiri** as far as one can see; as far as the eye can see; **me ga tsubureru** to lose one's sight; to become blind; **me ni amaru** to be innumerable; to be too much for; to be unpardonable; **me ni mienai** to be invisible, be unseen; **me ni tsuku** to attract (someone's) attention; to catch the eye; **me ga warui** to have poor eyesight; **me ga sameru** to wake up; to be awakened; to have one's eyes opened; **me o ageru** to lift one's eyes, look up; **me o maruku shite odoroku** to stare in wonder; **me o muku** to stare; to glare at; **me to me o miawasu** to exchange glances; **me ni hairu** to come into sight; to come into view; **me ni tatsu** to be conspicuous; **me ga kiku** to have an eye for; to be a good judge of. **Nagai me de mite ite kudasai.** Time will tell.

**me** bud, sprout, shoot; **me ga deru** to bud, to sprout; **me o tsumu** to nip (something) in the bud.

**-me** suffix denoting; order in which things are arranged; **sandome** the third time.

**meate** aim, object, end; **meate ni suru** to aim at, aim for.

**meboshi** objective, aim.

**mebunryoo** rough estimation (done by the eye).

**mechamecha ni** in disorder, in confusion; **mechamecha ni suru** to make a mess of, upset; to ruin, wreck; **mechamecha ni naru** to go to pieces; to be spoiled; to get mixed up.

**medatsu** to be conspicuous; to stand out; **medatsu iro** a loud, gay color; **medatta** striking, remarkable.

**medetai** happy; auspicious; successful; **medetai koto** happy event; matter for congratulations; **medetaku** happily, auspiciously; **medetaku owaru** to end happily. **Omedetoo!** Congratulations!

**meetoru** meter (measure); gauge; **meetoruboo** metric system.

**MEGANE** eyeglasses; insight; judgment; **meganeya** optician. **Megane nashi de yomemasen.** I can't read without glasses; **megane ni kanau** to find favorable.

**megurasu** to enclose with; surround.

**meguri** circumference, a tour; round; circulation; flow; **meisho meguri o suru** to make a tour of famous places.

**meguriau** to come across; to happen to meet.

**meguru** to go around; circulate.

**MEI** niece.

**meian** good idea, good suggestion; bright (brilliant) plan.

**meibo** register, roll of names, roster.

**meibutsu** specialty; noted product; attraction; feature. **Koko no meibutsu wa nan desu ka?** What is this place noted for?

**meichuu** hit; **meichuu suru** to hit the mark; to tell; **meichuu shinai** to miss, go wide (of the mark).

**meigetsu** full moon; **chuushuu no meigetsu** harvest moon.

**MEIGI** name; **meigijoo no** nominal, titular; **meigijoo wa** nominally; ostensibly.

**meihaku na** clear, distinct, explicit.

**meii** famous physician.

**meijin** expert; master.

**meijiru, meizuru** to command, to give orders.

**meikaku na** clear; definite; distinct; clear-cut; **meiki suru** to state clearly; to specify.

**meimei** christening, naming; **meimeishiki** christening ceremony; **meimei suru** to christen, name.

**meirei** command, order, injunction; **meireiteki na** imperative, peremptory; **meirei ni yotte** by order of; **meirei suru** to order, command, decree; to give orders to.

**meisai** particulars, details; **meisai na** detailed, minute; **meisai ni** minutely, in detail; fully; **meisaigaki** detailed description, statement, account.

**meisaku** masterpiece; fine piece of work.

**meisan** noted product.

**meisei** fame, reputation; **meisei aru** noted, renowned.

**meishi** calling card, visiting card; business card.

**meishin** superstition; **meishinteki na** superstitious.

**meisho** famous place; famous sight; **meisho o mawaru** to see the sights.

**meishoo** place of scenic beauty.

**meisoo** meditation, contemplation; dream, illusion; fallacy, erroneous idea; **meisoo suru** to meditate.

**meitei** drunkenness; **meiteisha** drunkard; **meitei suru** to get drunk.

**MEIWAKU** trouble; bother; nuisance; **meiwaku na** troublesome, annoying; **meiwaku suru** to be troubled; to have trouble; to get into trouble; **meiwaku o kakeru** to bother, annoy. **Gomeiwaku de wa arimasen ka?** (Are you sure) I'm not bothering you?

**meiyo** honor; glory; fame; **meiyo o hakusuru** to attain an honor; to attain a reputation; **meiyo o omonzuru** to have a sense of honor; **meiyoshin** ambition; desire for fame.

**meizuru** See meijiru.

**mejiri** corner of the eye.

**mejirushi** mark; landmark; sign; guide.

**mekakushi** blindfold; screen; blind.

**mekasu** to primp; deck oneself out; to dress elaborately; to dress up.

**MEKATA** weight; **mekata de uru** to sell by weight; **mekata o hakaru** to weigh (a thing).

**mekimeki** more and more; visibly; rapidly. **Nihongo ga mekimeki jootatsu shite imasu.** You are making rapid progress in Japanese.

**mekkiri** considerably, noticeably.

**mekubase suru** to wink meaningfully at.

**mekura** blindness; blind person; **mekura meppoo ni** recklessly; **mekura saguri o suru** to fumble; to grope. **Mekura hebi ni ojizu.** Fools rush in where angels fear to tread.

**memai** dizziness; **memai ga suru** to be dizzy.

**memeshii** effeminate, unmanly.

**memori** graduations (on a thermometer, etc.); graduations; markings.

**men** face; mask; surface; facet, aspect, phase, side; **men to mukatte** face to face; **men suru** to face, front on; to border on; to look out on. **Heya wa toori ni men shimasu.** The room looks out on the street; **menboku (menmoku)** face, countenance; honor; **menboku (menmoku) o isshin suru** to undergo a complete change.

**men** cotton (fabric); **menka** raw cotton; **menshi** cotton thread.

**mendoo** trouble, difficulty; troubles; complications; **mendoo na** complicated; troublesome; **mendoo o kakeru** to give trouble; **mendoo o miru** to take the trouble; to look after; **mendookusai** troublesome. **Mattaku mendookusai desu.** It's a great deal of trouble.

**men'eki** immunity (to disease); **men'eki ni natte iru** to be immune to; **men'eki chuusha** inoculation.

**menjo** exemption; excuse; discharge; **menjo suru** to exempt (from a tax); to release; to excuse.

**menjoo** diploma.

**menkai** interview; **menkai suru** to have an interview; **menkaibi** reception; visitors' day; office day.

**menkurau** to be confused; to be upset; to be at a loss.

**menkyo** = **menkyojoo** license; certificate; **menkyoryoo** license fee; **menkyojoo o motte iru** to hold a license.

**menmitsu na** detailed, minute; close; nice; meticulous; **menmitsu ni** minutely, etc.

**menshiki** acquaintance; **menshiki no aru hito** acquaintance; **ichi menshiki mo nai hito** complete stranger.

**menshoku** discharge, dismissal; **menshoku suru** to dismiss, discharge.

**menuki no** principal, main; **menuki no basho** busiest section; business center; **menuki no oodoori** main thoroughfare; busy street.

**merikomu** to cave in; to sink.

**mesaki** foresight; **mesaki ni** before one's eyes; under one's nose; **mesaki no mienai** stupid; **mesaki no** at hand; immediate.

**meshi** *(vulgar)* boiled rice; meal; food; **meshi o taku** to cook rice.

**MESHIAGARU** to eat; to drink *(respect)*. **Meshiagatte kudasai.** Please help yourself.

**meshita** inferior, subordinate.

**meshitsukai** servant.

**mesu** female (animal); **mesu neko** she-cat.

**metsuboo** downfall; ruin, destruction.

**metsuki** expression of the eyes; **kowai metsuki** menacing look.

**metta na** reckless; inconsiderate; **metta ni** rarely, seldom; recklessly; thoughtlessly.

**meue** superior, senior; **meue no hito o uyamau** to respect one's superiors.

**mezamashi dokei** alarm clock.

**mezamashii** remarkable; brilliant; admirable.

**mezawari** eyesore; offense to the eye.

**MEZURASHII** rare, unusual; new; curious; **mezurashii mono** novelty, curio.

**mi** body; person; self; oneself; **mi mo kokoro mo** body and soul; **mi o ayamaru** to lead a dissipated life; **mi no ue** one's station in life; **mi no mawari no mono** personal belongings.

**mi** fruit, nut, berry.

**miageta** admirable, praiseworthy; respectable.

**miawaseru** to exchange glances; to look at each other, to put off, postpone, defer; to abandon.

**miboojin** widow.

**mibun** social position, social standing; identity; **mibun o akasu** to reveal one's identity.

**miburi** gesture, motion; **miburi o suru** to gesture; make a motion.

**miburui** shivering, trembling; shiver; shudder; **miburui suru** to shiver (with cold), to tremble (with fear); to shudder (with horror). **Omotta dake de mo miburui ga suru.** The mere thought of it makes me shudder.

**MICHI** way, road, route, course; highway; **komichi** path, lane; **michi ni mayou** to lose one's way; **michi o kiku** to ask directions; **michibata** roadside, wayside; **michisuji** route, course.

**michibiju** to lead, guide.

**michigaeru** to mistake (by sight) one thing for another; **michigaeru hodo kawaru** to change beyond recognition.

**michi no** unknown, strange.

**michinori** distance, journey; **kisha de ichijikan hodo no michinori** about an hour's ride by train.

**michishirube** guidepost; street sign.

**michizure** fellow traveler, companion on a trip.

**midara na** indecent, obscene, lewd.

**midare** disorder; disturbance; irregularity.

**midareru** to be disordered; to go out of order.

**midashi** index; title; headline; heading.

**midasu** to put out of order; to turn upside down; to agitate, disturb; to demoralize.

**MIDORI, MIDORIIRO** green color; **midorigakatta** greenish; **midori no** green, verdant.

**mie** appearance, show, display; **mie no tame ni** for show; **mie ni suru** to do (something) for show or for the sake of appearance; **mie o haru** to show off.

**MIERU** to be visible; to see, catch sight of; to be in sight; to look like; to seem, appear; to be found; **mienaku naru** to disappear, become missing, become invisible. **Toshi no wari ni wakaku mieru.** He looks young for his age. **Me ga mieru yoo ni natta.** Now I can see things.

**miesuita** transparent; obvious, plain.

**migaki** polish; burnishing; **nihongo ni migaki o kakeru** to brush up one's Japanese.

**MIGAKU** to polish; to rub; to brush; to improve; to refine; **kutsu o migaku** to polish shoes; **ha o migaku** to brush one's teeth; **migakiageru** to polish (silver, etc.).

**migamae** attitude (posture) of being ready for action; **migamae o suru** to stand ready; to brace oneself.

**migawari** substitution; substitute; scapegoat; stand-in; **migawari o tateru** to put in one's place.

**MIGI** right, right-hand side; **migi e magaru** to turn to the right; **migi ni deru** to surpass, outdo. **Migigawa kootsuu.** Keep to the right.

**migiwa** waterside, water's edge.

**MIGOTO NA** beautiful; fine; pretty; brilliant; excellent; superb; **migoto ni** beautifully, etc. **Migoto migoto!** Well done!

**migurushii** ugly, unsightly; dishonorable, disgraceful.

**mihakarai** choice (at one's discretion). **Sore wa anata no omihakarai ni makasemasu.** I leave the choice to you.

**mihakarau** to choose (at one's discretion); to select (something) on one's own.

**miharai** outstanding (unpaid) account; **miharai no** outstanding, unpaid, unsettled.

**miharashi** view, prospect, outlook; **maharashi ga yoi** to have a fine view.

**mihari** watch, vigil, lookout; observation.

**miharu** to watch, keep watch, stand guard; **me o miharu** to open one's eyes wide; **me o mihatte** with wide-open eyes.

**mihon** sample, swatch, specimen.

**MIJIKAI** short, brief; **mijikaku suru** to curtail, shorten, abbreviate.

**mijime** misery; sadness; **mijime na** sad, miserable, pitiful.

**mijin** atoms; particles; **mijin ni naru** to be smashed to atoms.

**MIJITAKU** dress; equipment; preparation; **mijitaku o suru** to dress, get dressed; to equip; to prepare oneself.

**mijuku** immaturity, unripeness; **mijuku na** unripe, green, immature, inexperienced. **Watakushi no Eigo wa mijuku desu.** My English is far from perfect.

**mikai no** uncivilized, savage.

**mikake daoshi no** deceptive. **Sore wa mikake daoshi desu.** It's not as good as it looks.

**mikaku** sense of taste; palate; **mikaku o sosoru** to tempt the taste; **mikaku ni au** to suit one's taste.

**MIKAN** tangerine (popular fruit in Japan).

**mikan no** incomplete, unfinished.

**mikata** way of looking at things; point of view, viewpoint; **atarshii mikata o suru** to look at something in a new light; to see from a new point of view.

**mikawasu** to exchange looks.

**mikazuki** new, crescent moon.

**miki** trunk, stem.

**mikiri** abandonment; **mikiri o tsukeru** to wash one's hands of; to have nothing to do with; to give up; to desert.

**mikiru** to give up, abandon.

**MIKKA** three days; third day of the month; **mikkakan** three days; **Sangatsu mikka** March 3; **mikka ni agezu** almost every other day.

**mikkai** secret meeting, rendezvous.

**mikkoku suru** to inform against, betray; **mikkokusha** informer.

**MIKOMI** promise, hope, anticipation, prospect; **mikomi no aru** promising; **mikomi ga hazureru** to prove contrary to expectations.

**mikonsha** unmarried person.

**mikosu** to anticipate, foresee; to speculate (financially).

**mikubiru** to make light of; to think meanly of.

**mikudasu** to look down on; to despise.

**mimai** sympathy visit; **mimai ni iku** to visit a sick person.

**miman** under; below; less than; not more than; **hyakuen miman** less than one hundred yen; **jissai miman** under ten years of age; ten years and under.

**mimau** to visit a sick person.

**mime** features; face; looks; **mime yoi** good-looking; **mime uruwashii** beautiful, fair, pretty.

**MIMI** ear; hearing; **mimi ga yoi** to have a good ear; **mimi ni ireru** to inform; **mimi ni hairu** to reach one's ears; **mimi o katamukeru** to listen; **mimi o sobatateru** to strain one's ears; **mimi ni tako ga dekiru** to din into one's ears; **miminari** ringing in the ears; **mimi zawari no** grating, jarring (to the ears). **Miminari ga suru.** My ears are ringing.

**mimochi** conduct, behavior; **mimochi ga yoi** well-behaved, of good conduct; **mimochi ga warui** to lead a fast life, be of loose morals.

**mimono** sight, spectacle; attraction.

**mimoto** one's birth, parentage; identity; history; career.

**mimuki mo sezu** without looking around; without a look at; straight ahead.

**MINA, MINNA** all; everyone; everything; **mina de** in all; in a body; all told. **Mina de ikura desu ka?** How much for them all together? How much for the lot?

**minage suru** to drown oneself.

**minagoroshi** massacre, extermination, wholesale murder.

**minakami** source of a river or stream; headwaters.

**MINAMI** south; **minami no** southerly; southern; **minami ni** to the south; on the south.

**minamoto** source, fountainhead, origin, root.

**minaosu** to look at again; to have another look; to take a turn for the better, improve, look up.

**minarai** apprenticeship; apprentice; **minarau** to receive training, practice as an apprentice; to follow suit, copy; to learn from another.

**MINARI** dress, attire; personal appearance.

**minashigo** orphan.

**minasu** to regard as; to consider, think of; to suppose.

**minato** harbor, port.

**mine** peak, summit, top; back.

**minikui** indistinct, obscure; illegible; difficult to see.

**minikui** ugly.

**minji** civil affairs; civil case; **minji saibansho** civil court.

**minogasu** to neglect; to overlook; to forgive.

**minoo** nonpayment; default in payment; **minoo no** unpaid; in arrears.

**minoru** to bear fruit; to ripen.

**minu furi o suru** to pretend not to see; to wink at; to connive.

**min'yoo** ballad, folksong, popular song.

**MIOBOE** recognition; remembrance; **mioboe ga aru** to remember seeing before; to recollect; to recognize.

**MIOKURU** seeing someone off; **hito o miokuri ni iku** to go to see a person off. **Hikoojoo e tomodachi o miokuri ni ikimasu.** I am going to the airport to see a friend off.

**miosame** last look, farewell look.

**miotori** unfavorable comparison; **miotori ga suru** to compare unfavorably with; to suffer by comparison; to be eclipsed by.

**miotoshi** oversight, omission.

**MIRAI** (n.) future, time to come; future life; **mirai no** (adj.) future, prospective.

**miren** cowardice, attachment; regret; **miren ga aru** to be still attached to.

**MIRU** to see, look at, glance at, observe; to judge; to read; to look after, etc.; **yoku miru** to have a good look at; **chotto miru to** at first glance; **shinbun o miru** to read (look at) a newspaper. **Ima ni miro!** You'll soon see!

**miryoku** charm, fascination; (glamour) appeal; **miryoku ga nai** to have no appeal for; to have nothing attractive about.

**miryoo suru** to fascinate, charm.

**misadameru** to make sure of.

**misagehateta** mean, contemptible.

**misaki** cape, headland, promontory.

**MISE** store, shop; booth; **mise o hiraku** to open a store, to start a business.

**misekake** pretense, make-believe; appearance.

**misekakeru** to pretend, make a show of.

**MISERU** to show, let see, exhibit, display; to make something look like; to give an air of; **isha ni miseru** to consult a doctor, to be examined. **Anata no nooto o misete kudasai.** Please let me see your notebook.

**miseshime** lesson, object lesson, warning, example; **miseshime ni naru** to serve as a warning (lesson) to.

**mishimishi iu** to creak.

**MISO** soybean paste (food used in daily diet); **miso o tsukeru** to make a mess of; to make a poor showing; **miso shiru** soybean soup. **Soko ga miso da.** That's the beauty of it.

**misoka** last day of the month; **oomisoka** New Year's Eve.

**misokonai** misjudgment, mistaken impression.

**misokonau** to misjudge, make a mistake, make a wrong estimation.

**missetsu na** close, intimate; **missetsu na kankei ga aru** to be closely related to; to be in close connection with.

**misshiri, mitchiri** severely, seriously; closely, diligently; in earnest.

**misuborashii** shabby, ragged, seedy.

**misumisu** before one's very eyes; in full knowledge of the situation.

**mitasu** to fill, satisfy, appease, gratify; **kiboo o mitasu** to gratify a desire; **juyoo o mitasu** to meet a demand; to supply a need.

**mitate** diagnosis (medical); choice; **mitate chigai** wrong diagnosis; mistaken judgment.

**mitateru** to diagnose; to choose, select.

**mitchaku suru** to stick, adhere to; to be close together; to be interlocked.

**mitchiri** See **misshiri**.

**mitei no** unsettled, undecided.

**mitodokeru** to verify, make sure of; to satisfy oneself that.

**mitomein** private seal.

**MITOMERU** to see, witness; to catch sight of; to observe; to recognize; to admit.

**mitooshi** perspective, outlook; prospect; unobstructed view.

**mitoosu** to get an unobstructed view; to see through; to see into.

**mitsu** honey; **mitsubachi** honeybee; **mitsubachi no su** beehive; **mitsuzuki ryokoo** honeymoon.

**mitsudan** secret conversation, confidential talk; **mitsudan suru** to have a private (confidential) talk.

**mitsugi** secret; closed conference.

**MITSUKERU** to find out, discover; to detect; to sight, locate. **Uwagi o mitsukeru koto ga dekinai.** I can't find my coat.

**mitsumeru** to stare at, fix one's eyes on.

**mitsumori** estimate; assessment; evaluation.

**mitsumoru** to estimate; to calculate; evaluate.

**mitsurin** thick forest, dense woods.

**mitsu yunyuu** smuggling; **mitsu yunyuusha** smuggler; **mitsu yunyuu suru** to smuggle.

**mittomonai** indecent; disgraceful; unsightly; ugly; plain-looking; **mittomonai otoko** poorly dressed man. **Mittomonai koto o shite wa ikemasen.** Don't behave so disgracefully.

**MITTSU, SAN** three. (See also **mikka**.)

**miuchi** relations; relative; friends; followers.

**miwake** discrimination; judgment.

**miwakeru** to discriminate; to discern; to judge.

**miwatasu** to look over; to gaze out on; **miwatasu kagiri** as far as one can see.

**miyage, omiyage** souvenir; gift, present; **miyagebanashi** account of interesting or unusual things seen or heard on a trip.

**miyako** capital; metropolis.

**miyasui** evident, easily seen, clear.

**mizen ni** beforehand; before something happens; **mizen ni fusegu** to prevent (keep from) occurring; to take preventive action.

**mizo** ditch, drain, gutter; groove.

**mizore** sleet. **Mizore ga furimasu.** It's sleeting.

**mizou no** unheard of; unprecedented.

**MIZU** water; cold water; **mizu no tooranai** waterproof; watertight; **mizu de yusugu** to rinse with water; **mizu o waru** to dilute; **mizuirazu de kurasu** to live alone (without outsiders in the same house); **mizubukure** water blister; **MIZUGI** swimsuit; **mizugiwa** water's edge; **mizugiwadatte** splendidly; brilliantly; **mizugiwadatta** splendid; striking; beautiful; wheel; **mizugusuri** liquid medicine; **mizuhake** drainage; drain; **MIZUKE** dampness; moisture; **mizuke no aru** juicy; watery; **mizuke no nai** dry; parched; **mizukemuri** spray; **mizukoshi** filter; strainer; **mizukasai** watery; **mizusashi** water pitcher; **mizutame** reservoir; water tank; **mizutori** waterfowl.

**mizuhiki** colored paper cord used for tying up formal presents (red and white are chosen for ceremonious occasions).

**mizuiro** (n.) light blue; **muzuiro no** (adj.) light blue.

**mizukakeron** fruitless argument; endless dispute.

**mizumizushii** fresh-looking; ruddy.

**mizusaki annai, mizusaki annainin** pilot (of a boat).

**mizuumi** lake.

**MO** particle denoting: as well as; too; also; as many (much) as; no less (fewer) than; neither . . . nor; even; even if; although; in spite of; **donna ni ame ga hidokute mo** no matter how hard it may rain; **futte no tette mo** rain or shine. **Watakushi mo ikimasu.** I'll go too. **Hitori mo imasen.** There isn't even one person.

**mochi** durability; wear; **mochi ga yoi** to wear well, be durable.

**mochi** rice cake.

**mochiagaru** to be lifted, raised up; to arise; to take place; **MOCHIAGERU** to raise, lift up; to hold up; to praise; to flatter. **Kono hako wa omokute mochiageru koto ga dekimasen.** This box is too heavy for me to lift up. **Mochiagenaide kudasai.** Please don't lift it up.

**mochiau** to balance, keep balanced; to remain steady; to share; to pool (expenses).

**mochiawase** things on hand, in stock. **Mochiawase ga nai.** There isn't any on hand.

**mochiawaseru** to have on hand; to have in stock.

**mochiba** post, station; duty; round, beat, route.

**mochidasu** to take out, bring out; to carry out; to carry away; to remove; to save; to propose; to introduce.

**mochiiru** to use; to make use of, employ; to adopt; to apply.

**mochikaeru** to pass from one (hand or person) to another.

**mochikakeru** to propose; to court.

**mochikomi** delivery to the door.

**mochikomu** to carry in, bring in.

**mochikotaeru** to endure; to hold out; to stand.

**mochimono** property, possessions, belongings. **Kono hon wa Tanaka-san no mochimono desu.** This book is Mr. Tanaka's. This book belongs to Mr. Tanaka.

**mochinaosu** to improve; to pick up; to recover (usually used when speaking of illness).

**mochinige suru** to make off with, run away with.

**mochinushi** owner, proprietor, possessor.

**MOCHIRON, muron** of course; naturally; to be sure; certainly; no doubt; needless to say. **Mochiron suki desu.** Of course I like it! Certainly, I like it.

**mochiyoru** to contribute one's share; to bring one's quota.

**modaeru** to be in agony; to be worried; to suffer great agony.

**modokashigaru** to lose patience.

**modokashii** irritating; slow; slow-moving; not quick enough; unsatisfactory.

**modori** return; temporary recovery.

**modoru** to return, come back; to go back; to turn back; to recede.

**MODOSU** to return; to give; to send back; to throw up, vomit.

**moeagaru** to burst into flames, blaze up; **moegara** embers; cinders.

**moekiru** to burn out, be burned up.

**MOERU** to burn, blaze, be in flames; **moetsuku** to catch fire; to ignite; **moesashi** embers; half-burnt stump; **moeyasui** combustible, inflammable; **moenai** noncombustible; **moeru omoi** burning passion. **Ie ga moeru.** The house is on fire. **Hi ga yoku moete imasu.** The fire is burning briskly. (See also **hi.**)

**moeru** to sprout, to bud.

**mofuku** mourning clothes.

**mogaku** to struggle; to writhe; to wriggle.

**mogu** to break off; to tear off.

**moguri** diving; diver; unlicensed practitioner.

**moguru** to dive (into water); to dip; to creep (into bed); **toko ni moguru** to get into bed; to crawl into bed.

**moji** letter, character, ideograph; **moji doori no** literal; **moji no wakaru** literate, educated; **moji ni akarui** to be learned.

**mojimoji suru** to hesitate.

**mojiru** to twist, distort; to parody, mimic.

**mokei** model, pattern.

**MOKKA** now, at present, for the present, currently; **mokka no** present; existing; **mokka no tokoro** for the time being.

**mokkyo** tacit permission; **mokkyo suru** to give tacit permission.

**mokugeki** observation; **mokugeki suru** to observe, witness; **mokugekisha** eyewitness.

**MOKUHYOO** mark, sign; goal, target, objective: **-o mokuhyoo ni suru** to aim at; to have (something) as one's objective.

**mokuji** table of contents.

**mokumoku to** silently, in silence.

**mokumokutaru** silent, dumb; implicit.

**mokunin** tacit approval; passive consent; **mokunin suru** to tolerate; to give tacit approval; to connive.

**mokurei** nod; **mokurei suru** to nod; to greet with a nod.

**mokuroku** table of contents; list; catalogue.

**mokuromi** plan.

**mokusan** expectation; calculation; estimate; **mokusan ga hazureru** to be disappointed in one's expectations; to fail to come up to one's estimate.

**mokushi** revelation.

**mokushi suru** to overlook; to pass unnoticed.

**mokusoku suru** to measure with the eye.

**mokusoo** meditation.

**MOKUTEKI** aim, purpose, intention; **mokutekichi** destination, end of the journey.

**MOKUYOOBI** Thursday.

**mokuzai** wood, lumber, timber.

**mokuzen** before one's eyes; immediate; **mokuzen ni** before one's eyes; in the presence of; **mokuzen ni semaru** to be close at hand; to be right in front of one's eyes; to be imminent.

**momareru** to be tried; to be knocked around, tossed about.

**momegoto** trouble; dissension.

**MOMEN** cotton; cotton cloth; **momen ito** cotton thread; **momen mono** cotton goods; cotton clothes.

**momeru** to get into a dispute; to get into trouble; to have trouble; to feel discord; to be rumpled.

**momiau** to shove and push, jostle, to struggle with a person.

**momikesu** to rub out; to crush out; to smother; to hush up; to stifle.

**momiryooji** massage; **momiryooji suru** to massage.

**MOMO** peach.

**momohiki** underwear (shorts), drawers, trunks.

**momoiro** (n.) pink; **momoiro no** (adj.) pink, pinkish.

**momu** to rub, massage; to crumple up, to wrinkle.

**MON** gate; gateway; **mon'ei** gatekeeper.

**mon** crest.

**MONDAI** question, problem; subject, topic; **mondai to naru** to give rise to discussion; to be criticized; **mondai ni naranai** to be out of the question, to be insignificant; **roodoo mondai** labor problem.

**mondori utsu** to turn a somersault.

**mongen** closing time, lockup time.

**monjin** pupil, disciple, follower(s).

**monku** wording, words, terms, expression, complaint, grievance; objection; excuse; **monku o iu** to make a complaint; to grumble; **monku o iwazu ni** without question.

**MONO** thing, object; substance, matter; stuff, article; goods; possession; something; **mono ni suru** to secure; to take possession of; to make something of; **mono ni naru** to come to (anything) good; **mono ni naranai** to come to nothing; to get nowhere; to end in failure.

**mono** person, somebody.

**monohoshiba** place for drying clothes.

**monohoshizao** clothes pole.

**monomonoshii** showy, ostentatious; pretentious, pompous.

**MONO NO** though; although; only; but; about; some; **to wa iu mono no** for all that; in spite of all that is said; **mono no nifun to tatanu uchi ni** in less than two minutes.

**monooki** storeroom, storehouse.

**monoreeru** monorail.

**monosashi** ruler; footrule; yardstick.

**monoshiri** well-informed person; man of great knowledge; scholar.

**monosugoi** dreary, dismal; ghastly, grim, gruesome, terrible; **monosugoi arisama** horrible scene; **monosugoi hitode** a terribly large crowd of people.

**MOO** already; not any longer; by now; now; soon, before long; presently; **moo sukoshi** a little more, a few more; **moo ichido** once more. **Moo fuyu desu.** It's already winter. **Moo arimasen.** I haven't any more.

**moo** another. **Mizu o moo ippai kudasai.** May I have another cup of water?

**mooderu** to visit (a temple): to worship (at a temple or shrine).

**moofu** blanket.

**moojuu** wild beast; beast of prey.

**mooka** raging fire.

**mookaru** to be profitable; to make a profit; to pay; to be paying.

**mooke** profit, gains, earnings; **mooke ni naranai** to be unprofitable; **mookeguchi** profitable job, work, undertaking.

**mookeru** to make, earn profits; to make money; to set up, establish; to frame.

**moomoo to** dense, thick; dim; **moomoo to shite** thickly, in clouds.

**mooretsu** violence, fierceness; **mooretsu na** violent, fierce, furious, stormy; strong, intense; **mooretsu ni** violently, strongly, etc.; **mooretsu ni furu** to rain hard (furiously).

**mooshiawase** agreement; understanding; appointment.

**mooshiawaseru** to arrange; to agree upon; **mooshiawasete** by arrangement; **mooshiawaseta jikan ni** at the appointed (agreed-upon) hour.

**mooshideru** to make a proposal, make an offer.

**mooshikomi** offer, proposal; **mooshikomi yooshi** application form.

**mooshikomu** to apply for; to propose.

**mooshitate** statement, declaration; allegation; testimony; plea.

**mooshitateru** to state, declare; to testify.

**mooshon** motion; **mooshon o kakeru** to motion for (a person to do something); to make eyes at; to encourage.

**MOOSU** to say, tell (humble). **Hai, soo mooshimasu.** Yes, I'll tell him so. **Watakushi wa Yamada to mooshimasu.** My name is Yamada.

**MOPPARA** chiefly, mostly, principally; solely, exclusively; entirely. **Kare wa moppara shigoto ni seidashite imasu.** He devotes himself to his business.

**moraigo** adopted child.

**moraimono** present, gift (that is received).

**morasu** to let leak; to reveal, disclose; to let out, omit, leave out.

**MORAU** to receive; to get, obtain; to be given; to be presented with; to get a person to do, have a person do (following a **-te**

form). **Kono hon o morau koto ga dekimasen ka?** Can't I get this book? Couldn't you give me this book? **Tanaka-san ni katte moraimashita.** I had Mr. Tanaka buy it.

**more** leak, leakage, omission; oversight; **more o fusagu** to stop a leak.

**moreru** to leak; to escape; to come through; to get out; to get wind of; to be omitted; to be excluded.

**mori** leak.

**mori** nursemaid; taking care of a baby.

**mori** forest; wood.

**morikaesu** to regain, recover.

**MOSHI MO** in case of; if; provided that; **moshi mo no koto ga attara** if anything should happen; in case of emergency.

**MOSHI MOSHI** I say; say; if you please; please. **Moshi moshi.** Hello! Are you there (in a telephone conversation)?

**MOSHIYA** by any chance; by some possibility. **Moshiya to omotte kiite mita.** I chanced asking her.

**mosu, moyasu** to burn (transitive).

**mosurin** muslin.

**motareru** to lean on, lean against; to rest against; to recline on; to sit heavily on; to lie heavily on.

**motaseru** to let (someone) have, let (someone) take; to get (someone) to carry.

**moteamasu** to be embarrassed at, by; not to know what to do with.

**moteru** to be welcomed, made much of; to be popular; to receive attention.

**MOTO** origin, source, cause, root; investment price; cost price; **moto wa** originally, at first; **moto kara** from the beginning; **moto yori** from the first; originally; **motomoto** from the beginning, originally; **motone** original cost; cost price; **motone de uru** to sell at cost.

**moto** under; **oya no moto de** under parental supervision: **-no shusai no moto de** under the auspices of.

**motode** capital, funds; stock; **motode o orosu** to invest capital.

**MOTOMERU** to ask for, request, demand; to look for, search for.

**MOTSU** to hold; to carry; to have in hand; to possess, own; **shikkari to motsu** to grasp firmly; to take firm hold of.

**motsure** tangle; entanglement; trouble; complications.

**motsureru** to get entangled, be in a knot; to become complicated.

**mottai** artificial importance; **mottai o tsukeru** to exaggerate the importance of.

**mottaiburu** to put on airs.

**mottainai** wasteful; extravagant; impious; sacrilegious; gracious; more than one deserves. **Maa, mottainai!** What a waste! **Kare ni wa mottainai hodo no chii da.** The position is too good for him.

**MOTTE** with; by means of; by, through, because, on account of; **tegami de motte toiawaseru** to inquire by letter.

**motte iku** to take, carry (away).

**motte kuru** to bring; to fetch; to take along.

**motte no hoka** out of the question; outrageous; unpardonable.

**MOTTO** more; much; still more. **Motto kudasai.** Give me some more.

**MOTTOMO** most, exceedingly, extremely. **Mottomo juuyoo desu.** It is most important.

**MOTTOMO** indeed; it is true; but; **mottomo na** reasonable; right; rational; natural.

**mottomorashii** plausible.

**moya** haze, mist.

**moyasu** See **mosu.**

**moyoo** pattern; design; appearance, aspect.

**moyooshi** meeting; gathering.

**moyoosu** to organize, arrange; to hold (a meeting); to feel; to show signs of; to look like.

**MOYORI NO** nearest; adjacent, nearby. **Moyori no keisatsusho e shirasete kudasai.** Please notify any police station in your neighborhood.

**mozoo** imitation; **mozoo suru** to imitate, copy; **mozoohin** imitation, counterfeit.

**muboo** recklessness; thoughtlessness; **muboo na** reckless, rash; thoughtless, inconsiderate, ill-advised.

**mucha** nonsense; disorder; **mucha na** disorderly, confused; absurd, unreasonable; thoughtless; **mucha ni** recklessly; excessively, blindly; **muchakucha** unreasonable, absurd; mixed up, jumbled.

**muchi** ignorance; stupidity; **muchi na** ignorant, illiterate, etc.

**muchuu** unconsciousness; ecstasy; **muchuu ni naru** to become unconscious; to be carried away; to become ecstatic; **muchuu de** as in a dream; unknowingly; wildly, madly.

**muda** futility, uselessness; **muda na** fruitless, futile, no good, of no use; **muda ni naru** to get wasted; to be thrown away; to be in vain; **muda ni suru** to waste, throw away, etc.; **mudaashi** to go for nothing; **mudaashi o suru** to go in vain; to go on a fool's errand.

**mudabanashi** idle talk, gossip.

**mudan** without warning; without permission.

**muden** wireless communication.

**mueki no** useless, futile.

**MUGI** barley, oats, rye, wheat (general term for grain); **mugicha** barley tea; **komugiko** wheat flour; **mugimeshi** rice cooked with barley; **mugiwara booshi** straw hat.

**mugon** silence, muteness; **mugon no** silent, speechless, dumb; **mugon de** silently, in silence.

**muhi** uniqueness; **muhi no** unequaled, matchless, unique.

**muhon** rebellion, revolt, insurrection; treason; **muhon suru** to rebel, revolt; **muhonnin** rebel, insurgent; traitor.

**muhoo na** unlawful, unjust, outrageous.

**muhooshuu** without remuneration; **muhooshuu no** free; **muhooshuu de** free of charge, without recompense; **muhooshuu de hataraku** to work without pay.

**muigi, muimi** senselessness; **muigi na** senseless, absurd, meaningless.

**MUIKA** sixth day of the month; six days.

**muimi** See **muigi.**

**muishiki** unconsciousness; **muishiki ni** unconsciously; mechanically, automatically.

**mujaki** innocence, naïveté; **mujaki na** naive, innocent.

**mujin** See **mujinzoo.**

**muji no** plain, unfigured.

**mujinzoo, mujin** limitlessness.

**mujoo** heartlessness; **mujoo no** heartless, inhuman; highest; best; supreme.

**mujooken de** unconditionally; **mujooken no** unconditional; absolute.

**mujun** contradiction; inconsistency; **mujun no** contradictory; conflicting, inconsistent; **mujun suru** to be inconsistent.

**mukae** meeting (someone).

**MUKAERU** to meet, go to meet; to greet, welcome, receive; to invite, call for, send for; **Tookyoo eki de hito o mukaeru** to meet a person at the Tokyo station.

**mukaiau** to confront someone, to face each other.

**mukaikaze** head wind, adverse wind.

**mukamuka suru** to feel sick (nauseous); to feel offended; to get angry.

**mukankaku** insensibility; unconsciousness; lack of feeling; **mukankaku no** insensible; numb; unconscious.

**mukankei no** unrelated; unconcerned, disinterested.

**mukanshoo** non-intervention.

**mukashi** ancient times, old days, long ago, remote antiquity; **mukashibanashi** an old tale.

**MUKAU** to face, look out on; to be opposite; to meet, confront; to get toward; to turn toward; **kagami ni mukau** to look in a mirror; **Beikoku ni mukau** to head for (leave for, go to) America.

**mukeiken** inexperience; **mukeiken no** green, inexperienced.

**mukeru** to point at; to turn; to face; **me o mukeru** to turn one's eyes to.

**mukeru** to peel, to come off.

**muki** direction; quarter; situation; aspect; exposure; suitability; **kaze no muki** direction of the wind.

**muki** without limit in time; **muki no** unlimited, indefinite (service); **muki enki** indefinite postponement.

**mukidashi** nakedness; **mukidashi no** naked, uncovered, bare; **mukidashi ni** frankly, openly; **mukidashi ni suru** to expose.

**mukimi** shellfish stripped of their shells; hulled shellfish.

**muki ni naru** to become spirited.

**mukiryoku** enervation, lethargy.

**mukizu** spotlessness; **mukizu no** blameless; flawless; spotless; sound, perfect.

**MUKO** son-in-law; bridegroom.

**MUKOO** yonder; opposite direction; next to come; other party; **mukoo no** opposite, over there; **mukoo ni** on the opposite side, across; **MUKOOGAWA** the opposite side.

**mukoo** ineffectiveness; **mukoo no** invalid, ineffective, void; **mukoo ni naru** to become void.

**mukoomizu** recklessness; **mukoomizu no** reckless, foolhardy, rash; **mukoomizu ni** recklessly, head over heels.

**muku** to face, turn (one's face to); to look, look out on; to point to; to tend toward.

**muku** to suit, to be fit for.

**muku** to skin, to peel, to pare, to strip.

**mukuchi** reticence; **mukuchi no** reticent, closemouthed.

**mukui** retribution, punishment; reward, compensation.

**mukuiru** to reward, repay; to revenge; to retaliate.

**mukumu** to swell; to become swollen.

**mukyoka de** without permission.

**mukyooiku** illiteracy, lack of education; **mukyooiku na** uneducated.

**mukyuu** without salary; without pay; **mukyuu de** gratuitously, freely, without pay, for nothing; **mukyuu no** unpaid, unsalaried.

**mumenkyo no** unlicensed; without a license.

**MUNE** breast, chest; heart; mind; **mune ni ukabu** to occur, come to mind; **mune o uchiakeru** to open one's heart (or mind); to unburden oneself.

**mune** effect, purport, intention, principle. **Ashita kuru mune shirase ga arimashita.** There was a report that she intended to arrive tomorrow.

**munoo, munooryoku** incompetency, lack of ability; **munoo na** incapable, incompetent; **munoo na hito** a good-for-nothing.

**MURA** village, hamlet, rural community; **mura yakuba** village (municipal) office; **mura hazure de** on the outskirts of the village.

**mura** unevenness, capriciousness; cluster, clump; **mura no aru** uneven, irregular, lacking in uniformity; capricious, fickle.

**muragaru** to crowd, swarm, flock.

**muragi** caprice; **muragi na hito** fickle person.

**MURASAKI** (*n.*) purple; **murasaki no** (*adj.*) purple.

**murasu** to steam; to cook by steam; **gohan o murasu** to steam boiled rice.

**mure** group; crowd; herd; flock.

**murekusai** stuffy, musty, moldy.

**mureru** to be steamed; to be stuffy, to get musty, get moldy; **mureta** moldy, musty; stuffy.

**MURI** compulsion; coercion; unjustness, unreasonableness; **muri na** unreasonable, unjustifiable; unnatural; **muri ni** by force, forcibly; compulsorily; **muri yari ni** by force; **muri no nai** reasonable; natural; **muri na onegai** unreasonable request.

**murikai** lack of understanding; **murikai na** unsympathetic, unfeeling, heartless.

**murishi de** without interest, interest-free (money).

**muron** See **mochiron.**

**murui** matchlessness; **murui no** matchless, unique; unsurpassable.

**muryoku** weakness; debility, helplessness; **muryoku na** powerless, helpless, impotent; incompetent.

**muryoo** without charge; **muryoo no** free of charge, gratis; **muryoo de** free, for nothing, without charge; **muryoo shinryoojo** free clinic or infirmary.

**musabetsu** making no distinction; indifference; **musabetsu no** indiscriminate; equal; **musabetsu ni** indiscriminately; indifferently; equally.

**musaboru** to covet, be greedy for; **boori o musaboru** to profiteer, make an excess profit.

**musakurushii** filthy, dirty; shabby.

**musan no** having no property, unpropertied; **musansha** a proletarian; person without property; the "have-nots"; **musan kaikyuu** proletariat.

**musebu** to get choked (with tears).

**museifu** anarchy; **museifu shugi** anarchism; **museifu shugisha** anarchist.

**museigen** limitlessness; boundlessness; **museigen no** unlimited, limitless; free, unrestricted; **museigen ni** freely.

**musekinin** irresponsibility; **musekinan na** irresponsible.

**musendenshin** wireless telegraph; radiogram; **musendenshin de** by radiogram; **musendenshinkyoku** wireless telegraph office; wireless station; **musendenwa** radio-telephone.

**museru** to be choked (with).

**musessoo** inconstancy; **musessoo na** unprincipled; inconstant; unchaste.

**mushaburitsuku** to seize violently, pounce on; to grapple with.

**mushakusha suru** to be irritated; to be in an ugly mood; **mushakusha shita** irritated; shaggy, bushy; ragged.

**musha musha** munching, gobbling; **musha musha taberu** to munch, to eat greedily.

**MUSHI** insect, bug; worm; moth, caterpillar; temper; feeling; **mushi no sukanu** disagreeable; **mushi o korosu** to keep one's temper; **mushi no shirase** hunch, premonition; **mushi ni sasareru** to be bitten by an insect.

**mushi** disregard; **mushi suru** to disregard, ignore, take no account of, close one's eyes to; **-o mushi shite** in defiance of; disregarding.

**mushiatsui** hot and close, sultry.

**mushikaku** disqualification; incompetence; **mushikaku no** disqualified; uncertified; unlicensed.

**mushin** innocence; request; **mushin no** innocent; involuntary; mechanical; **mushin suru** to make a request; to beg for.

**mushinkei** apathy; **mushinkei na** dull, apathetic; insensible; **mushinkei de aru** to be insensible to; to be apathetic.

**mushiro** rather (than); better (than); sooner (than).

**mushiru** to pull off; to take off; to pluck.

**mushoku** lack of color; **mushoku no** colorless; transparent.

**mushoku no** unemployed, out of work.

**mushozoku** independence; being unattached; **mushozoku no** independent; unaffiliated, unattached; neutral.

**mushuu no** odorless.

**musoo** dream; dreaming; daydream; **musoo suru** to dream of; to fancy.

**musu** to steam; to heat with steam; to be sultry.

**musubi** knot, tie; end, conclusion, close; **musubi no kotoba** closing remarks; **mushubime** knot, tie.

**MUSUBU** to tie, knot; to close (a bargain); to conclude; to enter into; to join, link; to form; **himo de musubu** to tie with a cord.

**MUSUKO** son.

**MUSUME** daughter; young woman; girl.

**musuu** countless number; **musuu no** numberless, countless, innumerable; **musuu ni** without number; innumerably.

**muteikoo** nonresistance.

**muteppoo** recklessness; **muteppoo na** reckless, rash.

**mutsumajii** harmonious; intimate, friendly, on good terms; **mutsumajiku** harmoniously; happily.

**mutto suru** to get offended, take offense; to be stuffy, muggy.

**MUTTSU, ROKU** six.

**muttsuri** moodiness; moody person; **muttsuri shita** moody; sullen; grim.

**muyami na** excessive; indiscreet, thoughtless; rash; unreasonable.

**muyoku** unselfishness, **muyoku na** unselfish.

**muyoo no** unnecessary, needless; useless.

**muzai** innocence (of a crime); **muzai hoomen** acquittal; **muzai no** guiltless, innocent; **muzai ni naru** to be found innocent; to be acquitted.

**muzamuza** helplessly; recklessly; without much fuss; without regret.

**muzei no** tax free, duty free, untaxed; **muzeihin** duty-free goods.

**muzukaru** to fret; to be peevish (said of an infant).

**MUZUKASHII** hard, difficult, troublesome; delicate; doubtful; **muzukashii mondai** tough (touchy) question; hard problem; **muzukashii byooki** illness difficult to cure; **muzukashii tachiba** difficult situation.

**muzumuzu suru** to be itchy; to be irritated; to be impatient.

**MYOO** strangeness; cleverness; **myoo na** strange, queer, curious; miraculous; mysterious; **myoo na hito** strange person; **myoo na koto o iu** to say strange things; **myoo ni kikoeru** to sound funny.

**myooasa, myoochoo** tomorrow morning. **Myooasa mairimasu.** I will come tomorrow morning.

**myooban** tomorrow evening, tomorrow night.

**MYOOGONICHI** the day after tomorrow.

**myooji** surname, family name.

**myoonichi** tomorrow. (See also **ASHITA**.)

# N

**NA, NAMAE** name; title; designation; surname; personal name; reputation; fame; pretext, pretense; **na bakari no** nominal, in name only; **na mo nai** nameless, unknown; **na no aru** famous, celebrated; **na ga nai** to be nameless; **na ga shirete iru** to be well known, to be famous; to be popular; **na o kataru** to impersonate; **na o otosu** to lose one's reputation; **na o tsukeru** to name; **nadakai** famous, well known; **nafuda** nameplate; name card.

**na** green, leafy vegetables.

**NABE** pot, pan.

**nadameru** to soothe, calm.

**naderu** to pat; to smooth.

**nadetsukeru** to comb (hair); **kami o nadetsukeru** to smooth down one's hair.

**NADO** and so forth; and the like, etc.; **watakushi nado** the like of me; a person like myself.

**nae** seedling, shoot, sapling; **naedoko** seedbed; nursery.

**nagabiku** to be prolonged; to drag on. **Ano hito no byooki wa nagabiite iru.** Her illness is dragging on.

**nagagutsu** high boots.

**NAGAI** long, lengthy; **nagai aida ni wa** in the long run; **nagai aida** for a long time; **nagaku** for a long time; for many years; **nagaiki** longevity, long life; **nagaiki suru** to live to a great age.

**nagame** view, scenery, landscape.

**NAGAMERU** to look at; to watch; **keshiki o nagameru** to gaze at the landscape; **sora o nagameru** to look up at the sky; **hito no kao o nagameru** to gaze into someone's face.

**nagamochi** oblong Japanese chest.

**nagamochi** endurance, durability; **nagamochi suru** to last long, endure.

**naganaga** very long; **naganaga to kataru** to speak at great length.

**NAGANEN** many years; **naganen no** long; long standing; **naganen no tomodachi** a friend of long standing.

**-NAGARA** suffix denoting: while; as; at the same time that; during. **Asagohan o tabenagara rajio o kiita.** I listened to the radio while eating breakfast. **Nenagara hon o yonde wa ikemasen.** Don't read books [while] in bed.

**NAGARAKU** for a long time.

**nagare** stream, current; lineage.

**nagarekomu** to flow into.

**nagareru** to flow; to run.

**nagasa** length; measure. **Nagasa wa dono gurai desu ka?** How long is it? What is its length?

**nagasareru** to drift; to be swept away; **umi e nagasareru** to be washed out to sea.

**nagashi** kitchen sink.

**nagashime** sidelong glance; **nagashime ni miru** to look askance at; to look at (someone) out of the corner of one's eyes.

**NAGASU** to let flow; to drain; to wash away; **mizu o nagasu** to pour water; to drain off; **se o nagasu** to wash one's back.

**nagatarashii** lengthy; tedious.

**nagawazurai** lingering illness.

**nagaya** house of Edo period.

**nagedasu** to throw out, discard; **ashi o nagedasu** to stretch one's legs.

**nagekawashii** sad, lamentable.

**nageki** grief, sorrow; **nageki o kakeru** to be a source of constant trouble to others.

**nagekomu** to throw into.

**nageku** to weep; to grieve.

**NAGERU** to throw, fling, toss.

**nagetsukeru** to throw at.

**nageyari** neglect, negligence; **nageyari ni suru** to neglect; **shigoto o nageyari ni suru** to do sloppy work.

**nagi** lull, calm.

**nagori** traces, remains; parting; **mukashi no nagori** remains of the past; **nagori o oshimu** to grieve at parting.

**naguriai** fight, scuffle; **naguriai ni naru** to come to blows; **naguriai o suru** to fight.

**naguriau** to fight.

**naguru** to strike; to beat.

**nagusame** comfort, consolation.

**naguasameru** to comfort; **mizukara nagusameru** to comfort oneself.

**nagusami** amusement, sport, diversion, recreation; **nagusami ni** for fun.

**NAI** there is not; does not exist; be gone, missing; not to be found; have not (no); lack, be devoid of. **Nani mo nai.** There is nothing. **Okane ga nai.** I've no money.

**-NAI** suffix denoting; not; negative ending. **Shinaide kudasai.** Please don't do it. **Konaide kudasai.** Please don't come.

**naibu** (*n.*) inside, interior.

**naichi** homeland; mainland; interior.

**NAIFU** knife; penknife.

**naigai** inside and outside; domestic and foreign; home and abroad.

**naijoo** internal conditions; real state of affairs. **Ano hito wa sono kaisha no naijoo o yoku shitte imasu.** He knows the internal conditions of that company very well.

**naika** internal medicine; **naikai** physician.

**naikaku** cabinet; ministry; **Naikaku Sooridaijin** Premier; Prime Minister.

**naimen** (*n.*) inside, interior.

**nainai de** secretly; privately; **nainai no** secret; confidential; **nainai ni suru** to keep something secret.

**naishi** from . . . to; between . . . and . . . **Sore wa sen en naishi ni sen en shimasu.** It costs from one to two thousand yen.

**naishin** inner feelings; **naishin de wa** at heart; inwardly. **Naishin wa goku ii hito desu.** He is a good man at heart.

**naisho** secrecy; privacy; secret; **naisho de** in private; **naishobanashi** confidential talk.

**naishoku** private occupation; outside work; sideline.

**naishukketsu** hemorrhage.

**naitei** unofficial decision; **naitei suru** to decide unofficially; to arrange tentatively.

**naiyoo** contents.

**najimi** familiarity; acquaintance; intimate friend; **najimi no** familiar; **najimi ni naru** to make friends with.

**najimu** to become familiar with; to become attached to.

**najiru** to reprove, rebuke.

**NAKA** interior; inside; center; **naka ni** within; **ie no naka ni** in the house, indoors; **hako no naka e ireru** to put in a box.

**naka** relations; relationship; **naka no ii** to be on good terms; to be friendly; **naka no warui** to be on bad terms; to be unfriendly; **naka yoku suru** to keep on good terms with.

**nakaba** half; middle; **natsu no nakaba ni** in the middle of summer.

**nakadachinin** broker.

**nakagai, nakagaigyoo** brokerage; **nakagainin** broker; commission merchant; **nakagaiten** brokerage house.

**nakairi** recess, intermission.

**nakama** companion; member; (social) set; circle; **nakama ni hairu** to take part (join) in.

**nakamahazure ni sareru** to be shunned, to be left out.

**nakami** inside, interior; contents.

**NAKANAKA** very; considerably; rather, quite; easily; **nakanaka juudai na koto** (thing) of no small importance; **nakanaka dooshite** on the contrary.

**nakanaori** reconciliation; **nakanaori o suru** to become reconciled; to settle differences; **kenka no nakanaori o saseru** to patch up a quarrel.

**nakaniwa** courtyard.

**nakaore booshi** man's felt hat.

**nakaseru** to move to tears; to make someone cry.

**nakayasumi** rest, respite (in the middle of

work); **nakayasumi suru** to take a rest; to take a coffee break.

**nakayoshi** good friend, pal, chum; **nakayoshi de aru** to be good friends with.

**NAKAYUBI** middle finger.

**nakenashi no** small amount (of money) one has. **Nakenashi no kane o yarimashita.** I gave her what little money I had.

**naki** deceased; late (lately deceased); **naki haha** my late mother; **ima wa naki Tanaka-shi** the late Mr. Tanaka.

**nakigara** remains, corpse.

**nakigoe** cry; scream; **nakigoe de iu** to talk while sobbing.

**nakigoto** complaint; whimper; **nakigoto o lu** to grumble.

**nakitsuku** to implore, entreat.

**nakoodo** matchmaker.

**NAKU** to weep, cry; **nakunaku** tearfully; **naite me o harasu** to cry one's eyes out; **nakitai dake naku** to have a good cry.

**NAKUNARU** to get used up; to run out of. **Moo kane ga nakunarimashita.** I am short of funds. My money ran out. **Watakushi no tokei ga nakunarimashita.** My watch is missing.

**NAMAE, NA** name. **Onamae wa?** What is your name?

**namahanka** incomplete; superficial; **namahanka no Eigo** superficial knowledge of English.

**namahenji** vague reply; **namahenji o suru** to give an evasive reply.

**namaiki** conceit; **namaiki na** conceited; affected.

**namajii** halfheartedly; indifferently; rashly; **namajii na** halfhearted.

**namajikka ni** thoughtlessly; rashly; halfheartedly; **namajikka na koto o suru** to leave something half done.

**namakemono** lazy person.

**NAMAKERU** to be lazy. **Kyoo wa ichinichi namakete shimatta.** I've loafed all day.

**namakizu** fresh bruise.

**namamekashii** charming; coquettish.

**namanamashii** vivid.

**NAMA NO** fresh; raw; unripe; **namazakana** raw fish.

**namanurui** lukewarm; **namanurui henji** halfhearted answer.

**namari** lead (metal).

**namari** dialect, provincial speech.

**NAMATAMAGO** raw egg.

**namauo** raw fish.

**NAMERAKA** smoothness; **nameraka na** smooth, glassy; **nameraka ni** smoothly.

**NAMERU** to lick; to lap up; to experience; **nameru yoo ni kawaigaru** to dote on; **kuroo o nameru** to experience a hardship.

**NAMI** wave; sea; **nami no oto** roar of the waves. **Nami ga takai.** The sea is rough.

**nami** average; **nami no** average, common; **namihazurete** out of the ordinary, uncommon.

**namida** tears; **namida o nagasu** to weep; **namida ni musebu** to be choked with tears; **namidagumu** to be moved to tears.

**namiutsu** to undulate, wave.

**NAN, NANI** prefix or pronoun denoting: what, which, how many. **Nannin imasu ka?** How many persons are there?

**nan** difficulty; trouble; accident, defect; **nan naku** easily, without difficulty; **nan ni au** to have difficulty.

**naname no** diagonal; **naname ni** diagonally.

**NANATSU, SHICHI** seven.

**NANBAN** what number; what size. **Nanban desu ka?** What is your (telephone) number? **Nanban?** Number, please (asked by a telephone operator).

**NANBEN** how often, how many times; **nanben mo** often; many times; over and over.

**nanbutsu** tough customer; difficult person.

**NANDAKA** somehow or other; somewhat. **Nandaka tsukareta.** I don't know why, but I'm somewhat tired.

**NAN DE** why; how.

**nan de mo** any; whatever; anything, everything, by all means; probably; **nani ga nan de mo** at any rate; **nan de mo ka de mo** anything and everything. **Nan de mo soo iu uwasa desu.** So they say. So I hear.

**NANDO** how many times.

**NANDOKI, ITSU** when; **nandoki demo** whenever.

**nando mo** many times, often.

**NANGATSU** what month.

**nangi** trouble; hardship; **nangi na** difficult, troublesome; **nangi suru** to suffer hardship; **nangi o kakeru** to cause trouble.

**NANI** what? why? which, some, any, something; what!; well!; **nani wa tomo are** at all events, in any case; **nani ka ni tsukete** in one way or another; **nani yori** more than anything else; **nani yori na** the most desirable; the nicest; **nani ka taberu mono** something to eat. **Nani kuso.** Damn it! (See also **NAN.**)

**nanige naku** unintentionally; accidentally; **nanige naku yosoou** to look innocent; to look unconcerned.

**NANIGOTO** what; **nanigoto ni mo** in everything; **nanigoto ga aroo to** no matter what happens. **Nanigoto desu ka?** What's the matter? **Nanigoto mo nai** [Nothing has happened.] It's O.K.

**NANISHIRO** anyhow; at any rate, for. **Nanishiro taihen isogashii desu.** I am really very busy.

**nanitozo** please *(formal)*.

**NANJI** what time. **Nanji desu ka?** What time is it?

**nankinmame** peanut.

**nankuse** fault; **nankuse o tsukeru** to find fault with.

**Nankyoku** South Pole.

**nankyoku** crisis, difficult situation; **nankyoku ni ataru** to deal with the situation.

**Nankyokukai** Antarctic Ocean.

**nanmon** difficult problem; puzzle; ticklish question.

**NANNEN** what year; how many years. **Nan nen koko ni sunde imasu ka?** How many years have you lived here?

**NANNICHI** what day; how many days. **Kyoo wa nannichi desu ka?** What date is it?

**NAN NO** what; what kind; no; not at all; **nan no tame ni** why; **nan no yooji de** on what business. **Nan no koto mo nakatta.** Nothing has happened.

**NANOKA** seventh day of the month; seven days.

**nanpa** shipwreck.

**nanpasen** wrecked ship; **nansen** shipwreck; **nansen suru** to be shipwrecked.

**NAN TO** how; what; **nan to itte mo** after all; when all is said and done; **nan to shite mo** at any cost. **Nan to maa!** What! **Nihongo de sore o nan to iimasu ka?** How do you say it in Japanese?

**nanushi** village head.

**nao** more; still; yet; all the more; less; **nao ichido** once again; **nao mata** furthermore; in addition. **Nao machigatte imasu.** It is still wrong.

**NAORU** to be repaired; to be corrected; to recover, get well; **byooki ga naoru** to recover from an illness. **Kono tokei wa sugu naorimasu.** This watch can be repaired easily.

**NAOSARA** more; still more; less; still less; **naosara ii** to be so much better.

**naoshi** correction; mending, repair.

**NAOSU** to repair, mend; to correct; to cure. **Kono kutsu o naoshite kudasai.** I want these shoes repaired.

**napukin** napkin.

**NARA** if; in case; provided. **Hitsuyoo nara sugu mairimasu.** I will come if necessary. **Hoshii nara agemasu.** If you want it. I will give it to you.

**NARABERU** to arrange, put in order; to line up; to compare with; **kata o naraberu** to be (someone's) equal; **mihon o naraberu** to show samples.

**narabi** row, line; equal; **narabi naki** unequaled; **narabi ni** together with; besides.

**NARABU** to be in a row, stand side by side; **itchokusen ni narabu** to stand in a straight line.

**narai** custom, habit; **narai to naru** to form a habit.

**narasu** to ring; to blow; to sound; to complain; to be famous.

**narasu** to level; to smooth out; to tame; to domesticate; to train; to get used to; **inu o narasu** to train a dog; **konnan ni narasu** to inure (someone) to trouble.

**NARAU** to learn; to take lessons; to imitate, copy; **ikebana o narau** to take lessons in flower arrangement. **Anata wa okaasan ni naratte ryoori ga joozu desu ne.** You are following in your mother's steps as a good cook, aren't you?

**narazumono** rascal.

**NARERU** to become familiar with; to get used to; to become overly familiar; to become tame; **nareta** domestic; familiar. **Tookyoo no kuuki ni nareru koto wa muzukashii.** It is hard for me to adjust myself to the atmosphere of Tokyo.

**nari** sound; ring; **nari o shizumeru** to be silent, to watch breathlessly.

**nari** form, shape; size; personal appearance; **nari ga ookii** to be tall.

**naritachi** origin; organization.

**naritatsu** to consist of, be composed of.

**nariyuki** result, consequence; course (of events); **nariyuki ni makaseru** to let (something) take its own course; **koto no nariyuki** course of events.

**NARU** to become; to make; to get; to grow; to come; to set in; to pass; to attain; to begin to; to come to; to get to; to consist of; to be made of; to result in; to turn out; **byooki ga waruku naru** to take a turn for the worse (in an illness); **byooki ni naru** to fall ill; **hontoo ni naru** to come true; **suki ni naru** to begin to like; to develop a fondness for; **toshi ni naru** to come of age. **Samuku narimashita.** It is getting cold. **Naru yoo ni shika naranai yo.** Let things go their own way. Take things as they come.

**NARU** to sound; to ring; to roar; to strike; to resound; to be famous; **mimi ga naru** to have a ringing in one's ears.

**naru** to bear fruit, to grow (on a tree). **Ie no ringo ga yoku narimashita.** My apple tree is laden with apples.

**NARUBEKU, narutake** as . . . as possible; if possible; as . . . as one can; **narubeku hayaku** as quickly as possible; at the first opportunity. **Narubeku kuru yoo ni shimasu.** I'll try my best to come.

**NARUHODO** really; indeed; I see; certainly. **Naruhodo hontoo desu.** I see it is true. Indeed, you are right.

**narutake** See **narubeku.**

**nasake** sympathy; compassion; benevolence; affection; **nasake aru hito** charitable person; **nasake o kakeru** to show sympathy for; **nasakebukai** compassionate; benevolent; charitable.

**NASAKENAI** unsympathetic; heartless; cruel; miserable; pitiful; shameful; deplorable; **nasakenai arisama** a wretched condition. **Nan to iu nasakenai koto da!** What a shame!

**nasaru** to do *(respect).*

**nasu** to do, accomplish; to perform; to achieve; to form; to constitute; to make; to practice; to commit; **aku o nasu** to do wrong; **kokorozashi o nasu** to accomplish one's purpose; **en o nasu** to form a circle. (See also **suru.**)

**nasuru** to smear; to rub on; to blame.

**nata** hatchet.

**NATSU** summer; **natsubooshi** summer hat; **natsufuku, natsumono** summer clothes; **natsuyasumi** summer vacation.

**natsukashigaru** to long for; to pine for; to languish; **mukashi o natsukashigaru** to think fondly of the past.

**natsukashii** dear; beloved; longed for; **natsukashiku** longingly; fondly; **natsukashii kokyoo** one's beloved home; one's dear native place; **natsukashii omoide** fond memories; **natsukashisooni** longingly; yearningly. **Watakushi wa kokyoo ga natsukashii.** I long for home. I'm homesick.

**natsumikan** Chinese citron; bitter orange (similar to grapefruit).

**nawa** rope, cord; **nawa ni kakaru** to be arrested; **nawabari** roping off; **nawabari o suru** to rope off; **nawabari shita zaseki** roped-off seats; **nawabari o arasu** to trespass upon; to encroach upon; **nawatobi o suru** to jump (skip) rope.

**naya** outbuildings; shed; barn.

**nayami** suffering, pain, anguish, distress, trouble; **nayami ga aru** to have troubles; **nayami ga nai** to have no troubles; to be carefree.

**nayamu** to be worried about; to be troubled with; to suffer from; **nayande iru** to be in pain, to be in distress.

**nazashi** designation; calling by name.

**nazasu** to name; to call by name.

**NAZE** why; for what reason; **naze da ka** somehow; without knowing why. **Naze soo ka?** Why so? **Naze ka shiranai.** I don't know why.

**nazo** puzzle; riddle; **nazo o kakeru** to drop a hint; **nazo o satoru** to take a hint; **nazo o toku** to solve a riddle.

**nazukeru** to tame; to domesticate; to win over.

**nazukeru** to name; to call.

**nazuku** to be tamed; to become attached to; to take kindly to.

**NE** root, origin, source, base, foundation, nature; **ne mo nai uwasa** a groundless rumor; **ne mo ha mo nai koto** a pure fabrication; **ne ga tsuku** to take root; **ne ni motsu** to bear a grudge; **ne o haru** to spread roots.

**NE, NEDAN** price, cost; value; **ne ga deru** to increase in price; **ne o kiku** to ask the price; **ne o tsukeru** to set a price on. **Ne ga takai.** The price is high. It is high priced. **Ne ga yasui.** The price is low. It is moderately priced.

**ne** sound, tone; **fue no ne** tone of a flute; **kane no ne** sound of a bell.

**ne** *(n.)* sleep; **ne ga tarinai** to not get enough sleep.

**neage** price rise; price hike; **neage suru** to raise prices.

**nebaneba suru** sticky, gluey, gummy, clammy.

**nebari** stickiness, adhesiveness, perseverance; tenacity; **nebarizuyoi** persistent, tenacious; **nebarizuyosa** perseverance, stick-to-itiveness. **Ano hito wa nebari ga nai.** He lacks perseverance. He doesn't stick to it.

**nebaru** to be sticky, be adhesive; to persevere, to stick to a job.

**neboo** oversleeping; late riser, sleepyhead; **neboo suru** to oversleep, to get up late.

**nebumi** appraisal; estimation; **nebumi suru** to appraise, assess, value.

**NEDAN** price, cost, terms. **Nedan wa ikura desu ka?** What is the price? (See also **NE.**)

**nedaru** to tease; to coax; to extort; to demand.

**nedoko** bed; **nedoko ni hairu** to go to bed, to get into bed; **nedoko o koshiraeru** to make a bed.

**neesan** older sister.

**NEGAI** desire, wish; request; **negai ni yori** at one's request; **negai ga kanau** to receive a wish, to have a desire fulfilled.

**negaideru** to apply for; to send in (make) a petition.

**negaisage** withdrawal (of a petition or application); **negaisage ni suru** to withdraw a petition or application.

**negau** to petition, to beg, to wish; to hope for. **Onegai shitai koto ga aru.** I have a favor to ask of you. **Sore wa negatte mo nai**

**koto desu.** Nothing suits (pleases) me more than your proposal.

**negawashii** desirable.

**negi** leek, green onion.

**negiru** to haggle, beat down the price.

**neiro** tone; tone quality (of music).

**neji** screw; **neji de shimeru** to screw down.

**nejiau** to contend; to struggle with someone.

**nejifuseru** to get (someone) down, to overpower (someone).

**nejikeru** to be crooked, twisted; to become perverse; **nejiketa** perverse, twisted.

**nejikiru** to twist; to wrench off.

**nejikomu** to screw in; to stuff into, to demand an apology.

**NEJIMAWASHI** screwdriver.

**nejiru** to twist; to screw; to distort.

**nejitoru** to wrench off; to twist (someone's) arm (and take something from him).

**nekasu, nekaseru** to put to sleep; to send to bed; to make (someone) lie down; to lay (something) on the side; to let (something) lie idle; to keep idle; **nekashimono** unsold goods; merchandise that does not sell.

**nekkyoo** enthusiasm; fanaticism, craze; rage; passion; **nekkyoo shite** frantically, mad with excitement; **nekkyoo saseru** to create excitement, stir up enthusiasm; to thrill; **nekkyoo suru** to go wild over, go crazy over; to grow excited; **nekkyooteki** wild; enthusiastic; mad; hotheaded.

**NEKO** cat, kitten; **neko zuki** cat lover; **neko mo shakushi mo** everyone; anybody and everybody.

**nekoze** hunchback; **nekoze no** stooping, hunchbacked.

**NEKUTAI** necktie; **nekutai o shimeru** to tie a necktie; **nekutai o toku** to untie a necktie.

**nema** bedroom.

**nemaki** sleeping apparel, nightgown, pajamas.

**NEMUI, nemutai** sleepy, drowsy; **nemuku naru** to feel sleepy.

**nemuke** sleepiness, drowsiness.

**nemuri** sleep, nap; **fukai nemuri** deep sleep.

**NEMURU** to sleep; to fall asleep; **yoku nemutte iru** to be fast asleep. (See also **neru**.)

**nemutai,** See **NEMUI.**

**nen** sense, feeling; idea, notion, thought, desire, wish; concern; **fuan no nen** feeling of uneasiness; **nen o irete** carefully; **nen o osu** to call one's attention to; to remind one of something.

**NEN** year; **nen ni** yearly; per annum; **nen ni ichido** once a year; **nen ni ichido no** yearly, annual; **nenjuu** all year round, every day of the year; the whole year, the year through; **nengara nenjuu** all year

round; year after year; **nendo** business year, fiscal year; school year; **nenmatsu** at the end of the year; **nenpoo** annual salary.

**nendaijun** chronological order; **nendaijun no** chronological; **nendaijun ni** chronologically.

**nenga** New Year's greetings; **nenga ni iku** to make a New Year's call; **nengajoo** New Year's card.

**nen'iri** carefulness; **nen'iri ni** carefully, scrupulously, minutely; **nen'iri na** careful, conscientious, attentive.

**nenjiru** = **nenzuru** to pray.

**nenpyoo** chronology, chronological table.

**nenryoo** fuel; **ekitai nenryoo** liquid fuel; **nenryoo kiki** energy crisis.

**nenshi** New Year's Day; **nenshikyaku** New Year's caller; **nenshi mawari** New Year's calls.

**nenzuru** See **nenjiru.**

**neon** neon; **neonsain** neon sign.

**nerai** aim, objective; **nerai o sadameru** to take careful aim. **neraidokoro** one's objective, point aimed at.

**nerau** to aim at; to watch for.

**neri** *(n.)* kneading; **neru** to knead; to soften; to train.

**NERU** to sleep; to go to sleep; fall asleep; to take a nap; to lie down; **nerarenai** to lie awake, to sleep poorly; **yoku neru** to sleep well. **Neru jikan da.** It's time to go to bed. It's time to go to sleep. (See also **NEMURU.**)

**nesage** price reduction.

**nesshin** zeal, enthusiasm; **nesshin na** enthusiastic; **nesshin ni** eagerly, enthusiastically; earnestly.

**nessuru** to heat, make hot; to ignite; to get excited.

**netamu** to be jealous; to be envious of.

**netchuu** enthusiasm, zeal; **netchuu suru** to be enthusiastic about; **netchuu shite iru** to be devoted to, to be immersed in.

**netsu** heat; fever, temperature; craze, fad; enthusiasm; **netsu ga deru** to become feverish; **netsu ga aru** to be feverish; to be enthusiastic: **-ni netsu o ageru** to be deeply involved in; **netsuai** passionate love; **netsuai suru** to be madly in love; **netsujoo** fervor, zeal.

**nettai** tropics; **nettai koku** tropical country; **nettai no** tropical.

**netto** (tennis) net.

**nettoo** boiling water; **nettoo o abiru** to be scalded.

**NEUCHI** value, worth; price; estimation; **neuchi no aru** valuable; **neuchi no nai** worthless; **neuchi ga agaru** to rise in value; to rise in one's estimation; **neuchi**

**ga ochiru** to fall in value; **neuchi ga aru** to be worthy of; to be worth.

**nezumi** rat; mouse; **nezumitori** mousetrap.

**NEZUMIIRO** *(n.)* gray; **nezumiiro no** *(adj.)* gray.

**nezumizan** geometrical progression. **Jinkoo ga nezumizan de fueru.** The population increases by geometrical progression.

**NI** particle denoting: in; at; on; into; for; to; by; and; with; of; **asa ni** in the morning; **gozen sanji ni** at 3:00 A.M.; **hako ni ireru** to put into a box; **hito ni hanashikakeru** to speak to a person; **inu ni kamareru** to be bitten by a dog; **mado ni** at the window; in the window: **-ni chiyahoya suru** to make much of; **tana ni noseru** to put on the shelf; **Tookyoo ni iku** to go to Tokyo.

**NI, FUTATSU** two. (See also **FUTSUKA**.)

**ni** load, burden; package; luggage; freight; **ni ni naru** to be a burden to; **ni o tsumu** to load; **ni o orosu** to unload; **ni o koshiraeru** to pack; **ni o toku** to unpack.

**niau** to suit; to become; to match; **niawanai** unsuitable, unbecoming. **Kono kimono wa kimi ni niau.** This dress (suit) is becoming to you. **Sono tebukuro wa booshi ni niau.** Those gloves match the hat.

**nibui** dull; dense; slow; thickheaded.

**niburu** to become dull, become blunt; to weaken; **kesshin ga niburu** to weaken in one's resolve.

**nichanicha suru** to be slimy; to be sticky; to be greasy.

**nichibotsu** sunset; **nichibotsu ni** at sunset; **nichibotsu no nochi** after sunset; after dark.

**NICHIJOO** every day; usually; always; **nichijoo no** daily; usual; ordinary; **nichijoo no koto** everyday occurrence; **nichijoo no shigoto** daily routine; everyday work; **nichijoo go** everyday speech; ordinary language.

**NICHIYOO, NICHIYOOBI** Sunday; **Nichiyoo gakkoo** Sunday school.

**nichiyoohin** everyday necessity; articles used daily.

**nidashi** broth.

**NIDO** twice, two times; second time; **nido to shinai** never again; **nidome** second time; **nidome no** second.

**nieagaru** well done (cooking).

**niekiranai** vague; undetermined; indecisive; irresolute; **niekiranai henji** vague answer; noncommittal reply; **niekiranai hito** irresolute (undecided) person.

**NIERU** to boil; to cook; to be boiled; to be cooked. **Yoku niete imasu ka?** Is it well done? **Kono niku wa yoku niete inai**

**desu.** This meat is not well done. This meat is half cooked.

**nietatsu** to boil.

**nieyu** boiling water; **nieyu o nomaseru** to betray; to deceive; **nieyu o nomasareru** to be betrayed.

**NIGAI** bitter; **nigai keiken** bitter experience; **nigai keiken o shite me ga sameru** to learn by bitter experience; to have one's eyes opened; **nigai kao o suru** to make a (sour) face; to frown.

**nigami** bitterness, bitter taste. **Nigami ga aru.** It is bitter. It tastes bitter.

**niganigashii** bitter; painful; unpleasant; disgusting; shameful. **Niganigashii koto da!** What a shame!

**nigao** portrait; likeness.

**nigasu** to release, set free; to let escape; to miss; **tomodachi o nigasu** to miss a friend. (See also **nigeru**.)

**nigate** tough customer; difficult person, weak point.

**NIGATSU** February.

**nige** escape; retreat; **nige o utsu** to try to escape; to prepare an escape; to excuse oneself from; to shirk, evade; **nigeshi** flight; retreat; **nigeashi ni naru** to be ready to quit; to be inclined to run away. **Ano hito wa itsumo nigeashi ni natte iru.** He is always ready to quit. **Nige o utte mo dame desu.** Such an excuse is no good.

**NIGERU** to run away, flee; to escape; **motte nigeru** to make off with something.

**nigiru** to grasp, take hold of; to grip, seize.

**nigiwai** prosperity; bustle, activity, stir.

**nigiwashii** to be flourishing, prosperous; to be bustling; to be animated.

**NIGIWAU** to flourish, be prosperous; to be lively, be astir; to be crowded. **Tookyoo no machi wa nigiwatte iru.** The streets of Tokyo are crowded. **Mise wa minna nigiwatte iru.** All the stores are doing good business. All the stores are prospering.

**NIGIYAKA NA** prosperous, flourishing, animated, lively; cheerful, gay; **nigiyaka na hito** happy fellow; **nigiyaka na basho** bustling section (place); **nigiyaka ni** gaily; animatedly; **nigiyaka ni asobu** to make merry.

**nigori** muddiness; impurity; voiced consonant; **nigori mizu** muddy water.

**nigoru** to become muddy; to become impure; **nigotta** muddy; cloudy; voiced. **Ame ga futta no de ike ga nigorimashita.** The rain has made the pond muddy.

**nigosu** to make muddy; to answer vaguely, to speak ambiguously; **kotoba o nigosu** to say something ambiguously.

**niguruma** cart, wagon.

**NIHON** Japan; **NIHONGO** Japanese (language); **NIHONJIN** Japanese (person). (See also **NIPPON**.)

**niisan** older brother.

**nijimu** to blot; to run; to spread; to smudge; **inki no nijinde iru** ink-stained. **Arau to iro ga nijimu.** If you wash it, the color will run.

**nijinda** blurred, smudged, smeared; stained.

**NIJUU** twenty. (See also **HATSUKA**.)

**nijuu** duplication; **nijuu no** double, duplicate; **nijuu no imi** double meaning; **nijuu ni** doubly; twice; **nijuu ni sakusei suru** to make out in duplicate.

**NIKAI** second floor; twice, two times; **nikai ni** upstairs; **nikai ni agaru** to go upstairs; **nikaidate** two-story house.

**NIKKI** diary, journal; **nikki ni tsukeru** to record in a diary, make an entry in a diary; **nikki o tsukeru** to keep a diary.

**nikkoo** sunshine, sunlight.

**nikkyuu** daily wage; **nikkyuu de hataraku** to work by the day; **nikkyuu de harau** to pay by the day; to hire someone by the day.

**NIKU** meat; flesh; muscle; **niku no atsui** thick; **niku no usui** thin; **niku ga tsuku** to get fat; to gain weight; **niku ga ochiru** to get thin; to lose weight; **niku o kiru** to carve meat; **nikuya** butcher shop; **nikurui** meat; **nikushoku** meat-eating; meat diet.

**-NIKUI** suffix denoting: difficult; troublesome; awkward. **Nihongo de wa omou koto o iiarawashinikui.** It is difficult to express my thought in Japanese.

**nikui** hateful, detestable; abominable.

**nikumu** to hate, abhor, detest; **nikumu beki** hateful, detestable.

**NIMOTSU** baggage, luggage; load; belongings, personal effects; **nimotsu no mekata o hakaru** to weigh one's baggage; **nimotsu o azukeru** to check one's baggage.

**-NIN** suffix used as a counter for people; **sanjuunin** thirty people.

**nin** duty; responsibility; task; office; post; **nin ni ataru** to undertake a responsibility; to take on a duty; **nin ni taenai** to be unequal to the task; to be incompetent; **nin ni tsuku** to assume one's post; take up one's duties; **nin o mattoo suru** to fulfill one's duty.

**NINGEN, HITO** human being; **ningen no** human, mortal.

**ningyoo** doll; puppet; **ningyoo no yoo ni** like a doll (charming, beautiful, handsome);

**ningyooshibai** puppet show; **ningyootsukai** puppeteer.

**NINJIN** carrot.

**ninjoo** humanity; humaneness; kindness; sympathy; **ninjoo no aru hito** humane person, kindhearted person; **ninjoo ga aru** to be humane; to be sympathetic; **ninjoo ga nai** to be inhuman, be heartless.

**ninki** popular feeling, popular sentiment; popularity; business (conditions); **ninki ni joojiru** to catch the popular fancy; **ninki no aru** popular; **ninki no nai** unpopular; **ninki o toru** to win popularity; to gain favor. **Ninki ga yoi** Business is brisk. **Ninki ga warui.** Business is slack.

**ninpu** laborer; **ninpugashira** foreman.

**ninshiki** recognition; **ninshiki suru** to recognize; to perceive.

**nintai** patience; endurance; perseverance; **nintai suru** to be patient; to persevere; **nintai ga dekinai** to have no patience with; to be impatient with; **nintai shite** patiently.

**nintei** recognition; conclusion; presumption; authorization, sanction; **nintei suru** to admit; to presume; to authorize.

**nin'yoo** appointment; employment; **nin'yoo suru** to appoint to a post.

**ninzuu** number of persons; **ninzuu no ooi ie** large family.

**NIOI** smell, odor, scent; perfume, fragrance; **ii nioi** sweet smell; fragrant odor; **nioi ga ii** to be sweet smelling, be fragrant; **warui nioi** bad smell; foul odor; **nioi ga warui** to be foul smelling.

**niou** to smell; to be fragrant. **Gasu ga niou.** I smell gas.

**NIPPON** Japan; **Nippon no** (*adj.*) Japanese; of Japan; **Nippongo** Japanese (language); **Nipponjin** Japanese (person). **Nippongo ga dekimasu ka?** Can you speak Japanese? (See also **NIHON**.)

**nirami** glare; sharp look; influence; authority; **nirami ga kiku** to have authority over; to have influence over; **nirami ga kikanai** to have no authority over; to have no influence over.

**niramu** to glare at, scowl; **jitto niramu** to stare fixedly.

**NIRU** to boil; to cook. **Watakushi wa niku wa yoku nita hoo ga ii desu.** I like my meat well done.

**niru** resemble, be like, be similar to; **totemo yoku nite iru** to be very similar to; to resemble closely; **nite inai** to have no resemblance to; to be dissimilar.

**nise** (*n.*) imitation, sham; counterfeit, forgery; **nise no** (*adj.*) counterfeit, forged, false;

**nisemono** imitation, fake, counterfeit article.

**NISHI** west; **nishi no** western; **nishi ni** in the west; **nishi gawa ni** on the west (side).

**nita** like; similar.

**NI TSUITE** of; about; with; on; over; as to; concerning; regarding; on the subject of; in connection with; relating to; in the case of; **kono koto ni tsuite** about this; with regard to this matter; **kono ten ni tsuite** on this point.

**nittei** daily routine; day's agenda.

**NITTOO** daily wages; **nittoo o harau** to pay daily wages.

**NIWA** garden; yard; courtyard; **niwashi** gardener.

**niwakaame** sudden shower, downpour.

**niwaka no** sudden; abrupt; unexpected; **niwaka ni** suddenly, abruptly; unexpectedly; all at once.

**NIWATORI** chicken, hen; cock.

**nizukuri** packing; crating; **nizukuri suru** to pack; to crate; **nizukuri ga yoku dekite iru** to be well packed; **nizukuri ga fukanzen da** to be badly packed.

**NO** particle denoting: pertaining to: —'s; of—; —'s own; in; at; on; for; by; **eigo no sensei** teacher of English; English teacher; **Goya no e** a painting by Goya; **ie no iriguchi** entrance to the house; **ishi no hashi** stone bridge; bridge made of stone; **kawa no hashi** bridge over the river; **kyoo no shinbun** today's newspaper; **mondai no hito** man in question; **otooto no hon** my brother's book; **yuki no hi** snowy day.

**no** field, plain.

**nobasu** to extend, lengthen, stretch, draw out, prolong; to postpone; to straighten; **kanjoo o nobasu** to defer (payment) on a bill.

**noberu** to express, state; to explain; **iken o noberu** to express an opinion; **kansoo o noberu** to give one's impression; **riyuu o noberu** to state one's reason.

**nobetsu ni** ceaselessly, perpetually, continuously.

**nobi** postponement; spread, growth; **nobi o suru** to stretch oneself.

**nobiru** to extend, stretch; to be prolonged; to be deferred; to increase, grow, develop. **Watakushi no shuppatsu ga nobita.** My departure has been delayed.

**nobori** rise, ascent; uphill road.

**nobori** streamer, banner.

**NOBORU** to climb; to go up, rise; to be prompted; **yama ni noboru** to climb a mountain. **Taiyoo ga noboru.** The sun rises.

**nobose** dizziness, vertigo.

**noboseru** to be dizzy; to get excited; to be infatuated with; to be absorbed in; **nobosete** in the excitement. **Ano hito wa nobosete iru.** The blood has rushed to his head.

**NOCHI** future time; forthcoming time; **sono nochi** thereafter, since then; **mikka nochi** three days later; **nochi no** subsequent; future; **nochi ni** later on; afterward.

**-NODE** because of. **Kaze o hiita node atama ga itai desu.** My headache is due to my cold. [I have a headache because of a cold.]

**NODO** throat voice; **nodo ga yoi** to have a sweet voice; **nodo o itameru** to have a sore throat. **Nodo ga kawakimashita.** I'm thirsty.

**nodoka na** quiet, calm; pleasant; **nodoka na tenki** mild weather; **nodoka na kokoro** peace of mind; **nodoka ni** quietly; peacefully.

**nogareru** to escape; to flee, get away; to avoid, evade; **abunai tokoro o nogareru** to have a narrow escape; **nogarerarenai** unavoidable, inevitable. **Watakushi wa nogareru koto ga dekinai.** I'm in for it; it's inevitable.

**nohara** field, plain.

**nojuku** camping outdoors; **nojuku suru** to camp out.

**noki** eaves (of a house); **noki o naraberu** to stand side by side; to stand in a row.

**nokogiri** saw; **nokogiri de hiku** to saw.

**nokorazu** all, entirely, wholly, without exception; **issen mo nokorazu** to the last cent.

**NOKORI** remainder, rest, balance; **nokori no** remaining; **nokori naku** all, entirely; **nokorimono** remains, leavings, leftovers, remnants, scraps (of food).

**NOKORU** to be left, to remain, to linger. **Okane ga ikura ka nokotte iru.** I have some money left.

**NOKOSU** to leave behind; to keep in; to leave over; to save; **kane o nokosu** to save money; **shigoto o nokosu** to leave the work (partly done).

**nomareru** to be swallowed up, to be drunk up; to be awed by; to cower.

**nomaseru** to give a drink, serve a drink; to let (someone) drink, to treat (someone) to a drink; **ippai nomaseru** to entertain with liquor. **Doozo mizu o ippai nomasete kudasai.** Please give me a drink of water.

**nomikomu** to swallow; to drink, to gulp; to understand; to take in, to know. **Anata no iu koto ga yoku nomikomenai.** I can't grasp your meaning. I don't follow what you say.

119

**nomimizu** drinking water.

**NOMIMONO** beverage; **tsumetai nomimono** cold beverage.

**nominikui** distasteful, disagreeable (to drink), undrinkable.

**NOMU** to drink; to take (in); to swallow; to smoke; **ocha o nomu** to drink tea; **tabako o nomu** to smoke.

**NONBIRI** easily; **nonbiri to shita** carefree; easy; quiet; **nonbiri to shita seikatsu** carefree life, quiet life; **nonbiri suru** to feel at leisure, to be at ease.

**-NONI** particle denoting: although, though; in spite of, despite. **Wakai noni yoku hatarakimasu.** He works hard despite his young age.

**nonki na** carefree; easygoing; happy-go-lucky; **nonki ni** leisurely; **nonki ni kurasu** to take life easy.

**noo** brain; talent; ability; skill; **noo o itameru** to rack one's brains; **noo nashi no** good for nothing.

**noo** Noh play (also spelled No).

**nooen, noojoo** farm; **nooen ni kurasu** to live on a farm.

**nooen na** charming; engaging; bewitching; voluptuous.

**noofu** farmer; farmhand.

**noogu** farm equipment.

**noogyoo** farming, agriculture; **noogyoo no** agricultural.

**nooikketsu** cerebral hemorrhage.

**noojoo** See **hooen.**

**nooka** farmhouse; farmer.

**nookoo** density, thickness; **nookoo na** thick, dense; heavy; rich; **nookoo ni** thickly, densely; richly; **nookoo na tabemono** rich food.

**noomu** dense fog.

**nooritsu** efficiency; capability; **nooritsu no aru** efficient; capable; **nooritsu no agaranai** inefficient; **nooritsu o ageru** to increase efficiency, raise efficiency.

**nooryoku** ability; facility; competency; capability; faculty.

**noosakubutsu, noosanbutsu** crops, farm produce, agricultural products.

**nooson** rural area; farm village; agricultural district; **nooson no** rural; agricultural.

**nootan** shading; tinting; light and shade.

**nooten** scalp; crown of the head.

**noozei** tax payment; **noozei suru** to pay taxes; **noozeisha** taxpayer.

**nori** dried seaweed (a food).

**nori** paste; glue; starch; **nori de haru** to paste; to glue; **nori o tsukeru** to starch. **Kore ni nori o tsukete hoshii.** I'd like this starched.

**norikae** transfer; change; changing; **norikaeeki** junction, transfer point; **norikaeba** transfer point; **norikaekippu** transfer ticket. **Oosaka iki wa koko de norikae desu.** You must transfer here for Osaka.

**NORIKAERU** transfer; change (for a train, car, ship, etc.). **Shinjuku de basu ni norikaeru hoo ga yoi deshoo.** It will be better to transfer to a bus at Shinjuku.

**NORIMONO** vehicle, conveyance.

**noroi** (n.) curse.

**noroi** slow; lagging; tardy; dull; dense; **noroi kisha** slow train; **shigoto ga noroi** to be slow at one's work. **Ano hito wa banji ni noroi otoko da.** He is dense about everything.

**norou** to curse; to wish (someone) ill.

**NORU** to ride (in, on); to get (in, on); to go on board; to join; to take part in; to be taken in; to be recorded; **kisha ni notte iku** to go by train; **shinbun ni noru** to appear (be reported) in the newspaper; **soodan ni noru** to take part in a consultation; **uma ni noru** to mount a horse.

**noseru** to put on top of; to place on, set on; to carry; to load; to take on board; to impose upon; to publish; to record; **jidoosha ni hito o nosete yaru** to give (someone) a lift in a car; **jookyaku o noseru** to take on passengers.

**notto** nautical mile, knot.

**nottoru** to follow; to conform to; to go by; to be in accord with.

**NOZOITE** except, excepting; with the exception of; but; **hitotsu nozoite minna** all but one; **-o nozoite** with the exception of; excluding; **shoosuu o nozoite** with a few exceptions. **Nichiyoobi o nozoite mainichi benkyoo suru.** I study every day, except Sunday.

**nozoku** to eliminate, remove, exclude; to abolish; to omit.

**nozoku** to peep in, to look in.

**nozomi** wish, desire, hope; expectation, aspiration, ambition; **nozomi o kakeru** to set one's heart on.

**nozomu** face; to meet; to attend; to be present; **shiki ni nozomu** to attend a ceremony. **Niwa wa yama ni nozonde iru.** The garden faces the mountains.

**nozomu** to wish, to desire, to hope for, to aspire to; to expect; to look out on.

**nugeru** to come off; to slip down.

**NUGU** to take off; to pull off; to undress. **Kutsu o nugu no desu ka?** Shall I take off my shoes?

**nuibari** needle.

**nuka** rice bran; **nukamiso** salt and rice bran paste (for pickling).

**nukaru** to be muddy; to be slushy; to blunder, make a mistake.

**nukarumi** mud; mud puddle.

**nukasu** to omit, exclude, leave out; to overlook.

**nukedasu** to get loose; to sneak out, steal out.

**nukigaki** selection; excerpt.

**nukitoru** to pull out, extract; to abstract; to steal.

**NUKU** to pull out, take out, draw out; to extract (a tooth); to uncork; to unscrew; to select; to leave out, omit.

**numa** swamp, bog; **numachi** swampy place.

**nurasu** to wet; to dampen; to soak; to drench. **Ashi o nurasu na.** Don't get your feet wet!

**NURERU** to become wet, get wet. **Kao ga namida ni nurete iru.** Her face is wet with tears.

**nuri** coating; varnishing; lacquering; painting; plastering.

**NURU** to apply; to spread on; to paint; to plaster; to coat; **pan ni bataa o nuru** to spread butter on bread.

**nurui** lukewarm; dull; sluggish.

**nurumayu** lukewarm water.

**nusumimiru** to steal looks at, look furtively at.

**nusumu** to steal; to rob; to snatch a minute's rest; to elude the eyes of others; **hitome o nusunde au** to meet (someone) secretly; **nusubito** thief. **Okane o nusumareta.** My money has been stolen.

**NUU** to sew; **hitogomi o nuu** to go through a crowd; **kimono o nuu** to sew clothes.

**nyooboo** (*colloq.*) wife.

**nyuubai** beginning of the rainy season.

**nyuuden** telegram (cable) received; **-no mune nyuuden ga atta.** A telegram has been received to the effect that.

**NYUUGAKU** (school) admission, matriculation; **nyuugaku suru** to enter school; to matriculate; **nyuugakushiken** entrance examination.

**nyuugoku** imprisonment.

**nyuuhi** cost; expenditure; expenses.

**nyuuin suru** to enter a hospital; to be hospitalized.

**NYUUJOO** entrance; admission; **nyuujoo suru** to enter; to be admitted; **nyuujoo muryoo** free admission; **nyuujooken** admission ticket; **nyuujooryoo** admission fee.

**nyuukai** joining (an organization); admission; **nyuukai suru** to become a member (in an organization); **nyuukai o mooshikomu** to apply for membership.

**nyuukoo** entry (into port); docking; **nyuukoo suru** to enter port; to dock.

**nyuumon** entering private school; primer; **Nippongo nyuumon** Japanese (language) primer.

**nyuusatsu** bid; bidding; **nyuusatsu suru** to bid, make a bid.

**nyuusen suru** to be selected; be accepted.

**nyuusha suru** to enter a firm.

**NYUUSU** news; **kaigai nyuusu** foreign news.

**nyuutoo suru** to join a political party.

**nyuuwa na** gentle; tender.

**nyuuyoku** bath; bathing; **nyuuyoku suru** to bathe.

**nyuuyoo** need, necessity; requirement; **nyuuyoo na** necessary; required; **nyuuyoo de aru** to be in need of; to want.

**o** tail, brush; **o o furu** to wag the tail; **o hire o tsukete hanasu** to exaggerate.

**oashisu** oasis.

**OBA** aunt; **obachan** auntie.

**OBAASAN** grandmother; old woman.

**OBI** belt, sash (worn with a kimono); **obi o shimeru** to do up a sash; **obi o toku** to take off an obi; **obiage** sash-bustle; **obidome** sashband.

**obieru** to become frightened; to have a nightmare.

**obikidasu** to lure, entice.

**obitadashii** immense, vast; **obitadashiku** abundantly, profusely, in large numbers.

**obiyakasu** to threaten, intimidate; to scare.

**oboe** learning; memory; feeling; recollection; experience; **oboe ga yoi** to have a good memory; to be quick to learn.

**OBOERU** to remember; to keep in mind; to memorize; to learn; to recollect; **samusa o oboeru** to feel chilly. **Yoku oboete imasu.** I remember it well.

**obon** See **bon.**

**oboreru** to drown; to be drowned; to indulge in, to be addicted to.

**obotsukanai** uncertain, doubtful, almost hopeless; uneasy, weak.

**obusaru** to ride on someone's shoulders; to ride piggyback; to rely on.

**obuu** to take (carry) on one's back; **kodomo o obuu** to carry a child on one's back.

**OCHA, CHA** tea (usually Japanese). (See also **koocha.**)

**ochiau** to meet, rendezvous; to come (across) someone.

**ochibureru** to be ruined, to be reduced to poverty.

**ochido** fault, error; blame; **ochido ga nai** to be blameless; **hito no ochido ni suru** to lay the blame on someone else.

**ochiiru** to fall; to be reduced. **kiken ni ochiiru** to be in danger. **kukyoo ni ochiiru** to get into trouble.

**ochikomu** to fall in, fall into; to be depressed. **Kare wa kawa ni ochikonda.** He fell into the river. **Shiken ni ochite ochikonda.** I was depressed when I failed the exam.

**OCHIRU** to fall; to drop; to come down; to collapse; to be left out; to fall short of. **Yane kara ochite ashi o otta.** I fell from the roof and broke my leg. **Seiseki ga ochite kimashita.** My marks are going down.

**ochitsuki** composure, self-possession. **ochitsuki no aru** calm, self-composed; **ochitsuki no nai** fidgety, restless; **ochitsuki haratte** calmly.

**ochitsuku** to settle down, become quiet; **ki ga ochitsuku** to feel relieved; to recover one's composure.

**odayaka na** quiet, calm, peaceful, gentle; moderate; **odayaka de nai** alarming, threatening; upsetting, serious. **odayaka ni naru** to calm down, become calm.

**odokashi** threat, menace.

**odokasu** to threaten, menace; to browbeat; to scare.

**odori** dance; dancing; **odoriagaru** to jump; to dance for joy.

**odoroite** in astonishment, in amazement.

**odorokasu** to astonish, surprise, amaze; to startle, frighten.

**odoroki** amazement, wonder, surprise.

**ODOROKU** to be surprised, be amazed, to be frightened. **Kare wa odoroite tobiagatta.** He jumped up in surprise. **Odoroku koto wa nai.** Nothing is surprising about it. Don't be surprised.

**odoru** to dance; to step; **bando ni awasete odoru** to dance to a band.

**odoshi** threat, menace.

**odosu** to frighten, intimidate; to browbeat.

**oeru** to end, conclude, finish; **kai o oeru** to bring a meeting to a close; **gyoo o oeru** to finish a course.

**ogamu** to worship, venerate; to pray for.

**ogawa** brook, stream.

**oginau** to make good, make up for, supplement; **ketsuin o oginau** to fill a vacancy; **sonshitsu o oginau** to make up a loss.

**ogosoka na** grave, solemn, austere; **ogosoka ni** with solemnity.

**OHAYOO** Good morning! **OHAYOO GOZAIMASU.** Good morning (vulgar).

**OI** nephew.

**oi** (colloq.) hello! hey! look here!

**oichirasu** to drive out; to scatter.

**oidasu** to drive out, expel, turn out, evict.

**oihagi** highway robber.

**oiharau** to drive away; to send away.

**OIKAKERU** to chase, run after. **Inu ga neko o oikakete iru.** A dog is chasing a cat.

**oikomu** to corner; to drive in.

**oikosu** to outrun; to pass, to outdistance. **Hoka no kuruma o oikoshimashita.** She passed another car.

**oimawasu** to run after; to chase around.

**oioi** gradually, little by little; step by step; eventually.

**OISHII** delicious, tasty, sweet. **Aa oishii!** It tastes good! **Gohan wa oishikatta.** The meal was good.

**oitateru** to evict; to urge; to drive away.

**oitsuku** to overtake, catch up with.

**oitsumeru** to corner, get into a corner.

**OJI** uncle.

**ojigi** bow (inclination of the head or body); **ojigi o suru** to bow.

**OJIISAN** grandfather; old man.

**ojike** fear, fright; **ojike ga tsuku** to be seized with fear, be frightened.

**OJOOSAN** miss; daughter (respect).

**OKA** hill, mound; land; shore.

**OKAASAN** mother, mama (used by children in the family); mother (somebody else's).

**OKAGE** indebtedness, favor. **Okage sama de.** Thanks to your kindness.

**okami** landlady; mistress; hostess (at a restaurant).

**OKANE, kane** money.

**OKASHI, kashi** cake.

**OKASHII** amusing, laughable, funny; ridiculous; strange. **Nani mo okashii koto wa nai.** There is nothing funny. **Okashii hanashi da.** The story is strange.

**okashiya, kashiya** cake shop, candy shop.

**okasu** to commit; to violate; to rape; to infringe on; to desecrate; **kokuhoo o okasu** to break the laws of the land.

**okasu** to defy; to risk; to damage.

**okawari** second helping; another cup; **okawari suru** to ask for a second helping.

**oke** tub, tank, pail; **oke ippai no mizu** pailful of water.

**oki** open sea.

**okiagaru** to get up; to sit up; **toko no ue ni okiagaru** to sit up in bed.

**okidokei** table clock.

**okikaeru** to rearrange; to displace.

**okimono** small, decorative ornament.

**okinaoru** to sit up, sit erect.

**okinaosu** to replace; to rearrange.

**-OKI NI** at intervals of; **gofun oki ni** at five-minute intervals; **ichinichi oki ni** every other day.

**OKIRU** to get up; to rise; to raise oneself; **asa hayaku okiru** to get up early in the morning; **kan ga okiru** to have hysterics.

**okite** law, regulation, decree.

**okizari** desertion; **okizari ni suru** to desert; to leave behind.

**okkuu na** troublesome.

**okonai** act, deed; conduct; **okonai no yoi** well-behaved.

**okonau** to act, perform; to carry out; to conduct. **Kekkonshiki wa mikka ni okonaimasu.** We will hold the wedding on the third.

**okoraseru** to offend; to anger; to irritate (someone).

**okori** origin, source, cause, root.

**okorippoi** touchy, peevish, short-tempered.

**OKORU** to happen, occur, come about; to take place; to arise in; to originate. **Sensoo ga okoru ka mo shirenai.** A war may break out.

**okoru** to get angry; to lose one's temper; **okotte iru** to be angry. **Tanaka-san wa sono hanashi o kiite taihen okorimashita.** Ms. Tanaka got very angry at hearing that story. **Yamada-san ga konai node okotte imasu.** She is mad because Mr. Yamada hasn't come. **Sonna ni okotte wa ikemasen.** Don't be angry so much.

**OKOSU** to start, begin; to bring about; to establish; to promote; to improve, to awaken; to raise up, lift; to cause; to give rise to; **byooki o okosu** to fall ill; **shindai o okosu** to make a fortune. **Nanji ni anata o okoshimashoo ka?** When shall I wake you?

**okotari** negligence; **okotarigachi no** negligent, neglectful; **okotari naku** diligently, carefully.

**okotaru** to neglect; to fail to do.

**OKU** to put, place, lay, set; to keep; to establish, set up; to open; **fude o oku** to lay down a pen; **otetsudai o hitori oku** to hire domestic help; **nokoshite oku** to leave; **sono mama ni shite oku** to leave alone. **Kasa wa koko ni oite kudasai.** Please leave your umbrella here.

**OKU** back part; inner part; back; inner room; **oku e toosu** to show a person to the guest room; **yamaoku** the heart of (that part deep inside) a mountain.

**OKU** one hundred million.

**okubyoo** cowardice, timidity; **okubyoomono** coward.

**okufukai** deep, profound; of great depth.

**okugai** outdoors, in the open air.

**okujoo** rooftop.

**okunai** interior of a house, indoors.

**okurasu** to delay; to put off.

**okure** lag; **okure o toru** to be beaten; to be outstripped; **ki okure ga suru** to feel shy; to lose heart.

**OKURERU** to be late for; to be behind time; to get (fall) behind; to be left behind; **densha ni okureru** to miss a train.

**okuridasu** to send out; to forward; to see (someone) off; to show a person to the door.

**okurikomu** to see a person home; to escort (someone).

**OKURIMONO** present, gift; **okurimono o suru** to give (send) a gift.

**OKURU** to send; to see off; to send off; to escort; to spend, pass (time); **nimotsu o okuru** to send a package; **tanoshii seikatsu o okuru** to live a happy life. **Eki made ookuri shimashoo.** I will escort you to the station.

**OKURU** to present, to bestow; **gakui o okuru** to confer an academic degree. **Kare no sotsugyooiwai ni tokei o okurimashoo.** Let's give him a watch for a graduation gift.

**OKUSAMA, OKUSAN** madam, Mrs.

**okusoko** depth, bottom; **kokoro no okusoko de wa** in the back of one's mind; in the depths of one's heart.

**okusoku** guess, supposition; **okusoku suru** to guess, suppose.

**okusuru** to fear; to shrink; to hesitate; to be shy.

**okuyukashii** graceful; refined.

**okuyuki** depth; length.

**okuzashiki** inner room; back parlor.

**Omachidoo sama.** I'm sorry to have kept you waiting.

**omae** you *(impolite)*.

**omedeta** happy event.

**Omedetoo.** Congratulations!

**omei** slur; bad name; **omei o kiru** to get a bad name; to be dishonored; to have a bad name.

**omiyage, miyage** souvenir; parting present; gift.

**OMOCHA** toy; **omocha ni suru** to trifle with, toy with.

**OMOI** heavy; wealthy; serious, severe; important; **omoi byooki** serious illness; **ki ga omoi** to have a heavy heart.

**OMOI** thought, idea, mind; sense; heart; feeling; love; care, worry; will, wish; **omoi o kakeru** to take a fancy to; **omoi o kogasu** to burn with love; **omoi o korasu** to tax one's brain.

**omoiataru** to occur to; to call to mind.

**omoiawaseru** to consider (together); put two and two together. **Karekore omoiawasete yamemashita.** Taking everything into consideration, I gave up the idea.

**omoichigai** misunderstanding; **omoichigai o suru** to misunderstand.

**OMOIDASU** to recall, bring to mind, remember. **Dooshitemo omoidasenai.** Try as I may, I can't recall it.

**omoide** recollections, memories.

**omoigakenai** unexpected, unforeseen; least expected; chance, accidental; **omoigakenaku** unexpectedly.

**omoikiri** resolution.

**omoikiru** to resign oneself to; to give up; **omoikitte** boldly, resolutely.

**omoikitta** radical, bold, daring.

**omoikomu** to be under the impression that, to be possessed with (an idea).

**omoinokosu** to leave with regret.

**omoiomoi** each in one's own way; as one pleases.

**omoishiraseru** to teach someone (make someone learn) a lesson.

**omoitsuki** plan, suggestion. **Yoi omoitsuki desu.** That's a great idea.

**omoitsuku** to recall; to think of, to hit on. **Umai shukoo o omoitsuita.** I got a brilliant idea.

**omoitsumeru** to brood over; to love passionately.

**omoiyari** sympathy, consideration; **omoiyari no aru** sympathetic; considerate, kind.

**omoiyaru** to sympathize with.

**omokage** features, looks; image, likeness.

**omokurushii** heavy, ponderous; clumsy, oppressed.

**omomi** weight, emphasis, importance.

**omomuki** effect; taste, elegance, air, appearance; **omomuki no aru** refined. elegant; **omomuki no nai** tasteless, vulgar.

**omomuku** to go; to proceed to; to grow, to get.

**omomuro ni** slowly; gently; softly.

**OMO NA** chief, major, leading; **omo na hitobito** important persons; **omo na sangyoo** principal industries.

**omoni** heavy load.

**omonjiru** See **omonzuru.**

**omonzuru, omonjiru** to honor, respect, think much of.

**omoomoshii** serious; imposing; dignified; **omoomoshiku** solemnly, seriously.

**omori** weight, plumb, sinker.

**omosa** weight, heaviness.

**omoshi** weight (heavy object used to put pressure on something); **omoshi o oku** to place a weight on.

**omoshirogaru** to amuse oneself, to be amused; to think (something) funny.

**omoshirohanbun** half in fun.

**OMOSHIROI** interesting; pleasant, diverting; funny, odd; amusing; **omoshiroku** pleasantly; interestingly, delightfully, etc.; **omoshiroku nai** uninteresting, dull, stupid; unpleasant; unsatisfactory; undesirable.

**omoshiromi** interest; enjoyment; fun.

**omoshirosoo ni** with seeming (apparent) interest, enjoyment; like fun. **Kodomotachi wa omoshirosoo ni asonde imasu.** The children are playing, apparently enjoying themselves.

**OMOTE** face; obverse; right side; exterior; front; first half; **omote ni** outdoors; **omote no to** front door; **omote o dashite** right side up; **Omote Nihon** the Pacific side of Japan.

**omotemon** front gate.

**omotemuki** openly, publicly; officially; **omotemuki no** public, open.

**omotezashiki** front parlor.

**OMOU** to think; to consider; to believe; to wish, desire; to yearn for; to feel; to feel like; to regard (as); to expect; to hope; to imagine; **yoku omou** to think well of. **Kimi ga koko ni iru to wa omowanakkatta.** I had no idea you were here. **Maa omotte mo minasai.** Just think of it!

**omowareru** to seem, appear; to look; to be thought of (as). **Ame ga furisoo ni omowareru.** It looks like rain.

**omowaseburi** suggestive manner, coquetry; **omowaseburi na** suggestive, coquettish.

**omowaseru** to make (one) think; to remind (one) of; to be suggestive of.

**omowashii** satisfactory, desirable; **omowashiku nai** unsatisfactory.

**omowazu** unexpectedly; unconsciously, unintentionally.

**omoya** main house.

**on** kindness, goodness; favor; obligation; **on ni kanjiru** to feel indebted to; **on ni kiru** to be deeply grateful to; **on o kaesu** to repay a kindness.

**on** sound; tone; voice.

**onaidoshi** same age; **onaidoshi de aru** to be the same age.

**ONAJI** same, identical; equal, equivalent to, similar, like; **onaji yoo na** of the same kind; **onaji yoo ni** alike; **onaji ni** equally, etc.

**ONAKA** stomach, belly, abdomen. **Onaka ga suita.** I'm hungry. **Onaka ga itai.** I have a stomachache.

**ONDO** temperature.

**ongaeshi** repayment of a favor; **ongaeshi o suru** to repay a kindness (or favor).

**ONGAKU** music; **ongakuteki** musical; **ongaku no sensei** music teacher; **ongaku zuki** music lover.

**ongi** favor, obligation.

**oni** fiend, devil; ghost; **oni no yoo na** fiendish, inhuman.

**onjin** patron, benefactor.

**onjoo** warm heart, warm feeling; **onjoo aru** warmhearted.

**onjooshugi** paternalism.

**onjun na** gentle, meek.

**onkei** favor.

**onken** moderation; **onken na** moderate, temperate; sensible; **onken na setsu** a sensible opinion.

**onkoo na** gentle, courteous.

**onkyoo** sound, noise.

**onkyuu** pension; **onkyuu o ukeru** to receive a pension.

**ONNA** woman, female; female sex; mistress; **onna no** woman's; feminine; **onnarashii** womanly; ladylike; **ONNA NO KO** young girl; daughter; **onnashujin** landlady.

**ono** ax.

**onoono** each, everyone; all; respectively.

**onsen, onsenba** hot springs, spa; **onsenyado** hot springs inn.

**onshi** (highly respected) teacher (to whom a special indebtedness is felt).

**onshin** correspondence; **onshin suru** to correspond with.

**onshirazu** ingratitude; **onshirazu na** ungrateful.

**onshitsu** hothouse, greenhouse.

**onsu** ounce.

**onwa na** mild, gentle; genial.

**oo** oh! how!

**ooame** heavy rain, downpour.

**ooarashi, ooare** severe storm.

**oobo** subscription; application; **oobo suru** to subscribe to; to apply, make application; **oobosha** applicant; subscriber.

**ooboo** oppression, tyranny; **ooboo na** arbitrary; tyrannical; **ooboo o kiwameru** to tyrannize; to be high-handed.

**oobun** English or any Occidental written language or alphabet; **oobundenpoo** telegram written in the English (or any Occidental) alphabet.

**oobun no** appropriate, suitable; reasonable.

**ooburi** heavy downpour.

**oochaku** dishonesty; cunning; laziness; **oochaku na** dishonest; cunning; selfish; lazy.

**ooda** assault and battery; **ooda suru** to assault.

**oodan** crossing, intersection; **oodan suru** to cross, run across.

**oodeki** triumph, great success.

**ooen** aid, assistance; **ooen suru** to aid, support.

**OOFUKU** going and returning, round trip; **oofuku ryokoo** round trip; **oofuku suru** to go and return; **oofukuhagaki** return (post) card; **oofukukippu** round-trip ticket.

**oogesa** exaggeration; **oogesa na** exaggerated; **oogesa na hanashi** tall story, exaggeration; **oogesa na koto o iu** to exaggerate.

**oogi** folding fan; **oogi o tsukau** to fan oneself.

**oogoe** loud voice; **oogoe de** in a loud voice, loudly.

**oohei** arrogance; **oohei na** arrogant; **oohei ni** arrogantly.

**oohiroma** large, grand hall.

**OOI** lots of, heaps of, plenty, many, numerous, much. **Nihon ni wa yama ga ooi.** There are many mountains in Japan. **Nihonjin ni wa Eigo o hanasu hito ga ooi.** There are lots of Japanese who speak English. **Ano hito wa kodomo ga ooi.** He has many children.

**ooi** cover, covering; shade; screen; **ooi o suru** to cover, to wrap.

**ooi** yoo hoo!, hello!

**ooisogi** urgency; **ooisogi de** in great haste, hurriedly; **ooisogi de iku** to hurry to, rush to.

**oojikake** large scale; **oojikake de** on a large scale.

**oojiru** See **oozuru.**

**oojite** in proportion to; according to; in reply to; **hitsuyoo ni oojite** according to the need; according to the demand.

**oojoo** death; **oojoo suru** to die; to submit to, give in.

**OOKATA** probably, perhaps, maybe, almost, in general.

**OOKEI** O.K.

**OOKII, OOKINA** big, large, great; heavy; powerful; huge, massive; **hijoo ni ookii** huge, of great proportions; **ookina koto o iu** to talk big, brag, **ookiku naru** to grow larger, be enlarged; **ookiku suru** to enlarge, make larger.

**ookina** See **ookii.**

**ookisa** size, dimension, volume, bulk; **ookisa ga onaji** to be the same size; **ookisa ga chigau** to differ in size; **-kurai no ookisa de aru** to be about the size of.

**ookoo** being rampant; **ookoo suru** to overrun; to be rampant; to swagger; to go sideways.

**ooku** in many cases, in numerous cases; **ooku wa** mostly; for the most part; largely; **ooku no** a great many; plenty of; lots of; **ooku tomo** at most; generally.

**Ookura Daijin** Finance Minister; **Ookurashoo** Finance Ministry.

**ookyuu** emergency; first aid; **ookyuu teate** first-aid treatment.

**oomata** big strides; **oomata ni aruku** to stride; to walk with long steps.

**oome** overlooking; **oome ni miru** to overlook; to close one's eyes to; to let (something) pass.

**oomisoka** New Year's Eve.

**oomizu** heavy flood.

**oomukashi** remote antiquity; primitive ages; **oomukashi kara** from time immemorial.

**oonoo** anguish, agony; worry; **oonoo suru** to suffer anguish; to be in agony.

**oo-oo** often, frequently; sometimes.

**ooppira ni** openly, publicly.

**oorai** (street) traffic, comings and goings; **oorai suru** to come and go; to rise and fall. **Oorai ga ooi.** Traffic is heavy.

**ooryoo** usurpation, embezzlement; **ooryoo suru** to appropriate unlawfully; **ooryoosha** embezzler; **ooryoozai** embezzlement.

**oosen** response; acceptance; **oosen suru** to accept the challenge.

**oosetsu** reception; **oosetsu suru** to receive visitors; **oosetsuma** reception room, drawing room.

**ooshin** doctor's visit to a patient; house call.

**ooshuu** seizure, confiscation; **ooshuu suru** to seize.

**ooshuu** answer, reply; **ooshuu suru** to answer.

**oosooji** general cleaning; **oosooji o suru** to give a general cleaning.

**ootai** reception; **ootai suru** to receive, to wait on (a customer).

**ooto** vomiting; **ooto suru** to vomit.

**ootobai** motorcycle.

**ootome** automation.

**ootoo** answer, reply.

**oou** to reply; to veil; to wrap; to envelop, to hide, conceal; to shelter.

**oouridashi** large bargain sale.

**ooutsushi** close-up (in a movie).

**ooyake** (n.) public; government, **ooyake no** (adj.) public, open; official; **ooyake ni suru** to publish; to make known. **ooyake ni naru** to be made known.

**ooyasuuri** bargain sale.

**ooyoo** generosity; **ooyoo na** bighearted, generous.

**ooyoo** practical application; **ooyoo dekiru** applicable; **ooyoo suru** to put into use, to apply; to put to practical use.

**oozappa na** rough, loose, **oozappa na hanashi** rough, outline of a story.

**OOZEI** crowd, large number of people; **oozei de** in large numbers; **oozei no** many, large crowd of; **oozei no kazoku** large family.

**oozora** sky; heavens.

**oozuru, oojiru** to respond, reply, to comply with; to apply for.

**opera** opera.

**Oranda** Holland; **Orandago** Dutch (language); **Orandajin** Dutch (person).

**OREI, REI** etiquette, thanks, appreciation; remuneration.

**oreru** to break, snap, give way, yield; to be folded; **orete deru** to meet halfway. **Tsue ga oreta** The stick was broken.

**ori** cage, pen.

**origami** paper folding (popular Japanese pastime).

**origamitsuki no** certified, guaranteed.

**oriibu** olive.

**orikasanaru** to overlap; to lie one on another; **orikasanatte** overlapped; (stacked) in piles.

**orimono** cloth, textile.

**ORIRU** to go down; to come down; to get down; get off; to leave; to get out of; to alight, land; **densha o oriru** to get off a streetcar; **kaidan o oriru** to descend the staircase.

**oroka** not to mention; to say nothing of.

**oroshi** wholesale business; **oroshi de uru** to sell wholesale, at wholesale price; **oroshine** wholesale price(s).

**orosoka** careless, negligent; **orosoka ni suru** to neglect.

**OROSU** to take down; to lower; to bring down, to drop, let fall; to hand down; to unload; to let (someone) get off; to sell at wholesale. **Koko de oroshite kudasai.** Please let me get off here.

**ORU** to break; to bend, fold; to pick; **hana o oru** to pick a flower.

**oru** to weave.

**orugan** organ.

**osaeru** to stop; to curb, check, hold down, suppress.

**osamaru** to be at peace; to be calmed down, be pacified. **Kaze ga osamarismashita.** The wind has died down.

**osameru** to govern, rule; **ie o osameru** to manage a household.

**osanai** infant; young; childish; **osanai koro ni** in childhood.

**osen** pollution; **taiki osen** air pollution.

**oshaberi** chattering; gossip; gossiper; **oshaberi na** gossipy, talkative; **oshaberi suru** to chatter; to gossip.

**oshi** deaf-mute.

**oshi** weight; influence; **oshi no tsuyoi** overbearing, brazen; **oshi ga kiku** to have influence.

**oshiageru** to push; to thrust up.

**oshiau** to push, jostle.

**oshidashi** presence, appearance, look; **oshidashi no yoi** of fine appearance.

**oshidasu** to push out; to press forward; to force out.

**oshie** teaching, instruction; lesson; **oshiego** pupil.

**OSHIERU** to teach, give lessons; to show; to tell; **Nihongo o oshieru** to teach Japanese.

**oshihiromeru** to extend, expand, spread.

**OSHII** regrettable; precious, valuable; wasteful. **Sore wa oshii koto desu.** That's a pity! **Suteru no wa oshii desu.** It's too good to throw away.

**OSHIIRE** closet.

**oshikakeru** to force oneself into; to go uninvited.

**oshikomeru, oshikomu** to force in; to stuff into.

**oshimazu** liberally, freely.

**oshime** diaper.

**oshimu** to value, prize; to spare; to grudge; to be stingy of; to regret; **kane o oshimu** to be stingy with money; **wakare o oshimu** to be reluctant to leave.

**oshinabete** generally, in general.

**oshinokeru** to push away, to push aside.

**oshiroi** face powder.

**oshitaosu** to fell; to push down.

**oshitateru** to raise; set up, erect.

**oshitoosu** to push through; to persist to the end.

**oshitsubusu** to crush, smash, squash.

**oshitsukeru** to press, push against; to compel.

**oshitsumaru** to be jammed; to get near the end of the year. **Kotoshi mo oshitsumatte mairimashita.** It's getting near the end of the year.

**oshiuri** forcing a sale; **oshiuri suru** to force a person to buy.

**oshiwakeru** to push apart; to push through.

**oshiyaru** to push aside.

**oshiyoseru** to push to one side; to advance on.

**OSOI** late, tardy; behind time; slow; **ashi ga osoi** to walk slowly; **kaeri ga osoi** to be late in returning.

**OSORAKU** perhaps, maybe; in all probability; I'm afraid. **Osoraku moo Amerika e kaetta no deshoo.** I suppose he has already returned to the United States.

**osore** fear, terror; horror; awe, reverence; **osore o idaku** to be afraid of.

**osoreiru** to be overwhelmed, be awed. **Osoreirimasu.** I'm much obliged to you. **Osoreirimasu ga, kore o doko ni okimashoo ka?** Excuse me—where shall I put this?

**osoreooi** gracious, awe-inspiring; **osoreooku mo** graciously.

**OSOROSHII** fearful, awful, terrible, tremendous; **osoroshiku** terribly, etc; **osoroshiku atsui** terribly hot; **osoroshisa** fear, terror, horror.

**osou** to attack, assault.

**osowaru** to be taught.

**ossharu** to say, to speak, to tell, to relay, to mention *(respect)*.

**OSU** to push, shove, press; to infer, deduce, guess; to recommend. **Yamada-san o oshimashita.** I recommended Mr. Yamada.

**osu** (n.) male (animal); **osu no** male *(adj.)*; **osu neko** tomcat.

**osui** sewage; filthy water.

**otafukukaze** mumps.

**otaku** your house.

**OTEARAI** See TEARAI.

**oten** stain; blot; blemish; **oten o tsukeru** to stain; to spot; **oten no nai** spotless.

**OTO** sound, noise; roar; tone, note; fame; **oto ni kikoeta** celebrated, noted; **oto o tatete** noisily; **oto o tateru** to make a sound; to make noise.

**OTOKO** man, male; male adult; manly person; **otokorashii** manly; **otokorashiku** like a man; **otoko ni naru** to come of age; to become a man; **OTOKO NO KO** boy; **otokoyamome** widower.

**OTONA** adult (male or female).

**OTONASHII** gentle, good, quiet; **otonashiku suru** to keep quiet.

**OTOOSAN** father (used as term of address by the wife as well as children in the family); father (somebody else's).

**OTOOTO** younger brother.

**otoroeru** to decline; to fall.

**otoru** to be inferior; to fall behind.

**otoshiireru** to trap, capture.

**OTOSU** to drop, let fall; to lose; to dump; to remove; to take; to omit; to depreciate; **chikara o otosu** to lose strength, weaken. **Koppu o otoshite watta.** I dropped a cup and broke it.

**OTOTOI** day before yesterday.

**OTOTOSHI** year before last.

**otozureru** to call on, visit.

**OTSURI = tsurisen** small change (money).

**otte** later on; afterward.

**OTTO** husband.

**OU** to drive away, shoo; to pursue, to run after; **hi o otte** day by day; **jun o otte** gradually, in order; **hae o ou** to shoo flies.

**ou** to bear; to carry on one's back; to owe; to be due. **Watakushi wa ano hito ni ou tokoro ga ooi desu.** I owe him a lot. **Kodomo o senaka ni otte ikimashita.** She went there, carrying her child on her back.

**OWARI** end, termination, conclusion; **owari made** to the last; **owari ni** in the end; **owari no** final, last; **owari o tsugeru** to come to an end.

**OWARU** to end, come to an end, finish, complete. **Shigoto ga owatta.** The job is done.

**owaseru** to make carry; to lay a burden on.

**OYA** parent(s); dealer (of cards); **oya no** parental; **oya o uyamau** to respect one's parents.

**OYA** oh!; oh dear!; my!

**oyabun** boss; master.

**OYAJI** *(vulgar)* old man; chap; father.

**oyakata** boss, chief.

**oyako** parent and child.

**oyama** female impersonator (actor).

**oyashiro** Shinto shrine.

**OYAYUBI** thumb; big toe.

**oyayuzuri** inheritance; **oyayuzuri no** inherited (from one's parents).

**oyobosu** to influence, affect; exert; **kooeikyoo o oyobosu** to have a good influence on, to produce a good effect.

**oyobu** to reach; to amount to; to come up to; to extend; to cover; to match, equal; **oyobanai** to be no match (for); to be inferior (to); **oyobi mo tsukanai** not to begin to compare (to). **Sore ni wa oyobimasen.** Don't bother about that. **Watakushi wa kare ni oyobanai.** I'm no match for him.

**oyogi** *(n.)* swimming; swim; **oyogi ni iku** to go swimming.

**OYOGU** to swim; **yoku oyogu** to swim well. **Hitotsu oyogoo.** Let's go for a swim.

**OYOSO** about; roughly; as a rule; generally speaking; **oyoso gojuu en** approximately 50 yen. **Oyoso kare hodo atama no yoi mono wa nai.** It's not too much to say that there is no one as sharp as he.

**OYU, YU** hot water; warm water; bath; **oyu ni hairu** to take a bath.

## P

**paatonaa** partner.

**PAN** bread; **panko** bread crumbs; **pan o eru** to earn one's living (bread); **pan o yaku** to bake bread; **pan'ya** bakery.

**panama boo** panama hat.

**panku** puncture; **panku suru** to puncture.

**panorama** panorama.

**parapara** with a clatter; scattering as it falls; pitapat.

**pasokon** personal computer.

**pasu** pass, free ticket.

**patapata** with a pattering sound; **patapata suru** to patter; to flutter.

**patchi** Japanese-style close-fitting trousers (worn by workmen).

**pachiri** with a click.

**pattari** suddenly; all of a sudden.

**patto** suddenly; **patto suru** to be gay; to be showy; **patto moeru** to flare up.

**pechanko** flattened; crushed; **pechanako ni naru** to be flattened or crushed.

**peeji** page.

**pekopeko** cringing; **pekopeko suru** to cringe; to fawn upon.

**pekopeko** hungry. **Onaka ga pekopeko desu.** I'm awfully hungry.

**PEN** fountain pen; pen; **penga** pen-and-ink drawing; **penjiku** penholder; **pensaki** pen point; **pen shuuji** penmanship.

**pengin** penguin.

**penki** paint; **penki o nuru** to paint; **penkiya** painter.

**perapera** fluently, glibly; **perapera hanasu** to speak fluently; **perapera shaberu** to chatter, jabber.

**perori to** with a quick motion of the tongue; **perori to nameru** to lick; **shita o perori to dasu** to stick out the tongue; **perori to taberu** to eat rapidly; to make short work of a meal.

**pesuto** pest; black plague.

**PIANO** piano; **piano o hiku** to play the piano.

**piipii** whistling; piping; **piipii naku** to cheep, chirp (said of birds); **piipii shite iru** to be hard up (for money).

**pikaichi** number one. *(colloq.)* ace, star.

**pikapika** glitteringly; **pikapika suru** to glitter, sparkle, flash, twinkle.

**PIN** pin; hairpin; **anzenpin** safety pin.

**pinpin** in a lively manner; **pinpin shite iru** to be full of life, to be in the pink, to be well and sound.

**pinsetto** tweezers.

**pinto** focus; **pinto o awaseru** to focus, adjust the focus (of a camera).

**pirapira** flapping.

**piripiri** smarting; **piripiri suru** to smart, sting, burn.

**pishari** with a bang; **pishari to to o shimeru** to slam the door shut.

**pisutoru** pistol, revolver.

**pitari, pittari** suddenly, closely, flatly; **pittari goji ni** at (five o'clock) sharp; **pittari to au** to fit to a T; **pitari to tomaru** to come to a dead stop, to stop suddenly.

**pitchaa** pitcher (in a ball game).

**pitchi** pitch (vocal or in a game).

**pointo** point; decimal point; (railroad) switch.

**pokan to** vacantly; absentmindedly; **pokan to shite iru** to look blank.

**pokapoka** growing warmer; **pokapoka shite kuru** to grow warmer; **pokapoka suru** to feel warm.

**POKETTO** pocket; **poketto manee** pocket money.

**pondo** pound.

**ponpu** pump; **ponpu de mizu o kumiageru** to pump up water (from a well).

**pooru** pole.

**poroporo** in drops, tricklingly.

**POSUTO** postbox, mailbox; **posuto ni ireru** to mail.

**potapota** drop by drop; **potapota to tareru** to fall in drops; to trickle; to drip.

**potsupotsu** little by little; in drops; bit by bit. **Potsupotsu furu.** It rains in small drops.

**potto** in a glow; **potto kao o akarameru** to blush.

**punpun** piquantly; **punpun niou** to smell piquant; to smell fragrant; to stink, reek; **punpun okoru** to be in a huff; to fume.

**puremiamu** premium; **puremiamu o tsukeru** to place a premium (on); **puremiamu ga tsuite iru** to be at a premium.

**puro** pro, professional athlete.

**puropaganda** propaganda; **puropaganda o suru** to publicize; to spread propaganda.

**puropera** propeller.

**puroretaria** proletariat; proletarians.

**pyuu to** whizzing, whistling; **pyuu to fuku** to whistle; **pyuu to tobu** to whiz through the air.

# R

**-RA** suffix denoting: and others; and the like, etc. **Kimira ni wa ienai desu.** I can't tell it to you people.

**rachi** picket-fence; limit; **rachi mo nai** foolish, silly; **rachi ga aku** to reach a settlement; **rachi ga akanai** to make little headway, remain unsettled; **rachigai ni deru** to go beyond bounds.

**ragubii** rugby.

**-rai** suffix denoting: since, the past; **sakunenrai** since last year.

**raichoo suru** to arrive in Japan.

**RAIGETSU** next month; **saraigetsu** the month after next.

**raiharu** = **raishun** next spring.

**raihin** guest; **raihinseki** visitor's seats.

**raihoo** visit, call; **raihoo suru** to visit.

**raikai** attendance; **raikai suru** to attend a meeting; **raikaisha** audience; attendance.

**raikyaku** visitor, guest.

**raimei** thunderclap.

**RAINEN** next year; **sarainen** the year after next.

**raion** lion.

**rairaku** frankness; **rairaku na** frank; openhearted; broad-minded.

**raireki** career, history, origin (personal); **raireki o tadasu** to inquire into one's past.

**raishun** = **raiharu** next spring.

**RAISHUU** next week; **saraishuu** the week after next.

**raisukaree** curried rice.

**raiu** thunderstorm. **Raiu ga aru daroo.** There will be a thunderstorm.

**raiyuu** visit (from abroad); **raiyuusha** visitor; **raiyuu gaijin** foreign visitor.

**RAJIO** radio; **rajio hoosoo** radio broadcasting; **rajio o kiku** to listen to the radio; **rajio o tomeru** to turn off the radio; **keitai rajio** portable radio.

**raketto** racket (tennis, etc.).

**rakka** falling; **rakka suru** to fall; to drop.

**rakkan** optimism; **rakkanteki** optimistic; **rakkan suru** to be optimistic.

**rakkasan** parachute.

**rakkasei** peanut.

**RAKU** comfort, ease; pleasure; **raku na** comfortable, easy; **raku o suru** to take it easy. **Oraku ni nasatte kudasai.** Make yourself comfortable.

**rakuchaku** settlement; **rakuchaku saseru** to settle, bring to a conclusion; **rakuchaku suru** to be settled.

**rakudai** rejection; failure in an exam; **rakudai suru** to fail (flunk) an exam; to be rejected.

**rakuen** paradise.

**rakugaki** scribbling.

**rakugo** comic story.

**rakugosha** straggler.

**rakuseishiki** inauguration ceremony; completion ceremony.

**rakusen** defeat in an election; failure; rejection; **rakusensha** defeated candidate.

**rakutan** discouragement; despair; **rakutan saseru** to discourage; **rakutan suru** to be discouraged; to be disappointed.

**rakutenka** optimist; **rakutenshugi** optimism.

**ranboo** violence, outrage; **ranboo na** violent; rude; rowdy; disorderly; **ranboo suru** to behave rudely; **ranboomono** ruffian, rowdy.

**RANCHI** lunch; **ranchi o taberu** to have lunch.

**randoku** desultory reading.

**rankan** railing, handrail.

**ranpu** lamp.

**ran'yoo** abuse; misuse; **ran'yoo suru** to abuse.

**ranzatsu** disorder, confusion; **ranzatsu na** disorderly, untidy; **ranzatsu ni naru** to get confused; to be in disorder.

**ranzoo** overproduction; **ranzoo suru** to overproduce.

**rappa** trumpet, cornet, horn; **rappa o fuku** to blow a horn; **rappa nomi o yaru** to drink (something) directly from the bottle.

**rasen** screw; spiral spring; **rasenkei** spiral form; **rasenkei no** spiral-shaped.

**rasha** woolen cloth.

**-RASHII** -like; becoming; looking (like); appear, seem; it seems to me; probably; **kodomorashii** childlike. **Soo rashii.** I guess so. **Ame rashii.** It looks like rain. **Kuru rashii desu.** It seems he is coming.

**rashinban** compass.

**rasshu awaa** rush hour.

**reesu** lace; race.

**REI** custom, usage, habit, precedent; instance, case, example; **rei ni yotte** as usual; **rei no** usual, customary; **rei o ageru to** for instance; **rei o ageru** to give an instance; **rei ni naru** to set a precedent.

**REI** zero.

**REI, OREI** thanks, appreciation; **rei o noberu** to express thankfulness.

**rei** soul, spirit.

**rei** salutation; **rei o suru** to bow.

**reidai** example; exercise.

**reido** zero; freezing point (Centigrade); **reido ika** below zero.

**reifuku** evening dress.

**reigai** exception; **reigai no** exceptional; **reigai ni suru** to except, make an exception of.

**reigi** courtesy, etiquette; **reigi tadashii** courteous. **Kare wa reigi ga tadashii.** He has good manners.

**reihai** worship; **reihai suru** to worship; **reihaidoo** chapel; church.

**reijoo** letter of thanks; **reijoo o dasu** to send a letter of thanks.

**reikai** regular meeting.

**reikoku** cruelty; **reikoku na** cruel; coldhearted.

**reikoo** strict enforcement; **reikoo suru** to enforce strictly.

**reikyaku** refrigeration; cooling; **reikyaku suru** to cool; to refrigerate.

**reimeiki** dawn of a new age.

**reinen** ordinary year, average year; annually, every year; **reinen matsuri** annual festival; **reinen no toori** as usual; as every year.

**reiraku** ruin, downfall; **reiraku suru** to be ruined, go to ruin.

**reisei** coolness, calmness; **reisei na** cool, calm; **reisei na hito** coldhearted person; **reisei ni kangaeru** to think about something calmly.

**reishoo** cold smile, sneer; **reishoo suru** to sneer at; to mock; to give a mocking laugh.

**reisoo** formal wear; ceremonial dress.

**reisui** cold water; **reisuimasatsu** rubdown with a cold wet towel; **reisuiyoku** cold bath; **reisuiyoku suru** to take a cold bath.

**reitan** indifference, coolness; **reitan na** cool; cold; indifferent; **seiji ni reitan de aru** to be indifferent to politics.

**reiten** zero, zero point; **reiten o toru** to get a zero.

**reitooniku** frozen meat.

**reizen** offering to the spirits of the dead.

**reizoo** cold storage; refrigeration; **reizoo suru** to refrigerate; **reizooko** refrigerator; **reizoosha** refrigerated freight car.

**rekidai** successive generations.

**rekishi** history; **Nippon no rekishi** Japanese history; **rekishijoo yuumei na tokoro** place of historical interest; **rekishijoo no jinbutsu** historical personage; **rekishika** historian.

**rekizen to** clearly, plainly; **rekizen to shite akiraka desu.** It's as plain as day.

**rekkoku** nations (of the world).

**rekkyo** enumeration; **rekkyo suru** to enumerate, list.

**rekkyoo** great (world) powers (countries).

**rekoodo** phonograph record; **rekoodo o kakeru** to play a record (on a phonograph).

**REN'AI** love; **ren'ai jiken** love affair; **ren'ai kankei ni naru** to fall in love; to have a love affair.

**renchuu** party, company.

**renga** brick(s).

**rengoo** combination, union, confederation, amalgamation; alliance, coalition; **rengoo suru** to combine, etc.; **rengoo no** allied, associated, etc.; **rengookoku** allied countries; **Kokusai Rengoo** United Nations.

**renketsu suru** to couple, join, connect.

**renmei** joint signature; **renmei suru** to sign jointly.

**renpoo** federation (of states); union; commonwealth; **renpoo no** united, federated, etc.

**renraku** connection; traffic; communication; **renraku suru** to make contact; **renraku o toru** to get in touch with; **renraku o ushinau** to lose touch, lose contact; **renrakusen** ferryboat (connected with a train).

**renshuu** practice, training, drill, rehearsal; **renshuu o tsunda** well-trained; **renshuu suru** to practice, etc.

**rensoo** association (of ideas); **rensoo suru** to be reminded of; to associate (one) with (another).

**rentaisekinin** joint responsibility.

**Rentogen** X-ray; **Rentogen ni kakaru** to be X-rayed.

**renzoku** continuity; succession; **renzoku suru** to continue; to last; **renzoku teki** continuous; consecutive; **renzokuteki ni** continuously.

**renzu** lens.

**reppuu** heavy wind, hurricane. **Reppuu ga fuite iru.** There's a heavy wind blowing.

**resseki** attendance; **-ni resseki suru** to attend, be present at.

**resserareru** to be ranked with.

**ressha** railway train.

**ressuru** to attend, to present; to rank with, take one's place among.

**retsu** row, rank, tier, column, line; **retsu o tsukuru** to form a row, line up.

**rettoo** archipelago, chain of islands; **Chishima rettoo** the Kuriles.

**rettoo** inferiority; **rettoo na otoko** man of bad moral character; **rettoo no** inferior, of poor quality; **rettoohin** low-quality goods.

**rezubian** lesbian

**ri** advantage; benefit; interest; **rokubu no ri** 6 percent interest; **ri no aru** advantageous, beneficial; **ri ga aru** to be profitable; **ri o eru** to profit from, gain by.

**ri** reason, right, truth, principle; **ri no aru** reasonable, justifiable; **ri ni somuku** to be against reason.

**ribon** ribbon; **ribon de musubu** to tie with a ribbon.

**richi** intellect; **richiteki na** intellectual.

**richigimono** upright person.

**rieki** benefit, gain, profit; **rieki no aru** profitable, lucrative; **rieki o hogo suru** to protect one's interests; **riekikin** profits, proceeds.

**rien, RIKON** divorce; **rien suru** to divorce.

**rifujin** unreasonableness; **rifujin na** unreasonable, unjust.

**rigai** advantages and disadvantages; interests; **rigai ni kankei ga aru** to have an effect on one's interests; to have an interest in.

**rigaku hakushi** Doctor of Science.

**rigakushi** Bachelor of Science.

**rihatsu** haircutting; hairdressing; **RIHATSUTEN** barber shop; **rihatsushi** barber.

**riido** (n.) leading; **riido suru** to lead.

**riji** director; manager; **rijichoo** chairman of a board of directors; **rijikai** board of directors.

**rika** science.

**rikai** understanding, comprehension; **rikai dekiru** understandable. comprehensible; **rikai no nai** without understanding; **rikai no aru hito** sensible person; **rikai suru** to understand; to grasp; to appreciate; **rikairyoku** understanding, comprehension.

**rikimu** to strain oneself; to brag; to swagger.

**rikisaku** masterpiece; elaborate work.

**rikisetsu suru** to emphasize, to lay stress on; to be emphatic.

**rikkooho** candidacy (for an election); **rikkooho suru** to run as a candidate; **rikkooho o happyoo suru** to announce one's candidacy; **rikkoohosha** candidate.

**RIKON, rien** divorce; **rikon suru** to divorce.

**rikoo** cleverness, smartness; **rikoo na** clever, shrewd, bright, intelligent; **rikoo soo na** bright, intelligent looking.

**rikoo suru** to carry out, to fulfill.

**rikoshugi** egoism.

**rikoteki** egoistic, selfish.

**riku, rikuchi** land; **riku o iku** to go by land; **rikuro** land journey, land road (route). (See also **rikujoo**.)

**rikugun** army.

**rikujoo** land, ground; **rikujoo de** on land. (See also **riku**.)

**rikutsu** theory; argument; pretext; reason, logic; **rikutsu ni au** to stand to reason; **rikutsu ga tatanai** to be unreasonable, be illogical; **rikutsuppoi** argumentative; **rikutsuzeme** persuasive reasoning; **nan toka kan toka rikutsu o tsukete** on one pretext or another; **rikutsuzeme ni suru** to persuade (someone) by reason.

**rikuzoku** in succession, one after another.

**rimen** back, reverse, other side; **rimen de** behind the scenes, in secret; **rimen de ayatsuru** to pull strings; **rimen o kansatsu suru** to look at the other side.

**rimokon** remote control.

**RINGO** apple; **ringo no ki** apple tree.

**ringoku** neighboring country.

**rinjin** neighbor; **rinjin no yoshimi** neighborliness.

**rinjuu** one's last (deathbed) moment; **rinjuu no kotoba** dying words.

**rinka** neighboring house, house next door.

**rinkaku** contours, outline; **rinkaku o noberu** to give an outline, sketch.

**rinri** ethics, morality.

**rinyuu suru** to wean.

**RIPPA** fineness, richness; **rippa na** fine, splendid, good, nice, excellent, stately; **rippa ni** superbly, admirably, sufficiently; **rippa ni seikatsu suru** to make a decent living. **Rippa desu.** It's splendid.

**rippoo** legislation; **rippoo no** legislative.

**rippuku** anger, rage; **rippuku suru** to get angry; **rippuku saseru** to make angry.

**rirei** relay race.

**rireki** personal history, career; **rireki ga yoi** to have a good record of service; **rireki ga warui** to have a poor record of service; **rirekisho** personal history, record of one's life.

**ririku** takeoff; **ririku suru** to take off; to get afloat.

**ririshii** imposing; majestic.

**riron** theory.

**riroseizen** logical, valid.

**risaichi** stricken locality.

**risaisha** victim, sufferer.

**risan** dispersion; **risan suru** to be dispersed.

**rishi** interest; **yasui rishi** low interest; **takai rishi** high interest; **rishi o toru** to charge interest; **rishi o shoo zuru** to accrue.

**risoo** ideal; **takai risoo** high ideal; **risoo shugi** idealism; **risooteki** ideal; idealistic.

**risookyoo** utopia.

**risshoo** proof; **risshoo suru** to prove, demonstrate, bear out.

**risshun** first day of spring.

**risurin** glycerine.

**ritei** mileage, distance; **riteihyoo** milestone.

**ritsu** rate, proportion; **ritsu o ageru** to raise the rate.

**ritsuan** plan, device; **ritsuan suru** to plan, design, devise.

**riyoo** utilization; **riyoo suru** to use; to make use of, utilize; to take advantage of; **kikai o riyoo suru** to take advantage of an opportunity.

**riyuu** reason, cause; **riyuu de** for reasons of; **riyuu naku** without cause, without provocation; **riyuu no aru** reasonable; **riyuu no nai** groundless; **riyuu o noberu** to state one's reason.

**rizai** finance, economy.

**ro** hearth, fireplace; **robata** fireside.

**ro** oar.

**roboo** roadside, wayside; **roboo no chaya** wayside teahouse; **roboo no hito** passerby; **roboo ni tatsu** to stand by the roadside.

**robotto** robot.

**rodai** balcony (outdoor).

**roji** alley, lane.

**roken** discovery, exposure; **roken suru** to be found out; to be detected.

**rokotsu** frankness; **rokotsu na** frank, candid; plain; naked; **rokotsu na atekosuri** broad hint; **rokotsu ni ieba** frankly speaking.

**ROKU, MUTTSU** six; **dai roku** the sixth; **ROKUJUU** sixty; **rokumai byoobu** sixfold screen.

**rokudenashi** (n.) good-for-nothing.

**ROKUGATSU** June.

**rokuon** recording, transcription; **rokuonki** recorder (sound recording machine);

**rokuon suru** to record; to make a recording.

**ron** argument; discussion; essay; opinion; **ron o matanu** to be beyond argument; **ronbun** essay, article; thesis; **rongai** out of the question; irrelevant; **ronri** logic; **ronriteki** logical; **ronriteki ni** logically; **ronri ni awanai** to be illogical; **ronsetsu** essay; editorial, dissertation; **ronsetsu kisha** editorial writer.

**ronjiru, ronzuru** to discuss; to argue.

**ronkoku** prosecution; **ronkoku suru** to prosecute.

**ronzuru** See **ronjiru.**

**roo** wax; **roo o hiku** to wax; **roobiki** waxing; **roobiki no** waxed; **roogami** wax paper.

**rooa** deaf and dumb.

**rooba** old woman.

**roobo** aged mother.

**roobai** confusion, panic; **roobai suru** to be confused; to be in a panic.

**rooden** short circuit.

**roodoku** recitation; **roodoku suru** to recite, read aloud.

**roodoo** manual labor, work; **jikangai roodoo** overtime work; **roodoo jikan** working hours; **roodoo kaikyuu** laboring class; **roodoo kumiai** labor union; **roodoo kumiai yakuin** labor leader; **roodoo mondai** labor problem; **roodosha** laborer; **roodoo soogi** labor dispute; **roodoo undoo** labor movement; **roodoo suru** to labor, work. (See also **rooryoku.**)

**roogo** old age.

**roohi** waste (of time, energy); extravagance; **roohi suru** to waste, squander; **jikan o roohi suru** to waste time.

**ROOJIN** aged person.

**rooka** corridor, passageway, hall.

**ROOMAJI** Roman letters; romanization (anglicization); **roomaji de tsuzuru** to spell in Roman letters.

**romansu** romance.

**ROOMA SUUJI** Roman numerals.

**roonen** old age.

**roonin** unemployed person; **roonin shite iru** to be out of work; to be studying for an entrance examination to a college.

**rooren** expert; **rooren na** experienced.

**rooryoku** labor, effort; **rooryoku busoku** labor shortage. (See also **roodoo.**)

**roosoku** candle, **roosokutate** candlestick.

**roosu** sirloin.

**rootai** old person's body.

**Rootarii Kurabu** Rotary Club.

**rooya, keimusho** prison, jail.

**ROSHIA. Roshia no** (adj.) Russian; **Roshiago** Russian language. **Roshiajin** Russian (person).

**roten** open air; **roten no** outdoor.

**rui** kind, sort, variety; description; similar case; parallel. **rui no nai** unique; unparalleled; **ano rui no hito** people of that sort.

**ruibetsu** classification; **ruibetsu suru** to classify.

**ruiji** resemblance, similarity, likeness; **ruiji no** similar, analogous; **ruijiten** point of resemblance. **-ni ruiji suru** to be like, be similar to.

**ruikei** total sum. **ruikei suru** to total.

**ruirei** similar case, analogy; **ruirei no nai** unique; exceptional.

**runpen** tramp, hobo.

**RUSU** absence; **rusuchuu ni** during (one's) absence; **rusu ni suru** to be out (not at home); **rusu o tsukau** to pretend not to be in. **Sanpo ni itte rusu desu.** She has gone out for a walk.

**rusuban** temporary caretaker (while a person is away from home).

**ryaku** abbreviation; abridgment; **ryaku sazu ni** in detail (without abbreviating); **ryaku shite** in short; **ryaku suru** to abridge; to abbreviate; **ryakugo** abbreviation; **ryakuji** simplified character; simpler substitute; abbreviation.

**ryakudatsu suru** to loot; to plunder.

**ryakushiki** informal way; **ryakushiki no** informal; **ryakushiki de, ryakushiki ni** informally.

**ryakuzu** rough sketch; **ryakuzu o toru** to make a rough sketch of.

**ryohi** traveling expenses.

**RYOKAKU** traveler; passenger; tourist; **ryokaku annaijo** travelers' aid.

**RYOKAN** Japanese-style hotel or inn.

**ryoken** passport; **ryoken o hakko suru** to issue a passport; **ryoken o shinsei suru** to apply for a passport.

**RYOKOO** travel; trip; tour; **ryokoo suru** to travel; **ryokoo ni dekakeru** to start on a journey; **RYOKOO ANNAI** guidebook; **ryokoo annaisho** travel agency.

**ryoo-** prefix denoting: both, two; **ryooashi** both legs; both feet; **RYOOGAWA** both sides; **RYOOHOO** both; both sides; **ryoogan** both banks of a river; **ryoomen** both sides; **ryoomen o kansatsu suru** to examine both sides; **ryooshin** both parents; **ryootan** both ends; **ryoote** both hands; **ryoote de motsu** to hold in both hands. **Ryoohoo tomo shitte iru.** I know both of them.

**ryoo** hunting; shooting; game; fishing; **ryoo ni iku** to go hunting; to go fishing.

**ryoo** quantity, volume.

**ryoodo** territory, possession.

**ryoogae** money-changing, exchange of money; **Beika o Nihon no okane ni ryoogae suru** to change American money into Japanese money.

**ryoohoo** remedy; method of treatment.

**ryooji** consul; **ryoojikan** consulate; **soo ryoojikan** consulate general.

**ryooji** medical treatment.

**ryookai** comprehension; **ryookai suru** to comprehend, grasp; to see. **Sore wa watakushi ni wa ryookai dekinai.** It's beyond my comprehension.

**ryooken** idea, thought, notion; intention; view; direction; **ryooken o kiku** to ask (someone) his intention; **ryooken o sueru** to make up one's mind. **Doo iu ryooken de sonna koto o shita no desu ka?** What made you do such a thing?

**RYOOKIN** charge, fee; fare; **ryookin o torazu ni** free of charge; **ryookin o toru** to charge.

**ryookoo na** successful; favorable.

**RYOORI** cooking, cuisine; dish; food; **ryoori suru** to cook; to prepare food; **Nippon ryoori o taberu** to have a Japanese meal.

**ryooritsu** compatibility; coexistence; **ryooritsu suru** to be compatible with; to be consistent with; **ryooritsu shigatai** to be incompatible with, to be inconsistent with.

**ryooriya** restaurant (Japanese-style).

**ryooshin** conscience; **ryooshinteki** conscientious. **Ryooshin ga togameru.** My conscience bothers me.

**ryooshuusho** receipt.

**ryooyoo** convalescence; **ryooyoo suru** to convalesce.

**ryuuchoo** fluency; **ryuuchoo na** fluent; **ryuuchoo ni** fluently, eloquently; **ryuuchoo ni Nihongo o hanasu** to speak Japanese fluently.

**ryuudoobutsu** liquid diet.

**ryuugakusei** student studying abroad.

**ryuugaku suru** to study abroad.

**ryuugi** style; method.

**ryuukan** influenza.

**RYUUKOO** fashion, fad; popularity; **ryuukoo no** fashionable, in fashion; **ryuukoo suru** to be in fashion; to come into fashion; **ryuukoo ni okureru** to be out of fashion, out of style.

**ryuumachi** rheumatism.

**-SA** suffix added to the stem of an adjective to make a noun (comparable to English -ty, -ness); **bakabakashisa** stupidity, stupidness; **shitashisa** familiarity.

**sa** difference; margin. **Sa ga aru.** There is a difference.

**SAA** come; now; well; let me see. **Saa taihen na koto o shita.** Oh, what have I done! **Saa ikimashoo.** Let's go now.

**saabisu** service (at a restaurant, store, etc.). **Saabisu ga yoi.** The service is good.

**saachiraito** searchlight.

**saakasu** circus.

**sabaketa** sensible; frank; **sabaketa hito** person of the world.

**sabaku** desert.

**sabaku** to judge; to decide; to settle. **Hito o sabaku na.** Don't judge others.

**sabaku** to sell, to deal with.

**sabasaba shita** refreshing; agreeable.

**saaberu** Occidental-style sword; saber.

**sabetsu** distinction; discrimination; differentiation; difference; **sabetsu no aru** discriminating; **sabetsu naku** without discrimination; **sabetsu o suru** to discriminate.

**sabi** rust; patina; antique look; maturity; **sabi ga tsuku** to become rusty.

**sabireru** to cease to flourish.

**SABISHII** lonely, lonesome; deserted, desolate.

**saboru** to go slow; to sabotage; to cut classes.

**sabotaaju** sabotage; going slow.

**sadamaru** to fix; to become settled; to be determined; to be subjugated; **sadamatta** regular, fixed, definite. **Hi ga sadamarimashita.** The date is fixed. **Sadamatta jikan ni kimasu.** He comes at a regular time.

**sadameru** to establish, to lay down; to decide, to settle; **Shuppatsu no hi o sadamemashita.** I decided on a date of departure.

**sadamete** surely; to be sure.

**SAE** even; only. **Ano hito sae shitte imasu.** Even he knows it. **Okane sae areba kaimasu.** I'll buy it if only I have the money for it.

**saegiru** to cut off; to stop; to interrupt; to hinder, to obstruct, block; **me o saegiru** to obstruct a view; **hito no hanashi o saegiru** to cut in; to interrupt (someone's) conversation.

**saeru** to be bright, be clear; to attain a rare skill; **me ga saeru** to be wakeful. **Tsuki ga saeru.** The moon shines clearly. **Nakanaka saeta ude desu.** She is quite expert in it.

**saezuru** to sing, warble (a bird).

**safuran** saffron.

**sagaku** balance; difference.

**SAGARU** to hang down; to fall; to go down (in price); to leave; to retire. **Nichiyoohin**

**no ne ga sagarimashita.** The prices of ordinary commodities have come down.

**sagashidasu** to find out, discover.

**SAGASU** to seek, search for.

**SAGERU** to hang down; to lower, let down; to clear away; to wear (a sword); **akari o sageru** to lower a lamp; **nedan o sageru** to lower a price; **ozen o sageru** to clear a table.

**sagi** fraud; imposture; deceit, cheating; **sagi o hataraku** to defraud; **sagishi** swindler.

**saguri** probe; **saguri o ireru** to probe.

**saguru** to search for; to grope for; to probe; **iken o saguru** to feel out (someone's) view; **poketto o saguru** to fumble in one's pocket.

**sagyoo** work, operation; **sagyoo chuu** while working; **sagyoo o hajimeru** to begin work; **sagyooshitsu** workroom.

**sahodo** so; so much; much *(often used in the negative sense);* **sahodo ni mo nai** not so much as you think.

**sahoo** good manners, etiquette; **sahoo o shiranai** ill-mannered.

**SAI** talent; ability; difference; **sai no aru** talented; **gogaku no sai ga aru** to have an aptitude for languages; **sai o tanomu** to put too much confidence in one's own talents.

**-sai** year (as a counter for age); **san sai** three years old; **juugo sai** fifteen years old.

**saiai no** dearest, beloved.

**saibai** cultivation (of plants); **saibai suru** to cultivate.

**SAIBAN** judgment; trial; **saiban suru** to judge; **saibanchoo** chief judge; **saibankan** judge, bench (legal); **saibansho** court of justice, law court; **Saikoo Saibansho** Supreme Court.

**saiboo** cell.

**saichi** wit and intellect.

**SAICHUU** in the midst of; in the course of; at the height of; **shokuji no saichuu ni** in the middle of the meal. **Ima ga atsui saichuu da.** The summer heat is now at its height.

**saidaa** soda pop, soda water.

**saidai** greatest; maximum; **saidai no koofuku** to greatest happiness; **saidai sokuryoku** the maximum speed.

**saidan** altar.

**saien** talented woman.

**SAIFU** purse; wallet.

**saigai** calamity; **saigai o koomuru** to suffer a disaster.

**saigen** reappearance; **saigen suru** to reappear.

**saigen** limitation; **saigen ga nai** to be endless.

**saigetsu** time; years. **Saigetsu hito o matazu.** Time and tide wait for no man.

**SAIGO** last; **saigo no** last, closing; **saigo ni** lastly; **saigo no toshi** the last year; **saigo tsuuchoo** an ultimatum.

**saigo** one's last moment in life; **hisan na saigo o togeru** to die a sad death.

**saihai** (baton of) command; direction, leadership. **saihai o furu** to command.

**saihan** reprinting, second edition; **saihan suru** to reprint; **saihan ni naru** to run into a second edition.

**saihatsu** reappearance, **saihatsu suru** to appear again, have a second attack (of a disease).

**saihi** adoption or rejection; **saihi o kimeru** to decide on the adoption or rejection.

**saihoo** sewing; needlework; **saihoo suru** to sew; **saihooshi** tailor.

**saijin** sharp-witted person.

**SAIJITSU** national holiday.

**SAIJOO** (n.) best, highest; superlative; **saijoo no** (adj.) best, highest; **saijoohin** article of the best quality; **saijookyuu** the superlative degree.

**saikai** meeting again; **saikai o yakusuru** to promise to meet again.

**saikasoo** lowest layer.

**saiken** debenture; **saikensha** creditor.

**saiketsu** verdict, decision; **saiketsu suru** to bring in a verdict; to decide.

**saiki** pressing creditor.

**SAIKIN** latest; **saikin no joohoo** latest information.

**saikin** bacterium.

**saikon** second marriage; **saikon suru** to marry again.

**saikoo** maximum, **saikoo no** highest; supreme; **Saikoo Saibansho** Supreme Court.

**saikoo** revival, restoration; **saikoo suru** to reestablish, to renew.

**saikoo** reconsideration; **saikoo suru** to reconsider; **saikoo no ue de** on reflection.

**saikooten** highest point.

**saikoro** dice.

**saiku** workmanship; **saiku o suru** to work; to make; to patch up; to manipulate.

**saikuru** cycle.

**saikutsu** mining; **saikutsu suru** to work a mine.

**saimatsu** close of the year; **saimatsu no uridashi** year-end bargain.

**saiminjutsu** hypnotism; **saiminjutsu o kakeru** to hypnotize (someone).

**saimitsu** smallness; minuteness; **saimitsu na** minute; detailed; **saimitsu ni** in detail.

**saimoku** details; items; **saimoku ni wataru** to go into detail.

**saimu** debt; **saimu o hatasu** to settle one's debts; **saimusha** debtor.

**sain** signature; **sain suru** to sign.

**sainan** misfortune, calamity, accident; **sainan ni au** to meet with an accident (mishap); **sainan o manugareru** to escape a disaster.

**sainin** reappointment.

**sairai** second coming; reincarnation.

**sairei** festival.

**saisai** again and again; **saisai no** repeated; frequent.

**saisan** over and over again.

**saisei** regeneration; resuscitation; **saisei suru** to come to life again.

**saisen** offertory; sacred pennies; **saisen bako** offertory box (at a Shinto shrine).

**saishi** one's wife and children.

**saishiki** coloring; painting; **saishiki shita** colored; **saishiki suru** to paint.

**saishin** rehearing, retrial; **saishin suru** to rehear; to reexamine.

**saishin no** latest; **saishinshiki** latest model.

**saishin no** careful, prudent; **saishin no chuui o haratte** most carefully.

**SAISHO** beginning; **saisho no** first, original; **saisho wa** at first; **saisho ni** at the outset; in the first place; **saisho kara** from the very first.

**saishoku** living on vegetables only; vegetarian diet; **saishoku suru** to live on vegetables; **saishokushugisha** vegetarian.

**saishoo** (n.) minimum; smallest; **saishoo no** (adj.) smallest; least.

**saishuu** (n.) last, final; collection; **saishuu no** (adj.) last, final; **saishuu ressha** last train of the day.

**saishuu** collection; **saishuu suru** to collect, to gather samples.

**saisoku** urging; calling upon; **saisoku suru** to urge, press; **kane o saisoku suru** to call upon a person in order to pay off one's debts.

**saisoku** detailed rules.

**saitei no** lowest, minimum.

**saiten** marking, scoring.

**saiwai** good fortune; happiness; **saiwai na** happy, fortunate; **saiwai ni** happily, fortunately.

**saiyoo** adoption; appointment; **saiyoo suru** to adopt; to use, employ.

**saizen** (n.) best; one's best; **saizen no** (adj.) best; utmost; **saizen o tsukusu** to do one's best.

**SAJI** spoon; **saji de sukuu** to spoon up; **saji o nageru** to give up.

**sajiki** stand; gallery; upper boxes (in a theater).

**SAKA** sloping hill; slope; ascent; **saka ni naru** to slope; **saka o noboru** to go up a slope; **saka o kudaru** to go down a slope.

**sakadachi o suru** to stand on one's head.

**sakaeru** to prosper, flourish.

**sakai** boundary, border, frontier.

**sakamichi** a sloping way (road); sloping grade.

**SAKANA** fish; **sakana tsuri ni iku** to go fishing; **sakanaya** fishmonger; fish dealer.

**sakan na** prosperous; splendid; vigorous; **sakan ni** actively; vigorously; **sakan ni naru** to become active.

**sakanoboru** to go up; to go back, retrace.

**sakaratte** against; in the face of.

**sakarau** to oppose, go against.

**sakari** height, climax; rut, heat; **sakari de aru** to be in full bloom; to be in the prime of.

**sakasa, sakasama** inversion, inverted order; **sakasa no** inverted; **sakasa ni** wrong side up; upside down; **sakasa ni naru** to be inverted.

**sakasama** See **sakasa.**

**sakaya** sake shop.

**sakazuki** cup; wine cup; **sakazuki o sasu** to offer a cup (of wine); **sakazuki o hosu** to drink up (a cup of wine or sake); **sakazuki o mawasu** to pass around a cup.

**SAKE** Japanese liquor, wine.

**sake** salmon.

**sakebi** shout; cry.

**sakebu** to shout; to cry.

**sakei** leaning toward the left; **sakei suru** to lean toward the left; to become communistic.

**sakeme** crack.

**sakenomi** drinker.

**sakeru** to split; to be torn. **Kinomo ga sakemashita.** My dress was torn.

**sakeru** to avoid, to keep away.

**SAKI** point; tip; future; destination; front; **saki e itte** later on; **saki no** *(adj.)* future; coming; former; **saki ni** beyond; previously; **saki ga nagai** to have a long future; **yubi no saki** tip of the finger. **Saki ni itte kudasai.** Please go ahead.

**sakidatsu** to precede.

**sakigake** pioneer; **sakigake no** the foremost; **sakigake o suru** to lead.

**SAKIHODO, SAKKI** little while ago; **sakihodo kara** for some time.

**sakimawari** preoccupation, forestallment; **sakimawari o suru** to get ahead of.

**sakiototoi** three days back, three days ago.

**sakiototoshi** three years ago.

**sakisohon** saxophone.

**sakka** writer, author; literary person.

**sakkaku** illusion.

**SAKKI** See **SAKIHODO.**

**sakki** thirst for blood; menace; **sakki datsu** to look menacing.

**sakku** sack; case.

**sakkyoku** musical composition, musical piece; **sakkyoku suru** to set to music; **sakkyokuka** composer of music.

**SAKU** to rend, split, tear; **naka o saku** to sever the two.

**saku** device; plan; **saku o megurasu** to devise a scheme; **saku ga tsukiru** to be at wit's end.

**saku** to bloom.

**SAKUBAN** last evening, last night. (See also **YUUBE.**)

**sakubun** composition.

**sakudoo** maneuvers; artful management.

**sakugen** curtailment; retrenchment; **sakugen suru** to cut down.

**sakuhin** work (literary, musical, etc.).

**sakui** design; motif.

**sakuin** index; **sakuin o tsukuru** to provide with an index.

**sakujitsu** See **KINOO.**

**sakujo** omission; **sakujo suru** to strike out; to omit.

**SAKUNEN** See **KYONEN.**

**SAKURA** cherry tree.

**sakuranbo** cherry (fruit).

**sakurasoo** Japanese primrose.

**sakuryaku** artifice; device; stratagem; scheme; **sakuryaku ni tomu** to be resourceful in scheming.

**sakusei** manufacture, production.

**sakusen** military or naval operation; strategy.

**sakusha** author; dramatist; poet; composer; maker.

**SAKUYA** last night.

**sakyuu** sandhill, dune.

**-SAMA** See **-SAN.**

**samasu** to wake up, awaken; to make sober; to cool; to bring down. **Kono ocha wa moo sukoshi samashite kara nomimashoo.** I will drink this tea after it has cooled a bit.

**samatage** disturbance; hindrance.

**samatageru** to obstruct, hinder.

**samayou** to wander about; to stray.

**samazama** various; **samazama na hito** all sorts of people; **samazama ni** in many ways.

**SAMERU** to wake up; to come to oneself; to become sober; **me ga sameru** to be awakened; **yoi ga sameru** to become sober.

**samezame to** bitterly; without restraint; **samezame to naku** to weep bitterly.

**SAMO** as though, as if; **samo manzoku soo ni** with evident satisfaction. **Samo ureshisoo desu.** She looks quite pleased.

**samon** inquisition, inquiry; **samon suru** to interrogate; **samon kai** court of inquiry.

**samugari** person who is oversensitive to cold.

**samugaru** to complain of the cold; to be sensitive to the cold.

**SAMUI** cold, chilly.

**samuke** chill, fit of cold, cold shiver.

**samurai** knight.

**SAMUSA** coldness. **Samusa ga kibishiku narimashita.** The cold has worsened.

**SAN, MITTSU** three.

**-SAN** Mr., Ms. **Yamada-san** Mr. (Mrs., Miss) Yamada.

**sanba** midwife.

**sanbashi** landing pier.

**sanbi** praise; adoration; **sanbi suru** to praise.

**sanbika** hymn; **sanbika o utau** to sing a hymn.

**sanbun** prose.

**sanbutsu** product.

**sanchi** mountainous region; highlands.

**sanchi** place of production.

**sanchoo** summit (peak) of a mountain.

**sandan** devising ways and means; **sandan suru** to find a means; **kane o sandan suru** to manage to raise money.

**sandoitchi** sandwiches.

**sangai** three stories, third floor.

**sangai** damage; disaster; **sensoo no sangai** the evils of war.

**SANGATSU** March.

**sangyoo** (manufacturing) industry; **sangyoo no** industrial.

**sangyoo kookoku** classified advertisement.

**SANJUU** thirty.

**sanjuu no** threefold, triple; **sanjuu no hako** nest (set) of three boxes.

**sanjutsu** arithmetic; **sanjutsu o suru** to do sums.

**sanka** participation. **-ni sanka suru** to take part in.

**sankaku** triangle; **sankaku no** triangular.

**sankan** visit; **sankan suru** to visit and see.

**sankei** visiting a temple; **sankei suru** to go and worship (at a Buddhist temple or a Shinto shrine); **sankeinin** visitor to a temple, worshiper; pilgrim.

**sankoo** reference; comparison; **sankoo ni suru** to refer to; **sankoo ni naru** to serve as a reference; **sankoo no tame ni** for reference; **sankoonin** witness; **sankoosho** book of reference.

**sanmai** three sheets (of paper, or anything flat and thin); **sakana o sanmai ni orosu** to fillet fish (to make three pieces, i.e., 2 pieces of fish and the bone).

**sanmenkiji** third-page items of a newspaper; general news.

**sanmyaku** mountain range.

**sanpai** worship; **sanpai suru** to visit and worship (at a Shinto shrine).

**SANPO** a walk; **sanpo suru** to take a walk; **sanpo ni iku** to go for a walk.

**sanpu** scattering; **sanpu suru** to spread, scatter.

**sanpuku** side of a mountain.

**sanretsu** attendance; **sanretsu suru** to attend, be present at.

**sanrin** forest.

**sanrinsha** tricycle.

**sansei** seconding, approval; **-ni sansei suru** to support; to approve of.

**sanseiken** suffrage; political right.

**sanseisha** supporter; seconder.

**sanshoo** comparison; reference; **sanshoo suru** to refer to.

**sanshutsu** production, output; **sanshutsu suru** to produce.

**sanso** oxygen.

**sanson** mountain village.

**sansui** hills and streams; landscape; landscape painting of mountains and rivers.

**santan** pitifulness; **santan taru** pitiful; tragic.

**santoo** third class.

**san'yaku** powdered medicine.

**sanzai** (n.) spending (money); squandering; **sanzai suru** to spend money.

**sanzai** lying scattered; **sanzai suru** to lie scattered.

**SANZAN** severely; terribly; **sanzan matsu** to wait a long time; **sanzan na me ni au** to have a bitter experience.

**sao** pole, rod; **saodake** bamboo pole.

**SAPPARI** at all; quite; entirely; **sappari shita** refreshing. **Sappari wakarimasen.** I don't understand at all.

**sappuukei** tastelessness; **sappuukei na** tasteless; dry.

**SARA** dish, plate.

**sarada** salad; **saradayu** salad oil.

**SARAIGETSU** month after next.

**SARAINEN** year after next.

**SARAISHUU** week after next.

**sarakedasu** to reveal; to bring shamelessly into view; to lay bare; **muchi o sarake dasu** to expose one's ignorance.

**sara ni** anew, afresh; once more, again; furthermore.

**sararii** salary; **saraiiman** salaried man.

**sarasara** in the least; smoothly; rustling; murmuring.

**sarashi** bleaching; refining; exposure; **sarashiko** bleaching powder; **sarashimomen** bleached cotton.

**sarasu** to bleach.

**sarasu** to expose; **haji o sarasu** to be put to shame.

**sarau** dredge; to clean; to sweep away; **ninki o sarau** to win (popularity) by a clean sweep.

**sarau** to kidnap, to spirit away, to snatch.

**sarau** (colloq.) to review; to repeat; to practice; **piano o sarau** to practice the piano.

**saru** to go away, to leave; to take off; to

divorce; **gakkoo o saru** to leave school; **shoku o saru** to retire from a post.

**saru** monkey.

**sasaeru** to support, maintain; **ikka o sasaeru** to support one's family.

**sasageru** to offer; to sacrifice; to lift up.

**sasai na** trifling; small; **sasai na koto** trivial matter.

**sasayaki** whispering.

**sasayaku** to whisper.

**sasen** degradation; **sasen suru** to degrade; demote.

**saseru** to make; to let; to force; to cause; to get; **kodomo ni benkyoo o saseru** to make a child study.

**-(S)ASERU** causative ending denoting; cause to, make to, force to, allow to, let; **ikaseru** to make (someone) go; **tabesaseru** to make eat; to allow to eat; to let eat; to force to eat.

**SASHIAGERU** to present, offer *(humble)*.

**sashiatari** for the present.

**sashidashinin** sender (of mail, etc.).

**sashidasu** to present, offer; to send.

**sashidegamashii** impertinent.

**sashie** illustration; cut.

**sashigane** instigation; carpenter's square; **-no sashigane de** at the instigation of.

**sashihiki** deduction; balance; excess; ebb and flow; **sashihiki suru** to balance; to deduct.

**sashihiku** to subtract, take away.

**sashikakaru** to come upon; to approach.

**sashikomu** to insert; to push in; to have a fit of acute pain. **Tsuki no hikari ga mado kara sashikomu.** The moonlight floods through the window.

**SASHIMI** sliced raw fish (popular Japanese food).

**sashimukai** face to face; facing each other; **sashimukai de** sitting face to face; **sashimukai ni naru** to sit face to face.

**sashimukeru** to send, dispatch.

**sashioku** to set aside; to leave; to leave out of consideration.

**sashiosae** attachment; seizure; **sashiosaeru** to seize; to attach. **Zaisan ga sashiosaerarete iru.** Her property is under attachment.

**sashisematta** pressing, urgent; imminent; **sashisematta yooji ga aru** to have urgent business.

**sashitomeru** to prohibit, place a ban on.

**sashitsukae** engagement; hindrance; trouble; inconvenience; objection; **sashitsukae ga nakereba** if you have no objection; **sashitsukae ga nai** to be disengaged.

**sashitsukaeru** to be hindered.

**sashiwatashi** diameter.

**SASHIZU** direction; instruction; **sashizu suru** to direct; to instruct; **sashizu no moto ni** under (someone's) direction.

**sasoi** invitation; temptation; **sasoi ni yoru** to call for; **sasoi o kakeru** to sound out (someone) on a subject.

**SASOU** to invite (someone) to call for; to tempt.

**sassato** quickly; promptly.

**sasshi** sympathy; consideration; **sasshi ga tsuku** to make out; to guess; **sasshi no aru** sympathetic.

**SASSOKU** immediately; directly; **sassoku no henji** quick answer.

**sassuru** to perceive; to surmise; to sympathize with.

**SASU** to point at; to pour in; to put in; to hold over one's head; to wear; to measure; to rise; to stream in; to play; to be tinged; to offer a cup (of sake); to stick; to put in; **kita o sasu** to point to the north; **kabin ni mizu o sasu** to pour water into a vase; **kabin ni hana o sasu** to put flowers in a vase; **higasa o sasu** to hold a parasol over one's head; **katana o sasu** to wear a sword; **sake o sasu** to offer a cup of sake.

**sasu** to stab; to stitch, to sting. **Hachi ga sashimashita.** A bee has stung me.

**sasuga ni** indeed; as one might have expected; true to one's reputation. **Ano hito wa sasuga ni erai desu.** He is indeed a great man.

**sasuru** to rub; to pat; to strike.

**sata** notice; news; report; instruction; order; **sata ga aru** to get news from; **sata o suru** to give notice.

**sate** well; now; **sate mata** again; **nani wa sate oki** first of all.

**sato** village; parent's home (of a married woman); **sato ni kaeru** to come back to one's home village; to come back home.

**SATOO** sugar (often used with prefix **o-**); **satoo o ireru** to sugar; **satoo de katameta** candied. **Osatoo o kudasai.** Please give me some sugar.

**satori** comprehension; understanding; spiritual awakening (Buddhist term). **satori o hiraku** to be enlightened.

**satoru** to comprehend; to perceive; **hi o satoru** to be convinced of one's error.

**satosu** to admonish; to counsel.

**-SATSU** (counter for books) volume; copy.

**satsu, osatsu** paper money.

**satsubatsu na** rough; warlike; violent; bloody.

**satsuei** taking a photograph; **satsuei suru** to take a photograph of.

**satsui** murderous intent; **satsui o okosu** to seek to kill a person.

**satsujin** homicide.

**SATTO** in a quick motion; **satto yuderu** to boil briefly in hot water.

**sattoo** pouring in; **sattoo suru** to rush in; **mooshikomi ga sattoo suru** to have a crowd of applicants.

**sawagashii** noisy, unquiet; **seken ga sawagashii** things look dark and ominous.

**sawagasu** to disturb, agitate.

**sawagi** noise; shouts.

**SAWAGU** to get noisy; to become agitated; **chiisai koto ni sawagu** to make a fuss over trifles.

**sawari** hindrance; impediment; affection; harm.

**SAWARU** to hinder; to be injurious to; **jikoo ga sawaru** to be affected by the weather; to touch; to feel; **kenkoo ni sawaru** to affect one's health; **hito no ki ni sawaru** to hurt (someone's) feelings.

**sawaru** to touch.

**sawayaka** delightful; refreshing; clear; sweet; fluent, eloquent; **benzetsu sawayaka na hito** a fluent speaker; **kibun ga sawayaka ni naru** to feel refreshed.

**sayoku** left wing.

**SAYONARA, SAYOONARA** good-bye.

**sayoo** action, process, operation; **-ni sayoo suru** to act upon.

**SAYOONARA** See **SAYONARA.**

**sayuu** (*n.*) right and left; **sayuu suru** to influence; **sayuu ni** from side to side; on the right and left.

**SAZO** surely; indeed; how; **sazo otsukare deshoo.** You must be tired.

**sazukaru** to receive; to be granted; to be taught.

**sazukeru** to grant; to confer on; **hiden o sazukeru** to teach the secrets.

**se** back; ridge. **Se ni hara wa kaerarenu.** Necessity is a hard master.

**se, sei** height (of the body). **Se ga takai desu.** She is tall.

**sebameru** to narrow; to reduce; **seken o sebameru** to be humiliated.

**sebiro** man's suit.

**sebiru** to importune, to tease into.

**sebone** backbone, spine.

**sechigarai** stern; hard; **sechigarai yononaka** hard life.

**SEETAA** sweater.

**segamu** to importune.

**segare** my son, our son.

**sehyoo** public opinion, popular judgment; **sehyoo ni noboru** to be talked about.

**SEI** essence; spirit; vital power; **sei ga deru** to work hard; **sei o dasu** to work hard; **Sei ga tsukiru.** His energy is gone.

**sei** See **se** (height).

**sei** family name, surname.

**sei** sex, gender.

**sei** cause, effect; **-no sei de** owing to, because of.

**sei** life, existence; **sei o ukeru** to be born.

**-sei** suffix denoting: student; **ichinensei** first-year student; **bunkasei** student of literature.

**seibo** present given at the end of the year (as a token of thanks for favors).

**seibun** ingredient; a component.

**seibutsu** living things.

**seichoo** growth; growing; **seichoo shita** grown-up; **seichoo suru** to grow up; to be brought up.

**seidai** splendor; prosperity; **seidai na** prosperous; **seidai ni** splendidly; on a grand scale.

**seido** system; institution; **seido no ue no** institutional.

**seien** encouragement; **seien suru** to encourage.

**SEIFU** government.

**seifuku** conquest; **seifuku suru** to subjugate.

**seifuku** uniform.

**seigaku** vocal music.

**seigan** petition; application.

**seigen** restriction; limit; **seigen suru** to restrict; **seigen naku** without limitations.

**seigi** righteousness; justice; **seigi no** righteous.

**seigo** correction of (typographical) errors in printing.

**seigyo** control; **seigyo suru** to control.

**seigyoo** occupation; livelihood.

**seihantai** direct opposition; **seihantai no** diametrically opposed; **seihantai ni** in direct opposition; conversely.

**seiheki** predisposition; inclination.

**seihen** political change.

**seihi** success or failure; result.

**seihin** manufactured goods; products.

**SEIHOKU** northwest; **seihoku no** northwesterly.

**seihon** bookbinding; **seihon suru** to bind a book.

**seihoo** method of manufacture.

**seihoo** west; **seihoo no** western. (See also **NISHI.**)

**seihookei** (*n.*) square; **seihookei no** (*adj.*) square.

**seii** sincerity; faith; **seii aru** sincere; faithful.

**seiippai** to the best of one's ability; as hard as possible.

**seija** right and wrong; good and evil; **seija o wakeru** to discriminate between right and wrong.

**SEIJI** government; politics; **seijigaku** politics;

the study of politics; **seijika** statesman; politician.

**seijin** adult; attaining the age of maturity; **seijin shita** grown-up; **seijin suru** to grow up.

**seijin** sage, saint; **seijin buru** to give oneself a sanctimonious air.

**seijitsu** sincerity; faithfulness; **seijitsu na** sincere, honest; **seijitsu ni** sincerely.

**seijuku** ripeness; maturity; **seijuku shita** ripe; mature; **seijuku suru** to ripen.

**seika** parental home.

**seikai** political world; **seikai ni hairu** to enter upon a political career.

**seikaku** accuracy; **seikaku na** correct, accurate.

**seikaku** character, personality.

**SEIKATSU** life; livelihood; **seikatsu ga yutaka de aru** to be well off; **seikatsu o tateru** to earn one's living; **seikatsu suru** to live; to support oneself.

**seiken** political power; **seiken o nigiru** to take the reins of government.

**seiken** political view; **seiken o happyoo suru** to announce one's political views.

**seiketsu** cleanliness; purity; **seiketsu na** clean; pure; **seiketsu ni** cleanly; **seiketsu ni suru** to clean.

**seiki** vitality, vigor, life; **seiki ga michite iru** to be full of life.

**seiki** century.

**seikoo** success; exquisiteness.

**seikoo na** fine.

**seikoo shita** successful; prosperous.

**seikoo suru** to succeed in.

**seikyoo** prosperity, boom.

**seikyuu** claim; demand; **seikyuu suru** to claim; to demand.

**SEIMEI** life; **seimei hoken** life insurance; **seimei hoken o kakeru** to insure one's life. **Kono byooki wa seimei ni kakawaru koto wa arimasen.** This disease will never prove fatal.

**seimei** declaration, statement; **seimei suru** to declare.

**seimitsu** precision; minuteness; **seimitsu na** minute, detailed; **seimitsu ni** minutely, in detail.

**seimon** front gate.

**seimu** government business; administration.

**SEINAN** southwest; **seinan no** southwestern.

**seinen** youth, young man; young manhood; **seinen no** young, youthful.

**seinen** full age; **seinen ni tassuru** to come of age.

**seinengappi** date of one's birth.

**seirai** by birth, by nature; **seirai no** natural, innate.

**seirei** diligence; **seirei suru** to be diligent.

**SEIREKI** Christian era; year according to the Christian calendar; A.D. **Kotoshi wa seireki sen kyuuhyaku kyuujuu ninen desu.** This year is 1992.

**seiri** adjustment; readjustment; putting things into order; **seiri suru** to adjust; to regulate.

**seiritsu** completion, conclusion; coming into existence; **seiritsu saseru** to bring into existence; **seiritsu suru** to come into being.

**seiryaku** policy; state policy.

**seiryoku** energy, vigor; influence, power; **seiryoku no aru** influential, powerful; **seiryoku no nai** uninfluential, powerless; **seiryoku no oosei na** energetic, vigorous; **seiryoku o furuu** to wield power; **seiryoku o ushinau** to lose power; **seiryokuka** energetic person.

**seisai** restraint; sanctions; **seisai o kuwaeru** to restrain, punish.

**seisaku** policy; fabrication, manufacture; **seisaku suru** to fabricate, manufacture, produce, make.

**seisan** feasible plan; **juubun seisan ga aru** to be confident of success.

**seisan** liquidation; **seisan suru** to liquidate.

**seisan** production; **seisan suru** to produce; **seisan kajoo** overproduction; **seisan-ryoku** productive power.

**seisei doodoo** with dignity and impartiality; fair and square.

**seisei suru** to be refreshed; to feel revived.

**seiseki** results; marks; **seiseki ga yoi** to be successful.

**seishi** life and death; life or death; **seishi fumei no** missing; **seishi no sakai ni aru** to hover between life and death.

**seishi** rest, repose; stillness; **seishi no** stationary, static, still.

**seishi** restraint, repression; **seishi suru** to restrain, to check.

**seishi** paper manufacturer.

**seishiki** due form; formality; **seishiki no** formal; regular; **seishiki ni** formally; duly.

**seishin** soul, spirit; mind; will; **seishin shinkei anteizai** tranquilizer; **seishinbyoo** mental disease.

**seishin seii** with sincerity; with faithfulness.

**seishitsu** nature, character; property, quality.

**seisho** fair copy; **seisho suru** to make a fair copy of.

**seisho** Holy Bible.

**seishuku** silence, quiet; **seishuku na** silent; **seishuku ni** silently; in an orderly manner.

**SEISHUN** youth; **seishun jidai** youthful days.

**seisoo** formal dress; **seisoo suru** to dress up.

**seisoo** political strife.

**seisuru** to control; to restrain.

**seitai** system of administration.

**seitei** enactment; establishment by law; **seitei suru** to pass a law; to establish.

**seiten** fine weather; clear sky.

**SEITO** student, pupil.

**seiton** arrangement; regulation; **seiton shita** orderly; well-organized; **seiton suru** to put in order; arrange; **seiton yoku shite iru** to be in good order.

**seitoo** justice; **seitoo booei** legal defense; reasonable self-defense; **seitoo na** proper; legal; fair and proper; **seitoo ni** legally.

**seitoo** political party.

**seitsuu suru** to have a thorough knowledge of.

**seiyaku** oath; covenant; **seiyaku suru** to swear; **seiyakusho** written oath.

**Seiyoo** Western (Occidental) countries; **Seiyoo no** Occidental; **Seiyoojin** *(n.)* Westerner; European; Occidental.

**seizei** to the best of one's power; at most.

**seizen taru** orderly; regular; well-organized; **seizen to** in good order.

**seizon** existence; **seizon suru** to exist.

**seizoo** manufacture, fabrication; **seizoo suru** to make, manufacture.

**seizu** drawing; cartography.

**seji, oseji** compliments; **seji no yoi, oseji no yoi,** affable.

**SEKAI** world, earth; **sekaiteki** being worldwide, international.

**sekaseka suru** to bustle; to hustle.

**seken** public; people; world.

**sekennami** commonness; **sekennami no** common, ordinary; **sekennami ni** according to custom.

**SEKI** seat; **seki ni tsuku** to sit down, take a seat.

**seki** census register, domicile.

**seki** dam, weir, barrier.

**seki** cough; **seki o suru,** to cough; **seki ga deru** to suffer from a cough; **sekibarai** cough for clearing the throat; **sekibarai o suru** to clear one's throat.

**sekidoo** equator; **sekidoo no** equatorial.

**sekihi** tombstone; stone tablet.

**sekihin** extreme poverty; **sekihin no** very poor.

**sekiji** seating order, seniority; precedence.

**sekijitsu** former days; old times.

**sekikomu** to be excited; to be agitated.

**sekikonde** impatiently; in haste.

**sekimen** blush (of embarrassment); **sekimen saseru** to make a person blush; **sekimen suru** to blush; to be ashamed.

**sekinin** responsibility; duty; obligation; **sekinin ga aru** to be responsible for; **sekinin o hatasu** to discharge one's duty; **sekinin o ou** to take the responsibility.

**sekiryoo** lonesomeness; desolation.

**sekisetsu** accumulated snow.

**sekitan** coal.

**sekitateru** to hurry; to press.

**sekitomeru** to dam up; to check.

**sekiyu** petroleum; kerosene.

**sekizui** spine.

**sekkachi** impetuosity; impetuousness; **sekkachi na** hasty; impetuous.

**sekkai** incision; operation; **sekkai suru** to incise.

**SEKKAKU** with much trouble; with great pains; especially; kindly. **Sekkaku kita noni.** I came in vain.

**sekkei** plan, design; **sekkei suru** to plan, lay out; to draw up plans for the construction of.

**SEKKEN** soap.

**sekkin** approach; proximity; **sekkin suru** to approach.

**sekkyokuteki** positive; **sekkyokuteki ni** positively.

**sekkyoo** sermon; preaching; **sekkyoo suru** to preach; to admonish.

**SEMAI** narrow; limited.

**semakurushii** narrow and close.

**semaru** to press; to urge.

**semento** cement.

**semeru** to attack; to torture; to call to account.

**SEMETE** at least; at best. **Semete moo ichinichi otomari kudasai.** Please stay at least one more day.

**SEN** line; route; **sen ni natte** in a line; **Tookaidoosen** Tookaidoo Railroad (line); **sen o hiku** to draw a line.

**SEN** thousand; **sanzen** three thousand.

**sen** stopper, plug; **sen o suru** to stop with a cork; **mimi ni sen o suru** to stuff (something) in one's ears.

**sen** choice, selection; **sen ni hairu** to be selected; **sen ni moreru** to be left out.

**SENAKA** back (of the body).

**senbai** monopoly (of sales); **senbai suru** to monopolize (business).

**senbatsu** selection, choice; **senbatsu suru** to select; **senbatsu sareta** selected. (See also **sentei.**)

**senbetsu** parting present; farewell gift.

**senboo** envy; **senboo suru** to feel envy; **senboo no mato ni naru** to become the envy of.

**sencha** green tea.

**senchaku** first arrival.

**senchimeetoru** centimeter.

**senchoo** captain; master of a ship.

**sendan** arbitrary action; **sendan de** arbitrarily; at one's own discretion.

**SENDEN** publicity; propaganda; advertisement; **senden suru** to propagandize; to publicize.

**sendoo** guidance, leadership.

**SENGETSU** last month.

**senkyooshi** missionary.

**SENMENJO** washroom.

**senmon no** special; profession; **-o senmon ni atsukau** to specialize in.

**senmu torishimari yaku** managing director.

**senpai** *(n.)* senior; superior.

**senpatsu** starting out in advance of someone else; **senpatsu suru** to start in advance; **senpatsutai** advance party.

**senpoo** other person; one's destination.

**senpuku** concealment; state of being latent; **senpuku suru** to lie hidden; to go into hiding. (See also **senzai.**)

**senpukuki** period of incubation; latent period.

**senpuu** whirlwind; cyclone, tornado.

**senpuuki** electric fan.

**senrei** previous instance; precedence; **senrei no nai** unprecedented.

**senrei** baptism; christening; **senrei o hodokosu** to baptize; **senrei o ukeru** to be baptized.

**senren** polish; refinement; **senren sareta** refined; **senren suru** to refine.

**senritsu** melody; rhythm.

**senro** railway line; railroad track.

**senryaku** strategy; **senryakuka** strategist.

**senryoo** capture; occupancy; **senryoo suru** to take a position; to occupy.

**senryoo** dyestuff, dye.

**sensai** one's former wife.

**sensaku** search; investigation; **sensaku suru** to search into.

**SENSEI** teacher; an instructor; honorific for professional people (doctors, lawyers, etc.).

**sensei** oath; **sensei suru** to swear; to take an oath.

**SENSENGETSU** month before last.

**sensen kyookyoo** with great fear, with fear and trembling; **sensen kyookyoo to shite** living in constant fear.

**SENSENSHUU** week before last.

**senshi** death in military action; death on the battlefield.

**senshinkoku** advanced nation (in technology).

**senshitsu** cabin.

**senshu** champion; (sports) player.

**senshutsu** election; **senshutsu suru** to elect.

**SENSHUU** last week.

**sensoo** war; battle; **sensoo ni iku** to go to the front; **sensoo ni katsu** to win a battle; **sensoo suru** to make war; to fight.

**sensu** fan; folding fan.

**sensui** diving into water; submergence; **sensui suru** to dive; to submerge; **sensuikan** submarine.

**SENTAKU** wash, washing; laundry; **sentaku suru** to wash; **sentaku ni dasu** to send to be washed; **sentaku ga kiku** to stand and wash; **sentakuya** laundry (shop); laundryman.

**sentaku** selection, choice; **sentaku ni makaseru** to leave it a matter of choice.

**sentan** extreme point; extremity.

**sente** forestalling; the first move (in a game); **sente o utsu** to take the initiative; have the first move.

**sentei** selection, choice; **sentei suru** to select, choose.

**sententeki** inherent, congenital.

**sentoo** head, lead; **sentoo ni tatsu** to head, lead.

**sen'ya** other night; few nights ago.

**sen'yaku** previous engagement; **sen'yaku no tame** owing to a previous engagement.

**sen'yoo** exclusive use, private use; **sen'yoo no** exclusive, private.

**sen'yuu** exclusive possession; **sen'yuu suru** to enjoy sole possession of.

**senzai** being latent; **senzai ishiki** subconscious; **senzai no** latent, dormant; **senzai suru** to be latent.

**senzo** ancestor, forefather; **senzo no** ancestral, hereditary.

**senzoku** specially attached; **-ni senzoku suru** to belong exclusively to.

**seou** to carry on one's back; to bear; to shoulder; **omoni o seou** to be burdened with a grave duty; **sekinin o seou** to take a responsibility on one's own shoulders.

**seppaku** pressure; urgency; imminence; **seppaku shita** urgent, imminent; **seppaku suru** to draw near; to be pressed.

**seppun** kiss; kissing; **seppun o nageru** to send a kiss; **seppun suru** to kiss, press one's lips upon.

**serifu** speech, dialogue (in a play).

**sero** cello, violoncello.

**serori** celery.

**seru** light serge.

**serufutaimaa** self-timer.

**sessei** temperance, moderation; **sessei suru** to be temperate.

**sessen** fighting at close quarters; **sessen suru** to fight hand to hand.

**SESSE TO** as much as one can; diligently; **sesse to hataraku** to be busy at work.

**sesshi** Centigrade thermometer.

**SESSHOKU** contact, touch; **sesshoku suru** to touch; to come in contact with; **sesshoku o tamotsu** to keep in touch with.

**sesshoo** negotiation; **sesshoo suru** to negotiate with.

**sessuru** to touch; to have a contract with.

**setchi** establishment; **setchi suru** to establish.

**setchuu** compromise; **setchuu suru** to compromise.

**setomono** porcelain; chinaware.

**setsu** opinion, view; theory, doctrine.

**setsubi** equipment, arrangement; **setsubi o suru** to equip; to provide for.

**setsudan** cutting off, trimming; **setsudan suru** to cut off; to trim.

**SETSUMEI** explanation, elucidation; **setsumei suru** to explain; **setsumeisho** instruction booklet.

**setsuna** moment, instant; **setsuna no** momentary; **sono setsuna** at the very moment.

**setsu ni** eagerly, earnestly.

**setsuretsu** poorness; clumsiness; **setsuretsu na** poor; clumsy; unskillful.

**setsuritsu** establishment, foundation; **setsuritsu suru** to establish, institute, found.

**setsuyaku** economy; saving; thrift; **setsuyaku suru** to save; to economize.

**setsuyu** admonition, reproof; **setsuyu suru** to admonish, warn, reprove.

**setsuzoku** connection, joining; **setsuzoku suru** to join, connect, link.

**settai** reception; entertainment; **settai suru** to receive; to entertain.

**settei** establishment, creation; **settei suru** to found, institute (a corporation, etc.).

**setto** set.

**settoku** persuasion; **settoku suru** to persuade, convince.

**settoo** theft, larceny; **settoo o hataraku** to commit a theft.

**SEWA** help, aid, assistance; good offices; service, care; trouble; **sewa no yakeru** troublesome; **-no sewa ni naru** to be under the care of; **yokei na sewa o yaku** to poke one's nose where one is not wanted; **sewa suru** to help, aid; to do a kind office; to take care of. **Osewani narimashita.** Thank you for all your kindness.

**sewashii** busy; busily engaged.

**shaba** this world.

**shaberu** shovel.

**shaberu** to chatter; to prattle.

**shabon, SEKKEN** soap.

**shaburu** to suck; to chew.

**shachoo** president of a company.

**shadan** interception; isolation; **shadan suru** to cut off from.

**shadoo** roadway.

**shagamu** to squat; to crouch.

**shagareta** hoarse (voice); grating (laugh).

**shageki suru** to shoot, fire at; **shagekijoo** rifle-range.

**shain** member of a company.

**shajitsuteki** realistic, true to life.

**shakai** society; **shaki no tame ni** for the good of the public; **shakaigaku** sociology,

social science; **shakai-shugi** socialism; **shakai-shugisha** socialist.

**shakkin** debt; loan; **shakkin o kaesu** to pay a debt; **shakkin o koshiraeru** to fall into debt; **shakkin suru** to borrow money; **shakkintori** creditor.

**shakkuri** hiccup, hiccough; **shakkuri suru** to hiccup.

**shakoo** social life.

**shaku** Japanese foot; unit of measure corresponding to 3.30 cm. or 1.287 (American) foot. (No longer used.)

**shakuchi** leased land; rented ground.

**shakudo** measure, gauge, scale.

**shakushi** wooden spoon.

**shakuya** rented house; **shakuya suru** to rent a house; **shakuyanin** tenant.

**shamen** slanting surface; slope.

**shanpen** champagne.

**share** play upon words, pun; joke; **share o iu** to crack jokes.

**sharei** remuneration, reward; thanks; **sharei suru** to reward; to remunerate.

**shareru** to adorn oneself, to try to look pretty.

**shareta** stylish, tasteful.

**sharin** wheel.

**sharyoo** vehicles, cars.

**shasai** debentures; bond.

**shasei** sketching; **shasei suru** to sketch; to make a sketch.

**shasetsu** editorial, leading article.

**shashi** cross-eye.

**SHASHIN** photograph, **shashin no** photographic; **shashin ni toru** to take a photograph of; **shashin o hikinobasu** to enlarge a photograph; **shashin o toru** to have a photograph taken; to take a photograph; **shashin o yakitsukeru** to print a photograph; **SHASHINKI** camera.

**SHASHOO** conductor.

**shatai** body of a car.

**SHATSU** shirt, undershirt.

**shattaa** shutter.

**shazai** apology, **shazai suru** to acknowledge being at fault, apologize.

**shazetsu** refusal, denial; **shazetsu suru** to refuse, decline.

**SHI** city, municipality; **shi no** city, municipal; **shiyakusho** municipal building; City Hall.

**SHI** four (see also **YO, YON, YOTTSU**).

**shi** death; **shi ni hinshite iru** to be at the point of death; **shi o osorenai** to face death with calmness.

**shi** poetry, verse.

**-SHI** particle denoting: in addition to it. **Kane mo aru shi chii mo aru.** He has wealth and, in addition, high position.

**-shi** Mr., Ms. *(used mostly in writing).*

**shiage** finish, finishing; **shiage o suru** to give the finishing touches to.

**shiageru** to finish, complete.

**shiai** contest of skill, match; **shiai o suru** to play a match; **shiai o mooshikomu** to challenge to a game; **shiai o shoodaku suru** to accept a challenge (to a game).

**shian** meditation, consideration; **shian suru** to think; to consider.

**SHIASATTE** two days after tomorrow.

**shiawase** good fortune, happiness.

**shibafu** lawn; turf.

**shibai** play, drama; theater; **shibai ni iku** to go to the theater; **shibai o utsu** to give a performance; to trick someone.

**SHIBARAKU** for a while, for some time; **shibaraku shite** after a while.

**shibaru** to bind; to tie up; **kizu o shibaru** to bind up a wound; **kisoku de shibaru** to restrict (someone) by a rule.

**SHIBASHIBA** often, many times, repeatedly.

**shibatataku** to blink.

**shibire** numbness; insensibility.

**shibireru** to numb; to be numbed.

**shibomu** to fade, wither.

**SHIBOO** death; **shiboo suru** to die.

**shiboo** wish, desire; **shiboo suru** to wish, to desire.

**shiboo** fat, grease, suet.

**shiboosha** applicant, candidate.

**shiboru** to press out, wring out, squeeze; **chie o shiboru** to rack one's brains; **namida ni sode o shiboru** to weep bitterly; **ushi no chichi o shiboru** to milk a cow.

**shibu** branch; subdivision.

**shibui** astringent; austere; glum; sullen; chaste; simple yet refined (in taste); quiet, sober; **shibui kao** glum face; **shibui konomi** quiet taste.

**shibuki** spray; **shibuki o tobasu** to spray, to splash.

**shiburu** to be reluctant, be unwilling; to become loose with gripping pain (of bowels); not to go smoothly.

**shibushibu** reluctantly, unwillingly.

**shibutoi** churlish; stubborn.

**SHICHI, NANATSU** seven.

**shichi** fatal position; **shichi o dassuru** to have a hairbreadth escape.

**shichi** pawn; **-o shichi ni ireru o** to pawn personal property.

**SHICHIGATSU** July.

**SHICHIJUU** seventy.

**shichiya** pawnbroker, pawnshop.

**shichoo** city administration building.

**shichoo** mayor.

**shichuu** inside a city or town; **shichuu o neriaruku** to walk the streets in a procession.

**shichuu** stew.

**shichuu** support.

**shida** fern.

**SHIDAI** order; the state of things; as soon as; **shidai ni** gradually; **shidai ni yotte wa** according to circumstances; **tsuki shidai ni** as soon as it comes. **Tenki shidai desu.** It depends upon the state of the weather.

**shidoo** guidance, leading; **shidoo suru** to guide; to lead.

**shidoosha** leader, director.

**shiei** private management; **shiei no** private.

**shiei** municipal management.

**shieki** employment; service; **shieki suru** to employ.

**shifuku** private clothes.

**shigai** outskirts of a city, suburbs.

**shigai** streets.

**shigai** dead body, corpse.

**shigaisen** ultraviolet rays.

**shigamitsuku** to clasp, cling to.

**shigan** desire; application; volunteering; **shiganhei** volunteer; enlisted soldier; **shigansha** applicant; **shigan suru** to apply for.

**SHIGATSU** April.

**shigeki** stimulus, stimulation; **shigeki suru** to stimulate.

**shigemi** thicket, bush.

**shigeru** to become dense; to grow thick and rank.

**shigo** after death.

**shigoku** very, extremely.

**shigoku** to draw through the hand; to stroke (as a beard).

**SHIGOTO** work, task; job; **shigoto o suru** to work; **shigoto o toru** to get a job; **shigotoba** workshop.

**shigure** wintertime rain; wintry shower.

**shigusa** manners, behaviors; gesture.

**shihai** rule, control, management; **shihai suru** to govern, rule, manage; **kanjoo ni shihai sareru;** to be influenced by personal feelings; **shihaikaikyuu** governing class; **shihainin** manager, director.

**SHIHARAI** payment; **shiharai suru** to pay; **shiharai o seikyuu suru** to ask for payment; **shiharainin** payer (one who pays); **shiharaisaki** payee.

**shiharau** to pay; to discharge; **shiharau beki** payable.

**shihei** paper currency.

**shihen** volume of poems; Book of Psalms.

**shihoo** four sides; **shihoo ni** on all sides; **shihoo happoo** all directions; **shihoo happoo e** in all directions.

**shihooken** jurisdiction; judicial authority.

**shihon** capital; fund; **shihon o toozuru** to

invest one's capital in; **shihonka** capitalist; **shihonkin** capital; **shihonshugi** capitalism.

**shiin** cause of death.

**shiin** scene.

**shiire** stocking; laying in, buying up (of goods); **shiire o suru** to stock goods.

**shiireru** to stock goods, lay in (goods), to buy up (goods).

**shiiru** to compel; to force upon.

**shiitageru** to oppress, tyrannize.

**shiite** against one's will, by force.

**shiitsu** bed sheets, linen.

**shiji** support, maintenance; **shiji suru** to support; to maintain.

**shijin** poet, poetess.

**shijitsu** historical facts.

**shijoo** market, fair; **shijoo ni deru** to appear in a market; **shijoo ni dasu** to bring to market; **shijoo dookoo** market trends; **shijoo kakaku** market value; **shijoo no jissei** market forces; **shijoo shisuu** market index; **shika** market price.

**SHIJUU** the whole time, all the time, always.

**shijuu** forty. (See also **YONJUU**.)

**SHIKA** only *(used with a negative)*. **Osakana shika arimasen.** We have only fish. **Eigo shika hanasemasen.** I can speak only English.

**shika** market price.

**shikaeshi** tit for tat; revenge; **shikaeshi o suru** to take revenge.

**shikai** municipal assembly; town assembly.

**shikai** chairmanship.

**shikake** device, mechanism.

**shikakeru** to begin; to set to work; to fasten upon; to make advances.

**SHIKAKU** *(n.)* square; **shikaku na** *(adj.)* square; **shikakui hako** square box.

**shikaku** (sense of) sight, eyesight; **shikaku** qualification; capacity; **shikaku no aru** qualified; **-no shikaku de** in the capacity of; **shikaku o ushinau** to be disqualified for.

**shikaku** assassin.

**shikakubaru** to be formal; to stand on ceremony.

**shikamo** moreover, furthermore.

**shikaru** to scold; to reprove.

**shikaruni** however, nevertheless, but, yet *(formal);* **shikaruni mata** on the other hand.

**SHIKASHI** however, nevertheless.

**SHIKATA** method, way, means; **shikata ga naku (shikata nashi ni)** having no other choice. **Shikata ga nai desu.** I cannot help it.

**shike** stormy weather; scarcity of fish; **shike o kuu** to be overtaken by a storm.

**shikei** death penalty, capital punishment;

**shikei o senkoku suru** to pass sentence of death; **shikei o shikkoo suru** to execute.

**SHIKEN** examination, test; trial; **shiken ni tooru** to pass the examination; **shiken o okonau** to give an examination; **shiken suru** to examine, test; **shiken o ukeru** to take an examination.

**shiki** command, order; **shiki suru** to command, give an order; **-no shiki no moto ni** under the command of.

**shiki** ceremony; **shiki o ageru** to celebrate.

**shiki** four seasons.

**-shiki** suffix denoting: style; **seiyooshiki** Western style; Occidental style; **suisenshiki** flush style (toilet).

**shikibetsu** discrimination; discernment; **shikibetsu suru** to discern, distinguish.

**shikibuton** quiltlike mattress; bedding.

**shikichi** site, ground.

**shikifu** bed sheet.

**shikii** threshold, sill; **shikii o matagu** to cross the threshold.

**shikiishi** paving stone; pavement.

**shikikan** commander.

**shikikin** deposit, key money (for renting a house); **shikikin o ireru** to make a deposit on a house; to give key money.

**shikimono** matting; carpet; **shikimono o shiku** to lay a carpet.

**shikin** fund.

**shikiri** partition; settlement of accounts.

**SHIKIRI NI** frequently; continually; eagerly.

**shikisai** color, tint.

**shikisha** intelligent people; persons of good sense.

**shikitsumeru** to spread all over.

**shikka** at one's lap *(honorific address to parents, mostly used in letters);* **-no shikka ni** under the care of.

**SHIKKARI** firmly, tightly; strongly; exactly; **shikkari shita** strong; substantial.

**shikkei** disrespect; impoliteness; **shikkei na** impolite, rude; **shikkei suru** to say good-bye. **Shikkei shimashita.** I beg your pardon *(in men's talk).*

**shikki** damp; moisture; **shikki no aru** wet, damp, moist.

**shikki** lacquerware.

**shikkoo** execution, enforcement; **shikkoo suru** to execute, carry out, enforce; **shikkoo yuuyo** probation; suspension of execution; **shikkoo yuuyo to naru** to be released on probation.

**shikkoo** losing effect; invalidation.

**shikkui** mortar; plaster; **shikkui de nuru** to plaster.

**shikomi** training; teaching.

**shikomu** to train, to teach.

**shikoo** enforcement, carrying out; **shikoo**

sareru to take effect; **shikoo suru** to enforce.

**shikoo** taste; **shikoo ni tekisuru** to suit one's taste.

**shikooryoku** contemplative faculty, power to think.

**shikori** stiffness; bump.

**shiku** to spread, lay; to pave; to issue; to proclaim.

**shikujiru** to fail; to make a blunder; to be cashiered.

**shikyo** death.

**shikyoku** branch office.

**shikyoo** condition of the market.

**shikyoo** bishop.

**shikyuu** urgency; **shikyuu no** urgent; **shikyuu ni** at once, promptly.

**shikyuu** supply, allowance; **shikyuu suru** to provide; to supply.

**SHIMA** island.

**shima** stripes.

**SHIMAI** end, termination; **shimai ni** at last; **shimai ni naru** to come to an end; **shimai ni suru** to finish.

**SHIMAI** sisters.

**shimai** informal No dance (performed without wearing the formal standard costume).

**SHIMARI** tightness; locking, fastening, prudence; **shimari no aru** firm, locked; prudent; **shimari no nai** loose, impudent; stupid.

**SHIMARU** to shut, to close; to grow tight; to tighten, to sober down.

**shimatsu** management; circumstances, result, economy; **shimatsu no oenai** unmanageable; **shimatsu suru** to manage; to put in order.

**shimatta** compact; firm, well set.

**shimau** to close; to finish; to put away.

**shimedasu** to shut out, exclude.

**SHIMEI** full name.

**shimei** naming; nomination; **shimei suru** to name; to nominate.

**shimei** mission; errand; **shimei o mattoo suru** to fulfill a duty.

**shimekiri** close; closed; deadline.

**shimekomu** to lock in, shut in.

**shimekorosu** to strangle to death.

**shimen** space (in a magazine or newspaper).

**shimeppoi** damp; wet; **shimeppoi hanashi** tearful story.

**SHIMERU** to tie, to bind; to close, to shut.

**shimeru** to occupy; **jooseki o shimeru** to occupy the top seat.

**shimeru** to get damp; to get wet.

**shimesu** to point out; to show; to indicate.

**shimesu** to wet, moisten.

**shimete** altogether; in all.

**shimi** stain, blot; **shimi no aru** stained; **shimi darake no** spotty. **Shimi ga demashita.** There is a stain.

**shimijimi** carefully; fully; heartily; **shimijimi kao o miru** to look searchingly into (someone's) face; **shimijimi kiku** to listen attentively to.

**shimin** citizen.

**shiminken** citizenship.

**shimiru** to penetrate; to soak into; to smart; to be touched with; **shinsetsu ga mi ni shimiru** to appreciate (someone's) kindness fully. **Kaze ga mi ni shimiru.** The wind is penetrating. **Kono rooshon wa shimiru.** This lotion smarts.

**shimizu** spring water.

**SHIMO** frost; **shimo de kareru** to be nipped by frost; **shimoyake** frostbite.

**shimon** trial; inquiry; examination; **shimon suru** to try (hear) a case.

**shimon** fingerprints; **shimon o toru** to take (someone's) fingerprints.

**shimuke** one's behavior toward; one's attitude.

**shimukeru** to act toward; to treat; to send.

**SHIN** heart; mind; core; **shin kara** heartily, sincerely; **shin made** to the core.

**shin** truth, reality; **shin ni** truly, really, actually; **shin no** true, real; **shin ni semaru** to be true to one's nature.

**shina** coquetry; **shina o tsukuru** to be coquettish.

**shina** article; goods, stuff.

**shinabiru** to wither; to droop.

**shinagire** out of stock; sold out.

**shinai** city; inside the city.

**shin'ai** affection, love; **shin'ai naru** dear, beloved.

**shinamono** article; goods.

**shin'an** new idea; new design.

**shinario** scenario.

**shinayaka na** pliant, flexible, supple.

**shinboku** friendship, intimacy; **shinboku o hakaru** to cultivate a friendship.

**shinboo** patience, endurance, forbearance; **shinboo no nai** impatient; **shinboo no yoi** patient; **shinboo suru** to endure; to be patient.

**shinboo** axle, shaft.

**SHINBUN** newspaper; journal; **shinbundane** news matter; **shinbun kisha** journalist.

**shinchiku** new building; **shinchiku no** newly built; **shinchiku suru** to build, rebuild.

**shinchintaisha** replacing the old with new; replacement; metabolism; **shinchintaisha suru** to be renewed; to be replaced.

**shinchishiki** new knowledge; advanced idea.

**shincho** books newly published.

**shinchoo** care; prudence; **shinchoo na** careful, cautious; **imi shinchoo** having deep meaning; to be of profound significance.

shinchoo height, stature; **shinchoo ga takai** to be tall.

shinchuu brass.

shinchuu true motive; mind; **shinchuu o sassuru** to share (someone's) feelings.

shindai sleeper (on a train).

shindai fortune, property.

shindan diagnosis; **shindan suru** to diagnose.

shinden sanctuary (in a Shinto shrine).

shindoo tremor, shock, vibration; oscillation; **shindoo suru** to shake, vibrate (from an earthquake or collision); to swing, oscillate, move to and fro.

shingai infringement, encroachment; **shingai suru** to infringe; to make an attack upon.

shingaku theology.

shingari rear; rearguard; **shingari o tsutomeru** to bring up the rear.

shingata new style; new design.

shingenchi seismic center; center of disturbance.

shingetsu new moon.

shingi genuineness, authenticity; **shingi o tashikameru** to ascertain the truth.

shingi consideration, discussion, investigation; **shingi suru** to consider, to investigate.

shingoo signal; **kiken shingoo** danger signal; **shingoo suru** to signal, give a signal.

shingu bedding and bedclothes.

shin'i real intentions; true meaning.

shinikakatta dying; at the point of death.

shinime moment of death.

shinimonogurui death struggle; desperation; **shinimonogurui de** desperately; **shinimonogurui no** desperate; **shinimonogurui ni naru** to make a desperate effort.

shinin dead person.

shinitaeru to die out.

shiniwakareru to be parted by death.

shinja believer; faithful (person).

shinjin divine worship; devotion; **shinijin bukai** pious, devout; **shinjin suru** to worship; to regard with adoration.

shinjiru See **shinzuru.**

shinjitsu truth; reality; **shinjitsu na** true, real; **shinjitsu ni** truly, really.

shinjitsu sincerity; faithfulness; **shinjitsu na** sincere; faithful.

shinjoo article of faith; creed; (one's) true feelings.

shinju pearl.

shinjuu double suicide; suicide for love.

shinka real value, true worth; **shinka o mitomeru** to appreciate the true value.

shinka evolution; **shinka suru** to evolve.

shinkaichi newly developed district.

shinkan, shinkansho new publication; new book.

shinkei nerves; **shinkei kabin** nervousness; being overly sensitive; **shinkei no** nervous; **shinkeishitsu** nervous temperament; **shinkeishitsu no** nervous; **shinkei suijaku** nervous breakdown; **shinkeitsuu** neuralgia; **shinkei seishin anteizai** tranquilizer.

shinken na earnest; **shinken ni naru** to be earnest; to become earnest.

shinkijiku new device; originality; **shinkijiku o dasu** to introduce a new method.

shinkoku declaration; report (tax return, etc.); **shinkoku suru** to state; to report.

shinkoku na deep, serious.

shinkon new marriage; **shinkon no** newly married; **shinkon ryokoo** honeymoon; **shinkon ryokoo o suru** to go on a honeymoon.

shinkoo faith; belief; **shinkoo no jiyuu** freedom of faith; **shinkoo no nai** unbelieving; **shinkoo suru** to believe in.

shinkoo advance, progress; **shinkoo suru** to advance, to progress.

shinkoo friendship, cordiality.

shinku hardship; tribulation; **shinku suru** to suffer hardship.

shinkuukan vacuum tube.

shinkyuu promotion; **shinkyuu suru** to win a promotion; to be promoted.

shinme sprout, shoot; **shinme o dasu** to bud, sprout.

shinmi blood relation; **shinmi ni natte sewa o suru** to look after with great kindness.

shinmiri heart to heart; earnestly; **shinmiri hanasu** to have a heart-to-heart talk.

shinmitsu intimacy; familiarity; close friendship; **shinmitsu na** intimate; familiar; **shinmitsu na aidagara de aru** to have a strong friendship.

shinmotsu present, gift.

shinmyoo na fair; commendable, conscientious; docile; **shinmyoo ni** commendably; quietly; meekly; fairly.

shinnen new year. **Shinnen omedetoo.** I wish you a Happy New Year.

shinnen faith, belief; deeply rooted conviction.

shinnin confidence, trust; **shinnin suru** to confide in, believe in.

shinninjoo credentials.

shinnyuu invasion; inroad; trespass; intrusion; **shinnyuu suru** to invade; to intrude into; **shinnyuusha** invader; trespasser.

shinnyuusei new student; freshman.

shinobi stealthy movement; going in disguise.

shinobu to bear, endure; to conceal; to hide oneself; to steal along one's way; **fujiyuu o shinobu** to suffer privation; **hitome o shinobu** to elude observation; **yo o shinobu** to live in concealment.

**shinogiyoi** genial; nice; mild.

**shinogu** to endure, bear; to rise above.

**shinonde** patiently; meekly; secretly.

**SHINPAI** uneasiness; apprehension; anxiety; worry; care; fear; **shinpai na koto** trouble, difficulty; **shinpai no amari** overcome with anxiety; **shinpai suru** to fear; to be anxious.

**shinpan** judgment; **shinpan suru** to judge; to umpire; **shinpansha** umpire; judge.

**shinpan** new edition, new publication; **shinpan no** newly edited, newly published.

**shinpi** mystery; **shinpi na** mysterious, mystic.

**shinpo** progress, advance, improvement. **shinpo suru** to make progress.

**shinpu** Catholic priest.

**shinpu** bride.

**shinpuku** admiration and devotion, honest submission; **shinpuku suru** to acknowledge another's superiority; to obey faithfully.

**shinrai** trust, reliance; confidence; **shinrai suru** to trust, to place confidence in.

**shinratsu** severity; poignance; **shinratsu na** severe; poignant.

**shinreki** new calendar; Gregorian calendar, solar calendar (as distinguished from the lunar calendar used in the past).

**shinri** examination, trial; **shinri suru** to try, to examine.

**shinri** truth, truism; **shinri o motomeru** to seek truth.

**shinri** psychic state; **shinrigaku** psychology.

**shinrin** forest, wood.

**shinroo** bridegroom.

**SHINRUI** relation, relative.

**shinryaku** aggression; invasion; **shinryaku suru** to invade.

**shinryoku** fresh green.

**shinsa** examination, investigation, inspection; **shinsa suru** to examine, inquire into; **shinsain** jury, committee of inquiry.

**shinsai** disaster caused by earthquake.

**shinsatsu** medical examination; **shinsatsu o ukeru** to consult a physician; **shinsatsu suru** to examine a patient.

**shinsei** sacredness, sanctity; **shinsei na** holy, sacred, hallowed; **shinsei ni suru** to make holy; **shinsei o kegasu** to defile the sacredness.

**shinsei** application, petition; **shinsei suru** to apply; **shinseinin** applicant, petitioner, claimant.

**shinseki** relative.

**shinsen na** fresh, new.

**SHINSETSU** kindness; goodness; friendliness; **shinsetsu na** kind, good, cordial; **shinsetsu o suru** to do a kindness.

**shinsetsu** new establishment; **shinsetsu no** newly organized, newly formed; **shinsetsu suru** to establish newly.

**shinshaku** consideration, allowance; **nan no shinshaku mo naku** without any consideration; **shinshaku suru** to take into consideration.

**shinshi** gentleman; man of position; **shinshi kyooyaku** gentleman's agreement; **shinshirashii** gentlemanlike.

**shinshiki** new style; new system; **shinshiki no** of a new style; modern.

**shinshin no** rising.

**shinshitsu** bedchamber, bedroom.

**shinshoku** food and sleep; **shinshoku o wasurete** forgetful of sleep and other comforts; regardless of oneself.

**shinshoku** erosion; **shinshoku suru** to erode.

**shinshuku** expansion and contraction; elasticity; **shinshuku suru** to expand and contract; **shinshuku jizai** elasticity; **shinshuku jizai no** elastic.

**shinshutsu** marching out; emergence; **shinshutsu suru** to march out; emerge.

**shinsoo** true state; **shinsoo o akiraka ni suru** to disclose the real state of affairs; **shinsoo o kataru** to lay bare the truth of a matter.

**shinsui** launching; **shinsui suru** to launch; to be launched; **shinsuishiki** launching (ceremony).

**shinsui** fascination, infatuation; **shinsui suru** to be fascinated.

**shinsui** flooding, inundation; **shinsui suru** to be flooded.

**shintai** image of a god.

**shintai** body; person; constitution; **shintai kensa** physical examination; **shintai no** bodily, corporal.

**shintai** advance and retreat; movement; **shintai suru** to move, to act.

**shintaku** trust; **shintaku suru** to entrust with; to leave in trust (property, etc.); **shintaku gaisha** trust company; **shintaku shikin** trust fund.

**shintei** presentation; **shintei suru** to present, give.

**shinten** personal; confidential (written on the envelope of a letter); **shinten no** private, confidential; **shintensho** confidential letter.

**shinto** believer (religious).

**shin to shita** silent, still; deserted.

**shin to suru** prevailing silence.

**shintsuu** mental suffering; anxiety.

**SHINU** to die, pass away, expire; **shinu made** to the end; **shinu kakugo de** at the risk of one's life.

**shinwa** myth, mythology.

**shin'ya** dead of night, midnight; **shin'ya ni** late at night.

**Shin'yaku Seisho** New Testament.

**shin'yoo** confidence, trust; credit; **shin'yoo ga aru** to be trusted by; **shin'yoo o eru** to have credit with; **shin'yoo suru** to trust; to credit; **shin'yoojoo** letter of credit; **shin'yoo kumiai** credit association, credit union.

**shin'yuu** intimate friend.

**shinzen** amity, goodwill; **shinzen shisetsu** goodwill mission.

**shinzoku** relation, relative.

**SHINZOO** heart; **shinzoobyoo** heart disease; **shinzoomahi** heart failure.

**shinzui** essence.

**shinzuru, shinjiru** to believe in; to accept (something) as true; to trust.

**SHIO** salt (often used with the prefix o-); **shiokarai** salty; **shio de aji o tsukeru** to season with salt; **shio ni tsukeru** to salt; to pickle in salt.

**shioki** punishment; execution; **shioki o suru** to punish; to execute.

**shiokuri** supply; allowance; **shiokuri o suru** to furnish a person with money (for living expenses, schooling, etc.).

**shiorashii** moving, touching; plausible; **shiorashii koto o iu** to say pretty things.

**shioreru** to wither, droop; to be in low spirits.

**shippai** failure; defeat; **shippai suru** to fail; to be unsuccessful.

**shippi** useless expenses.

**shippitsu** writing; **shippitsu suru** to write.

**shippo** tail; **shippo o dasu** to give (someone) away; to disclose (someone's) identity; **shippo o maku** to acknowledge defeat; **shippo o osaeru** to find fault (with someone).

**shippuu** violent wind; gale.

**shirabakkureru** (*colloq.*) to dissemble; to pretend not to understand.

**SHIRABERU** to investigate; to examine; to prepare a lesson for.

**shirafu** soberness; sobriety; state of not being drunk.

**shirakeru** to become chilled; to be spoiled. **Ano hito ga kuru to itsumo za ga shirakemasu** He is always a wet blanket.

**shiranu** unknown, unfamiliar; **shiranu kao o suru** to look on with indifference.

**shirase** information; news; sign; notice.

**SHIRASERU** to notify; to send a notice; **kekkon o shiraseru** to send a notice of marriage.

**shirazu shirazu** unawares; unconsciously.

**shirei** instructions; order, notice.

**shiren** trial, test; **shiren ni taeru** to stand the test; **shiren o ukeru** to be tried, be tested.

**shireru** to become known.

**shiri** private gain; self-interest; **shiri o hakaru** to look to one's own interests.

**shiri** buttocks; rump; bottom; **shiri ga nagai** to wear out one's welcome; **shiri ga wareru** to be brought to light; to be found out; **shiri o mukeru** to turn one's back upon.

**shirikon** silicon.

**shirime** contemptuous glance; **shirime ni kakeru** to look disdainfully at.

**shirioshi** backing, support; **shirioshi o suru** to back, support.

**shiritsu** private establishment (school, welfare agency, etc.); **shiritsu no** (*adj.*) private.

**shiritsu** municipal establishment; **shiritsu no** municipal, city.

**shirizokeru** to refuse; to reject; to repel, to drive back.

**shirizoku** to retreat, retire, withdraw; to leave; **ippo shirizoku** to take a step backward.

**shiro** fortress; castle.

**shiro** (*n.*) white.

**SHIROI** (*adj.*) white; **shiroku suru** to whiten.

**shirooto** amateur.

**shirozatoo** white sugar, granulated sugar.

**SHIRU** to learn; to become acquainted with; **shitte iru** to know. **Nihongo mo Chuugokugo mo shitte imasu.** He knows both Japanese and Chinese.

**shiru** juice, sap; fluid; soup, broth; **shiru no ooi** juicy, succulent.

**shirushi** sign, mark, symbol, badge; **shirushi o tsukeru** to mark, to tick.

**shirusu** to write down; to describe.

**shiryo** consideration; thought; **shiryo no aru** thoughtful; **shiryo no nai** thoughtless.

**shiryoku** desperate effort; **shiryoku o tsukushite** with desperate courage.

**shiryoku** funds, resources, means.

**shiryoku** eyesight, sight, vision.

**shiryoo** materials, data.

**shiryuu** branch stream.

**shisai** reason; circumstances; details, particulars; **shisai no** minute, detailed; **shisai ni** minutely, in detail.

**shisaku** speculation; meditation; **shisaku ni fukeru** to be engrossed in thought; **shisaku suru** to think; to speculate.

**shisaku** trial production; **shisaku suru** to manufacture on a trial (experimental) basis.

**shisan** property; fortune; assets.

**shisatsu** inspection; examination; **shisatsu shite aruku** to make a tour of inspection; **shisatsu suru** to visit; to inspect.

**shisei** carriage, posture, pose; **shisei o tadasu** to hold oneself up.

**shisei** municipal organization; **shisei choosa** municipal census.

**shiseiji** illegitimate child.

**shiseki** place of historical interest.

**shisen** line of vision (sight); **shisen o sakeru** to avoid the public gaze.

**shisen** branch line.

**shisetsu** institution; institute; **shisetsu suru** to institute; to equip.

**shisetsu** mission; envoy.

**shisha** dead person.

**shisha** branch office.

**shisha** preview; **shisha o okonau** to hold a preview.

**shishokan** post office box.

**shishoo** teacher, master (of traditional arts and sports).

**shishoo** casualties; number of killed and wounded; **shishoosha** dead and injured.

**shishunki** adolescence, puberty; **shishunki no** adolescent.

**shishutsu** expenditure; payment; **shishutsu suru** to pay; to disburse.

**shishuu** collection of poems.

**shishuu** embroidery; **shishuu suru** to embroider.

**shisoo** thought, idea.

**shissaku** error, mistake; **shissaku suru** to do (anything) amiss; to make a mistake.

**shisseki** reproof, reprimand; **shisseki suru** to reprove.

**shisshoku** unemployment; **shisshoku suru** to become unemployed.

**shisso** simplicity, plainness, frugality; **shisso na** simple, plain; **shisso ni kurasu** to live a simple life; to live plainly.

**shissoo** running fast; going at full speed; **shissoo suru** to run away; to run at full speed.

**shissoo** disappearance (of a person); **shissoo suru** to disappear.

**SHITA** tongue; **shita o dasu** to put out one's tongue; **shita o maku** to be astonished.

**SHITA** foot; bottom; lower place; **-no shita de** under, below; **-no shita ni** under, below; **shita e** down, downward; **shita kara** from below, from the bottom; **shita no** lower; downward, subordinate; inferior.

**shitabi** burning with less intensity; **shitabi ni naru** to reach a low mark, to wane.

**shitagaeru** to be attended by, to bring under subjection.

**shitagaki** rough copy, draft; **shitagaki o suru** to draft; to make a rough copy.

**SHITAGATTE** accordingly, consequently; correspondingly.

**shitagau** to follow; to accompany; to obey.

**shitageiko** preparation; rehearsal; **shitageiko o suru** to prepare.

**SHITAGI** underwear, undergarment.

**shitagokoro** secret desire, intention; **shitagokoro ga aru** to have a secret desire.

**shitagoshirae** preparation, arrangement.

**shitai** dead body.

**shitaji** ground; groundwork, preparation.

**shitakensa** previous examination.

**SHITAKU** preparation; arrangement; **shitaku o suru** to prepare.

**shitamachi** downtown.

**shitami** preliminary inspection.

**shitamuki** downward look, downward tendency; **shitamuki no** downward; prone; **shitamuki ni naru** to look down.

**shitanuri** undercoating, prime; **shitanuri o suru** to put on the first coat (of paint).

**SHITASHII** intimate; familiar; **shitashii aidagara de aru** to be on intimate terms; **shitashiku** intimately; personally; **shitashiku suru** to be great friends.

**shitashimi** friendship, friendly feeling; **shitashimi no aru** familiar, close, affectionate; **shitashimi no nai** unfamiliar; strange; cold.

**shitashimu** to become friendly with; to become a great friend of.

**shitashirabe** preliminary inquiry; preparation; doing homework; **shitashirabe o suru** to inquire beforehand.

**shitataru** to drip; to drop.

**shitate** cut; tailoring; getting ready; **shitate no yoi** well-tailored; **shitatemono** sewing; tailoring; **shitateya** dressmaker; tailor.

**shitate ni deru** to treat (someone) with deference; to behave humbly.

**shitateru** to make (clothes); to train for a trade.

**shitatsuzumi** smacking one's lips; **shitatsuzumi o utsu** to smack one's lips; **shitatsuzumi o utte taberu** to eat with much relish.

**shitau** to yearn after; to long for.

**shitauchi** tut.

**shitauke** subcontract; **shitauke ni dasu** to sublet.

**shitayaku** subordinate employee.

**shitayomi** preparation of one's lessons; rehearsal; **shitayomi o suru** to prepare one's lessons.

**shitazumi** being in the lower layer of something; **shitazumi ni naru** to be in the lower layer; to be placed under something; **shitazumi no seikatsu o suru** to be low in the social scale.

**shitchi** swampy land; damp ground.

**shitei** designation; **shitei no** recognized; appointed; **shitei suru** to designate; to name; to appoint.

**shitei** private mansion.

**shiteki** pointing out; **shiteki suru** to point out; to show; to indicate.

**shiteki** poetic.

**shiteki** private, personal.

**shiten** branch store.

**shitogeru** to bring about; to complete.

**shitoo na** right and proper; fair; reasonable.

**shitoshito** gently; softly; damp; wet.

**shitoyaka na** gentle, graceful.

**SHITSU** nature, character; quality.

**-shitsu** suffix denoting: room, chamber; **kyooshitsu** classroom; **shinshitsu** bedroom.

**shitsuboku na** simpleminded.

**shitsuboo** disappointment; despair; **shitsuboo shite** disappointedly; **shitsuboo saseru** to disappoint; **shitsuboo suru** to be disappointed at.

**shitsugen** slip of the tongue; blunder in speech.

**shitsugyoo** unemployment; **shitsugyoo suru** to be thrown out of work.

**shitsuji** steward; manager; butler.

**shitsuke** discipline; breeding; training; **shitsuke no yoi** disciplined, well-bred.

**shitsukeru** to train, bring up.

**shitsukkoi, shitsukoi** obstinate, persistent.

**shitsumei** loss of eyesight; **shitsumei suru** to lose one's sight.

**SHITSUMON** question; interrogation; **shitsumon suru** to question.

**shitsumu** attending to one's business.

**shitsunai** interior of a room; **shitsunai de** in a room; **shitsunai sooshoku** interior decoration.

**SHITSUREI** breach of etiquette, discourtesy; **shitsurei na** impolite; **shitsurei na koto o iu** to say rude things.

**shitsuren** broken heart; disappointment in love; **shitsuren suru** to be crossed in love; to become heartbroken.

**shittakaburi** pretension to knowledge; **shittakaburi o suru** to pretend to know.

**SHITTE IRU** See **SHIRU**.

**shitto** jealousy; **shitto suru** to be jealous.

**shiwa** wrinkles; lines on one's face; creases; rumples; **shiwa ga yoru** to become wrinkled; **shiwa ni naru** to be crumpled; **shiwa o nobasu** to smooth the creases.

**shiwaza** act, action, deed.

**shiyoo** use, employ; **shiyoo suru** to use; to make use of; **shiyoohoo** directions for use; **shiyoonin** employee.

**shiyoo** private business, private use; **shiyoo de** for private use, on private business; **shiyoo suru** to turn to private use.

**shizai** private fortune, money; **shizai o toojite** out of one's own purse, at one's own expense.

**shizen** nature; **shizen no** natural, instinctive; **shizen ni** naturally, spontaneously.

**SHIZUKA NA** silent, quiet, still, peaceful; **shizuka ni kurasu** to live in peace; **shizuka ni naru** to become still, get calm.

**shizuku** drop; **shizuku ga tareru** to drip.

**shizumaru** to become quiet.

**shizumeru** to quiet, calm, pacify; to quell; to subdue; to sink, send to the bottom.

**shizumu** to sink; to go to the bottom; to feel depressed.

**sho** writing; document; calligraphy, penmanship; book.

**-sho** suffix denoting: public office; **keisatsusho** police station; **Zeimusho** Office of Internal Revenue.

**shobatsu** punishment; **shobatsu suru** to punish; to impose a punishment.

**shobun** disposition; management; punishment; **shobun suru** to dispose of; to punish.

**shochi** management, action; **shochi suru** to manage; to dispose of; to deal with.

**shochuu kyuuka** summer vacation.

**shoen** first public performance of a play.

**shoga** pictures and writings.

**shogen** preface, introduction.

**shogeru** to be dejected, cast down.

**shohan** first edition of a book.

**shoho** first step; elements; **shoho no** elementary, rudimentary.

**shohoo** prescription.

**shojo** (*n.*) virgin, maiden; **shojo no** (*adj.*) virgin.

**shoka** early summer.

**shokan** letter; **shokansen** letter paper.

**shokatsu** jurisdiction.

**shokei** punishment.

**shoki** expectation, anticipation; **shoki no** expected.

**shoki** heat, hot weather; **shoki ni ataru** to be affected by the heat.

**shoki** first stage, beginning.

**shoki** clerk.

**shokikan** secretary.

**shokken** authority; official power; **shokken o ran'yoo suru** to abuse one's official authority.

**shokki** tableware.

**shokkoo** workman.

**shoku** office; situation, position; occupation, employment, job; **shoku ni tsuku** to take a post; **shoku o motomeru** to look for employment.

**shoku** eating; food; appetite; **shoku ga susumu** to have a good appetite.

**shokuatari** attack of indigestion, food poisoning.

**shokuba** workshop; place of work.

**shokubutsu** plant; **shokubutsugaku** botany; **shokubutsuen** botanical garden.

**shokudai** candle-stand.

**SHOKUDOO** dining room; **shokudoosha** dining car.

**SHOKUEN** table salt.

**shokugo** after a meal.

**shokugyoo** occupation, employment.

**shokuhi** charge for boarding; board.

**shukuin** staff; personnel.

**SHOKUJI** meal; diet; **shokuji o suru** to eat; **shokujidoki** mealtime.

**shokuji** typesetting; typography; composition; **shokuji o suru** to compose; **shokujikoo** typesetter.

**shokumin** colonization, settlement; colonists; **shokumin suru** to colonize; to found a colony; **shokuminchi** colony; **shokuminchi no** colonial.

**shokumotsu** food.

**shokumu** duties, functions; **shokumu o hatasu** to discharge a duty; **shokumujoo** officially, in the line of duty; **shokumujoo no** official.

**shokun** Ladies and gentlemen! *(used in a speech).*

**shokunin** workman; artisan.

**shokupan** bread; loaf of bread.

**shokuryoohin** articles of food, foodstuffs.

**shokushi, hitosashiyubi** forefinger; index finger; **shokushi o ugokasu** to be desirous of.

**shokutaku** person with nonofficial status; person employed without tenure.

**shokutaku** dinner table; **shokutaku ni tsuku** to take one's seat at the table.

**shokuyoku** appetite; relish; **shokuyoku ga nai** to have no appetite; **shokuyoku o susumaseru** to stimulate one's appetite.

**shokuyoo** no used for food; **shokuyoo ni teki suru** to be fit for the table.

**shomei** signature; **shomei suru** to sign.

**shomen** document; letter.

**shomotsu** book.

**shonbori** lonely, solitarily.

**shonichi** first day; opening day.

**shoo** nature, disposition; character; quality; **shoo no yoi** of good quality; **shoo ga au** to be congenial; **shoo ga awanai** to be incompatible.

**shoo** chapter, section.

**shoo** prize, reward; **shoo o ataeru** to give a prize; **shoo o eru** to get a prize.

**shoo** quotient (math).

**shoo** ministry.

**SHOOBAI** trade, business; **shoobai ni narana** not to be paying; **shoobai o suru** to do business; **shoobainin** merchant.

**shoobatsu** rewards (honors) and punishment.

**Gakkoo de shoobatsu o uketa koto wa arimasen.** I have received no honors or punishment in my school days.

**shooben** urine; **shooben o suru** to urinate.

**shoobi** admiration; appreciation; **shoobi suru** to praise; to applaud.

**shooboo** prevention and extinction of fires; **shoobooshi** fireman; **shooboosho** firehouse; **shoobootai** fire company. (See also **hi**.)

**shoobu** match, contest; game; **shoobu o kimeru** to fight to a finish; **shoobu o suru** to have a match (game, sport).

**shoobun** innate disposition; temperament.

**shoochi** consent, acceptance; **shoochi no ue de** by mutual agreement; **shoochi suru** to consent; to agree to; to understand, to know.

**shoochoo** symbol; symbolism.

**shoodaku** consent, acceptance; **shoodaku suru** to consent to; to comply with.

**shoodoku** disinfection, sterilization; **shoodoku suru** to disinfect; **shoodokuzai** disinfectant; antidote.

**shoodoo** impulse; impetus.

**shoofuda** price tag; **shoofuda tsuki no** marked with a price tag; genuine.

**SHOOGAI** life; lifetime; all one's days; to the end of one's life; **shoogai no** lifelong; **shoogai o oeru** to end one's days.

**shoogai** injury, harm.

**shoogaibutsu** obstacle.

**SHOOGAKKOO** grade school, elementary school.

**shoogaku** small sum.

**shoogakukin** scholarship.

**SHOOGATSU** New Year; January.

**shoogen** testimony, evidence; **shoogen suru** to testify to.

**shoogi** game of Japanese chess; **shoogi o sasu** to play chess.

**shoogidaoshi** falling in rapid succession one after another; **shoogidaoshi ni naru** to fall forward, one upon another as when a train makes a sudden stop; to fall like ninepins.

**SHOOGO** noon, midday.

**shoogyoo** commerce, trade; **shoogyoo no** commercial.

**shoohai** prize cup; medal.

**shoohai** victory or defeat; **shoohai o arasou** to contend for victory.

**shoohei** engagement (for a position); employment; **shoohei suru** to engage; to employ.

**shoohi** consumption; spending; **shoohi suru** to consume; to spend; **shoohisha** consumer.

**shoohin** short piece; sketch.

**shoohin** goods; commodity; **shoohinken** gift certificate (issued by retail stores).

**shoohyoo** trademark.

**shooji** paper sliding door.

**shoojiki** honesty, uprightness; **shoojiki na** honest, upright; **shoojiki ni** honestly, frankly.

**shoojin** devotion; aspiration; religious purification; abstinence from animal food; vegetable diet; **shoojin suru** to devote oneself to.

**shoojiru** See **shoozuru.**

**shoojo** young girl; little girl.

**shoojoo** certificate of merit; honorary certificate.

**shoojoo** condition of illness; symptom.

**shooka** digestion; **shooka furyoo** indigestion; **shooka suru** to digest; **shookaki** digestive organ.

**SHOOKAI** introduction; recommendation; **shookai suru** to introduce, recommend; **shookaijoo** a letter of introduction; **shookaisha** introducer.

**shookai** minute explanation.

**shookai** company, firm.

**shookai** inquiry, reference; **shookai suru** to inquire.

**shookaki** fire extinguisher.

**shookaku** raising to a higher status; **shookaku suru** to be raised to higher ranks.

**shookan** summons; call to appear; **shookan suru** to summon, call up; **shookanjoo** summons; a written summons.

**shookaryoku** digestion.

**shookasen** fireplug, hydrant.

**shooken** securities; bond.

**shooki** soberness; **shooki ni kaeru** to come to one's senses; **shooki o ushinau** to lose one's senses; to faint.

**shookibo** small scale.

**shookin** prize (in money); **shookin o kakeru** to offer a cash prize.

**shookizuku** to come to one's senses.

**shooko** proof, evidence; **shookohin** evidence (thing).

**shookodateru** to prove; to testify.

**shookoo** brief tranquility; temporary ease.

**shookoogyoo** commerce and industry.

**Shookoo Kaigisho** Chamber of Commerce and Industry.

**shookyokuteki** negative; passive.

**shookyuu** promotion; **shookyuu suru** to be promoted.

**shookyuu** raise in wages.

**shoomei** proof; certification; **shoomei suru** to prove; to certify; **shoomeisho** certificate; **mimoto shoomeisho** identification card (or other document).

**shoomei** illumination, lighting.

**shoomen** front; **shoomen kara miru** to take a front view; **shoomen shoototsu** head-on collision.

**shoometsu** extinction; disappearance; **shoometsu suru** to disappear; to be extinguished.

**shoomi** net; **shoomi gokiro aru** to weigh five kilograms net.

**shoomon** bond; deed; **shoomon o ireru** to give bond; to sign a written agreement.

**shoomoo** consumption; waste; **shoomoo suru** to consume; to waste; to tire out.

**shoonen** youth, boy; boyhood.

**shooni** infant, baby; **shoonika** pediatrics.

**shoonin** recognition; acknowledgment; witness; surety; **shoonin suru** to recognize; to admit; **shoonin ni tatsu** to be a witness to.

**shoonin** merchant, trader; **shoonin ni naru** to become a merchant.

**shoorai** (n.) future; (adj.) **shoorai no** future; prospective.

**shoorei** encouragement; promotion; **shoorei suru** to encourage; to promote; to urge.

**shoori** victory, triumph; **shoori o eru** to win a victory.

**shooryaku** abbreviation, omission; **shooryaku suru** to eliminate; to omit.

**shooryoo** small quantity.

**shoosai** details, particulars; **shoosai ni** in detail; **shoosai no** minute, detailed.

**shoosan** praise; admiration; **shoosan suru** to praise; to admire.

**shoosen** merchant vessel.

**shoosetsu** fiction; romance; novel; **shoosetsuka** novelist, novel writer; **shoosetsuteki** fictitious, romantic.

**shooshi** death by fire.

**shooshin** promotion, advancement; **shooshin suru** to rise in rank.

**shooshin** prudence, caution, timidity; **shooshin na** timid, cautious, prudent.

**shoosho** bond; document; certificate; diploma.

**shooshoku** light eating; **shooshokuka** light eater.

**shooshoo** little, few; in a small degree.

**shooshuu** calling out; summons; convocation; draft (into military service); **shooshuu suru** to call out; to summon; to assemble.

**shoosoku** news; **shoosoku o kiku** to hear from; to have news of (someone); **shoosoku ni tsuujiru** to be well informed; **shoosokutsuu** well-informed person.

**shoosoo** irritation, fretfulness; impatience; **shoosoo suru** to fret; to fidget, be impatient.

**shoosui** emaciation, haggardness; **shoosui suru** to become emaciated.

**shoosuru** to call; to name.

**shoosuu** decimal, fraction; small number; minority; **shoosuu de aru** to be very few.

**shootai** true character; **shootai naku** out of one's senses; **shootai o arawasu** to reveal one's true character; **shootai o tsukamu** to get at the bottom of an affair.

**shootai** invitation; **shootai suru** to invite.

**shooten** focus; **shooten o awaseru** to focus; to bring into focus.

**shooten** shop, store.

**shootoo** putting out lights; **shootoo suru** to put out the light; **shootoorei** curfew.

**shoototsu** collision, crash; conflict; **iken no shoototsu** conflict of opinions; **shoototsu suru** to run into; to collide.

**shoouindoo** show window.

**shooyo** reward; giving a reward; **shooyo o ataeru** to give a reward.

**shooyoo** commerce, business; **shooyoo no** commercial; pertaining to business.

**SHOOYU** soy sauce.

**shoozen** sadly, sorrowfully; **shoozen to** with a heavy heart, sadly.

**shoozoo** portrait; likeness; **shoozoo o kakeru** to have one's portrait painted.

**shoozuru** to produce; to yield; to grow; to arise; to spring up.

**shori** management; transaction; treatment; **shori suru** to manage; to treat.

**shoron** preface, introduction.

**shorui** documents, papers.

**shosai** study, library.

**shoseki, HON** books.

**shosen** in the end; after all.

**shoshin** belief, conviction.

**shoshinsha** beginner, novice.

**shosuru** to conduct oneself; to deal with; to condemn, sentence.

**shotai** household; **shotaidoogu** household necessities; **shotaijimiru** to be sobered down by household cares; **shotaimochi** family person; **shotaimochi ga ii** to be a good housekeeper; **shotainushi** head of a household.

**shotaimen** first interview; **shotaimen no hito** a stranger.

**SHOTCHUU** (colloq.) always; often; all the time. **Shotchuu kaze o hikimasu.** I catch cold often.

**shoten** bookshop.

**shotoku** income; earnings; **shotokuzei** income tax.

**shotoo** elementary.

**shou** to carry on the back.

**shoyoo no** necessary, requisite, needed.

**shoyuu** possession; **shoyuu suru** to have; to possess; **shoyuuchi** one's land; one's estate; **shoyuuhin** belongings; **shoyuuken**
property; proprietorship, ownership; **shoyuusha** proprietor.

**shozai** whereabouts; site, position; situation. **shozai o hakken suru** to discover (someone's) whereabouts; **shozai o kuramasu** to conceal (one's own) whereabouts.

**shozaichi** site, locality.

**shozaifumei no** missing.

**shozoku** one's post, one's attachment; **shozoku no** attached to, belonging to, **shozoku saseru** to attach; to put under the control of.

**shozon** opinion; view; intention; **shozon o akasu** to tell one's real intention; **shozon o tazuneru** to ask (someone's) opinion about.

**shu** lord; chief; principal; master; **shu to shite** mainly, chiefly.

**shubi** course of an event; **shubi yoku** successfully; luckily.

**shuchoo** assertion; maintenance; opinion; **shuchoo o toosu** to impose one's opinion on someone else; **shuchoo suru** to assert, to maintain; to advocate; to insist upon.

**shudai** subject, theme.

**SHUDAN** means, way; measures, steps. **shudan o miidasu** to find the means to; **shudan o toru** to take means.

**shuei** guard; **shuei suru** to keep guard.

**shuen** feast, banquet; cocktail party; **shuen o moyoosu** to hold a cocktail party.

**shuen** starring, playing the leading part.

**SHUFU** housewife.

**shufu** capital, metropolis.

**shugei** manual arts; handicraft.

**shugi** principle; ism; **shugi o mamoru** to stick to one's principles.

**shugo** protection, guard; **shugo suru** to protect, watch over.

**shuhitsu** chief editor.

**shuisho** prospectus.

**SHUJIN** master; employer; one's husband.

**shujinkoo** hero, heroine (in a novel).

**shujin'yaku** host, hostess.

**shuju no** various, several, sundry.

**shujutsu** surgical operation.

**shukan** subjectivity; subjective view; **shukanteki** subjective.

**shukei** paymaster; accountant.

**shuken** sovereignty; **shukensha** supreme ruler; chief of state.

**shuki** memorandum, note; **shuki o kaku** to make a memorandum of.

**shukka** outbreak of fire; **shukka suru** to start a fire.

**shukke** (Buddhist) priest.

**shukketsu** bleeding, hemorrhage; **shukketsu**

**suru** to bleed; **shukketsu o tomeru** to stop bleeding.

**shukkin** attendance (at the office); **shukkin suru** to go to work; **shukkinbo** attendance record, time book; **shukkin jikan** office-going hour.

**shukkoo** departure of a ship from a port; **shukkoo suru** to sail.

**shukoo** plan, idea, contrivance; **shukoo o korasu** to devise a plan.

**shukoo** handiwork, handicraft, manual work.

**shukuboo** cherished desire.

**shukuboo o tassuru** to attain a cherished desire.

**shukuchoku** night duty; **shukuchoku suru** to keep night watch; to be on night duty; **shukuchokuin** person on night duty.

**shukudai** homework; **shukadai ni suru** to reserve for future discussion; to keep in abeyance.

**shukuden** congratulatory telegram.

**shukufuku** blessing; **shukufuku sareta** blessed, happy; **shukufuku suru** to bless.

**shukuhai** toast (congratulatory cup); **shukuhai o ageru** to drink a toast.

**shukuhaku** lodging, accommodation; **shukuhaku suru** to put up for the night; to lodge; **shukuhakunin** lodger; **shukuhakuryoo** room and board; lodging charge; hotel bill.

**shukujitsu** holiday.

**shukumei** fate, destiny; predestination; **shukumei no** predestined; **shukumeiron** fatalism; **shukumerion sha** fatalist.

**shukun** distinguished service; meritorious deeds.

**shukusatsuban** pocket-sized edition of a book; monthly bound edition of newspapers.

**shukusha** residence; lodging house; billet.

**shukusha** drawing on a small scale.

**shukushoo** reduction, curtailment; **shukushoo suru** to reduce; to retrench; to curtail.

**shukusuru** to congratulate.

**shukuten** celebration; commemoration; **shukuten o ageru** to celebrate.

**shukutoo** benediction.

**shukuzu** reduced drawing; reduced copy.

**SHUMI** taste; interest; **shumi no aru** tasteful; **shumi no nai** tasteless, dull; **shumi o motsu** to have taste for; to like.

**shumoku** items; article.

**shun** season; **shun no yasai** vegetables in season.

**shunin** person in charge; responsible official.

**shunkan** moment, instant; **shunkan ni** in a moment; **shunkan no** momentary, instantaneous.

**shunoo** brains; soul; leader. **Tanaka-san wa sono jigyoo no shunoo to natte iru.** Mr. Tanaka is the driving force of that enterprise.

**shunretsu na** unrelenting; rigorous; drastic.

**shuppan** publication; **shuppan suru** to publish, issue; **shuppansha** publisher.

**shuppan** sailing; **shuppan suru** to sail, to set sail.

**shuppatsu** departure; starting; **shuppatsu suru** to depart; to leave; to start; **shuppatsuten** starting point.

**shuppei** dispatch of troops.

**shuren** dexterity.

**shurui** kind, sort, variety; **arayuru shurui no** all kinds of; **onaji shurui no** of the same kind.

**shuryoku** main force; main body.

**shuryoo** hunting; shooting; **shuryooka** hunter.

**shusai** sponsorship; **-no shusai de** under the auspices of.

**SHUU** week.

**shuukyoku** end, conclusion; **shuukyoku no** last, final; **shuukyoku o tsugeru** to come to an end.

**shuunyuu** income; receipts; revenue; **shuunyuu ga ooi** to enjoy a comfortable income.

**shuuressha** last train.

**shuuri** repair; **shuuri suru** to repair, mend.

**shuuryoo** completion; **shuuryoo suru** to complete the course of.

**shuusai** genius; talented person.

**shuusaku** study.

**shuusan** gathering and dispersion.

**shuusanchi** distributing center.

**shuusei** amendment; revision; modification; **shuusei suru** to amend; to revise; to modify; **shuuseian** amendment (to a bill).

**shuusen** recommendation; mediation; **shuusen suru** to recommend; to mediate.

**shuusen** end of war; **shuusen ni naru** to come to the end of a war.

**shuusengyoo** brokerage; commission agency; **shuusenryoo** commission; brokerage; **shuusenya** broker, commission agent; real estate agency; employment agency.

**shuusennin** go-between; middleman.

**shuushi** religion; sect, denomination.

**shuushi** income and expenditure. **Shuushi ga tsugunawanai.** We cannot make ends meet.

**shuushi** from beginning to end.

**shuushin** morality, ethics.

**shuushin** lifetime; all one's life; **shuushin chooeki** penal servitude for life; **shuushin kaiin** life member.

**shuushoku** securing employment; **shuushoku**

**suru** to secure a position in an office; to enter into service.

**shuushuku** contraction, shrinking; **shuushuku suru** to contract; to shrink.

**shuushuu** collection; **shuushuu suru** to collect; to gather.

**shuutai** unseemly sight; shameful conduct; scandalous condition; **shuutai o enzuru** to behave disgracefully.

**shuuten** terminal point.

**SHUUTO** father-in-law; **SHUUTOME** mother-in-law.

**shuutoo na** cautious; scrupulous, thorough; **shuutoo na chuui** scrupulous (meticulous) care.

**shuuu** shower; **shuuu ni au** to be caught in a shower.

**shuuwai** acceptance of a bribe; graft; **shuuwai suru** to take a bribe.

**shuuya** all night; whole night through; **shuuya unten** all-night service (for trolley cars, buses).

**shuuyoo** culture; cultivation; **shuuyoo o tsumu** to make a constant effort to improve oneself; **shuuyoo suru** to cultivate.

**shuuyoo** accommodation, reception; **shuuyoo suru** to take in; to quarter.

**shuuyooryoku** capacity.

**shuuzei** collection of taxes; **shuuzei suru** to collect taxes; **shuuzeiri** tax collector.

**shuuzen** repair; mending; **shuuzen suru** to repair; to mend.

**shuwan** ability, skill, talent; **shuwan no aru** able, capable, talented.

**shuyoo na** chief; important; essential.

**shuzoku** race; family; class.

**shuzooka** sake brewer.

**soaku na** crude, coarse; inferior.

**SOBA** buckwheat; dark buckwheat noodles; **kake soba** buckwheat noodles served in soup; **mori soba** buckwheat noodles served with soup but in a separate container.

**SOBA** side; neighborhood, proximity; **soba ni, soba de** at hand, beside; **soba no** neighboring.

**sobadateru** to prick up one's ears; **mimi o sobadatete kiku** to strain one's ears to listen.

**sobieru** to rise; to tower; to soar. **Yama ga takaku sobieru.** The mountain towers.

**SOBO** grandmother.

**soboku** simplicity, artlessness; **soboku na** simple, artless.

**soburi** behavior; bearing; manner; **soburi o suru** to behave oneself; to assume the air of.

**sobyoo** rough sketch.

**sochi** management; disposal; dealing.

**SOCHIRA, SOTCHI** there; that way.

**sodachi** breeding, bringing up; **sodachi no warui** ill-bred; of slow growth; **sodachi no yoi** well-bred; of good social background.

**SODATERU** to bring up, raise; to train; **hana o sodateru** to grow flowers; **kodomo o sodateru** to bring up a child.

**SODATSU** to grow; to be brought up.

**SODE** sleeve; **sode ni sugaru** to hang on a person's sleeve; to beg for mercy; **sode o hiku** to pull (someone) by the sleeve.

**soen** long negligence; **soen ni naru** to neglect to visit.

**soeru** to add; to affix, attach; **chikara o soeru** to give a person assistance; **kyoo o soeru** to liven up the entertainment.

**SOFU** grandfather; **SOFUBO** grandparents.

**sogai** check; obstruction, impediment; **sogai suru** to check; to obstruct, impede.

**sogeki** sniping; **sogeki suru** to aim and shoot; to fire at; to snipe.

**sogo** discrepancy; disappointment, failure; **sogo suru** to go wrong; to be in disagreement.

**sogu** to chip; to cut aslant; to diminish, reduce; **kyoomi o sogu** to spoil the pleasure.

**sokkenai** cold; blunt; dry; curt; **sokkenai aisatsu** curt salutation.

**sokki** shorthand, stenography; **sokkiroku** shorthand records; stenographic transcript; **sokkisha** stenographer.

**sokkin** spot cash; **sokkin de harau** to pay cash.

**sokkoojo** meteorological station, weather bureau.

**SOKKURI** whole; just as it is; altogether; **jitsubutsu sokkuri** to be true to life.

**sokkyookyoku** improvisation (in music).

**SOKO** that place, there; **soko e** there, to that place; **soko kara** from there; **soko ni, soko de** there, in that place.

**soko** bottom, depth; sole (shoe); **sokoshirenu** bottomless, unpredictable; **kokoro no soko kara** from the bottom of one's heart.

**sokode** now; then; thereupon; accordingly.

**sokoi** underlying motive; true intention.

**sokoiji** spite, malice; **sokoiji no warui** malicious, spiteful.

**sokojikara** latent (potential) energy; reserve of force; **sokojikara no aru** strong; energetic **sokojikara no aru koe** deep (tone of) voice.

**sokoku** one's native land; **sokokuai** love of the native land.

**sokonau** to harm, hurt, injure, damage, spoil, ruin.

**sokonuke sawagi** boisterous merrymaking.

**sokoo** conduct, behavior; **sokoo ga osamaranai** to conduct oneself improperly.

**SOKORA, SOKORA ATARI** thereabouts; about there.

**soko soko ni** hastily, hurriedly.

**sokotsu** carelessness, heedlessness; **sokotsu na** careless, heedless.

**-SOKU** counter denoting: pair (for shoes, socks, and stockings); **kutsu issoku** one pair of shoes.

**sokubai suru** to sell on the spot.

**sokubaku** restriction, restraint; **sokubaku sareru** to be restricted; **sokubaku suru** to restrict.

**sokudo** speed, velocity.

**sokui** accession to the throne.

**sokuji** at once, immediately.

**sokujitsu** same day; on the very same day.

**sokumen** side, flank; **sokumen no** lateral, flanking.

**sokuryoku** speed, velocity; **sokuryoku o choosetsu suru** to regulate the speed.

**sokuryoo** land survey; **sokuryoo suru** to measure; to survey; **sokuryooshi** surveyor.

**sokusei** rapid completion; quick mastery; **sokusei kooza** intensive course.

**sokuseki** footprint.

**sokushi** instantaneous death; **sokushi suru** to die instantly.

**sokushin** promotion; acceleration, hastening; **sokushin suru** to promote; to further; **shokuyoku o sokushin suru** to stimulate the appetite.

**sokutatsu, sokutatsu yuubin** special delivery; **sokutatsu de** by special delivery; **sokutatsu de dasu** to send by special delivery.

**sokutei** measurement; **sokutei suru** to measure.

**sokutoo** prompt answer, ready reply; **sokutoo suru** to reply at once.

**SOKUZA NI** at once, immediately, instantly.

**somaru** to be dyed, be colored; to be infected with.

**SOMATSU** crudeness, coarseness; **somatsu na** crude; coarse; poor; **somatsu ni suru** to treat lightly; to handle roughly.

**some** dye; dyeing; **some ga yoi** to be well dyed, **someko** dyestuff, dye.

**someru** to dye; to stain.

**sometsuke** dyeing; printing; blue-and-white porcelain.

**SOMOSOMO** in the first place.

**somukeru** to turn away, avert; **kao o somukeru** to turn one's face away.

**SOMUKU** to revolt against; to rise against; to act contrary to; to disobey; to violate; **ryooshin ni somuku** to go against one's principles.

**son** loss, damage; disadvantage; **son na** disadvantageous; **son ni naru** to be disadvantageous to; **son o suru** to suffer a loss.

**sonaeru** to prepare; to provide for; **igen o sonaeru** to possess great dignity; **man'ichi ni sonaeru** to prepare for the worst.

**sonaeru** to offer (to the altar).

**sonaetsukeru** to provide with; to equip with.

**sonawaru** to be furnished with, be supplied with.

**sonboo** existence; life or death fate; **sonboo ni kansuru mondai** a question of life or death; **sonboo ni kansuru** to decide the fate.

**sonchoo** esteem, respect; appreciation; **sonchoo suru** to esteem, respect.

**sonchoo** village headman; mayor.

**sondai** haughtiness, arrogance; **sondai na** arrogant, haughty; **sondai ni kamaeru** to have a haughty bearing.

**son'eki** profit and loss; loss and gain; **son'eki o keisan suru** to calculate profit and loss.

**songai** damage, injury; loss; **songai baishoo** compensation for damages; **songai baishoo o yookyuu suru** to sue for damages; **songai o ataeru** to do damage; **songai o koomuru** to suffer a loss.

**sonjiru** See **sonzuru.**

**sonkai** village assembly.

**SONKEI** respect; high regard; honor; **sonkei suru** to respect, esteem, honor; **sonkei sareru** to be respected.

**sonmin** villagers.

**SONNA** that sort of, such; of the kind, of the sort; **sonna hito** such a person; a person like that; **sonna ni** so; in that way; so much; particularly.

**SONO** that, those; **sono ba** that place; **sono ba de** then and there; on the spot; **sono go** after that, afterward; from that time on; **sono go no** later; **sono hen** about, thereabouts; **sono hoka** besides, beyond, moreover; **sono hoka no** other, another; **sono hoka wa** the rest, the others; **sono koro** around that time; in those days; **sono koro no** of that time; **sono kuse** and yet, notwithstanding; **sono mama** as it is, in that condition; **sono mama ni shite oku** to leave as it is; **sono ta** besides, moreover; beyond; **sono te** that trick [that hand]; that device; **sono toori** just so; exactly in that way; **sono uchi ni** before long; by and by; in the meantime; **Sono te wa kuwanu.** None of your games! I'm not so easily cheated. **Sono ue no koto wa yakusoku**

**dekimasen.** I can't promise any more than that.

**sonryoo** hire, rent (tools, articles); **sonryoo de kariru** to hire; **sonryoo de kasu** to hire out; to rent out.

**sonshitsu** loss, damage; disadvantage.

**sonshoo** injury, damage, casualty; **sonshoo o koomuru** to be damaged; **sonshoo suru** to injure, damage.

**sonsuru** to exist; to remain.

**sontoku** loss and gain, profit and loss; **sontoku no mondai de wa nai** not to be a question of money.

**sonzai** existence; **sonzai suru** to exist; to remain.

**sonzoku** continuance; **sonzoku suru** to continue; to last.

**sonzuru** to be worn out, be damaged.

**SOO** that way; so; idea; **soo iu** that sort of; **soo iu wake de** for that reason. **Soo desu.** That is so. **Soo shite kudasai.** Please do so.

**soo** thought, conception; **soo o neru** to meditate, to work on a plan.

**soo** bonze; priest, monk.

**soo** layer, stratum, seam.

**sooan** draft; rough cast.

**sooba** current price; quotation; speculation; **sooba ni te o dasu** to engage in speculation; **soobashi** speculator.

**sooban** sooner or later; by and by.

**soobetsukai** farewell meeting; farewell dinner.

**soochi** arrangement, equipment; **soochi suru** to equip with; to arrange.

**soochoo** university president.

**soochoo** early morning; **soochoo ni** early in the morning.

**soochoo na** solemn; sublime.

**sooda** soda; bicarbonate of soda.

**soodai** representative; deputy; **soodai ni naru** to represent.

**soodan** consultation, conference; **soodan no ue** after consultation; **soodan suru** to consult, confer; **soodan ni noru** to take part in a consultation.

**soodasui** soda water.

**soodoo** confusion, disorder; disturbance; **soodoo o okosu** to raise a disturbance.

**soodooin** general mobilization.

**soofu** sending; **soofu suru** to send; to forward.

**soogakari de** full force; with a united force; everybody participating.

**soogaku** musical performance; music.

**soogaku** total amount; sum total.

**soogankyoo** binoculars.

**soogawa** whole leather.

**soogei** sending off and welcoming (people).

**soogi** funeral service; **soogi o okonau** to hold

a funeral service; **soogisha, soogiya** undertaker.

**soogi** dispute; quarrel; conflict; (labor) strike; **soogidan** strikers.

**soogo** reciprocity; **soogo no** mutual, reciprocal.

**soogon** grandeur; solemnity; **soogon na** magnificent; grand; solemn.

**soogoo** looks, features; **soogoo o kuzushite warau** to smile gleefully; to be radiant with joy.

**soogoo** synthesis; putting together; **soogoo suru** to put together.

**soogoo daigaku** university.

**soogyoo** start of an enterprise.

**soohaku** paleness; **soohaku na** deadly pale.

**soohoo** both parties; both sides; each side; **soohoo no** either; both; mutual.

**sooi** difference, disparity; **-ni sooi nai** must be, it is certain that; **sooi naku** certainly; without fail; **-to sooi suru** to differ; to disagree; to be contrary to.

**sooi** new device; novel idea; originality.

**SOOJI** cleaning; sweeping; **sooji o suru** to clean; to sweep.

**soojishoku** general resignation; **soojishoku o suru** to resign in a body.

**soojite** generally; in general; for the most part.

**soojuku** premature growth, precocity; **soojuku no** precocious.

**soojuu** management; control; manipulation; **soojuu suru** to manage; to handle; to control; **kikai o soojuu suru** to operate a machine; **otto o soojuu suru** to manage one's husband; **soojuushi** pilot; manipulator.

**sookai** freshness; exhilaration; **sookai na** refreshing, enlivening; **sookai ni suru** to refresh; to exhilarate, enliven; **sookai ni naru** to be refreshed.

**sookai** general meeting; general assembly.

**sookan** first publication (of a new magazine, paper, etc.); **sookangoo** initial number (issue) of a magazine.

**sookan** deportation; **sookan suru** to send back; to deport.

**sookan** grand sight.

**sookatsu** summary; **sookatsu suru** to sum up; to summarize.

**SOOKEI** total; sum total; **sookei de** in all, as a total; **sookei suru** to sum up; to total.

**sooken** healthiness; **sooken na** healthy, sound, stout.

**sookin** remittance; **sookin suru** to remit money; to send money.

**sooko** warehouse; **sooko ni azukeru** to store in a warehouse; **sooko ni hokan suru** to store.

**sookon** early marriage.

**sookoo** manuscript; copy; **sookoo o tsukuru** to draft; to make a draft.

**SOO KOO SURU UCHI NI** in the meantime; meanwhile.

**sookutsu** den, lair; nest; **doroboo no sookutsu** den of thieves.

**sookuzure** collapse, complete rout; **sookuzure ni naru** to be routed.

**sookyo** daring enterprise.

**soomei** wisdom, sagacity; **soomei na** wise, clearheaded.

**soomen** Japanese noodle (popular in summer).

**soomoku** plants and trees.

**soomokuroku** general table of contents.

**soomu** general affairs; director; manager.

**soonan** meeting with an accident; mishap. **soonan suru** to meet with an accident; **soonansha** victim of an accident; **soonan shingoo** signal of distress.

**soonen** prime of life.

**soonyuu** insertion; **sooyuu suru** to insert, put in.

**sooon** noise, hubbub.

**soooo** fitness, suitability; **soooo na** appropriate, adequate; **soooo suru** to be suitable, to be fitting.

**sooran** superintendence, control; **sooran suru** to superintend, manage.

**soorei** splendor, magnificence; **soorei na** magnificent, splendid.

**sooretsu** funeral procession.

**sooretsu na** heroic, tragic; **sooretsu na saigo o togeru** to die a heroic death.

**sooritsu** establishment, foundation; institution; organization; **sooritsu suru** to establish, institute, found; **sooritsusha** founder.

**sooron** introduction; general remarks; quarrel, dispute; **sooron suru** to quarrel; to argue.

**sooryo** priest, monk, bonze.

**sooryooji** consul-general; **sooryoojikan** consulate-general.

**soosa** search, investigation; **soosa suru** to search, look for, hunt for.

**soosa** process, operation, management.

**soosai** general manager; president; governor.

**soosaku** creation; original work; **soosaku suru** to create; to originate; to write an original work; **soosakuka** person of originality; fiction writer; **soosakuteki** creative, original.

**soosaku** search, investigation; **soosaku suru** to search, to look for, to hunt for; **soosakutai** search party.

**soosenkyo** general election.

**sooshihainin** general manager.

**sooshiki** funeral; funeral services.

**sooshin** transmission of a message; telegraphic service.

**sooshingu** personal ornaments, furnishings.

**SOOSHITE, SOSHITE** and then; and in addition.

**sooshitsu** loss; forfeiture; **sooshitsu suru** to lose; to be lost.

**soosho** series (of books); collected works.

**sooshoku** ornamentation, decoration, adornment; **sooshoku no nai** plain, unadorned; **sooshoku suru** to ornament, adorn, decorate.

**sooshuunyuu** total income.

**soosoo** early; as soon as possible; without delay.

**soosu** Worcestershire sauce.

**soosuu** total number.

**sootaiteki** relative; correlative.

**sootatsu** conveyance; delivery; **sootatsu suru** to send; to forward; to convey.

**sootei** binding; design; **sootei suru** to bind; to design.

**sooto** daring enterprise.

**sootoku** governor-general; viceroy.

**SOOTOO** fitness, suitability; **sootoo na, sootoo no** suitable; respectable; reasonable; moderate; considerable; **sootoo ni kurashite iru** to be comfortably off; **sootoo suru** to be fit for.

**sootoo** sweeping away; **sootoo suru** to sweep away.

**soowa** episode.

**soozai** daily dishes.

**soozen** noisily; uproariously; **soozen to** in a noisy manner.

**soozoku** succession; inheritance; **soozoku suru** to inherit; to succeed; **zaisan o soozoku suru** to inherit an estate.

**soozokunin** heir, heiress.

**soozoo** creation; **soozoo suru** to create.

**soozoo** imagination; fancy; **soozoo ni tomu** imaginative; **soozoo suru** to imagine, fancy; **soozooryoku** power of imagination.

**soozooshii** noisy, full of noise.

**sopurano** soprano.

**SORA!** there! **Sora miro!** There! You see! I told you so *(colloq.)*!

**SORA** sky; air; heavens; **sora de** by heart, by memory; **sora takaku** high up in the sky; **sora de oboeru** to learn by heart; **sora de yomu** to recite from memory.

**soradanomi** hoping against hope; vain hope.

**sorairo** sky blue, azure.

**soramoyoo** look of the sky; weather; situation.

**sorasu** to evade, elude, dodge; to turn aside; to draw off; **hanashi o waki ni sorasu** to turn the talk away; **me o sorasu** to look away;

to avert one's eyes from; **shitsumon o sorasu** to parry a question.

**sorasu** to bend, to curve; to turn backward.

**sorazorashii** feigned; false; hypocritical; **sorazorashiku** in obvious dissimulation, hypocritically.

**SORE** it, that; **sore da kara** therefore, accordingly; **sore dake** that much, so much; **sore na noni** yet, in spite of that; **sore demo** still, yet; **sore hodo** so much, so; **sore kara** and then, after that; **sore made** till that time; **sore nara** then, if so; **sore ni** besides that; **sore tomo** or else.

**soreru** to stray; to glance off.

**sori** warp; curve; bend; **sori ga au** to get along (with each other) very well; **sori ga awanai** not to be on good terms (with someone).

**sorimi** straightening oneself up; holding one's head high; **sorimi ni naru** to throw back one's head.

**soroban** abacus; finance; **soroban o toreru** to pay; to be profitable; **soroban o hajiku** to move counters of an abacus; to calculate. **Soroban ga awanai.** The accounts do not square.

**soroeru** to put in order, arrange in order.

**soroi** set; suit; **soroi mo sorotte** without exception; **soroi no** of the same pattern, uniform.

**SOROSORO** slowly, gradually; gently.

**sorou** to become complete; to be arranged in order; to gather, assemble; to agree, be in accord.

**soru** to bend; to warp; to bend backward. **Hi ni atatte ita ga sorimashita.** The sun has warped the board.

**soru** to shave; **kao o soru** to shave oneself.

**soryaku** roughness; **soryaku no** rough, cursory; **soryaku ni** roughly.

**sosei** resuscitation; reanimation; revival; **sosei suru** to revive, come to life again; **sosei no omoi o suru** to feel revived, to feel a great relief.

**soseihin** article of inferior quality.

**sosen** ancestor.

**soshaku** chewing, mastication; **soshaku suru** to chew, masticate.

**soshakuchi** leased ground.

**soshakuken** lease.

**soshi** obstruction; check, prevention; **soshi suru** to check; to hold in check; to hinder, impede.

**soshiki** system; organization; formation; composition; **soshiki suru** to form; to organize; to constitute; **soshikiteki** systematic; methodical; **soshikiteki ni suru** to systematize.

**soshiru** to slander; to blame, speak ill of.

**SOSHITE** See **SOOSHITE.**

**soshitsu** predisposition; nature; makings. **Ano hito ni wa shijin no soshitsu ga aru.** He is very poetic. (He has the poet in him.)

**soshoku** plain diet; **soshoku suru** to eat poorly (live on poor fare).

**soshoo** lawsuit; action; case; **soshoo o okosu** to sue; **soshoo suru** to sue; to start a lawsuit; to go to law.

**sosogu** to pour into; to pour on; to water; to pour (itself) into.

**sosokkashii** hasty; careless; heedless; **sosokkashii koto o suru** to act carelessly; to make a stupid mistake.

**sosonokasu** to tempt, entice; to stir up.

**sosoru** to incite, stir up, to excite.

**sossen suru** to take the lead; to take the initiative.

**sosui** drainage.

**SOTCHI, SOCHIRA** there; that way.

**sotchinoke** laying aside; neglecting; **sotchinoke ni suru** to neglect; to leave out in the cold.

**sotchoku** plainness, frankness, candidness; **sotchoku na** simple and honest; **sotchoku ni hanasu** to speak frankly.

**SOTO** out of doors, outside; **soto e iku** go outside.

**sotobori** outer moat (around Japanese castles).

**sotogawa** outer side; outside.

**sotoumi** open sea.

**sotsu** waste; bungling; fault; **sotsu ga nai** to be faultless.

**sotsugyoo** graduation; completion of a course of study; **sotsugyoo suru** to complete a course; to graduate from; **sotsugyoosei** graduate, alumnus; **sotsugyoo shiki** graduation ceremony; commencement; **sotsugyoo shoosho** certificate; diploma.

**sotsuu** understanding; **sotsuu suru** to understand (each other); **ishi ga sotsuu suru** to come to a good mutual understanding.

**SOTTO** quietly; softly; gently; secretly; **sotto shite oku** to leave it as it is.

**sottoo** fainting; **sottoo suru** to faint.

**sowasowa** nervously; restlessly; **sowasowa suru** to be restless; to be nervous.

**soyogu** to rustle; to wave.

**soyoo** grounding; elementary knowledge; culture; **soyoo ga aru** to be well grounded in.

**soyosoyo to** softly, gently (said only of the blowing of the wind); **soyosoyo fuku kaze** gentle breeze.

**sozei** taxes; taxation.

**su** sandbank; shallow; **su ni noriageru** to run aground.

**su** vinegar.

**su** nest; den; **su ni tsuku** to brood, incubate; **su o tsukuru** to build a nest.

**suashi** barefoot; **suashi de** barefoot(ed).

**subarashii** splendid, magnificent.

**subashikkoi, subayai** nimble; active, smart; quick-witted.

**subayai** See **subashikkoi**.

**subekkoi** smooth; slippery; velvety.

**suberikomu** to slide into; to slip into.

**suberu** to slide; to slip; to glide.

**subesube shita** smooth; velvety.

**SUBETE** whole, all; altogether; **subete no** all; whole; every.

**sudare** bamboo blind; **sudare o kakeru** to hang a bamboo blind; **sudare o maku** to roll up a bamboo blind.

**sude** empty hand; **sude de** unarmed, empty-handed.

**SUDENI** already.

**sudoori** passing by without calling; **sudoori suru** to pass by without calling (at someone's house).

**SUE** end; future; **sue ni wa** in the long run, **sue no** last; final; youngest; **sue no aru wakamono** a promising youth.

**suekko** youngest son, youngest daughter.

**sueru** to set, place, lay.

**suetsuke** fitting up; installation; **suetsuke no** fixed, stationary.

**suetsukeru** to fit up; to set, place in position.

**sugao** unpainted face.

**sugaru** to cling to; to lean on.

**sugata** form, figure, shape; **sugata o kaeru** to disguise oneself; **sugata o kakusu** to disappear.

**sugenai** cold; rough; flat; **sugenaku** coldly, roughly; flatly; **sugenaku kotowaru** to refuse flatly.

**sugi** cryptomeria; Japanese cedar.

**-SUGIRU** suffix denoting: be excessively, do (something) excessively; **omosugiru** to be too heavy; **tabesugiru** to eat excessively.

**sugiru** to pass by; to go too far.

**SUGOI** uncanny, weird; ghastly, lurid; **sugoi hikari** lurid light.

**sugosu** to pass, spend (time); to take too much.

**sugosugo** dejectedly; disconsolately; with a heavy heart.

**SUGU** soon; immediately; close by; near; **sugu hana no saki ni** just under one's nose; **sugu ni** immediately, instantly.

**sugureru** to surpass, excel; to be excellent; to be strong.

**sugurete** eminently; conspicuously; by far.

**suhada** bare skin; **suhada ni naru** to bare oneself; **suhada ni kiru** to wear next to the skin.

**suhadaka** nudity; state of being stark naked; **suhadaka de** stark naked.

**sui** essence; pith; elegance; fashion; **sui na** fashionable; refined, tasteful; **sui o kikasu** to pardon (someone else's) folly.

**sui** sour, acid; **sui mo amai mo shirinuita hito** person who has tasted the bitter and the sweet of life.

**suiageru** to suck up.

**suichoku no** perpendicular, vertical.

**suichuu** (*n.*) being in the water; **suichuu no** (*adj.*) underwater; **suichuu ni** (*adv.*) underwater.

**suidasu** to suck out.

**suiden** paddy field, rice field.

**SUIDOO** water service; waterworks; city water; channel; **suidoo o hiku** to have water pipes laid; to have water supplied; **suidookan** water pipe.

**suiei** swimming; **suieigi** bathing suit; **suieijoo** swimming place.

**suifu** sailor, seaman; **suifu ni naru** to become a sailor.

**suigai** damage by flood; flood disaster; **suigaichi** flooded district.

**suigen, suigenchi** source of a river; fountainhead.

**suihei** water level; horizon; **suihei no** level, horizontal; **suihei ni** horizontally.

**suihei** sailor (in the navy); **suiheifuku** seaman's uniform.

**suiheisen** horizon; sealine; horizontal line.

**suihen** waterside.

**suijaku** emaciation, debility; **suijaku suru** to be weakened; to grow weak.

**suiji** cooking, cookery; **suiji gakari** person in charge of cooking; cook; **suiji suru** to cook; **suijiba** kitchen.

**suijooki** vapor, steam.

**suijun** water level.

**suika** watermelon.

**suikan** drunken fellow.

**suiki** moisture, humidity; dropsy; **suiki no aru** moist, humid; **suiki ga dekiru** to become dropsical.

**suikomu** to inhale; to draw in; to absorb; to suck in.

**suikoo** execution; **suikoo suru** to execute, carry out.

**suikuchi** mouthpiece; cigar holder.

**suikyo** recommendation; **suikyo ni yotte** through (someone's) recommendation. **suikyo suru** to recommend.

**suikyoo** drunken frenzy; whim, vagary; **suikyoo de** out of mere pique; just for kicks; **suikyoo na** frenzied with drink.

**suimen** water surface; **suimen kara ichi meetoru ue** one meter above the water; **suimen ni ukabu** to rise to the surface.

**SUIMIN** sleep; **suiminbusoku** want of sleep.
**suimon** floodgate.
**SUIMONO** soup (Japanese style); **suimono wan** soup bowl. (See also **suupu**.)
**suinan** calamity by water; casualty at sea.
**suiri** reasoning; induction; **suiri suru** to reason; to induce.
**suiro** waterway; watercourse.
**suiron** reasoning; **suiron suru** to reason; to deduce.
**suiryoku** hydraulic power; **suiryoku denki** hydroelectricity.
**suiryoo** guess, conjecture; **suiryoo suru** to guess; to presume; to consider.
**suiryoo** quantity of water, volume of water.
**suiryuu** stream; water current.
**suisaiga** watercolor painting; **suisaigaka** watercolor painter.
**suisanbutsu** marine products: fish, crabs, lobsters, clams, oysters, seaweeds.
**suisangyoo** fishery; marine products industry. (See also **suisanbutsu**.)
**suisatsu** guess, conjecture; sympathy; **suisatsu suru** to conjecture, to guess, to infer from.
**suisentoire** flush toilet.
**suisen** recommendation; **suisen suru** to recommend; **suisenjoo** letter of recommendation.
**suisen** daffodil.
**suisha** water mill, water wheel.
**suishin** depth of water.
**suishinki** propeller; screw.
**suishoo** recommendation; approval; praise; **suishoo suru** to recommend; to praise.
**suishoo** crystal; **suishoo no yoo na** crystalline, crystal-like.
**suisoku** conjecture, supposition; inference; **suisoku suru** to conjecture; to suppose.
**suisoo** water tank, cistern.
**Suisu** Switzerland; **Suisu no** (*adj.*) Swiss; **Suisujin** Swiss (person).
**suitai** decline; decay; **suitai suru** to decline; to decay; to fall.
**suitchi** switch.
**suitei** presumption; conclusion; **suitei suru** to presume; to conclude.
**suitoo** canteen.
**suitoo gakari** cashier, teller.
**suitorigami** blotting paper, blotter.
**suitoru** to suck up; to absorb.
**suitsuku** to stick fast to, adhere.
**suiun** transportation by water; **suiun no ben** facilities for transportation by water.
**Oosaka wa suiun no ben ga ii desu.** Osaka City has very good facilities for marine transportation.
**suiyaku** liquid medicine.
**suiyoku** cold water bath.
**SUIYOOBI** Wednesday.

**suizokukan** aquarium.
**SUJI** line; strips; muscle; sinew, tendon; fiber; plot; source, quarter.
**sujigaki** plot of a play.
**sujimukai no** See **sujimukoo no**.
**sujimukoo no** diagonally opposite; **sujimukoo no ie** a house diagonally across the street.
**sujoo** past career; one's past; birth; blood; origin; **sujoo no iyashii** of low birth; **sujoo no shirenai** of unknown character; **sujoo no yoi** of good family; of good birth.
**sukaafu** scarf.
**sukaato** skirt.
**sukashi** watermark; transparency; openwork; **sukashi no** watermarked.
**sukasu** to look through; to hold to the light; to thin out; to leave an opening.
**SUKEETO** skating; pair of skates; **sukeeto o suru** to skate.
**suketchi** sketch, sketching; **suketchi ni iku** to go sketching; **suketchi suru** to make a sketch.
**SUKI** fondness; love; fancy; taste; **suki na** (*adj.*) favorite, pet; **suki ni** as one pleases; at one's pleasure; **suki ni naru** to become fond of; **suki ni saseru** to let (someone) do as he or she pleases. **Suki desu.** I like it.
**suki** opening; crack; chance, opportunity; leisure; unguarded point; **suki ga nai** to find no chance; **suki o nerau** to watch for a chance.
**suki** spade, plow.
**sukihara** empty stomach.
**sukii** ski.
**sukikirai** likes and dislikes; **sukikirai no ooi** squeamish; finical, finicky, too particular.
**sukima** space; crevice; intermission; **sukima naku** leaving no space; compactly.
**sukitooru** to be transparent, be clear; **sukitootta** clear, transparent.
**SUKIYAKI** Japanese dish of meat and vegetables usually cooked on the table.
**sukizuki** taste, liking, fondness; matter of taste; **sukizuki ga aru** each to one's own taste. **Sore wa sukizuki desu.** It is a matter of taste.
**SUKKARI** completely, entirely.
**sukoburu** very, highly, extremely, awfully.
**SUKOSHI** little, few, bit; **sukoshi demo** any, even a little; **sukoshi no** a little, a few, slight; **sukoshi mo** not in the least (*used with a negative verb*); **sukoshi zutsu** little by little.
**Sukottorando** Scotland; **Sukottorando no** (*adj.*) Scots; of Scotland; **Sukottorandojin** Scot (person).
**SUKU** become empty; become sparse; **aida ga suku** to become separated; **te ga suku**

to be disengaged. **Onaka ga sukimashita.** I'm hungry. **Kono densha wa suite imasu.** This streetcar isn't crowded.

**sukui** help, rescue, relief, salvation; **sukui o motomeru** to ask for help, call for help; to seek salvation; **sukuinushi** savior, deliverer.

**sukuidasu** to help (someone) out of; to rescue.

**sukumu** to be cramped; to be paralyzed with fear.

**SUKUNAI** to be few, little, scanty, scarce. **Shuunyuu ga sukunai desu.** Her income is small.

**sukunakaranu** not a little; not small; considerable; much; **sukunakaranu meiwaku** considerable inconvenience; much trouble.

**SUKUNAKUTOMO** at least, to say the least.

**sukuramu** scrimmage; **sukuramu o kumu** to line up for a scrimmage.

**sukurin** movie screen.

**SUKUU** to help, save, rescue; to relieve; **sukuu koto no dekinai** hopeless.

**sukuu** to scoop, to ladle; to trip up.

**sumai** dwelling, residence, abode.

**sumanai** to be sorry for; to have no excuse for.

**sumaseru** to bring to an end.

**sumashita** affected, stuck-up; indifferent.

**SUMASU** to finish, conclude, get through. **Gohan wa sumasemashita.** We have finished our meal.

**sumasu** to clear, to clarify; to look demure, to be affected.

**sumau** to live, dwell.

**SUMI** India ink; ink stick (cake of ink used to prepare ink for brush writing); **sumi o suru** to rub an ink stick; **sumi o tsukeru** to dip in ink; to smear with ink.

**SUMI** charcoal; **sumiya** charcoal dealer.

**sumi** corner, nook; **sumi kara sumi made** every nook and corner; **sumi ni oku** to put in the corner.

**sumika** dwelling, residence.

**sumikomu** to live in an employer's house.

**SUMIMASEN** pardon me; I'm sorry. **Sumimasen ga enpitsu o kashite kudasai.** Pardon me—may I borrow your pencil?

**sumiyaka na** quick, rapid, swift, speedy, prompt.

**sumizumi** all the corners; every nook and corner. **Kono hen wa sumizumi made shitte imasu.** I know every nook and corner of this neighborhood.

**sumoo** Japanese wrestling; **sumoo o toru** to wrestle.

**SUMU** to reside, live. **Kono machi ni sunde imasu.** I live in this town. **Doko ni sunde imasu ka?** Where do you live?

**sumu** to end; to come to an end.

**sumu** to become clear (liquid).

**sun** Japanese inch (corresponds to 1.193 American inches). (No longer used.)

**SUNA** sand; **suna de migaku** to polish with sand; **suna o maku** to scatter sand.

**sunao** meekness, gentleness; **sunao ni** obediently, meekly; **sunao na** meek, gentle; **sunao ni suru** to obey; to be obedient.

**SUNAWACHI** namely, that is to say; nothing but; neither more nor less; thereupon.

**sune** leg; shin; **sune ni kizu o motsu mi** someone having a guilty conscience; **oya no sune o kajiru** to sponge off one's parents.

**suneru** to be peevish; to sulk; to be in a snit.

**sunka** moment's leisure; little time to spare; **sunka mo nai** to have no time to spare.

**su no mono** vinegary dish; vegetables seasoned with vinegar.

**sunpoo** measure, dimensions; **sunpoo o toru** to take measurements (for a new suit); **sunpoo no toori ni** according to the measurements; **sunpoogaki** measurement, specification.

**Supein** Spain; **Supeingo** Spanish (language); **Supeinjin** Spaniard.

**supootsu** sports; **supootsubangumi** sports program.

**suppadaka** nudity, nakedness.

**SUPPAI** sour, acid, tart. **Kono miruku wa suppaku natte imasu.** This milk has turned sour.

**suppanuku** to expose; to disclose.

**suppokasu** to leave undone; to neglect.

**suppon** snapping turtle.

**SUPUUN** spoon.

**-sura** particle denoting: even, so much as. **Kodomo sura shitte imasu.** Even a child knows it.

**surari to shita** slender, graceful.

**surasura** smoothly; without a hitch.

**surechigau** to pass by each other.

**surekkarashi** pert person.

**sureru** to rub; to graze; to be worn out.

**suri** pickpocket, cutpurse.

**suriherasu** to wear down; to wear away.

**surikireru** to get worn out; to become threadbare.

**surikomu** to rub in.

**surimono** printed matter; **surimono ni suru** to print.

**surimuku** to rub off; to chafe.

**surippu** slip (woman's undergarment).

**suriru** thrill.

**suritsubusu** to grind down; to rub out of shape; to dissipate one's fortune.

**SURU** to do; to play; to practice; to make; to

change one thing into another; to act as, officiate as. **Suru koto ga nai desu.** I have nothing to do. **Nihongo no benkyoo o shimashita.** I have studied Japanese. **Kyooto e iku koto ni shimashita.** I have decided to go to Kyoto. **Ano hito wa kyooshi o shite imasu.** He is a teacher. **Sore wa sen en shimasu.** It costs one thousand yen.

**suru** to print; to duplicate. **Meishi o sutte moraitai desu.** I would like to have visiting cards printed.

**suru** to pick (someone's) pocket.

**suru** to grind, to bray.

**suru** to rub, to file.

**suru** to lose one's fortune. **Kabu de okame o surimashita.** She lost her fortune on the stock market.

**surudoi** sharp, acute, keen, cutting.

**SURUTO** whereupon, just then; then; well. **Suruto minna de goman en desu ne?** Then the total will be fifty thousand yen, won't it?

**susamajii** alarming, dreadful, fearful, terrible.

**susamu** to grow in intensity or violence; to go to ruin; to grow wild; to be addicted to.

**susanda** ruined, desolate, dreary. **Susanda seikatsu o shite imasu.** He is living a wild life.

**suso** skirt (of a dress); bottom (of a mountain); **zubon no suso** trouser cuff.

**susu** soot; **susu darake no** sooty.

**susugu** to rinse; to wash.

**susukeru** to be stained with soot; **susuboketa, susuketa** smutty.

**susumeru** to promote; to advance, put forward; to put on (a watch); **kooshoo o susumeru** to proceed with the negotiations.

**susumeru** to recommend; to advise, to counsel; to encourage, to present, to offer.

**susumu** to progress, advance, go forward.

**susunde** of one's own accord; willingly.

**susurinaki** sobbing; **susurinaki o suru** to sob.

**susurinaku** to sob; to whimper.

**sutaa** star (of movies or stage).

**sutaato** (*n.*) start (in a sport); **sutaato o kiru** to start.

**sutajio** studio (for movies, broadcasting).

**sutanpu** stamp; datemark.

**sutareru** to fall into disuse; to go out of use or fashion.

**sutasuta to** quickly, hurriedly.

**sutebachi** despair; self-abandonment; **sutebachi ni naru** to abandon oneself to despair.

**sutebasho** dumping ground.

**sutego** deserted child; foundling.

**SUTEKI NA** splendid, brilliant, fine, remarkable, superb; **SUTEKI NI** exceedingly, remarkably; **suteki na gochisoo** a fine dinner.

**sutekki** walking stick, cane.

**sutemi** disregard of one's life; desperation; **sutemi ni naru** to abandon oneself to despair.

**sutene** bargain price; **sutene no** ridiculously cheap; **sutene de uru** to sell at a sacrifice; to sell dirt cheap.

**SUTERU** to throw away, abandon; to give up.

**suteuri** sacrifice sale; a less-than-cost bargain; **suteuri ni suru** to sell at a sacrifice.

**sutezerifu** menace; parting shot; **sutezerifu o nokosu** to leave with a parting remark.

**suto** See **sutoraiki.**

**sutoobu** stove.

**sutoraiki, suto** strike (walkout of labor).

**sutoraiku** strike (baseball).

**sutoroo** (beverage) straw.

**SUU** to breathe; to inhale; to sip; to absorb; to smoke; **iki o suu** to breathe the air; **tabako o suu** to smoke a cigarette.

**SUU-** prefix denoting: several; **suujitsu** several days; **suunin** several persons.

**suu** number, figure; **daitasuu** majority.

**suugaku** mathematics; **suugaku no** mathematical; **suugakusha** mathematician.

**suuhai** worship; adoration; **suuhai suru** to worship, venerate.

**SUUJI** figure, numeral; **suuji no** numerical; **suujijoo** numerically.

**suukoo** loftiness, sublimity; **suukoo na** lofty, sublime.

**SUUPU** soup (Occidental style); **suupu zara** soup plate. (See also **shiru** and **tsuyu.**)

**suusei** trend; drift; tendency; tide, current; **yo no suusei ni tomonatte** with the trend of the times.

**suwari** stability; **suwari ga yoi** to sit well; to be stable.

**SUWARU** to sit; to squat; to be set; **chan to suwaru** to sit straight; **raku ni suwaru** to sit comfortably.

**suyaki** unglazed pottery; **suyaki no** unglazed.

**suyasuya to** quietly, gently, peacefully; **suyasuya to nemuru** to sleep quietly.

**suzu** tin.

**suzu** bell, handbell; **suzu no oto** tinkle of a bell; **suzu o narasu** to ring a bell.

**suzume** sparrow.

**suzumi** enjoying the cool air; **suzumi ni iku** to go out to cool off.

**suzumu** to cool oneself; to enjoy the cool breeze.

**suzunari** cluster (of fruit); **suzunari ni natte iru** to hang in clusters.

**suzuri** ink stone (used in preparing ink for brush writing) (see also **sumi**); **suzuribako** ink-stone case.

**SUZUSHII** cool, refreshing; **suzushii kao o suru** to assume a nonchalant air; to appear calm and unconcerned.

# T

**ta** rice field, paddy field; **ta o tagayasu** to till a rice field; **ta ni mizu o hiku** to irrigate a rice field.

**ta** others, rest; **ta no** other, another.

**ta-** prefix denoting: many, much; **tagaku no okane** large amount of money.

**TABAKO** cigarette; **tabako ire** cigarette case; **tabako o suu** to smoke a cigarette; **tabakoya** cigar store (stand).

**tabaneru** to bundle; to tie up in a bundle.

**tabeakiru** to become tired of (a food).

**tabehajimeru** to begin to eat.

**tabekata** how to eat. **Nihonshoku no tabekata o setsumei shite kudasai.** Please explain how to eat Japanese food.

**TABEMONO** food; provisions; edibles. **Nani ka tabemono wa arimasu ka?** Can we get something to eat? **Nihon de wa omo na tabemono wa okome desu.** In Japan, rice is the staple food.

**TABERU** to eat; to take; to live on; **gekkyuu de taberu** to live on the salary; **hitokuchi taberu** to have a mouthful (of food). **Yooshoku bakari tabete imasu.** I am eating only foreign (Occidental) food.

**tabesugi** overeating, surfeit.

**tabesugiru** to overeat.

**tabetsukeru** to be accustomed to eat. **Chuuka ryoori wa tabetsukete imasen.** I am not accustomed to Chinese food.

**tabezu girai** disliking (a food) without tasting; food prejudice.

**tabi** socks worn with kimono; **tabi issoku** pair of tabi; **tabi o haku** to put on socks; **tabihadashi** wearing socks but no shoes; **tabihadashi de** in one's socks.

**tabi** journey; **tabi o suru** to travel; **jinsei no tabi** life's journey.

**-tabi** times, occasion; **-tabi goto ni** whenever, every time when.

**tabikoogyoo** local performances (of a theatrical company); road performances.

**tabisaki** while on journey. **Sono tegami wa tabisaki de uketorimashita.** I received that letter while I was on a trip.

**TABITABI** often, many times, repeatedly. **Sono koto wa tabitabi hanashi ni demashita.** That subject came up often in our conversation.

**taboo** being fully occupied with; being busy; **taboo na** busy; **taboo ni torimagire** on account of the pressure of business; **taboo de aru** to be busy.

**TABUN** perhaps, probably. **Kon'ya tabun kuru deshoo.** He will probably come tonight.

**tabun** reaching (others') ears; **tabun o habakaru** to be afraid of publicity.

**tabyoo** being sickly; being weak and feeble.

**TACHI** nature, character, quality, disposition, **tachi no yoi** of good quality; **tachi no warui** of bad quality.

**tachiagaru** to stand up, rise to one's feet.

**tachiai** presence, attendance; **-ni tachiai o motomeru** to request (someone's) presence as a witness.

**tachiau** to stand by; to fight with; **-ni tachiau** to attend; **-to tachiau** to fight with.

**tachibanashi o suru** to talk standing; to stand chattering together.

**tachidokoro ni** on the spot, instantly. **Tachidokoro ni kesshin shimashita.** He made up his mind in an instant.

**tachidomaru** to stop short, to halt, stand still; **kyuu ni tachidomaru** to come to a sudden halt.

**tachidooshi** (n.) standing the whole way. **Ueno made tachidooshi deshita.** We had to stand the whole way to Ueno.

**tachifusagaru** to block (someone's) passage.

**tachigie** going out (said of a charcoal fire, etc.); being dropped (said of matters); half-burned. **Sono keikaku wa tachigie ni narimashita.** The plan has fallen through.

**tachigiki** eavesdropping, overhearing; **tachigiki o suru** to eavesdrop.

**tachigui** eating while standing; **tachigui o suru** to eat standing.

**tachigusare** dilapidation (of a building); **tachigusare ni naru** to fall into ruin.

**tachiiru** to enter; to penetrate; to interfere. **Shibafu ni tachiiranaide de kudasai.** Keep off the grass. **Tachiitta koto o otazune shimasu ga ...** It might be too personal, but may I ask ...

**tachiki** standing tree.

**tachikomeru** to screen, envelop. **Kasumi ga tachikomeru.** The mist envelops all things.

**tachimachi** at once; in an instant. **Nihon ni kuru to tachimachi yuumei ni narimashita.** As soon as he came to Japan, he became prominent.

**tachimawaru** to go round; to play one's part; to maneuver; **joozu ni tachimawaru** to

play one's part well; **zuruku**
**tachimawaru** to act in a cunning way.
**tachimi** seeing a play from the gallery (from standing room).
**tachimukau** to fight against.
**tachinaoru** to regain one's footing; to recover.
**tachinoki** removal; vacation; evacuation; **-ni tachinoki o meizuru** to order to vacate; **tachinoki meirei** order for removal; deportation order; an eviction order; **tachinokisaki** refuge.
**tachinoku** to quit; to leave; to vacate.
**tachiokure** being late in getting started.
**tachiokureru** to be tardy, be behind time.
**tachioojoo** standstill, deadlock, being kept standing; **tachioojoo o suru** to come to a standstill; to be in a dilemma.
**tachisukumu** to stand petrified with fear.
**tachiyoru** to call at; **-no uchi ni tachiyoru** to drop in.
**tachizume** being kept standing.
**tada** merely, only, simply; free of charge.
**tadachi ni** at once, immediately, directly; without delay. **Tadachi ni kite kudasai.** Please come immediately.
**tadagoto** trivial matter; commonplace (thing). **Tadagoto de nai.** It is no trivial matter.
**TADAIMA** now, just now; I'm home (greeting); **tadaima no tokoro** for the present; **tadaima de wa** now, nowadays.
**tadai no** heavy, great; serious; **tadai no songai** heavy loss; **tadai no eikyoo o koomuru** to be seriously affected.
**tadanori** free ride; stealing a ride.
**tadare** sore; inflammation; **tadareru** to break out in sores; to be inflamed.
**TADASHI** however; provided that. **Tadashi kodomo wa hangaku desu.** (But) children are (charged) half-price.
**TADASHII** right, proper.
**tadasu** to examine, investigate; to inquire into; to question.
**tadayou** to drift about; to wander; **kao ni urei o tadayowasete** with a worried look; **nami ni tadayou fune** a boat drifting at the mercy of the waves.
**tadooshi** transitive verb (one which can take the particle o).
**tadoru** to go on wearily.
**taedae** brokenly; feebly, faintly.
**taegatai** intolerable, unbearable.
**taema** break; gap; pause.
**taeru** to bear; to bear up; **konku ni taeru** to bear up under privation; **nin ni taeru** to be equal to one's duty; **juunen no shiyoo ni taeru** to be good for ten years.
**taeru** to become extinct; **onshin ga taeru** to hear nothing from (someone). **Kyookyuu ga taeru.** The supply is cut off.

**taezu** constantly; **taezu doryoku suru** to make a constant effort.
**taga** hoop; **taga o hazushite sawaide iru** to go on a spree.
**tagaeru** to break; to violate; **yakusoku o tagaeru** to break a promise.
**tagai ni** with one another; with each other; mutually.
**tagaku** large sum.
**tagayasu** to till, plow, cultivate; **hatake o tagayasu** to farm; to work on a farm.
**tagei** varied accomplishments; **tagei na** highly accomplished; **tagei na hito** versatile person; **tagei no** many-sided.
**tagon** telling others; **tagon suru** to tell others.
**tagui** kind, class, sort; **tagui naki** matchless, unique.
**taguru** to haul in (hand over hand); to follow up; to trace to its source.
**tahata** farm; field; cultivated land.
**tahoo** another side; other side; **tahoo de wa** on the other side; **tahoomen** many directions; many sides; different subjects.
**tai** opposite; even, equal; versus, against; **-ni tai suru** versus, against, toward, to; **san tai go no seiseki** a score of 3 to 5; **tai Bei booeki** trade with the U.S.A.
**tai** body, form; **tai o kawasu** to dodge; **tai o nasanai** to be in bad form.
**tai** party, corps, band; **tai o kumu** to form in a line, to form a party; **tai o toku** to disband.
**tai-** prefix denoting: great, large, grand; general, main, principal; serious; **tainin** important mission; **taiyaku** important task.
**-tai** suffix denoting: be desirous of, want to do (something). **Tabetai desu.** I want to eat. **Mitai desu.** I want to see it.
**taibetsu** general classification; **taibetsu suru** to classify roughly.
**taibu** bulkiness; greater part; **taibu no** voluminous.
**taibyoo** serious illness.
**taida** idleness, laziness; **taida na** idle, lazy.
**taido** attitude; **taido o ippen suru** to change one's attitude completely.
**taifuu** gale, typhoon.
**TAIGAI** generally; almost; probably. **Doyoobi wa taigai uchi ni imasu.** I am usually at home on Saturdays.
**taigaku, taikoo** leaving school.
**taigan** opposite bank of a river.
**taigen, taigen soogo** bragging, boasting; **taigen soogo o suru** to boast.
**taigi** toil, exertion, labor; **taigi sooni** languidly; **taigi desu** to feel tired.
**taigo** ranks; **taigo o midashite** in confusion.
**taigotettei** spiritual awakening.
**taigun** large crowd (herd, flock, school, etc.); **kujira no taigun** large school of whales.

**taigun** large force, great army.

**taiguu** treatment; service; rating; **taiguu ga warui** to treat coldly; to be paid poorly; **taiguu ga yoi** to treat well, be hospitable, pay well.

**taigyoo** slowdown strike.

**taihai** crushing defeat; **taihai suru** to meet with a crushing defeat.

**taihai** decay, corruption; **taihai suru** to be ruined.

**taihan** for the most part.

**taihei** peace, tranquility.

**TAIHEIYOO** Pacific Ocean.

**TAIHEN** very, extremely, remarkably; **taihen na** serious, dreadful; innumerable; **taihen ni** very. **Taihen omoshiroi desu.** It is very interesting.

**taiho** arrest; apprehension; **taihojoo** warrant of arrest.

**taiho** deterioration; retrogression, going backward.

**taihoo** gun; cannon; **taihoo o utsu** to fire a gun.

**taii** general idea; résumé; outline.

**taii** abdication.

**taiiku** physical education.

**taiin suru** to be released from (leave) a hospital.

**taiji** subjugation; wiping out; control.

**taijoo** leaving, exit; **-ni taijoo o meizuru** to order (a person) out of the room; **taijoo suru** to leave.

**taijuu** weight (of the body); **taijuu ga masu** to gain weight.

**taika** authority, distinguished person (in any circle, i.e., master painter, great musician, eminent scholar, etc.).

**taika** great fire.

**taika** degeneration.

**taika** fireproof; **taika kenchiku** fireproof building.

**taikai** withdrawal of membership (from an association or society).

**taikau, taiku** physique; **taikaku kensa** physical examination.

**taikan** high official.

**taikanshiki** coronation.

**taika renga** firebrick.

**taikei** system; **taikei o tateru** to systematize.

**taiken** personal experience; **taiken suru** to experience.

**taiketsu** confrontation; **-to . . . o taiketsu saseru** to confront (someone) with (another).

**taiki** standing by; being ready; **taiki no shisei** in a position of readiness.

**taiki** atmosphere.

**taikin** large sum of money.

**taiko** drum.

**taikobara** potbelly, paunch, bay window.

**taikoo** opposition; rivalry, confrontation; **taikoo undoo** a countermovement; **taikoo suru** to oppose; to face; to counteract; **taikoosaku** counterplan, countermeasures; **taikoosha** rival, antagonist.

**taikoo** fundamental principle, code.

**taikoo** See **taigaku.**

**taiku** See **taikaku.**

**taikutsu** ennui; dullness; **-ni taikutsu suru** to be bored; to become weary of; **taikutsu saseru** to bore.

**taikyaku** retreat; **taikyaku suru** to retreat.

**taikyo, taishutsu** leaving, quitting; **taikyo suru** to leave, quit; **taikyo meirei o dasu** to issue an order for departure.

**taikyoku** general state; general situation; **taikyoku ni me o tsukeru** to take a large view of things.

**taikyoo** leaving the capital.

**taikyuuryoku** durability; endurance.

**taiman** negligence.

**taimen** dignity, honor, reputation; **-no taimen o sonjiru** to bring disgrace on; **taimen o omonzuru** to have a sense of honor; to make much of one's dignity; **taimen o tamotsu** to keep one's reputation.

**taimen** interview, meeting; **taimen suru** to interview, to meet.

**taimoo** great ambition; **taimoo o idaku** to harbor an ambition.

**tainin** important mission; **tainin o hatasu** to carry out an important mission.

**tainoo** nonpayment; **tainoo suru** to be delinquent in payment; **tainookin** arrears; **tainoosha** delinquent payer.

**taion** body temperature; **taion o hakaru** to take the (body) temperature; **taionkei** clinical thermometer.

**taipisuto** typist.

**taipuraitaa** typewriter.

**taira** evenness; level; flatness; **taira na** flat; **taira ni suru** to level, flatten.

**tairageru** to subdue; to subjugate.

**tairiku** continent; **tairiku no** continental.

**tairitsu** opposition; rivalry.

**tairyaku** outline; summary; **tairyaku o noberu** to give an outline.

**tairyoo** large quantity; **tairyoo seisan** mass production.

**tairyoo** big catch (of fish).

**taisa** great difference; **taisa o shoojiru** to make a great difference; **taisa ga aru** there is a great difference.

**taisai** grand festival; great fete.

**taisan** dispersion; **taisan saseru** to break up; **taisan suru** to take flight; to be dispersed.

**taisei** structure; system; organization; trend of affairs; general situation; **sekai no taisei**

international situation; **taisei ni tsuujiru** to be conversant with the trend.

**taisei** completion, accomplishment; **taisei suru** to complete.

**TAISEIYOO** Atlantic Ocean.

**taiseki** accumulation; heap; **taiseki suru** to accumulate.

**taisen** great war; **Dai niji sekai taisen** World War II.

**TAISETSU NA** important, precious. **Hakkiri kaku koto ga taisetsu desu.** It is important to write clearly. **Taisetsu ni shite kudasai.** Please take good care of it.

**taishaku** loan; **taishakuhyoo** balance sheet.

**taishikan** embassy; **taishikan'in** embassy attaché.

**taishin kenchiku** earthquake-proof building.

**taishita** great; important; remarkable.

**taishite** very, greatly; importantly; remarkably (used with negative expressions).

**taishitsu** physical constitution.

**taishoku** gluttony; **taishoku no** gluttonous, greedy; **taishoku suru** to eat (too) much.

**taishoku** resignation; **taishoku teate** retirement allowance; **-o taishoku suru** to resign from an office; to retire from service.

**taishoo** object.

**taishoo** title of the highest officers of the army and navy; general, admiral; leader; head.

**taishuka** heavy drinker.

**taishutsu** leaving; **taishutsu suru** to leave, retire from. (See also **taikyo.**)

**TAISOO** very; exceedingly; many; much. **Taisoo omoshiroi shibai desu.** It is an exceedingly enjoyable play.

**TAISOO** physical exercise, gymnastics; **taisoo o suru** to exercise.

**taisuru** to front; to oppose; to be opposite to; to correspond to.

**TAITEI** generally; usually; mostly; **taitei no hito** most people. **Taitei wa arukimasu.** Usually I walk. **Nichiyoobi wa taitei uchi ni imasu.** Generally I stay at home on Sundays.

**taiteki** powerful enemy. **Yudan taiteki.** False security is a great foe.

**taitoku suru** to master; to comprehend.

**taitoo** equality, equal footing; **taitoo ni** on equal terms; **taitoo no** equal.

**taitoru** title.

**taiu** heavy rain, downpour.

**taiwa** dialogue; conversation; **to taiwa suru** talk with.

**TAIWAN** Taiwan; **Taiwan no** Taiwanese.

**taiya** tire.

**taiyaku** important task; heavy role.

**TAIYOO** sun; **taiyooreki** the solar calendar; Gregorian calendar.

**taiyoo** summary; general principle; résumé.

**taiyoo** ocean; **taiyoo no** oceanic.

**taizai** stay; **taizai suru** to stay.

**taizen** calmness, composure; **taizen to shite** calmly, composedly.

**tajitsu** one day in the future; some day.

**tajoo na** amorous; wanton; of loose morals.

**takaburu** to be proud; to be haughty; to hold up one's head.

**takadai** height; upland.

**takadaka** at the height; **takadaka to** aloft, proudly.

**TAKAI** high, tall; **takai tatemono** tall building; **takai yama** tall mountain. **Nedan ga takai.** The price is high.

**takai** another world; **takai suru** to die.

**takaibiki** loud snore.

**takamaru** to rise; to swell; to be raised.

**takara** treasure.

**takaru** to swarm; to gather, assemble; to crowd.

**takasa** height.

**takatobi** high jump; running away; **takatobi suru** to run away (to avoid).

**takawarai** loud laugh; ringing laughter.

**take** bamboo.

**take** length; measure; height; **take ga takai** to be tall.

**takenawa** being at its height, being in full swing.

**taki** waterfall.

**takibi** bonfire; wood fire; **takibi o suru** to make a fire.

**takidashi** boiling rice for sufferers in an emergency.

**takimono** fuel; firewood.

**takitsuke** kindling wood.

**takitsukeru** to light, kindle; **kenka o takitsukeru** to fan a quarrel; to incite; **sutoobu ni hi o takitsukeru** to make a fire in the stove.

**takkuru** tackle; **takkuru suru** to tackle.

**tako** kite; **tako o ageru** to fly a kite.

**takokujin** foreigner.

**TAKU** to boil rice or other food.

**takuchi** house lot; residential land.

**takuetsu** excellence; superiority; **takuetsu suru** to be distinguished, exceed in.

**takuhatsu** religious begging.

**takujisho** day nursery.

**takujoo denwa** desk telephone.

**takumashii** robust, strong.

**takumi** skill, adroitness, cleverness; **takumi na** skillful, dexterous.

**takuramu** to scheme, plan; to play a trick; to design, devise; to invent; **muhon o takuramu** to conspire.

**TAKUSAN** much, many, a lot; **takusan no** numerous. **Moo takusan desu.** No, thank you (I've had enough). **Takusan tabemashita.** I ate a lot.

**takusetsu** excellent opinion; enlightened views.

**TAKUSHII** taxicab.

**takusuru** to trust; to entrust.

**takuwae** store, reserve, savings; **issen no takuwae mo nai** to have not a penny saved.

**takuwaeru** to save, amass, lay by, hoard; **hige o takuwaeru** to wear a mustache; **kane o takuwaeru** to save money.

**TAMA** rare; seldom, not often; **tama ni** rarely, once in a while.

**tama** ball; globe; bead; jewel; **tama no ase** beads of perspiration; **me no tama** eyeball; **teppoo no tama** bullets; **tama o nageru** to throw a ball.

**TAMAGO** egg; **tamago no kimi** yolk of an egg; **tamago no shiromi** white of an egg; **tamago o kaesu** to hatch an egg.

**TAMANEGI** onion.

**tamaranai** to be unbearable; cannot help; be dying for.

**tamari** pool; waiting room.

**tamarimizu** stagnant water.

**tamaru** to collect, accumulate, gather; **harai ga tamaru** to be in arrears; **shakkin ga tamaru** to run up debts.

**tamashii** soul; spirit; **tamashii o ubau** to enchant.

**tamatama** by chance. **Tamatama kare wa byooki deshita.** It so happened that he was ill.

**tamatsuki** billiards.

**tamazan** calculation on the **soroban** (an abacus).

**TAME** benefit; consequence; aim; reason; for the purpose of; for the sake of; because of; **hoomon shita tame ni** as a result of his visit; **tame ni naranai** to be of no good; **tame ni naru** to do good.

**tameike** irrigation pond; reservoir.

**tameiki** sigh; **tameiki o tsuku** to heave a sigh.

**tamerau** to hesitate, waver.

**tameru** to save, put by, store; to accumulate, collect.

**tameshi** experiment; attempt; **tameshi ni** by way of experiment.

**tameshi** example, precedent. **Sonna tameshi wa nai.** There is no precedent for this.

**TAMESU** to try, attempt; to make a trial of; to put to the test; **yuuki o tamesu** to put one's courage to test.

**tamoto** sleeve of Japanese dress; foot; **hashi no tamoto** foot of a bridge.

**tan** phlegm; **tan o haku** to expectorate; to spit out.

**-tan** measure of land (about .245 acres); roll of cloth (about 12 yards).

**TANA** shelf, rack; **jibun no koto wa tana ni ageru** to criticize others without recognizing one's own defects; **tana ni ageru** to put up on a shelf.

**tanaoroshi** inventory; stock-taking; fault-finding; **tanaoroshi suru** to take stock; to pick holes in (someone else's) character.

**tanazarashi** shopworn merchandise; secondhand merchandise; **tanazarashi ni naru** to be shopworn.

**tanbe** field, rice field.

**tanchoo** monotony, lack of variety; **tanchoo na** monotonous, dull.

**tandoku** being by oneself; **tandoku hikoo** solo flight.

**tane** seed; stone or pit of a fruit; breed; child; cause, sources; secret of a trick; **tane o maku, tanemaki o suru** to sow (seeds); **namida no tane** source of grief.

**taneabura** seed oil, canola oil (used in cooking).

**tanegire** being incapable of supplying something, being exhausted; **tanegire ni naru** to run short of (something).

**tanen** many years.

**tangan** entreaty, supplication, petition; **tangan suru** to entreat, supplicate, petition; appeal.

**tan'i** unit.

**tani, tanima** valley.

**tanigawa** stream running through a valley.

**tanin** stranger; (other) person.

**tanin gyoogi** standing on ceremony. **Tanin gyoogi ni naranaide kudasai.** Please don't stand on ceremony.

**tanisoko** bottom of a valley.

**tan'itsu** singleness; **tan'itsu no** single, sole, simple.

**tan'itsuka** unification.

**TANJOO** birth; **tanjoo o iwau** to celebrate a birth; **tanjoo suru** to be born; **TANJOOBI** birthday.

**tanjun** simplicity, plainness; **tanjun na** simple, naïve, unsophisticated.

**tanjuu** pistol; revolver.

**tanka, waka** Japanese verse of 31 syllables.

**tanken** exploration; expedition; **tanken suru** to explore; **tankenryokoo** an expedition.

**tanki** quick temper; **tanki na** irritable, quick-tempered; **tanki o okosu** to become impatient.

**tankoo** coal mine; **tankoofu** coal miner.

**tankoobon** separate volume; **tankoobon to shite shuppan suru** to publish in book form.

**tanmei** short life, early death.

**tanmono** cloth, piece goods, drapery.

**tannin** charge, duty; **tannin suru** to take charge of.

**tanomi** request; solicitation, reliance; **-o hito no tanomi de suru** to do something at the request of (someone else); **tanomi ni naranai** to be unreliable.

**tanomoshii** reliable, trusty; **sue tanomoshii wakamono** promising youngster.

**TANOMU** to ask; to beg, to desire; to trust to; to rely on (someone to do something); **isha o tanomu** to call a doctor; **kodomo o tanomu** to entrust someone with the care of a child. **Yamada-san ni tanonde kudasai.** Please ask Mr. Yamada to do it.

**TANOSHII** to be pleasant, delightful, enjoyable.

**tanoshimi** pleasure, enjoyment, amusement.

**tanoshimu** to take pleasure in; to enjoy oneself; to amuse oneself with; **jinsei o tanoshimu** to enjoy life.

**tanpaku** quality of being simple; frankness; **tanpaku na** simple, unaffected, plain (as a diet).

**tanpen** short piece; **tanpen shoosetsu** short story.

**tanrei na** graceful.

**tanren** temper; forge; training; **seinen no ishi o tanren suru** to train the mind of a young person; **tetsu o tanren suru** to temper metal; **tanren suru** to temper; to forge; to train.

**tansei** sigh; groan; lamentation; **tansei o morasu** to lament; to sigh deeply.

**TANSHIN** alone.

**tansho** weak point or defect (in personality); **tansho o oginau** to remedy a defect; **-ga tansho de aru** -is one's weak point.

**tanshuku** shortening, curtailment; **tanshuku suru** to shorten, cut off.

**TANSU** Japanese-style chest of drawers.

**tantei** detective, undercover person; **himitsu tantei** private detective; **tantei shoosetsu** detective story.

**tantoo** dagger.

**tantoo suru** to take charge of.

**taoreru** to fall; to fall down, tumble down; **taoreta ie** tumbledown house; **taorekakatta ginkoo** insecure financial institution.

**TAORU** towel.

**taosu** to throw down; to bring down; to beat; **ki o kiritaosu** to fell a tree; **shakkin o taosu** to fail to pay a debt.

**tappitsu** elegant penmanship.

**TAPPURI** much, great deal, plentifully, full. **Go fiito tappuri aru.** It is a good five feet.

**-tara** suffix denoting; if, when, in case; **ame ga futtara** if (in case) it rains; **Yamada-san ga kitara** if Mr. Yamada should come.

**tarasu** to drop; to let drop; to dribble; to let fall; to hang down; to suspend; **maku o tarasu** to hang a curtain; **yodare o tarasu** to drool; **yuka e mizu o tarasu** to spill water on the floor.

**tarazu** not enough, insufficient, short of; **ni man en tarazu de** for less than 20,000 yen.

**tareru** to drip, trickle down, fall in drops. **Amadare ga noki kara tareru.** The rain drops from the eaves. **Ki no eda ga hikuku tarete iru.** The branches of the tree are drooping low.

**tariru, taru** to be enough, be sufficient; **shinrai suru ni tariru** to be worthy; to be trusted.

**taru** barrel, cask.

**tarumu** to become slack, loose, lax. **Nawa ga tarunde imasu.** The rope is slackening.

**tasatsu** murder.

**TASHIKA** if I remember right; **tashika na** certain, sure. **Tashika desu.** It is certain. **Tashika soo iimashita.** I think (I'm pretty sure) he said so.

**tashikameru** to make certain, authenticate, verify.

**tashinami** circumspection; self-control; accomplishments secretly enjoyed; **tashinami ga nai** lack of self-control. **Ano hito wa e no tashinami ga aru.** She can paint.

**TASHOO** more or less; in some measure, a little; somewhat. **Tashoo no chigai wa aru deshoo.** There will be some difference, but not much.

**tasogare** evening, twilight.

**TASSHA** healthiness; **tassha na** healthy, strong; **tassha ni kurasu** to enjoy vigorous health; **tassha ni naru** to get well. **Otassha desu ka?** Are you well?

**tassuru** to reach, arrive at, get to, attain; **mokutekichi ni tassuru** to arrive at a destination; **sen en ni tassuru** to run into 1000 yen.

**TASU** to add; **ni ni san o tasu** two plus three; **moo sukoshi mizu o tasu** to add a little more water.

**tasukaru** to be saved, be rescued; to be of help; **fushigi ni tasukaru** to have a miraculous escape; **taihen tasukaru** to be greatly relieved.

**tasuke** salvation; preservation; deliverance; succor, help, aid, assistance; **kami no tasuke** help from God; **tasukebune** lifeboat.

**TASUKERU** to help, aid, assist; to reinforce; **komatte iru hito o tasukeru** to help a person in need.

**tasuu** large number, majority; **tasuu no**

many; **tasuu o shimeru** to command a majority; **tasuuketsu** decision by the majority.

**tatakau** to fight with; to fight against; to fight a battle; **yuuwaku to tatakau** to struggle with temptation.

**tataki** striking, beating, pounding, chopping fine; concrete.

**tatakiau** to scuffle.

**tatakifuseru** to knock down.

**tatakikomu** to strike into; to train hard.

**tatakikowasu** to knock to pieces.

**tatakinomesu** to knock down.

**tatakiotosu** to strike (fruit) from a tree; to attack (someone) so violently that s(he) is obliged to resign her/his post.

**tatakitsukeru** to throw a thing against something; to throw to.

**TATAKU** to strike, beat, hit; to knock; **taiko o tataku** to beat a drum; **to o tataku** to tap at the door.

**TATAMI** floor mat made of rice straw tightly bound together and covered on the upper surface with matting; **tatami o shiku** to lay down a **tatami.**

**TATAMU** to fold; to shut up; to wind up; to do away with; **ie o tatamu** to shut up one's house; **kami o yottsu ni tatamu** to fold a paper into four.

**tatari** evil consequence.

**tataru** to bring evil upon, to cast an evil spell on; to inflict a calamity on.

**TATE** length, height; **tate no** lengthwise.

**tate** shield; **-ni tate o tsuku** to set oneself against, oppose, defy (someone).

**-tate** suffix denoting: just; fresh from; **takitate** just boiled; **kitate** just arrived; **dekitate** just completed.

**tatefuda** sign, signboard.

**tategu** furnishings (of a house); fixture; **tategu o ireru** to furnish a house.

**tateguya** shop where house furnishings are made and sold.

**tatekae** defraying the expense for another person; **tatekaekin** the sum defrayed temporarily for another person; advance (payment).

**tatekakeru** to rest, stand, lean, set, place something against.

**tatekomoru** to shut oneself up, confine oneself, remain in seclusion.

**tatekomu** to be crowded (with people); to be pressed with business; to be crowded with buildings; **shigoto ga tatekonde iru** to be pressed (with business).

**tatemae** ceremony of putting the framework in a Japanese house or other building.

**tatemae** principle; policy; rule; **-o tatemae to suru** to make a point of.

**tatemashi** extension of a building.

**TATEMONO** building, house. **Nihonshiki no tatemono ni sunde imasu.** I live in a Japanese-style house.

**tatenaosu** to build again; to reconstruct.

**TATERU** to build, construct, erect, set up; to shut, close; **hata o tateru** to hoist a flag; **ie o tateru** to build a house; **kinenhi o tateru** to erect a monument; **to o tateru** to shut the door.

**tatetsubo** floor space of a building. **Kono uchi wa tatetsubo ga hyaku tsubo aru.** The floor space of this house is 100 **tsubo** (**tsubo:** about 6 feet by 6 feet).

**tatetsuke** opening and shutting of doors and windows. **Kono uchi wa tatetsuke ga yoi.** The doors and windows of this house open and shut smoothly.

**tateyoko** length and breadth; lengthwise and crosswise.

**TATOE** even if, even though; **tatoe donna koto ga atte mo** whatever may happen; **tatoe joodan ni mo sey o** even in jest.

**tatoe** simile, metaphor, example; **tatoe ni iu yooni** as the saying goes.

**TATOEBA** for instance, for example.

**tatoeru** to compare; to give an example.

**TATSU** to sever, cut off; to chop off; to break; **futatsu ni tatsu** to cut in two; **sake o tatsu** to abstain from sake.

**TATSU** to stand up, to rise, to get on one's feet; to leave; **asu Tookyoo o tatsu** to leave Tokyo tomorrow; **seki o tatsu** to leave the seat. **Kemuri ga tatsu.** The smoke rises.

**tatsujin** master; expert; one who is adept; **yumi no tatsujin** archery expert.

**tatsumaki** waterspout, sand pillar.

**TATTA** only, merely; **tatta ima** just now, a moment ago.

**tatte** earnestly; **tatte no negai** earnest request.

**tattobu** to value; to set a value on.

**tattoi** noble, august, high (in rank); valuable.

**taue** rice transplantation; **taue doki** the rice-planting season; **taue uta** the rice-planting song; **taue o suru** to transplant rice.

**tawagoto** silly talk, nonsense.

**tawainai** easy; innocent; droll.

**tawamureru** to play; to frolic; to jest; to dally; **onna ni tawamureru** to flirt with a woman.

**tawara** straw bag for rice; bale.

**tawashi** scrubbing brush.

**tayasu** to exterminate; to eradicate; to put an end to.

**TAYASUI** easy, simple. **Tayasui goyoo desu.** It's an easy thing. I'll be glad to do it for you.

**tayoo** pressure of business; many things to do.

**tayori** intelligence, news, tidings; letter; **tayori ga nai** to hear nothing from; **tayori o suru** to write a letter.

**tayori** reliance, dependence; **tayori to naru hito** one's second self, a reliable person.

**tayoru** to rely on, depend on.

**tayumu** to flag, slacken one's efforts, relax one's attention.

**tazei** great number.

**tazuna** rein, bridle; **tazuna o shimeru** to tighten the reins; **tazuna o yurumeru** to slacken the reins.

**TAZUNERU** to look for, search for, hunt for; ask; **anpi o tazuneru** to inquire after a person; **michi o tazuneru** to ask the way to.

**TE** hand; arm; paw; helping hand, possession; handwriting; means, way, trick; hand (in card playing); **te ga aite iru** to be free; to have no work on hand; **te ga tarinai** to be shorthanded.

**-te** suffix denoting: one who performs; direction; **kamite** upper part; **shimote** lower part; **yarite** clever fellow, cunning fellow; **yomite** one who reads.

**teaka** dirt from the hands; **teaka ga tsuku** to become soiled from handling.

**TEARAI, OTEARAI** toilet, bathroom.

**tearai** rough, violent; **tearai koto o suru** to act violently.

**teashi** hand and foot. **Watakushi no teashi to natte hataraite kuremashita.** He was my right-hand man.

**teatari shidai ni** at random.

**teate** recompense; allowance; medical care; **rinji teate** temporary allowance; **kizu no teate o suru** to dress a wound; **teate o dasu** to give an allowance.

**teatsui** hospitable; courteous.

**tebanashi de** with the hands free; openly; broadly; **kodomo o tebanshi de asobaseru** to leave children by themselves; **tebanashi de jitensha ni noru** to ride a bicycle without using the handlebars.

**tebanasu** to let go of, release.

**tebayaku** quickly, rapidly.

**tebikae** note, memo.

**tebikaeru** to withhold from, hold off (buying goods, etc.).

**tebiki** leading another by the hand to show the way; guidance; guidebook; **Yamada-san no tebiki de** through Mr. Yamada's good offices.

**tebiroi** wide, roomy; on a large scale; **tebiroku shoobai o suru** to carry on a large trade, do a big business.

**tebukuro** gloves; **tebukuro o hameru** to put on gloves.

**tebura** empty hands; naked fist; **tubura de hoomon suru** to call on (someone) without bringing a present.

**teburi** gesture; customs.

**tebusoku** too short of helping hands.

**techigai** something amiss, something wrong; **techigai ni naru** to go wrong.

**techoo** notebook, memorandum book.

**tedashi** meddling; interference; **tedashi o suru** to poke one's nose into.

**tedasuke** aid, assistance; **tedasuke ni naru** to be of help to.

**tedate** means, measures, steps; method.

**tedori** net receipts; **tedori juuman en to** receive 100,000 yen net.

**TEEBURU** table (Occidental).

**teepu** tape; **teepu rekoodaa** tape recorder.

**tefuki** hand towel.

**tegai no** self-sustained, self-fed; **tegai no inu ni te o kamareru** to be bitten by a pet dog; to be betrayed by a favorite person.

**tegakari** hold; clue, trace; **tegakari o eru** to find a clue to.

**tegakeru** to engage in; to have experience in; to bring up.

**TEGAMI** letter, note, correspondence; **tegami o dasu** to send a letter, write to; **tegami o morau** to receive a letter.

**tegara** merit; achievement, distinguished service.

**tegaru na** easy (not difficult) to do; **tegaru na shokuji** light meal; **tegaru ni hoomon suru** to make an informal call.

**tegata** draft, bill, note; sign; **hyakuman en no tegata** draft for one million yen; **yakusoku tegata** promissory note.

**tegatai** safe; steady and honest, reliable; prudent; of good reputation (said of a shop).

**tegawari** substitute. **Watakushi wa tegawari o sagashite imasu.** I am looking for someone to relieve me. I am looking for someone to take my place.

**tegiwa** workmanship, skill (in doing or making); **tegiwa yoku** cleverly, skillfully; **tegiwa ga warui** unskillful.

**tegokoro** discretion, consideration; **tegokoro o kuwaeru** to use one's discretion.

**tegoro** handy; convenient; moderate (in price or size); just right. **Tegoro na uchi ga mitsukarimashita.** We've found a house just right for us.

**tegotae** reaction, response; resistance; **tegotae ga aru** to be responsive; to be effective.

**tegowai** strong; handy.

**teguchi** way, means.

**tehai** arrangement.

**tehajime** beginning; **tehajime ni** first, to begin with; **tehajime no** opening, first.

**tehazu** order, arrangement, plan; **tehazu o suru** to make arrangements.

**tehodoki** rudimentary lesson.

**tehon** model, pattern.

**tei** appearance, style; **tei yoku kotowaru** to decline politely.

**teiboo** dike; bank, embankment.

**teichi** lowland, low ground.

**teiden** power failure.

**teido** degree, standard, measure, extent; **teido no takai** of high standard; **teido no mondai** a question of degree.

**TEIEN** formal garden.

**teigi** definition.

**teigi** proposal; **teigi suru** to propose.

**teihaku** anchorage, mooring; **teihaku chuu no fune** vessels in the harbor; **teihaku suru** to be at anchor.

**teihyoo** settled opinion; reputation; **-to no teihyoo ga aru** to have the reputation of.

**teiin** regular staff; capacity (of a car); quorum.

**TEIJIKA NA** nearby; **teijika na tokoro** place nearby.

**teijuu suru** to live (at a permanent address).

**teika** fixed price, list price; **teikahyoo** price list.

**teika suru** to grow worse, deteriorate.

**teikei** cooperation; **teikei suru** to join hands with; to act in concert with.

**teiken** definite view, fixed opinion.

**teiketsu** conclusion, contract; **shakkan o teiketsu suru** to arrange a loan.

**teiki** fixed (regular) time, definite period, time; **teiki jooshaken** season ticket; commutation ticket; **teiki kankoobutsu** periodical; **teiki ni** periodically.

**teikiatsu** low atmospheric pressure.

**teikoku** fixed time, appointed time.

**teikoku** empire; **teikoku no** imperial.

**teikoo** resistance, opposition; **-ni teikoo suru** to resist, oppose, fight.

**teikyoo** offer; **teikyoo suru** to offer; to put at (someone's) disposal.

**teikyuu, tenisu** tennis; **teikyuu o suru** to play tennis.

**teikyuubi** periodic holiday observed by stores.

**teikyuu na** low; cheap; vulgar.

**TEINEI NA** polite, courteous; careful, scrupulous. **Teinei na taido de hanashimashita.** He spoke very courteously. **Teinei na shigoto o shimashita.** He did a very careful job.

**teinen** retirement age.

**teinoo** feeblemindedness, imbecility; **teinooji** imbecile child, idiot.

**teippai** one's utmost.

**teiraku** fall; depression; **teiraku suru** to fall, go down.

**teire** care; keeping; repairing; trimming (a garden); **teire no ikitodoita uchi** carefully kept house; **teire o suru** to repair, to renovate.

**teiri** low rate of interest.

**teiryoo** fixed quantity.

**TEIRYUUJOO** bus stop, streetcar stop.

**teisai** appearance, show; style; **teisai o tsukuru** to keep up appearances; **teisai ga yoi** pleasing in appearance.

**teisatsu** reconnaissance.

**teisei** correction; revision; **teisei suru** to correct, revise.

**teisetsu** faithfulness, constancy, devotion.

**teisha** stopping a vehicle (car, train, etc.); **hijoo teisha** emergency stop; **teisha suru** to stop at; **teisha o meizuru** to order a vehicle to stop.

**teishaba, teishajoo, EKI** railway station.

**teishi** stop, stoppage, suspension; **shiharai o teishi suru** to suspend payment; to stop payment.

**teishoku** regular occupation.

**teishoo** discourse; lecture.

**teishu** head of a family; husband; innkeeper.

**teishuku** virtue; **teishuku na** virtuous and refined (woman).

**teishutsu** presentation (in the formal, official sense); **teishutsusha** introducer, presenter.

**teishuu** regular income; **teishuu ga nai** to have no regular income.

**teisoo** chastity, faithfulness.

**teisuru** to present, offer; to pass; **ikan o teisuru** to be a grand sight.

**teitai** accumulation, piling up; indigestion; **teitai suru** to accumulate, pile up.

**teitaku** mansion.

**teito** metropolis; imperial capital.

**teiton** standstill; stagnation; **teiton suru** to come to a standstill.

**teitoo** mortgage, security; **teitoo ni toru** to hold (something) as security.

**tejina** parlor tricks, conjuring tricks; **tejinashi** juggler, magician.

**tejoo** handcuff.

**tejun** order; systematic plan; **tejun ga kuruu** to go out of order; **tejun o sadameru** to arrange for.

**tekagen** discretion, consideration; **tekagen ga wakaranai** to be little used to; **tekagen o suru** to use one's discretion; to make allowances.

**tekazu** trouble; **tekazu o kakeru** to give trouble.

**teki** enemy, opponent, antagonist; **teki mikata** friend and foe; **tekichi** enemy's land.

**tekibishii** severe, strict, stern, rigorous, intense.

**tekichuu** hit, hitting the mark.

**tekigaishin** hostile feeling.

**tekigi** suitability for an occasion; **tekigi na** suitable; **tekigi ni** suitably; **tekigi no shochi o suru** to act as one thinks fit.

**tekigoo** conformity, agreement; **tekigoo suru** to conform to.

**tekihatsu** disclosure, exposure; **tekihatsu suru** to disclose, expose; **fusei jiken o tekihatsu suru** expose.

**tekihi** fitness, suitability. **Tekihi wa wakarimasen.** I cannot tell whether it is suitable or not.

**tekihoo** proper method; legality.

**tekihyoo** apt remark; **tekihyoo o kudasu** to make a pertinent comment.

**tekikaku, tekkaku** exactness; acuteness; **tekikaku na** exact, acute.

**TEKIMEN NI** immediately.

**tekin** security (money), deposit; **tekin o utsu** to give a deposit.

**tekinin** competence, fitness.

**tekioo** fitness; adaptability.

**tekipaki** actively; briskly; promptly.

**tekirei** good example.

**tekiryoo** proper quantity.

**tekisei kensa** test for quality; aptitude test.

**tekisetsu** fitness, appropriateness; **tekisetsu na** appropriate.

**tekishi, tekitai** hostility, animosity.

**tekishutsu** extraction; quotation; **tekishutsu suru** to extract.

**tekisuru** to fit, suit, agree; **kenkoo ni tekisuru** to be good for one's health; **shokuyoo ni tekisuru** to be fit to eat.

**tekisuto** text, textbook.

**tekitai** (see **tekishi**) **ni tekitai suru** to stand against.

**TEKITOO NA** appropriate, suitable; **tekitoo ni** in an appropriate fashion. (See also **tekisetsu.**)

**tekiyoo** summary, résumé; application; **tekiyoo suru** to apply.

**tekizai tekisho** right person in the right place. **Kare wa tekizai tekisho desu.** He is the right man for that place.

**tekizu** wound; **tekizu o ou** to be wounded (in a fight).

**tekkai** withdrawal; **takkai suru** to withdraw.

**tekkaku** See **tekikaku.**

**tekkan** iron pipe.

**tekken** clenched fist.

**tekkin konkuriito** concrete reinforced with steel.

**tekkiri** surely, without doubt.

**tekkoojo** iron foundry, ironworks.

**tekkotsu** iron frame, steel skeleton.

**tekkyoo** iron bridge.

**tekozuru** to be at one's wit's end; to have much trouble with. **Ano hito ni wa zuibun tekozurimashita.** He was an awkward customer to deal with.

**tekubari** preparation.

**TEKUBI** wrist.

**tekuse no warui** light-fingered, thievish.

**TEMA** time; wages; **temachin** wages, service charge. **Kono shigoto wa tema ga kakaru.** This job takes a lot of time. **Tema wa ikura desu ka?** How much do I owe you (for your services)?

**temae** this side.

**temaegatte** willfulness, selfishness; **temaegatte na yatsu** selfish fellow.

**temane** gesture; **temane o suru** to gesticulate.

**temaneki** beckoning.

**temawari** one's personal effects.

**temawashi** preparation, arrangement; **temawashi ga yoi** to be fully prepared in advance; **temawashi suru** to get ready.

**TEMIJIKA NI** in short; **temijika ni ieba** in short, in brief.

**temochibusata** feeling awkward, or ill at ease.

**temoto** money on hand; **temoto ga kurushii** to be short of cash.

**TEMPURA** See **TENPURA.**

**temukai** resistance.

**ten** dot; mark; point; **ten no uchidokoro no nai** faultless; **ookisa no ten de** in point of size.

**ten** heaven, sky.

**tenami** skill; **tenami o miseru** to show one's skill.

**tenboo** view, observation; **tenboo suru** to view, look upon; **tenbookyoo** periscope; telescope; **tenboosha** observation car; parlor car.

**tenbun** natural endowment; **tenbun no yutaka na** highly gifted.

**tenchi** change of air; **tenchi suru** to go (to another place) for a change of air.

**tenchi** heaven and earth; universe; sphere.

**TENDE** (always used with a negative) at all; altogether; **tende hanashi ni naranai** to leave no room for negotiation. **Tende yoku nai.** It is no good at all.

**tengoku** heaven, paradise.

**tengu** long-nosed goblin in Japanese mythology.

**tenimotsu** luggage, hand baggage; **tenimotsu toriatsukaijo** baggage room.

**ten'in** store clerk.

**tenioha** grammatical particles such as **wa, ga, o, ni,** etc.

**tenisu** See **teikyuu.**

**tenji** braille (dots).

**tenjoo** ceiling.

**tenka** entire country.

**tenkai** development, expansion; **tenkai suru** to develop, expand.

**tenkan** conversion; **tenkan suru** to convert, divert, turn.

**tenkei** model, specimen; **tenkeiteki Amerikajin** typical American.

**tenken** inspection; **tenken suru** to inspect.

**TENKI, tenkoo** weather; humor; **TENKI YOHOO** weather forecast. **Kyoo wa tenki ga warui.** The weather is bad today. He is ill-tempered today.

**tenki** turning point.

**tenkin** change of office; **-ni tenkin ni naru** to be transferred to.

**tenko** roll call.

**tenkoo** weather (see also **tenki**); **tenkoo fujun** unseasonable weather.

**tenkoo** turn, shift; **tenkoo suru** to turn.

**tenkyo** change of residence; **-ni tenkyo suru** to move to.

**tenmatsu** details (of an event).

**tenmei** providence, fate; **tenmei o shiru** to resign oneself to fate.

**tenmon** astronomy; **tenmondai** astronomical observatory; **tenmongakusha** astronomer.

**tennen** nature; **tennen no bi** natural beauty; **tennen gasu** natural gas.

**tennentoo** smallpox.

**tennin** transfer; change of post.

**tennoo** emperor; **Tennoo Heika** His Majesty the Emperor.

**tennyo** heavenly maiden.

**TENOHIRA** palm of the hand.

**tenpen chii** natural disaster (earthquake, flood, typhoon, etc.).

**tenpin** gift of heaven; innate nature; **tenpin o hakki suru** to bring all one's talents into play.

**tenpuku** downfall; **tenpuku suru** to turn over, capsize.

**TENPURA, TEMPURA** deep-fried fish, shrimps, and vegetables.

**tenrankai** exhibition.

**tensai** genius; natural gift. **Tensai hada no hito desu.** He is something of a genius.

**tensai** calamity.

**tensai** reproduction of something which was once published.

**tensaku** correction (of a composition, poem, etc.).

**tensei** nature; by nature. **Tensei shoojiki desu.** He is honest by nature.

**tenseki suru** to transfer one's legal domicile. (See also **tentaku**.)

**tensen** dotted line.

**tensha** transcription; **tensha suru** to copy, transcribe.

**tenshi** angel.

**tenshin ranman** naïvete; artlessness, innocence.

**tensho** letter of introduction.

**tenshu** shopkeeper, storekeeper.

**tenshukaku** castle tower.

**tensoo** transmission; forwarding; **yuubinbutso o Kyooto ni tensoo suru** to forward mail to Kyoto.

**tensui oke** rainwater tank.

**tentai** heavenly bodies.

**tentaku, tenseki** change of residence.

**tentan** unselfishness.

**tentekomai o suru** to be in a business boom.

**tentoo** overturning; fall; **ki ga tentoo suru** to lose one's presence of mind; **tentoo suru** to fall; to overturn.

**tentoo** shop; **tentoo ni dasu** to put something on sale.

**tenugui** Japanese towel; **tenugui kake** towel rack.

**tenukari** fault; oversight.

**tenurui** slow, dilatory.

**tenzai suru** to be dotted with.

**teochi** fault; slip; omission.

**teoke** wooden pail.

**teokure ni naru** to be too late.

**teppen** top, summit; **atama no teppen** crown (of the head).

**teppitsu** stylus (for handwritten mimeograph work).

**tera** Buddhist temple.

**terasu** to shine on, shed light on; to refer to; **jijitsu ni terashite** in the light of the facts.

**TEREBI** television.

**terekkusu** telex.

**terikaesu** to reflect.

**terikomu** to shine into.

**teritsukeru** to shine down upon.

**tero** terrorism.

**TERU** to shine; to be fine; **tette mo futte mo** rain or shine. (See also **terasu**.)

**teryoori** homemade dish.

**tesage** handbag.

**tesaguri** groping; **tesaguri de iku** to grope (in the dark).

**TESAKI** hand; finger; agent; follower; tool; **tesaki no kiyoo na** dexterous.

**tesei** handmade; homemade.

**teshita** follower; agent, vassal. (See also **tesaki**.)

**tesoo** line in the palm; **tesoo o miru** to read a palm.

**tessaku** iron railing.

**tessuru** to pierce, penetrate.

**tesuri** handrail.

**tesuu** trouble, care; **tesuu ga kakaru** to require care, be troublesome.

**tesuuryoo** fee, commission.

**tetsu** iron; **tetsubin** iron kettle.

**TETSUDAI** help, assistance; assistant, helper.

**TETSUDAU** to help, assist, lend a hand;
　**shigoto o tetsudau** to help (someone) with
　work.

**TETSUDOO** railway, railroad.

**tetsugaku** philosophy; **tetsugaku joo**
　philosophically.

**tetsujoomoo** wire entanglements; barbed-wire
　entanglements.

**tetsuke(kin)** advance (money), deposit;
　**tetsukekin o utsu** to pay a deposit.

**tetsuya** all night through; **tetsuya suru** to be
　up all night.

**tetsuzuki** process, formalities, proceedings;
　**tetsuzuki o suru** to take steps.

**tettei suru** to get to the bottom; to be
　thorough.

**tetteiteki na** thoroughgoing.

**tettoo tetsubi** thoroughly (from beginning to
　end).

**tettoribayai** quick; rough and ready.

**tewake o suru** to divide work.

**tewatashi** handing over personally.

**tezaiku** handiwork.

**tezema** narrowness; smallness. **Koko wa
　tezema de komarimasu.** We are cramped
　for space here.

**tezukami ni suru** to take with the fingers.

**tezuru** connection; **tezuru o motomeru** to
　hunt up a connection.

**tezuyoi** firm, resolute.

**TO** particle denoting: and; with; along with;
　if, when; as soon as. **Asoko wa haru ni
　naru to komimasu.** That place gets very
　crowded in spring. **Kyooto e Yamada-san
　to ikimashita.** I went to Kyoto with Mr.
　Yamada. **Tookyoo to Kyooto e
　ikimashita.** I went to Tokyo and Kyoto.

**TO** door.

**tobaku** gambling.

**tobasu** to let fly; to omit; to hurry; **kaze ni
　booshi o tobasu** to have one's hat blown
　off by the wind.

**tobiagaru** to fly up; to take wing, take flight;
　to jump to one's feet.

**tobiaruku** to run about.

**tobidasu** to fly out; to take wing; to run out.

**tobidoogu** firearm.

**tobihi** flying sparks; leap of flames; chicken
　pox.

**tobiiri** open contest.

**tobikakaru** to spring (leap, jump) upon.

**tobikiri** extra fine; best, choicest; **tobikiri
　jooto no shina** top-grade article.

**tobikomu** to jump (spring) into; to rush; **heya
　ni tobikomu** to burst into the room; **mizu
　ni tobikomu** to dive into water.

**tobikosu** to jump over, leap over.

**tobimawaru** to fly about; to jump about.

**tobinoku** to jump back; to spring aside.

**tobiokiru** to jump out of bed; to start up; to
　jump for.

**tobioriru** to jump down, leap down.

**tobira** leaf of a gate (or door); title page of a
　book.

**tobisaru** to fly away.

**TOBI TOBI NI** here and there; at intervals; at
　random, without order; **tobi tobi no**
　sporadic.

**tobitsuku** to fly at, spring at, leap at.

**tobokeru** to pretend ignorance.

**toboshii** to be scarce; to be short.

**TOBU** to fly; to jump, leap, bound.

**tochi** ground, land; **tochi no mono** native,
　villager.

**TOCHUU** on the way; halfway; **tochuu de
　yameru** to give up halfway; **tochuu gesha
　suru** to stop over (on a train trip).

**todaeru** to cease, stop, end; to drop.

**TODANA** cupboard, closet.

**TODOKERU** to report; to send. **Okome o
　todokete kudasai.** Please send me the rice.

**todokoori** hitch, hindrance; being in arrears;
　**todokoori naku** duly, regularly; smoothly.

**todokooru** to be in arrears; to be left undone;
　to be stagnant. **Shigoto ga takusan
　todokootte imasu.** There is a good deal of
　work left undone.

**todoku** to reach, get to; to attain; **me no
　todoku kagiri** so far as (anyone) can see;
　**omoi ga todoku** to realize one's objective.

**todomaru** to stop, halt, stand still.

**todome** finishing stroke, *coup de grace*.

**todomeru** to stop, cease, put an end to.

**togameru** to censure, to rebuke; to disapprove;
　**ki ga togameru** to feel uneasy.

**togarasu** to sharpen; to point; to pout; **enpitsu
　o togarasu** to sharpen a pencil.

**togaru** to be pointed, come to a point; **togatta
　hana** hawk nose.

**toge** splinter; thorn; **toge ga aru kotoba**
　stinging words; **yubi ni toge ga sasaru** to
　get a splinter in one's finger.

**togeru** to accomplish, achieve; to attain, gain,
　realize; to commit; **yakusoku o togeru** to
　fulfill one's promise.

**togireru** to break; to pause; to be interrupted.

**togu** to whet, grind, sharpen; **naifu o togu** to
　sharpen a knife.

**toguchi** doorway.

**toho** going on foot.

**tohoo ni kureru** to be bewildered.

**toiawaseru** to inquire, to refer. **Taishikan de
　toiawasete kudasai.** Please inquire at the
　Embassy.

**toitsumeru** to press for an answer.

**tojikomeru** to confine, shut in; **ame ni tojikomerareru** to be housebound by rain.

**tojikomoru** to confine oneself to; to shut oneself up.

**tojimari o suru** to lock a door.

**TOJIRU** to bind; to file; to sew up.

**TOJIRU** to shut, close.

**tokai** city, town; **tokaijin** city people, townsfolk.

**tokaku** (to be) apt to; in one way or other; **tokaku suru uchi ni** in the meantime. **Wakai mono wa tokaku keisotsu de aru.** Young people are apt to act hastily.

**tokasu** to melt, liquefy; to fuse; **koori o takasu** to melt ice; **satoo o mizu ni tokasu** to dissolve sugar in water.

**tokeau** to be melted together; to come to a mutual understanding.

**TOKEI** clock, watch; **oki dokei** clock; **ude dokei** wristwatch; **tokeiya** a watchmaker.

**tokeru** to melt; dissolve; **mizu ni tokeru** to be soluble in water; **netsu de tokeru** to melt by heat.

**tokeru** to get loose, come untied. **Musubime ga toketa.** The knot has come untied.

**TOKI** time; hour; moment; time when; **toki hazure no** out of season; **toki o eta** seasonable, timely. **Kyooto e itta toki kaimashita.** I bought it when I went to Kyoto.

**TOKIDOKI** now and then; occasionally. **Tokidoki aimashita.** I met him occasionally.

**tokifuseru** to persuade; to convince; to argue down; to prevail upon.

**tokitsukeru** to persuade, prevail upon.

**tokka** special prices; **tokka hanbai** sale at reduced prices.

**tokken** exclusive right or privilege.

**tokki** projection; **tokki suru** to project.

**tokkoo** special virtue, efficacy.

**tukkumiau** to grapple with each other.

**tokku ni** (adv.) a long time ago.

**tokku no** (adj.) a long time ago; **tokku no mukashi** long ago, ages ago.

**tokkuri** sake bottle.

**tokkyuu** special express (train).

**TOKO** alcove; floor; bed; bedding; **toko no ma** guest room alcove in a Japanese house where hanging scrolls, flower arrangements, etc., are displayed; **toko o shiku** to spread out bedding, make a bed; **toko ni tsuite iru** to be in bed; **tokokazari** alcove ornament.

**tokoage** to leave a sickbed.

**tokoo** voyage, passage; **-e tokoo suru** to make a voyage to; **tokoosha** passenger, emigrant.

**TOKORO** address, place; **tokoro o eru** to find a right place.

**tokorode** then, well, now.

**TOKOROGA** but, however, on the contrary.

**tokoya** barbershop, barber.

**toku** profit, gain; **toku na** profitable, advantageous; **toku o suru** to gain, profit, benefit.

**toku** virtue, morality.

**toku** to untie, undo, unbind; to melt; to fuse; to smelt.

**TOKUBETSU NO** special, particular, exceptional; **TOKUBETSU NI** specially.

**tokuchoo** characteristic.

**tokudane** exclusive news, scoop (newspaper).

**tokuden** special telegram.

**tokugi** morality; **tokugijoo** morally; from the moral point of view.

**tokuhain** special representative, special correspondent (of a newspaper).

**tokui** pride, self-complacency; one's forte; customer, patron.

**tokumei** anonymity; **tokumei de** anonymously.

**TOKU NI** especially. **Ashita wa toku ni hayaku kite kudasai.** Please come especially early tomorrow.

**tokusaku** better way, wiser way.

**tokusan** specialty of a locality.

**tokusei** special make; deluxe.

**tokusetsu** specially set up, specially organized.

**tokushi** benevolence, charity; **tokushika** charitable or self-sacrificing person.

**tokushi** special envoy.

**tokushoku** special feature, specialty.

**tokushu na** special.

**tokuten** score (sports).

**tokuto** carefully, attentively.

**tokutokuto** proudly; with a triumphant air.

**tokutooseki** special seat.

**tokuyaku** special contract.

**tokuyuu no** peculiar; characteristic.

**tomadoi suru** to be bewildered.

**TOMARU** to stop (at or in). **Itami wa tomarimashita.** The pain is gone. **Kono densha wa shinagawa de tomarimasu ka?** Does this train stop at Shinagawa Station?

**tomaru** to lodge; **hitoban tomaru** to stay overnight.

**tomasu** to enrich, make wealthy.

**TOMATO** tomato.

**tomeru** to stop, bring to stop; **gasu o tomeru** to turn off the gas; **kuruma o tomeru** to stop a car.

**tomeru** to give lodging (to a person), give shelter.

**-TOMO** of course; even though; **donna koto ga okoroo tomo** whatever may happen. **Ikimasu tomo.** Of course I will go.

**tomo** attendant; suite; **tomo ni** together with; including; **tomo o suru** to follow (someone). **Daika sooryoo tomo ni sen en desu.** The price is 1000 yen, including postage.

**TOMODACHI** friend. **Tomodachi ni ai ni ikimasu.** I am going to see a friend.

**tomodaore** common ruin.

**tomokaku** at all events, at any rate.

**tomokasegi suru** to work (both husband and wife) for a living.

**tomonau** to accompany, go with; **heigai ga tomonau** to be attended with evil.

**tomosu** to burn, light, turn on (a lamp).

**tomu** to grow rich. **Ano hito wa keiken ni tonde imasu.** He has great experience.

**tomurai** funeral, burial.

**tomurau** to mourn for the dead.

**ton** ton, tonnage.

**tonaeru** to recite; to repeat; to chant.

**TONARI** neighboring house; next-door neighbor; **tonari no** adjoining, next; **tonari atte iru** to be next door to each other; **tonari no hito** next-door neighbor.

**tonbo** dragonfly.

**tonda** surprising; extraordinary; shocking, terrible; unexpected; **tonda me ni au** to meet with a misfortune.

**tondemonai** surprising; extraordinary; unexpected; awful; abused; **tondemonai koto ni naru** to become serious; to take an unexpected turn.

**TONIKAKU** in any case.

**tonjaku** care, heed, regard; **jikan ni tonjaku naku** regardless of time.

**tonkatsu** pork cutlet.

**tonkyoo** ludicrousness; wild screech or act (to scare or make others laugh); **tonkyoo na** freakish.

**tonneru** tunnel.

**tonogata** men, gentlemen; **tonogata no** men's, gentlemen's.

**tonto** not at all, not in the least; entirely. **Ano hito wa ton to konai.** She does not come at all.

**tonton byooshi** without a hitch. **Koto ga tonton byooshi ni hakonde imasu.** Things are going along swimmingly.

**ton'ya** wholesale shop, wholesale dealer.

**TOO** ten, ten years old.

**too** political party; **Shakaitoo** Socialist Party.

**too** counter for cattle (denoting: head); **ushi hattoo** eight cows.

**too** rightness, propriety, justness; this; **too no honnin** person in question; **toogetsu** this month.

**-too** tower, pagoda.

**-too** suffix denoting: grade, class; **ittoo** first class.

**tooa** East Asia.

**tooben** answer; explanation; defense.

**tooboe** howling; **inu no tooboe** the howling of dogs; **tooboe suru** to howl.

**tooboo** flight, desertion; **tooboo suru** to run away; **tooboosha** a fugitive.

**TOOBUN** for the time being. **Toobun ame wa furanai deshoo.** It won't rain for a while.

**toobun** sugar content; **toobun o fukunda** sugary.

**toochaku** arrival; **toochaku jun ni** in order of arrival; **toochaku shidai** immediately on arrival; **toochaku suru** to arrive.

**toochi** this place, here.

**toochoku** being on duty; on watch.

**toodai** lighthouse.

**toodori** president, director.

**tooen** distant (blood) relation.

**tooge** mountain pass, defile; crisis; **Hakone no tooge** Hakone Pass; **tooge o kosu** to pass the critical stage.

**toogi** debate, discussion; **toogi suru** to discuss, debate.

**toogoku** imprisonment.

**Tooguu** Crown Prince.

**toogyo** rule, management.

**tooha** party, faction; school; clique.

**tooha suru** to traverse; to travel on foot; to tramp.

**tooheki** thievishness; kleptomania.

**toohi** escape, flight; **toohi suru** to escape, fly.

**toohyoo** voting; poll; **-ni toohyoo suru** to vote for; **toohyoo de kimeru** to decide by vote; **toohyoo ni iku** to go to the polls.

**TOOI** far, far away. **Tanaka-san no uchi wa koko kara tooi desu.** Mr. Tanaka's house is far from here.

**tooin** party member.

**tooitsu** unification, uniformity; **tooitsuteki** unifying.

**tooji** at that time; at this time.

**toojiru** See **toozuru.**

**toojisha** person concerned; **toojisha ni kakeau** to negotiate with the persons concerned.

**toojitsu** day in question; appointed day; day of issue (for a ticket, etc.).

**toojoo suru** to get on board a ship or plane.

**toojoo** stage entrance; **toojoo suru** to go on the stage.

**TOOKA** ten days; tenth day of the month.

**tookan** mailing, posting; **tegami o tookan suru** to mail a letter.

**tookarazu** before long, in the near future.

**tookei** statistics; **tookei o toru** to make a survey.

**tooki** registration; **tooki suru** to register.

**tooki** earthenware.

**tookoo suru** to contribute to a periodical.

**tookoo suru** to go to school.

**tookoo suru** to surrender.

**tooku** a distant place; **ki ga tooku naru** to faint, swoon.

**tookyokusha** authorities concerned.

**tookyori** equal distance.

**tookyuu** class, grade; **tookyuu o tsukeru** to grade.

**toomawari** detour; roundabout way; **toomawari o suru** to detour.

**toomawashi na** roundabout, indirect; **toomawashi ni** indirectly; in a roundabout way.

**toome** distant view; **toome ga kiku** to be able to see a long way off.

**toomei na** transparent.

**toomen no** present; urgent; immediate; **toomen no mondai** matter in hand.

**toomichi** long way, great distance.

**toonan** robbery, burglary.

**tooni** long ago; already.

**toonin** person in question.

**toonoku** to recede; to get away. **Ashi ga toonoku.** Her visits are becoming rarer.

**toonori** long ride, long drive; **toonori o suru** to take a long drive; **jitensha no toonori o suru** to go on a long cycling excursion.

**toorai suru** to come, arrive; to occur; to come to hand. **Kikai ga toorai shita.** An opportunity presented itself.

**toorei** returning a salute; returning a call.

**TOORI** road, street; traffic; **toori o yoku suru** to clear a passage; **toori ippen no** casual; indifferent.

**-TOORI** like, as; **watakushi no iu toori** as I say.

**-toori** kinds. **Iku toori mo aru.** There are many kinds.

**toorigakari** passing, chance; **toorigakari no hito** passersby.

**toorikakaru** to happen to pass (come by).

**toorikosu** to go beyond; to walk past; to pass.

**toorinuke** passing through.

**tooroku** registration; **tooroku suru** to register.

**tooron** debate, discussion; **tooron suru** to debate; **tooronkai** forum.

**tooroo** fixed stone lantern, dedicatory lantern.

**TOORU** to go along; to pass; to go by the name of; to be admissible; to get through; **shiken ni tooru** to pass an examination; **sujimichi ga tootte iru** to be consistent; to be logical. **Kono basu wa Ginza o toorimasu.** This bus goes through Ginza.

**tooryuu suru** to stay at.

**toosa** exploration; survey.

**toosei** management, control; regulation; **toosei suru** to bring under government control; to regulate, govern.

**toosen** winning a prize; success in a lottery; **toosen bangoo** winning numbers; **toosensha** successful candidate.

**tooshaban** mimeograph, duplicator.

**tooshi** investment; **-ni tooshi suru** to invest in; **tooshika** investor.

**toosho** contribution; **tooshoran** letters-to-the-editor column.

**tooshu** present master; head of a family.

**toosoo** escape.

**TOOSU** to let (someone) pass through; to admit; to carry; to realize; to make; to usher in; **me o toosu** to run over, glance over; **mon o toosu** to admit a person within the gates.

**toosutaa** toaster.

**toosuto** toast (bread).

**TOOTEI** by no means (used with a negative); after all. **Sonna koto wa tootei dekimasen.** I can't possibly do such a thing.

**tootoi** precious, valuable; high; noble; sacred, holy. **Tootoi ojikan o saite kudasaimashite arigatoo gozaimashita.** Thank you for spending your precious time on me.

**TOOTOO** at last, at length, finally. **Tootoo sono shigoto o shite shimaimashita.** I've finally finished that work.

**tootoo to** flowing in torrents; eloquently; **tootoo to nagareru** to flow majestically (as a river); **tootoo to noberu** to speak fluently.

**toowaku suru** to be perplexed, be puzzled; to be embarrassed; to be at a loss.

**TOOYOO** Orient; **Tooyoo no** (adj.) Oriental; **Tooyoojin** (n.) Oriental.

**tooyoo** appointment, promotion; **tooyoo suru** to appoint, promote.

**tooyoo kanji** (ideographic) characters included in the official list of 1850 (**Tooyoo Kanji Hyoo**) designated by the Japanese Government as the basic symbols in writing (replaced by **jooyoo kanji** in 1981).

**tooza** present time; current deposit; **tooza no kozukai** pocket money adequate for the present.

**toozakaru** to become more distant; to go away; **akuyuu kara toozakaru** to keep away from bad companions.

**toozakeru** to keep clear of, away from; to keep at a distance.

**toozen** matter of course; naturally.

**toozoku** thief, robber, burglar.

**toozuru** to throw; to throw away, throw off; to abandon; **ippyoo o toozuru** to cast a vote.

**toppatsu** outbreak; **toppatsuteki** unexpected, sudden.

**toppi na** extravagant, fantastic, venturesome.

**toppuu** gust of wind.

**tora** tiger.

**toraeru** to catch, seize, take hold of; **erikubi o toraeru** to seize (someone) by the neck.

**torahoomu** trachoma.

**torai suru** to come over the sea; to visit (a country).

**TORAKKU** truck; track field.

**toranpu** playing cards; **toranpu o suru** to play cards.

**TORI** bird, fowl; **TORINIKU** chicken meat, poultry.

**toriaezu** in haste; for the time being.

**toriageru** to take up, take in one's hand; **fuhei o toriageru** to listen to a complaint.

**toriatsukai** handling (of a thing); arrangement (of a business); treatment (of a guest). **Toriatsukai chuui.** Handle with care.

**toriau** to hold each other; to struggle for; to take notice of.

**toriawase** assortment; combination.

**torichigaeru** to mistake; to misunderstand; to misapprehend.

**torie** worth, merit, useful (strong) point; **torie no aru** useful, valuable, worthy; **torie no nai** worthless, good for nothing.

**torihakarau** to manage; to arrange; to dispose of; to settle; to deal with.

**toriharau** to remove, take away, clear away; to clear by taking (things) away.

**torihazusu** to remove; to take to pieces.

**torihiki** transaction, dealing; **torihiki o suru** to do business with; **torihiki o hajimeru** to open an account with; **torihikisaki** customer; business connection.

**torii** open front gate of a shrine, often painted red.

**toriire** harvest, crop; **toriire doki** harvesttime.

**toriireru** to take in; to harvest, gather in; to accept; to adopt.

**toriisogi** in a hurry; with dispatch.

**torikaeru** to change, exchange; to renew.

**torikaeshi** recovery, retrieval; **torikaeshi ga tsukanai** irrevocable.

**torikaesu** to get back; to regain, recover; to recall.

**torikakaru** to begin, commence; to set about.

**torikawasu** to exchange.

**torikesu** to cancel, revoke; **chuumon o torikesu** to cancel an order; **zenhanketsu o torikesu** to revoke a former decision.

**torikimeru** to arrange; to agree upon, settle, decide upon.

**toriko** captive, prisoner of war.

**torikomu** to take in; to bring over; to be in confusion; to get in favor with; **sentakumono o torikomu** to take in

washing. **Kyoo wa sukoshi torikonde imasu.** This place is upset today.

**torikoshiguroo** unnecessary worry; **torikoshiguroo o suru** to run to meet trouble; to be overanxious.

**torikowasu** to pull down; to take down; to break down; to break up.

**torikumu** to wrestle with; to grapple with; to be matched against.

**torimagireru** to be in confusion; **zatsumu ni torimagireru** to be under the pressure of routine business.

**torimaku** to surround, hem in, encircle, enclose; to fawn upon.

**torimatomeru** to gather all together; to collect; to pack; **kazai doogu o torimatomeru** to collect one's household goods.

**torimidasu** to disturb; to lose one's composure. **Heya wa torimidashite atta.** The room was in disorder.

**torimodosu** to take back; to regain, recover; to resume.

**torimotsu** to treat; to receive; to entertain.

**torinaosu** to recover; to mend; to alter.

**torinashi** mediation, intercession.

**torinasu** to plead for; to mediate; to recommend.

**torinigasu** to fail to catch; **kikai o torinigasu** to miss an opportunity.

**torinokeru** to remove, take away; to clear away, get rid of.

**toriotosu** to let fall, slip, drop; to miss one's hold.

**torishimari** management, supervision, control; **torishimariyaku** manager, director.

**torishimaru** to manage, control, superintend, oversee.

**torisoroeru** to put together; to gather; to assort.

**toritate no** fresh (from); **toritate no momo** fresh peaches; **toritate no sakana** fish fresh from the sea.

**toritateru** to collect; to promote; to patronize; **kashikin o toritateru** to collect loans; **yakunin ni toritateru** to appoint (someone) to a post.

**toritomeru** to ascertain, make sure; to make definite; **inochi o toritomeru** to have a narrow escape.

**toritsugi** intermediation; receiving a thing and handing it to another; agency; agent; answering a knock (or bell); usher; **toritsugi o suru** to act as an agent, to transmit; to convey.

**toritsuke** run on a bank.

**toritsukeru** to fit; to furnish; to install; to draw out (of the bank); **kikai o toritsukeru** to set up an apparatus.

**toritsuku** to hold fast to, cling to; to catch hold of; **toritsuku shima mo nai** to be left helpless.

**toritsukurou** to mend, repair, patch; **teisai o toritsukurou** to keep up appearances.

**toriya** bird fancier; poultry dealer.

**toriyoseru** to get, obtain, procure.

**tororo** grated yam.

**torotoro suru** to doze; to take a nap.

**TORU** to take; to take in one's hand, take hold of; to get; to fetch; to hand; to pass; to receive; to gain; to accept; to adopt; to choose; to buy; to gather; to pick; to eat; to charge; to manage; to interpret; to take away; to catch; to deprive a person of; to possess; to take possession of; to need, require; to preserve; to engage; to subscribe to; to insist; **eiyoobutsu o toru** to take nourishing food; **fude o toru** to take a pen in hand; to write; **jikan o toru** to take time; **jimu o toru** to do business; **ichiban chiisai no o toru** to pick the smallest one; **kane o torareru** to have one's money stolen; **ki no mi o toru** to pick fruit from trees; **kusa o toru** to weed; **hyaku man en no gekkyuu o toru** to receive a salary of one million yen; **rishi o toru** to charge interest; **sakana o toru** to catch fish; **shashin o toru** to have a picture taken; **shibai no seki o totte oku** to reserve a seat at a theater; **shinbun o toru** to subscribe to a newspaper; **tsuyoi taido o toru** to assume a fair attitude toward; **wairo o toru** to accept a bribe; **waruku toru** to take amiss. **Heya o totte okimashita.** I have engaged a room for you. **Kare wa kataku totte ugokanai.** He tries to carry his point and won't yield. **Shio o totte kudasai.** Will you pass me the salt? **Yasai wa ano mise kara torimasu.** We buy vegetables from that store.

**Toruko** Turkey; **Torukogo** Turkish (language); **Torukojin** Turk.

**toryoo** paints.

**TOSHI** year; age; **toshi to tomo ni** with age; **toshi o mukaeru** to welcome the New Year; **toshi o okuru** to pass the years; **toshi o toru** to grow old; **toshigoro** marriageable age; **onaji toshigoro no** of about the same age; **toshigoro no musume** daughter of marriageable age; **toshishita** younger; junior; **toshiue** senior; older; **TOSHIYORI** old person. **Tanaka-san yori mittsu toshi shita desu.** He is three years younger than Mr. Tanaka. **Yamada-san yori mittsu toshi ue desu.** He is three years older than Mr. Yamada.

**toshi** towns and cities; **toshi keikaku** city planning.

**toshikoshi** New Year's Eve.

**toshimawari** luck attending one's age. **Kotoshi wa toshimawari ga warui.** This year is an unlucky one for me.

**-to shite** as; for; in the capacity of; **orei to shite** as a token of thanks; **soodai to shite shusseki suru** to attend as a representative.

**tosho** books; **tosho gakari** librarian; **toshokan** library; **tosho etsuranshitsu** reading room.

**TOSSA NO AIDA NI** in a moment; quick as thought; on the spur of the moment.

**tosshin suru** to rush; to dash; to charge.

**totan** zinc.

**totan'ita** galvanized iron sheets.

**-totan ni** just as; in the act of. **Watakushi ga hairu totan ni kare wa dete itta.** He went out just as I entered.

**TOTEMO** very, awfully; extraordinarily.

**totonoeru** to prepare, get ready; to arrange.

**totonou** to be prepared; to be arranged; to be in good order; to be ready, be settled.

**TOTSUZEN** suddenly, abruptly; all of a sudden; **totsuzen no** sudden, abrupt. **Totsuzen jishoku shimashita.** She resigned without giving notice.

**totte** handle; knob; **totte o tsukeru** to fix a handle.

**tottei** jetty, breakwater.

**TOU** to ask, question.

**tozan** mountain climbing.

**tozetsu** stoppage, cessation; interruption; **tozetsu suru** to be stopped; to be interrupted.

**tsuba** saliva; **tsuba o kakeru** to spit at.

**tsubasa** wings.

**tsubo** land measure of six **shaku** (Japanese feet) square. **Kono niwa wa sanbyaku tsubo arimasu.** This garden has an area of three hundred **tsubo.**

**tsubo** jar; **tsubo ni ireru** to pot (plant).

**tsubomeru** to make narrow; to pucker up; **kasa o tsubomeru** to shut an umbrella; **kuchi o tsubomeru** to pucker up the lips.

**tsubomi** flower bud.

**tsubu** grain; drop (of liquid).

**tsubureru** to be crushed; to be smashed, be broken; to break; **menboku ga tsubureru** to be put out of countenance. **Ginkoo ga tsubureta.** The bank failed.

**tsubusu** to crush; to smash, break; **shindai o tsubusu** to dissipate one's fortune; **jikan o tsubusu** to kill time.

**tsubuyaku** to mutter, grumble; to murmur.

**TSUCHI** ground, earth; mud; clay.

**tsuchikusai** rustic; boorish.

**tsue** cane, walking stick; **tsue o tomeru** to make a stopover; **tsue o tsuku** to walk with a walking stick.

**tsugeguchi** talebearing; **tsugeguchi suru** to carry tales.

**tsugeru** to tell; to inform; to bid; **itoma o tsugeru** to bid farewell.

**TSUGI** next, succeeding, adjacent; **tsugi no ma** next room. **Kono tsugi wa dare desu ka?** Who comes next to her?

**tsugi** patch; **tsugi o ateru** to patch.

**tsugime** joint; seam; **tsugime nashi no** seamless.

**TSUGOO** circumstances; **tsugoo ni yori** for certain reasons; **tsugoo yoku** fortunately; **tsugoo ga yoi** to be convenient; **tsugoo suru** to arrange; to manage.

**tsugoo** in all; together.

**tsugu** to pour out; to fill; **ocha o ippai tsugu** to pour a cup of tea.

**tsugu** to join, to piece together; **ki ni take o tsugu** to graft bamboo onto a tree; to be incongruous.

**tsugu** to rank next to, to be next to, to rank second to.

**tsugu** to succeed, to accede; to inherit.

**TSUI** unintentionally; by mistake.

**tsui** pair, couple.

**tsuide** order, sequence; **tsuide ni** by way of, incidentally, when, as; **tsuide no setsu** at your convenience.

**tsuihoo** banishment, exile.

**tsuika** supplement, appendix; **tsuika suru** to add, supplement.

**tsuikyuu** investigation; **tsuikyuu suru** to inquire closely into (a matter).

**TSUINI** at last, finally; at length.

**tsuiraku** crash; fall; **tsuiraku suru** to fall; to crash.

**tsuiseki** pursuit, chase; **tsuiseki suru** to pursue.

**TSUITACHI** first day of the month.

**tsuitate** screen.

**TSUITE** (always used following **ni**) of, about, concerning; **kono ten ni tsuite** on this point. **Kono mondai ni tsuite doo omoimasu ka?** What do you think about this?

**tsuitoo** mourning; **tsuitoo suru** to mourn (a death); **tsuitoo no kotoba** memorial address; eulogy.

**tsuitotsu** bumping into the rear; **tsuitotsu suru** to collide (from behind).

**tsuiyasu** to spend, expend, lay out; **mono o mueki ni tsuiyasu** to be wasteful.

**tsujitsuma** consistency; **tsujitsuma no awanu** inconsistent.

**tsukaeru** to be clogged, be obstructed, be blocked; to be barred; **kotoba ga tsukaeru** to stammer, to stick in one's throat; **mune ga tsukaeru** to feel heavy in the stomach. **Kuda ga tsukaete iru.** The pipe is choked.

**tsukai** message; errand; messenger.

**tsukaihatasu** to squander, spend all (one's money).

**tsukaikata** usage, application. **Kono kikai no tsukaikata ga wakarimasen.** I don't know how to use this machine.

**tsukaikomu** to embezzle.

**tsukaimichi** employment, use.

**tsukainareru** to be accustomed to using.

**tsukaisugiru** to use excessively; to spend too much.

**tsukamaeru** to catch; to seize; to take hold of.

**tsukamaru** to be caught, be taken; to be arrested.

**tsukamaseru** to let (someone) grasp; to bribe.

**tsukamiai** grappling, fighting (without a weapon).

**tsukamu** to seize, catch, grasp, hold.

**tsukare** weariness, fatigue.

**TSUKARERU** to get tired, grow weary, become fatigued.

**tsukaru** to soak in; to be soaked in, be steeped in; **kaisui ni tsukaru** to take a dip (in the sea).

**tsukasadoru** to rule, govern, administer; to take charge of.

**TSUKAU** to use, put to use, employ; to take; to spend; **atama o tsukau** to use one's brain; **yu o tsukau** to take a hot bath. **Ano hito wa rippa na Nihongo o tsukaimasu.** He speaks good Japanese.

**tsukeiru** to take advantage of (someone); to presume on (someone's) good nature; to impose on (someone's) kindness.

**tsukekomu** to enter; to take advantage of another's weakness.

**tsukemono** pickles; pickled vegetables.

**tsukenerau** to prowl, to dog, shadow; to hang about.

**TSUKERU** to attach one thing to another, to set one thing on another, to stick on, to sew on; to wear, to make an entry (in a book); **kata o tsukeru** to make an end (of something); **ki o tsukeru** to take care; **mikomi o tsukeru** to form a judgment; **kusuri o tsukeru** to apply a medicine; **na o tsukeru** to name; **pan ni bataa o tsukeru** to spread butter on bread; **te o tsukeru** to put one's hand to a task; to eat.

**tsukeru** to soak in, steep in.

**TSUKI** moon; month; **mikazuki** crescent; **tsuki ni nikai** twice a month; **tsuki no de** rising of the moon.

**-tsuki** suffix denoting: assigned to; attached to; per. **Hitori ni tsuki gosen en desu.** The charge is 5000 yen per person.

**tsukiageru** to thrust up; to push up; to toss.

**tsukiai** keeping company; association; intercourse; **tsukiai no tame ni** for the sake of friendship; **tsukiai nikui** to be difficult to get along with; **tsukiai o suru** to keep company with.

**tsukiatari** dead end (street); collision, crash.

**tsukiau** to keep company with, associate with.

**tsukidasu** to thrust out, stick out, push out, stretch out.

**tsukihajime** beginning of a month.

**tsukihi** days and months; time; years; date.

**tsukikaesu** to thrust back.

**tsukimatou** to follow, shadow (someone); to hang on; to pursue.

**tsukimono** accessory, adjunct, appendage; part; anything which is attached to or is an indispensable part of something.

**tsukinami na** commonplace; conventional.

**tsukinuku** to thrust through, pierce, penetrate.

**tsukiokure no** of the previous month; **tsukiokure no zasshi** back numbers of a magazine.

**tsukiotosu** to throw or push (someone) down or off.

**tsukiru** to become exhausted; to be used up, be consumed. **Okane ga tsukimashita.** I ran out of money.

**tsukisoi** attendant; nurse; chaperon.

**tsukisou** to attend (someone); to accompany.

**tsukitaosu** to knock down.

**tsukitomeru** to ascertain, make sure of; to assure, convince, satisfy oneself of.

**tsukitoosu** to thrust, pierce.

**tsukitsukeru** to thrust before; to put (place) under (someone's) nose; to point at.

**tsukiyo** moonlit night.

**tsukizue** end of a month.

**tsukizuki no** monthly; **tsukizuki no teate** monthly allowance.

**tsukkakaru** to fall on, pick a quarrel with (someone).

**tsukkakeru** to slip on.

**tsukkiru** to cross; to go (run) across; to go through.

**tsukkomu** to thrust in; to plunge in; to poke into.

**TSUKU** to arrive at. **Fune wa ima tsukimashita.** The ship has just arrived. **Koobe ni tsukimashita.** He arrived at Kobe.

**tsuku** to adhere to, to stick to. **Te ni penki ga tsuite iru.** There is paint on her hand.

**tsuku** to pierce, to thrust, to stab; **tantoo de tsuku** to stab (someone) with a dagger.

**TSUKUE** table, desk.

**TSUKURU** to make, manufacture; to prepare, produce; to turn out; to frame; to build, erect; to form; to raise; to cultivate; to

constitute; **ie o tsukuru** to build a house; **kane o tsukuru** to make a fortune; **rajio o tsukuru** to make a radio; **retsu o tsukuru** to form in line.

**tsukusu** to exhaust; to come to the end of; to serve (someone); to make efforts.

**tsukuzuku** thoroughly, utterly, quite; **tsukuzuku iya ni naru** to become utterly disgusted; **tsukuzuku kangaeru** to reflect carefully.

**TSUMA** wife.

**tsumadatsu** to stand on tiptoe.

**tsumahajiki ni suru** to flick; to disdain; to shun; to scorn.

**tsumamidasu** to pick out, drag out, turn out.

**tsumamu** to pick, pinch, take a pinch of.

**TSUMARANAI** trifling, worthless, commonplace; **tsumaranai koto** matter of no importance; **tsumaranai mono** trifling thing.

**TSUMARI** in the end; in the long run; finally; in a word.

**tsumaru** to be blocked up; to be full, be packed; to be shortened; **hentoo ni tsumaru** to be at a loss for a reply; **kane ni tsumaru** to be pressed for money; **ki ga tsumaru** to be oppressive.

**tsumashii** frugal, thrifty, economical.

**tsumazuku** to take a false step; to lose one's footing, stumble, fall.

**TSUME** nail; claw; hoof; hook; **tsume o kiru** to cut one's nails.

**tsumekakeru** to crowd (a house); to throng to (the door).

**tsumekiri** constant attendance; staying at one's post without a break.

**tsumekomu** to cram; to stuff; to jam; to pack; **heya ni hito o tsumekomu** to crowd people into a room.

**tsumemono o suru** to stuff, pack.

**tsumeru** to cram; to stuff; to fill; to pack; to charge; **kaban ni tsumeru** to pack a suitcase.

**TSUMETAI** cold (to the touch), chilly; icy; **tsumetai kokoro** cold heart; **tsumetai mizu** cold water.

**tsumi** crime, offense; sin; fault; **tsumi na** sinful, cruel, inhuman.

**tsumiageru** to heap up, make a pile; to accumulate.

**tsumidasu** to send off, ship off.

**tsumihoroboshi** atonement of sins, expiation.

**tsumikaeru** to reship.

**tsumikomu** to load; to put on board; to take in.

**tsumini** cargo, freight.

**tsumitateru** to save up (money); to lay by; to reserve, amass, accumulate.

**TSUMORI** intention; motive, expectation;

understanding. **Haratta tsumori desu.** I
believe I've paid for it. **Iku tsumori desu.**
I intend to go.

**tsumorigaki** written estimate; written
measurement.

**tsumoru** to accumulate; to be piled up; to
amount to. **Tsumoru hanashi ni yo o
fukashita.** We had much to talk about and
sat up far into the night. **Yuki ga tsumoru.**
Snow is piled up on the ground.

**tsumu** to pile up, heap up; to load; to
accumulate; to take on board; to pick; to
pluck; to pull out.

**tsumujikaze** whirlwind, tornado.

**tsuna** cord, rope, line. **Tanomi no tsuna mo
kireta.** The last ray of hope is gone.

**tsunagi** connection, link.

**tsunagu** to tie, fasten, chain, connect, join.

**tsunami** tidal waves.

**tsune** usual state; **tsune no** usual, ordinary,
common; **tsune ni** always.

**tsuneru** to pinch.

**tsuno** horn; **tsuno o hayasu** to become
jealous.

**tsunoru** to solicit (a subscription); to collect;
to grow violent, severe, intense, fierce; to
become worse.

**tsunzaku** to rend, break; to pierce; to split.

**tsupparu** to stretch (an arm or leg against
something); to plant one's feet on the
ground.

**TSURAI** hard; painful; bitter; **tsuraku**
bitterly, harshly.

**tsuranaru** to range; to lie in a row; to be
present at. **Matsuda-san no kekkonshiki
ni tsuranatta.** I attended Mr. Matsuda's
wedding.

**tsuranuku** to pierce; to pass through.

**tsurara** icicle.

**tsurasa** pain, painfulness.

**tsure** companion.

**tsureai** (*colloq.*) spouse, husband, wife.

**tsuredatsu** to go along with.

**TSURERU** to take (with). **Tomodachi o
tsurete ikimashita.** I took a friend of mine
with me.

**tsuresou** to be married, be husband and wife.

**tsuri** change. **Gohyaku en no tsuri o
moraimashita.** I received change of 500
yen.

**tsuri** fishing (with a hook and line). **Tsuri o
shi ni ikimashita.** I went fishing.

**tsuriai** balance, equilibrium; harmony; **tsurial
o toru** to balance oneself.

**tsurusu** to hang, suspend; to swing.

**tsutaeru** to convey; to report; to deliver; to
communicate.

**tsutawaru** to be handed down; to be
transmitted.

**tsute** intermediary; good offices; **tsute o
motomeru** to hunt up connections.

**tsutomaru** to be fit for; to be equal to (a
position).

**TSUTOME** duty; service; **tsutome o hatasu**
to discharge one's duties; **tsutomeguchi**
place of employment.

**TSUTOMERU** to serve, to hold (fill) a post;
to exert oneself; to make an effort; to
endeavor; to labor, work; **tsutomesaki**
one's place of employment. **Takagi-san
wa ginkoo ni tsutomete imasu.** Takagi
works for a bank.

**tsutsu** pipe, tube; gun barrel; gun.

**tsutsuku** to poke at; to pick at, to peck.

**tsutsumashii** modest, reserved.

**TSUTSUMI** package, parcel; **tsutsumigami**
wrapping paper, packing sheet.

**tsutsumi** dike, embankment.

**TSUTSUMU** to wrap, to do up, to pack.

**tsutsushimi** prudence, discretion, caution;
**tsutsushimi no nai** immodest, indiscreet;
**tsutsushimi o wasureru** to lose one's self-
control.

**tsutsushimu** to be discreet; to be careful, be
prudent; to restrain oneself.

**tsuttatsu** to stand; to stand up straight.

**tsuu** connoisseur, authority, expert judge.

**-tsuu** counter for letters, telegrams; **tegami o
ittsuu dasu** to send a letter.

**tsuuchi** information; **tsuuchi suru** to inform.

**tsuuchoo** official communication,
notification.

**tsuufuu** ventilation.

**tsuugaku suru** to go to school.

**tsuuji** bowel movement; **tsuuji ga tomaru** to
become constipated; **tsuuji o tsukeru** to
loosen the bowels.

**tsuujiru** to pass; to run; to be opened (to
traffic); to be understood.

**tsuujoo** usually; ordinarily; as a rule.

**tsuukai na** extremely delightful; pleasant;
**tsuukai na otoko** a man of spirit. **Sore wa
tsuukai de atta.** It was a delightful
sensation.

**tsuukan** passing through customs.

**tsuukan suru** to feel keenly, feel acutely.

**tsuukin suru** to go to the office.

**tsuukoku** announcement, notice, information;
**tsuukoku suru** to notify.

**tsuukoo** passing; transit; **tsuukoodome no**
thoroughfare; **tsuukoodome ni suru** to
close a road; to stop traffic.

**TSUUREI** as a rule; commonly.

**tsuusan** sum total.

**tsuusetsu na** keen, acute.

**tsuushin** correspondence, communication;
**tsuushinsha** news agency.

**tsuushoo** common name.

**tsuutatsu** notification; **tsuutatsu suru** to notify.

**tsuuun** transportation, moving van; **tsuuun gaisha** mover.

**-TSUUWA** counter denoting: phone call unit. **Ittsuuwa wa sanpun desu.** One telephone call unit is based on three minutes' conversation.

**tsuuwaryoo** charge for a telephone call.

**tsuuyaku** interpretation, interpreter; **tsuuyaku suru** to interpret.

**tsuuyoomon** public gate; side gate.

**tsuuyoo suru** to pass for; to circulate; to be current; to hold good.

**tsuya** gloss, luster.

**TSUYOI** strong, powerful, robust, healthy.

**tsuyoki** firmness; **tsuyoki o shimesu** to show firmness.

**tsuyomeru** to strengthen; to invigorate; to intensify; **imi o tsuyomeru** to emphasize.

**tsuyomi** strength, power; strong point.

**tsuyosa** strength, power.

**tsuyu** rainy season (June–July); **tsuyu no iri** start of the rainy season; **tsuyu no ake** end of the rainy season.

**tsuyu, otsuyu** soup, broth; gravy (Japanese style).

**tsuyu** dew, dewdrop. **Tsuyu ga oriru.** The dew falls.

**TSUZUKERU** to continue; to keep on.

**tsuzuki** continuation; connection; succession.

**TSUZUKU** to go on; to follow, go in succession; to last. **Ame wa mikka tsuzukimashita.** The rain continued to fall for three days.

**tsuzuri** spelling.

**tsuzuru** to spell words; to compose (a tune); **bun o tsuzuru** to write.

# U

**uba** wet nurse.

**ubaguruma** baby carriage.

**ubau** to take by force, snatch; to rob (someone of something).

**ubu** naïveté; greenness.

**UCHI** house; home; inside, interior; **sono hi no uchi ni** in the course of that day; **uchi no koto** household matters; **uchi de asobu** to play indoors.

**uchiageru** to shoot up; to send up; to set off.

**uchiakeru** to disclose, reveal; to confide (a secret); **himitsu o uchiakeru** to give secret information; to disclose secrets.

**uchiau** to exchange blows.

**uchiawase** previous arrangement; consultation; **uchiawase o suru** to make arrangements for.

**uchiawaseru** to strike (one thing against another); to make arrangements for something.

**uchidasu** to begin to beat; to strike out; to close.

**uchideshi** apprentice; private pupil.

**uchigawa** inside.

**uchikaesu** to strike, beat, hit back, return a blow.

**uchikesu** to deny; to negate; to contradict.

**uchiki** retiring disposition; shyness.

**uchikiru** to close; to discontinue; **kooshoo o uchikiru** to drop negotiations.

**uchikomu** to drive in; to strike into; to shoot into; to fall deeply in love with; to be absorbed in; **kugi o uchikomu** to drive a nail into; **tama o uchikomu** to send bullets into.

**uchimaku** real state of things; inside facts; **uchimaku o abaku** to see behind the scenes.

**uchiotosu** to strike down, knock down, floor; to shoot down.

**uchitaosu** to knock down, strike down, overthrow.

**uchitokeru** to open one's heart; to be frank, to be candid.

**uchitomeru, uchitoru** to kill, slay, shoot dead.

**uchiumi** inland sea.

**uchiwa** family circle; private circle (of friends); **uchiwa dooshi** those who are of the same party (or family, etc.); member of the inner circle.

**uchiwake** item breakdown (of an account); details.

**uchooten ni naru** to be in ecstasy.

**uchuu** universe, cosmos; **uchuu hikooshi** astronaut; **uchuu kaihatsu** space development; **uchuusen** spacecraft.

**UDE** arm; ability; **ude o furuu** to exercise a talent; **ude o kasu** to lend a helping hand; **ude o tamesu** to test one's ability; **udekiki** able man; man of ability.

**udon** noodle; **udonko** wheat flour; **udonya** restaurant where Japanese noodles are the specialty.

**UE** upper part, surface, topside; top, summit, head; after, on, upon; **ichiban ue no** uppermost; **shiken no ue de** on examination; **ue ni tatsu hito** one who stands in authority over others; **ue no** higher; upper; superior.

**ue** hunger; starvation; **uejini** death by starvation.

**uekaeru** to transplant, replant; **hoka no hachi ni uekaeru** to transplant into another pot.

**ueki** plant; potted plant; **uekiya** gardener.

**uekomi** thicket, shrubbery.

**ueru** to plant.

**ueru** to become hungry; to starve; to be famished; to hunger for.

**ueshita** up and down; shirts and trousers; **ueshita ni naru** to be upside down; **ueshita ni suru** to turn upside down.

**uetsuke** planting; transplanting.

**ugai** gargling, rinsing the mouth; **ugai suru** to gargle; **ugaigusuri** a gargle.

**ugatsu** to dig; to cut through; to pierce; **ugatta koto o iu** to make a pointed remark.

**UGOKASU** to move; to shift; to remove, to set in motion; **chooshuu o ugokasu** to move an audience; **hito no kokoro o ugokasu** to touch the heart.

**ugoki** movement, motion.

**UGOKU** to move; to shift; to sway; to work; to be transferred to another position. **Ugoite wa ikemasen.** Don't move.

**ugomeku** to wriggle, squirm.

**uisukii** whiskey.

**ukaberu** to float, keep afloat.

**ukabu** to float; to come to the surface, appear. **Ii kangae ga ukanda.** I hit upon a good idea.

**UKAGAU** to pay a visit; to inquire *(humble)*. **Sono koto wa Yamada-san ni ukagaimashita.** I asked Mr. Yamada about it. **Yamada-san no otaku ni ukagaimashita.** I visited Yamada's house.

**ukagau** to watch for, to look for, to be on the lookout for; **hito no kaoiro o ukagau** to study a person's face; **kikai o ukagau** to look for a chance.

**ukareru** to make merry; to be gay.

**ukasareru** to be carried away, be captivated; **netsu ni ukasareru** to be delirious with fever.

**ukatsu** carelessness, thoughtlessness; stupidity.

**uke** reputation, popularity; acceptance, assent, consent. **Ano hito wa uke ga ii.** She has a good reputation.

**ukedasu, ukemodosu** to redeem, take (something) out of pawn.

**ukekotae** reply, answer; **ukekotae o suru** to reply, answer.

**ukemi** acting on the defensive; passive (in grammar).

**ukemochi** charge.

**ukemodosu** See **ukedasu.**

**ukenagasu** to ward off, turn aside; **shitsumon o takumi ni ukenagasu** to ignore a question diplomatically.

**ukeoi** contract for work.

**ukeou** to undertake; to take upon oneself; to assume.

**UKERU** to receive; to accept; to have, to obtain; to take; **hoomon o ukeru** to receive a visit; **shujutsu o ukeru** to have an operation (surgical). (See also **uketoru.**)

**uketomeru** to stop; to catch; to ward off; **tama o uketomeru** to catch a ball.

**UKETORI** receipt; acceptance; **uketorinin** receiver, recipient.

**UKETORU** (see **UKERU**) to receive; to accept. **Tegami o uketorimashita.** I received a letter.

**uketsugi** succession; inheritance.

**UKETSUKE** receiving; accepting; reception desk; **uketsuke gakari** receptionist.

**ukewatashi** delivery, transfer; **ukewatashi o suru** to deliver, transfer.

**uki** float, buoy.

**ukiagaru** to rise to the surface; to float.

**ukiashi** unsteadiness; wavering, faltering; **ukiashi ni naru** to waver, become unsteady.

**ukibukuro** air bladder (of a fish), life buoy, life belt.

**UKKARI** vacantly; carelessly; without attention.

**uku** to float; to come to the surface; to be left over; to be saved; **ki ga uku** to be gay, to be exhilarated.

**UMA** horse, mount; **umakata** driver of a pack horse; **umaya** horse stable.

**UMAI** good; nice; tasty; skillful; successful; profitable; **umai mono** delicious, dainty food.

**umami** deliciousness, flavor; **umami no aru hanashi** a nice speech.

**umare** birth, lineage; **umare no yoi** to be well-born, be high-born.

**UMARERU** to be born; **hinka ni umareru** to come from a poor family; **umareru to sugu** at birth.

**umaretsuki** by nature; by temperament.

**umaru** to be filled up; to be hurried.

**umeawase** amends, compensation; **sonshitsu no umeawase o suru** to make up for a loss.

**umeki** moan, groan.

**umeku** to groan, moan.

**umeru** to bury; to reclaim; to fill up.

**umetate** reclamation; filling up; **umetatechi** reclaimed land; **umetate kooji** reclamation work.

**UMI** sea; ocean; **hi no umi** vast sheet of fire; sea of fire; **umi de oyogu** to swim in the ocean; **umibe** beach, seashore.

**umi** pus; **umi o motsu** to form pus.

**umi no haha** one's natural mother.

**umitate** fresh (said of an egg).

**UMU** to bear, give birth to, be delivered of. **Anzuru yori umu ga yasui.** Fear often exaggerates danger.

**umu** existence, presence; yes or no; **umu o iwasezu** forcibly; whether one will or not. **Ayamari no umu o shirasete kudasai.** Let me know whether there is any mistake.

**umu** to form pus, fester.

**un** fortune, lot, destiny, fate; **un no warui** unlucky; **un no yoi** lucky.

**un** (colloq.) yes; hmm; well; groan.

**unadareru** to hang one's head.

**unagasu** to urge, press, demand, to call upon; to stimulate.

**unari** groan; roar; humming.

**unaru** to groan; to roar; to howl, to hum.

**unasareru** to have a nightmare, have bad dreams.

**unazuku** to nod, bow one's head in assent.

**unchin** freight; portage; shipping expenses.

**undei no sa** all the difference in the world.

**UNDOO** movement, motion; physical exercise; **undoo suru** to move; to exercise; to walk; to campaign; **undooka** athlete.

**une** furrow.

**uneru** to wind; to undulate; **nami ga uneru** to swell.

**unga** canal; **ungachitai** canal zone.

**unmei** destiny, fate, fortune; doom.

**unomi ni suru** to gulp down.

**unpan** transportation; **unpan suru** to transport.

**unsoo** carrying, transport; **unsoo suru** to carry, transport; **unsooya** mover, forwarding agent.

**UNTEN** operation; driving; working; **unten suru** to drive, operate, work; **untenshu** engineer (operator of an engine); chauffeur; motorman; **unten menkyo** driver's license.

**unto** (colloq.) with great force; with all one's might; soundly; liberally; **kane ga unto aru** to have lots of money; **unto osu** to push with all one's might.

**unubore** self-conceit; **unubore ga tsuyoi** to be full of conceit.

**unuboreru** to be vain; to be conceited, to think highly of oneself.

**un'yu** traffic; transport.

**unzan** operation, calculation; **unzan suru** to calculate.

**unzari suru** to be disgusted with.

**UO** fish; **uogashi** fish market.

**uppun** resentment, grudge, enmity.

**URA** reverse side; back, sole of the foot; lining of clothes; hidden meaning of an expression; second half of baseball inning.

**uradana** house in an alley.

**uradoori** back street.

**uragaki** endorsement; **uragaki suru** to endorse.

**uragiri** treachery, perfidy.

**uragiru** to betray, turn traitor, go over to the enemy.

**uraguchi** back entrance.

**uraji** lining; cloth for lining.

**urameshii** reproachful; resentful; hateful.

**urami** resentment; grudge; hatred; malice; **urami o idaku** to bear a grudge.

**uramichi** byway; back road.

**uramon** back gate.

**uramu** to bear a grudge; to feel bitter against; to think ill of.

**uranai** fortune-telling; fortune-teller.

**uranau** to divine, forecast; **minoue o uranau** to tell (someone's) fortune.

**uraniwa** backyard; rear garden.

**urate** rear of a building.

**URAYAMASHII** enviable. **Anata ga urayamashii desu.** I envy you.

**urayamu** to envy, be envious of, be jealous of; **hito no koofuku o urayamu** to envy a person his good luck.

**urekko** popular person; social lion; **bundan no urekko** popular writer.

**urekuchi** market.

**ureshigaru** to be glad; to take delight in; to feel happy.

**URESHII** glad, joyous, delighted, happy. **Ome ni kakarete ureshii desu.** I'm glad to be able to see you.

**uriage** proceeds (returns) of a sale.

**URIBA** sales counter.

**uribagakari** sales clerk.

**uridame** proceeds, cash in a money box.

**uridashi** bargain sale; opening sale.

**uridasu** to offer for sale, place on the market, put on sale.

**urikire** sold out.

**uriko** salespeople.

**urimono** for sale; **urimono ni dasu** to put up for sale.

**URINE** sale price.

**urioshimi** holding (hoarding) goods for future sale; **urioshimi o suru** to hoard goods for future sale.

**urotaeru** to be confused, be thrown into confusion; to be upset.

**urotsuku** to loiter, hang about; to wander about.

**URU** to sell; to deal in; to offer for sale. **Sore wa doko de utte imasu ka?** Where is it sold?

**uru** to gain; to get.

**urumu** to be wet; to be moist; to be blurred; to be dimmed.

**uruoi** moisture, damp; enrichment; grace, charm; **uruoi no aru** moist; profitable; tasteful.

**uruosu** to wet, moisten; to dip; to be moistened, be wet; to benefit (someone).

**URUSAI** annoying, tiresome, harassing, irksome; noisy. **Urusai!** Pipe down!

**uruudoshi** leap year.

**uruwashii** beautiful, pretty; fine; **gokigen uruwashiku** in good humor; in excellent health.

**uryoo** rainfall; **uryookei** rain gauge.

**usagi** rabbit.

**usankusai** suspicious-looking; uncanny.

**USHI** cattle; cow; bull; ox.

**USHINAU** to lose; to miss; to part with; to be deprived of.

**USHIRO** *(n.)* back, rear; *(adj.)* **ushiro no** back, hind, rear; **ushiroashi** hind legs; **ushiro ni** behind; **ushiro e mawaru** to get behind.

**ushirogurai** shady; not aboveboard; **ushirogurai koto** underhanded, shady transaction.

**ushiromuki** standing with the back toward another.

**ushiroyubi o sasu** to point a finger of scorn at; **ushiroyubi o sasareru** to be talked about as an object of scorn.

**uso** lie, falsehood; **makka na uso** a pack of lies; **uso no** false; **uso o tsuku** to lie; **uso happyaku o naraberu** to tell all sorts of lies.

**usugurai** gloomy, dim, dusky, dark.

**USUI** thin; light; weak; **ninjoo no usui hito** coldhearted person.

**usukimi warui** dismal; weird, eerie.

**usuppera na** thin; flimsy; superficial.

**usuragu** to thin; to fade, grow pale; to be toned down; to become dim.

**usurasamui** chilly; rather cold.

**UTA** ode, poem; song; **uta o utau** to sing a song; **uta o yomu** to compose a poem.

**utagai** doubt; **utagai naku** beyond doubt; **utagai o harasu** to clear away suspicion; **utagai o idaku** to harbor suspicion; **utagai o toku** to clear up all doubts.

**utagau** to doubt; to be doubtful of. **Utagau yochi ga nai.** There is no room for doubt.

**UTAU** to sing, chant, carol; to recite; **hanauta o utau** to hum a song.

**uten** rainy weather; rainy day.

**utouto suru** to doze off, to slumber.

**UTSU** to strike, hit, beat; to fire, shoot; to drive in; to give a performance; to attack, assault; to send a telegram; **denpoo o utsu** to send a telegram; **fui o utsu** to make a sudden attack; **kugi o utsu** to drive in a nail; **pisutoru de utsu** to shoot with a

revolver; **shibai o utsu** to give a play; to play a trick. **Tokei ga niji o utta.** The clock struck two.

**utsubuse ni** on one's face.

**UTSUKUSHII** beautiful, fair; **utsukushii hanashi** a beautiful story; **utsukushii keshiki** beautiful scenery.

**utsumuku** to look down; to stoop; **utsumuite aruku** to walk with one's head bent.

**utsurigi** caprice, whim; **utsurigi no** capricious, changeable.

**utsuru** to be reflected; to fall upon; to be becoming; to be taken; **kagami ni utsuru** to be reflected in a mirror; **shashin ni utsuru** to be photographed. **Ano kata ni wa ano kimono ga yoku utsuru.** That dress is very becoming to her.

**utsuru** to remove; to change, shift; to be infectious.

**utsushi** copy.

**UTSUSU** to remove; to transfer; to pour; to carry; to turn; to direct; **jimusho o utsusu** to move the office; **miruku o hoka no bin ni utsusu** to pour milk from one bottle into another.

**utsusu** to copy, to transcribe; to describe, to picture; to photograph; **sashin o uteusu** to have one's picture taken.

**utsuwa** vessel; caliber; **sono utsuwa de nai** to be by no means qualified.

**uttae** accusation, charge; lawsuit; complaint; petition; **uttae o kiku** to hear a case.

**uttaeru** to sue; to complain to; **hootei ni uttaeru** to take legal proceedings against someone; **risei ni uttaeru** to appeal to reason; **yoron ni uttaeru** to appeal to public opinion.

**uttooshii** depressing, oppressive, gloomy.

**uwabe** surface, exterior.

**UWAGI** upper or outer garment; coat; jacket.

**uwagoto o iu** to be delirious.

**uwaki** fickleness, inconstancy; flirtation; **uwaki na** fickle, flirtatious; **uwakimono** licentious man, wanton woman.

**uwame** upward glance.

**uwamuki** upward trend. **Sooba ga uwamuki de aru.** Prices show an upward trend.

**uwamuku** to look up, to turn one's face upward.

**uwanosora** absentmindedness; **uwanosora de kiku** to listen absently.

**uwanuri** final coating (of plaster or paint); **son no uwanuri o suru** to add to one's loss; to suffer loss upon loss.

**uwasa** rumor, report, talk; **uwasa o suru** to spread a rumor.

**uwate** better hand; **uwate ni deru** to get the upper hand.

**uwayaku** superior official.

**uyamau** to respect; to honor.

**uyamuya** ambiguity; vagueness; **uyamuya ni suru** to obscure an issue; **uyamuya ni hoomuru** to suppress a matter.

**uyauyashiku** respectfully.

**uyoku** right wing; right field (in baseball).

**uyo kyokusetsu** much meandering; **uyo kyokusetsu o hete** after aimless wandering.

**uzoo muzoo** rabble; all sorts and conditions of men.

**uzukumaru** to crouch, squat down.

**uzumaki** eddy, whirlpool.

**uzumaku** to whirl, swirl; to flow in whirls; to curl.

**uzumaru** to be filled up; to be buried.

**uzumeru** to bury.

**uzumoreru** to be covered with; to live in obscurity.

# W

**WA** particle denoting: sentence topic: = as for. **Doitsugo wa benkyoo shimashita.** [As far as German is concerned] I studied German. **Kinoo wa ikimashita.** I went yesterday (but not today). **Watakushi wa ikimasen.** As for me, I'm not going.

**wa** circle; ring; wheel; **wa ni wa o kakeru** to exaggerate.

**waapuro** word processor.

**wabiru** to apologize for; to make an excuse; to beg pardon.

**wabishii** miserable, poor, wretched; **wabishii kurashi o suru** to lead a lonely life.

**wabun** text in Japanese; **wabun eiyaku** translating into English from Japanese; **wabun denpoo** telegram in Japanese.

**wadachi** rut, wheel track.

**wadai** topic, subject; **wadai ni noboru** to be talked about.

**wadakamari** ill feeling; reserve; **wadakamari ga aru** to be vexed at something.

**wadakamaru** to be coiled up (as a snake); to be rooted; to be harbored.

**Wa-Ei jisho, Wa-Ei jiten** Japanese-English dictionary.

**wafuku** Japanese clothes; kimono.

**wagamama** willfulness; waywardness; **wagamama na** willful, wayward; **wagamama o suru** to have one's own way; **wagamamamono** self-willed person.

**wagoo suru** to harmonize with; to agree with each other.

**wairo** bribery, bribe; **wairo o tsukau** to bribe, corrupt; **wairo o toru** to be bribed, to take a bribe.

**waishatsu** man's dress shirt.

**waiwai** noisily, clamorously.

**waka, tanka** Japanese verse of 31 syllables; Japanese verse.

**wakagaeri** rejuvenation.

**wakage** youthful spirit.

**WAKAI** young, youthful; **wakai hito** young person; **wakakatta toki** when she was young; **wakamono** young man.

**wakai suru** to make up, settle amicably; to accommodate with.

**wakarazuya** blockhead; incorrigible person.

**WAKARE** farewell, parting; division; branch; **wakare no sakazuki** a parting cup; **wakare o oshimu** to be reluctant to part; **wakare o tsugeru** to say good-bye.

**WAKARERU** to branch off, split, part; to break up, be divided; to get separated; **eikyuu ni wakareru** to part forever.

**wakari** understanding; **wakari no yoi** intelligent, sensible; **wakari no warui** slow to understand.

**wakarikitta** well-known; obvious.

**WAKARU** to understand, realize, comprehend; **wakari nikui** hard to understand.

**wakasu** to boil; to heat; **cha o wakasu** to make tea; **yu o wakasu** to boil water.

**WAKE** reason; ground; meaning; circumstance; **wake no wakaranai hanashi** a strange story; senseless talk; **wake no wakatta hito** a person amenable to reason; **wake o tazuneru** to ask the reason. **Sore wa doo iu wake desu ka.** What do you mean by that?

**wakehedate** partiality, favoritism; **wakehedate no nai** impartial, fair; **wakehedate o suru** to be partial, to discriminate.

**wakemae** share, portion.

**wakeme** dividing line, decisive event.

**WAKERU** to divide, separate; to distribute; to distinguish; **itsutsu ni wakeru** to divide into five parts. **Tochi o kodomo ni wakemashita.** He divided his estate among his children.

**waki** side; other way; supporting role; **waki no** other, another; side, lateral; **waki ni yoru** to step aside; **waki e oku** to lay aside; **waki o tsutomeru** to support the leading actor (in a No play).

**wakimae** discernment, discrimination; judgment; understanding; **wakimae no nai** thoughtless, indiscreet.

**wakime** sidelong glance; **wakime mo furazu** without looking aside, devoting oneself entirely to.

**wakimi o suru** to look aside; to look off.

**WAKU** to boil. **Furo ga wakimashita.** The

bath is ready. **Yu ga waite imasu.** The water is boiling.

**waku** to gush out; to spring; to grow.

**waku** frame, embroidery frame.

**wameku** to cry; to scream, yell, shriek.

**wan** bay; inlet; gulf.

**wanpaku kozoo** spoiled child; naughty boy.

**wanpaku na** willful; naughty.

**wanryoku** physical strength.

**warai** laughter; smile; ridicule; **waraigao** smiling face; smile; **waraigusa** laughingstock, butt of ridicule; **warai joogo** ticklish person.

**waraji** straw sandals; **waraji o haku** to put on straw sandals; to fly from (official) pursuit; **waraji o nugu** to take off straw sandals; to settle down.

**WARAU** to laugh; to smile; to chuckle; to deride, jeer.

**wareme** crack, crevice, fissure.

**wari** rate, proportion, percentage; 10%; **wari no yoi** profitable; **wari ni** comparatively; **nen ichiwari no risoku** interest of 10 percent annually.

**wariai** rate, proportion; **wariai ni** comparatively.

**waribiki** discount, price reduction; **waribiki suru** to allow a discount.

**waridasu** to calculate, compute; to deduce from, conclude from.

**warikireru** to be divisible. **Sanjuuku wa juusan de warikireru.** Thirty-nine can be divided by 13.

**WARU** to split; to crush; to divide; to get lower than; to dilute; to open one's heart; to cut; to halve; to cleave; to rend; **juuni o roku de waru** to divide 12 by 6; **maki o waru** to split wood for fuel. **Kono sake wa mizu de watte aru.** This sake is mixed with water.

**warubireru** to act timidly; to fear; **warubirezu** with good grace; without fear.

**warudakumi** evil design, machination; **warudakumi o suru** to conspire.

**warugashikoi** cunning, artful.

**warugi** ill will; **warugi no nai** without malice; **warugi no nai hito** good-natured person. **Watashi wa warugi de shita no de wa arimasen.** I meant no offense at all.

**WARUI** bad, ill, evil; unlucky; wormy, rotten; wrong; defective; detrimental, slanderous; **waruku natta tabemono** spoiled food; **warui koto o suru** to do wrong; to commit a sin, commit a crime; **karada ni warui** to be injurious to the health; **waruku suru** to make a thing worse; **waruku suru to** if things go wrong; **waruku toru** to take amiss. **Ano hito wa me ga warui.** He has poor eyesight.

**warujie** *(n.)* craftiness, cunning; **warujie no aru** *(adj.)* cunning; **hito ni warujie o tsukeru** to put a person up to mischief.

**warukuchi** abuse, abusive language; **kage de warukuchi o iu** to backbite; **warukuchi o iu** to speak ill of.

**warumono** bad fellow; rogue.

**warusa** mischief; trick.

**wasei** of Japanese make.

**wasen** Japanese rowboat.

**washizukami** grasping, clutching; **washizukami ni suru** to grasp, clutch.

**wasuregachi na** forgetful.

**wasuremono** thing left behind; **wasuremono o suru** to leave (something) behind.

**wasureppoi** to have a poor memory.

**WASURERU** to forget; to lose sight of; to leave behind; **shinshoku o wasureru** to forget sleep and food, be devoted to.

**WATA** cotton; cotton wool; **wata ire** padded clothes; **wata no ki** a cotton plant; **wata no yoo ni tsukareru** to get dog tired.

**WATAKUSHI I;** secrecy; privacy; **watakushi no** my; private; personal; **watakushi no nai** disinterested, unselfish; **watakushitachi** we.

**watari** passing; crossing; **watari ni fune** timely help/offer; **watari o tsukeru** to pave the way; to establish some connection.

**watariau** to cross swords with; to quarrel with.

**wataru** to go over; to go; **Chuugoku kara Nippon ni wataru** to come from China to Japan; **hashi o wataru** to cross a bridge; **umi o wataru** to sail across the sea.

**WATASHI I** *(more informal than* **WATAKUSHI**).

**watashi** ferry; place where passengers take a ferryboat; **watashibune** ferryboat.

**WATASU** to pass (a person) over; to carry across; to take over; to ferry over; to hand deliver; to transfer; to make over; to pay; **kyuuryoo o watasu** to pay wages; **mukoogawa ni watasu** to take over to the other side (of the river).

**watto** with a sudden outcry; **watto nakidasu** to burst into tears.

**wayaku suru** to translate into Japanese.

**waza to** purposely, on purpose; **wazatorashii** artificial, unnatural; studied; **wazatorashiku** artificially.

**wazawai** misfortune, adversity, calamity.

**WAZAWAZA** intentionally, on purpose; **wazawaza iku** to take the trouble to go.

**WAZUKA NA** small (quantity); few (in number); slight.

**wazurawashii** vexatious, troublesome, wearisome; **yononaka ga wazurawashii** to be weary of life.

**wazurawasu** to trouble; to keep a person busy; to exercise; to cause inconvenience.

# Y

**-YA** particle denoting: and (used when a list is incomplete); or; as soon as; **are ya kore ya de** with one thing or another; **tori ya kemono** birds and beasts; **Tookyoo ni tsuku ya** as soon as I got to Tokyo.

**-ya** suffix denoting: store, dealer; **sakanaya** fish market; fishmonger.

**yaa** oh; hallo.

**yaado** yard.

**yabo** boorishness; want of taste; **yabo na** uncouth, vulgar, unrefined; senseless; rusty; **yabo na otoko** boor, silly fellow.

**yabuisha** quack doctor.

**yabun** evening, nighttime. **Yabun ni demashite osoreirimasu.** I must apologize for calling on you so late at night.

**yabunirami** squint; cross-eye; **yabunirami no** cross-eyed.

**yabure** rupture, breach; rent, tear; **kimono no yabure** tear in a garment; **yabure kabure** desperation, self-abandonment.

**yabureru** to be torn, be rent; to be broken; to be beaten; to fail in one's design. **Kare no keikaku wa yabureta.** His attempt had failed. **Kimono ga yaburete iru.** The clothes are torn.

**YABURU** to tear, rend; to break, destroy, crush; **heiwa o yaburu** to disturb the peace; **kami o yaburu** to tear a sheet of paper.

**yachin** house rent; **yachin no todokoori** rent arrears. **Yachin ga agarimashita.** The rent has been raised.

**yado, yadoya** hotel, inn, lodging; **ichiya no yado o kasu** to give a night's lodging; **yado o kou** to ask for lodging; **yado o toru** to stay at an inn for the night.

**yadonashi** homelessness; homeless person, vagrant.

**yadoya, yado** inn, hotel; **yadoya ni tomaru** to stay at an inn; **yadoya no hiyoo** hotel expenses.

**yagai** field; **yagai undoo** outdoor exercise; **yagai no** open air, outdoors.

**yagaku** night study; evening school; **yagakkoo** night school.

**yagate** presently, soon; before long.

**yagoo** shop name; firm name.

**yagu** bedclothes, bedding.

**yagura** tower, turret; **hinomiyagura** fire tower.

**yagyoo** night work; **yagyoo teate** overtime (for night work); **yagyoo o suru** to work at night.

**YAHARI** too, also; as well; still; all the same; after all. **Demo yahari yamemashoo.** I won't do it, notwithstanding your persuasion. **Yahari dame desu.** That won't do, either.

**yaiyai** hey!; hard; pressingly; **yaiyai itte saisoku suru** to press (someone) for.

**yaji** heckling; cheering; rooting.

**yajiru** to cheer; to support; to disturb; to heckle; to interrupt; to obstruct. **Benshi o yajiritaoshita.** The speaker was hissed down.

**yajiuma** mob, busybodies, bystander.

**yakai** evening party; ball; **yakai o moyoosu** to give a party.

**YAKAMASHII** noisy, uproarious; rigorous, strict. **Ano heya wa taihen yakamashii desu.** That room is very noisy.

**yakan** night, nighttime.

**yakan** kettle.

**yake** despair, desperation.

**yakeato** ruins left after a fire.

**yakedo** scald, burn.

**yakei** night view; **Koobe no yakei** the view by night of Kobe.

**yakei** night watch.

**YAKERU** to burn; to be burned; to be destroyed; to be roasted; to be broiled; to be scorched; **hi ni yaketa kao** sunburned face; **yakeru yoo na atsusa** burning heat of day; **mune ga yakeru** to have heartburn.

**yakeshinu** to perish by fire.

**yaketsuku** to scorch, burn; **yaketsuku yoo na taiyoo** burning sun.

**yaki** baking, roasting; firing of porcelain; tempering of a sword. **Kono tooki wa yaki ga ii desu.** This porcelain is well fired.

**yakimashi** further copies (prints) of a photograph.

**yakimochi** toasted *mochi* (rice cake); jealousy; **yakimochi yaki** jealous person; **yakimochi o yaku** to be jealous.

**yakimoki suru** to be impatient; to be nervous.

**yakimono** ceramic ware, pottery; broiled, baked, or roasted dish.

**yakin** night duty, night work; **yakin o suru** to be on night duty.

**yakinaoshi** warming (of cooked food); literary rehash, adaptation; **yakinaoshi suru** to adapt from, to rehash. **Kore wa furui Nihon no shoosetsu no yakinaoshi desu.** This is an adaptation from an old Japanese story.

**yakinaosu** to bake for the second time; to roast again; to imitate.

**yakiniku** roast meat.

**yakitori** roast fowl.

**yakizakana** broiled fish.

**yakkai** trouble; support; dependence; **yakkai o kakeru** to give trouble; to be under the care of; to be welcomed by; **yakkai na** troublesome, difficult, annoying; **yakkaimono** burden, drag, nuisance. **Yakkaibarai.** Good riddance to bad rubbish.

**yakki to naru** to get warm; to become excited.

**YAKKYOKU** pharmacy; dispensary.

**yakoo ressha** night train.

**YAKU** to burn; to set something on fire; to broil; to roast; **imo o yaku** to bake potatoes; **niku o yaku** to roast meat; **sakana o yaku** to broil fish; **sumi o yaku** to make charcoal; **te o yaku** to burn one's fingers or hand; to be at a loss.

**YAKU** translation, version; **yakusha** translator; **yakusu, yaku suru** to translate.

**YAKU** about, approximately.

**yaku** office; duty; part in a drama; **yakuba** public office; **yakume** duty; business; mission; **yakume o hatasu** to discharge one's duties; **yakunin** government official; **yakusha** actor, actress; **yakusho** public office; **yaku ni tatsu** to be of use; **yaku o tsutomeru** to play the part of.

**yakuhin** drugs, chemicals.

**yakusoku** promise; engagement; appointment; **yakusoku suru** to promise.

**yakyuu** baseball; **yakyuu o suru** to play baseball.

**YAMA** mountain; hill; mine; crown (of a hat); pile; speculation; climax (of a drama); **yama no yoo na** mountainous; **yamakuzure** landslide; **yamamichi** mountain road; **yamanobori** mountain climbing; **yamabiraki** the opening of a mountain to pilgrims or climbers for the year; **yamadera** temple in the mountains; **yamaguni** mountainous country. **Koko ga kono shoosetsu no yama desu.** Here is the climax of this novel. **Yama ga atatta.** The speculation has turned out well.

**yamadashi** bumpkin, rustic.

**yamai** illness; **yamai ni kakaru** to become ill.

**yamakaji** forest fire.

**yamamori** heap; heaping up anything in measuring; heaping full; **yamamori ni suru** to heap up; to fill to overflowing.

**yamashii** to feel ashamed; to have qualms of conscience.

**yamawake ni suru** to divide equally into two parts.

**yame** end, conclusion, finish; abolition, stop, discontinuance; **yame ni suru** to be discontinued.

**YAMERU** to stop; to break; to give up, abandon; to resign; to discontinue; **gakkoo o yameru** to leave school; **hanashi o yameru** to cease talking; **shoku o yameru** to retire from office; **torihiki o yameru** to close an account.

**yamiagari** convalescence; **yamiagari no** convalescent.

**yamitsuki** infatuation; feeling ill; **yamitsuki ni naru** (*colloq.*) to develop into a passion; to be wholly given up to.

**yamitsuku** (*colloq.*) to be taken ill; to be wholly given up to; to run madly after.

**yamiyo** dark night.

**yamome** widow.

**YAMU** to stop, cease, abate; to clamp down; to drop down; **yamu o enai** unavoidable; necessary; **yamu o ezu** unavoidably. **Ame ga yamimashita.** The rain has stopped.

**yanami** row of houses.

**yane** roof; **yaneura** attic.

**yanushi** owner of a house; landlord.

**yanwari** softly; gently.

**YAOYA** fruit and vegetable market; greengrocer.

**-YARA** and so on; and the like; **nani yara ka yara de** with one thing or other.

**yariba** disposal place; **yariba ga nai** to be at a loss as to where to put (something); **yariba ni komaru** to be at a loss as to what to do with (something).

**yaridasu** to begin to do.

**yarikake** half-done, half-finished.

**yarikakeru** to begin; to set about; to proceed to make.

**yarikaneru** to hesitate to do. **Ano hito wa donna koto demo yarikanenai otoko da.** He is up to all sorts of things. He will go to any extreme.

**yarikata** manner of doing; **yarikata ga ii** to go about one's task in the right way. **Sore wa yarikata shidai desu.** It depends on how you do it.

**yarikomeru** to silence; to snub; to put down; to argue down.

**yarikuchi** manner of acting; policy. **Yarikuchi ga shaku da.** I am displeased with his way of doing things.

**yarikuri** to make shift; **yarikuri o suru** to live by one's wits.

**yarinaosu** to do over again; to try again; to start over again; to resume.

**yarippanashi ni suru** to neglect; to leave in disorder.

**yarisokonai** failure.

**yarisugiru** to overdo; to go too far; to do too much.

**yarisugosu** to go past.

**yaritogeru** to accomplish, perform, achieve; to finish.

**yaritori** exchange; **yaritori suru** to exchange.

**YARU** to give, present (something to someone in one's in group). **Inu ni mizu o yatta.** I gave water to the dog.

**yaru** to do, to undertake.

**YASAI** vegetables.

**YASASHII** gentle, tender; easy, simple; **yasashii mondai** easy question; **yasashii kotoba o kakeru** to speak kindly (words) to (someone).

**yasegaman suru** to endure (anything) because of pride.

**yasei** wildness; **yasei suru** to grow wild (without being cultivated).

**YASERU** to become lean (thin); to lose freshness.

**yashiki** mansion; premises; grounds; home site.

**yashin** ambition, aspiration; schemes; **yashin manman** highly ambitious; **yashin o idaku** to be ambitious; **yashinka** ambitious person.

**yashinai** nutrition; bringing up; **karada no yashinai ni naru** to be nutritious.

**yashinau** to bring up; to support; to subsist; to maintain; to feed.

**yashinaioya** foster father; foster mother.

**yashiro, oyashiro** Shinto shrine.

**yasuagari** (n.) inexpensiveness, cheapness, economy.

**yasubushin** flimsily constructed building.

**YASUI** cheap, inexpensive; **yasui hon** cheap book; **yasumono** low priced (cheaply made) article. **Bukka ga yasuku narimashita.** Prices have come down. **Yasumonokai no zeni ushinai.** Penny wise and pound foolish.

**-YASUI** suffix denoting: easy to, simple to; **kowareyasui** to be easy to break; **yomiyasui** to be easy to read.

**yasumaru** to be rested; to feel at rest; **karada no yasumaru toki ga nai** to be too busy to relax for a moment.

**yasumeru** to rest (oneself); to give rest; to ease; **karada o yasumeru** to rest from work; **ki o yasumeru** to set (one's mind) at ease.

**YASUMI** rest; recess; holiday; vacation: **natsuyasumi** summer vacation.

**YASUMU** to rest; to go to bed; to take a vacation; **gakkoo o yasumu** to be absent from school; **yoru hayaku yasumu** to go to bed early in the evening.

**yasuppoi** cheap, flashy; mean; **yasuppoku mieru** to look cheap.

**yasuraka na** peaceful, calm; **yasuraka ni** peacefully, at rest.

**yasuri** file, rasp; **yasuri o kakeru** to file.

**yasuukeai** ready promise; irresponsible promise; **yasuukeai o suru** to promise readily; to promise without due consideration.

**yasuuri** bargain sale; **yasuuri o suru** to sell at a bargain price.

**yasuyado** lodging house; cheap inn.

**yasuyasu** easily, with ease.

**yatai** float (in a festival); one's fortune; **yatai mise** open-air stall (or booth).

**yatara na** careless; indiscriminate.

**YATOI** employment; employee; **yatoi gaikokujin** foreign employees; **yatoiire** employment, hire; **yatoinin** employee; servant; **yatoinushi** employer.

**yatou** to engage, employ, hire.

**yatsuatari ni** indiscriminately, recklessly.

**yatsugibaya ni** in rapid succession.

**yatsureru** to get thin; to be worn out, to waste away; **miru kage mo naku yatsurete iru** to be a mere shadow of one's former self.

**yatte miru** to try, attempt.

**YATTO** at last; with difficulty; **yatto kurashite iku** to have great difficulty making both ends meet. **Yatto kippu ga kaeta.** I could buy a ticket only with difficulty.

**yattoko** pincers, nippers; wrench.

**YATTSU, HACHI** eight. (See also **yooka, hachigatsu.**)

**yattsukeru** to attack.

**yawarageru** to soften, lessen, lighten; to moderate; to relax; **koe o yawarageru** to speak softly; **kotoba o yawarageru** to speak gently (with soft words).

**yawaragu** to soften; to be softened; to become mild, become moderate. **Arashi ga yawaragimashita.** The storm has abated.

**YAWARAKAI** soft, gentle, tender, mild; **yawarakai niku** tender meat.

**yaya** to some degree, somewhat. **Yaya shina ga ochiru.** It is somewhat inferior in quality.

**YAYAKOSHII** difficult, complicated, intricate. **Yayakoshii hanashi desu.** It is a complicated story.

**yayamo sureba** to be apt to, be liable to.

**YO** night; **yo o akasu** to pass a night without sleep. **Yo ga akeru.** The day is breaking.

**YO** world, age, times; **yo ni deru** to see the light, to rise in the world; **yo o itou** to be weary of life; **yo o saru** to depart this life, to die.

**-yo** above, over; more; **san mairu yo** over three miles; three miles plus.

**yoakashi** sitting up all night.

**YOAKE** dawn, daybreak; **yoake ni** at dawn, at daybreak.

**yobawari** calling (someone) by name; **doroboo yobawari suru** to brand as a thief.

**yobi** reserve; preparation; **yobi no** reserve, spare; **yobihin** spare store, reserve supply; **yobikin** reserve fund, emergency fund.

**yobiageru** to call out, call up; **namae o yobiageru** to call out (someone's) name.

**yobiatsumeru** to call together, assemble, summon.

**yobidashi** subpoena; calling out; summoning.

**yobidasu** to call out; to call up.

**yobigoe** cry; cry of street hucksters.

**yobiireru** to call (someone) in; to hail (someone) into.

**yobikakeru** to call (out) to; to speak to, address.

**yobiko** whistle; birdcall; **yobikobue** (police) whistle.

**yobikomu** to call a person in.

**yobimono** chief attraction; feature attraction; **kyoogi chuu no yobimono** feature attraction of the tournament.

**yobiokosu** to wake, rouse; to call; **kioku o yobiokosu** to call to mind.

**yobirin** (call) bell; buzzer.

**yobitateru** to call out; to call to; to ask to come.

**yobitomeru** to call and stop; to call to (someone) to stop; to call (someone) back.

**yobiuri** hawking.

**yobiyoseru** to call, summon, send for; to call together, assemble.

**yoboo** prevention, precaution; **yoboo chuusha** preventive injection, inoculation; **yoboo suru** to prevent; to keep as a precaution against.

**yoboyobo** tottering.

**YOBU** to call; to call out to; to call after; to send for; to invite; **isha o yobu** to send for a doctor.

**yobun** (n.) surplus, extra; **yobun no** (adj.) surplus, extra, remaining.

**yobyoo** complication.

**yochi** foresight; **yochi suru** to know beforehand.

**yochi** room, space.

**yodan** digression; **yodan ni wataru** to digress; **yodan wa shibaraku oki** to return to the main subject.

**yodare** saliva; **yodare o tarasu** to slobber.

**yodooshi** all night, all night through.

**yofukashi o suru** to keep late hours; to sit up late at night.

**yofuke** late hours; **yofuke ni** late at night.

**yogen** prediction, prophecy; **yogen suru** to foretell, predict.

**yogi** bedcover.

**yogi nai** unavoidable.

**yogisha** night train.

**yogore** dirt, filth, soil; **yogoreme** visible stain.

**yogoreru** to become dirty, become filthy; to be stained; **yogoreppoi** easily soiled; liable to be soiled.

**YOGOSU** to make unclean; to stain; to soil, foul.

**yoha** aftermath; tail end; **taifuu no yoha** the end of a typhoon.

**yohaku** space; margin.

**YOHODO** to a great degree; very greatly; for a good while; **yohodo mae** quite a while ago; **yohodo no** large number of, great deal of.

**yohoo** forecast, prediction; **tenki yohoo** weather forecast; **yohoo suru** to forecast, predict.

**YOI, II** good, right, fine; **yoi kangae** a good idea. **Sore de yoi.** That will do. **Itte yoi.** You may go.

**yoi** evening; **yoi no kuchi ni** in the early evening; **yoi no myoojoo** evening star; Venus.

**yoi** intoxication; **yoi ga deru** to become intoxicated; **yoi ga mawaru** to get tipsy; **yoi ga sameru** to sober up; **yoidore** drunkard; **yoidore ni naru** to be drunk.

**yoigoshi** overnight.

**yoin** trailing note, reverberation; agreeable aftertaste, suggestion; **yoin no aru** trailing; suggestive; pregnant.

**yoippari** sitting (staying) up very late; **yoippari no asaneboo** late to bed and late to rise.

**yoizame** sobering up.

**yojireru** to be twisted, be contorted.

**yojiru** to twist.

**yoka** spare time; **yoka ni** in spare time; **yoka ga aru** to have leisure; **yoka o riyoo suru** to take advantage of spare time.

**yokan** presentiment, premonition; **yokan ga suru** to have a premonition.

**yokan** chill in the air (early spring).

**yokare ashikare** right or wrong; rightly or wrongly.

**yokaze** night wind.

**-yoke** suffix denoting: shelter; screen; **hiyoke** sunshade.

**YOKEI NA** extra; unnecessary; enough and then some; superfluous; **yokei na mono** unnecessary (thing); **yokei na hiyoo** extra expenses. **Yokei na osewa desu.** Mind your own business.

**yokeru** to avoid, shun; to keep off from; to keep aloof.

**yoki** expectation, anticipation; **yoki ni hanshite** contrary to expectation; **yoki shinai** unexpected; unlooked for; **yoki suru** to expect, anticipate.

**yokin** money deposited; **yokin suru** to deposit money in the bank.

**YOKKA** four days, fourth day of the month.

**yokkaku** bathers; visitors at a spa (or hot spring).

**yokkyuu** craving, desire.

**YOKO** width; side; flank; **yoko no** sidelong; horizontal; **yoko ni** across, crossways; **yoko kara kuchi o dasu** to cut in; to put in a word; **yoko ni naru** to be down; **yokobai ni naru** to lie on one's side.

**yokochoo** lane; side street.

**yokodori suru** to snatch.

**yokogiru** to cross, traverse; to sail across; **toori o mukoo e yokogiru** to go across the street.

**yokoku** notice, announcement; **yokoku nashi ni** without warning; **yokoku no toori** as previously announced; **yokoku suru** to give notice in advance.

**yokome** sidelong glance; **yokome de miru** to look askance at; **yokome o tsukau** to cast a sidelong glance.

**yokomichi** byroad; wrong direction; digression; **yokomichi ni hairu** to deviate from.

**yokomoji** Occidental script or letters.

**yokoo** rehearsal; preliminary exercise.

**yokoppara** side (of the body).

**yokoshima** wickedness; **yokoshima na** wicked.

**YOKOSU** to send; to forward; to hand over, give over, deliver.

**yokotaeru** to lay down; **mi o byooshoo ni yokotaeru** to become ill; to lie down in a sickbed.

**yokotaoshi ni naru** to fall sideways.

**yokotawaru** to lie down; to lie across; **nagaisu ni yokotawaru** to lie on a sofa.

**yokoyari** interruption (of conversation); **-ni yokoyari o ireru** to break in; to cut in.

**yokozuke ni suru** to bring alongside (a pier, etc.).

**YOKU** well; often; thoroughly. **Kono hon wa yoku kakete iru.** This book is written well.

**yoku** greed, desire; **yoku no fukai** avaricious, greedy; **yoku o hanarete** without ulterior motive; **yoku toku zuku de** for gain; for self-interest; **yokubari** greedy person.

**YOKUASA** following (next) morning.

**YOKUBAN** following (next) evening.

**yokubaru** to be avaricious, be greedy.

**yokuboo** desire, ambition.

**YOKUCHOO** next morning.

**YOKUGETSU** next month.

**YOKUJITSU** next day.

**yokujoo** public bath.

**yokume** partiality, prejudice; **yokume de miru** to show prejudice. **Ikura yokume de mite mo.** Even if I give it the benefit of the doubt.

**YOKUNEN** next year.

**yokusei** control, suppression; **yokusei dekinai** uncontrollable; **yokusei suru** to control; to suppress.

**YOKUSHITSU** bathroom.

**YOKUSOO** bathtub.

**yokusuru** to bathe; to take a bath; **onkei ni yokusuru** to be favored with; **onten ni yokusuru** to receive a special favor.

**yokuyoku** very, extremely; carefully; **yokuyoku iya ni natta** being quite sick of; **yokuyoku no koto de nakereba** unless driven to extremes; **yokuyoku no riyuu** a very strong reason.

**yokuyokujitsu** next day but one; two days later.

**yokuyokunen** next year but one; two years later.

**yokuyoo** intonation, modulation; **yokuyoo no aru** modulated; **yokuyoo no nai** monotonous; **yokuyoo o tsukeru** to modulate.

**yokyoo** entertainment; extra show, side show.

**yomawari** night watch; night watchmen.

**yomei** remainder of one's life; **yomei ikubaku mo nai** to have only a few years left (to live).

**yomeru** to be able to read; to read well; to see; to understand; to see through. **Kono shoosetsu wa chotto yomeru.** This novel is rather interesting (reading).

**yomi** reading, Japanese reading of a Chinese character (**kun** reading).

**yomiageru** to read out, read aloud; to finish reading, read through; **hon o yomiageru** to read through a book.

**yomiayamari** misreading; mispronunciation.

**yomiayamaru** to misread; to mispronounce.

**yomichi** night journey; **yomichi o iku** to go by night.

**yomigaeru** to come to one's senses; to be freshened; to be brought to life; to rise from the dead. **Yomigaetta yoo na kokochi ga suru.** I feel like myself again (a new man).

**yomikaki** reading and writing; **yomikaki ga dekiru** to be able to read and write.

**yomikata** reading, pronunciation; reading lesson.

**yomikikaseru** to read (a book) to (someone).

**yomikonasu** to digest what one reads.

**yomimono** reading, reading matter; **kodomo no yomimono** children's books; juvenile literature.

**yominaosu** to reread.

**yominikui** illegible; difficult to read; **yominikui ji** illegible handwriting.

**yomiotosu** to overlook (miss) in reading; to skip (over).

**yomiowaru** to read through; to finish reading.

**yomite** poet; reader.

**yomiyoi** easy to read; legible; **yomiyoi ji** legible handwriting.

**YOMU** to read; to recite; to understand; to see; **hito no kaoiro o yomu** to read (someone's) face; **hito no shinchuu o yomu** to guess what a person means; **musabori yomu** to devour (a book); **uta o yomu** to recite a poem; to compose a poem; **zatto yomu** to run one's eyes over; to scan.

**YON, YOTTSU, SHI** four; **juuyon** fourteen; **yonjuu** forty.

**yonabe** night work; **yonabe o suru** to do night work.

**YONAKA** midnight; **yonaka ni** in the dead of night; in the middle of the night.

**yonareru** to get used to the world; to grow accustomed to the ways of the world; to grow worldly; **yonarenu** inexperienced; green; **yonareta hito** man (woman) of the world. **Kare wa mada yonarenai.** He has seen little of life.

**yondokoronai** unavoidable; urgent, pressing; necessary; **yondokoronaku** unavoidably; out of necessity; unwillingly.

**yonen nai** wholly engrossed; earnest; eager; **kenkyuu ni yonen nai** to be absorbed in study.

**yononaka** world; public; times; **yononaka e deru** to start life; **yononaka ga iya ni naru** to be sick of the world.

**-YOO** manner, style, way, appearance; **-no yoo na** in the manner of, like; **-no yoo ni** in the manner of; **-no yoo desu** it's like. **Kuru yoo desu.** It appears that he is coming.

**yoo** main point; essence; **yoo wa** in brief.

**yoo** business; task; use; service; **yoo ga aru** to have business on hand; **yoo o tasu** to go to the bathroom.

**yoobo** foster mother.

**yooboo** expectation; urgent request; **yooboo suru** to demand.

**YOOCHIEN** kindergarten.

**yoodan** business talk.

**yoodateru** to lend, advance (money); to accommodate.

**yoodo** iodine.

**yoofubo** foster parents.

**YOOFUKU** Western-style clothes.

**yoogisha** suspect, suspected person.

**yoogo** protection, safeguard; **yoogo suru** to protect, defend.

**yoogo** wording; terms.

**yoogu** tools, implements.

**yooguruto** yogurt.

**yoohinten** haberdashery.

**yoohoo** directions for use; uses.

**YOOI** easiness, simplicity; **yooi de nai** difficult; **yooi na** easy, simple.

**yooi** preparation, provision; prudence; **man'ichi no yooi o suru** to prepare for an emergency; **yooi suru** to get ready.

**yooiku suru** to bring up; to rear.

**YOOJI, YOO** business. (See also **yooken**.)

**yooji** infant, baby.

**yoojin** care, prudence; **yoojin bukai** careful; **yoojin no tame** as a precaution; **yoojin suru** to be careful; **yoojinboo** bodyguard.

**yoojin** high official.

**yoojo** adopted daughter.

**yoojoo suru** to take care of one's health.

**YOOKA** eight days; eighth day of the month.

**yooka** adoptive family.

**yookai** dissolution; melting, smelting, fusion; **yookai suru** to dissolve; melt; to smelt; to fuse.

**yookan** Occidental-style building.

**yookan** bittersweet jelly of beans (popular snack or dessert item).

**yooken, YOOJI** business; matter of business. **Nani ka goyooken ga arimasu ka?** Do you have any business to transact?

**yooki** weather; gaiety; **yooki na** bright; cheerful (of disposition); **yooki ni atarareru** to be affected by the weather; **yooki ni naru** to be merry, become lively.

**yooki** receptacle; vessel.

**yookoo** traveling abroad; **yookoo suru** to go abroad.

**yookyuu** claim; demand; request; **yookyuu suru** to claim; to demand; **yookyuusha** claimant.

**yoomu** important mission.

**yoomuki** business; mission; errand; **yoomuki o tazuneru** to inquire into (someone's) business; to ask (someone) his or her business.

**yoorei** example.

**yooro** important position; high office; **yooro ni tatsu** to occupy an important position.

**yoorooin** old-age home, nursing home.

**yoorookin** old-age pension.

**YOOROPPA** Europe; **Yooroppajin** European.

**yoosen** letter paper.

**yoosha naku** without ceremony; mercilessly.

**yooshi** point, gist; essential (important) points;

summary; blank printed forms; **denpoo yooshi** telegraph form.

**yooshi** adopted son; **yooshi ni suru** to adopt a child.

**yooshiki** mode; form; style.

**yoosho** Western books.

**yooshoku** Western food; **yooshokuya** restaurant serving Western food.

**yooshoku shinju** cultured pearl.

**yooshu** Western wine.

**yooso** essential element; important factor.

**yoosoo** Western-style books, clothes, dress; **yoosoo suru** to be dressed in European style.

**YOOSU** condition; circumstances; appearance; **-no yoosu o suru** to show signs of; **yoosu o ukagau** to observe; to see how things stand.

**yoosuru** require; need.

**yootashi** transacting business; **yootashi ni iku** to go out on an errand.

**yooten** gist; main point.

**yooto** use; **yooto ga hiroi** to have various (many) uses.

**YOOYAKU** at last; at length; gradually; narrowly; **yooyaku ma ni au** to be barely on time. **Yooyaku ame ga yanda.** At last the rain stopped.

**yopparai** drunkard, drunk.

**yoreru** to be twisted, get twisted.

**yoreyore no** worn out; seedy; threadbare.

**-YORI** from; out of; at; in; since; than; before; **umi no kanata yori** from beyond the sea. **A wa B yori se ga takai.** A is taller than B. **Kai wa gogo yoji yori hajimaru.** The party is to begin at four in the afternoon.

**yori** twist, ply; **yori ito** twisted thread; **yori o kakeru** to give a twist.

**yoriai** meeting; gathering.

**yoridasu** to pick out, single out; to sort out.

**yoridokoro** ground; source; authority; reliance; **yoridokoro no aru** sure, reliable, authentic; **yoridokoro no nai** groundless, unfounded, unreliable.

**yorikakaru** to lean (stand) against.

**yorimichi** stop (on the way); **yorimichi o suru** to visit on the way; to break a journey.

**yorinuki no** (adj.) choice, select.

**yorinuku** to choose, select, pick out; **tasuu no uchi kara yorinuku** to pick (a few) out of a large number.

**yorisou** to draw close, draw near; to nestle.

**yoritoru** to choose.

**yoriwakeru** to sort out, assort, classify; to pick out; to separate.

**yorokeru** to totter; to stagger.

**yorokobashii** glad, joyous, delighted. **Konna**

**yorokobashii koto wa arimasen.** Nothing gives me as much pleasure.

**yorokobasu** to delight, rejoice; to bring joy, gladden.

**YOROKOBI** joy, delight; congratulations; **yorokobi o noberu** to congratulate.

**YOROKOBU** to be glad; to rejoice; to be delighted (at). **Yorokonde.** Gladly. With pleasure.

**yoron** public opinion.

**YOROSHII** to be good; to be permissible; to be acceptable.

**YOROSHIKU** well; properly; in an appropriate way; best regards. **Aoki-san ni yoroshiku.** Please remember me to Aoki.

**yoroyoro** unsteadily; **yoroyoro to aruku** to walk unsteadily (feebly or drunkenly).

**yorozuya** general store.

**YORU** night.

**yoru** to depend on; to hang on; to be based upon, be founded on; **goirai ni yori** at your request; **saikin no choosa ni yoreba** according to the latest information.

**yoseru** to let approach, let come near; to bring near; to draw near; to add; **isu o yoseru** to draw up one's chair; **-ni mi o yoseru** to become dependent on.

**yoshi** all right; well; good; now; even if, though; **yoshi nanigoto ga okoroo tomo** whatever may happen. **Yoshi boku ga yatte miyoo.** Now I'll try.

**-no yoshi** I hear . . .

**yoshin** preliminary tremors.

**yoshin** preliminary examination.

**yoshuu** preparation; rehearsal; **yoshuu suru** to prepare lessons; to rehearse.

**YOSO** somewhere else; another place; **yoso de** elsewhere, somewhere else; **yoso goto** another's affair; **yoso mi** looking off, aside, away.

**yosoku** estimation, estimate; forecast; **yosoku suru** to estimate, to forecast, predict.

**yosoo** anticipation, expectation; **yosoo suru** to expect, anticipate; **yosoogai ni** unexpectedly; **yosoogai no** unexpected.

**yosoou** to dress (attire, equip) oneself in.

**YOSU** to stop, to drop; to leave off; to give up; to cut off; **tabako o yosu** to stop smoking. **Joodan wa yose.** None of your jokes.

**yosutebito** hermit; monk.

**yotayota** unsteadily.

**yotei** plan; schedule; **yotei no toori** as prearranged.

**yotsugi** heir; heiress.

**yotsukado** crossroads; corner of the street.

**YOTTE** and so, consequently, therefore.

**yotto** yacht.

**YOTTSU, YON, SHI** four. **Yottsu kaimashita.** I bought four of them.

**you** to get drunk; to feel sick (from motion); **fune ni you** to get seasick; **hikooki ni you** to get airsick; **sake ni you** to get drunk.

**YOWAI** weak; feeble (in body); poor-spirited; delicate (things); mild, gentle; **ki no yowai** fainthearted; softhearted, limited; **karada ga yowai** to have a weak constitution; to be in poor health.

**yowaki** (stock market term) bears; shorts; selling spirit.

**yowami** weakness, feebleness; **yowami ni tsukekomu** to take advantage of (someone's) weak point; **yowami o miseru** to display cowardice.

**yowamushi** weak person; crybaby.

**yowane** weakness; confession of weakness; **yowane o haku** to betray weakness; to complain.

**yowatari** going through the world; living; **yowatari no heta na** dull-witted, shiftless; **yowatari no joozu na** shrewd, hardheaded.

**yoyaku** reservation; advance booking; **yoyaku suru** to book in advance; to subscribe to; **yoyaku mooshikomikin** subscription (money); initial installment; **yoyakusha** subscriber.

**yoyuu** spare, reserve (money, time, etc.); **yoyuu shakushaku** to have a good deal in reserve.

**YU, OYU** hot water; **yu ni hairu** to take a bath; **yu o tsukawaseru** to bathe (a child or invalid); **yu o sasu** to pour hot water; **yu o wakasu** to boil water.

**YUBI** finger, toe; **yubi o kuwaeru** to look with envy; **yubiwa o yubi ni hameru** to put a ring on a finger.

**YUBUNE** bathtub.

**yudan** negligence; inattention; carelessness; imprudence; unguarded moment; **sukoshi mo yudan ga nai** to be always on one's guard; **yudan suru** to be negligent. **Yudan taiteki.** Danger comes soonest when it is despised.

**YUDAYAJIN** Jew, Jewish person.

**yuderu** to boil; to seethe.

**yudono** bathroom (for bathing only).

**yuen** lampsoot, lampblack; **yuen ga tatsu** to smoke.

**yugameru** to distort; to contort; to crook, bend; to curve; to warp; **kao o yugameru** to make a wry face.

**yugamu** to warp; to swerve, deflect; to be crooked, be distorted.

**yuge** jet of stream, vapor; **yuge o tatete okoru** to fume (with anger).

**yuigon** testament, will; one's dying wish, **yuigon o kaku** to make a will; **yuigon o sezu ni shinu** to die intestate; **yuigon suru** to leave a will.

**yuiitsu** only, sole; unique.

**yuisho** lineage, blood; history.

**YUKA** floor; **yuka o haku** to sweep the floor; **yukaita** floorboard.

**yukai** pleasure; happiness; merriment; **yukai na** pleasant, happy, merry, joyful.

**yukashii** attractive, amiable; winning, engaging.

**yukata** light, unlined cotton garment worn in summer.

**yuketsu** blood transfusion.

**YUKI, IKI** going; bound for; **Oosaka yuki no densha** the Osaka train.

**YUKI** snow; **yuki o itadaku** snowcapped; **yuki o kaku** to shovel away the snow; **yukidoke** thawing (of ice and snow); **yukidoke suru** to thaw; **yuki ga furu** to snow. **Yuki ga tsumoru.** The snow covers the ground.

**yukiatari battari** rashly; impetuously; on the spur of the moment; **yukiatari battari ni yaru** to take chances, to act impetuously.

**yukichigai** crossing. **Kimi no tegami wa boku no to yukichigai ni natta.** Your letter crossed mine.

**yukidomari** blind alley; dead end (of a street); impasse.

**yukigakari** circumstances; convention.

**yukigake ni** on one's way to.

**yukiki** going and coming; traffic; **yukiki no hito** passersby; acquaintances; **yukiki suru** to come and go; to associate.

**yukisaki** one's destination.

**yukitodoku** to be scrupulous; to be prudent; be careful; to be attentive.

**yukitsuke no** favorite; regular; **yukitsuke no mise** one's favorite shop.

**yukiwataru** to extend; to prevail; to spread; to penetrate; to pervade.

**yukizumaru** to stand still; to arrive at a deadlock; **kotoba ga yukizumaru** to be at a loss for words.

**YUKKURI** slowly, at leisure, leisurely; **yukkuri suru** to enjoy one's free time. **Yukkuri nasai.** Stay as long as you can.

**YUKU, IKU** to go, proceed; to travel; **kisha de yuku** to go by train; **umaku yuku** to go well; to be successful.

**yukue** whereabouts; **yukue fumei** missing; **yukue o kuramasu** to conceal oneself; **yukue o sagasu** to trace (someone).

**yukusaki** destination; future.

**yukusue** future.

**yukute** way; path; **yukute o saegiru** to stand in the way; **yukute o terasu** to light the way.

**yukuyuku** on the way; **yukuyuku wa** in the end, in the course of time.

**yume** dream; **yume no yo** dream world; **-o yume ni miru** to see in a dream; **yume kara sameru** to wake from a dream; to be disillusioned; **yume o miru** to dream.

**YUNOMI** mug, cup.

**YUNYUUHIN** imports, imported goods.

**yurai** origin; history; **yurai suru** to originate.

**yure** shake, sway, rock, jolt, roll, pitch.

**yureru** to shake, rock, pitch; to tremble.

**yuriokosu** to shake up; to wake up by shaking.

**yuru** to shake; to swing; to joggle.

**yurui** relaxed, loosening, slack.

**yurumeru** to loosen, unloose; to unbend, relax; **te o yurumeru** to loosen one's hold of.

**yurumu** to loosen, become (get) loose; to abate. **Ki ga yurunde iru.** His attention is wandering.

**yurushi** permission, leave; license; initiation; pardon, forgiveness; **yurushi o ete** with permission; **yurushi o kou** to ask permission.

**YURUSU** to permit, allow; to approve; **jikan no yurusu kagiri** so far as time permits.

**yuruyaka na** lenient; mild; **yuruyaka na saka** gentle slope.

**yuruyuru** slowly, leisurely.

**YUSHUTSU** export, exportation; **yushutsu suru** to export; **yushutsuhin** exports.

**yusoo** transportation, conveyance; **yusoo suru** to convey, transport.

**yusuburu** to shake; to swing.

**YUSUGU** to wash out; to rinse.

**yusuri** extortion, blackmail; blackmailer; **yusuru** to extort (money), blackmail; to squeeze.

**yutaka na** abundant, plentiful, copious; **yutaka na seikatsu** rich living.

**yutanpo** hot water bottle. **Yutanpo o irete oyasuminasai.** Get into bed with a hot water bottle.

**yutori** room, margin; elbow room; spare (money), time; **yutori o toru** to leave some room for.

**yuttari shita** easy; composed; **yuttari shita kimochi ni naru** to feel easy; to feel at home.

**YUU, IU** to speak, talk; to mention.

**yuu** to tie; to dress; to arrange; **kami o yuu** to dress one's hair.

**YUUBE** last night; yesterday evening. (See also **sakuban.**)

**yuuben** eloquence; **yuuben na** eloquent, fluent; **yuuben o furuu** to speak eloquently; **yuubenka** eloquent speaker.

**yuubi** grace, elegance; refinement; **yuubi na** graceful, elegant.

**YUUBIN** mail, post; **gaikoku yuubin** foreign mail; **yuubin chokin** postal savings; **yuubin haitatsunin** letter carrier; **yuubin kawase** money order; **YUUBIN KITTE** postage stamp; **sokutatsu yuubin** special delivery; **yuubin o dasu** to send a letter by mail; **YUUBINBAKO** mailbox, letter box; **yuubinbutsu** mail, postal matter; **dai isshu yuubinbutsu** first-class mail; **dai nishu yuubinbutsu** second-class mail; **YUUBINKYOKU** post office. (See also **yuusooryoo.**)

**yuuboo** hopefulness; **yuuboo na** hopeful, promising; **zento yuuboo na seinen** a promising youth.

**yuuchoo na** sedate, calm, composed; tedious, wearisome, slow.

**YUUDACHI** shower; **yuudachi ga kuru** to have a shower; **yuudachi ni au** to be caught in a shower.

**yuudai na** magnificent, imposing.

**yuudoku na** poisonous, venomous.

**yuudoo** inducement; **yuudoo suru** to draw, lure, lead.

**yuueki** usefulness; benefit, advantage, instructiveness; **yuueki na** useful, advantageous; **yuueki desu** to be useful; to be beneficial; **yuueki ni tsukau** to make the best use of.

**yuuenchi** recreation ground, public playground.

**yuuetsu** superiority, supremacy; **yuuetsu suru** to be superior to, to surpass; **yuuetsukan** sense of superiority.

**yuugai na** bad, harmful, injurious; **kenkoo ni yuugai de aru** to be bad for the health.

**YUUGATA** evening.

**yuugi** play, game, amusement; **yuugi o suru** to play a game.

**yuugoo** melting, fusion, union, harmony; **yuugoo suru** to melt down, to harmonize; to fuse, unite.

**yuuguu** warm treatment; **-ni yuuguu sareru** to be received cordially by; **-o yuuguu suru** to give a warm reception to.

**YUUHAN** supper, evening meal.

**yuuhi** setting sun.

**yuui na** capable, able, efficient; **shoorai yuui na** promising.

**YUUJIN** friend, companion.

**yuujoo** friendliness; friendly feelings.

**yuujuufudan** irresolution, indecision; **yuujuufudan no** irresolute.

**yuukai** abduction, kidnapping; **yuukai suru** to kidnap; **yuukaisha** kidnapper.

**yuukan** evening issue, evening paper.

**yuukan na** brave, courageous, daring; **yuukan ni** courageously.

**yuukensha** elector, voter.

**yuuki** courage, valor; **yuuki rinrin** spiritedly, bravely; **yuuki o dasu** to gather one's courage; **yuuki o ushinau** to lose courage.

**yuukoo na** efficient; meritorious, **yuukoo de aru** to be effective, to hold good; **yuukoo ni tsukau** to make good use of.

**yuukyuu no** salaried.

**yuumei na** famous, noted, celebrated; **yuumei ni naru** to become famous.

**yuumoa** humor; **yuumoa ni tomu** to have a sense of humor.

**YUURANBASU** sight-seeing bus.

**yuuretsu** superiority; inferiority; merits; difference; **yuuretsu ga nai** to be equal; **yuuretsu o arasou** to strive for superiority.

**yuuri** profitable; profitability.

**yuuryo** anxiety, concern; **yuuryo subeki** serious, grave; **yuuryo suru** to become anxious about, become troubled.

**yuuryoku na** powerful, influential; controlling; **yuuryokusha** influential person.

**yuuryoo na** superior, excellent, choice; **yuuryoo na seiseki** excellent result.

**yuusenken** priority, first claim.

**yuushi** volunteer; supporter; interested person.

**yuushoo** victory; superiority.

**yuushuu** superiority; sublimity, excellence; **yuushuu na** superior, best, excellent.

**yuusooryoo** postage. (See also **yuubin, yuuzei.**)

**yuutai** generous treatment; hospitality, welcome; **yuutai o ukeru** to be welcomed at.

**yuutai** voluntary resignation, voluntary retirement; **-o yuutai suru** to resign or retire voluntarily from . . .

**yuutoo** superiority; excellency; top grade; **yuutoo no** high-grade, superior, excellent, first-rate; **yuutoo de sotsugyoo suru** to graduate with honors.

**yuuutsu na** melancholy, cheerless, gloomy.

**yuuwa suru** to melt; to soften; to soothe; to conciliate, placate, propitiate; to be reconciled with.

**yuuwaku** temptation, enticement; **yuuwaku suru** to tempt, entice; **yuuwaku to tatakau** to resist temptation.

**yuuyake** evening glow; afterglow.

**yuuyami** twilight, dusk; **yuuyami semaru koro** in the gathering dusk.

**yuuyo** delay; hesitation; extension of time, grace, reprieve; **yuuyo naku** without delay; without allowing an extension; **yuuyo o ataeru** to give an extension; **yuuyo suru** to hesitate, give time.

**yuuyoo** usefulness; **yuuyoo na** useful, serviceable; **yuuyoo ni** usefully, effectively.

**yuuyuu** leisurely; deliberately; serenely, placidly, calmly.

**yuuzai** guiltiness; conviction; culpability; **yuuzai no** guilty.

**yuuzei** postage. (See also **yuubin, yuusooryoo.**)

**yuuzuu** circulation (of a bill or note); accommodation; versatility; adaptability; **yuuzuu o kikasu** to adapt oneself; **yuuzuu suru** to advance money.

**yuzuriau** to compromise, concede mutually, meet halfway.

**yuzuriukeru** to obtain by transfer; to take over; to inherit.

**yuzuriwatashi** alienation; conveyance; transfer.

**yuzuru** to make over; to hand over; to transfer; to part with; **hito ni seki o yuzuru** to make room for; **ippo mo yuzuranai** not to yield a step.

# Z

**zaazaa** plenty, freely, profusely (said of rain or water); **zaazaa mizu o nagasu** to let water run freely. **Ame ga zaazaa futte iru.** It is pouring.

**ZABUTON** cushion to sit on; **zabuton o shiku** to seat oneself on a cushion.

**zadan** familiar conversation, table talk; **zadankai** (discussion) meeting.

**zaiaku** sin, transgression, offense, crime; **zaiaku o okasu** to commit a sin; to commit a crime.

**zaibatsu** powerful financial group.

**zaichuu** containing. **Insatsubutsu zaichuu.** Printed matter only.

**zaidan** foundation; financial group.

**zaigai** abroad, overseas; **zaigai nipponjin** Japanese residents abroad.

**zaigaku** in school; **zaigaku chuu** while in school; **zaigaku suru** to be in school, at school.

**zaigen** source of revenue; resources; **zaigen ni toboshii** to lack financial resources.

**zaigoo** sins, sinful acts; **zaigoo no fukai** sinful.

**ZAIJUU** residence; **Nyuuyooku zaijuu no Nipponjin** Japanese residents in New York.

**zaikyoo** being in the capital; staying in Tokyo; **zaikyoo no yuujin** a friend in the capital (in Tokyo).

**zaimoku** wood, timber, lumber.

**zainin** criminal, offender, malefactor.

**zairai** existing hitherto; **zairai no** usual, ordinary, conventional.

**zairyoku** financial status.

**zairyoo** raw material; data.

**zairyuu** residing, dwelling; **-ni zairyuu suru** to reside in.

**zaisan** property; fortune; **zaisan o tsukuru** to make a fortune; **zaisanka** wealthy person.

**zaisei** finance; financial affairs; **zaisei joo** financially, from a financial point of view; **zaisei joo no** fiscal.

**zaishoku** service; tenure (of office); **zaishoku chuu** during one's term of office.

**ZAITAKU** being at home. **Myoonichi wa gozaitaku deshoo ka?** Will you be at home tomorrow?

**zakka** miscellaneous goods; **zakkashoo** grocer; general dealer.

**zakkubaran na** frank, plain, outspoken; **zakkubaran ni** frankly, plainly; **zakkubaran ni hanasu** to speak plainly.

**zanbu** remainder, rest, balance.

**zanbu to** with a great splash.

**zange** repentence; penitence; confession of sins; **zange suru** to repent, be penitent.

**zangen** slander; false charge.

**zankoku** cruelty, brutality; harshness, coldheartedness; inhumanity; **zankoku na** cruel, brutal, merciless, harsh; **zankoku ni atsukau** to treat cruelly.

**zanmu** remaining business; **zanmu o seiri suru** to wind up affairs.

**zannen** regret, chagrin; mortification; **zannen na** regrettable; mortifying; **zannen ni omou** to regret; to be sorry for.

**zannin** brutality, cruelty; coldheartedness; **zannin na** brutal, cruel; **zannin ni mo** brutally, cruelly; **zanninsei** cruel nature.

**zanpai** rout, crushing defeat; **zanpai suru** to be routed, be beaten to the ground.

**zanshi suru** to be killed in an accident.

**zansho** heat of late summer, lingering summer, Indian summer.

**zansonsha** survivor.

**zanson suru** to survive; to subsist; to remain, be left.

**zappi** miscellaneous expense; incidental expense.

**zappoo** general news; **zappooran** news columns.

**ZARA NI** in plenty; plentifully; everywhere; **zara ni aru** to be very common; to be found everywhere.

**zarazara** rough feeling; **zarazara suru** to feel rough.

**ZASEKI** seat; room.

**zasetsu** breakdown; setback; collapse; discouragement; **zasetsu suru** to break down, receive a setback; to become discouraged; to collapse. **Keikaku wa chuuto de zasetsu shita.** The plan collapsed before it was completed.

**ZASHIKI** room; living room in a Japanese house; **kyaku o zashiki e toosu** to show a visitor into the living room.

**zashoo suru** to run ashore, run aground; to be stranded.

**ZASSHI** magazine, periodical, journal; **zasshi o toru** to subscribe to a magazine.

**zasshu** crossbreed, hybrid; variety; various kinds; **zasshu no** mixed, crossbred, hybrid; **zasshu o tsukuru** to cross, interbreed.

**zatsudan** chatting, gossiping; **zatsudan suru** to gossip, chat.

**zatsuji** miscellaneous affairs.

**zatsumu** routine work; miscellaneous business; **zatsumu ni owareru** to be kept busy with miscellaneous business.

**zatsu na** rough, coarse; miscellaneous; **zatsu ni kaku** to write carelessly, scribble; to draw roughly; **zatsu na kotoba o tsukau** to speak roughly; **zatsu na tatekata** crude (flimsy) construction.

**zatsuon** hubbub; murmur; static (on the radio).

**zatsuyoo** miscellaneous business.

**zatsuzen** disorder, confusion; indiscriminately, desultorily; **zatsuzen to shita** disorderly; desultory; indiscriminate. **Zatsuzen to tsumikasanete aru.** They are heaped in disorderly fashion.

**zatta no** sundry, miscellaneous, various, diverse; all sorts of; **zatta no mono** all sorts of things.

**ZATTO** roughly; hastily; briefly; approximately; **zatto shita** rough, cursory, coarse; **zatto shita mitsumori** rough estimate; **zatto me o toosu** to glance cursorily through (a book); **zatto setsumei suru** to explain briefly.

**zattoo** bustle; congestion; confusion; **zattoo shita machi** busy street; **zattoo suru** to bustle; to be crowded (with).

**zawameki** to be noisy; to rustle.

**zawatsuku** to be noisy; to rustle; to murmur, to be agitated.

**zawazawa** murmuringly, rustlingly; noisily; **zawazawa suru** to be noisy; to be agitated.

**ze ga hi demo** whether right or wrong; by hook or by crook; by all means. **Ze ga hi demo sore o te ni irenakereba naranai.** By hook or by crook, I must get it.

**ZEHI** by all means; under any circumstance.

**ZEI** tax, duty; rate; **zei o chooshuu suru** to collect taxes; **zei o kasuru** to impose a tax (on); to levy a tax; **zei o osameru** to pay taxes; **zeikan** customs, customhouse.

**zeitaku, zeitakuhin** luxury; extravagance; **zeitaku na** luxuriant, extravagant; **zeitaku**

**ni** luxuriantly, extravagantly; **zeitaku ni kurasu** to live in luxury; **zeitaku o iu** to ask too much; **zeitaku o suru** to indulge in luxury.

**zekkoo** severance of a friendship or acquaintanceship.

**zekkoo no** finest, best; capital, splendid; **zekkoo no kikai** splendid opportunity, golden opportunity.

**zekkyoo** exclamation, ejaculation; **zekkyoo suru** to exclaim; to shout, yell.

**zen** Buddhist sect emphasizing religious meditation.

**zen'aku** good and bad; right and wrong.

**ZENBU** all parts, whole, entire lot; **zenbu de** altogether; in all.

**zenbu** first part; front; forepart.

**zenbun** complete sentence; full text.

**zenchi** complete recovery; perfect cure; **zenchi suru** to be completely cured or recovered.

**zenchoo** presage, omen; sign, symptom.

**zendai mimon no** unprecedented, unheard of, record-breaking.

**ZENGAKU** total amount, sum total.

**ZENGO** before and after; order; thereabouts, somewhere about; **zengo no kankei** context (of a sentence); **zengo o tsuujite** from the first to the last.

**zengo fukaku** being unconscious; **zengo fukaku ni** quite unconsciously.

**zengosaku** remedial measures; **zengosaku o koozuru** to consider the remedies.

**zen'i** good intention; good faith; **zen'i no** well-meant, well-intentioned, in good faith.

**zenin** approval; **zenin suru** to approve.

**zen'in** everybody present; all members.

**ZENJITSU** previous day, day before.

**zenjutsu no** previously mentioned, above mentioned.

**zenka** previous criminal record; **zenkamono** ex-convict.

**zenkai** complete recovery of health.

**zenkai** last occasion; previous installment; **zenkai ni** last time, previously; **zenkai no** last, previous.

**zenkan** whole volume, entire book.

**zenkei** whole view; panoramic view; bird's-eye view.

**zenken** full power; full authority; **zenken o inin suru** to entrust a person with full power (or authority).

**zenki** previous period; first term; first half of the year.

**zenki no** aforementioned, above mentioned; **zenki no toori** as mentioned above.

**zenkoku** whole country, whole land; **zenkoku**

**ni** throughout the country; **zenkokuteki no** national, country-wide.

**zenkoo** good conduct, good deed.

**zenkoo** whole school; **zenkoo seito** the whole student body.

**zenmai** spring (of clocks, etc.).

**zenmai** flowering fern.

**zenmetsu** annihilation, extermination; **-o zenmetsu saseru** to annihilate.

**zennan zennyo** pious men and women, pious people.

**zennin** virtuous person.

**zennoo** advance payment; **zennoo suru** to pay in advance.

**zenpai** complete defeat, crushing defeat; **zenpai suru** to suffer a crushing defeat.

**zenpai** total abolition; **zenpai suru** to abolish, to make a clean sweep of.

**zenpan** first half.

**ZENPOO** front; **zenpoo ni** ahead, in front; **zenpoo no** front, forward.

**zenpuku no** utmost, greatest; wholehearted; **zenpuku no doryoku o suru** to exert oneself to the utmost.

**zenrei** precedent; previous example; **zenrei no nai** unprecedented.

**zenretsu** front rank.

**zenryoku** all one's energy (strength, power); **zenryoku o tsukusu** to do one's best.

**zenryoo** goodness, integrity; **zenryoo na** good, virtuous, honest.

**zensei** height of prosperity; zenith of power; **zensei jidai** golden age; age of prosperity; **zensei o kiwameru** to be at the height of prosperity.

**zensekai** whole world; world at large; **zensekai ni** all over the world.

**zensha no** former, prior.

**zenshi** whole city; all over the city; **zenshi itaru tokoro ni** everywhere in the city; **zenshimin** all the citizens; all the residents of the city.

**zenshin** whole body; full-length photo (of the body); all over the body; **zenshin fuzui** total paralysis; **zenshin fuzui ni naru** to become paralyzed.

**zenshin** advance, progress; **zenshin suru** to advance.

**zenshin** gradual (slow but steady) advance; **zenshin suru** to move step by step.

**zenshin** antecedents; (one's) past.

**zenshin** one's whole heart; **zenshin o komete** with all of one's heart.

**zensho** taking proper measures; **zensho suru** to manage tactfully.

**zenshoo** complete destruction by fire; **zenshoo suru** to be entirely destroyed by fire.

**zenshoo** complete victory, unbroken series of

victories; **zenshoo suru** to win a complete victory.

**zenshoogai** one's whole life; **zenshoogai o tsuujite** throughout one's life.

**zensokuryoku** full speed, top speed; **zensokuryoku o dasu** to go at full speed.

**ZENTAI** whole body; entirety; naturally; as a matter of course; on earth; **zentai de** in all, altogether; **zentai to shite** in general; **zentai ni** wholly, entirely, generally; **zentai no** whole, entire, complete.

**zento** future; prospect; future career; **zento ni nozomi o kakeru** to pin one's hopes on one's future; **zento ryooen** distant goal.

**ZEN'YA** previous night; **sono zen'ya** night before.

**zen'yaku** complete translation.

**ZENZEN** entirely, completely, wholly; thoroughly; exactly; at all. **Zenzen shiranai.** I don't know at all.

**zeppan** out of print.

**zeppeki** precipice, cliff.

**zero** zero, nought, nothing.

**zessei** matchless, peerless.

**zesshoku** fasting, abstention from food; **zesshoku suru** to go without food.

**zessoku** cessation of breathing; expiration; **zessoku suru** to die, expire.

**zessuru** to go out of existence, become extinct; to exceed, be beyond (something).

**zetchoo** highest point, summit, zenith; **zetchoo ni tassuru** to reach the summit.

**zetsuboo** despair, hopelessness; **zetsubooteki no** hopeless, desperate; **mattaku zetsuboo de aru** to be utterly hopeless; **zetsuboo suru** to despair, give up hope.

**zetsudai no** gigantic, colossal, enormous; **zetsudai no doryoku o suru** to make a supreme effort.

**zetsuen** isolation; insulation; **zetsuen suru** to sever connections with; to insulate; **zetsuensen** insulated wire.

**zetsumei** death; **zetsumei suru** to die, expire.

**zetsumetsu** extermination; extinction; **zetsumetsu suru** to exterminate, stamp out; to die out.

**zetsumu** nil, nought, nothing; **-wa zetsumu de aru** there can be no such.

**ZETTAI** absoluteness; positiveness; **zettai ni** decidedly, absolutely; **zettai no** absolute, positive; **zettai zetsumei** desperation, last extremity.

**zokkai** world; life; laity; **zokkoo no** worldly, mundane.

**zokkoku** dependency; subject state, tributary.

**zokkoo** continuation; **zokko suru** to continue, proceed with.

**zokuaku na** being coarse, vulgar, gross, unrefined.

**zokuhatsu, zokushutsu** successive occurrence; **zokuhatsu suru** to occur in succession.

**zokuhen** sequel.

**zoku na** worldly; popular; common; vulgar; **zoku ni** commonly, popularly.

**zokusetsu** common saying; popular view; tradition.

**zokushoo** popular designation; popular name.

**zoku suru** to belong to; to pertain to; to come under. **Beikoku ni zoku suru.** It belongs to the United States.

**zokuzoku** successively, in rapid succession.

**zokuzoku suru** to feel chilly; to shiver; to thrill.

**zonbun** to the full; to one's heart's content; **omou zonbun naku** to cry to one's heart's content.

**zonjiru** See **zonzuru.**

**zonmei** living, being alive; existence; **zonmei chuu ni** during one's lifetime; **zonmeisha** survivor.

**zonzai na** careless, inattentive; rough; rude; **zonzai ni** roughly, crudely, carelessly; **zonzai na mono no iikata o suru** to be rough spoken; **zonzai ni kaku** to write carelessly.

**zonzuru** to know; to be aware of, be conscious of; to think; to be acquainted with. **Kono fukin wa yoku zonjite imasu.** I know this neighborhood well. **Sono hito o go-zonji desu ka?** Are you acquainted with him?

**zoo** image, statue, statuette; figure.

**zoo** elephant.

**zoochiku** extension; addition; **zoochiku suru** to enlarge; to build an extension.

**zoochoo** presumption; **zoochoo suru** to become arrogant.

**zooen** reinforcements; **zooen suru** to reinforce.

**zoofuku ki** amplifier.

**zoogaku** increase, augmentation; **zoogaku o suru** to increase, raise (money, salary, etc.).

**zoogen** increase and/or decrease.

**zooheikyoku** mint (for money).

**zooho** supplement, enlargement; **-o zooho suru** to enlarge, supplement.

**zooin** increase in personnel; increased staff.

**zooka** increase, augmentation; **zooka suru** to increase, augment; **zookaritsu** the rate of increase.

**ZOOKIN** cleaning rag; mop.

**zookyuu** wage increase, pay increase; **zookyuu suru** to increase wages.

**zooo** hatred, spite, antipathy.

**ZOORI** sandals; **zoori o haku** to wear sandals.

**zoosaku** fittings; furniture; alterations, features; **zoosaku no sorotta kao** regular features, comely face; **zoosaku o suru** to make alterations in a house. **Zoosakuzuki kashiya.** Furnished house to let.

**ZOOSA NAI** not difficult, easy, simple; **zoosa naku** easily, without difficulty.

**zoosen** shipbuilding; **zoosenjo** shipyard, dockyard.

**zooshi** increase in capital; **zooshi suru** to increase the capital.

**zooshin** promotion; betterment, increase; **zooshin suru** to promote; to increase; to be conducive to; **nooritsu o zooshin suru** to increase efficiency.

**zoosho** collection of books.

**zooshuu** additional income, increase of receipts.

**zoosui** rise (swelling) of a river.

**zootei** presentation, offer; **zootei suru** to present; to give a present; **zooteihin** gift, present; **zooteisha** giver.

**zootoo** exchange of presents; **zootoo suru** to exchange presents; **zootoohin** presents, gifts.

**zoowai** bribery, corruption; **zoowai suru** to bribe; to offer a bribe; **zoowai jiken** bribery case; **zoowaisha** briber.

**zooyo** presentation; donation, present; **zooyo suru** to present; to donate; **zooyosha** donor.

**zoozei** increase in taxation, tax increase; **zoozei an** bill for an increase in taxation; **ichiwari no zoozei** a 10 percent increase in taxation; **zoozei suru** to increase taxes.

**zorozoro** dragging along, trailing along, going with many followers. **Minna ga zorozoro tsuite aruku.** They follow at her heels.

**zotto suru** to shudder, shiver, to feel shocked; **hito o zotto saseru** to make (someone) shudder; **kangaete mo zotto suru** to shudder at the thought of.

**zu** drawing, picture; diagram; map; **zu de setsumei suru** to illustrate by a diagram; **zu ni noru** to be puffed up; **zu o hiku** to draw a diagram.

**-zu** a negative ending denoting: not, without. **Gohan o tabezu ni ikimashita.** She went there without eating.

**zuan** plan, design; sketch; **zuan o tsukuru** to prepare a design; **zuanka** designer, draftsperson.

**zubazuba** *(colloq.)* frankly, candidly; **zubazuba itte shimau** to speak frankly.

**ZUBON** trousers, pants.

**zubora** negligence; nonchalance; slovenliness; **zubora na** negligent, slovenly; **zubora ni** negligently; with nonchalance; **zubora ni naru** to become negligent.

**zuboshi** bull's-eye, mark; **zuboshi o sasu** to hit the mark.

**zubunure ni naru** to become soaked (drenched) to the skin.

**zubutoi** bold, daring, audacious; impudent; **zubutoi hito** bold fellow; **zubutoi koto o suru** to do a bold thing.

**zudon to** with a bang, with a thud. **Zudon to teppoo no oto ga shita.** Bang! went the gun.

**zugayooshi** drawing paper.

**ZUIBUN** fairly, pretty, tolerably; extremely; **zuibun na** awful, nasty, very disagreeable; **zuibun samui** very cold.

**zuihitsu** stray notes; essay; jottings; miscellaneous writings.

**ZUII** liberty, freedom; absence of restraint; **zuii ni** freely, voluntarily; **zuii no** free, voluntary, optional. **Gozuii ni meshiagatte kudasai.** Please help yourself.

**zuiichi** *(n.)* best; foremost; **Nippon zuiichi no sakura no meisho** the most famous place for cherry blossoms in Japan. **Sekai zuiichi desu.** It is the largest in the world.

**zuiji** at any time; as occasion demands.

**zuikoo** accompanying; attendance on a journey; **zuikoo suru** to accompany (someone); **zuikooin** staff (personnel), attendants.

**zujoo** overhead; over one's head; **zujoo ni ochite kuru** to fall on one's head; **zujoo o tobu** to fly overhead.

**zukai** illustration, graphic representation; **zukai suru** to illustrate; **zukai shite setsumei suru** to illustrate with a diagram.

**zukazuka** straightly, directly.

**zukizuki itamu, zukizuki suru** to throb with pain.

**zumen** drawing, plan, map.

**-zumi** suffix denoting: maximum weight capacity of; shipment by; **kisenzumi** shipment by freight; **kyuutonzumi kasha** nine-ton freight car.

**zunguri shita** dumpy, stocky.

**ZUNOO** head, brains; **zunoo meiseki no** clearheaded; **zunoo o yoosuru shigoto** brain work.

**zunukete** exceptionally, extraordinarily; far above the average; **zunukete se no takai kodomo** an exceptionally tall child.

**zunzun** rapidly; apace; in leaps and bounds; **zunzun saki e iku** to go ahead at a rapid pace; **zunzun susumu** to proceed rapidly.

# zurari to          zuuzuushii

**zurari to** all in a row; in a long row; **zurari to narabu** to stand in a long row; to sit in a long row.

**zureru** to slip down; to slip off.

**zuru** to slip down. **Zubon ga zuru.** His trousers are slipping.

**zuru** cheating.

**zurui** sly, crafty; unfair; **zurui otoko** foxy fellow; **zurui koto o suru** to do a tricky thing.

**zurukeru** to shirk (neglect) one's duty; to be tardy; to be idle; **gakkoo o zurukeru** to play truant from school.

**zushin to** with a thud; with a heavy sound.

**zutazuta** pieces; **zutazuta ni** in pieces, stripes; **zutazuta ni hikisaku** to tear to shreds; **zutazuta ni kiru** to cut to pieces.

**-ZUTSU** each, apiece; **hi ni sankai zutsu** three times a day; **hitori ni mittsu zutsu** three pieces to each person; **ni sannin**
zutsu by twos and threes; **sukoshi zutsu** little by little, bit by bit.

**ZUTSUU** headache; **wareru yoo na zutsuu** a splitting headache; **zutsuu no tane** a cause of worry; **zutsuu ga suru** to have a headache.

**ZUTTO** directly to the point; straight to the spot; very much; by far; all the time; **zutto ii** very much better; **zutto izen** long time ago; **zutto tsuzuite** all the time. **Zutto massugu itte kudasai.** Keep straight on.

**zuutai** body, frame, physique.

**zuuzuuben** dialect spoken in the northeastern part of Japan.

**zuuzuushii** impudent, audacious; shameless; **zuuzuushiku** impudently, audaciously, shamelessly; **zuuzuushiku naru** to become impudent; **zuuzuushisa** impudence, audacity, effrontery; shamelessness. **Zuuzuushii otoko da.** He is impudent.

# GLOSSARY OF
# GEOGRAPHICAL NAMES

**Afurika** Africa.
**Ajia** Asia.
**Airurando** Ireland.
**Aisurando** Iceland.
**Amerika** America.
**Amerika Gasshuukoku** U.S.A.
**Arasuka** Alaska.
**Arujeria** Algeria.
**Arupusu** Alps.
**Aruzenchin** Argentina.
**Beikoku** America/U.S.A.
**Biruma** Burma.
**Bonbei** Bombay.
**Burajiru** Brazil.
**Chiri** Chile.
**Chuubei** Central America.
**Chuugoku** China.
**Chuuoo Amerika** Central America.
**Denmaaku** Denmark.
**Doitsu** Germany.
**Eikoku** England.
**Ejiputo** Egypt.
**Firipin** Phillippines.
**Furansu** France.
**Gasshuukoku** United States.
**Girisha** Greece.
**Hangarii** Hungary.
**Hawai** Hawaii.
**Hokkaidoo** Hokkaido.
**Hokubei** North America.
**Honkon** Hong Kong.
**Igirisu** England/Great Britain.
**Indo** India.
**Indoneshia** Indonesia.
**Indo shina** Indochina.
**Iraku** Iraq.
**Iran** Iran.
**Isuraeru** Israel.
**Itaria** Italy.
**Juneebu** Geneva.
**Kanada** Canada.
**Kankoku** South Korea.
**Kita Amerika** North America.

**Kita Choosen** North Korea.
**Koobe** Kobe.
**Kyooto** Kyoto.
**Kyuuba** Cuba.
**Kyuushuu** Kyushu.
**Manira** Manila.
**Maree** Malaya.
**Mekishiko** Mexico.
**Minami Afurika** South Africa.
**Minami Amerika** South America.
**Mosukuwa** Moscow.
**Nanbei** South America.
**Nihon** Japan.
**Nihonkai** Japan Sea.
**Nippon** Japan.
**Noruee** Norway.
**Nyuu Jirando** New Zealand.
**Nyuu Yooku** New York.
**Oosaka** Osaka.
**Ooshuu** Europe.
**Oosutorariya** Australia.
**Oosutoria** Austria.
**Oranda** Holland/Netherlands.
**Pakisutan** Pakistan.
**Pekin** Beijing.
**Perushawan** Persian Gulf.
**Poorando** Poland.
**Porutogaru** Portugal.
**Rondon** London.
**Roshia** Russia.
**San Furanshisuko** San Francisco.
**Shiberia** Siberia.
**Shingapooru** Singapore.
**Sueeden** Sweden.
**Suisu** Switzerland.
**Supein** Spain.
**Suriranka** Sri Lanka.
**Tai** Thailand.
**Taiheiyoo** Pacific Ocean.
**Taipee** Taipei.
**Taiseiyoo** Atlantic Ocean.
**Taiwan** Taiwan.
**Tookyoo** Tokyo.
**Toonan-Ajia** Southeast Asia.
**Toruko** Turkey.
**Washinton** Washington, DC.
**Yooroppa** Europe.

# English-Japanese

# A

**a, an** hitotsu, ichi (but no word is usually used
  for this).
  **There is a man.** Otoko no hito ga imasu.
  **He is a policeman.** Junsa desu.
**abandon (to)** suteru *(give up);* misuteru
  *(forsake, desert);* yameru *(relinquish).*
**abbreviate (to)** ryaku suru *(simplify);*
  shooryaku suru *(omit, cut out).*
**abbreviation** ryaku, ryakugo.
**ability** shuwan *(capacity);* giryoo *(skill);*
  nooryoku, sainoo *(talent).*
**able** dekiru; binwan na, yuunoo na.
**able (to be)** dekiru.
**abolish (to)** haishi suru.
**abortion** datai.
**about** goro *(point in time);* kurai, gurai, hodo,
  bakari *(quantity);* mawari *(nearness of a
  place);* -ni tsuite *(concerning).*
**above** -no ue *(higher than, over);* -ijoo *(more
  than).*
**abroad** kaigai ni *(overseas).*
**absence** rusu *(from home, from the office);*
  kesseki *(from school, from a meeting).*
**absent** rusu no, kesseki no.
**absolute** zettaiteki.
**absorb (to)** suiageru *(suck up);* suitoru *(take
  in).*
**abstain (to)** kiken suru *(from voting).*
**abstract** chuushooteki.
**absurd** okashii, baka na.
**abundant** takusan no.
**abuse** akuyoo.
**abuse (to)** akuyoo suru.
**academy** akademii, gakkai.
**accent** akusento.
**accent (to)** kyoochoo suru *(emphasize).*
**accept (to)** ukeru, osameru *(take in);*
  shoodaku suru *(agree to).*
**acceptance** shoodaku.
**accident** jiko.
  **by accident** guuzen ni.
**accidental** guuzen no.
**accidentally** guuzen ni; omoi gake naku
  *(unexpectedly).*
**accommodate (to)** tekioo saseru *(adapt,
  adjust);* shuuyoo suru *(take in).*
**accommodation** tekioo *(adaptation);* shisetsu
  *(facilities).*
**accompany (to)** isshoni tsuite iku.
**accomplish (to)** shitogeru, kansei suru.
**accord** itchi, choowa *(harmony);* ishi *(choice,
  will).*
**according to** -ni yoreba; -ni yotte *(depending
  on).*
**account** kanjoo *(statement of money);* hanashi
  *(narration).*

**accountant** kaikei gakari.
**accrue (to)** rishi o **shoozuru.**
**accuracy** seikaku sa.
**accurate** seikaku na.
**accuse (to)** hinan suru.
**accustom (to)** narasu; shuukan o tsukeru
  *(habituate).*
**ache** itami
**ache (to)** itamu
**achieve (to)** shitogeru *(accomplish).*
**achievement** kooseki.
**acid** *adj.* suppai. *-n.* san.
**acknowledge (to)** mitomeru.
**acknowledgment** uketori *(receipt).*
**acquaintance** shiriai.
**acquire (to)** eru *(gain);* te ni ireru *(acquire
  property or rights).*
**across** mukoogawa *(across the street).*
  **go across** yokogiru.
  **come across** mitsukeru *(happen to find).*
**act** maku *(of a play);* okonai *(deed).*
**act (to)** suru *(do);* furumau *(behave).*
**active** katsudooteki, sakan na.
**activity** katsudoo.
**actor** yakusha; eiga haiyuu *(movie actor).*
**actress** joyuu.
**actual** hontoo no.
**actually** hontoo ni.
**acute** surudoi *(sharp);* kyuusei no *(opp. of
  chronic).*
**adapt (to)** tekigoo saseru *(make fit).*
**add (to)** kuwaeru.
**addition** tashizan *(math.);* kuwaeta mono
  *(thing added).*
**address** juusho *(of a place);* hanashi
  *(speech).*
**address (to)** hanashikakeru *(speak to).*
  **to address a letter** tegami ni atena o
  kaku.
**adequate** tekitoo na.
**adjective** keiyooshi.
**adjoining** tonari no.
**administer (to)** kanri suru.
**admiral** kaigun taishoo.
**admiration** kanpuku, kanshin.
**admire (to)** kanshin suru, uyamau.
**admission** nyuujooryoo *(charge).*
**admit (to)** mitomeru *(recognize);* ireru *(let in).*
**admittance** nyuujoo *(entrance).*
  **No admittance.** Tachiiri kinshi.
**adopt (to)** toriireru.
**adult** otona.
**advance (to)** susumeru.
**advanced technology** sentan gijutsu.
**advantage** rieki *(benefit).*
**adventure** booken.
**adverb** fukushi.
**advertise (to)** kookoku suru.
**advertisement** kookoku.

    **classified ad** sangyoo kookoku.
**advertising** kookoku.
    **agency** kookoku dairi ten.
    **campaign** kookoku sen.
    **research** kookoku choosa.
**advice** chuukoku.
**advise (to)** chuukoku suru.
**affair** koto, kotogara.
**affect (to)** eikyoo suru *(influence)*.
**affected** kidotta *(in manner)*.
**affection** aijoo.
**affectionate** aijoo no aru.
**affirm (to)** dangen suru *(state as a fact)*.
**affirmation** dangen.
**afloat (to be)** ukabiagaru.
**afraid** kowai.
**after** ato de *(later)*; ato *(next to)*; sorekara *(and then)*.
**afternoon** gogo.
**afterward** sono go.
**again** mata, moo ichido.
**against** -ni taishite.
**age (to)** toshi o toru *(said of a person)*; furuku naru *(said of a thing)*.
**agency** dairiten *(office of an agent)*.
**agent** dairinin *(person)*.
**aggravate (to)** motto waruku suru *(make worse)*.
**ago** mae.
**agree (to)** sansei suru.
**agreeable** kokoroyoi *(pleasing)*.
**agreement** keiyaku, kyootei, dooi.
**agricultural** noogyoo no.
**agriculture** noogyoo.
**ahead** mae ni *(in front of)*; saki ni *(of time or place)*.
**aid** enjo.
    **first aid** ookyuu teate.
    **first-aid station** ookyuu teatesho.
**aid (to)** enjo suru.
**aim** mokuteki *(purpose)*.
**aim at (to)** nerau.
**air** kuuki.
**airfield** hikoojoo.
**air force** kuugun.
**airmail** kookuubin.
**airplane** hikooki.
**airport** kuukoo.
**aisle** toorimichi.
**alarm** odoroki *(sudden fear)*; keihoo *(warning)*.
    **alarm clock** mezamashi-dokei.
**alcohol** arukooru.
**alike** onaji yoo ni *(in a similar way)*.
**all** minna, subete, zenbu.
**alliance** doomei.
**allow (to)** yurusu *(permit)*; ataeru *(give)*.
**ally** mikata.

**almost** taitei, hotondo.
**alone** hitori de; tandoku de.
**along** -ni sotte *(parallel to)*; issho ni *(together with)*.
**already** sude ni, moo.
**also** yahari, mata, -mo.
**altar** saidan.
**alter (to)** kaeru.
**alternate** *adj.* hitotsu oki no. *-n.* kawari no hito *(person)*; kawari no mono *(thing)*.
**alternate (to)** hitotsu oki ni suru; koogo ni suru.
**although** keredomo.
**altitude** takasa.
**altogether** mina de *(in all)*, mattaku *(completely)*.
    **It's five hundred yen altogether.** Mina de gohyaku en desu.
**always** itsu mo *(at all times)*; itsu demo *(at any time)*.
**amaze (to)** odorokaseru.
**amazement** odoroki.
**ambassador** taishi.
**ambitious** haki no aru, yashin no aru.
**amend (to)** teisei suru.
**America** Beikoku, Amerika.
    **American** Beikokujin, Amerikajin *(person)*; Amerika no *(pertaining to the U.S.A.)*.
**among** -no naka no, -no naka ni, -no naka de.
**amount** gaku; soogaku *(total)*.
**ample** juubun na.
**amplifier** zoofuku ki; anpu.
**amuse (to)** tanoshimaseru, omoshirogaraseru.
**amusement** goraku.
**amusing** omoshiroi.
**analyze (to)** bunseki suru, kentoo suru.
**ancestor** sosen.
**anchor** ikari.
**ancient** furui, mukashi no.
**and** to, ya, soshite.
**anecdote** itsuwa.
**angel** tenshi.
**anger** ikari.
**anger (to)** okoru, okoraseru.
**angry (to be)** okotte iru.
    **to get angry** okoru.
**animal** doobutsu.
**animate (to)** kappatsu ni suru.
**annex** bekkan *(building)*.
**annihilate (to)** zenmetsu saseru.
**anniversary** kinenbi.
**announce (to)** koohyoo suru *(publish)*; seimei suru *(declare)*.
**annoy (to)** komaraseru.
**annual** maitoshi no.
**annul (to)** torikesu.
**anonymous** tokumei no.

**another** hoka no.
**answer** henji, kotae.
**answer (to)** kotaeru, henji o suru.
**antenna** antena.
**anticipate (to)** yosoo suru.
**antique** kottoohin.
**anxiety** shinpai.
**anxious (to get)** shinpai suru.
**any** nani ka, dare ka; sukoshi mo *(not even a little).*
**anybody** dare ka, dare demo.
**anyhow** tomokaku, tonikaku.
**anything** nani ka, nan demo.
**anywhere** doko demo.
**apart** betsu, betsu ni.
**apartment** apaato.
**apiece** -zutsu.
**apologize (to)** ayamaru.
**apparent** akiraka na *(obvious).*
**appeal (to)** uttaeru.
**appear (to)** arawareru *(make an appearance).*
**appearance** mikake *(mien).*
**appease (to)** nadameru.
**appendix** furoku *(of a book);* moochoo *(of the body).*
**appetite** shokuyoku.
**applaud (to)** hakushu kassai suru.
**applause** kassai.
**apple** ringo.
**application** mooshikomi *(request).*
**apply (to)** mooshikomu.
**appoint (to)** ninmei suru.
**appointment** ninmei *(assignment to office);* yakusoku *(engagement).*
**appreciate (to)** kansha suru *(thank);* arigataku omou *(feel gratified).*
**appreciation** kansha.
**appropriate** *adj.* tekitoo na.
**approve (to)** sansei suru *(agree);* yoi to omou *(think well of).*
**April** Shigatsu.
**apron** epuron, maekake.
**arbitrary** dokudanteki na.
**arcade** aakeedo.
**architect** kenchikuka.
**architecture** kenchiku.
**ardent** nesshin na.
**area** akichi *(open space);* chiiki *(region).*
**argue (to)** iiarasou; giron suru.
**argument** iiarasoi, ronsoo.
**arithmetic** sanjutsu.
**arm** ude *(of the body);* buki *(weapon).*
    **armaments** buki.
    **arms reduction** gunshuku.
**arm (to)** *v.t.* busoo saseru; *v.i.* busoo suru.
**army** rikugun.
**around** -no mawari ni.

**arouse (to)** me o samasaseru *(awaken);* sawagaseru *(stir up).*
**arrange (to)** seiton suru *(set in order);* uchiawaseru *(make an arrangement).*
**arrangement** uchiawase *(plan).*
**arrest** taiho.
**arrest (to)** taiho suru, tsukamaeru.
**arrival** toochaku.
**arrive (to)** toochaku suru, tsuku.
**art** geijutsu *(art in general);* bijutsu *(fine arts).*
**article** shinamono *(commodity);* kiji *(writing).*
**artificial** jinzoo no *(not natural).*
**artist** geijutsuka, geinoojin *(performing artist);* bijutsuka *(person skilled in one of the fine arts).*
**artistic** geijutsuteki.
**as** -to shite *(in the capacity of);* -no yoo ni *(in such a manner);* -hodo *(as . . . as).*
**ascertain (to)** tashikameru, kakutei suru *(determine).*
**ash** hai.
**ashamed (to feel)** hazukashiku omou.
**aside** soba ni; waki e *(nearby).*
**ask (to)** kiku, tazuneru.
**asleep (to be)** nemutte iru.
**aspire (to)** netsuboo suru.
**aspirin** asupirin.
**assault** shuugeki, bookoo.
**assemble (to)** atsumeru *(bring together);* atsumaru *(come together).*
**assembly** shuukai, kumitate.
**asset** shisan.
**assign (to)** ategau *(allot);* shitei suru *(designate).*
**assist (to)** tetsudau, tasukeru.
**assistant** tetsudai, joshu.
**associate (to)** koosai suru *(mingle with);* rensoo suru *(relate in thinking).*
**assume (to)** hikiukeru *(undertake);* katei suru *(suppose).*
**assurance** hoshoo, ukeai.
**assure (to)** hoshoo suru.
**astonish (to)** odorokasu, bikkuri saseru.
**astound (to)** bikkuri gyooten saseru.
**astronaut** uchuu hikooshi.
**asylum** seishin byooin.
**at** ni, de.
**athlete** undooka.
**athletics** undoo.
**atmosphere** fun'iki.
**attach (to)** tsukeru.
**attack (to)** koogeki suru, semeru, osou.
**attain (to)** tassuru *(gain);* toochaku suru *(reach).*
**attempt (to)** kokoromiru.
**attend (to)** -ni shusseki suru *(be present at).*

**attention** chuui.

**attic** yane ura.

**attitude** taido.

**attorney** bengoshi *(lawyer)*.
   **power of attorney** ininken, dairinin.

**attract (to)** chuui o hiku *(draw attention);* miwaku suru *(entice)*.

**attraction** miwaku.

**attractive** miryokuteki, aikyoo ga aru.

**audience** choshuu.

**audit** kaikei kansa suru.

**August** Hachigatsu.

**aunt** oba, obasan.

**author** chosha *(writer of a book)*.

**authority** taika *(great expert);* tookyokusha *(government)*.

**authorize (to)** kengen o ataeru.

**automatic** jidooteki.

**automobile** jidoosha.

**autumn** aki.

**average** heikin.

**avoid (to)** sakeru.

**awake (to be)** me ga samete iru.

**awaken (to)** okosu *(arouse)*.

**award** shoohin, shooyo.

**award (to)** shooyo a dasu.

**aware (to be)** shoochi shite iru.

**away** achira ni, atchi ni.
   **Go away.** Atchi e itte.

**awful** osoroshii, taihen na.

**awkward** fuben na, bukiyoo na.

**baby** akanboo.

**back** senaka *(of the body);* ura *(of a house, etc.)*.

**background** haikei.

**backward** ushiro ni *(toward the back);* gyaku ni *(in a reverse direction)*.

**bacon** beekon.

**bad** warui.

**badge** kishoo.

**bag** fukuro.

**baggage** nimotsu *(heavy, such as trunks);* tenimotsu *(hand luggage)*.

**bake (to)** yaku.

**baker** pan'ya.

**bakery** pan'ya.

**balance** tsuriai; nokori *(remainder)*.

**balcony** barukonii.

**ball** tama *(sphere);* mari, booru *(for a game)*.

**balloon** keikikyuu *(aircraft);* fuusen *(toy)*.

**banana** banana.

**band** bando, gakudan.

**bandage** hootai.

**banister** tesuri.

**bank** ginkoo *(financial institution);* dote *(of a river)*.
   **bank account** ginkoo yokin kooza.
   **bank balance** ginkoo yokin zandaka.
   **bank charge** ginkoo tesuu ryoo.
   **bank check** ginkoo kogitte.
   **bank letter of credit** ginkoo shin-yoo joo.
   **bank loan** ginkoo kashitsuke.
   **bank note** satsu.
   **bank statement** ginkoo kanjoo hookoku sho.

**banker** ginkooka.

**bankruptcy** hasan.

**banquet** enkai.

**bar** baa *(for drinks);* kanaboo *(rod)*.

**barber** rihatsushi, tokoya.

**barbershop** rihatsuten.

**bare** hadaka no.

**barefoot** suashi no.

**barn** ushigoya.

**barrel** taru.

**barren** ko o umanai *(sterile);* fumoo no *(land)*.

**basin** tarai.

**basis** kiso, konkyo.

**basket** kago.
   **wastepaper basket** kuzu-kago.

**bath** o-furo *(hot);* mizu-buro *(cold)*.
   **to take a bath** furo ni hairu.

**bathe (to)** kaisuiyoku o suru *(in the sea);* mizu o abiru *(in running water)*.

**bathroom** furoba; tearai *(toilet)*, toire.

**battle** ikusa, sensoo.

**bay** wan.

**be (to)** iru, oru *(there is: animate);* aru *(there is: inanimate);* da *(it is—)*.

**beach** umibe, kaigan.

**bean** mame.

**bear** kuma.

**bear (to)** gaman suru *(endure);* umu *(give birth to)*.

**beard** hige.

**beat (to)** utsu.

**beautiful** utsukushii, kirei na.

**beauty** utsukushisa; bijin *(beautiful woman)*.

**beauty parlor** biyooin.

**because** kara, node *(used after a sentence or clause)*.

**become (to)** -ni naru.

**becoming (be)** niau *(befitting)*.

**bed** nedoko, beddo; shindai *(berth)*.

**beef** gyuuniku.

**beer** biiru.

**beet** biitsu, kabu.

**before** mae, mae ni.

**beg (to)** tanomu.

**beggar** kojiki.

**begin (to)** *v.t.* hajimeru; *v.i.* hajimaru.

**beginning** hajime.

**behave (to)** furumau.

**behavior** furumai.

**behind** ushiro ni, ato ni.

**belief** kakushin *(conviction)*; shinkoo *(faith)*; iken *(opinion)*.

**believe (to)** shinjiru.

**bell** kane, beru.

**belong to** -ni zokusuru.

**below** shita ni.

**belt** beruto; obi *(sash)*; kawa-obi *(leather)*.

**bench** benchi.

**bend (to)** *v.t.* mageru; *v.i.* magaru.

**beneath** shita ni.

**benefit** rieki *(good advantage)*; onkei *(favor)*.

**bequest** izoo.

**beside** -no soba ni, -no soba de.

**besides** -no hoka ni, sono ue *(moreover)*.

**best** ichiban ii.

**bet** kake.

**bet (to)** kakeru.

**betray (to)** uragiru *(act treacherously)*.

**better** motto ii.

    **better than** yori ii.

**between** -no aida ni.

**beware (to)** yoojin suru.

**beyond** -no mukoo ni.

**bicycle** jitensha.

**bid (to)** ne o tsukeru *(offer a price)*; nyuusatsu suru *(make a bid)*.

**big** ookii, ooki na.

**bill** denpyoo *(grocer's bill, restaurant bill of fare)*.

**billion** juu-oku.

**bind (to)** yuwaeru, shibaru *(tie)*.

**bird** tori.

**birth** tanjoo.

    **to give birth** umu.

**birthday** tanjoobi.

**biscuit** bisuketto *(tea biscuit, cookie)*.

**bishop** kantoku *(Protestant)*; shikyoo *(Catholic)*.

**bit** sukoshi.

**bite** kamikizu *(dog bite)*; sashikizu *(mosquito bite)*.

**bite (to)** kamu *(chew)*; sasu *(said of insects)*.

**bitter** nigai.

**bitterness** nigami.

**black** kuroi.

**black person** kokujin.

**blade** ha.

**blame** seme *(censure)*; tsumi *(crime, sin)*.

**blame (to)** semeru; hihan suru *(criticize)*.

**blank** hakushi *(blank sheet of paper)*.

**fill in a blank form** yooshi.

**blanket** moofu.

**bleed (to)** shukketsu suru.

**bless (to)** kiyomeru *(consecrate)*; agameru *(praise, glorify)*.

**blessing** shukufuku *(benediction)*; kami no megumi *(God's blessing)*.

**blind** *adj.* moomoku no.

**blindness** moomoku.

**block** katamari *(bulky piece)*; kukaku *(row of houses)*.

**block (to)** fusagu, samatageru.

**blood** chi.

**bloom (to)** saku.

    **hana ga saku** the flowers are blooming.

**blossom** hana.

**blotter** suitorigami.

**blouse** burausu.

**blow (to)** fuku *(wind)*.

**blue** aoi.

**blush (to)** sekimen suru, akaku naru.

**board** ita *(plank)*; makanai *(food)*.

**boardinghouse** geshukuya.

**boarding pass** toojooken.

**boast (to)** jiman suru.

**boat** booto *(rowboat)*; fune *(powered by motor)*.

**body** karada *(living or dead person)*; shigai *(corpse)*.

**boil (to)** wakasu *(water)*; yuderu *(cook in water)*.

**boiler** boiraa.

**bold** daitan na.

**bomb** bakudan.

**bomb (to)** bakugeki suru.

**bond** shooken *(document)*.

**bone** hone.

**book** hon.

    **textbook** kyookasho.

**bookseller** hon'ya.

**bookstore** hon'ya.

**border** kokkyoo *(frontier of a country)*; kyookai *(boundary, limit)*.

**boring** omoshiroku nai *(uninteresting)*.

**born (to be)** umareru.

**borrow (to)** kariru.

**boss** uwayaku.

**both** futari tomo *(people)*; ryoohoo *(things)*.

**bother (to)** nayamasu *(annoy)*; jama suru *(trouble)*.

**bottle** bin.

**bottom** soko.

**bounce (to)** hanekaeru.

**bowl** donburi, booru.

**box** hako.

**boy** shoonen, otoko no ko.

**bracelet** udewa.

**braid** uchihimo, amigami.

**brain** noo; atama *(intellectual ability)*.
**brake** bureeki.
**branch** eda *(of tree)*; shiten *(office, etc.)*.
**brassière** burajaa.
**brave** yuukan na.
**bread** pan.
**break (to)** kowasu *(destroy)*; yaburu *(tear, rip)*.
**breakfast** asagohan.
**breast** mune *(human)*.
**breath** iki.
**breathe (to)** iki o suru.
**breeze** soyokaze.
**bribe** wairo.
    **to take a bribe** wairo o toru.
**brick** renga.
**bride** hanayome.
**bridegroom** hanamuko.
**bridge** hashi.
**brief** mijikai *(short)*.
**bright** akarui *(with light)*; hade na *(of color)*.
**brighten (to)** akaruku suru *(with light)*.
**brilliant** migoto na.
**bring (to)** motte kuru.
    **to bring up** sodateru *(a child)*; mochidasu *(for discussion)*.
**Britain** Eikoku, Igirisu. (See also **English.**)
    **British** Eikoku no, Igirisu no.
**broad** hiroi.
**broadcast** hoosoo.
**broadcast (to)** hoosoo suru.
**broil (to)** yaku.
**broken** kowareta.
**brook** ogawa.
**broom** hooki.
**brother** niisan, oniisan, ani *(older)*; otooto *(younger)*.
**brother-in-law** gi-kei, giri no ani *(older)*; gitei, giri no otooto *(younger)*.
**brown** chairo.
**bruise** uchikizu.
**bruise (to)** *v.t.* uchikizu o ukeru.
**brush** fude *(for writing)*; hake, burashi *(for sweeping)*.
**bubble** awa.
**buckle** bakkuru, bijoo.
**bud** tsubomi.
**Buddha** Hotoke.
    **statue of the Buddha** Butsuzoo.
**Buddhism** Bukkyoo.
**budget** yosan.
**build (to)** tateru.
**building** tatemono.
**bulletin** keiji *(pinned on a board)*; kaihoo *(publication)*.
    **bulletin board** keijiban.
**bundle** tsutsumi.
**burn (to)** yaku; moyasu *(throw into a fire)*.

**burst (to)** sakeru *(pipes, etc.)*.
**bus** basu.
**bush** shigemi.
**business** yooji *(errand)*; shigoto *(work)*; shoobai *(profession)*.
**businessperson** kaishain.
**busy** isogashii.
**but** ga, shikashi, keredomo *(however)*.
**butcher** nikuya.
**butcher shop** nikuya.
**butter** bataa.
**button** botan.
**buy (to)** kau.
**buyer** kaite, baiyaa.
**by** soba ni *(nearby)*; de *(by means of)*.

# C

**cab** takushii *(taxi)*.
**cabbage** kyabetsu.
**cable** keeburu *(rope, wire)*; kaigai denshin *(cablegram)*.
**cage** tori kago *(for birds)*; ori *(for animals)*.
**cake** keeki.
**calculator** keisanki.
**calendar** karendaa, koyomi.
**calf** koushi.
**call (to)** hoomon suru *(to make a call, visit)*; yobu *(to summon)*.
**calm** shizuka na, odayaka na.
**calm (to)** shizuka ni suru.
**camera** kamera.
**camp** kyanpu.
**camp (to)** kyanpu suru.
**can** kan.
**can (be able)** dekiru *(can do)*; -koto ga dekiru *(can—)*.
**can opener** kan-kiri.
**cancel (to)** torikesu *(revoke)*; sakujo suru *(delete)*.
**candidate** koohosha.
**candle** roosoku.
**candy** kyandii, ame.
**cap** booshi *(hat)*; futa *(lid)*.
**capital** shuto *(city)*; shihon *(money)*.
    **capital punishment** shikei.
**capricious** kimagure na.
**captain** rikugun taii *(army)*; senchoo *(merchant ship)*; kaigun taisa *(navy)*.
**captive** toriko.
**capture (to)** toriko ni suru, tsukamaeru.
**car** kuruma *(vehicle)*; jidoosha *(automobile)*.
**carbon paper** kaabon peepaa.
**card** hagaki *(postcard)*; e-hagaki *(illustrated postcard)*; toranpu *(playing card)*.
**care (to)** kamau *(be concerned)*; sewa o suru *(care for a child)*.

**to take care** daiji ni suru.
**careful** chuuibukai.
**careless** fuchuui na.
**caress** aibu; hooyoo.
**carpenter** daiku.
**carpet** juutan.
**carry (to)** motte iku *(take to);* hakobu *(transport).*
**carve (to)** kiru *(meat);* chookoku suru *(sculpture).*
**case** hako *(box);* jiken *(matter).*
**cash** genkin.
    **to cash a check** kogitte o genkin ni kaeru.
**cashier** genkin gakari, genkin suitoo gakari.
**cassette** kasetto.
**castle** shiro.
**cat** neko.
**catch (to)** toraeru.
    **I have caught a cold.** Kaze o hikimashita.
    **I could not catch the train.** Densha ni ma ni aimasen deshita.
**category** shurui *(kind);* burui *(class).*
**cathedral** jiin.
**Catholic** Kyuukyoo, Katorikku.
**cattle** ushi *(cow, ox);* kachiku *(livestock).*
**cause** gen'in.
    **without cause** gen'in nashi ni.
**cause (to)** gen'in to naru *(bring about);* -saseru *(cause a person to do . . .).*
**cease (to)** yamu, owaru *(come to an end).*
**ceiling** tenjoo.
**celebrate (to)** iwau.
**cellar** chikashitsu.
**cement** semento.
**cemetery** bochi, hakaba.
**censorship** ken'etsu.
**center** chuushin *(of a circle).*
**central** chuushin no, chuuoo no.
    **central heating** danboo-soochi *(heating system).*
**century** seiki.
**ceremony** shiki.
**certain** tashika na *(without doubt);* aru *(a certain).*
**certainty** tashika na koto.
**certificate** shoomeisho.
**chain** kusari.
**chair** isu, koshikake.
**chairperson** gichoo.
**chalk** hakuboku, chooku.
**challenge** choosen.
**challenge (to)** choosen suru.
**champion** chanpion, senshu *(athletic);* tooshi *(fighter);* yoogosha *(defender).*
**chance** chansu *(opportunity);* guuzen *(coincidence);* unmei *(luck, fortune).*
    **to take a chance** chansu o toru.

**change** henka, kawari *(alteration);* komakai okane *(small change);* otsuri *(money returned as change).*
**change (to)** kaeru *(make different);* kawaru *(become different).*
**chapel** reihaidoo *(place of worship).*
**chapter** shoo.
**character** tokuchoo *(unique feature, distinctive mark);* seishitsu *(disposition).*
**characteristic** *adj.* dokutoku no.
**charge (to)** tsumu *(load);* kokuhatsu suru *(accuse);* tsuke ni suru *(charge to an account).*
**charitable** omoiyari no aru *(sympathetic).*
**charity** jizen.
**charming** miwakuteki na *(fascinating);* taihen utsukushii *(very attractive);* aikyoo no aru *(engaging).*
**chase (to)** oikakeru.
**chat (to)** shaberu, uchikutsuroide hanasu.
**cheap** yasui.
**cheat (to)** damasu.
**check** chikki *(claim check);* kogitte *(bank check).*
**check (to)** kuitomeru *(hold back, hamper).*
**cheer (to)** nagusameru *(comfort);* genkizukeru *(enliven).*
**cheerful** akarui *(disposition);* genki na *(lively).*
**cheese** chiizu.
**chemical** *n.* kagaku seihin. *-adj.* kagaku no.
**chemistry** kagaku.
**cherish (to)** daiji ni suru.
**cherry** sakura no hana *(blossom);* sakura no ki *(tree);* sakuranbo *(fruit).*
**chest** mune *(of the body);* hako *(box).*
**chestnut** kuri.
**chew (to)** kamu.
**chicken** niwatori, chikin.
**chief** *n.* shunin *(head person). -adj.* omo na.
**chimney** entotsu.
**chin** ago.
**China** Chuugoku.
    **Communist China** Chuukyoo.
    **Chinese** Chuugokujin *(person);* Chuugoku no *(pertaining to the country).*
**chip** kirehashi, kakera.
**chocolate** chokoreeto.
**choice** sentaku *(selection);* yorigonomi *(preference).*
**choke (to)** *v.t.* chissoku saseru *(suffocate);* *v.i.* chissoku suru.
**choose (to)** erabu *(make a choice of);* yoru *(pick out).*
**chop (to)** kizamu *(mince).*
**chopsticks** hashi.
**Christian** Kirisutokyoo-shinja *(person).*
    **Christianity** Kirisutokyoo.
**Christmas** Kurisumasu.

**church** kyookai.
**cigar** hamaki, shigaa.
   **cigar store** tabakoya.
**cigarette** makitabako, shigaretto.
**circle** maru; enshuu *(circumference)*.
**circular** *adj.* marui. *-n.* kaijoo.
**circulate (to)** kubaru *(distribute)*.
**circumstances** jijoo *(conditions)*; baai
   *(case)*.
**citizen** shimin.
**city** shi.
**city hall** kookaidoo.
**civilization** bunmei.
**civilize (to)** bunmeika suru.
**claim** seikyuu *(demand)*; yookyuu *(request)*;
   shuchoo *(insistence)*.
**claim (to)** seikyuu suru *(demand)*; shuchoo
   suru *(insist)*.
**clamor** sawagi *(loud noise)*.
**clap (to)** hakushu suru *(applaud)*.
**class** shurui *(kind)*; kaikyuu *(social status)*;
   kurasu *(school)*.
   **first class** ittoo *(in plane, etc.)*.
**classic** koten.
**classify (to)** bunrui suru.
   **classified ad** sangyoo kookoku.
**clause** jookoo, setsu *(grammar)*.
**clean** kirei na.
**clean (to)** sooji suru *(rooms, etc.)*.
   **to make clean** kirei ni suru.
**cleaner** kuriininguya *(laundry)*.
**cleanliness** seiketsu sa.
**clear** kirei na.
   **The sky is clear today.** Kyoo wa sora ga
   harete imasu.
   **This is clear.** Kore wa kirei desu.
   **clear soup** osumashi.
**clerk** jimuin *(office)*; ginkooin *(bank)*.
**clever** rikoo na *(intelligent)*; joozu na
   *(dexterous)*; kayoo na *(skillful)*.
**climate** kikoo.
**climb (to)** noboru.
**clip** kurippu.
**clip (to)** karu.
**clock** tokei.
   **alarm clock** mezamashi dokei.
**close** -no soba ni *(nearby)*; no chikaku ni
   *(close to)*; kinjo ni *(in the
   neighborhood)*.
**close (to)** *v.t.* shimeru; *v.i.* shimaru.
**closed** kyuugyoo *(business)*; heiten *(store)*.
**closet** todana *(cupboard)*; oshiire *(for storage)*.
**cloth** kire, nuno *(general term)*.
   **cotton cloth** momen mono.
   **silk cloth** kinu mono.
**clothes** kimono *(Japanese)*; yoofuku
   *(Occidental)*.
**cloud** kumo.

**cloudy** kumotte iru.
**clover** kuroobaa.
**club** boo *(heavy stick)*; kurabu *(association)*.
**coal** sekitan.
**coarse** arai, somatsu na *(roughly made)*; katoo
   na *(rude)*.
**coast** kaigan *(beach)*; engan *(shore)*.
**coat** kooto *(Japanese)*; uwagi *(Occidental-
   style jacket)*.
**cocktail** kakuteru.
**code** kisoku *(set of rules)*.
**coffee** koohii.
**coffin** hitsugi, kan'oke.
**coin** kahei.
**cold** samui *(weather)*; tsumetai *(to the
   touch)*.
   **to catch a cold** kaze o hiku.
   **It is cold.** Samui desu.
   **I am cold.** Watashi wa samui desu.
**coldness** samusa, tsumetasa.
**collaborate (to)** kyoodoo de hataraku *(work
   together)*.
**collar** karaa *(for men)*; kubiwa *(for animals)*,
   eri.
**collect (to)** *v.t.* atsumeru *(gather, get together)*;
   *v.i.* atsumaru *(come together)*.
**collection** shuushuu *(of stamps, etc.)*; kashikin
   chooshuu *(of debts)*.
**college** daigaku *(university)*.
**colonial** shokuminchi no.
**colony** shokuminchi.
**color** iro.
**color (to)** iro o tsukeru *(add color)*.
**column** enchuu *(pillar)*; ran *(newspaper)*.
**comb** kushi.
**comb (to)** kushi de toku, kushi o kakeru
   *(one's hair)*.
**combination** kumiawase.
**combine (to)** kumiawaseru *(join together)*.
**come (to)** kuru.
   **to come around** yatte kuru.
   **to come back** kaette kuru.
   **to come in** hairu.
**comedy** kigeki.
**comet** suisei.
**comfort** nagusame *(consolation)*.
**comfort (to)** nagusameru *(console)*.
**comfortable** kokochi yoi, raku na.
**comma** konma, kuten.
**command** shiki *(military direction)*; meirei
   *(order)*.
**command (to)** meizuru *(direct)*; shihai suru
   *(control)*; meirei suru *(give orders)*.
**commander** shikisha.
**commercial** *adj.* shoobai no, shoogyoo no; *n.*
   komaasharu *(advertisement)*.
**commission** ninmu *(charge, duty)*; toritsugi
   *(agency)*; tesuuryoo *(for service)*.

**commit (to)** okasu *(a crime)*.
**common** futsuu no *(ordinary)*; atarimae no *(usual)*.
  **common sense** jooshiki.
**communicate (to)** renraku suru *(contact)*; tsuushin suru *(correspond with)*.
**communication** renraku, tsuushin; shomen *(written message)*.
  **mass communication** masukomi.
**community** shakai *(society)*.
**compact disk** konpakuto disuku.
**companion** nakama *(comrade)*; aite *(partner)*; tsure *(traveling)*.
**company** kyaku *(social)*; kaisha *(firm)*.
**compare (to)** hikaku suru, kuraberu.
**comparison** hikaku.
**compete (to)** kyoosoo suru, kisou.
**competition** kyoosoo *(rivalry)*; shiai *(contest)*.
**complain (to)** fuhei o iu *(make a complaint)*.
**complaint** fuhei, kujoo.
**complete** zenbu no *(entire)*; kanzen na *(perfect)*.
**complex** fukuzatsu na *(complicated)*.
**complexion** kaoiro.
**complicate (to)** fukuzatsu ni suru.
  **to get complicated** fukuzatsu ni naru.
**compliment** sanji *(praise)*; oseji *(flattering speech)*.
**compose (to)** sakkyoku suru *(music)*; shi o tsukuru *(poetry)*.
**composer** sakkyokuka *(of music)*.
**composition** sakubun *(as a school subject)*; sakuhin *(prose or poetry)*; sakkyoku *(music)*; haigoo *(arrangement)*.
**comprise** naritatsu, fukumu.
**compromise** jooho *(concession)*; dakyoo *(agreement)*.
**compromise (to)** dakyoo suru.
**computer** konpyuutaa.
  **computer language** konpyuutaa gengo.
  **computer program** konpyuutaa puroguramu.
  **digital computer** dejitaru konpyuutaa.
  **personal computer** pasokon.
**conceit** unubore *(overweening, excessive self-importance)*.
**conceited** unuboreta.
**conceive (to)** jutai suru *(become pregnant)*; kokoro ni idaku *(form a conception of, imagine)*.
**concentrate (to)** shuuchuu suru.
**concern** jigyoo *(enterprise)*; shinpai *(anxiety)*.
  **a matter of great concern** juudai na mondai.
  **to be concerned** shinpai suru.

**concerning** -ni tsuite.
**concert** ongakukai.
**concrete** konkuriito *(for building)*.
**condemn (to)** hinan suru *(censure)*; senkoku suru *(sentence)*.
**condense (to)** asshuku suru *(compress)*; mijikaku suru *(shorten)*.
**condition** jootai *(aspect)*; jooken *(terms)*.
  **critical condition** kiken jootai.
  **on condition that** -no jooken de.
**conduct** furumai *(behavior)*; okonai *(deed)*.
  **bad conduct** warui okonai.
  **good conduct** yoi okonai.
**conduct (to)** okonau *(perform)*.
  **to conduct a business** shoobai o keiei suru.
  **to conduct an orchestra** ookesutora o shiki suru.
**conductor** shashoo *(of trains, etc.)*; shikisha *(of an orchestra)*.
**confess (to)** jinin suru *(acknowledge)*; mitomeru *(admit)*; hakujoo suru *(make a confession)*.
**confession** kokuhaku, hakujoo.
**confidence** shin'yoo, shinrai *(trust)*; jishin *(self-confidence)*.
**confident** jishin no aru.
**confidential** himitsu no.
**confirm (to)** tashikameru *(establish firmly)*; kakushoo suru *(verify)*.
**confirmation** kakunin *(corroboration)*; kakushoo *(proof)*.
**congratulate (to)** iwau, shukusu.
**congratulations** omedetoo gozaimasu.
**connect (to)** tsunagu *(join)*.
**connection** kankei *(relation)*; tsunagari *(link)*.
**conquer (to)** seifuku suru.
**conquest** seifuku.
**conscience** ryooshin.
**conscientious** ryooshinteki na.
**conscious** kizuite iru *(aware)*.
**consent** dooi *(assent)*; itchi *(unanimity)*.
**conservative** hoshuteki na.
**consider (to)** yoku kangaete miru *(contemplate)*; kooryo ni ireru *(to take into account)*; kangaeru *(think)*.
**considerable** kanari no *(much)*.
**consideration** kooryo *(careful thought)*; omoiyari *(thoughtful regard)*.
**consistent** shubi ikkan shita.
**consist of (to)** -kara naru *(be composed of)*.
**constant** kawaranai *(unchanging)*; chuujitsu na *(faithful)*.
**constitution** kenpoo *(of a state)*; taikaku *(of the body)*.
**constitutional** kenpoojoo no.
**consul** ryooji.

**consulate** ryoojikan.

**contagious** densensei no.

   **a contagious disease** densenbyoo.

**contain (to)** ireru *(include);* haitte iru *(have within);* fukurude.

**container** iremono.

**contemporary** gendai no *(of the day);* doojidai no *(existing at the same time).*

**contented** manzoku shita.

**contentment** manzoku *(satisfaction).*

**contents** naiyoo.

**continent** *n.* tairiku.

**continual** taema no nai *(unceasing).*

**continue (to)** *v.t.* tsuzukeru; *v.i.* tsuzuku.

**contraception** hinin *(birth control).*

**contract** keiyaku *(agreement);* keiyakusho *(written document of an agreement).*

**contractor** keiyakunin, ukeoinin.

**contradict (to)** hanbaku suru *(rebut);* mujun suru *(conflict with).*

**contradiction** hanbaku *(rebuttal);* mujun *(inconsistency).*

**contradictory** mujun shite iru.

**contrary** hantai no.

   **on the contrary** hantai ni, kaette.

**contrast** taishoo.

**contrast (to)** taishoo suru.

**contribute (to)** kifu suru *(money, etc.);* kikoo suru *(to a publication).*

**contribution** kifu *(donation);* kikoo *(something written for a publication).*

**control** toosei *(government);* yokusei *(restraint).*

   **birth control** sanji seigen.

**control (to)** toogyo suru *(govern);* toosei suru *(regulate).*

**controversy** ronsoo, giron *(dispute).*

**convenience** benri, tsugoo.

**convenient** tsugoo no yoi, benri na.

**convent** shuudooin.

**convention** kyoogikai, kaigi, shuukai.

**conversation** kaiwa *(dialogue);* hanashi *(talk).*

**converse (to)** hanasu.

**convert (to)** kaeru *(change into);* kaishuu saseru *(to a religion).*

**convict (to)** yuuzai to senkoku suru *(declare guilty).*

**conviction** kakushin *(firm belief);* yuuzai hanketsu *(verdict of guilty).*

**cook** ryoorinin *(of Japanese or any other kind of food);* kokku *(for other than Japanese food).*

**cook (to)** ryoori suru, ryoori o tsukuru.

**cool** suzushii *(temperature);* tsumetai *(to the touch);* reisei na *(unexcited);* reitan na *(lacking in zeal).*

**cool (to)** tsumetaku suru.

**copy** utsushi, kopii *(of a letter, etc.);* mosha *(of a picture).*

**corporation** kaisha *(firm);* shadan-hoojin *(corporate body).*

**correct** tadashii *(right);* tashika na *(sure);* seikaku na *(accurate);* machigai no nai *(without error).*

**correct (to)** naosu; koosei suru *(proofread),* tensaku suru *(school papers).*

**correction** teisei *(of an error);* koosei *(in proofreading);* tensaku *(of a school composition).*

**correspond (to)** buntsuu suru, tsuushin suru *(exchange letters);* itchi suru *(agree).*

**correspondence** tsuushin; buntsuu.

**correspondent** tsuushin'in *(of a periodical);* tokuhain *(mass media).*

**corrupt (to)** fuhai suru *(rot);* daraku suru *(morally).*

**corruption** daraku *(moral deterioration).*

**cost** nedan *(price);* hiyoo *(expense).*

**costume** fukusoo, kimono; yoofuku *(Western);* ishoo *(fancy dress).*

**cotton** wata *(raw);* momen *(woven).*

**cough** seki.

**count** keisan *(reckoning).*

**count (to)** kazoeru.

**counter** kauntaa *(restaurant, etc.);* chooba *(in Japanese-style hotel).*

**countless** kazoekirenai.

**country** inaka *(rural region);* kuni *(nation).*

**countryman** inaka mono *(a rustic);* dookokujin *(compatriot).*

**couple** futatsu *(of things);* futari *(of people);* futsuka *(of days);* fuufu *(husband and wife).*

**courage** yuuki.

   **to have courage** yuuki ga aru.

**course** kamoku, katei *(of study);* koosu, michi *(road followed);* yarikata *(line of conduct or action).*

**court** saibansho *(tribunal).*

   **law court** hootei.

**courteous** teinei na; teichoo na *(polite).*

**courtesy** teinei *(politeness);* kooi *(favor);* reigi *(civility).*

**courtyard** nakaniwa.

**cousin** itoko

   **second cousin** mata itoko.

**cover** futa, kabaa.

**cow** meushi.

**co-worker** shigoto nakama.

**crack** wareme *(split);* sukima *(chink);* hibi *(flaw).*

**crack (to)** *v.t.* waru; *v.i.* wareru; hibi ga hairu *(break without separating).*

   **to crack a nut** kurumi o waru.

   **to crack a joke** joodan o tobasu.

   **a hard nut to crack** nan mondai.

**cradle** yurikago.

**crash** shoototsu *(collision)*.
**crash (to)** shoototsu suru.
**crazy** kichigai jimita *(half-crazed)*.
  **crazy about** muchuu ni natta.
**cream** kuriimu.
**create (to)** tsukuru *(bring into being)*; soosaku suru *(produce)*.
**creature** ikimono *(living thing)*.
**credit** kurejitto, shin'yoo *(trust)*.
**creditor** kashi nushi, saikensha.
**crime** tsumi.
  **to commit a crime** hanzai o okasu.
**crisis** kiki *(crucial time)*; tooge *(of a sickness, etc.)*.
  **political crisis** seiji no kiki.
  **financial crisis** keizai no kiki.
**critic** hihyooka *(reviewer)*.
**critical** hihyooteki *(inclined to criticize)*; kiki no *(serious)*.
**criticism** hihyoo, hihan.
**criticize (to)** hihyoo suru *(discuss critically)*; hinan suru *(find fault with)*.
**crooked** magatte iru *(bent)*; nejireta *(twisted)*; fushoojiki na *(dishonest)*.
**crop** shuukaku *(yield)*; toriire *(harvest)*.
**cross** juuji *(lines that intersect)*; juujika *(religious symbol)*.
**crossing** tokoo *(ocean)*; koosaten *(intersection)*.
**crossroads** koosaten; yotsukado.
**crouch (to)** kagamu.
**crow** karasu.
**crowd** hito gomi.
  **to be crowded** konde iru.
**crown** kanmuri.
**crown (to)** eikan o sazukeru *(reward or honor)*.
**cruel** zankoku na.
**cruelty** zangyaku.
**crumb** pan kuzu.
**crumble (to)** kuzureru *(collapse)*; mu ni kisuru *(come to nothing)*; kona ni suru *(break into crumbs)*.
**crust** pan no kawa.
**crutch** matsubazue.
**cry** sakebi goe *(shout)*; naki goe *(weeping)*.
**cry (to)** sakebu *(shout)*; naku *(weep)*.
**cunning** warugashikoi *(sly)*; zurui *(crafty)*.
**cup** yunomi *(teacup)*; koppu *(glass)*; kappu *(trophy)*.
  **a cup of coffee** koohii ippai.
  **a cup of tea** o-cha ippai.
**cure (to)** naosu.
  **to be cured of** naoru.
**curiosity** kookishin.
**curious** kookishin ga tsuyoi *(inquisitive)*; kimyoo na *(strange)*.
**curl** kaaru *(of hair)*.
**current** *adj.* genzai no *(present)*; ryuutsuu

shite iru *(in general circulation)*. *-n.* nagare *(stream)*.
**curtain** mado kake, kaaten *(for a window)*; maku *(theater)*.
**curve** yumi nari *(arched shape)*; kyokusen *(curved line)*.
**curve (to)** *v.t.* mageru; *v.i.* magaru.
**cushion** kusshon; zabuton *(for sitting)*.
**custom** shuukan *(habit)*; fuuzoku *(convention)*.
**customary** futsuu no *(ordinary)*.
**customer** kyaku.
**customhouse** zeikan.
**customs official** zeikanri.
**cut** kirikizu *(wound)*; kirehashi *(a piece of something)*.
**cut (to)** *v.t.* kiru; *v.i.* kireru.

**dagger** tantoo.
**daily** mainichi no.
  **daily newspaper** nikkan shinbun.
**dainty** kyasha na.
**dam** damu, seki.
**damage** songai *(loss)*; higai *(injury, harm)*.
**damage (to)** dame ni suru.
**damp** shimeppoi *(of things)*; shikki no ooi *(of atmosphere)*.
**dance** dansu *(foreign)*; odori *(Japanese)*.
**dance (to)** odoru.
**danger** kiken.
**dangerous** abunai.
**dark** kurai *(little light)*; koi *(color)*; kuroi *(person)*.
**dash (to)** tosshin suru *(rush)*.
**data** deeta.
  **data processor** deeta purosessa.
**date** yakusoku *(appointment)*; hizuke *(on a letter)*.
**daughter** musume *(plain form)*, ojoosan *(respect form)*.
**dawn** yoake.
**day** hi, hiru *(daytime)*.
  **day after tomorrow** asatte.
  **day before yesterday** ototoi.
  **yesterday** kinoo.
  **today** kyoo.
**dazzle (to)** me o kuramasu.
**dead** shinda *(lacking life)*.
  **dead leaves** kareha.
**deaf** mimi no kikoenai.
**deal** torihiki *(business)*.
  **a great deal** hijoo ni takusan.
**deal (to)** torihiki suru *(trade)*; tsukiau *(associate with)*.
**dealer** shoonin.

**dear** takai *(price)*; kawaii *(beloved)*.

**death** shi *(loss of life)*; shiboo *(act or fact of dying)*.

**debate** ronsoo.

**debit** karigata.

**debt** shakkin *(sum due)*; saimu *(liability)*.

**debtor** karinushi.

**decanter** tokkuri.

**decay** fuhai *(rot)*.

**decay (to)** kusaru *(rot)*; otoroeru *(decline)*; taika suru *(deteriorate)*.

**deceased** shiboo.

**deceit** azamuki.

**deceive (to)** damasu *(cheat)*; azamuku *(delude)*.

**December** Juunigatsu.

**decent** ontoo na *(proper)*; joohin na *(modest)*; kanari rippa na *(respectable)*.

**decide (to)** kimeru.

**decision** kettei.

**decisive** ketteiteki.

**deck** kanpan, dekki *(of a ship)*; hito kumi *(of playing cards)*.

**declare (to)** shinkoku suru *(report)*; mooshitateru *(state)*.

**decline** jitai *(refuse)*.

**decline (to)** jitai suru.

**decrease** genshoo.

**decrease (to)** *v.t.* herasu, sukunaku suru; *v.i.* heru.

**decree** hanketsu *(judicial decision)*; hoorei *(ordinance)*.

**dedicate (to)** sasageru *(consecrate)*; yudaneru *(devote oneself to one's work)*.

**deed** kooi *(action)*; jikkoo *(performance)*; okonai *(act)*; shoosho *(document)*.

**deep** fukai *(opp. of shallow)*; koi *(color)*.

**deer** shika.

**defeat** haisen *(military)*; shippai *(failure)*.

**defeat (to)** *v.t.* makasu;
     **to be defeated** *v.i.* makeru.

**defect** ketten.

**defend (to)** mamoru.

**defense** booei.

**defiance** choosen *(challenge)*; mushi *(disregarding)*.

**define (to)** teigi suru.

**definite** hakkiri shita.

**defy (to)** choosen suru *(challenge)*; mushi suru *(disregard)*.

**degree** do *(on a thermometer, etc.)*; gakui *(diploma)*.
     **by degrees** dandan.

**delay** chien.

**delay (to)** *v.i.* okureru.

**delegate** daihyoo *(representative)*.

**delegate (to)** haken suru *(depute)*; inin suru *(entrust)*; daihyoo suru *(represent)*.

**deliberate (to)** shian suru *(consider)*; shingi suru *(discuss)*.

**deliberately** shinchoo ni, yuuyuu to.

**delicacy** bimyoosa *(of coloring, etc.)*.

**delicate** yowai *(in health)*; kowareyasui *(fragile)*.
     **a delicate situation** muzukashii tachiba.

**delicious** oishii.

**delight** ureshisa.

**deliver (to)** todokeru *(goods)*; watasu *(hand over)*.

**deliverance** kyuushutsu *(from bondage, etc.)*; sukui dasu koto.

**delivery** haitatsu *(forwarding)*.

**demand** yookyuu, motome *(request)*; juyoo *(for goods)*.
     **to be in demand** juyoo ga aru.

**democracy** minshushugi, demokurashii.

**demonstrate (to)** jitsuen suru.

**demonstration** jitsuen *(exhibition)*; jii undoo, demo *(mass meeting, protest parade)*.

**denial** hitei *(negation)*; hinin *(disavowal)*; kyohi *(refusal)*.

**denounce (to)** kokuhatsu suru *(inform against)*; haki suru *(repudiate)*.

**dense** fukai *(as fog)*; oishigetta *(as forest)*; konda *(crowded)*.

**density** mitsudo.

**dentist** haisha.

**deny (to)** uchikesu.

**depart (to)** deru.

**department** bumon *(section)*; depaato *(department store)*.

**departure** shuppatsu.

**depend (to)** tayoru *(for support)*; tanomi ni suru *(rely on)*.

**dependent** tayotte iru *(on one's parents, etc.)*.

**deplore (to)** nageku *(lament)*.

**deposit** tetsukekin *(as a binder)*; yokin *(in a bank)*.

**depreciation** genka shookyaku.

**depress (to)** kiochi suru.

**depression** fukeiki *(in business)*; yuuutsu *(of mind)*.

**deprive (to)** ubaitoru.

**depth** fukasa.

**deride (to)** azakeru.

**descend (to)** kudaru *(go down)*; oriru *(alight from)*; kudari ni naru *(slope down)*.

**descendant** shison.

**describe (to)** setsumei suru, noberu *(give an account of)*.

**description** setsumei, jojutsu *(of a person)*.

**desert** sabaku.

**desert (to)** suteru *(one's family or friend)*; dassoo suru *(from the army or prison)*.

**deserve (to)** shikaku ga aru *(be entitled to)*; kachi ga aru *(be worthy of)*.

**design** zuan *(sketch);* kooan *(idea, scheme);* dezdin *(dress, etc.).*

**designer** zuanka *(of patterns);* kooansha *(of ideas);* dezainaa *(of dresses).*

**desirable** nozomashii.

**desire** yokuboo *(craving);* nozomi *(wish, hope).*

**desire (to)** nozomu *(long for);* kiboo suru *(wish).*

**desk** tsukue, desuku.

**desolate** wabishii, sabishii.

**despair** zetsuboo, rakutan *(despondency).*

**despair (to)** zetsuboo suru *(lose hope);* rakutan suru *(be disappointed).*

**desperate** zetsuboo teki na *(beyond hope);* kiken na *(dangerous);* hisshi no *(frantic);* mukoomizu no *(reckless).*

**despise (to)** misageru.

**despite** akui *(malice);* bujoku *(insult);* keibetsu *(scorn).*

   **despite** -ni mo kakawarazu.

**dessert** dezaato.

**destiny** unmei.

**destroy (to)** kowasu; hakai suru *(demolish);* dainashi ni suru *(ruin);* zenmetsu saseru *(annihilate).*

**destruction** hakai.

**detach (to)** hikihanasu *(unfasten, separate).*

**detail** saimoku *(item);* kuwashii koto, shoosai *(particulars).*

   **in detail** kuwashiku.

**detain (to)** hikitomeru.

**detect (to)** tantei suru.

**detective** tantei.

   **detective story** tantei shoosetsu.

**determination** saiketsu *(decision);* kesshin *(resolution);* ketsudan ryoku *(firmness of purpose).*

**determine (to)** kakutei suru *(ascertain);* kimeru *(decide).*

**detest (to)** kirau.

**detour** mawari michi.

**detrimental** furieki na, yoku nai.

**develop (to)** hatten saseru *(cause to grow);* keihatsu suru *(unfold);* genzoo suru *(photo negatives).*

**development** seichoo *(growth);* hatten *(gradual progress);* kakuchoo *(expansion).*

**device** kufuu.

**devil** oni, akuma.

**devise (to)** kufuu suru.

**devoid** kakete iru *(lacking in).*

**devote (to)** sasageru *(give up, direct).*

**devour** gatsugatsu taberu *(eat hungrily and greedily);* horobosu *(destroy).*

   **devour a book** musabori yomu.

**dew** tsuyu.

**dial** daiyaru, mojiban.

   **telephone dial** daiyaru.

**dial (to)** diayaru o mawasu.

**dialect** hoogen.

**dialogue** kaiwa, taiwa.

**diameter** chokkei.

**diamond** daiyamondo.

**diary** nikki.

   **to keep a diary** nikki o tsukeru.

**dictate (to)** kakitoraseru *(a letter).*

**dictation** kakitori *(practice in spelling);* koojutsu *(business).*

**dictionary** jisho, jiten, jibiki *(lexicon).*

   **English-Japanese dictionary** Ei-Wa jiten.

   **Japanese-English dictionary** Wa-Ei jiten.

**die (to)** shinu.

**diesel** diizeru.

**Diet** gikai *(Japanese Parliament).*

**diet** shokuji ryoohoo *(prescribed allowance of food);* daietto *(for weight loss).*

**difference** chigai *(dissimilarity);* sabetsu *(distinction);* iken no sooi *(disagreement).*

**different (be)** chigau.

**differ from (to)** chigau.

**difficult** muzukashii.

**difficulty** konnan, mendoo.

**dig (to)** horu.

**digest (to)** shooka suru *(food);* kanryaku ni suru *(abbreviate).*

**dignity** igen *(of bearing).*

**dim** usugurai.

**dimension** menseki *(area);* ookisa *(size).*

**diminish (to)** *v.i.* chiisaku naru *(in size);* sukunaku naru *(in number).*

**dine (to)** shokuji o suru.

**dining room** shokudoo.

**dinner** hiru no shokuji, hirugohan *(noon meal);* ban no shokuji, yuuhan *(evening meal).*

**dip (to)** tsukeru, hitasu.

**diplomacy** gaikoo *(between nations);* kakehiki *(tactful dealing).*

**diplomat** gaikookan.

**direct** massugu na *(straight);* jika no *(direct rays, etc.).*

**direct (to)** shiiji suru *(point the way);* sashizu suru *(order).*

**direction** hoogaku *(way);* shidoo *(guidance);* kanri *(control);* sashizu *(instruction).*

**director** shihainin *(manager);* juuyaku *(of a company);* shunin *(chief).*

**directory** juushoroku.

   **telephone directory** denwachoo.

**dirt** obutsu *(filth);* doro *(mud);* hokori *(dust).*

dirty kitanai.

disability muryoku.

disabled muryoku ni natta.

disadvantage furi.

disagree (to) itchi shinai.

disagreeable fuyukai na.

disagreement fuitchi *(discord);* fuchoowa *(disharmony);* iken no sooi *(dissent);* fuwa *(quarrel).*

disappear (to) mienaku naru.

disappearance mienaku naru koto, shooshitsu.

disappoint (to) shitsuboo saseru.

disapprove (to) sansei shinai.

disaster tensai *(calamity).*

disastrous hisan na, saigai no ookii *(flood, etc.).*

discharge kaiko *(release from duty);* jotai *(army).*

discharge (to) funaoroshi o suru *(cargo);* hassha suru *(a gun);* hima o dasu *(dismiss).*

discipline kunren *(drill);* kiritsu *(order).*

disclaim (to) hooki suru.

disclose (to) arawasu *(expose);* abaku *(reveal);* happyoo suru *(make known).*

disclosure bakuro.

discomfort fukai.

disconnect (to) kiru *(sever a connection).*

discontent fumanzoku na.

discontinue (to) chuushi suru.

discord fuwa.

discotheque disuko.

discount waribiki.

discount (to) waribiki suru.

discourage (to) rakutan saseru
  to be discouraged gakkari suru.

discouragement rakutan.

discover (to) mitsukeru *(find small things);* hakken suru *(find more important things).*

discovery hakken.

discreet shiryo no aru *(judicious);* shinchoo na *(prudent);* yoojinbukai *(wary).*

discretion shiryo *(prudence).*

discuss (to) toogi suru *(talk over);* tooron suru *(argue).*

discussion toogi *(debate);* tooron *(argument).*

disdain keibetsu.

disdain (to) keibetsu suru.

disease byooki.

disgrace fumeiyo *(dishonor);* haji *(shame).*

disguise hensoo.
  in disguise hensoo shite.

disguise (to) hensoo suru.

disgust iyake.

disgust (to) mune o waruku suru *(nauseate);* kimochi waruku saseru *(create an aversion).*

be disgusted unzari suru.

dish sara.

dishonest fushoojiki na.

disk enban.

dislike kirai.

dislike (to) kirau.

dismiss (to) ikaseru *(allow to go);* menshoku suru *(expel);* hima o dasu *(discharge).*

dismissal hima.

disobey (to) somuku.

disorder ranzatsu *(lack of order);* konzatsu *(confusion).*

dispense with (to) shobun suru *(dispose of).*

display chinretsu *(show);* hyoogen *(manifestation);* misebirakashi *(ostentation).*

displease (to) ki ni sawaraseru *(offend).*

displeasure fuman *(dissatisfaction).*

disposal shobun.

dispose (to) naraberu *(arrange);* -ki ni naru *(be inclined to).*
  to dispose of shobun suru.

dispute kooron *(debate);* soogi *(controversy);* kenka *(altercation).*

dispute (to) toogi suru *(argue about);* hanbaku suru *(contest);* teikoo suru *(oppose).*

dissolve (to) tokasu *(melt);* torikesu *(annul).*

distance kyori.

distant tooi *(far off).*

distinct hakkiri shita *(clear);* tokushu na *(different).*

distinction tokuchoo *(individuality).*

distinguish (to) miwakeru *(visually);* kikiwakeru *(by sound).*

distort (to) yugameru *(twist);* kojitsukeru *(pervert).*

distract (to) ki o torareru.

distress nayami *(worry);* nageki *(grief);* kutsuu *(pain).*

distribute (to) wariateru *(allot);* makichirasu *(spread out);* bunpai suru *(apportion);* kubaru *(deal out).*

district chihoo *(region);* ku *(city ward).*

distrust fushin'yoo.

distrust (to) shinjinai.

disturb (to) jama suru.

disturbance jama.

ditch mizo.

dive (to) tobikomu.

divide (to) wakeru *(separate, part);* waru *(by cutting);* shikiru *(by partition).*

divine shinsei na.
  divine being kami.
  divine service reihaishiki.

division warizan *(math.);* bunkatsu *(separation).*

divorce (to) rikon suru.
  divorced rikon shita hito.

**dizziness** memai.

**dizzy** memai ga suru.

**do (to)** suru *(act)*; tsukuru *(make)*.

**dock** hatoba, dokku.

**doctor** isha *(medical)*; hakase *(academic)*.

**doctrine** shugi.

**document** shorui *(papers)*; shoosho *(deed)*; bunsho *(official letter)*.

**dog** inu.

**doll** ningyoo.

**dome** maru tenjoo, doomu.

**domestic** katei no *(household)*; kainarasareta *(domesticated, tame)*; kokunai no *(native, pertaining to one's country)*.

    **domestic affairs** kaji *(of a household)*.

    **domestic animal** kachiku.

**dominate (to)** shihai suru *(govern)*.

**door** to, doa *(Western-style)*.

    **Japanese sliding door** shooji.

    **entrance door** genkan no doa.

    **back door** uraguchi no doa.

**dose** fukuyooryoo *(medicine)*.

**dot** ten.

**double** nibai.

**double (to)** nibai ni suru.

**doubt** utagai *(lack of certainty)*; fushin *(misgiving)*.

**doubt (to)** utagau *(disbelieve)*; fushin ni omou *(question)*.

**doubtful** tashika de nai *(uncertain)*; hakkiri shinai *(ambiguous)*; utagawashii *(questionable)*.

**doubtless** utagai nai.

**down** shita.

**dozen** daasu.

**draft** kawase tegata *(bank order)*; shitae *(sketch)*; shitagaki *(of a plan)*.

    **draft (draught) of wind** sukima kaze.

**drag (to)** hiku *(draw forcibly)*; hikizuru *(pull)*.

**drain (to)** haisui suru *(carry away water)*; nomihosu *(drink up)*.

**drama** engeki, dorama *(a play)*; gekiteki jiken *(event)*.

**draw (to)** kaku *(pictures)*; hikitsukeru *(attention)*.

    **to draw back** shirizoku.

**drawer** hikidashi *(of a table, etc.)*.

**drawing room** zashiki.

**dread** osore.

**dread (to)** osoreru.

**dreadful** osoroshii.

**dream** yume.

**dream (to)** yume o miru.

**dreamer** kuusooka, musooka.

**dress** kimono *(Japanese)*; doresu, yoofuku *(Western)*.

**dress (to)** *v.t.* kimono o kiseru; *v.i.* kimono o kiru.

**dressmaker** yoofukuya, yoosaishi *(of Western clothes)*; shitateya.

**drink** nomimono.

    **drinking water** nomimizu.

**drink (to)** nomu.

**drip (to)** shitataru.

**drive (to)** unten suru.

**driver** untenshu.

**drop** itteki *(of liquid)*.

**drop (to)** *v.t.* otosu *(let fall)*; *v.i.* ochiru *(from a height)*.

**drown (to)** oboreru.

**drug** kusuri *(medicine)*; mayaku *(narcotics)*.

**drugstore** kusuriya.

**drum** taiko; doramu *(Occidental-style)*.

**drunk** yotte iru.

    **drunken person** yopparai.

**dry** kawaita *(of things)*; kansoo shita *(of climate)*.

**dry (to)** kawakasu *(make dry)*; nuguu *(wipe one's eyes, etc.)*; kawaku *(become dry)*.

**dryness** kawaki *(thirst)*.

**duck** ahiru *(domestic)*; kamo *(wild)*.

**due** manki *(payable)*; toozen no *(fit, proper)*.

    **due to** -no tame ni.

**dull** nibui *(blunt)*; bonyari shita *(stupid)*; omoshiroku nai *(uninteresting)*.

**during** -no aida, -kan, -chuu (juu).

    **during ten years** juunen kan.

    **during one's absence** rusu no aida, rusu chuu.

**dust** chiri; hokori *(a finer dust than chiri)*.

**dust (to)** sooji suru, hokori o harau.

**dusty** hokori no ooi.

**Dutch** Oranda no.

**duty** tsutome *(work to be done)*; gimu *(moral or legal obligation)*; kanzei *(on imported goods)*.

**duty free** muzei no.

**dwarf** kobito *(person)*; kogata no *(undersized)*.

    **dwarf trees** bonsai no ki.

**dwell (to)** sumu.

**dye** senryoo.

**dye (to)** someru.

# E

**each** kaku-: *(prefix)* -zutsu: *(suffix)*.

    **each person** meimei; kakuji

    **each person or thing** sorezore *(of several)*.

    **each other** otagai ni.

    **each time** -tabi ni.

**eager** nesshin na *(ardent)*.

**eagle** washi.

**ear** mimi.
**early** *adj.* hayai. *-adv.* hayaku.
**earn (to)** kasegu *(by labor)*.
**earnest** majime na *(serious)*; nesshin na *(intense)*.
**earth** tsuchi *(soil)*; chikyuu *(world)*.
**ease** raku, kiraku.
**ease (to)** raku ni suru.
**easily** yasashiku; tegaru ni *(readily)*; surasura to *(smoothly)*.
**east** higashi.
    **the East** Tooyoo.
    **East Asia** Higashi Ajia.
**Easter** fukkatsusai, iisutaa.
**eastern** higashi no.
**easy** yasashii.
**eat (to)** taberu; meshiagaru *(honorific: respect)*.
**echo** yamabiko *(a phenomenon of nature)*; hankyoo *(in other cases)*.
**echo (to)** hankyoo suru.
**economical** keizaijoo no, keizaiteki na.
**economize (to)** setsuyaku suru *(use economically)*.
**economy class** ekonomii kurasu.
**edge** ha *(of blade)*; hashi *(of cloth)*; kishi *(of cliff, etc.)*.
**edition** han.
    **first edition** shohan.
    **new edition** shinpan.
    **revised edition** kaiteiban.
**editor** henshuusha *(of books or magazines)*; shuhitsu *(of newspaper)*.
**editorial** shasetsu.
**education** kyooiku.
    **to receive an education** kyooiku o ukeru.
**effect** kekka *(consequence)*.
**effective** yuukoo na *(operative)*; yuunoo na *(efficient)*.
**efficiency** nooritsu.
**effort** doryoku *(strenuous attempt)*; honeori *(exertion)*; rooku *(strain)*.
    **with an effort** hone otte.
    **without any effort** doryoku sezu ni.
**egg** tamago.
**egoism** jiko chuushin shugi.
**eight** yattsu, hachi.
**eighteen** juuhachi.
**eighteenth** juuhachi ban.
**eighth** dai hachi.
**eightieth** hachijuu ban.
**eighty** hachijuu.
**either** dochiraka no *(one of the two)*; dochira mo *(each of two)*.
    **either . . . or** -ka . . . ka, -ka aruiwa . . . ka
**elastic** shinshukusei no aru, shinayaka na *(flexible)*.
**elbow** hiji.

**elder** toshiue no.
**elderly** nenpai no.
**eldest** ichiban toshi ue no.
**elect (to)** erabu *(choose)*; senkyo suru *(by vote)*.
**election** senkyo.
**electric** denki no.
**electrical** denki no.
**electricity** denki.
**elegant** yuuga na *(graceful)*; joohin na *(tasteful)*.
**element** yooso *(component part)*.
**elementary** shoho no.
**elephant** zoo.
**elevator** erebeetaa.
**eleven** juuichi.
**eleventh** dai juuichi.
**eliminate (to)** nozoku *(exclude)*; sakujo suru *(get rid of)*; habuku *(omit)*.
**eloquence** yuuben.
**eloquent** yuuben na.
**else** hoka ni.
    **anyone else** hoka ni dare ka.
    **something else** hoka ni nani ka.
**elsewhere** hoka ni doko ka.
**elude (to)** nogareru *(evade)*; sakeru *(escape adroitly from)*.
**embark (to)** joosen suru *(board a ship)*; shuppan suru *(depart)*.
**embarrass (to)** komaraseru.
    **I was embarrassed.** Komarimashita.
**embarrassing** toowaku saseru.
**embarrassment** toowaku *(perplexity)*.
**embassy** taishikan.
**embody** gutaika suru *(make concrete)*.
**embrace (to)** daku *(a person)*; torimaku *(encircle)*; hoogan suru *(contain)*.
**embroidery** nuitori, shisuu.
**emerge (to)** arawareru *(come out into view)*.
**emergency** hijooji.
**eminent** kencho na *(distinguished)*.
**emotion** kanjoo *(feeling)*.
    **appeal to the emotions** kanjoo ni uttaeru.
    **with emotion** kandoo shite.
**emperor** tennoo.
**emphasis** kyoochoo.
**emphasize (to)** kyoochoo suru.
**emphatic** tsuyoi.
**empire** teikoku.
**employee** yatoinin, shiyoonin, juugyoo in.
**employer** yatoinushi.
**employment** shokugyoo *(occupation)*; shigoto *(work)*; koyoo.
**empty** kara no.
**enable (to)** -ga dekiru.
**enamel** enameru.
**enclose (to)** kakomu *(surround)*; kakou *(shut in)*, doofuu suru *(in a letter)*.

**enclosure** kakoi *(fence);* doofuubutsu *(enclosed materials).*

**encourage (to)** genki zukeru *(hearten);* yuuki zukeru *(put courage into).*

**encouragement** hagemashi.

**end** sue *(latter part);* owari *(the close);* ketsumatsu *(conclusion);* shimai *(finish).*

**end (to)** owaru, shimau.

**endeavor** jinryoku, doryoku.

**endeavor (to)** doryoku suru *(try hard);* kokoromiru *(attempt).*

**endorse (to)** uragaki suru.

**endure (to)** gaman suru *(bear bravely);* mochikotaeru *(hold out).*

**enemy** teki.

**energy** chikara *(power);* genki *(vigor).*
  **atomic energy** genshiryoku.
  **energy crisis** nenryoo kiki
  **mental energy** seishin nooryoku.
  **solar energy** taiyoo enerugii.

**enforce (to)** shiiru *(press).*

**engage (to)** yatou *(hire).*

**engaged** isogashii *(busy);* kon'yaku shite iru *(betrothed).*

**engagement** yakusoku *(formal promise);* kon'yaku *(betrothal);* yooji *(business).*

**engine** kikai *(machine);* kikan *(boiler),* enjin *(of car, etc.).*

**engineer** gishi *(of factory).*

**English** eigo *(pertaining to the language);* Igirisu (Eikoku) no *(pertaining to the country);* Igirisujin (Eikokujin) *(pertaining to the people).*

**engrave (to)** horu; insatsu suru *(print).*

**enjoy (to)** tanoshimu.

**enjoyment** tanoshimi.

**enlarge (to)** ookiku suru *(make bigger);* hikinobasu *(a photograph, etc.).*

**enlist (to)** guntai ni hairu *(in the army);* hito no shiji o eru *(secure one's support).*

**enormous** kyodai na.

**enough** juubun.

**enter (to)** hairu.

**entertain (to)** tanoshimaseru *(amuse);* motenasu *(guests).*

**entertainment** goraku *(amusement);* yokyoo *(public show).*

**enthusiasm** nesshin.

**enthusiastic** nesshin na.

**entire** kanzen na *(complete);* zentai no *(whole).*

**entitle (to)** na o tsukeru.

**entrance** iriguchi.

**entrust (to)** makaseru *(a duty, etc.);* azukeru *(a thing to another person).*

**enumerate (to)** kazoeru *(count).*

**envelope** fuutoo *(for letters).*

**envious** urayamashii.

**envy** urayami, shitto *(jealousy).*

**envy (to)** urayamu *(feel envy of);* shitto suru *(begrudge).*

**episode** soowa, episoodo.

**equal** onaji *(the same);* byoodoo no *(equitable).*

**equal (to)** -ni hitoshii.
  **A equals B.** A wa B desu.

**equality** byoodoo.

**equator** sekidoo.

**equilibrium** tsuriai.

**equip (to)** yooi suru *(supply);* soobi suru *(fit);* mijitaku suru *(array).*

**equipment** shitaku, junbi, soochi.

**era** jidai.

**erase (to)** kesu nuguikesu *(wipe out).*

**eraser** keshi gomu.

**erect (to)** tateru *(set up).*

**err (to)** machigaeru.

**errand** tsukai.

**error** machigai.

**escalator** esukareetaa.

**escape** toosoo *(running away);* datsugoku *(from prison).*

**escape (to)** nigeru *(get free);* nogareru *(get off safely).*

**escort (to)** goei suru *(with military);* tsukisou *(accompany).*

**especially** tokuni.

**essay** ronbun, zuihitsu.

**essence** yooten *(main points);* hontai *(a thing in itself);* yooso *(element).*

**essential** kanarazu iru, nakute wa naranai *(necessary);* honshitsuteki no *(of essential character).*

**establish** tateru, setsuritsu suru *(found);* kakutei suru *(ascertain);* seitei suru *(prove).*

**establishment** setsuritsu *(business firm).*

**estate** shoyuuchi *(property);* jisho *(ground).*

**esteem** sonkei *(respect form).*

**esteem (to)** sonkei suru.

**esthetic** fuuryuu na, biteki na.

**estimate** mitsumori *(of the cost);* hyooka *(of the value).*

**estimate (to)** hyooka suru *(appraise);* mitsumoru *(compute);* handan suru *(judge).*

**estimation** mitsumori, hyooka.

**eternal** eikyuu no *(everlasting);* huhen no *(immutable).*

**eternity** eikyuu, eien *(infinite time);* fumetsu *(immortality).*

**ether** eeteru.

**European** Yoorappajin *(people);* Yooroppa no *(pertaining to Europe).*

**evade** sakeru.

**evasion** kaihi.

**eve** yuugata *(evening);* zenya *(the evening or day before a festival).*

**even** mo, demo *(also)*; taira na *(level)*; choodo *(just)*.

**evening** ban, yoru, yuugata.
    **Good evening!** Konban wa.
    **yesterday evening** sakuban, yuube.
    **tomorrow evening** myooban, ashita no ban.

**event** dekigoto, jiken.

**ever** itsu demo *(always)*; taezu *(incessantly)*; ima made ni *(up to now)*; itsu ka *(on any occasion)*.

**every** mai-, donna -demo; zenbu *(all)*.
    **everyday** mainichi.
    **every year** maitoshi.

**everybody** dare mo *(referring to members of a group)*; dare demo *(no matter who)*; minna *(all)*.

**everything** nan demo *(no matter what)*; zenbu, minna *(all things)*.

**everywhere** doko de mo *(no matter where)*; hooboo *(all over)*.

**evidence** shooko *(proof)*.

**evident** akiraka na *(obvious)*.

**evil** *adj.* warui, akushitsu na *(wicked)*; fukitsu na *(unlucky)*. *-n.* aku *(vice)*; jaaku *(wickedness)*; warui koto *(bad thing)*.

**evoke (to)** hikiokosu *(draw forth)*.

**evolve (to)** tenkai suru *(unfold, unroll)*; hatten suru *(develop)*.

**exact** seikaku na *(accurate)*; genmitsu na *(precise)*; genkaku na *(rigorous)*.

**exaggerate (to)** kochoo suru, oogesa ni iu.

**exaggeration** kochoo, oogesa.

**exalt (to)** takameru *(raise high)*; homesoyasu *(extol)*.

**exaltation** takameru koto.

**examination** kensa *(inspection)*; choosa *(investigation)*; koosatsu *(consideration)*; shiken *(test)*.

**examine (to)** shiraberu *(inspect)*; shiken suru *(give a test)*.

**example** rei *(illustration)*; tehon *(model, pattern)*.

**exceed** sugiru, kosu *(go over)*.

**excel (to)** sugureru.
    **She excels in English.** Eigo ni sugurete iru.

**excellence** subarashisa, kesshutsu *(superiority)*; choosho *(great merit)*.

**excellent** sugureta.

**except** -no hoka wa.

**except (to)** nozoku *(omit)*.

**exception** reigai.

**exceptional** reigaiteki na.

**exceptionally** reigaiteki ni *(unusually)*; hijoo ni *(very)*.

**excess** yobun.

**excessive** yobun no *(surplus)*; hoogai na *(exorbitant)*.

**exchange** kookan *(of things in general)*; ryoogae *(of coins)*.

**exchange (to)** torikaeru, kookan suru *(barter)*.
    **exchange rate** kawase sooba.

**excite (to)** *v.i.* sawagu *(a body of people)*; *v.t.* ugokasu *(arouse a feeling)*.
    **to get excited** koofun suru.

**excitement** koofun.

**exclaim** sakebu *(cry out)*; zekkyoo suru *(speak vehemently)*.

**exclamation** zekkyoo *(outcry)*; kantanshi *(an interjection)*.
    **exclamation mark** kantanfu.

**exclude (to)** nozoku.

**exclusive** dokusenteki *(monopolistic)*; -o nozoite *(not including)*.

**excursion** ensoku *(picnic)*; yuuran ryokoo *(pleasure tour)*.

**excuse** koojitsu *(bad)*; iiwake *(apology)*.

**excuse (to)** yurusu *(forgive)*; benkai suru *(vindicate)*.
    **Excuse me.** Gomen nasai.

**execute (to)** jikkoo suru *(carry out)*; suikoo suru *(perform)*.

**execution** shikkoo, suikoo.

**exempt (to)** menzuru *(free)*.

**exercise** undoo *(of the body)*; renshuu *(lesson)*.

**exercise (to)** undoo suru *(engage in athletics)*; renshuu suru *(practice)*.

**exert (to)** tsukusu *(put forth)*; mochiiru *(use)*.

**exertion** doryoku, jinryoku *(vigorous effort)*.

**exhaust (to)** kara ni suru *(empty)*; tsukai tsukusu *(use up)*; tsukarehatesaseru *(tire out)*.

**exhaustion** hiroo *(extreme fatigue)*.

**exhibit (to)** tenji suru *(show publicly)*.

**exhibition** hakurankai *(exposition)*; tenjikai *(show)*.

**exile** tsuihoo *(banishment)*; tsuihoonin *(person in exile)*.

**exile (to)** tsuihoo suru.

**exist** sonzai suru, aru *(be)*.

**existence** sonzai *(being)*; seizon *(life)*.

**exit** deguchi.

**expand** hirogeru *(spread out)*; kakuchoo suru *(extend)*; kakudai saseru *(amplify)*.

**expansion** kakuchoo *(dilation)*; hirogari *(expanse)*.

**expansive** koodai na *(extensive)*; kokoro no hiroi *(comprehensive)*.

**expect (to)** kitai suru *(look forward to)*; -to omou *(suppose)*.

**expectation** kitai *(anticipation)*; yosoo *(probability)*.

**expedition** tanken *(for exploration)*.

**expel (to)** oiharau *(drive out)*; menshoku suru *(dismiss)*.

**expense** hiyoo.

**expensive** takai, kooka na *(costly)*.

**experience** keiken *(personal observation)*.

**experience (to)** keiken suru *(undergo)*.

**experiment (to)** shiken suru *(test)*, tamesu *(try out)*.

**expert** *adj.* kurooto *(in doing something)*. *-n.* senmonka *(specialist)*.

**expire (to)** kikan ga kireru *(come to an end)*, iki o hikitoru *(breathe one's last)*; kieru *(die out)*; shoometsu suru *(become extinct)*.

**explain (to)** setsumei suru *(give an explanation)*; kaishaku suru *(interpret)*; benmei suru *(justify by an explanation)*.

**explanation** setsumei.

**explanatory** setsumeiteki, setsumei no.

**explode (to)** bakuhatsu suru.

**exploit** tegara *(brilliant achievement)*.

**exploit (to)** kuimono ni suru *(take advantage of for one's own ends)*.

**explore (to)** tanken suru *(search through)*; choosa suru *(inquire into)*.

**explosion** bakuhatsu.

**export** yushutsu.

**export (to)** yushutsu suru.

**expose (to)** sarasu *(leave unprotected)*; chinretsu suru *(exhibit)*; roshutsu suru *(in photography)*; abaku *(disclose, reveal)*.

**express** sokutatsu *(special delivery)*; kyuukoo *(train)*.

**express (to)** iiarawasu *(state)*.

**expression** hyoojoo *(facial)*; hyoogen *(verbal)*.

**expressive** hyoojoo ni tomu.

**expulsion** hoochiku.

**exquisite** sensai na *(delicate)*.

**extend (to)** nobasu *(in length or term)*; hirogeru *(in breadth)*; okuru *(invitation, greetings)*.

**extensive** koodai na *(far-reaching)*.

**extent** han'i *(space, scope, degree)*.
  **to some extent** aru teido.

**exterior** soto, hyoomen *(surface)*.

**exterminate (to)** tayasu.

**external** gaibu no *(outside)*.

**extinct** horobite shimatta.

**extinction** shoometsu.

**extinguish** kesu *(put out)*; tayasu *(put an end to)*.

**extra** betsu no; googai *(edition of a newspaper)*.

**extract** bassui *(excerpt)*.

**extract (to)** nuku *(pull out)*; nuki-toru *(pull out with difficulty)*; tekishutsu suru *(draw forth)*.

**extraordinary** futsuu de nai *(exceptional)*; hibon na *(uncommon)*; ichijirushii *(remarkable)*.

**extravagance** zeitaku *(lavish wastefulness)*; hoojuu *(unrestrained excess)*.

**extravagant** zeitaku na *(profuse, wasteful)*; mucha na *(unreasonable)*; hoogai na *(exorbitant, excessive)*.

**extreme** kyokutan na *(utmost)*; ichiban tooi *(outermost)*.

**extremely** taihen, hijoo ni.

**extremity** hashi *(extreme point)*.

**eye** me.

**eyebrow** mayuge.

**eyeglasses** megane.

**eyelid** mabuta.

**fable** otogibanashi, guuwa.

**face** kao.

**face (to)** mukau.

**facilitate** raku ni suru.

**facility** yooi *(ease)*; bengi *(convenience)*.

**fact** koto; shidai *(of an occurrence)*; jikoo *(particulars)*.
  **in fact** jitsu wa.

**factory** kooba, koojoo.

**faculty** shuwan *(aptitude)*; gakubu *(of a university)*.

**fade** iro ga sameru.

**fail (to)** shippai suru *(be unsuccessful)*; hasan suru *(become bankrupt)*.
  **without fail** machigai naku, kitto, zehi.

**faint** usui *(of color)*; yowai *(wanting in courage)*; kasuka na *(of sound, etc.)*.

**faint (to)** kizetsu suru.

**fair** *adj.* kirei na *(pretty)*; iro no shiroi *(of complexion)*; koohei na *(impartial)*. *-n.* ichi *(market)*; jizen ichi *(bazaar)*.

**faith** shinkoo *(belief)*; shinjoo *(creed)*; kyoogi *(religious doctrine)*; shinrai *(trust)*.

**faithful** chuujitsu na.

**fall** tsuiraku *(drop)*; taki *(cascade)*; aki *(autumn)*; kanraku *(surrender)*; gakai *(of a government)*.

**fall (to)** ochiru *(drop)*; furu *(rain, snow)*; sagaru *(prices)*.
  **fall down** korobu.

**false** uso no, hontoo de nai *(not true)*; fujitsu na *(not faithful)*; sorazorashii *(feigned)*; nise *(counterfeit)*.

**fame** meisei.

**familiar** yoku shirarete iru *(well known)*; kikinareta *(to the ear)*; minareta *(to the*

*eye);* arifureta *(common);* shitashii
*(intimate).*
**family** kazoku.
   **family name** myooji.
**famine** busshi no ketsuboo *(scarcity of food);*
  kikin *(failure of crops);* kiga *(starvation).*
**famous** yuumei na.
**fan** sensu *(folding);* uchiwa *(nonfolding).*
  **electric fan** senpuuki.
**fancy** soozooryoku *(imagination);* kangae
  *(idea).*
**fantastic** kuusooteki na *(extravagant);* iyoo na
  *(grotesque);* soozoojoo no *(imaginary),*
  subarashii *(wonderful).*
**far** tooi.
  **as far as** made.
  **so far** ima made *(up to now).*
**fare** ryookin *(cost of transportation).*
  **one-way fare** katamichi ryookin.
**farm** hatake *(field);* noojoo *(ranch).*
**farmer** noofu, hyakushoo.
**farming** noogyoo *(agriculture).*
**farther** motto tooi.
**farthest** ichiban tooi.
**fashion** tsukuri kata *(shape);* ryuukoo, fasshon
  *(style).*
**fashionable (to become)** ryuukoo suru.
**fast** hayai.
**fasten (to)** shikkari tomeru *(make fast);* kukuri
  tsukeru *(attach securely).*
**fat** *adj.* futotta. *-n.* abura.
**fatal** inochi ni kakawaru.
  **fatal accident** chimeiteki jiko.
  **fatal disease** fuji no yamai.
  **fatal wound** chimeishoo.
**fate** unmei *(destiny);* un *(appointed lot).*
**father** otoosan *(respect);* chichi *(plain).*
**faucet** jaguchi.
**fault** ketten *(defect);* tansho *(weak point);*
  machigai *(mistake).*
**favor** onegai *(request).*
  **Could (will) you do me a favor?** Onegai
  dekimasu ka?
**favor (to)** ekohiiki o suru *(be partial to);* shiji
  suru *(support).*
**favorable** kooi aru *(well disposed);* shoodaku
  no *(consenting).*
**favorite** *adj.* ki ni iri no *(preferred);* daisuki
  na *(liked greatly). -n.* ninkimono *(person).*
**fax** fakkusu.
**fear** osore *(dread);* shinpai *(anxiety).*
**fear (to)** osoreru.
**fearless** daitan na.
**feather** hane.
**feature** tokuchoo *(characteristic);* yooten
  *(striking point);* kaodachi *(appearance).*
**February** Nigatsu.
**federal** chuuoo seifu no *(pertaining to the*
  *central government).*

**fee** gessha *(monthly);* shinsatsuryoo
  *(doctor's).*
**feeble** yowai *(weak);* bonyari shita
  *(indistinct).*
**feed (to)** tabesaseru.
**feel (to)** sawaru *(touch);* kanjiru *(perceive a*
  *sensation).*
**feeling** kankaku *(sense);* kimochi *(sensation);*
  kanjoo *(emotion).*
**fellow** *adj.* nakama no. *-n.* nakama
  *(associate).*
**fellowship** shoogakukin *(grant);* shinboku
  *(friendliness).*
**female** onna *(woman).*
  **female sex** josei.
**feminine** onna no.
**fence** kakine *(enclosure for garden);* kakoi
  *(for other purposes);* hei.
**fencing** kendoo *(Japanese-style);* fenshingu
  *(foreign).*
**ferocious** kyooboo na *(fierce);* yaban na
  *(savage).*
**ferry** watashibune *(ferryboat);* renrakusen
  *(connected with trains).*
**fertile** koeta *(productive).*
**fertilize (to)** hiryoo o hodokosu.
**fertilizer** hiryoo *(manure);* kagaku hiryoo
  *(chemical).*
**fervent** netsuretsu na *(ardent).*
**fervor** netsu joo *(ardor).*
**festival** saijitsu *(feast day);* omatsuri, matsuri
  *(of shrine or temple).*
**fetch** motte kuru.
**fever** netsu.
**few** ni san *(two or three);* sukoshi *(not*
  *many).*
**fiber** sen'i.
**fiberoptic communication** hikari tsuushin.
**fiction** shoosetsu, fikushon.
**field** nohara *(open country);* bokusoochi
  *(meadow).*
  **rice field** ta.
**fierce** araarashii *(ferocious);* mooretsu na
  *(violent);* hageshii *(furious).*
**fiery** hi no yoo na *(glowing).*
**fifteen** juugo.
**fifteenth** dai juugo; juugo nichi *(of the*
  *month);* juugo ban.
**fifth** dai go.
**fiftieth** dai gojuu.
**fifty** gojuu.
**fig** ichijiku.
**fight** kenka *(brawl);* sensoo *(battle).*
**fight (to)** sensoo suru *(wage war);* doryoku
  suru *(struggle for);* kenka suru *(quarrel).*
**figure** suuji *(number);* katachi *(form);* sugata
  *(body);* moyoo *(design, pattern).*
**file** yasuri *(tool);* retsu *(row);* fairu *(official*
  *file);* tojikomi *(for letters).*

**fill (to)** *v.t.* ippai ni suru; *v.i.* ippai ni naru *(become full).*

**film** fuirumu *(for camera);* eiga *(motion picture).*

**filthy** kitanai *(unclean);* gehin na *(obscene).*

**final** saigo no *(last);* shuukyoku no *(conclusive).*
  **finally** tootoo.

**finance** zaisei.

**finance (to)** kane o dasu.

**financial** zaiseijoo no.

**find (to)** mitsukeru.

**fine** *adj.* komakai *(small);* hosoi *(slender);* usui *(thin);* utsukushii *(beautiful);* ii *(good);* genki na *(healthy).*

**fine** *n.* bakkin *(penalty).*

**finger** yubi.

**finish (to)** shimau, oeru; dekiagaru *(complete a piece of work);* shiageru *(get a thing done).*

**fire** hi; kaji *(conflagration).*

**fireworks** hanabi.

**firm** *adj.* katai *(compact);* shikkari shita *(rigid).*

**firm** *n.* shookai, kaisha *(commercial).*

**first** *adj.* dai ichi no, ichi ban no *(ordinal number).* -*adv.* hajime.
  **at first** hajime wa.
  **for the first time** hajimete.

**fish** sakana, uo; sashimi *(slices of raw fish).*
  **raw fish** namazakana.

**fish (to)** tsuri o suru.
  **go out fishing** tsuri ni iku.

**fisherman** ryooshi.

**fist** nigiri kobushi.

**fit** *adj.* tekitoo na *(appropriate);* datoo na *(proper, right).* -*n.* hossa *(convulsion).*

**fit (to)** tekigoo suru *(be fit for);* awaseru *(make to suit);* junbi suru *(qualify);* au *(be adjusted to fit).*

**fitness** tekitoo.

**five** itsutsu, go.

**fix (to)** kimeru *(determine);* toritsukeru *(arrange);* naosu *(mend).*

**flag** hata.

**flame** honoo.

**flank** sokumen *(side).*

**flank (to)** sokumen o mamoru.

**flash** hirameki *(lightning).*

**flat** hiratai *(level);* kin'itsu no *(unvarying);* ki no nuketa *(stale).*

**flatter** oseji o iu.

**flattery** oseji *(insincere compliment).*

**flavor** aji *(taste);* kaori *(smell).*

**fleet** kantai *(navy).*

**flesh** niku *(meat for eating);* nikutai *(of the human body).*

**flexibility** shinayakasa.

**flexible** shinayaka na *(pliable).*

**flight** hikoo *(trip by air);* tooboo *(fleeing);* kaidan *(of stairs).*

**fling (to)** tosshin suru *(dash, rush);* nagetsukeru *(hurl, toss).*

**flint** hiuchi ishi.

**float (to)** uku *(on water);* ukabu *(on water or in air).*

**flood** oomizu, koozui.

**flood (to)** shinsui saseru *(inundate);* shinsui suru *(be inundated);* hanran suru *(overflow).*

**floor** yuka *(of a room).*

**floppy disk** furoppii disuku.

**flourish (to)** sakaeru *(thrive).*

**flow** nagareru.

**flower** hana.
  **flower arrangement** ikebana, kadoo.

**fluid** ekitai.

**fly** hae.

**fly (to)** tobu.

**foam** awa.

**foam (to)** awa ga tatsu.

**fog** kiri *(mist);* moya *(haze).*
  **thick fog** noomu.

**fold** hida *(in a garment).*

**fold (to)** tatamu, oru.

**foliage** ha.

**follow (to)** -ni shitagau *(go or come after);* -ni tsuite kuru *(come traveling with someone);* -ni tsuite iku *(go accompanying someone);* issho ni iku *(accompany).*

**following** sono tsugi no *(next).*
  **the following day** akuru hi.

**fond (be)** konomu.

**fondness** suki.

**food** tabemono.

**fool** baka.

**foolish** baka na *(silly);* bakarashii *(nonsensical);* bakageta *(ridiculous).*

**foot** ashi *(of the body);* fiito *(measure).*

**football** futtobooru, shuukyuu.

**footstep** ashidori *(tread);* ashiato *(footprint).*

**for** -no kawari ni *(in place of);* -o daihyoo shite *(representing);* -ni taishite *(in return for, in contrast with);* -no tsugunai ni *(in compensation for);* -no tame ni *(on behalf of, in support of, for the purpose of, because of);* -ni mukatte *(in the direction of);* -no wari ni wa *(in respect of).*
  **for example** tatoeba.
  **for the first time** hajimete.
  **for the most part** daibubun.
  **for the present** ima no tokoro.

**forbid** kinjiru.

**force** chikara *(strength);* guntai *(troops).*
  **by force** muri ni.

**force (to)** bookoo suru *(use force upon);* kojiakeru *(break open);* oshiyaru *(impel);*

muri ni, shiite *(when followed by a causative verb)*.
  **I forced her to go.** Muri ni ikaseta.
**ford (to)** asase o wataru *(wade across)*.
**foreground** zenkei.
**forehead** hitai.
**foreign** gaikoku no *(pertaining to foreign countries in general)*; seiyoo no *(of the West)*.
**foreigner** gaikokujin, gaijin *(foreigners in general)*; oobeijin *(Western)*.
**forest** hayashi, mori *(grove)*; shinrin *(dense growth)*.
**forget (to)** wasureru.
**forgetfulness** wasureppoi koto.
**forgive** yurusu.
**forgiveness** yurushi.
**fork** fooku *(for eating)*; wakaremichi *(parting of the ways)*; shiryuu *(of a river)*; mata *(of a tree)*.
**form** katachi *(shape)*; keishiki *(formality)*; yooshi *(blank)*.
**form (to)** katachizukuru *(shape)*; tsukuru *(organize)*; -ni naru *(constitute)*; tsukuriageru *(build up)*.
**formal** seishiki no.
**formation** soshiki.
**former** mae no, saki no *(previous)*.
**formerly** mae ni *(previously)*; moto *(originally)*.
**formula** hooshiki, yarikata *(method)*.
**forsake (to)** misuteru *(abandon)*.
**fort** yoosai.
**fortieth** yonjuu ban me no; dai yonjuu.
**fortunate** un ga ii.
**fortunately** un yoku, shiawase ni mo *(luckily)*.
**fortune** shiawase *(good luck)*; zaisan *(wealth)*; unsei *(fate)*.
**forty** shijuu, yonjuu.
**forward** zenpoo e *(onward)*.
  **move forward** zenshin suru.
**forward (to)** okuru *(goods)*; kaisoo suru, tensoo suru *(letters)*.
**foster** yoo—.
  **foster daughter** yoojo.
  **foster father** yoofu.
  **foster mother** yoobo.
  **foster son** yooshi.
**found (to)** setsuritsu suru *(establish, start)*; kiso o oku *(lay the base of)*.
**foundation** dodai *(groundwork)*; konkyo *(basis)*; shuppatsuten *(beginning)*; zaidan *(endowed institution)*.
**founder** sooritsusha *(one who establishes or lays a foundation)*.
**fountain** funsui.
**four** yottsu, shi, yon.

**fourteen** juushi, juuyon.
**fourteenth** juuyon ban me no *(place)*; juuyokka *(of the month)*.
**fourth** yottsu me, dai shi, dai yon; yokka *(of the month)*.
**fowl** tori *(bird)*.
**fox** kitsune.
**fragment** kakera, kirehashi.
**fragrance** yoi nioi.
**fragrant** nioi no ii.
**frail** yowayowashii.
**frame** gakubuchi.
**frame (to)** e o gaku ni ireru *(a picture)*.
**frank** sotchoku na *(openhearted)*; koozen no, akarasama na *(without guile)*.
**frankness** sotchoku.
**free** tada *(gratis)*; jiyuu na *(liberated)*; muzei *(without tax)*.
**free (to)** *v.t.* hanasu *(let go free)*; *v.i.* jiyuu ni naru *(be set free)*.
**freedom** jiyuu *(liberty)*; dokuritsu *(independence)*.
**freeze (to)** *v.t.* kooraseru; *v.i.* kooru.
**freight** kamotsu *(goods)*.
**French** furansu no *(pertaining to France)*; furansugo *(language)*; furansujin *(people)*.
**frequent** tabitabi no *(recurring often)*.
**frequent (to)** yoku iku *(visit often)*.
**frequently** tabitabi *(often)*; yoku *(at short intervals)*.
**fresh** mizumizushii *(newly grown)*; dekitate no *(just made)*; shinsen na, atarashii *(said of foods)*.
**friction** masatsu, atsureki.
**Friday** Kin'yoobi.
**friend** tomodachi; yuujin.
**friendly** aiso no ii.
**friendship** yuujoo *(friendly attachment)*; yuugi *(intimacy)*.
**frighten (to)** odorokasu;
  **be frightened** bikkuri suru, odoroku.
**frightening** kowai.
**fringe** fusa *(tuft)*; heri *(border)*.
**frivolity** fumajime.
**frivolous** fumajime na.
**frog** kaeru.
**from** -kara.
  **from now on** ima kara.
**front** mae, zenmen *(forward part)*; zenpoo *(forward place)*; shoomen *(of a building)*; sensen *(line of battle)*.
**frost** shimo.
**fruit** kudamono.
**fry (to)** furai ni suru, ageru.
**frying pan** furai pan, age nabe.
**fuel** nenryoo.
**fugitive** *n.* toosoosha *(runaway)*; boomeisha *(political refugee)*.

**fulfill (to)** hatasu *(perform);* jikkoo suru *(execute).*

**full** ippai no *(filled to capacity).*

**fully** mattaku.

**fun** tanoshimi *(amusement).*

**function** hataraki.

**function (to)** hataraku.

**fund** kikin.

**fundamental** kisoteki na.

**funds** shikin *(sum of money).*

**funny** kokkei na.

**fur** kegawa.

**furious** okotte iru *(angry).*

**furnace** ro.

**furnish (to)** kyookyuu suru *(provide);* sonaeru *(equip).*

**furniture** kagu.

**furrow** ato *(track);* wadachi *(rut);* fukai shiwa *(deep wrinkle).*

**furrow (to)** kao o shikameru *(make a wrinkle in the face).*

**further** sono ue *(besides).*

   **further away** motto saki.

   **further on** motto saki e.

**fury** gekido *(wild anger);* kyooboo *(violence).*

**future** *adj.* mirai no. *-n.* mirai *(time to come);* shoorai *(prospect).*

   **in the future** mirai ni, shoorai.

**gaiety** nigiyakasa *(mirth).*

**gain** rieki *(opposite of loss);* mooke *(earnings);* zooka *(increase).*

**gain (to)** te ni ireru, eru *(obtain);* masu *(increase).*

**gallant** isamashii.

**gallery** gyaraii *(of fine arts);* tachimi-seki *(standing room in a theater).*

**gamble (to)** kakegoto o suru, kakeru.

**game** yuugi *(amusement);* kyoogi *(sporting contest);* shoobugoto *(of chance).*

**garage** gareeji.

**garden** niwa.

   **public garden** kooen.

**gardener** uekiya, niwashi.

**garlic** ninniku.

**gas** gasu.

**gasoline** gasorin.

**gate** mon.

**gather** *v.t.* yoseatsumeru *(bring together);* atsumeru *(collect);* saishuu suru *(pick up);* tsumu *(as flowers); v.i.* atsumaru *(assemble).*

**gay** yooki na *(said of people);* hade na *(said of colors).*

**gem** hooseki *(jewel).*

**gender** sei.

**general** *adj.* ippan no, ippanteki no *(belonging to the whole);* taitei no *(common to many).*

   **in general, generally** ippan ni.

**general** *n.* taishoo *(military).*

**generalize (to)** ippanka shite kangaeru.

**generation** sedai *(used when referring to people, as in "young generation");* jidai *(period of time).*

**generosity** kandaisa, kimae no yosa.

**generous** ki no ookii, kandai na.

**genius** tensai.

**gentle** otonashii *(said of people);* yasashii *(said of manners);* odayaka na *(quiet).*

**gentleman** shinshi.

**genuine** honmono no *(authentic);* senjitsu na *(sincere).*

**geographical** chiriteki no.

**geography** chiri.

**germ** baikin.

**German** doitsu no *(pertaining to Germany);* doitsugo *(language);* doitsujin *(people).*

**gesture** miburi.

**get (to)** naru *(become, turn);* te ni ireru *(get hold of).*

**ghastly** zotto suru.

**giant** *adj.* ooki na, ookii. *-n.* oootoko *(big man).*

**gift** miyage *(souvenir);* okurimono, purezento *(present);* sainoo *(talent).*

**gifted** sainoo no aru *(talented).*

**girl** onna no ko.

**give (to)** sashiageru *(to others: humble);* ageru *(to others);* yaru *(to others: fam.);* watasu *(hand over);* kudasaru *(from others: respect);* kureru *(from others: fam.).*

   **give back** kaesu.

**glad** ureshii *(delighted, happy).*

   **be glad** yorokobu.

**gladly** yorokonde.

**glance** hitome.

   **at a glance** hitome de.

**glance (to)** chiratto miru *(look rapidly);* zatto me o toosu *(read rapidly).*

**glass** garasu *(material).*

   **looking glass** kagami.

   **drinking glass** koppu.

**gleam** kagayaki *(shine);* hirameki *(of intelligence).*

**gleam (to)** kagayaku.

**glitter** kagayaki.

**glitter (to)** pikapika hikaru.

**globe** tama *(round object);* chikyuu *(the earth).*

**gloomy** kurai *(dark);* usugurai *(somber);* inki na *(depressed).*

**glorious** kooei aru *(illustrious);* soogon na *(majestic);* subarashii *(delightful).*

**glory** kooei *(honor);* sookan *(splendor).*

**glove** tebukuro.

    **a pair of gloves** tebukuro hitokumi.

**go (to)** yuku, iku; mairu *(honorific: humble);* irassharu *(honorific: respect).*

    **to go away** itte shimau.

    **to go back** kaeru.

    **to go down** oriru *(stairs, etc.);* kudaru *(mountains, etc.).*

    **to go into** hairu.

    **to go out** deru.

    **to go up** noboru, agaru.

**god** kami *(deity);* guuzoo *(idol).*

**gold** kin.

**golden** kin'iro no.

**good** ii, yoi.

    **Good afternoon!** Konnichi wa.

    **Good evening!** Konban wa.

    **Good morning!** Ohayoo gozaimasu.

    **Good night!** Oyasumi nasai *(said when going to bed).*

**good-bye** sayonara.

**goods** shinamono.

**goodwill** kooi.

**goose** gachoo.

**gossip** goshippu, uwasabanashi.

**gossip (to)** uwasabanashi o suru, hito no uwasa o suru.

**govern (to)** osameru *(rule);* kanri suru *(control).*

**government** seiji *(politics);* seitai *(form of government);* kanri *(management);* toochi kikan *(governing body).*

**grace** shitoyakasa.

**graceful** shitoyaka na.

**grain** kokumotsu.

**grammar** bunpoo.

**grand** subarashii *(magnificent);* rippa na *(splendid).*

    **Grand!** migoto desu.

**grandchild** mago.

**granddaughter** mago musume.

**grandfather** ojiisan, sofu.

**grandmother** obaasan, sobo.

**grandson** mago musuko.

**grant** kyoka *(permission);* joseikin *(funds).*

**grant (to)** kikitodokeru *(consent to);* ataeru *(give);* juyo suru *(bestow);* yurusu *(allow, permit).*

**grape** budoo.

**grapefruit** gureepu furuutsu.

**grasp (to)** nigiru *(in the hand);* tsukamu *(with the hand or mind).*

**grass** kusa.

**grasshopper** inago.

**grateful** arigatai.

**gratitude** kansha.

**grave** *adj.* juudai na *(serious).*

**grave** *n.* haka *(place of burial).*

**gravel** jari.

**gray** nezumi iro, hai iro.

**grease** abura.

**great** ookii *(large);* idai na *(much above the average).*

**greatness** idaisa.

**greedy** kuishinboo na *(for food);* yokufukai *(for gain).*

**green** midori.

**greet (to)** aisatsu suru.

**greeting** aisatsu.

**grief** fukai kanashimi *(deep sorrow);* shintsuu *(distress).*

**grieve (to)** *v.t.* fukaku kanashimaseru *(cause grief to);* kurushimaseru *(distress); v.i.* fukaku kanashimu *(feel grief);* nageku *(lament).*

**grin (to)** niyatto warau.

**grind** surikudaku.

**groan** unari goe.

**groan (to)** unaru, umeku.

**grocer** shokuryoohin'ya.

**grocery store** shokuryoohin'ya.

**grope** tesaguri suru.

**gross** juuni daasu *(12 doz.).*

**ground** jimen *(surface of earth);* dodai *(foundation).*

**group** guruupu; shuudan *(assemblage).*

**group (to)** matomeru.

**grow (to)** hattatsu suru *(develop);* seichoo suru *(said of animate things);* haeru *(flourish in earth).*

**growth** seichoo.

**grudge** urami.

    **hold a grudge against** uramu.

**gruff** bukkiraboo na.

**guard** hoshoo *(sentry);* shashoo *(of a train);* bannin *(watchman).*

**guard (to)** mamoru.

**guardian** kookennin *(legal);* hogosha *(keeper).*

**guess** suiryoo, ate zuiryoo.

**guess (to)** soozoo suru.

    **guess right** iiateru.

**guide** annaisha *(tourist);* michi annaisha *(one who shows the way);* shidoosha *(leader).*

**guide (to)** annai suru *(lead the way).*

**guilt** tsumi.

**gum** nori, gomu.

    **chewing gum** chuuingamu.

**gun** juu *(firearm);* teppoo *(rifle, shotgun);* kenjuu *(revolver).*

**gush (to)** fukideru.

# H

**habit** shuukan.
**habitual** shuukanteki na *(customary)*; jooshuuteki *(regular)*.
**hail** arare *(small hailstone)*; hyoo *(large hailstone)*.
**hail (to)** arare ga furu.
**hair** ke *(in general)*; kami *(of the head)*.
**hairdo** heya sutairu.
**hairdresser** biyooshi.
**half** hanbun.
  **half-hour** hanjikan, sanjippun.
**hall** hiroma, hooru.
**ham** hamu.
**hammer** kanazuchi.
**hand** te.
**hand (to)** watasu *(hand over)*.
**handbag** handobaggu, tesage.
**handful** te ippai.
**handkerchief** hankachi.
**handle** te, hikite *(of a door)*; e, te *(of a tool)*.
**handle (to)** atsukau.
**handsome** tanrei na *(good-looking)*; yooboo no utsukushii *(beautiful)*.
**handy** kiyoo na *(said of persons)*; choohoo na, benri na *(said of things)*.
**hang** *v.t.* kakeru *(something)*; kubi o kukuru *(a person)*; *v.i.* sagaru *(hang down)*.
**happen (to)** furikakaru *(befall)*; okoru *(occur)*.
**happening** dekigoto *(event)*; jiken *(incident)*.
**happiness** koofuku *(well-being)*; shiawase *(fortune, luck)*.
**happy** ureshii, koofuku na *(felicitous, joyous)*; shiawase na *(favored by luck)*.
**harbor** minato.
**hard** katai *(solid, as opposed to soft)*; muzukashii *(difficult)*.
  **to study hard** isshookenmei benkyoo suru.
**harden** *v.t.* katameru, kataku suru *(solidify)*; katamaru *(become solid)*.
**hardly** hotondo *(used with a negative expression)*.
**hardness** kenroo.
**hardship** konnan.
**hardware** kanamono.
  **hardware store** kanamonoya.
**hardy** joobu na.
**hare** no-usagi.
**harm** gai *(damage)*; songai *(loss)*; sonshoo *(injury)*.
**harm (to)** gaisuru.
**harmful** warui.
**harmless** gai no nai.

**harmonious** tsuriai no toreta *(balanced)*.
**harmony** waon *(musical)*; haigoo *(of colors)*; enman, choowa *(between persons)*.
**harsh** soaku na *(coarse)*; fuchoowa na *(discordant)*; kibishii *(stern)*.
**harvest** shuukaku.
**haste** isogi.
**hasten (to)** isogu *(hurry)*; isogaseru *(hurry a person)*; hayameru *(a result)*; isoide suru *(hurry to)*.
**hat** booshi.
**hate** nikumi.
**hate (to)** nikumu, kirau.
**hateful** nikurashii.
**hatred** nikushimi.
**haughty** gooman na.
**have (to)** motsu *(possess, hold)*; nomu *(drink)*; taberu *(eat)*; uketoru *(receive)*.
**haven** minato, hinansho.
**hay** karekusa.
**he** kare, ano hito.
**head** atama *(of the body)*; kashiro *(leader)*, shunin *(chief)*.
**headache** zutsuu.
**heal** *v.t.* naosu *(mend)*; *v.i.* naoru *(be mended)*.
**health** kenkoo.
**healthy** kenkoo na, joobu na.
**heap** yama.
  **to heap up** tsumu.
**hear (to)** kiku.
**hearing** kiku chikara, chooryoku.
  **hard of hearing** mimi ga tooi.
**heart** shinzoo *(organ of the body)*; kokoro *(as seat of the emotions)*.
**heat (to)** atatameru, atsuku suru.
**heaven** tengoku *(Christian)*; gokuraku *(Buddhist)*.
  **Heavens!** oya maa!
**heavy** omoi.
**hedge** ike gaki.
**heed (to)** shitagau.
**heel** kakato.
**height** takasa.
**heir** soozokunin.
**heiress** soozokunin.
**helm** kaji.
**help** tetsudai.
**help (to)** tetsudau *(give a helping hand)*; sewa o suru *(take care of)*; tasukeru *(rescue)*.
**helper** tetsudai.
**helpful** yaku ni tatsu.
**hem** fuchi *(margin)*; heri *(edge)*; sakai *(border)*.
**hen** mendori.
**henceforth** kore kara.
**her, hers** kanojo no. (See also **him**.)
**herb** yakusoo *(medical)*.

**herd** mure.

**here** koko *(this place);* kotchi, kochira *(this side).*

**herewith** koko ni.

**hero** eiyuu *(of a battle);* shujinkoo *(of a novel).*

**heroic** eiyuuteki.

**heroine** jojoofu *(person of great deeds);* onna shujinkoo *(of a novel).*

**herring** nishin.

**herself** jibun *(self, same word is used for both male and female).*

    **by herself** hitori de, jibun de.

**hesitate (to)** tamerau, chuucho suru.

**hide (to)** kakusu *(conceal);* himitsu ni suru *(keep secret);* kakureru *(conceal oneself).*

**hideous** zotto suru yoo na.

**high** takai.

**higher** -yori mo takai.

**hill** oka *(small mountain);* saka (on a road).

**him** ano kata ni, ano hito ni *(to him);* ano kata o, ano hito o *(as object of sentence).*

**himself** jibun *(same word used also for "herself").*

    **by himself** jibun de.

**hind** ushiro no.

**hinder (to)** jama suru, samatageru.

**hinge** chootsugai.

**hint** hinto, honomekashi *(allusion);* atekosuri *(insinuation).*

**hint (to)** honomekasu *(allude to);* atekosuru *(insinuate).*

**hip** oshiri, koshi.

**hire (to)** yatou *(servants, etc.);* kariru *(cars).*

**his** ano hito no, kare no.

**historian** rekishika.

**historic** rekishijoo no, rekishiteki no.

**history** rekishi.

**hit (to)** utsu, tataku, naguru.

    **to hit against** butsukeru.

**hoarse** shagare goe no.

**hoe** kuwa.

**hold (to)** motsu *(have);* okonau *(a ceremony);* kaisai suru *(an exhibition or conference);* tamotsu *(maintain).*

**hole** ana.

**holiday** yasumi *(period of recreation or rest);* matsuri *(festival);* saijitsu *(national holiday).*

**hollow** *adj.* kara no *(empty).* *-n.* kubomi *(cavity).*

**holy** shinsei na *(sacred);* koogooshii *(divine);* shinkooshin no fukai *(deeply pious).*

**homage** keii *(respect).*

**home** uchi, katei *(family).*

    **hometown** kokyoo, kuni, furusato.

**honest** shoojiki na *(truthful);* seijitsu na *(sincere);* sotchoku na *(frank).*

**honesty** seijitsu.

**honey** hachimitsu.

**honor** meiyo *(fame);* shin'yoo *(credit);* sonkei *(esteem).*

**honor (to)** meiyo o ataeru *(exalt);* hijoo ni sonkei suru *(venerate).*

**honorable** tootoi, sonkei subeki.

**hood** zukin *(garment).*

**hoof** hizume.

**hook** kugi *(to hang things on).*

**hope** kiboo *(opp. of despair);* kitai *(confident anticipation);* mikomi *(probability).*

**hope (to)** nozomi o kakeru *(count on);* nozomu *(desire).*

**hopeful** kiboo ni michite iru, ate ni shite iru.

**hopeless** nozomi no nai.

**horizon** chiheisen *(of land);* suiheisen *(of sea).*

**horizontal** yoko no.

**horn** tsuno *(of animals);* tsuno bue *(wind instrument),* horun *(English horn).*

**horrible** osoroshii *(terrible);* monosugoi *(ghastly).*

**horror** kyoofu.

**horse** uma.

**horseback (on)** uma ni notte iru.

**hosiery** kutsushita.

**hospitable** motenashi no yoi.

**hospital** byooin.

**host** shujin *(one who entertains another, hotel keeper).*

**hostess** hosutesu, onna shujin *(in a hotel or restaurant);* okami *(in an inn);* shujin *(at home).*

**hostile** tekii no aru.

**hot** atsui.

**hotel** hoteru *(Western-style);* yadoya, ryokan *(Japanese-style).*

**hot spring** onsen.

**hour** jikan.

    **two hours** ni jikan.

**house** ie *(the structure);* uchi *(home, one's abode).*

**household** shotai, katei *(home).*

**housekeeper** kaseifu.

**how** doo, donna ni.

    **How are you?** Ogenki desu ka?

    **How beautiful!** Maa kirei desu ne.

    **how long** dono kurai nagaku.

    **how many** dono kurai, ikutsu.

    **how much** ikura.

    **how often** nando kurai.

**however** ga, keredomo; donna ni -mo, ikura -mo *(in whatever way, to whatever degree).*

**howl (to)** hoeru *(said of animals);* unaru *(said of the wind).*

**human** *adj.* ningen no *(characteristic of people).* *-n.* ningen, hito.

    **human being** ningen.

    **human nature** ningensei.

**human race** jinrui.

**humane** ninjoo no aru *(compassionate);* jihibukai *(merciful).*

**humanity** jindoo.

**humble** kenson na *(modest);* hikaeme na *(not pretentious).*

**humid** shimeppoi *(damp);* shikki no takai *(of high humidity).*

**humiliate** jisonshin o kizutsukeru, haji o kakaseru *(mortify).*

**humility** kenson *(humbleness).*

**humor** kishitsu *(disposition);* kibun *(mood);* kimagure *(caprice);* kokkei, yuumoa *(jocularity).*

    **in good humor** jookigen.

**hundred** hyaku.

**hundredth** hyakubanme no.

**hunger** ue *(famine);* kuufuku *(craving for food).*

**hungry (be)** onaka ga suita.

**hunt** kari ryoo *(hunting).*

**hunt (to)** kari o suru *(shoot animals);* sagasu *(look for).*

**hunter** ryooshi.

**hurry** *n.* isogu koto, isogi.

    **be in a hurry** isoide iru.

**hurry (to)** isogu.

**hurt (to)** *v.i.* itamu; *v.t.* itameru.

**husband** otto.

**hush (to)** shizuka ni saseru *(quiet);* damaraseru *(silence);* osaeru *(restrain).*

**hyphen** haifun.

**hypocrisy** gizen.

**hypocrite** gizensha.

**hypothesis** kasetsu.

# I

**I** watakushi, watashi, boku *(used by men among friends).*

**ice** koori.

**icy** koori de tsurutsuru shita.

**idea** kangae *(thought);* chishiki *(knowledge);* inshoo *(impression);* shinnen *(belief);* omoitsuki *(intention).*

**ideal** *n.* risoo. *-adj.* risooteki na.

**idealism** risooshugi.

**idealist** risooka.

**identical** dooitsu no.

**idiot** hakuchi.

**idle** shigoto no nai *(unemployed);* hima de aru *(not active);* namaketa *(lazy).*

**idleness** namakeru koto.

**if** moshi.

**ignoble** iyashii, gehin na.

**ignorance** mugaku *(lack of education);* muchi *(lack of knowledge).*

**ignorant** mugaku na *(without education);* muchi na *(unthinking, uninformed);* fuannai no *(unaware).*

**ignore (to)** mushi suru.

**ill** kagen ga warui, byooki no *(sick, unwell);* warui *(bad, evil).*

**illness** byooki.

**illusion** sakkaku *(optical);* moosoo *(delusion).*

**illustrate (to)** sashie o ireru *(pictures and diagrams);* rei o shimesu *(give examples).*

**illustration** sashie *(picture);* rei, tatoe *(example).*

**image** sugata *(form);* chookokuzoo *(carved statue);* guuzoo *(idol).*

**imaginary** soozoo no.

**imagination** soozoo.

**imagine (to)** soozoo suru *(form a mental picture);* omou *(think);* kangaeru *(suppose).*

**imitate (to)** maneru, mane o suru.

**imitation** mane *(copy);* magaimono, nisemono *(fake).*

**immediate** sugu no, chokusetsu no.

**immediately** sugu ni.

**imminent** sashisematta *(impending).*

**immobility** fudoosei.

**immoral** fudootoku na.

**immorality** fudootoku.

**immortal** fujimi no, shinu koto no nai.

**immortality** fushi, fukutsusei.

**impartial** koohei na.

**impatience** tanki.

**impatient (be)** ki ga hayai *(of character);* tanki na *(quick tempered).*

**imperfect** fukanzen na *(incomplete);* kekkan no aru *(faulty).*

**impertinence** shitsurei.

**impertinent** shitsurei na *(rude);* namaiki na *(insolent).*

**impetuosity** sekkachi.

**impetuous** gekiretsu na, nesshin na.

**impious** fushinjin na.

**import** yunyuuhin *(goods).*

**import (to)** yunyuu suru.

**importance** juuyoosei.

**important** daiji na *(of consequence);* kan'yoo na *(essential);* chomei na *(eminent).*

**impossible** fukanoo na.

**impress (to)** osu *(imprint);* inshoo zukeru *(produce a vivid impression);* kandoo saseru *(move deeply).*

**impression** inshoo

    **be under the impression that** -to omotte iru, ki ga suru.

**imprison (to)** keimusho ni ireru.

**improve (to)** *v.t.* jootatsu saseru *(ameliorate);* yoku suru *(better);* kairyoo suru *(reform); v.i.* jootatsu suru *(become better).*

**improvement** kairyoo *(reform)*.

**improvise (to)** sokkyoo de suru.

**imprudence** fukinshin.

**imprudent** fukinshin na.

**impulse** shoodoo *(propulsion)*; shigeki *(impetus)*.

**impure** fujun na *(adulterated)*.

**in** ni, de; -no nakani *(inside)*; -no uchi ni *(within)*.

   **in order to** tame ni.

**inadequate** fujuubun na, futekitoo na.

**inaugurate** *v.t.* hajimeru *(begin)*; *v.i.* hajimaru *(be inaugurated)*.

**incapable** -ga dekinai, muryoku na.

**incapacity** munoo, futekitoo.

**inch** inchi *(American measure)*.

**incident** dekigoto *(occurrence)*.

**include** fukumu, fukumeru

   **to be included** haitte iru.

**income** shuunyuu *(earnings)*.

**incomparable** hikaku no dekinai.

**incompatible** ki no awanai *(inharmonious)*; itchi shinai *(inconsistent)*; ryooritsu shinai *(not able to coexist)*.

**incompetent** chikara no nai, munoo na.

**incomplete** fukanzen na.

**incomprehensible** ryookai dekinai.

**inconvenience** fuben.

**inconvenient** fuben na *(not suitable)*; tsugoo ga warui *(troublesome)*.

**incorrect** machigatte iru *(inaccurate)*; datoo de nai *(improper)*.

**increase** zooka.

**increase (to)** *v.t.* fuyasu *(quantity)*; ookiku suru *(size)*; ageru *(price)*; *v.i.* fueru *(in quantity)*; ookiku naru *(in size)*; takaku naru *(in price)*.

**incredible** shinjirarenai.

**incur** ukeru *(meet with)*; au *(run into)*.

**indebted** kari no aru *(owing money)*; sewa ni natte iru *(obliged)*.

**indecision** fuketsudan.

**indecisive** niekiranai.

**indeed** hontoo ni *(in fact)*.

**independence** dokuritsu *(self-government)*.

**independent** dokuritsu no.

**index** sakuin *(of books)*.

**index finger** hitosashi yubi.

**indicate (to)** shimesu.

**indicative** -o shimesu *(giving an indication of)*; -o honomekasu *(giving a hint)*.

**indifference** mukanshin.

**indifferent** reitan na *(pertaining to feelings)*; mutonjaku na *(pertaining to appearance)*.

**indignant** fungai shita *(angered)*.

**indignation** fungai.

**indirect** toomawashi no *(devious)*; kansetsu no *(not straightforward)*.

   **indirect answer** kansetsu no henji.

**indirectly** kansetsu ni.

**indiscretion** shiryo no nai koto *(imprudence)*.

**indispensable** zettai hitsuyoo na *(absolutely necessary)*; sakerarenai *(unavoidable)*.

**individual** *adj.* koko no *(separate)*; dokutoku no *(peculiar)*. -n. kojin.

**indivisible** wakeru koto no dekinai *(entity)*.

**indolence** bushoo *(sloth, idleness)*.

**indolent** bushoo na *(idle, lazy, slothful)*; mukatsudoo no *(inactive)*.

**indoors** okunai.

   **to go indoors** naka e hairu.

**induce (to)** sasoikomu *(attract)*.

**induct (to)** hikiireru *(introduce into a place)*.

**indulge (in)** -ni fukeru.

**indulgence** kimama, wagamama.

**indulgent** tenurui *(not severe)*.

   **indulgent (parent)** yasashii.

**industrial** sangyoo no.

**industrious** kinben na *(hardworking)*.

**industry** sangyoo.

**inexhaustible** tsukinai *(limitless)*; taenai *(unfailing)*; tsukarenai *(unwearied)*.

**inexplicable** fukakai na *(incomprehensible)*.

**inexpressible** iiarawasenai *(indescribable)*.

**infallible** zenzen ayamari no nai *(free from error)*; kesshite machigawanai *(never mistaken)*.

**infamous** hyooban no warui *(notorious)*; fumenboku na *(shameful)*.

**infancy** akanboo no toki *(babyhood)*; shoki *(beginning of existence)*.

**infant** *n.* akanboo, chiisai kodomo *(very young baby)*. -adj. akanboo no *(pertaining to a baby)*.

**infantry** hohei.

**infection** kansen *(contagion)*.

**infer (to)** suiri suru *(conclude by reasoning)*; ketsuron o hikidasu *(draw conclusions)*.

**inference** ketsuron *(conclusion)*; suiron *(deduction)*.

**inferior** *adj.* shita no *(less important)*; somatsu na *(poor quality)*. -n. shita no kaikyuu *(lower in rank)*.

**infernal** meido no, jigoku no *(hellish)*; hidoo no *(inhuman, devilish)*.

**infinite** kagiri no nai *(endless)*; hijoo na *(very great)*.

**infinity** mugen *(boundlessness)*.

**inflation** infure.

**inflict (to)** ataeru *(impose)*.

**influence** eikyoo *(effect)*; seiryoku *(personal)*.

**influence (to)** eikyoo suru.

**inform (to)** shiraseru.

**information** shirase *(news)*; hoochi *(report)*; chishiki, joohoo *(knowledge)*.

**ingenious** rikoo na *(clever)*; kiyoo na *(skillful)*; koomyoo na *(cleverly contrived)*.

**ingenuity** rikoosa *(cleverness)*.

**ingratitude** onshirazu.

**inhabit** kyojuu suru *(reside)*; sumu, yadoru *(live in)*.

**inhabitant** kyojuusha.

**inherit (to)** soozoku suru.

**inheritance** isan *(thing inherited)*; soozoku *(an inheriting)*.

**inhuman** zannin na.

**initial** *adj.* hajime no *(beginning)*. *-n.* kashira mo ji *(letter)*.
    **initial stage** shoki.

**initiate (to)** hajimeru *(begin)*; seishiki ni kanyuu saseru *(admit)*.

**initiative** dokusooryoku *(originality)*.

**injurious** yuugai na *(harmful, hurtful)*.

**injury** kega *(wound)*; songai *(damage)*.

**injustice** fuhoo, fusei *(iniquity)*, fukoohei *(unjust act)*.

**ink** sumi *(Japanese only)*; inki, inku *(other)*.

**inkwell** inkitsubo.

**inland** kokunai no *(domestic)*.

**inn** yadoya, ryokan.

**innate** umaretsuki no *(inborn)*.

**innkeeper** ryokan no shujin, yadoya no shujin.

**innocence** mujaki *(freedom from wrong)*.

**innocent** muzai no *(not guilty)*; mujaki na *(guileless)*.

**inquire** tazuneru.

**inquiry** toiawase.

**inscription** kaite aru koto.

**insect** mushi.

**insensitive** mukankaku na *(not able to feel)*; heiki na *(callous)*.

**inseparable** hanasu koto ga dekinai.

**inside** naka.

**insight** kenshiki.
    **person of insight** kenshiki aru hito.

**insignificant** tsumaranai *(unimportant)*; muimi na *(meaningless)*.

**insincere** seii no nai.

**insinuate (to)** sore to naku iu *(hint)*.

**insist (to)** kyoochoo suru; iiharu.
    **He insisted on this point.** Kare wa kono ten o kyoochoo shita.

**insistence** kyoochoo; shuchoo.

**inspect (to)** shiraberu *(examine)*; ken'etsu suru *(view officially)*.

**inspection** ken'etsu *(official viewing)*; choosa *(critical examination)*.

**install (to)** ninmei suru *(place a person in office)*; soochi suru, toritsukeru *(put in position for use)*.

**installment** bunkatsubarai *(a portion of money paid at stated times)*.

**instance** rei *(example)*; baai *(occasion)*.

**instant** *adj.* kyuu na. *-n.* sokuji *(precise moment)*; shunkan *(moment)*.

**instantaneous** sokuza no.
    **instantaneous death** sokushi.

**instantly** sokuza ni, sugu.

**instead (of)** kawari ni.

**instigate (to)** sosonokasu *(incite)*.

**instinct** honnoo.

**instinctive** honnooteki na.

**institute** kyookai, gakkai *(institution, society)*.

**institute (to)** setsuritsu suru *(establish)*.

**institution** setsuritsu *(establishment)*; seitei *(of law)*; seido *(system)*; kanrei *(custom)*; gakkai *(learned society)*.

**instruct (to)** oshieru *(teach)*; kyooju suru *(educate)*.

**instruction** jugyoo *(a lesson)*; yoohoo *(a teaching or precept)*.

**instructor** kyooshi.

**instrument** doogu *(for work or means)*; gakki *(musical)*.

**insufficiency** fujuubun *(inadequacy)*; futekitoo *(incompetency)*.

**insufficient** fujuubun na *(not sufficient)*; futekitoo na *(inadequate)*.

**insult** bujoku *(insolence)*; burei *(impoliteness)*.

**insult (to)** bujoku suru.

**insuperable** uchikatenai *(insurmountable)*.

**insurance** hoken.
    **life insurance** seimei hoken.

**insure (to)** hoken o kakeru.

**integral** kanzen na.

**intellect** chishiki.

**intellectual** *adj.* chishiki no. *-n.* chishikijin.

**intelligence** chiryoku *(mental ability)*; chisei *(mentality)*; joohoo *(information)*.

**intelligent** kashikoi.

**intend (to)** -tsumori.
    **I intend to marry her.** Ano hito to kekkon suru tsumori desu.
    **I intend to go.** Iku tsumori desu.

**intense** nesshin na.

**intensity** kyoodo.

**intention** kangae.

**interest** kyoomi *(pleasurable concern)*; kanshin *(intellectual curiosity)*; riken *(pecuniary concern)*; rishi *(rate)*.
    **compound interest** fukuri.
    **have an interest in** kyoomi o motsu.

**interest (to)** kyoomi o okosaseru *(attract attention)*; kookishin o hiku *(excite the curiosity of)*; doojoo o hiku *(excite sympathy)*.

**interesting** omoshiroi.

**interfere (to)** kanshoo suru *(meddle)*; chootei suru *(mediate)*; jama suru *(interrupt)*.

**interference** boogai, jama.

**interior** naka, naibu.

**intermediate** chuukan no.

**international** kokusaiteki, kokusai.

international relations kokusai kankei.

interpose (to) -no aida ni ireru.

interpret (to) kaishaku suru, handan suru (construe).

interpretation kaishaku, setsumei (explanation); handan (judgment); tsuuyaku (translation).

interpreter tsuuyaku.

interrupt (to) saegiru (break in upon); jama o suru (hinder); chuushi saseru (break the continuity of).

interruption chuushi, jama.

interval kankaku.

interview menkai (meeting); mensetsu, intabyuu (job interview), kaiken (with reporters).

interview (to) menkai suru.

intimacy shinmitsu.

intimate shinmitsu na (very friendly); kojinteki no (personal); shitashii (friendly).

intimidate (to) obiyakasu.

into ni, no naka e.

intolerable gaman no dekinai.

intolerance kyooryoo.

intolerant kyooryoo na (bigoted).

intonation koe no taka hiku, intoneeshon.

introduce (to) shookai suru (a person).

introduction shookai (of a person); jobun (of a book).

intuition chokkan.

invade (to) shinnyuu suru (overrun); shinryaku suru (aggress); oshiyoseru (rush into).

invariable kawaranai.

invasion shinryaku.

invent (to) hatsumei suru (method, etc.); kangaedasu (a story).

invention hatsumei (something discovered after experimentation); tsukurigoto (a falsehood).

inventor hatsumeika.

invert (to) hantai ni suru (reverse).

invest (to) tooshi suru.

investment tooshi.

invisible me ni tsukanai.

invitation shootai.

invite (to) shootai suru, maneku.

invoice okurijoo, inboisu.

invoke (to) kami ni inoru.

involuntary muishiki no.

involve (to) hikikomu.

iron tetsu (metal); airon (for pressing).

iron (to) airon o kakeru (clothes).

irony hiniku.

irregular fukisoku na.

irreparable torikaeshi ga tsukanai.

irresistible tomeru koto no dekinai.

irritate (to) iraira saseru.

irritation shigeki (medical term); okoraseru koto (exasperation, annoyance).

island shima.

isolate (to) kakuri suru.

Israel Isuraeru.

issue hakkoo (of a newspaper or other publication); mondai ten (problem).

issue (to) hakkoo suru.

it sore (often omitted in Japanese).
   It's here. Koko ni arimasu.
   It's late. Osoi desu.

Italian adj. Itarii no. -n. Itariijin (people).

item koomoku.

its sono.

itself hitoride ni (by, of itself).

ivy tsuta.

# J

jacket uwagi; jaketto (sweater).

jam jamu.

January Ichigatsu.

Japan Nippon, Nihon.

Japanese adj. -Nippon no, Nihon no, Nipponjin, Nihonjin (person); Nippongo, Nihongo (language).

jar tsubo, kame.

jaw ago.

jealous shittobukai.

jealousy yakimochi, shitto.

jelly jerii.

jewel hooseki.

job shigoto (work); shokugyoo (occupation); chii (position).

join (to) awaseru (put together); kuttsukeru (fasten); renketsu saseru (connect, link); issho ni naru (become united).

joint n. kansetsu (of the body); awaseme (seam); tsugime (junction). -adj. kyoodoo no (common).

joke joodan.

joke (to) joodan o iu (jest); fuzakeru (be humorous).

jolly yukai na.

journal nikki (diary); nikkan shinbun (daily newspaper); zasshi (magazine).

journalism jaanarizumu (practice of); shinbungaku (study of).

journalist jaanarisuto, shinbunkisha (reporter).

journey ryokoo.

joy yorokobi.

joyous ureshii.

judge saibankan (public officer in a court of justice); shinpan (umpire); kanteika (connoisseur).

judge (to) handan suru (estimate, conclude); saiban suru (at court).

judgment handan (adjudication); hanketsu

*(court decision);* hihan *(criticism);*
handanryoku *(powers of
discrimination).*
**judicial** saibanjoo no.
**juice** shiru, juusu.
**July** Shichigatsu.
**jump** tobiagari.
**jump (to)** tobu, janpu suru.
**June** Rokugatsu.
**junior** *adj.* toshishita no. *(opp. to senior).*
**just** *adj.* tadashii *(upright);* koosei na
*(impartial);* seitoo na *(lawful);* tekitoo na
*(proper);* jissai no *(actual). -adv.* choodo
*(exactly);* hon no *(only);* yatto *(hardly).*
**justice** seigi *(righteousness);* kooketsu
*(integrity);* koosei *(fairness).*
**justify** seitooka suru.

## K

**keen** eibin na *(acute).*
**keep** kau *(animals);* motsu *(hold);* totte oku
*(hold on to).*
    **keep in mind** oboete oku.
    **keep quiet** shizuka ni suru.
    **Keep still!** Oshizuka ni.
**kettle** yakan.
**key** kagi.
**kick (to)** keru.
**kill (to)** korosu.
**kin** miyori.
**kind** *adj.* shinsetsu na *(gentle); -n.* shurui
*(class, variety, sort).*
**kindly** *adv.* shinsetsu ni.
**kindness** shinsetsu *(benevolence);* aijoo
*(love);* kooi *(goodwill).*
**king** oo.
**kingdom** ookoku *(monarchical state);* kuni
*(realm).*
**kiss** kisu, seppun.
**kiss (to)** kisu suru, seppun suru.
**kitchen** daidokoro.
**kite** tako.
**knee** hizagashira.
**kneel (to)** hizamazuku.
**knife** naifu.
**knit (to)** amu.
    **knitting** amimono.
**knock (to)** tataku.
    **knock against** -ni butsukaru.
    **knock at the door** to o tataku.
**knot** musubime.
**know (to)** shitte iru, zonjite iru *(humble).*
**knowledge** chishiki *(information);* gakumon
*(learning).*
**known** yuumei na.
    **make known** shiraseru.

**Korean** *adj.* Kankoku no, Choosen no. *-n.*
Choosenjin *(people);* Choosengo
*(language).*

## L

**label** fuda; raberu, retteru.
**labor** *n.* roodoo, shigoto.
**laboratory** jikkenjo.
**lace** reesu *(fabric);* himo *(of shoe).*
**lack (to)** fusoku suru.
**lacquer** urushi.
    **lacquerware** nuri mono.
**lady** fujin.
    **Ladies** Fujin tearaijo *(toilet).*
**lake** mizuumi; -ko *(in compound names).*
    **Lake Biwa** Biwako.
**lamb** kohitsuji.
**lame** bikko.
**lamp** dentoo *(electric).*
**land** riku *(solid part of the earth's surface);*
jimen *(ground).*
**land (to)** jooriku saseru, jooriku suru
*(disembark);* oriru *(alight).*
**landscape** keshiki.
**language** kotoba, gengo; -go *(in
compounds).*
    **Japanese language** Nihongo.
**lantern** choochin *(paper);* tooroo *(metal or
stone);* ishi dooroo *(stone).*
**large** ookii, ookina.
**laser** reezaa.
**last** *n.* ichiban ato *(end of something). -adj.*
saikin no *(most recent);* saigo no *(final). -
adv.* owari ni *(after all others);* saikin
*(most lately).*
    **last night** yuube, sakuban.
**last (to)** tsuzuku *(continue);* mochikotaeru
*(endure);* nagamochi suru *(wear well).*
**lasting** eizoku suru *(durable);* fuhen no,
eikyuu no *(permanent).*
**latch** kannuki.
**late** osoi *(opp. to early);* ko- *(prefixed to the
name of someone deceased).*
**lately** saikin.
**latter** ato no, koosha no.
**laugh** warai.
**laugh (to)** warau.
**laughter** warai.
**lavish** kimae no yoi.
**law** hooritsu.
**lawful** hooritsu ni kanatta.
**lawn** shibafu.
**lay (to)** oku *(put);* umu *(eggs).*
**layer** soo.
**lazy** namaketa; bushoo na.
**lead** namari *(mineral);* shidoo *(guidance).*

**lead (to)** annai suru *(guide)*.
**leader** shidoosha *(guide)*.
**leadership** shidooryoku.
**leaf** ha.
**leak (to)** moru.
**lean (to)** katamuku *(incline)*; yorikakaru *(lean against)*.
**leap** hiyaku.
**leap (to)** tobikoeru *(pass over)*; tobu *(jump)*.
**learn** narau, benkyoo suru *(study)*; kioku suru *(memorize)*.
**learned** hakugaku na, gakumon no aru.
**learning** gakumon *(knowledge)*; hakushiki *(erudition)*.
**least** ichiban chiisai *(in size)*; ichiban sukunai *(in number or amount)*.
    **at least** sukunaku tomo.
**leather** kawa.
**leave** yasumi *(holiday)*.
**leave (to)** deru *(depart)*; tatsu *(depart for a long trip)*; azukeru *(on deposit)*.
**lecture** koogi *(in classroom)*; kooen *(in public)*; setsuyu *(admonition)*.
**left** *n.* hidari.
**leg** ashi.
**legal** hooritsujoo no.
**legend** densetsu.
**legislation** hooritsu seitei *(enacting of laws)*; hooritsu *(laws)*.
**legislator** rippoosha.
**legislature** rippoobu.
**legitimate** goohoo no *(lawful)*, doori ni kanatta *(reasonable)*.
**leisure** hima.
**lemon** remon.
    **lemonade** remoneedo.
**lend (to)** kasu.
**length** nagasa.
**lengthen (to)** nagaku suru *(make longer)*; nobasu *(prolong)*.
**less** chiisai *(in size)*; sukoshi no, sukunai *(in quantity)*; yori chiisai *(smaller than)*; yori sukunai *(fewer than)*.
**lesson** jugyoo *(schoolwork)*; gakka *(subject)*; ka *(chapter)*.
**let (to)** saseru *(allow)*; kasu *(loan)*.
    **house for let** kashiya.
**letter** tegami *(epistle)*; ji *(in alphabet)*.
**level** *n.* heimen *(flat surface)*; heichi *(flat ground)*. *-adj.* taira na *(even)*; suihei no *(horizontal)*.
    **(at) the same level** onaji takasa *(said of height)*; onaji teido *(said of degree)*.
**liability** saimu.
**liable** seme o oubeki *(responsible)*; fukusubeki *(subject to)*; kakariyasui *(exposed to)*.
**liar** usotsuki.
**liberal** hoofu na, takusan no *(abundant)*; kechi

kechi shinai *(not sparing)*; kimae ga ii *(generous)*; shinpoteki na *(progressive)*.
**liberty** jiyuu.
**library** toshokan *(public)*; shosai, toshoshitsu *(private, home)*.
**license** kyoka *(permission)*; ninka *(authorization)*; kyokasho, menjoo *(certification)*.
    **driver's license** unten menkyo.
**lick (to)** nameru.
**lie** uso.
    **tell a lie** uso o tsuku.
**lie (to)** yoko ni naru *(rest)*.
**lieutenant** rikugun chuui *(army)*; kaigun taii *(navy)*.
**life** inochi *(animate existence)*; genki *(energy)*.
**lift (to)** ageru *(raise)*; mochiageru *(hold up)*.
**light** *adj.* karui *(weight)*; usui *(color)*; yasashii *(work)*. *-n.* hikari *(beam)*; akari *(of lamp, flame)*; kootaku *(brightness)*.
    **sunlight** hi no hikari.
**light (to)** hi o tsukeru.
    **light the fire** hi o tsukeru.
    **light the lamp** akari o tsukeru.
**lighten (to)** akaruku suru *(make bright)*; karuku suru *(diminish in weight)*.
**lighthouse** toodai.
**lighting** shoomei *(illumination)*.
**lightning** inabikari *(from cloud to cloud)*.
    **flash of lightning** denkoo.
**light up** terasu.
**like** *adj.* onajiyoo na *(similar)*; nite iru *(alike)*.
**like (to)** konomu, suku.
    **Would you like to go?** Ikitai desu ka?
**likely** tabun *(probably)*; tekitoo na *(suitable)*; tanomoshii *(promising)*; mottomo rashii *(credible)*.
**likewise** dooyoo ni *(similarly)*; mata *(too, also)*; nao mata *(moreover)*.
**liking** *n.* konomi.
**limb** te ashi *(hand or foot)*; eda *(branch)*.
**limit** seigen *(in the abstract sense)*; kyookai, sakai *(boundary)*.
**limit (to)** seigen suru.
**limp** bikko o hiku.
**line** kei, sen, ito *(thread)*; retsu *(row)*; kakei *(lineage)*; iegara *(family)*; michi *(course, route)*; -sen *(suffixed to the name of railroad)*, shoobai *(trade)*.
    **Tokaido Line** Tookaidoosen *(The Tokaido Railroad)*.
**line (to)** sen o hiku *(mark with lines)*; rinkaku o toru *(outline)*; ichiretsu ni suru *(align)*; ura o tsukeru *(cover with lining)*; retsu o tsukuru *(line up)*.
    **lining** ura *(of dresses)*.
**linen** rinneru.

**linger (to)** urouro suru; nagabiku.
**link** tsunagime.
**link (to)** tsunagu.
**lion** raion, shishi.
**lip** kuchibiru.
**liquid** ekitai.
**liquor** sake *(Japanese rice wine)*; yooshu *(foreign)*.
**list** mokuroku *(catalogue)*; kakakuhyoo *(price)*.
**list (to)** kakinaraberu.
**listen** kiku.
**literary** bungaku no.
**literature** bungaku.
**little** chiisai, chiisa na *(not big)*; sukoshi *(quantity)*; tsumaranai *(trivial)*; kechi na *(mean, petty)*.
**live** *adj.* ikite iru.
**live (to)** sumu *(dwell)*; ikiru *(exist)*; ikite iru *(be living)*; ikinagaraeru *(remain alive)*; kurasu *(spend one's days)*.
**lively** genki no yoi *(spirited)*; yooki na *(cheerful)*; kappatsu na *(brisk)*.
**liver** kanzoo *(organ of body)*; kimo, rebaa *(food)*.
**load** omoni *(burden)*; nimotsu *(on a conveyance)*.
**load (to)** tsumu.
**loan** kashikin *(money that is lent)*; shakkin *(borrowed money)*.
**loan (to)** kasu *(lend)*; kariru *(borrow)*.
**local** chihooteki na, chihoó no.
**locate (to)** mitsukeru.
**location** basho.
**lock** kagi.
**lock (to)** kagi o kakeru.
**locomotive** kikansha.
**log** maruta.
**logic** ronri.
**logical** ronriteki na.
**loneliness** sabishisa.
**lonely** kodoku no *(isolated)*; sabishii *(lonesome)*.
**long** nagai *(lengthy)*; hosonagai *(elongated)*; takai *(tall)*.
　　**a long time** nagai aida.
　　**before long** mamonaku.
　　**long ago** mukashi.
**longing** akogare.
**look** ichi moku *(glance)*; yooboo *(aspect)*; yoosu *(deportment)*; kaotsuki *(countenance)*.
**look (to)** miru *(oneself)*; goran nasaru *(respect: used in speaking of a person outside one's in group)*; mieru *(have the appearance, seem)*.
　　**Look out!** Abunai.
**loose** yurui *(not tight)*; darashi no nai *(lax)*;

fumimochi na *(wanton)*; fuseikaku na *(inexact)*.
**loosen (to)** toku *(undo)*; yurumeru *(slacken)*.
**lord** shihaisha *(ruler)*; shujin *(master)*; shu *(Christ)*.
**lose (to)** ushinau; nakusu *(cease to have)*; otosu *(by dropping)*; makeru *(be beaten)*.
**loss** son, sonshitsu.
**lost** nakushita *(gone out of one's possession)*; yukue fumei no *(missing)*.
**lot** *adv.* takusan *(great deal)*; oozei *(multitude)*.
　　**a lot of people** oozei no hito.
**loud** *adj.* oogoe no, ookina koe no *(said of a voice)*; ookina oto *(loud sound)*; soozooshii *(noisy)*; kebakebashii *(gaudy)*.
**love** ai *(parental fraternal)*; ren'ai *(between man and woman)*.
**love (to)** aisuru *(as a parent)*; koi suru, ren'ai suru *(one of the opposite sex)*.
　　**fall in love** koi ni ochiiru.
**lovely** utsukushii *(beautiful)*; kawairashii *(charming)*; subarashii *(wonderful)*.
**low** hikui *(not high)*; yowai *(weak)*; iyashii *(in society)*.
**lower (to)** sageru, orosu *(haul down)*; ichidan to sageru *(make less elevated)*.
**loyal** chuujitsu na; chuugi na.
**loyalty** chuusetsu; chuugi.
**luck** un, kooun.
　　**bad luck** un ga warui.
　　**good luck** un ga ii.
**lucky** un ga ii, kooun na.
**luggage** nimotsu.
**luminous** hikaru.
**lump** katamari.
**lunch** hirugohan, ranchi.
**lung** hai.
**luxurious** zeitaku na.
**luxury** zeitaku.

# M

**machine** kikai.
**mad** ki no kurutta, kichigai *(insane)*; muchuu no *(infatuated)*; okotta *(angry)*.
**madam** okusama.
**madness** kichigai.
**magazine** zasshi.
**magistrate** hanji.
**magnificent** rippa na *(grand, stately)*; subarashii *(splendid)*.
**maid** musume *(girl)*; otetsudai *(servant)*.
**mail** yuubin.
**main** omo na.
　　**mainland** hondo.

**main road** hondoo.
**main street** hondoori.
**maintain (to)** tamotsu, fji suru.
**majesty** igen *(dignity)*.
    **His Majesty** heika.
**major** *adj.* omo na.
**majority** daibubun *(opp. of minority);*
    kahansuu *(plurality);* daitasuu *(most of,*
    *greater part).*
**make (to)** tsukuru; koshiraeru *(construct,*
    *manufacture).*
**male** osu *(animal);* otoko *(human).*
**malice** tekii.
**man** otoko *(male human).*
**manage (to)** keiei suru *(a business).*
**management** toriatsukai *(handling);* soojuu,
    toogyo *(control);* keiei *(direction).*
**manager** shihainin, maneejaa.
**mankind** jinrui *(human race).*
**manner** gyoogi *(deportment);* taido *(attitude);*
    yarikata *(method).*
**manners** sahoo.
**manufacture** seizoo.
**manufacture (to)** seizoo suru.
**manufacturer** seizoosha; seisakusha,
    seizoogyoosha.
**manuscript** genkoo.
**many** *adj.* takusan no, oozei no.
**map** chizu.
**maple** momiji.
**March** Sangatsu.
**march** kooshin *(parade);* kooshin kyoku
    *(music).*
**march (to)** kooshin suru *(in a parade);*
    susumu *(proceed).*
**marine** umi no *(oceanic);* kookaijoo no
    *(nautical).*
**mark** shirushi, maaku; ato *(impression);* shimi
    *(stain);* kizuato *(scar);* kizu *(scratch).*
**mark (to)** maaku o tsukeru.
    **to make a mark** shirushi o tsukeru.
**market** ichiba, maaketto.
    **bear market** uri sooba.
    **bull market** kai sooba.
    **buyer's market** kaite shijoo.
    **market forces** shijoo no jissei.
    **market index** shijoo shisuu.
    **marketing** maaketingu.
    **market position** shikyoo.
    **market price** shika.
    **market share** shijoo sen-yuu ritsu.
    **market trends** shijoo dookoo.
    **market value** shijoo kakaku.
**marriage** kekkon.
**marry (to)** kekkon suru.
**marvel** fushigi.
**marvelous** fushigi na.
**masculine** otoko no.
**mask** men, masuku.

**mask (to)** men o kaburu.
**mason** ishiya.
**mass** *n.* taishuu.
    **mass communication** masukomi.
    **mass production** tairyoo seisan.
**mast** masuto, hobashira.
**master** shujin *(of the house);* shujin
    *(employer);* sensei *(teacher).*
**master (to)** joozu ni naru *(become skillful);*
    yoku oboeru *(learn well).*
**masterpiece** meisaku, kessaku.
**mat** tatami *(for floor of Japanese house).*
**match** matchi *(for fire);* shiai *(contest);*
    kyoogi *(game).*
**match (to)** niau *(be suitably associated, fit*
    *together).*
**material** *n.* zairyoo *(cloth, etc.).*
**maternal** haha kata no.
**mathematics** suugaku.
**matter** mondai *(problem);* jiken *(event);* koto
    *(thing).*
**matter (to)** kamau, mondai ni suru.
**mattress** mattoresu.
**mature (to)** otona ni naru *(reach adulthood);*
    jukusuru *(as a fruit).*
**maximum** saidaigen.
**May** Gogatsu.
**may** -ka mo shiremasen *(possibility).*
    **It may rain.** Ame ga furu ka mo
    shiremasen. -te mo ii desu *(have my*
    *permission to).*
    **You may go.** Itte mo ii desu. *(You have my*
    *permission to go.)*
**mayor** shichoo.
**me** watashi ni *(to me);* watashi o *(as obj. of*
    *verb).*
**meadow** bokujoo.
**meal** shokuji, gohan.
**mean** *adj.* iji no warui, hiretsu na *(base).*
**mean (to)** imi suru.
    **What does it mean?** Sore no imi wa nan
    desu ka?
**meaning** imi.
**meantime, meanwhile** sono aida ni.
    **in the meantime** soo shite iru uchi ni.
**measure** sunpoo *(dimension);* monosashi
    *(yardstick).*
**measure (to)** sunpoo o toru *(length),* hakaru
    *(reckon).*
**meat** niku.
**mechanic** kikaikoo *(worker in a factory).*
**mechanical** kikaiteki no; kikai no.
**mechanically** kikaiteki ni.
**medal** medaru, kunshoo *(military).*
**meddle (to)** kanshoo suru *(interfere).*
**mediate (to)** chootei suru *(arbitrate);* chuukai
    suru *(act as an intermediary);* tonnasu
    *(intercede).*
**medical** igakuteki no.

**medicine** kusuri *(a drug)*; igaku *(the science)*.

**mediocre** nami no, taishita koto no nai.

**mediocrity** heibon.

**meditate (to)** mokusoo suru.

**meditation** mokusoo *(contemplation)*.

**medium** *adj.* chuu kurai no. *-n.* chuu kurai.

**meet (to)** au, o me ni kakaru *(respect)*.

**meeting** kai *(assembly)*.

**melt (to)** *v.t.* tokasu; *v.i.* tokeru.

**member** kaiin *(of an association)*.

**memorize (to)** oboeru.

**memory** kioku.

**mend (to)** naosu *(repair)*; tsugu *(darn)*; tsukurou *(patch up)*.

**mental** seishin no.

**mention** genkyuu.

    **honorable mention** hoojoo.

**mention (to)** iu, hanasu *(in speaking)*; kaku *(in writing)*.

    **Don't mention it.** Doo itashimashite.

**merchandise** shoohin.

**merchant** shoonin.

**merciful** jihibukai *(compassionate)*.

**merciless** mujihi na.

**mercury** suigin.

**mercy** jihi *(compassion)*.

**merit** *n.* kachi *(worth)*; tegara *(deed)*.

**merry** yukai na; tanoshii *(joyous)*.

**message** kotozuke *(verbal)*.

**messenger** tsukai.

**metal** kane.

**metallic** kane no, kanamono no.

**method** hoohoo.

**metropolis** shuto *(capital)*; chuushin-chi *(central place)*.

**microphone** maikurohon, maiku.

**microscope** kenbikyoo.

**microwave oven** denshi renji.

**midday** hiru.

**middle** naka no, chuukan no *(intermediate)*; chuui no *(medium)*.

    **in the middle of** mannaka ni.

    **Middle Ages** Chuusei.

    **middle class** chuusan kaikyuu.

**midnight** mayonaka.

**might** *n.* chikara *(strength)*.

**mighty** chikara no tsuyoi, taishita.

**mild** otonashii *(gentle)*; kandai na *(not severe)*.

**mildness** odayakasa.

**military** rikugun no.

**milk** gyuunyuu *(cow's)*, miruku.

**milkman** gyuunyuu ya.

**mill** suisha *(water)*; fuusha *(wind)*; seifunjoo *(flour)*.

**million** hyakuman.

    **one hundred million** ichioku.

**millionaire** hyakuman chooja.

**mind** kokoro *(intention)*; kangae *(thought)*; atama *(brain, head)*.

    **frame of mind** kimochi.

**mind (to)** ki ni kakeru *(bear in mind)*; sewa o suru *(take care of)*.

**mine** *pron.* watashi no, watashi no mono; *-n.* koozan *(for minerals)*.

**miner** koofu.

**mineral** *n.* koobutsu. *-adj.* koobutsu no.

**minimum** saishoogen no.

**minister** daijin *(of state)*; kooshi *(diplomatic)*; bokushi *(of religion)*.

**ministry** -shoo *(suffix)*; seishoku *(of church)*.

    **Ministry of Foreign Affairs** Gaimushoo.

**mink** ten, minku.

**minor** miseinensha *(legal: less than 20 years old)*.

**minority** shoosuu *(smaller number)*; shoosuu too *(opp. of majority)*; miseinen *(legal infancy)*.

**minute** fun *(time)*.

    **Any minute now.** Moo sugu desu.

    **Wait a minute!** Chotto matte kudasai.

**miracle** kiseki *(religious)*.

**mirror** kagami.

**miscellaneous** iroiro na.

**mischief** itazura.

**mischievous** itazurazuki na.

**misdemeanor** fugyooseki.

**miser** kechinboo.

**miserable** fukoo na *(unfortunate)*; hisan na *(wretched)*; aware na *(pitiable)*.

**miserably** mijime ni.

**misery** komatte iru koto *(a state of being in distress)*.

**misfortune** fukoo *(unhappiness)*; sainan *(calamity)*.

**mishap** omoigakenai dekigoto.

**misprint** insatsu chigai, misupurinto.

**Miss** -san *(same suffix as for Mr. and Mrs.)*.

    **Miss Yamada.** Yamada-san.

**miss (to)** ma ni awanai *(fail to get on time)*; nakusuru *(lose)*; kizukanai *(fail to perceive)*.

**mission** dendoo kai, misshon *(religious)*; shisetsu *(official)*.

**missionary** senkyooshi, dendooshi.

**mist** kasumi.

**mistake** machigai.

**mistake (to)** machigau.

**Mister** -san. See **Miss.**

    **Mr. Yamada.** Yamada-san.

**mistrust** fushin'yoo.

**mistrust (to)** shinyoo shinai, ayashimu.

**mistrustful** utagaibukai.

**misunderstand (to)** gokai suru.

**misunderstanding** gokai *(mistake)*; iken no sooi *(disagreement)*.

**misuse** machigatte tsukau koto.

**misuse (to)** machigatte tsukau.

**mix (to)** *v.t.* mazeru *(put together); v.i.* mazaru, majiwaru *(associate).*

**mixture** mazeta mono.

**mob** gunshuu *(crowd).*

**mobilization** dooin.

**mobilize (to)** dooin suru.

**mock (to)** baka ni suru *(ridicule);* maneru *(mimic).*

**mockery** baka ni suru koto.

**mode** ryuukoo, moodo.

**model** moderu *(photography, fashion);* mokei *(copy);* tehon *(example);* hinagata *(miniature).*

**model (to)** kataduru *(to copy).*

**moderate** onken na *(temperate);* tegoro no *(medium).*

**moderate (to)** setsudo o mamoru *(keep within bounds);* yawarageru *(one's temper).*

**moderation** tekido, sessei.

**modern** kindai no; kindaiteki *(of the present time);* gendai no *(contemporary);* modan na *(new in fashion).*

**modest** kenson no *(unassuming);* shitoyaka na *(moderate, unaggressive).*

**modesty** kenson.

**modification** henkoo.

**modify (to)** aratameru *(alter);* kanwa suru *(lessen);* keigen suru *(tone down).*

**moist** *adj.* shikketa, shimeppoi. *-n.* shikke.

**moisten (to)** shimesu *(dampen);* shimeru *(become moist).*

**moment** shunkan.

　**Any moment now.** Moo sugu desu.

　**Just a moment!** Chotto matte kudasai.

**monarchy** kunshu seitai *(system);* kunshukoku *(nation).*

**monastery** shuudooin.

**Monday** Getsuyoobi.

**money** kane, okane.

　**money order** yuubin gawase.

　**paper money** satsu.

**monk** shuudoosoo.

**monkey** saru.

**monologue** hitorigoto.

　**to talk to oneself** hitorigoto o iu.

**monopoly** dokusen; senbai.

**monorail** monoreeru.

**monotonous** tanchoo na.

**monotony** tanchoo.

**monster** kaibutsu *(dragon, etc.).*

**monstrosity** kikai na koto.

**monstrous** kikai na.

**month** tsuki.

　**this month** kongetsu.

　**last month** sengetsu.

　**next month** raigetsu.

**monthly** *adj.* maigetsu no. *-adv.* maigetsu. *-n.* gekkanzasshi *(monthly magazine).*

**monument** kinenhi.

**monumental** kinen no.

**mood** kibun *(feeling);* kigen *(temper).*

**moody** muttsuri shita.

**moon** tsuki.

　**full moon** mangetsu.

**moonlight** tsuki no hikari.

**mop** moppu.

**moral** *adj.* dootokuteki na *(virtuous). -n.* kyookun *(maxim).*

**morale** shiki.

**moralist** dootoku shugisha.

**morality** dootoku.

**more** motto.

**morning** asa.

**morsel** hito kire *(a little piece).*

**mortal** *adj.* kanarazu shinu *(subject to death).*

**mortgage** teitoo.

**mortgage (to)** teitoo ni suru.

**mosquito** ka.

**most** *adj.* taitei no *(greatest number);* daitai *(the majority of);* ichiban *(used for the superlative).*

　**most numerous** ichiban ooi.

**mostly** taitei.

**moth** ga.

**mother** okaasan, okaasama *(respect);* haha.

**motion** undoo *(opp. of rest);* teburi, miburi *(gesture).*

**motionless** ugokanai.

**motive** dooki.

**motor** hatsudooki, mootaa.

**motor (to)** unten suru *(drive a car).*

**mount** yama *(mountain).*

**mount (to)** daishi ni haru *(pictures);* noboru *(ascend).*

　**mount a horse** uma ni noru.

**mountain** yama.

**mountainous** yama no ooi.

**mourn (to)** nageku, kanashimu *(lament).*

**mournful** kanashimi ni shizunda.

**mourning** mo.

**mouse** nezumi.

**mouth** kuchi.

**movable** ugokasu koto no dekiru.

**move** ugoki, idoo.

**move (to)** *v.t.* ugokasu; *v.i.* ugoku, hikkosu *(change one's dwelling).*

　**move back** hikkomeru, hikkomu.

　**move forward** *v.t.* mae e dasu; *v.i.* mae e deru.

**movement** koodoo *(action).*

**movies** eiga.

**moving** ugokasu, kandoo saseru *(evoking emotion);* hikkoshi *(changing one's dwelling).*

**much** takusan, takusan no.

　**much better** zutto ii.

**mud** doro.

**muddy** doro no ooi; doro darake no *(covered with mud)*.

**mule** raba.

**multiple** tasuu no.

**multiply** kakeru; masu *(increase)*.

**multitude** oozei, gunshuu.

**mumble (to)** butsu butsu iu.

**municipal** shi no, toshi no.

**municipality** jichiku, shi tookyoku.

**munitions** gunjuhin.

**murder** hitogoroshi, satsujin.

   **to commit a murder** hitogoroshi o suru.

**murder (to)** hito o korosu.

**murmur** zawameki, sasayaki.

**murmur (to)** sasayaku.

**muscle** kinniku.

**museum** hakubutsukan.

   **art museum** bijutsukan.

**mushroom** kinoko.

**music** ongaku.

**musical** *adj.* ongaku no. *-n.* myuujikaru.

**musician** ongakka.

**must** -nakereba naranai, -nakereba ikenai *(have to);* -ni chigai nai *(in the sense of an obvious inference).*

   **I must go.** Ikanakereba naranai. Ikanakereba ikenai.

   **You must have said so.** Soo itta ni chigai nai.

**mustard** karashi.

**mute** oshi no *(unable to speak).*

**mutter (to)** butsu butsu iu *(mumble);* sasayaku *(murmur).*

**mutton** hitsuji no niku.

**my** watashi no *(of or relating to me);* uchi no *(pertaining to things or persons of one's home or workplace).*

**myself** jibun, watakushi jishin.

**mysterious** fushigi na *(strange);* fukakai na *(inexplicable).*

**mystery** shinpi; fukakai na koto.

**myth** shinwa.

# N

**nail** tsume *(of a finger or toe);* kugi *(fastener).*

**nail (to)** kugi o utsu.

**naïve** mujaki na *(innocent);* adokenai *(unsophisticated).*

**naked** hadaka no.

**name** namae *(designation);* hyooban *(fame).*

   **first name** namae.

   **last name** myooji.

   **My name is . . .** Namae wa . . . to iimasu.

   **What is your name?** Onamae wa?

**name (to)** namae o tsukeru.

**nameless** na no nai.

**namely** sunawachi.

**nap** keba *(of wool);* hirune *(short sleep).*

**napkin** napukin.

**narrow** semai.

**narrow (to)** *v.t.* sebameru; *v.i.* semaku naru.

**nasty** iji no warui.

**nation** kokumin *(people);* kuni *(country).*

**national** kokumin no, kuni no.

**nationality** kokuseki.

**nationalization** kokkateki ni suru koto, kokueika.

**nationalize (to)** kokuei ni suru *(to have the state operate).*

**native** *adj.* naikoku no *(opp. of foreign);* dochaku no *(aboriginal). -n.* naikokujin *(opp. of foreigner);* dojin *(aborigine).*

**natural** shizen no, shizen no mama no *(nonartificial);* mikaikon no *(uncultivated).*

**naturalness** kazarike no nai koto.

**nature** seishitsu *(character);* shizen *(the physical universe).*

**naughty** itazura na.

**naval** kaigun no.

**navy** kaigun.

**near** soba no, chikai *(not far);* kinjo no *(around the corner).*

**nearly** hotondo *(almost);* kare kore *(about).*

**neat** kichinto shita *(tidy, orderly);* kozappari shita *(smart, dapper);* shumi no ii *(trim);* seizen to shita *(orderly).*

**neatness** sappari shite iru koto.

**necessarily** yamu naku, hitsuyoo ni kararete.

**necessary** hitsuyoo na.

**necessity** hitsuyoo.

**neck** kubi.

**necklace** kubi kazari, nekkuresu.

**necktie** nekutai.

**need** iriyoo *(want);* hitsuyoo *(necessity);* nyuuyoo *(demand);* kyuuboo *(destitution).*

   **be in need of** iriyoo desu.

**need (to)** iru *(want);* hoshii desu *(wish to have).*

**needle** hari.

**needless** fuhitsuyoo na.

**needy** konkyuu shite iru.

**negative** *n.* uchikeshi *(expression);* nega *(photograph). -adj.* insei no *(opp. of positive);* hantai no *(contrary).*

**neglect** kamawanai koto *(want of attention);* mushi *(disregard).*

**neglect (to)** namakeru, mushi suru.

**negotiate** kooshoo suru, danpan suru.

**negotiation** kooshoo, danpan.

**neighbor** tonari.

**neighborhood** kinjo.

**neither** dochira mo *(negative);* mo-mo . . . *(negative).*
> **Neither apples nor oranges are expensive.** Ringo mo mikan mo takaku nai.
> **Neither is delicious.** Dochira mo oishiku nai.

**nephew** oi.

**nerve** shinkei *(in anatomy);* daitan *(pluck);* yuuki *(courage).*

**nervous** shinkeishitsu na *(behavior);* shinkei no *(pertaining to nerves);* kurooshoo no *(apprehensive).*

**nest** su.

**net** ami.

**neuter** chuusei.

**neutral** chuuritsu no *(not involved in hostilities);* kooheimushi no *(impartial).*

**never** kesshite *(with a negative verb).*

**nevertheless** -ni mo kakawarazu.

**new** kondo no *(recently appointed);* atarashii *(recently acquired).*

**news** tayori *(tidings);* nyuusu, hoodoo *(newspaper news).*

**newspaper** shinbun.

**next** tsugi no, ichiban chikai *(nearest);* tonari no *(neighboring);* kondo *(after this).*

**nice** ii, yoi *(agreeable);* shinsetsu na *(kind).*

**nickname** adana.

**niece** mei.

**night** yoru.

**nightmare** warui yume, akumu.

**nine** kokonotsu, ku, kyuu.

**no** iie.
> *Note that when answering a question in the negative, the usage of yes and no in Japanese is opposite to their usage in English.*
> **Didn't you see it?**
> **No, I didn't.** Hai, mimasen deshita.
> **Yes, I did.** Iie, mimashita.

**nobility** kazoku, kizoku *(titled group).*

**noble** *adj.* kooketsu na *(high-minded);* yuudai na *(imposing);* kedakai *(dignified);* mibun no takai *(aristocratic).*

**nobody** dare mo, donata mo *(followed by a negative verb).*

**noise** oto *(sound);* urusai oto *(unpleasant sound).*

**noisy** soozooshii; urusai.

**nominate (to)** shimei suru.

**nomination** shimei.

**none** dare mo, donata mo *(of persons);* dore mo *(of things) (followed by a negative verb).*

**nonsense** bakageta koto, bakarashii koto.

**noon** hiru, shoogo.

**normal** *adj.* atarimae no *(not strange);*

hyoojunteki na *(standard);* futsuu no *(regular);* heikin no *(average).*

**north** kita.

**northeast** hokutoo, toohuko.

**northern** kita no.

**northwest** seihoku, hokusei.

**nose** hana.

**nostril** hana no ana.

**not** -nai, -masen.
> **I do not go.** Ikimasen *(polite).* Ikanai *(plain).*
> **It is not a station.** Eki de wa arimasen (ja arimasen).
> **It is not expensive.** Takaku arimasen.

**note** tegami *(a letter);* kiroku *(for later reference);* satsu *(paper money).*

**note (to)** shirusu *(mark down);* hikki suru *(take note of).*
> **note down** kakitomeru.

**nothing** nani mo *(with a negative verb).*

**notice** shirase, kokuchi *(public notice);* chuumoku *(observation).*

**notice (to)** ki o tsukeru, chuui suru *(pay attention to).*

**notify (to)** tsuuchi suru *(inform);* happyoo suru *(announce).*

**notion** ippanteki gainen *(general conception);* kangae *(idea);* iken *(opinion);* ikoo *(intention).*

**noun** meishi *(substantive).*

**nourish** jiyoo ga aru.

**nourishment** jiyoo, jiyoobutsu *(nutriment);* shokumotsu *(food).*

**novel** *adj.* atarashii *(new);* kawatta *(strange).* *-n.* shoosetsu.

**novelty** kawatta mono *(thing);* kawatta koto *(event).*

**November** Juuichigatsu.

**now** ima.
> **now and then** toki doki.

**nowadays** konogoro; chikagoro.

**nowhere** doko ni mo *(with a negative verb).*

**nuclear** kaka no.
> **nuclear energy** genshiryoku.
> **nuclear reactor** genshiro.

**nude** *adj.* hadaka no *(naked).* *-n.* nuudo, rataiga *(in art).*

**nuisance** meiwaku *(action);* yakkai na hito *(person).*

**nullify (to)** mukoo ni suru *(make invalid);* yameru *(cancel);* dame ni suru *(make useless).*

**numb (to become)** kogoeru *(from cold);* shibireru *(from pressure).*

**number** suuji *(numeral);* banchi *(indicating location);* ban *(turn);* bangoo *(for telephone or room);* -goo *(issue of a periodical).*

# number (to)                                    oldest

**number (to)** kazoeru *(count)*.
**numerous** takusan no.
**nun** ama.
**nurse** kangofu.
**nursery** kodomo beya *(for children)*; uekiya *(for plants)*.
**nut** kurumi.

## O

**oak** kashi.
**oar** kai.
**oat** karasu mugi.
**oath** chikai.
  **to take an oath** chikai o tateru.
**obedience** fukujuu *(submission)*; juujun *(dutifulness)*.
**obedient** juujun na, sunao na.
**obey** shitagau, iu koto o kiku.
**object** mono *(article)*; mokuteki *(aim)*.
**object (to)** hantai suru.
**objection** hantai *(adverse reason)*.
  **I have no objection to it.** Hantai shimasen.
**objectionable** iya na *(offensive)*; monku no desoo na *(open to objection)*; omoshiroku nai *(unpleasant)*.
**objective** *n.* mokuteki *(purpose)*. *-adj.* kyakkanteki na.
**objectively** kyakkanteki ni.
**objectivity** kyakkansei.
**obligation** gimu *(duty)*; on *(debt of gratitude)*; giri *(sense of duty)*.
**obligatory** gimuteki, hitsuyoo na.
**oblige (to)** muri ni saseru *(compel)*.
  **be much obliged** arigatoo zonjimasu.
**obliging** shinsetsu na.
**oblique** katamuita, aimai na.
**obscure** *adj.* bonyari shita.
**obscurity** aimaisa.
**observation** kansatsu *(notice)*; kanshi *(watching)*.
**observatory** tenmondai *(astronomical)*; sokkoojo *(meteorological)*.
**observe (to)** mokugeki suru *(catch sight of)*; miru *(see)*; ki ga tsuku *(notice)*.
**observer** bookansha; obuzaabaa *(at a conference)*.
**obstacle** shoogai *(hindrance)*; jama *(impediment)*.
**obstinacy** goojoo *(stubbornness)*; gankyoo *(persistence)*.
**obstinate** ganko na *(stubborn)*; gankyoo na *(persistent)*.
**obvious** akiraka na.
**obviously** akiraka ni.

**occasion** ori, kikai.
**occasionally** tama ni *(at times)*.
**occupation** shigoto *(employment)*; shokugyoo *(calling)*; gyoomu *(business)*; shoobai *(trade)*; senryoo *(military)*.
**occupy (to)** senryoo suru *(by force of arms)*; sumu *(live in)*; te ga fusagaru *(take up space)*.
  **to be occupied** fusagatte iru.
**occur (to)** okoru.
**occurrence** dekigoto.
**ocean** umi.
  **Indian Ocean** Indoyoo.
**October** Juugatsu.
**odd** hen na *(strange)*; hanpa no *(not paired)*.
  **odd number** kisuu.
**odor** kaori *(fragrance)*; nioi *(smell)*.
**of** no
  **roof of the house** ie no yane.
**off** *(usually expressed by verbs)*.
  **She cut it off.** Kirihanashite shimaimashita.
  **The button is off.** Botan ga hazurete imasu.
  **The train is off.** Densha wa dete shimaimashita.
**offend** *v.i.* ki ni sawaru *(displease)*; *v.t.* okoraseru *(make angry)*.
**offense** hansoku *(transgression)*; tsumi *(crime)*; bujoku *(insult)*.
**offensive** *adj.* fuyukai na *(unpleasant)*; burei na *(insolent)*; iya na *(disgusting)*; kooseiteki *(aggressive)*. *-n.* koogeki
**offer** mooshikomi, mooshiide.
**offer (to)** sonaeru *(as act of worship)*; sashiageru *(as a present)*; mooshideru *(make an offer)*; teikyoo suru *(propose to give)*; susumeru *(proffer)*.
**offering** sonaemono *(to a deity)*; kenkin *(gift of money to a church)*.
**office** jimusho *(in general)*; yakusho *(of govt.)*.
  **branch office** shiten.
  **head office** honsha, honten.
**officer** yakunin *(civil)*; shookoo *(military)*.
**official** *adj.* seishiki na *(formal)*; omote muki no *(public)*. *-n.* yakunin.
**often** tabi tabi, yoku.
**oil** abura.
**old** furui *(of things)*; toshiyori *(of persons)*.
**old age** roonen
**old man** ojiisan.
**old woman** obaasan.
**older** toshiue no.
  **older brother** niisan, oniisan; ani.
  **older sister** neesan, oneesan; ane.
**oldest** nenchoo no.
  **oldest daughter** *(among daughters)* choojo.

249

**oldest son** (*among sons*) choonan.
**olive** oriibu.
   **olive oil** oriibu oiru.
**ominous** fukitsu na (*inauspicious*); yochi suru (*prognostic*); ken'aku na (*threatening*).
**on** -no ue ni, -no ue de, -no ue no.
   **It is on the desk.** Tsukue no ue ni aru.
**once** ichi do (*one time*); moto (*formerly*); mae ni (*before*).
   **at once** sugu ni.
   **all at once** kyuu ni, totsuzen.
   **once in a while** tokidoki.
   **once a year** ichinen ni ichido.
   **once more** moo ichido.
**one** hitotsu, ichi (*a single person or thing*); katahoo (*one of a pair*); kata (*in paired compounds, such as*; kata me = *one eye*); *pron.* hito, jibun.
**oneself** jishin, jibun.
**onion** tamanegi.
**only** tada (*merely, but*); tatta (*emphatic*); honno (*nothing but*).
**open** *adj.* hiraita, hirobiro shita.
**open (to)** *v.t.* akeru; *v.i.* aku.
**opening** kuchi (*gap*); ana (*hole*); hajime (*beginning*); kuchi, kikai, chansu (*opportunity*).
**opera** opera, kageki.
**operate** *v.i.* ugoku (*function*); *v.t.* soojuu suru (*work*); kanri suru (*superintend*).
**operation** shujutsu (*surgical*); sagyoo (*working*); unten (*of a mechanism*).
**opinion** kangae, kenkai (*notion*).
**opponent** hantaisha (*in debate*); aite (*in sport*); kyoosoosha (*in business*).
**opportune** kootsugoo no.
**opportunity** kikai.
**oppose (to)** hantai suru.
**opposite** *adj.* -no mukoo no, -no mukai no (*facing*). -*n.* mukoogawa (*the other side*).
**opposition** hantai.
**oppress** shiitageru, osaeru.
**oppression** appaku (*tyranny*); konnan (*hardship*).
**optimism** rakutenshugi.
**optimistic** rakutenteki.
**oral** kootoo no, kuchi de iu, kuchi no.
   **oral examination** kootoo shiken.
**orange** *n.* mikan (*tangerine*); orenji.
**orator** enzetsusha.
**oratory** yuuben, enzetsu.
**orchard** kudamono batake, kajuen.
**orchestra** kangengaku, ookesutora.
**ordeal** shiren (*severe trial*).
**order** iitsuke, meirei (*injunction*); kunrei (*instruction*); jun (*regular arrangement*); chuumon (*commission to supply*).
   **in order to** -tame ni.

   **put in order** seiri suru.
**order (to)** iitsukeru (*command*); chuumon suru (*give an order for*).
**ordinary** futsuu no (*common*); atarimae no (*not special*).
**organ** orugan (*musical instrument*).
**organization** koosei (*formation*); soshiki (*system*); dantai (*body*).
**organize (to)** soshiki suru (*to form*); sooritsu suru (*to institute*).
**Orient** Tooyoo.
**oriental** *adj.* tooyoo no. -*n.* Tooyoojin.
**origin** moto, kigen.
**originality** dokusoosei.
**originate (to)** hajimeru, soosaku suru (*invent*).
**ornament** kazari.
**orphan** koji.
**other** hoka no (*not the same*); moo hitotsu no (*additional*).
**ought** -beki (*obligation*).
   **You ought to go to a doctor.** Isha e iku beki desu.
**ounce** onsu.
**our, ours** watashitachi no, watashidomo no.
**out** soto e (*outside*).
**outcome** kekka.
**outdo (to)** dashinuku.
**outer** soto no, sotogawa no.
**outlast (to)** -yori mochi ga ii.
   **This outlasts that one.** Kôre wa sore yori mochi ga ii desu.
**outlay** keihi (*expenses*); shuppi (*expenditure*).
**outlet** deguchi.
**outline** rinkaku (*contour*); aramashi (*essential points*).
**outline (to)** aramashi o noberu (*state the gist*); autorain o kaku (*write*).
**outlook** mikomi.
**output** sangaku (*product, yield*).
**outrage** ranboo.
**outrageous** ranboo na, hidoi.
**outside** soto, omote.
**oval** daen no, daenkei no.
**oven** obun.
**overcoat** oobaa, oobaakooto.
**overcome (to)** -ni uchikatsu; -ni makeru (*be overcome*).
**overflow (to)** hanran suru (*said of a river*); koboreru (*water in a vessel*).
**overlook (to)** miotosu (*omit seeing*); miwatasu (*view from a high place*); minogasu (*refrain from seeing*).
**overpower (to)** makasu, attoo suru.
**overrule (to)** iatsu suru, kyakka suru (*reject, decide against*).
**overrun (to)** habikoru, afureru.
**overseas** kaigai no.

**oversight** miotoshi *(failure to notice);* shissaku *(mistake).*

**overtake (to)** oitsuku.

**overthrow (to)** hikkurikaesu *(upset);* uchitaosu *(knock down);* seifuku suru *(vanquish);* kutsugaesu *(subvert).*

**overwhelm (to)** attoo suru *(crush);* seifuku suru *(defeat).*

**owe (to)** -ni kari ga aru *(be financially indebted to a person).*

**own** *adj.* jibun no.

**own (to)** motsu, shoyuu suru.

**owner** mochinushi *(proprietor);* ninushi *(of goods).*

**ox** ushi.

**oxygen** sanso.

**oyster** kaki.

# P

**pace** -ho, -po *(suffix: step).*
     **She took two paces.** Niho arukimashita.

**pace (to)** aruite hakaru.

**pacific** odayaka na *(quiet, calm);* shizuka na *(still, as water; placid, as the sea; serene, as the mind; peaceful, as sleep);* heiwateki na *(not warlike).*

**Pacific Ocean** Taiheiyoo.

**pack (to)** tsutsumu, nizukuri suru.

**page** *n.* peeji.

**pagoda** too.

**pain** kurushimi *(distress);* nayami *(suffering);* itami *(ache);* fuan *(uneasiness).*

**pain (to)** *v.t.* kurushimeru *(cause pain to); v.i.* itamu *(ache, smart).*

**painful** itai.

**paint** penki.

**paint (to)** penki o nuru *(a house, etc.);* e o kaku *(a picture).*

**painter** penkiya *(for houses);* ekaki *(artist).*

**painting** e o kaku koto *(art, hobby, vocation);* e *(that which is painted).*

**pair** ittsui *(of objects);* fuufu *(married couple);* hitokumi *(a set).*

**pair (to)** kumiawaseru.

**pale** usui *(of color);* aoi *(of the face).*

**palm** tenohira *(of the hand).*

**pamphlet** panfuretto.

**pan** nabe.

**pancake** pankeeki.

**pane** garasu ita.
     **windowpane** mado no garasu ita.

**pang** sashikomi *(sudden sharp pain);* uzuki *(twinge).*

**panic** kyookoo.

**panorama** panorama.

**pants** zubon.

**paper** kami.

**parachute** parashuuto, rakkasan.

**parade** kanpeishiki *(military);* pareedo, gyooretsu, kooshin *(for popular celebrations).*

**parade (to)** kooshin suru.

**paragraph** paragurafu.

**parallel** *adj.* heikoo no.

**parallel (to)** heikoo suru.

**paralysis** mahi.

**paralyze** mahi suru.

**parcel** tsutsumi *(package);* kozutsumi *(for mail).*
     **parcel post** kozutsumi yuubin.

**pardon** yurushi.

**pardon (to)** yoosha suru *(forgive);* yurusu *(excuse).*
     **Pardon me!** Shitsurei.

**parenthesis** kakko.

**parents** ryooshin.

**park** kooen.

**park (to)** chuusha suru.

**parliament** gikai.

**part** bun, bubun *(portion, piece);* bu *(of a book);* hen *(district).*
     **the greater part** daibubun.

**part (to)** wareru *(separate, divide, split);* kireru *(as a cable);* wakareru *(take leave).*
     **to part from** hanareru.
     **to part with** tebanasu.

**partial** hiiki na *(biased, not fair);* ichi bubun no *(not total).*

**partially** ichibubun.

**particular** *adj.* sore zore no, meimei no *(individual);* betsudan no, tokubetsu no *(special);* kichoomen na *(precise). -n.* kuwashii koto *(a detail).*

**particularly** toku ni, tokubetsu ni.

**party** seitoo *(political);* enkai, paatii *(entertainment).*

**pass** tooge *(over a mountain);* pasu, kippu *(ticket);* nyuujooken *(of admission).*

**pass (to)** tooru *(go beyond);* tatsu *(time).*

**passage** fune no ryokoo *(on a ship);* watashi *(across a river);* rooka *(corridor).*

**passenger** jookyaku *(train, etc.);* senkyaku *(ship).*

**passing** *adj.* ichijiteki no *(temporary). -n.* tsuuka *(passage).*

**passion** joonetsu *(emotion),* netsujoo *(intense emotion);* nekkyoo *(fervid devotion);* kanshaku *(fury).*

**passive** *adj.* ukemi no. *-n.* ukemi *(grammatical verb form).*

**past** *n.* kako *(time gone by);* rireki *(past life or career). adj.* kako no *(gone by);* sugita bakari no *(just passed);* izen no *(ago).*
     **half-past seven** shichiji han.
     **the past year** sakunen.

**paste** *n.* nori.

**patch** tsugi.

**patch (to)** tsugu.

**patent** tokkyo.

**paternal** chichi no, chichikata no.

**path** komichi.

**pathetic** kanashii.

**patience** gaman *(forbearance);* shinboo *(perseverance).*

**patient** *adj.* gaman zuyoi, shinboo zuyoi. *-n.* kanja *(sick person).*

**patriot** aikokusha.

**patriotism** aikokushin *(nationalism).*

**patron** hogosha *(protector);* kooensha, patoron *(backer);* hiiki kyaku *(regular customer).*

**patronize (to)** hiiki ni suru.

**pattern** gara, moyoo *(of fabric);* tehon *(model);* mihon *(sample).*

**pause** kyuushi *(short stop).*

**pause (to)** *v.i.* tomaru.

**pave (to)** hosoo suru.

**pavement** hodoo.

**pay** kyuuryoo *(salary);* chingin *(wages).*

**pay (to)** harau.

**payment** shiharai *(paying);* shiharaikin *(sum paid).*

**pea** endoomame.

    **green peas** guriin piisu.

**peace** heiwa *(opp. of war).*

**peaceful** heiwa na.

**peach** momo.

**peak** itadaki.

**pear** nashi.

**pearl** shinju.

**peasant** hyakushoo *(farmer);* inakamono *(rustic).*

**pebble** jari.

**peculiar** tokushu na *(characteristic);* hen na *(strange).*

**pecuniary** kinsenjoo no.

**pedal** pedaru.

**pedal (to)** pedaru o fumu.

**pedestrian** hokoosha.

**peel** kawa.

**peel (to)** kawa o muku.

**pen** pen *(for writing);* ori *(sty).*

    **fountain pen** mannenhitsu.

**penalty** bakkin *(fine);* kei *(punishment).*

**pencil** enpitsu.

**penetrate (to)** *v.t.* hairikomu *v.i.* tsukiiru.

**peninsula** hantoo.

**penitence** kookai *(repentance).*

**pension** onkyuu *(government);* nenkin *(annuity).*

**people** hitobito, hito, hitotachi *(individuals collectively);* kokumin *(a nation).*

**pepper** koshoo.

**perceive (to)** ryookai suru *(apprehend);* shikibetsu suru *(discern);* wakaru *(grasp).*

**percentage** hyakubun ritsu, paasenteeji.

**perfect** kanzen na.

**perfect (to)** kansei suru.

**perfection** kansei *(completion);* kanzen *(being unblemished);* jukutatsu *(proficiency).*

**perfectly** kanzen ni.

**perform (to)** suru *(do);* nashitogeru *(accomplish);* enjiru *(act, as in a play).*

**performance** suru koto *(doing);* jikkoo *(execution);* engeki *(of a drama);* yokyoo *(entertainment).*

**perfume** koosui.

**perfume (to)** koosui o tsukeru.

**perhaps** tabun *(probably);* hyotto suru to *(maybe).*

**peril** kiken.

**period** jidai *(era);* shuushifu *(in punctuation).*

**periodical** zasshi *(magazine).*

**perish (to)** horobiru *(suffer destruction);* kusaru *(spoil, decay);* shinu *(die).*

**permanent** eikyuu no *(lasting);* eikyuuteki na *(perpetual);* fuhen no *(unchanging).*

**permission** kyoka *(permitting);* menkyo *(license);* dooi *(consent).*

**permit** menkyo *(license);* menkyojoo *(written permission).*

**permit (to)** kyoka suru *(allow).*

**perplex (to)** *v.t.* komaraseru *(throw into confusion);* *v.i.* komaru *(be perplexed).*

**persecute (to)** hakugai suru.

**persecution** hakugai.

**perseverance** nintai.

**persist (to)** ganbaru *(insist on);* jizoku suru *(last).*

**person** hito; -nin *(suffix).*

    **three persons** sannin.

**personal** kojin no *(individual);* jibun no *(one's own);* shiyoo no *(private).*

**personality** jinkaku *(character);* kosei *(distinctive personal quality).*

**perspective** mikomi *(prospect).*

**persuade (to)** tokifuseru, settoku suru.

**pertaining to** -ni kan shite.

**petty** chiisai *(small in size);* sasai na *(trifling);* kechi na *(mean).*

**pharmacist** kusuriya.

**pharmacy** kusuriya.

**phenomenal** hijoo na.

**phenomenon** genshoo.

**philosopher** tetsugakusha.

**philosophical** tetsugakuteki.

**philosophy** tetsugaku.

**photograph** shashin.

**take a photograph** shashin o toru.
**photograph (to)** utsusu.
**phrase** ku.
**physical** shizen no *(natural);* nikutai no *(bodily).*
**physician** isha.
**physics** butsurigaku.
**piano** piano.
**pick (to)** tsumu *(flowers, grass);* erabu *(select).*
   **to pick up** hirou.
**picnic** pikunikku, ensoku.
**picture** shashin *(photo);* e *(painting).*
**picture (to)** egaku.
**picturesque** e no yoo na.
**pie** pai.
**piece** kire *(obtained by cutting);* kakera *(broken piece).*
**pig** buta.
**pigeon** hato.
**pile** yama *(heap).*
**pile (to)** tsumu.
   **to pile up** tsumiageru.
**pill** gan'yaku.
**pillar** hashira.
**pillow** makura.
**pilot** mizusaki annai *(of a ship);* soojuushi *(of a plane).*
**pin** pin.
**pin (to)** pin o sasu.
**pinch (to)** tsuneru.
**pine** matsu.
**pink** pinku.
**pious** keiken na *(devout);* shinjinbukai *(religious).*
**pipe** kiseru, paipu *(for smoking);* tekkan *(of iron).*
**pitiful** kawaisoo na *(touching);* mijime na *(miserable).*
**pity** doojoo.
**pity (to)** doojoo suru.
**place** tokoro.
**place (to)** oku.
   **to take place** okoru.
**plain** *adj.* akiraka na *(evident);* karui *(said of food);* jimi na *(unadorned);* futsuu no *(ordinary).* *-n.* heichi *(level ground).*
**plan** zumen *(drawing);* keikaku *(project).*
**plan (to)** keikaku suru *(devise a method or course).*
**plane** hikooki *(airplane);* heimen *(level surface).*
**plant** shokubutsu.
**plant (to)** ueru.
**plaster** kooyaku *(medical);* kabe *(mud);* shikkui *(sand and lime).*
**plate** sara *(for eating);* ita *(of metal).*
**platform** purattohoomu, hoomu *(for trains);* endan *(stage).*

**platter** oozara.
**play** asobi *(children's play);* shibai, engeki *(dramatic performance).*
**play (to)** asobu *(for amusement);* hiku *(a string or keyboard instrument);* fuku *(a wind instrument).*
**plea** negai.
**plead (to)** uttaeru.
**pleasant** kokoromochi no yoi *(giving pleasure);* yukai na *(cheerful).*
**please (to)** yorokobasu *(delight);* tanoshimaseru *(give pleasure to).*
   **Please.** Doozo.
**pleasure** tanoshimi *(delight);* yorokobi *(enjoyment).*
**pledge** yakusoku *(promise);* shirushi *(guarantee).*
**pledge (to)** teitoo ni ireru *(give as a pledge);* yakusoku suru *(promise).*
**plenty** takusan *(much);* juubun *(enough).*
**plot** jisho *(land);* inboo *(conspiracy).*
**plot (to)** takuramu *(scheme secretly);* inboo o megurasu *(conspire).*
**plow** suki.
**plow (to)** tagayasu.
**plum** ume.
**plunder (to)** ryakudatsu suru.
**plural** fukusuu.
**plus** purasu, tasu.
**pocket** poketto.
   **pocket money** kozukai.
**poem** shi; uta.
**poet** shijin.
**poetic** shiteki no.
**poetry** shi, uta.
**point** saki *(tapering end);* kangae *(opinion);* ten *(dot);* pointo *(prominent feature).*
**point (to)** togarasu.
   **to point out** yubi sasu *(with the hand);* chuui o hiku *(draw attention).*
**pointed** togatta.
**poison** doku.
**poison (to)** doku o ireru *(infect with poison);* dokusatsu suru *(kill with poison).*
**poisoning** chuudoku.
**polar** kyokuchi no.
**pole** sao.
**policeman** junsa, keikan.
**policy** shudan *(method);* hooshin *(guiding principle);* seisaku *(course of action in govt.).*
   **insurance policy** hoken shoosho.
**Polish** Poorandojin *(people);* Poorando no *(country).*
**polish** tsuya.
   **shoe polish** kutsuzumi.
**polish (to)** migaku.
**polite** teinei na.

**politeness** teinei.

**political** seijijoo no, seijiteki na.
   **political party** seitoo.

**politics** seiji.

**pollution** osen.
   **air pollution** kuuki osen.

**pond** ike.

**poor** binboo na *(opp. of rich);* warui *(in quality);* kawaisoo na *(worthy of pity).*

**popular** ninki no aru *(liked);* hyooban no ii *(famous, talked of);* taishuuteki na *(in general favor).*

**population** jinkoo.

**pork** butaniku.

**port** minato.

**porter** monban *(gatekeeper);* akaboo *(at railway stations);* booi *(at hotels).*

**portrait** shoozooga.

**position** tsutomeguchi *(employment);* tachiba *(circumstances);* oki dokoro *(place).*

**positive** *adj.* tashika na *(sure);* meikaku na *(definite);* utagai no nai *(unquestionable);* jishin no aru *(convinced). -n.* poji *(in photography).*

**possess (to)** motsu.

**possession** mochimono *(thing held).*

**possibility** kanoosei.

**possible** dekiru.

**post** hashira *(pillar);* kui *(stake);* yuubinbutsu *(mail);* posuto *(mailbox).*

**postage** yuubinryoo.
   **postage stamp** kitte.

**postcard** hagaki *(plain);* ehagaki *(picture).*

**poster** posutaa.

**posterity** shison.

**post office** yuubinkyoku.

**pot** nabe *(pan);* tsubo *(jar);* hachi *(bowl).*

**potato** jagaimo.

**pound** pondo.

**pour (to)** tsugu *(into glass);* hidoku furu *(said of rain).*

**poverty** binboo.

**powder** kona.

**power** chikara.

**powerful** tsuyoi *(strong);* yuuryoku na *(influential).*

**practical** jissaiteki na *(opp. of theoretical);* jitsuyooteki na *(useful).*

**practice** jitsuyoo *(opp. of theory);* keiko *(exercise).*

**practice (to)** jikkoo suru *(carry out);* keiko suru *(exercise).*

**praise** shoosan *(commendation).*

**praise (to)** homeru.

**prank** itazura.

**pray (to)** inoru.

**prayer** inori.

**preach (to)** sekkyoo suru.

**precaution** yoojin.

**precede (to)** sakidatsu.

**preceding** mae no.

**precept** kyookun.

**precious** kooka na *(costly);* taisetsu na *(highly esteemed).*

**precise** seikaku na *(exact);* kuwashii *(detailed);* kichoomen na *(regular).*

**precision** seikaku *(accuracy);* seimitsu *(exactitude).*

**predecessor** zenninsha.

**preface** jobun.

**prefer** -hoo ga suki desu *(one thing to another).*
   **I prefer this.** Kono hoo ga suki desu.

**pregnant** ninshin shite iru.

**prejudice** henken *(bias).*

**prejudice (to)** henken o motaseru.

**preliminary** kari no, yobiteki no.

**prepare (to)** shitaku o suru, junbi o suru.

**prescribe (to)** sashizu suru *(dictate);* shohoo o kaku *(medicine).*

**presence** shusseki *(at a meeting, etc.).*

**present** *adj.* shusseki shite iru *(opp. of absent);* ima no, genzai no *(now existing). -n.* genzai *(the present time);* ima *(now);* okurimono, purezento *(gift).*
   **to make a present** okurimono o suru.
   **for the present** toobun.

**present (to)** ageru, sashiageru *(a gift);* shookai suru *(introduce a person);* miseru *(exhibit);* teishutsu suru *(offer);* noberu *(state).*

**preserve (to)** hozon suru *(maintain);* satoozuke ni suru *(in sugar);* suzuke ni suru *(in vinegar).*

**preside (to)** shikai suru.

**president** shachoo *(of a company);* toodori *(of a bank);* daitooryoo *(of a country);* gakuchoo *(of a university).*

**press** shinbun *(newspaper);* assakuki *(machine).*

**press (to)** susumeru *(urge);* shimeru *(squeeze);* puresu suru *(iron);* osu *(push).*

**pressing** puresu.

**pressure** atsuryoku *(compulsion).*

**prestige** meisei *(fame);* ishin *(dignity).*

**presume (to)** suitei suru *(assume);* katei suru *(suppose);* omou *(guess).*

**pretend (to)** misekakeru *(lay claim);* -furi o suru *(make believe).*

**pretext** koojitsu *(pretense);* benkai *(excuse).*

**pretty** *adj.* kirei na *(beautiful). -adv.* kanari *(fairly).*

**prevail (to)** katsu *(be victorious);* yuusei de aru *(be predominant);* ryuukoo suru *(be prevalent).*

**prevent (to)** samatageru *(hinder);* mamoru *(guard against);* jama o suru *(stand in one's way).*

**prevention** booshi, yoboo.

**previous** saki no *(former)*; mae no *(prior to)*.
the previous year mae no toshi.

**prey** gisei *(victim)*.

**price** nedan *(charge)*; daika *(cost)*; bukka *(of commodities)*.
price index bukka shisuu.

**pride** hokori *(in something or someone)*; unubore *(self-conceit)*; kooman *(haughtiness)*.

**priest** sooryo *(Buddhist)*; kannushi *(Shinto)*; bokushi *(Protestant)*; shinpu *(Catholic)*.

**principal** *adj.* dai ichi no *(first)*; omo na *(main, most important)*. -*n.* gankin *(money)*; koochoo *(of a school)*.

**principle** gensoku *(fundamental rule)*; shugi *(doctrine, an -ism)*.

**print (to)** shuppan suru *(publish)*; insatsu suru *(to put into print)*.

**prison** keimusho.

**prisoner** shuujin *(criminal)*; horyo *(of war)*.

**private** *adj.* watakushi no, shiyoo no *(opp. of public)*; shiei no *(privately operated)*; kojin no *(personal)*.

**privilege** tokken *(prerogative)*; tokuten *(peculiar right)*.

**prize** shoohin.

**prize (to)** omonjiru *(esteem)*; daiji ni suru *(value highly)*.

**probable** arisoo na *(likely to be)*; yuuboo na *(promising)*.

**probably** tabun *(perhaps)*; taitei *(most likely)*.

**problem** mondai.

**procedure** tetsuzuki *(steps)*; junjo *(way of proceeding)*.

**proceed (to)** susumu *(move on)*; hajimeru *(begin)*; tsuzukeru *(continue)*.

**process** hoohoo *(method)*; katei *(course)*.

**procession** gyooretsu.

**proclaim (to)** koohyoo suru *(publish)*; fukoku suru *(promulgate)*; sengen suru *(declare officially)*.

**produce (to)** seisan suru *(yield)*; enshutsu suru *(as plays)*.

**product** sanbutsu *(agricultural produce)*; seisakuhin *(of industrial manufacture)*.

**production** seisaku *(through manufacture)*.

**productive** hoofu na *(producing abundantly)*; yoku tsukuridasu *(bringing forth)*.

**profess to** hakujoo suru.

**profession** shokugyoo *(a calling)*; koogen *(avowal)*; sengen *(declaration)*.

**professional** shokugyoo joo no *(pertaining to work)*; senmonteki *(technical)*.

**professor** kyooju *(of a university)*.

**profile** yokogao.

**profit** rieki *(pecuniary gain)*; eki *(advantage)*.

**profit (to)** eki o eru; toku o suru.

**program** puroguramu *(theatrical, computer, etc.)*; keikaku *(plan)*.
programming puroguramingu.

**progress** zenshin *(movement forward)*.

**progress (to)** shinpo suru *(improve)*; zenshin suru *(advance)*; tsugoo yoku iku *(get on well)*; hattatsu suru *(develop)*.

**prohibit** kinjiru *(forbid)*.

**prohibition** kinshi *(order forbidding)*.

**project** keikaku *(plan)*; kigyoo *(industrial)*.

**project (to)** keikaku suru *(devise)*; tsukidasu *(protrude)*.

**promise** yakusoku *(engagement)*; keiyaku *(contract)*; mikomi *(hope)*.

**promise (to)** yakusoku o suru.
to keep a promise yakusoku o mamoru.

**prompt** hayai, subayai *(quick)*; sumiyaka na *(speedy)*; sassoku no *(done quickly)*.

**prompt (to)** unagasu.

**promptness** binsoku.

**pronounce (to)** hatsuon suru *(articulate)*; senkoku suru *(announce formally)*; sengen suru *(declare)*.

**proof** shoomei *(demonstration)*; shooko *(evidence)*; kooseizuri *(printing)*.

**proper** tekitoo na *(appropriate)*; joohin na *(respectable)*; dokutoku no *(particular)*; tadashii *(correct)*.

**property** zaisan *(assets)*; jisho *(land)*.

**proportion** wari, wariai *(ratio)*; warimae *(share)*; tsuriai *(balance)*.

**proposal** mooshikomi, teian.

**propose (to)** teian suru *(propound)*; mooshikomu *(offer)*.

**prosaic** sanbun no *(of prose)*; omoshiroku nai *(dull, commonplace)*.

**prose** sanbun.

**prospect** mikomi *(outlook)*; nagame *(view)*; mitooshi *(mental view)*; yosoo *(expectation)*.

**prosper (to)** sakaeru, han'ei suru.

**prosperity** hanjoo *(of a business)*; ryuusei *(state of thriving)*; seikoo *(success)*.

**prosperous** sakan na *(thriving)*; rieki no aru *(profitable)*.

**protect (to)** hogo suru *(keep safe)*; fusegu *(defend)*.

**protection** hogo *(guarding from harm)*; kooen *(patronage)*.

**protector** hogosha.

**protest** koogi *(dissent)*; fufuku *(disapproval)*.

**protest (to)** koogi suru *(make a protest)*; hantai suru *(oppose)*; genmei suru *(declare formally)*.

**Protestant** Purotesutanto, Shinkyoo.

**proud** tokui na.

**prove (to)** shoomei suru *(demonstrate);* tashikameru *(make certain);* jikken suru *(experiment).*

**proverb** kotowaza.

**provide** yooi suru *(supply).*
  **provide with** kyookyuu suru.

**province** chihoo *(place at a distance from the capital);* han'i *(sphere or scope).*

**provision** chozoohin *(of food, etc.);* shokuryoohin *(supplies);* kitei *(stipulation);* junbi *(preparation);* yobi *(reserve).*

**provoke (to)** kanjoo o okosaseru *(call forth);* okoraseru *(rouse to anger);* fungai saseru *(exasperate);* okosu *(stimulate).*

**proximity** chikai koto; kinsetsu.

**prudence** yoojin, shinchoo na koto.

**prune** sumomo.

**psychological** shinrigaku joo no.

**psychology** shinrigaku.

**public** *adj.* ooyake no *(opp. of personal);* kookai no *(open to all). -n.* kokumin *(the people).*
  **to make public** koohyoo suru.

**publication** happyoo *(public notification);* shuppan *(publishing);* shuppanbutsu *(published materials).*

**publish (to)** shuppan suru *(books, etc.);* happyoo suru *(make known).*

**publisher** shuppansha.

**pull (to)** hiku.

**pulpit** koodan.

**pulse** myaku.

**pump** ponpu.

**punish (to)** bassuru.

**punishment** batsu *(act of punishing);* keibatsu *(penalty imposed by court).*

**pupil** seito *(school);* deshi *(disciple);* hitomi *(of the eye).*

**purchase** kaimono *(that which is bought);* torihiki *(act of buying).*

**purchase (to)** kau, koonyuu suru.

**pure** junsui no *(unmixed);* seijun na *(uncontaminated);* kirei na *(unsullied),* junketsu na *(chaste);* keppaku na *(guiltless).*

**purity** junketsu *(chastity).*

**purpose** mokuteki *(object);* -tsumori *(intention).*

**purse** saifu.

**pursue (to)** oikakeru *(chase);* tsukimatou *(follow closely);* jikkoo suru *(carry on).*

**pursuit** tsuiseki *(chase).*

**push (to)** osu *(opp. to pull);* oshiugokasu *(move by pushing);* tsukidasu *(thrust);* shiiru *(force).*

**put** *v.t.* oku.
  **put away** shimau.
  **put off** nobasu, enki suru.

**put on** kaburu *(hat);* kiru *(dress);* haku *(shoes).*

**puzzle** nazo *(enigma);* pazuru *(quiz);* nandai *(difficult problem).*

**puzzle (to)** toowaku saseru *(perplex).*
  **be puzzled** toowaku suru.

# Q

**quaint** fuugawari na.

**qualify (to)** tekioo saseru *(fit);* shikaku o eru *(have the qualifications for).*
  **be qualified for** shikaku ga aru.

**quality** hinshitsu *(degree of excellence);* seishitsu *(property).*

**quantity** ryoo, bunryoo *(amount);* suuryoo *(numbers).*

**quarrel (to)** kenka suru.

**quarter** yon bun no ichi *(one-fourth part);* hen *(district).*

**queen** jooo.

**queer** hen na, myoo na *(strange);* okashii *(funny);* okashi na *(unusual).*

**quench (to)** iyasu *(one's thirst);* kesu *(extinguish).*

**question** shitsumon *(interrogation);* koto *(matter);* mondai *(problem).*

**question (to)** shitsumon suru, tazuneru *(inquire);* tou *(ask);* gimon o okosu *(raise a doubt);* utagau *(doubt).*

**quick** hayai.

**quickly** hayaku.
  **Come quickly!** Hayaku kite kudasai.

**quiet** *adj.* shizuka na *(calm);* otonashii *(of character);* ochitsuita *(not showy). -n.* shizukesa *(stillness);* kyuusoku *(repose);* ochitsuki *(peace of mind).*
  **Keep quiet!** Shizuka ni shite kudasai!

**quiet (to)** *v.t.* shizuka ni saseru; *v.i.* shizuka ni naru.

**quit (to)** hanasu *(let go);* hooki suru *(abandon);* yameru *(cease).*

**quite** sukkari *(completely);* jijitsujoo *(actually);* kanari *(somewhat);* tashoo wa *(to a certain extent);* taihen *(very).*
  **quite good** totemo yoroshii.

**quote (to)** in'yoo suru *(cite);* hikiai ni dasu *(refer to);* mitsumoru *(estimate).*

# R

**rabbit** usagi.

**race** kyoosoo *(contest);* jinshu *(of human beings).*

**race (to)** kyoosoo suru.

**radio** rajio.

**rag** boro.

**rage** ikari.

**ragged** boro boro no.

**rail** reeru *(of railway);* tesuri *(of a fence).*

**railroad** tetsudoo.
> **railroad station** eki.
> **railroad train** kisha, densha.

**rain** ame.

**rain (to)** ame ga furu.

**rainbow** niji.

**rainy** ame furi no.
> **rainy season** baiu, tsuyu.
> **rainy weather** uten.

**raise (to)** ageru *(move upward);* mochiageru *(lift up);* kakageru *(hoist);* saibai suru *(grow).*

**raisin** hoshibudoo.

**rake** kumade.

**range** han'i *(scope);* narabi *(row);* dennetsuki *(electric cookstove);* gasu konro *(gas stove).*

**range (to)** *v.t.* naraberu.

**rank** retsu *(row);* kaikyuu *(military).*

**ransom** minoshirokin *(money demanded);* kaihoo *(release from captivity).*

**rapid** *adj.* hayai. *-n.* kyuuryuu *(swift current).*

**rapidity** sokudo.

**rapidly** kyuu ni, hayaku.

**rapture** uchooten.

**rash** *adj.* sekkachi na.

**rat** nezumi.

**rate** warai *(proportion);* sooba *(of exchange);* sokudo *(speed).*

**rate (to)** nedan o tsukeru, mitsumoru *(estimate).*

**rather** kanari *(tolerably, fairly);* mushiro *(instead of);* sukoshi *(somewhat).*
> **I'd rather go.** Watakushi wa dochira ka to ieba ikitai desu.
> **rather good** kanari yoi.
> **rather than** -yori mo.

**ration** haikyuu shokuryoohin.

**rational** rikutsu no aru.

**rave (to)** tawagoto o iu *(talk wildly);* donaru *(talk furiously).*

**raw** nama no *(uncooked).*

**ray** koosen, hikari.

**razor** kamisori.

**reach (to)** todoku *(come to);* oitsuku *(overtake);* -ni tassuru *(attain to).*

**react (to)** *v.i.* hannoo suru *(act in response).*

**reaction** handoo *(against);* hanpatsu *(repulsion).*

**read (to)** yomu.

**reading** dokusho.

**ready** yooi no totonotta *(completely prepared);* yorokonde . . . suru *(willing);*

kakugo no tsuita *(mentally prepared for);* tejika na *(handy).*

**real** hontoo no *(true);* jitsuzai suru *(actually existing);* jissai no *(opp. of imaginary);* honmono no *(genuine).*

**reality** shinjitsu *(opp. of fantasy);* genjitsu *(actuality).*

**realization** jitsugen.

**realize (to)** jitsugen suru *(effectuate);* ki ga tsuku *(come to understand).*

**really** hontoo ni.
> **Really!** Soo nan desu ka!

**rear** ushiro.

**rear (to)** *v.t.* sodateru *(bring up).*

**reason** risei ryoku *(intellectual faculty);* doori *(explanation);* riyuu *(cause);* dooki *(motive);* wake *(ground);* iiwake *(excuse).*

**reason (to)** suiri suru *(draw a conclusion);* handan o kudasu *(form a judgment);* kentoo suru *(examine critically).*
> **by reason of** -no tame ni.

**reasonable** risei no aru *(endowed with reason);* muri ga nai *(justifiable);* koohei na *(fair-minded);* gooriteki na *(rational).*

**reasoning** riron, ronkyuu.

**reassure (to)** anshin saseru.

**rebel** muhonnin *(person).*

**rebel (to)** boodo o okosu *(take up arms against);* shitagawanai *(disobey);* somuku *(act against).*

**rebellion** hanran *(revolt);* boodoo *(riot);* hankoo *(resistance);* muhon *(treason).*

**recall** torikeshi *(act of revoking);* kaisoo *(recollection).*

**recall (to)** omoidasu *(recollect);* torikesu *(revoke);* yobikaesu *(call back).*

**receipt** uketori.

**receive (to)** uketoru.

**receiver** reshiibaa *(radio);* uketorinin *(person).*

**recent** chikagoro no *(modern);* atarashii *(new);* saikin no *(the latest).*

**reception** kangei *(welcoming);* kangeikai, resepushon *(social entertainment).*

**recess** kyuuka *(vacation);* yasumi jikan *(school);* kyuukei *(conference).*

**reciprocal** soogo no *(mutual);* okaeshi no *(done in return).*

**recite (to)** anshoo suru *(repeat from memory);* roogin suru *(as a poem, etc.);* monogataru *(recount).*

**recognize (to)** wakaru, mitomeru.

**recoil (to)** handoo *(as a gun);* hanekaeri *(spring back).*

**recollect (to)** omoidasu.

**recollection** oboe *(reminiscence);* kaisoo *(remembrance);* tsuioku *(retrospection);* omoide *(that which is recollected).*

**recommend (to)** suisen suru.

**recommendation** suisen.

**reconcile (to)** wakai saseru.

**record** kiroku *(written note)*; rireki *(career)*; rekoodo *(phonograph)*.

**record (to)** kiroku suru *(in writing)*; rokuon suru *(in sound)*.

**recover (to)** torimodosu *(get back)*; zenkai suru *(from sickness)*.

**recruit** shinpei.

**rectangle** choohookei.

**red** *adj.* akai. *-n.* aka.

**redeem (to)** shookan suru.

**redouble (to)** issoo tsuyomeru.

**reduce (to)** *v.t.* -ni suru *(convert)*; herasu *(make small)*.

**reduction** waribiki *(discount)*.

**reed** ashi.

**refer (to)** sankoo ni suru *(consult)*; makaseru *(a matter to a person)*.

**reference** mimoto shoomeisho *(a statement of qualifications for someone)*; kikiawase *(inquiry)*; kankei *(relation)*.

**refine (to)** seisei suru *(oil, etc.)*.

**refinement** seisei *(of oil, etc.)*; joohinsa *(elegance)*.

**reflect (to)** hansha suru *(throw back light, etc.)*; arawasu *(show)*; kangaeru *(ponder)*.

**reflection** hansha.

**reform** kaikaku *(political)*; kanka *(of persons)*.

**reform (to)** kaizen suru *(amend)*; aratameru *(make better)*; kaikaku suru *(renovate)*.

**refrain** orikaeshi.

**refrain (to)** sashihikaeru *(abstain from)*; gaman suru *(forbear)*.

**refresh (to)** arata ni suru *(make new)*.

**refreshment** tabemono *(food)*; karui nomimono *(drink)*.

**refuge** hinan *(shelter)*; hinanjo *(place of retreat)*; hogo *(protection)*.
    **to take refuge** hinan suru.

**refund** harai modoshi.

**refund (to)** harai modosu.

**refusal** kotowari.

**refuse** kotowaru *(decline)*; jitai suru *(decline to receive)*; shoodaku shinai *(reject)*.

**refute (to)** hanbaku suru.

**regard** kooryo *(consideration)*; sonkei *(respect)*.
    **in regard to** -ni tsuite.

**regime** toochi *(administration)*; kanri *(control)*; seiken *(political power)*.

**regiment** rentai.

**register** choomen *(record book)*; meibo *(of names)*.

**register (to)** kaku *(a name)*; kakitome ni suru *(a letter)*.
    **registered letter** kakitome.

**regret** kookai *(repentance)*; shitsuboo *(disappointment)*; zannen *(remorse)*.

**regret (to)** zannen ni omou *(be sorry for)*; ki no doku ni omou *(deplore)*; ikan ni omou *(lament)*; kookai suru *(repent)*; oshiku omou *(be sorry for the loss of)*.

**regular** kimatta *(according to rule)*; futsuu no *(usual)*; teiki no *(at intervals)*.

**regulate (to)** choosetsu suru.

**regulation** kisoku.

**rehearsal** shitageiko, renshuu, rihaasaru.

**rehearse (to)** shitageiko suru, renshuu suru.

**reign** jidai *(period)*.

**reign (to)** osameru.

**reinforce (to)** hokyoo suru.

**reject (to)** kotowaru.

**rejoice (to)** yorokobu.

**relapse** burikaeshi *(recurrence of illness)*.

**relate (to)** hanasu *(narrate)*; kankei o tsukeru *(connect)*.

**relation** kankei *(connection)*; shinrui *(kinsman)*.

**relationship** kankei.

**relative** *adj.* hikakuteki, kankei aru. *n.* shinrui, shinseki *(kinsman)*.

**relax (to)** kitsurogu *(take one's ease)*; ochitsuku *(calm down)*; yurumu *(become loose)*; yawaragu *(become less strict)*.

**relaxation** kibarashi *(recreation)*; kyuuyoo *(rest)*; yurumi *(of muscles)*; tegokoro *(of regulations)*.

**release (to)** hanasu *(let go free)*; tooka suru *(let fall from)*; happyoo suru *(make public)*.

**relent (to)** yawaragu, kandai ni naru.

**relentless** mujihi na.

**relevant** kankei no aru.

**reliable** tashika na.

**reliance** shinrai *(trust)*; shin'yoo *(confidence)*.

**relic** ibutsu.

**relief** kyuujo *(help)*; keigen *(alleviation)*; anraku *(comfort)*.

**relieve (to)** tasukeru *(raid)*; raku ni suru *(give comfort)*.

**religion** shuukyoo.
    **Buddhist religion** Bukkyoo.
    **Shintoism** Shintoo.

**religious** shuukyooteki na *(of religion)*; shinkoo no *(devout)*; shinjin bukai, keikan na *(pious)*.

**relinquish (to)** suteru, hooki suru.

**relish** aji *(taste)*; kaori *(flavor)*; fuumi *(good taste)*.

**relish (to)** ajiwatte miru *(savor)*; oishiku taberu *(eat with pleasure)*; tanoshimu *(enjoy)*.

**reluctance** chuucho.

**reluctant** iyagaru, fushoo bushoo no.

**rely upon** tayoru *(depend upon)*.

**remain** todomaru, taizai suru *(stay)*.

**remainder** nokori *(remaining part)*; zanryuusha *(remaining person)*.

**remark** itta kotoba *(anything said)*; iken *(comment)*.

**remark (to)** -ni chuumoku suru *(take notice of)*; hihyoo suru *(comment)*.

**remarkable** chuumoku subeki *(noteworthy)*; sugureta *(exceptional)*; subarashii *(striking)*.

**remedy** kusuri *(medicine)*; chiryoo *(treatment)*.

**remember (to)** oboeru; omoidasu *(recollect)*.

**remembrance** omoide *(recollection)*; kiokuryoku *(memory)*; kinen *(commemoration)*.

**remind (to)** omoidasaseru *(bring something to mind)*.

**remorse** kookai *(regret)*; ryooshin no togame *(pangs of conscience)*.

**remote** tooi, hanareta.

   **remote control** rimokon.

**removal** iten *(of or from house)*; kaishoku *(position)*.

**remove (to)** dokeru, torinozoku.

**renew** atarashiku suru *(make new again)*; irekaeru *(replace)*; kurikaesu *(repeat)*.

**rent** yachin *(for a house)*.

**rent (to)** kasu *(to somebody)*; kariru *(from somebody)*.

**repair** shuuzen *(act of repairing)*; kaifuku *(restoration to a sound state)*.

**repair (to)** naosu *(mend)*; kaifuku suru *(restore)*; teisei suru *(remedy)*.

**repeat (to)** kurikaesu *(do once more)*; sono mama tsutaeru *(tell to another)*; kurikaeshite okonau *(do over again)*.

**repent (to)** kuiru, kookai suru.

**repetition** kurikaeshi, hanpuku.

**reply** henji.

**reply (to)** henji suru.

**report** hookoku, shirase *(account)*.

**report (to)** hookoku suru.

**represent (to)** dairi suru *(persons, etc.)*; arawasu *(as a symbol)*; egakidasu *(portray)*.

**representation** daihyoo *(delegate)*; mooshitate *(petition)*.

**representative** dairinin; daihyoo *(delegate)*.

**repress (to)** yokuatsu suru *(suppress)*; yokusei suru *(keep under control)*.

**reprimand** shisseki.

**reprimand (to)** shikaru, hinan suru.

**reprisal** shikaeshi, fukushuu.

**reproach** shisseki *(upbraiding)*; togame *(censure)*.

**reproach (to)** shikaru.

**reproduce (to)** fukusha suru *(make a copy)*; saisei suru *(remake)*.

**reputation** hyooban, meisei.

**request** negai, seikyuu.

**request (to)** negau *(beg)*; tanomu *(ask)*.

**require (to)** iru *(need)*.

**rescue** sukuidashi, kyuujo.

**rescue (to)** sukuidasu *(deliver from)*; kaihoo suru *(set free)*.

**research (to)** kenkyuu suru, shiraberu.

**resent (to)** okoru, hankan o motsu.

**resentment** urami *(animosity)*; fungai *(indignation)*.

**reservation** yoyaku *(at a hotel)*.

**reserve** junbi *(readiness)*; yobihin *(stock)*.

   **without reserve** fukuzoonaku *(freely)*.

**reserve (to)** totte oku *(set apart, keep in store)*.

**reside (to)** sumu.

**residence** sumai; juusho.

**resign (to)** yameru *(relinquish)*; dannen suru *(abandon)*; jishoku suru *(give up office)*; taishoku suru *(retire)*.

   **to resign oneself** shitagau, akirameru *(accept one's fate)*.

**resignation** jishoku.

**resist (to)** teikoo suru *(withstand)*; gekitai suru *(repel)*; hantai suru *(oppose)*.

**resistance** teikoo, hantai.

**resolute** shikkari shita.

**resolution** ketsudan *(firmness)*; kesshin *(formed purpose)*.

**resolve (to)** kesshin suru *(determine)*; kaiketsu suru *(settle)*.

**resort** hoyoochi *(for health)*.

   **summer resort** hishochi.

**resort (to)** -ni uttaeru.

**resources** shigen.

**respect** sonkei *(esteem)*; kankei *(relation)*.

   **in respect to** -ni kanshite.

**respect (to)** kooryo suru *(heed)*; sonchoo suru *(treat with deference)*; uyamau *(revere)*.

**respectful** teinei na, reigi tadashii *(well mannered)*.

**respective** kakuji no, sorezore no.

**respite** yuuyo *(delay)*; shikei no shikkoo yuuyo *(reprieve)*; ichijiteki chuushi *(temporary cessation)*.

**responsibility** sekinin.

**responsible** sekinin ga aru.

**rest** nokori *(remainder)*; yasumi *(repose)*; suimin *(sleep)*; teishi *(cessation of motion)*.

**rest (to)** yasumu; suimin o toru *(have some sleep)*.

**restaurant** ryooriya *(Japanese)*; resutoran *(Western-style)*.

**restless** ochitsukanai.

**restoration** fukkoo *(revival)*; kaifuku *(recovery)*.

**restore (to)** moto ni modosu *(bring back)*; kaesu *(give back)*; fukushoku saseru

*(reinstate);* fukkoo suru *(reestablish);*
  naosu *(reconstruct).*
**restrain (to)** yokusei suru.
**restraint** yokusei.
  **without restraint** enryo naku.
**restrict** seigen suru, kagiru.
**restriction** seigen *(limitation).*
**result** kekka.
**result (to)** -ni owaru *(end up in).*
**resume (to)** futatabi hajimeru.
**retail** kouri.
**retail (to)** kouri suru.
**retain (to)** hoji suru *(keep);* kioku suru
  *(memorize).*
**retaliate (to)** shikaeshi suru.
**retaliation** shikaeshi, fukushuu.
**retire (to)** intai suru *(from work);* yasumu
  *(rest).*
**retirement** intai.
**retract** torikesu.
**retreat** taikyaku *(military).*
**retreat (to)** taikyaku suru.
**retrieve (to)** torimodosu *(recover);* sukuidasu
  *(rescue).*
**return (to)** kaeru *(come back);* kaesu *(give
  back).*
**reveal (to)** shimesu *(disclose);* shiraseru *(make
  known);* bakuro suru *(divulge).*
**revelation** happyoo *(disclosure);* Mokushiroku
  *(Book of the Bible).*
**revenge** fukushuu.
**revenue** shotoku *(income of an individual);*
  sainyuu *(of the state).*
**reverence** suuhai *(veneration);* sonkei
  *(esteem).*
**reverend** bokushi *(Protestant clergyman);*
  shinpu *(Catholic clergyman).*
**reverse** abekobe, hantai.
**reverse (to)** abekobe ni suru.
**revert** ni moto ni modoru.
**review** hihyoo *(critical);* fukushuu *(study).*
**review (to)** saichoosa suru *(view again);*
  kansatsu suru *(survey);* kaisoo suru
  *(reconsider);* hihyoo o kaku *(books).*
**revise (to)** teisei suru *(correct).*
**revision** kaisei, kaitei.
**revive (to)** fukkatsu suru.
**revoke (to)** torikesu *(annul);* haishi suru
  *(abolish).*
**revolt** hanran.
**revolt (to)** hanran o okosu *(rebel).*
**revolution** kakumei.
**revolve (to)** mawaru, kaiten suru.
**reward** hoobi, hooshuu.
**reward (to)** -ni mukuiru *(repay);* hoobi o
  ataeru *(give a reward to).*
  **be rewarded** mukuirareru.
**rhyme** in.
**rib** abara bone.

**ribbon** ribon.
**rice** ine *(plant);* kome *(raw grain);* gohan
  *(cooked).*
**rich** kanemochi no *(wealthy);* yutaka na
  *(abundant).*
**richness** yuufuku.
**rid (get)** torinozoku.
**riddle** nazo.
**ride** noru koto.
**ride (to)** -ni noru.
**ridiculous** bakarashii.
**rifle** shoojuu.
**right** *adj.* tadashii *(correct);* mottomo na
  *(reasonable);* machigai no nai *(not wrong);*
  migi no *(direction).* -n. kenri *(privilege);*
  migi *(direction).*
  **have a right to** kenri ga aru.
  **to the right** migigawa ni.
**righteous** koohei na, tadashii.
**righteousness** seigi, koohei.
**rightful** tadashii.
**rigid** kyuukutsu na *(not flexible);* genkaku na
  *(strict).*
**rigor** genkaku.
**rigorous** genkaku na.
**ring** wa *(circle, link, wheel);* yubiwa *(for
  finger).*
**ring (to)** *v.t.* narasu; *v.i.* naru.
**rinse (to)** yusugu.
**riot** soodoo, boodoo.
**riot (to)** soodoo o okosu.
**ripe** jukushita.
**ripen (to)** jukusu *(become ripe);* jukusaseru
  *(make ripe).*
**rise** agari, shusse *(getting ahead).*
**rise (to)** agaru *(go up);* okiru *(from bed, etc.);*
  deru *(said of the sun).*
**risk** booken *(hazard);* kiken *(peril).*
  **run a risk** booken o suru.
**risk (to)** kiken ni sarasu *(expose to peril);*
  kakeru *(venture);* ichi ka bachi ka yatte
  miru *(take the chance of).*
**rite** gishiki.
**ritual** gishiki *(rite);* shikiten *(ceremony).*
**rival** kyoosoosha *(competitor);* teki *(enemy);*
  aite *(in sport).*
**rivalry** kyoosoo.
**river** kawa.
**road** michi, dooro.
  **main road** oodoori.
  **middle of the road** michi no mannaka.
**roar** unari *(of an animal);* todoroki *(of waves,
  etc.).*
**roar (to)** unaru *(of animals);* todoroku *(of
  waves, etc.);* donaru *(vociferate).*
**roast** roosuto.
**roast (to)** roosuto ni suru.
  **roast beef** roosuto biifu.
**rob (to)** nusumu.

**robber** doroboo, gootoo.
**robbery** nusumi.
**robe** gaun *(gown);* yukata *(Japanese bathrobe).*
**robot** robotto.
**robust** ganjoo na.
**rock** iwa.
**rock (to)** *v.t.* yusuru; *v.i.* yureru.
**rocky** iwa no ooi.
**rod** boo, sao.
**roll** maki gami *(of paper);* rooru pan *(bread).*
**roll (to)** korobasu *(roll over);* maku *(wind);* tsutsumu *(enwrap);* sayuu ni yusuru *(shake from side to side);* korobu *(tumble down).*
**romantic** romanchikku na.
**romanticism** roomanshugi.
**roof** yane.
**room** heya *(of a house);* basho *(space).*
   **make room for** basho o tsukuru.
   **There's no room.** Basho ga arimasen.
**root** ne.
**rope** nawa, tsuna.
**rose** bara.
**rot (to)** kusaru *(decay).*
**rough** zara zara shita *(opp. of smooth);* deko boko no *(opp. of level);* arai *(said of the sea);* ranboo na *(riotous);* gekiretsu na *(violent);* arappoi *(rude).*
**round** *adj.* marui. *-adv.* maruku. *-n.* maru, en *(circle).*
**round off (to)** shiageru.
**rouse** me o samasu.
**rout (to)** haisoo suru.
**route** tsuuro, ruuto.
**routine** kimatta junjo *(fixed procedure).*
**rove (to)** urotsuku.
**row** narabi *(line);* sawagi *(disturbance).*
   **be in a row** narande iru.
   **place in a row** ichiretsu ni oku.
**row (to)** kogu *(a boat).*
**royal** kooshitsu no.
**rub (to)** kosuru *(any object);* sasuru *(the body).*
**rubber** gomu.
**rubbish** garakuta, gomi.
**rude** busahoo na *(unmannerly);* soya na *(uncivil);* shitsurei na, burei na *(impolite);* ranboo na *(rough).*
**ruin** haikyo *(remains);* koseki *(historical site);* hakai *(destruction);* metsuboo *(decay).*
**ruin (to)** waruku suru *(damage);* dame ni suru *(make useless).*
**rule** monosashi *(measure);* joogi *(ruler for lines);* kisoku *(principle).*
   **as a rule** ippan ni.
**rule (to)** suji o hiku *(mark with lines);* osameru *(govern).*

**ruler** shihaisha *(sovereign);* joogi *(for drawing lines).*
**rumor** uwasa.
**run (to)** hashiru, kakeru.
   **run away** nigeru.
**rural** inaka no.
**rush** ooisogi *(great haste);* kyuugeki na zooka *(sudden increase).*
**rush (to)** isogu.
   **rush hour** rasshu awaa.
   **rush into** tobikomu.
   **rush out** tobidasu.
   **rush toward** hashitte iku.
**Russian** Roshiya no *(pertaining to Russia);* Roshiyajin *(person);* Roshiyago *(language);* Roshiya *(country).*
**rust** sabi.
**rust (to)** *v.t.* sabisaseru; *v.i.* sabiru.
**rustic** inaka no; inaka mono no *(person).*
**rusty** sabita.
**rye** raimugi.

**sacred** shinsei na *(hallowed).*
**sacrifice** gisei *(surrender of a desirable thing).*
**sacrifice (to)** gisei ni suru *(renounce something).*
**sacrilege** bootoku.
**sad** kanashii.
**sadden (to)** kanashimaseru.
**saddle** kura.
**sadness** kanashimi.
**safe** *adj.* buji na, anzen na *(free from danger);* tashika na *(reliable). -n.* kinko *(strongbox).*
**safely** buji ni.
**safety** buji, anzen.
**sail** ho.
**sail (to)** shuppan suru *(depart);* fune de iku *(go by boat);* kookai suru *(navigate).*
**saint** seija, seijin.
**sake** tame; mokuteki *(purpose).*
   **for the sake of** -no tame ni.
**salad** sarada.
**salary** gekkyuu *(monthly);* nenkyuu *(annual);* sarari.
**sale** uridashi *(bargain);* hanbai *(selling).*
   **sales analysis** hanbai bunseki.
   **sales estimate** yosoo uriage daka.
   **sales force** hanbai in.
   **sales promotion** hanbai sokushin.
   **sales quota** hanbai wariate.
   **sales territory** hanbai chiiki.
   **sales volume** hanbai ryoo.
**salt** shio, shokuen *(for the table).*
**salt (to)** shio de aji o tsukeru.

**salute** eshaku *(nod)*; aisatsu *(greeting)*; keirei *(military)*.

**salute (to)** aisatsu suru.

**salvation** sukui.

**same** onaji.

   **all the same** mattaku onaji.

**sample** mihon, sanpuru.

**sanctuary** reihaidoo *(in a church)*; shinden *(Shinto shrine)*.

**sand** suna.

**sandal** sandaru *(Occidental-style)*; zoori *(Japanese-style)*.

**sandwich** sandoitchi.

**sandy** suna no *(pertaining to sand)*; sunachi no *(land)*; usuchairo no *(in color)*.

**sane** shooki no.

**sanitary** eiseitekina.

**sap** jueki *(of trees)*; genki *(vitality)*.

**sap (to)** yowaraseru.

**sarcasm** hiniku, fuushi.

**sarcastic** hiniku na.

**sardine** iwashi.

**sash** obi.

**satellite** eisei.

**satiate (to)** akisaseru.

**satin** shusu.

**satisfaction** manzoku.

**satisfactory** manzoka na *(contented)*; juubun na *(sufficient)*; yoi *(adequate, good)*.

**satisfy (to)** manzoku saseru *(gratify)*; zenbu hensai suru *(discharge)*; baishoo suru *(recompense)*.

**saturate (to)** hitasu.

**Saturday** Doyoobi.

**sauce** soosu *(Worcestershire)*; shooyu *(soy sauce)*.

**saucer** koohii zara *(for coffee cup)*; chataku *(for Japanese teacups)*.

**sausage** sooseeji.

**savage** *adj.* yaban na. *-n.* yabanjin.

**save (to)** sukuu *(rescue)*; takuwaeru *(hoard)*; setsuyaku suru *(economize)*; tasukeru *(from injury)*; tameru *(put by)*.

   **be saved** tasukaru.

   **save time** jikan o setsuyaku suru.

**savings** chokin, ginkoo yokin *(bank)*.

**savior** sukuinushi.

**say (to)** iu, ossharu *(honorific; respect)*.

   **Say!** Chotto!

**scales** hakari *(weighing instrument)*; uroko *(of fish)*.

**scan (to)** kuwashiku shiraberu.

**scandal** shuubun, gigoku, oshoku.

**scanty** sukunai, toboshii.

**scar** kizu ato.

**scarce** sukunai, fusoku na; mare na.

**scarcely** karoojite *(with difficulty)*; yatto *(barely)*; hotondo *(with a negative verb; almost, not)*.

**scarcely know** hotondo zonjimasen *(honorific: humble)*.

**scare (to)** *v.t.* odokasu.

   **get scared** odoroku.

**scarf** sukaafu, erimaki.

**scatter** *v.t.* makichirasu *(strew)*; oichirasu *(disperse)*.

**scene** keshiki *(landscape)*; bamen *(movie, etc.)*.

**scenery** keshiki; kookei *(sight, spectacle)*.

**schedule** jikanhyoo *(timetable)*; ichiranhyoo *(catalogue)*.

**scheme** keikaku *(in a good sense)*; takurami *(in a bad sense)*.

**scholar** seito *(student)*; gakusha *(learned person)*.

**school** gakkoo.

   **go to school** tsuugaku suru.

   **junior high school** chuugakkoo.

   **leave school** taigaku suru.

   **primary school** shoogakkoo.

   **senior high school** kootoogakkoo.

**science** kagaku.

**scientific** kagakuteki.

**scientist** kagakusha.

**scissors** hasami.

**scold (to)** shikaru.

**scope** han'i.

**scorn** keibetsu.

**scorn (to)** keibetsu suru.

**scornful** keibetsuteki na.

**scrape (to)** kezuru, kaku.

**scratch** kakikizu *(made by nail or claw)*; kasurikizu *(wound)*.

**scratch (to)** kaku *(an itchy place)*; hikkaku *(cause a wound)*.

**scream** sakebigoe.

**scream (to)** sakebu *(cry out)*.

**screen** shikiri *(partition)*; maku *(curtain)*.

   **folding screen** byoobu.

   **paper screen** shooji *(in a Japanese house)*.

**screw** neji.

   **screwdriver** nejimawashi.

**scribble (to)** nagurigaki suru.

**scroll** makimono.

**scruple** chuucho, tamerai.

**scrupulous** ryooshin teki na.

**scrutinize (to)** sensaku suru.

**sculpture** chookoku.

**sea** umi.

**seal** han, in, fuuin *(impression)*; azarashi *(animal)*.

**seal (to)** han o osu; fuujiru *(close up)*.

**seam** nuime.

**search** soosaku *(quest)*; sensaku *(inquiry)*; tsuikyuu *(close inquiry)*; ginmi *(scrutiny)*.

**search (to)** sagasu *(explore)*; jitto mitsumeru

*(scrutinize carefully);* saguru *(probe);* shiraberu *(examine).*

**seashore** kaigan.

**seasickness** funayoi.

**season** kisetsu.

   **rainy season** baiu, tsuyu.

**season (to)** aji o tsukeru.

**seat** koshikake *(anything to sit on);* isu *(chair);* benchi *(bench);* seki *(place where one sits).*

**seat (to)** koshikakeru.

**second** *n.* dai ni *(in succession);* byoo *(in time);* futsuka *(of the month).* -*adj.* ni banme no.

**second (to)** sansei suru *(support).*

**secondary** dai ni no.

**secret** *adj.* himitsu no. -*n.* himitsu.

**secretary** hisho *(in a business office);* shoki *(recording officer; as a title).*

**sect** shuuha, ha.

**section** bun *(part);* kuiki *(area, zone).*

**secure** anshin na *(free from care);* buji na *(safe);* daijoobu na *(sure).*

**secure (to)** shikkari to suru *(make fast);* eru *(obtain);* hoshoo suru *(guarantee).*

**security** tanpo *(for debts);* teitoo *(deposited as a pledge);* anzen *(safety).*

**see** miru *(look at);* miseru *(show).* -ni au *(meet face to face);* wakaru *(comprehend);* tamesu *(try out).*

   **I see.** Wakarimashita.

**seed** tane.

**seek (to)** sagasu *(look for);* sagashimotomeru *(try to obtain).*

**seem (to)** mieru.

   **She seems not to know it.** Shiranai rashii.

**seize (to)** tsukamaeru.

**seldom** metta ni *(with negative).*

   **I seldom go.** Metta ni ikimasen.

**select (to)** erabu.

**selection** sentei.

**self** jibun, jishin.

   **by itself** shizen ni.

   **by oneself** hitori de.

   **myself** watashi jishin.

**selfish** migatte na *(concerned unduly with oneself);* rikoteki na *(egoistic).*

**selfishness** wagamama.

**self service** serufu saabisu

**sell (to)** uru.

**semicolon** semikoron.

**senate** jooin *(U.S.);* sangiin *(Japan).*

**senator** jooingiin *(U.S.);* sangiingiin *(Japanese).*

**send (to)** okuru *(to a distant place);* todokeru *(nearby);* dasu *(by mail).*

**senior** toshiue *(in age);* senpai *(old-timer).*

**sensation** kankaku *(perception by the senses);*

kimochi *(feeling);* kandoo *(excited feeling);* koofun *(excitement);* hyooban *(of gossip, etc.).*

**sense** chikaku *(perception);* ishiki *(consciousness);* kanji *(sensation);* kannen *(mental discernment);* funbetsu *(practical judgment);* imi *(meaning).*

**senseless** mukankaku na *(thoughtless);* bakageta *(foolish).*

**sensibility** kankaku.

**sensible** kenmei na *(wise);* kashikoi *(sagacious);* shiryo no aru *(thoughtful).*

**sensitive** kanjiyasui *(delicate);* shinkei kabin na *(overly sensitive);* sugu ki ni suru *(touchy).*

**sensitivity** shinkei kabin.

**sentence** bunshoo *(in writing);* bun *(gram.);* senkoku *(judgment).*

**sentiment** kanji, joosoo.

**sentimental** senchimentaru na; kanshooteki na.

**separate** wakareta *(disconnected);* betsu no *(distinct);* koko no *(individual);* hitori hitori no *(single);* kakuri shita *(isolated).*

**separate (to)** hanasu; wakeru; setsudan suru *(sever);* hikihanasu *(disconnect);* hanareru *(disunite);* bekkyo suru *(live apart, part company).*

**separately** betsu betsu ni, tandoku ni.

**separation** bunri, datsuri.

**September** Kugatsu.

**serene** ochitsuita *(tranquil);* hareta *(unclouded);* uraraka na *(bright and clear);* odayaka na *(placid).*

**sergeant** gunsoo *(army);* keibu *(in a police force).*

**series** shiriizu, renzoku.

**serious** majime na *(solemn);* juudai na *(important);* kitoku no *(dying, critically ill).*

**seriously** majime ni.

**sermon** sekkyoo.

**servant** meshitsukai.

   **maidservant** otetsudai.

**serve (to)** hookoo suru *(act as a servant);* kyuuji o suru *(wait on table);* yaku ni tatsu *(be of use);* tsugoo ga yoi *(be suitable);* -no tame ni hataraku *(give service to).*

**service** sewa *(assistance rendered);* hookoo *(servant's occupation);* saabisu *(treatment in hotels, etc.);* reihai *(religious).*

**session** kaiki *(period);* kaitei *(sitting of law court);* gakki *(school term).*

**set** *adj.* kimatta, kitei no. -*n.* kumi *(things of the same kind).*

   **complete set** hito kumi.

**set (to)** *v.t.* oku *(place);* tateru *(erect);* hajimeru *(begin);* totonoeru; kimeru *(fix);* *v.i.* shizumu *(as the sun).*

**settle (to)** kimeru *(fix);* kaiketsu suru *(solve);* ochitsuku *(settle down);* imin suru *(colonize).*

**settlement** kaiketsu *(of an affair);* jidan *(agreement);* seisan *(liquidation);* setsurumento *(social service).*

**seven** nanatsu, shichi.

**seventeen** juunana, juushichi.

**seventeenth** dai juunana; juushichi nichi *(of the month).*

**seventh** dai shichi; nanoka *(of the month).*

**seventieth** dai nanajuu.

**seventy** nanajuu, shichijuu.

**several** iro iro no *(diverse);* ikutsuka no *(various).*

    **several times** suukai.

**severe** hidoi *(harsh);* kibishii *(strict);* genkaku na *(stern);* gensei na *(rigidly accurate);* mooretsu na *(intense).*

**severity** gekiretsu *(harshness);* genkaku *(strictness).*

**sew (to)** nuu.

**sewer** gesui.

**sex** sei.

    **female sex** mesu *(animals);* josei *(humans).*

    **male sex** osu *(animals);* dansei *(humans).*

**sexual** seiteki na.

**shabby** misuborashii.

**shade** hikage *(of sun);* kage *(of trees, etc.).*

**shade (to)** kage ni suru *(cast shade upon);* hikari ga ataranai yoo ni suru *(protect from light);* kakusu *(screen from view).*

**shadow** kage.

**shady** kage no ooi.

**shake (to)** *v.t.* yusuru *(rock, swing);* furu *(by holding);* *v.i.* furueru *(tremble).*

**shallow** asai.

**sham** *adj.* nise no. *-n.* nise.

**sham (to)** -no furi o suru.

**shame** haji *(disgrace);* hazukashisa *(consciousness of shortcoming);* fumenboku *(ignominy);* fumeiyo *(dishonor).*

**shame (to)** haji saseru.

**shameful** hazukashii.

**shameless** haji shirazu no.

**shape** katachi *(form);* keijoo *(configuration);* sugata *(guise).*

**shape (to)** katachi o tsukeru.

**shapeless** katachi no nai.

**share** bun *(part);* wakemae *(portion);* kabu *(finance).*

**share (to)** wakeru *(divide);* buntan suru *(partake).*

**shareholder** kabunushi.

**sharp** *adj.* surudoi *(as blades, needles);* yoku kireru *(as edge for cutting);* saki no togatta *(pointed);* nukeme no nai *(shrewd).*

**sharpen (to)** togu *(an edge);* togarasu *(a point);* kezuru *(a pencil).*

**shatter (to)** konagona ni kowasu *(break in pieces);* kujiku *(hope).*

**shave (to)** soru *(blade);* kezuru *(plane).*

**she** ano onna no hito, kanojo.

**shed** koya.

**shed tears (to)** namida o nagasu.

**sheep** hitsuji.

**sheer** kewashii *(steep);* mattaku no *(utter).*

**sheet** shikifu *(for a bed);* ichi mai no kami *(of paper).*

**shelf** tana.

**shell** kara *(of mollusks);* koo *(of lobster, crab, etc.).*

**shelter** hinanjo *(refuge);* hinangoya *(shed);* hogo *(protection).*

**shelter (to)** *v.t.* hogo suru *(protect);* yadorasu *(lodge);* kakumau *(give refuge);* *v.i.* hinan suru *(take refuge).*

**shepherd** hitsuijikai.

**shield** tate.

**shield (to)** hogo suru.

**shift** kootai *(act of taking a turn).*

**shift (to)** *v.t.* utsusu, kaeru.

**shine (to)** hikaru *(glitter);* teru *(as sun or moon);* kagayaku *(sun).*

**ship** fune.

    **steamship** kisen.

**ship (to)** fune de okuru *(send by ship);* okuru *(send by any means).*

**shipment** funazumi *(ship's load);* ni *(cargo);* tsumini *(the goods shipped).*

**shirt** shatsu, waishatsu *(Western-style);* juban *(Japanese).*

**shiver** miburui.

**shiver (to)** furueru, miburui suru.

**shock** shokku, shoogeki *(impact);* shoototsu *(collision);* shindoo *(by earthquake);* kandoo *(of the mind).*

    **have a shock** bikkuri suru.

**shock (to)** odorokasu *(with fear);* odoroku *(be shocked).*

**shoe** kutsu.

**shoemaker** kutsuya.

**shoot** utsu *(as a gun).*

**shooting** shageki.

**shop** mise; -ya *(in compounds).*

    **butcher shop** nikuya.

**shopping** kaimono.

**shore** kaigan.

**short** mijikai *(not long);* hikui *(not tall).*

    **short distance** shookyori, tan kyori.

**shorten (to)** *v.t.* mijikaku suru *(make shorter);* tsumeru *(curtail);* *v.i.* mijikaku naru *(become shorter);* tsumaru *(be curtailed).*

**shorthand** sokki.

**shot** happoo *(of a gun)*; chuusha *(injection)*.
**shoulder** kata.
**shout** oogoe *(loud voice)*.
**shout (to)** oogoe de yobu *(call out)*; oogoe o
  dasu *(utter a loud cry)*; sakebu, donaru
  *(utter with a shout)*.
  **to shout at** donari tsukeru.
**shove (to)** oshiwakeru.
**shovel** shaberu.
**show** shibai, misemono *(public show)*.
**show (to)** miseru *(let see)*; oshieru *(point
  out)*.
**shower** niwaka ame *(of rain)*; yuudachi *(in
  summer)*.
**shrill** kandakai.
**shrimp** ebi.
**shrine** jinja *(Shinto)*.
**shrink (to)** chijimu.
**shrub** kanboku.
**shun (to)** sakeru.
**shut** *adj.* shimatta, tojita.
**shut (to)** *v.t.* shimeru *(a door, etc.)*; tojiru
  *(things with lids)*; *v.i.* shimaru *(be shut)*.
**shy** hazukashii *(bashful)*; uchiki na *(timid)*;
  kimari ga warui *(embarrassed)*.
**sick (be)** guai ga warui *(unwell)*.
  **She got sick.** Byooki ni narimashita.
**sickness** byooki.
**side** kawa (gawa).
**sidewalk** hodoo, jindoo.
**siege** kakomi.
**sigh** tameiki.
**sigh (to)** tameiki o tsuku.
**sight** shiryoku *(power of seeing)*; nagame
  *(view, scene)*; keshiki *(scenery)*.
  **out of sight** mienai.
**sign** sain *(signature)*; shirushi *(indication)*;
  chookoo *(symptom)*; zenchoo *(omen)*;
  fugoo *(mark)*; kanban *(signboard)*; miburi
  *(gesture)*.
**sign (to)** shomei suru *(one's name)*.
**signal** shingoo, keihoo.
**signal (to)** shingoo o okuru.
**signature** shomei, sain.
**significance** imi *(meaning)*; juuyoosei
  *(importance)*.
**significant** juuyoo na.
**signify (to)** -o imi suru.
**silence** seishuku, chinmoku.
**silence (to)** damaraseru.
**silent** shizuka na.
**silicon** keiso.
**silicone** shirikon.
**silk** kinu.
  **silk cloth** kenpu.
**silken** kinu no.
**silkworm** kaiko.
**silly** baka na.

**silver** gin.
**silvery** gin'iro no.
**similar** nite iru *(resembling)*; onaji yoo na
  *(same kind)*; ruiji shita *(alike)*.
**similarity** ruiji.
**simple** kantan na *(not complicated)*; tanjun na
  *(not combined)*; wake no nai, yasashii
  *(easy)*.
**simplicity** tanjun, kantan.
**simply** tan ni.
**simulate (to)** -no mane o suru.
**simultaneous** dooji no.
**sin** tsumi.
**sin (to)** tsumi o okasu.
**since** -kara *(because)*; -te kara *(after, follows
  verb in -te form)*.
**sincere** seijitsu na.
**sincerely** hontoo ni *(truly)*; seijitsu ni.
**sincerity** seijitsu.
**sinew** suji.
**sing** utau; naku *(birds)*.
  **sing a song** uta o utau.
**singer** kashu; utaite.
**single** tada hitotsu no *(one only)*; kokono
  *(individual)*; dokushin no *(unmarried)*.
**singular** mezurashii *(uncommon, rare)*; hen na
  *(strange)*; fushigi na *(wondrous)*.
**sinister** ninsoo no waruii *(person)*.
**sink** nagashi *(in a kitchen)*.
**sink (to)** *v.i.* shizumu *(be submerged)*; *v.t.*
  shizumeru *(submerge, go down)*.
**sinner** tsumibito.
**sip (to)** susuru.
**sir** sensei *(teacher, lawyer, title of respect)*.
  **Thank you, sir.** Arigatoo gozaimasu.
**sister** neesan, oneesan, ane *(older)*; imooto
  *(younger)*.
**sister-in-law** gi-shi, giri no ane *(older)*; gimai,
  giru no imooto *(younger)*.
**sit (to)** koshikakeru *(on a chair)*; suwaru.
**site** basho *(place)*; shikichi *(for a building)*.
**situation** tsutome guchi *(employment)*; jijoo
  *(circumstance)*.
**six** muttsu, roku.
**sixteen** juuroku.
**sixteenth** dai juuroku, juurokunichi *(of the
  month)*.
**sixth** dai roku; muika *(the sixth of the
  month)*.
**sixtieth** dai rokujuu.
**sixty** rokujuu.
**size** ookisa, saizu *(dimension)*; sunpoo
  *(measure)*.
**skate (to)** sukeeto o suru.
**skates** sukeeto.
**skeleton** gaikotsu.
**skeptic** *n.* utagai bukai hito.
**sketch** suketchi *(rough drawing)*; shitagaki

*(rough draft)*; gaiyoo *(outline)*; shasei *(from nature)*.

**ski, (skiing)** sukii.
   **a pair of skis** sukii hitokumi.

**skill** gijutsu.

**skillful** joozu na.

**skin** hifu *(human, animal)*; kawa *(of animals or fruit)*.

**skirt** sukaato *(Western dress)*; suso, hakama *(Japanese kimono)*.

**skull** zugaikotsu.

**sky** sora.
   **blue sky** aozora.

**slander (to)** waruku iu; chuushoo suru.

**slap** hirate uchi.
   **to slap (someone's) face** kao o hirate de utsu.

**slate** *n.* sekiban.

**slaughter** tosatsu *(butchering)*; gyakusatsu *(massacre)*.

**slave** dorei.

**slavery** dorei seido.

**sled** sori.

**sleep** nemuri.

**sleep (to)** nemuru *(slumber)*; yasumu *(rest, doze)*; neru.

**sleeve** sode.

**slender** hossori shita *(slim, opp. of stout)*; kabosoi *(slight)*; yowai *(weak, feeble)*; hinjaku na *(meager)*.

**slice** kire.

**slice (to)** usuku kiru.

**slide (to)** suberu.

**slight** kyasha na *(slender)*; karui *(not severe)*; sukoshi no *(small, not great)*.

**slight (to)** keibetsu suru.

**slip** surippu *(article of woman's clothing)*.

**slip (to)** subette korobu *(trip)*; tsumazuku *(stumble)*; fumihazusu *(miss one's footing)*.

**slipper** surippa.

**slippery** suberiyasui, tsuru tsuru shita.

**slope** keisha *(slant)*; koobai *(incline)*; saka *(hill)*; shamen *(inclined plane)*; keisachi *(sloping ground)*.

**slot** hosonagai ana.

**slovenly** bushoo na.

**slow** osoi.

**slow (to be)** okureru *(fall behind)*.

**slowly** yukkuri.

**slowness** osoi koto.

**slumber** karui nemuri, madoromi.

**slumber (to)** *v.i.* utouto suru *(sleep lightly)*; nemuru *(sleep)*; utatane suru *(doze)*; inemuri suru *(drowse)*.

**sly** zurui.

**small** chiisai *(not big)*; hosoi *(slender)*.

**smart** kashikoi *(clever)*; haikara na, sumaato na *(elegant in dress)*.

**smash (to)** kowasu.

**to be smashed** kowareru.

**smear (to)** nasuritsukeru.

**smell** nioi *(odor)*; kaori *(scent)*; akushuu *(stink)*.

**smell (to)** kagu *(get the odor of, exercise the sense of smell)*; nioi ga suru *(emit an odor)*; warui nioi ga aru *(be rank)*; hijoo ni kusai *(stink)*.

**smile** bishoo, hohoemi.

**smile (to)** niko niko suru, hohoemu.

**smoke** kemuri.

**smoke (to)** kemuri o haku *(emit smoke)*; tabako o suu *(cigarettes)*.

**smooth** sube sube shita *(not rough)*; taira na *(level, even)*; odayaka na *(not ruffled)*; dekoboko no nai *(not jagged)*.

**smooth (to)** nobasu, nadaraka ni suru.

**smother** chissoku saseru *(suffocate)*; akubi o kamikorosu *(a yawn)*; kanjoo o osaeru *(an emotion)*; kakusu *(conceal)*; momikesu *(stifle)*.

**smuggle (to)** mitsuyunyuu suru.

**snake** hebi.

**snapshot** sunappu shashin.

**snatch (to)** hittakuru *(grab)*; nusumu *(steal)*.

**sneer (to)** reishoo suru.

**sneeze (to)** kushami o suru.

**snore (to)** ibiki o kaku.

**snow** yuki.
   **snowfall** yukifuri.

**snow (to)** yuki ga furu.

**snowstorm** fubuki.

**so (thus)** desu kara.
   **and so on** -nado, -too.
   **It is so.** Soo desu.
   **I think so.** Soo omoimasu.

**soak (to)** shimitooru *(permeate)*; nurasu *(drench)*.

**soap** sekken.

**sob** susuri naki.

**sob (to)** susuri naku.

**sober** yotte inai *(not intoxicated)*; majime na *(serious)*.

**sociable** shakooteki na *(fond of company)*; koosai joozu na *(companionable)*.

**social** shakai no, shakaiteki na.

**society** shakai *(community)*; jooryuu shakai *(upper class)*; tsukiai *(companionship)*; dooseki *(company)*; kai *(association)*.

**sock(s)** kutsushita *(Western)*; tabi *(Japanese)*.

**socket** soketto *(electric)*.

**soft** yawarakai *(not hard)*; yasashii *(not harsh)*.

**soften (to)** yawarakaku suru *(as an object)*; yawarageru *(in feeling)*.

**soil** tsuchi *(earth)*; tochi *(ground)*.

**soil (to)** yogosu.

**soldier** heitai.

**sole** *adj.* tatta hitori no *(one and only; pertaining to persons);* tatta hitotsu no *(pertaining to inanimate things);* tandoku no *(exclusive to one);* dokutoku no *(unique).* *-n.* soko *(of a shoe);* ashi no ura *(of the foot).*

**solemn** genshuku na.

**solemnity** genshuku, soogon.

**solicit** segamu *(ask earnestly of);* kongan suru *(importune);* konsei suru *(entreat).*

**solid** joobu na *(strong);* katai *(hard).*

**solitary** hitori de kurasu *(living alone);* tsure nashi no *(without companions);* sabishii *(lonely);* hitodoori no mare na *(unfrequented).*

**solitude** kodoku *(being alone);* sabishisa *(loneliness).*

**soluble** tokeru.

**solution** kaishaku *(a solving);* setsumei *(explanation);* kaiketsu *(settlement).*

**solve (to)** kaiketsu suru *(clear up);* setsumei suru *(explain);* kaitoo suru *(find an answer);* toku *(a problem).*

**some** *(often omitted in Japanese)* ikuraka no *(an indefinite quantity);* sukoshi *(a little, a few);* ni-san *(two or three).*

    **Give me some water, please.** Mizu o kudasai.

**somebody** donata ka *(honorific: respect);* dare ka.

**somehow** doo ni ka *(in some way or other);* nan to ka shite *(in one way or another);* doomo *(for some reason or other).*

**someone** donata ka *(honorific: respect);* dare ka.

**something** nani ka.

**sometime** itsuka *(at an indefinite time);* sono uchi ni *(at a time hereafter);* shibaraku *(for a certain period).*

**sometimes** toki ni wa *(at times);* toki doki *(occasionally);* tama ni *(now and then).*

**somewhat** ikuraka *(in some measure);* sukoshi *(a little);* ikubun *(to some extent).*

**somewhere** doko ka ni, doko ka de *(in or at someplace);* doko ka e *(to someplace);* aru tokoro *(a certain place).*

**son** musuko.

**song** uta.

    **popular song** ryuukooka.

**soon** sugu.

**soot** susu.

**soothe (to)** nadameru *(calm down);* nagusameru *(comfort);* shizumeru *(assuage).*

**sore** *adj.* tadareta *(inflamed);* itamu *(painful to the touch).* *-n.* odeki *(boil);* tadare *(a festering).*

**sorrow** kanashimi, nageki.

**sorry (be)** kinodoku ni omou.

    **Excuse me.** Okinodoku desu *(I am sorry for you).*

    **I am sorry** Sumimasen. Gomen nasai.

**sort** shurui *(kind, class);* hinshitsu *(character, nature).*

**sort out (to)** yoriwakeru.

**soul** tamashii.

**sound** *adj.* kenkoo na, kenzen na *(of healthy mind);* itande inai *(undamaged);* tashika na *(reliable);* ronriteki na *(logical).* *-n.* oto *(that which is heard);* hibiki *(reverberation).*

**sound (to)** fuku *(a wind instrument);* narasu *(other musical instruments);* aizu suru *(give a signal);* oto o saseru *(make a sound).*

**soup** suupu *(Western style);* suimono *(Japanese).*

**sour** suppai.

**source** moto *(origin);* minamoto *(of a river).*

**south** minami.

**southeast** toonan.

    **Southeast Asia** Toonan Ajia.

**southern** minami no.

**southwest** nansei.

**sovereign** kunshu.

**sow (to)** maku *(scatter);* makichirasu *(disseminate);* hiromeru *(propagate).*

**space** aita basho *(room);* supeesu; tokoro *(place);* kankaku *(interval);* kyori *(distance).*

**space (to)** kankaku o oku.

**spacecraft** uchuusen.

**spacious** hirobiro to shita *(vast, broad);* ookii *(large).*

**spade** suki.

**spare** *adj.* yobi no *(held in reserve);* yobun no *(superfluous);* fuyoo no *(not required);* hinjaku na *(scanty);* kiritsumeta *(stinted).* *-n.* yobi *(reserve).*

**spare (to)** oshimu *(use grudgingly);* ken'yaku suru *(economize);* yurusu *(forbear);* sashi hikaeru *(refrain from);* tebanasu *(release).*

**spark** hi no ko, hibana *(of fire);* kirameki *(gleam);* kakki *(animating principle).*

**sparkle (to)** kagayaku.

**sparrow** suzume.

**speak (to)** hanasu *(narrate);* iu *(mention).*

**speaker** hanashite, enzetsusha *(one who delivers a speech);* kooensha, kooshi *(lecturer);* supiikaa *(radio loudspeaker).*

**special** tokubetsu no *(of a particular kind);* sen'yoo no *(private);* tokutei no *(definite);* namihazure no *(extraordinary);* tokushu no *(particular).*

**specialty** tokusanhin *(special product);* meisan *(famous product);* tokushoku *(special feature).*

**specific** tokushu na, tokutei na.

**specify (to)** shitei suru.

**spectacle** kookei *(sight)*; sookan *(noteworthy scene)*; misemono *(public show)*.

**spectator** kenbutsunin *(onlooker)*; bookansha *(bystander)*.

**speculate (to)** kangaeru *(consider)*; shisaku suru *(meditate)*; suisoku suru *(conjecture)*; tooshi suru *(invest)*.

**speech** hanashi *(talk)*; hanasu nooryoku *(faculty of speaking)*; kotoba *(language)*; enzetsu *(public address)*.

**speed** sokuryoku *(velocity)*; hayasa *(swiftness)*.

**speedy** sokuryoku no hayai.

**spell** majinai *(charm)*.

**spell (to)** tsuzuru.

**spelling** tsuzuri.

**spend (to)** tsukau *(pay out)*; kurasu *(time)*.

**sphere** tama *(globe)*; kyuumen *(spherical surface)*; tentai *(heavenly body)*.

**spice** yakumi *(condiment)*; kaori *(fragrance)*; kooryoo *(aromatic vegetable flavoring)*.

**spider** kumo.

**spill (to)** kobosu.

   **to get spilled** koboreru.

**spin (to)** tsumugu *(yarn)*; kakeru *(a web)*; mawasu *(a top)*; mayu o tsukuru *(silk; by a silkworm)*.

**spirit** tamashii *(as distinct from matter)*; seishin *(disposition of mind)*; kakki *(vigor)*; netsui *(ardor)*.

**spiritual** seishinteki na *(concerned with things of the mind or soul)*; kami no *(divine)*; shinsei na *(sacred)*; shuukyoojoo no *(religious)*.

**spit (to)** tsuba o haku.

**spite** ijiwaru *(malice)*; urami *(grudge)*.

   **in spite of** -ni mo kakawarazu.

**spite (to)** ijiwaru o suru.

**spiteful** ijiwarui.

**splash (to)** hanekakeru, haneageru.

**splendid** rippa na *(imposing)*; subarashii *(magnificent)*; migoto na *(admirable)*.

**splendor** kagayaki, migoto.

**split (to)** *v.t.* saku *(crack)*; waru *(divide)*; sogu *(cleave)*; *v.i.* wareru.

**spoil (to)** itameru *(damage)*; dame ni suru *(render useless by injury)*; waruku suru *(make bad)*.

**sponge** *n.* kaimen, suponji.

**spontaneous** shizen no *(natural)*; jihatsuteki no *(voluntary)*; jidooteki na *(self-acting)*.

**spoon** saji.

**spoonful** saji ippai no.

**sport** undoo, supootsu *(recreation)*; tanoshimi *(pastime)*; joodan *(jest)*.

**spot** tokoro *(place)*; ten *(speck)*; shimi *(stain)*.

**spread (to)** *v.t.* hirogeru *(in length and breadth)*; nuru *(butter)*; hiromaru *(news)*; *v.i.* hirogaru *(to be disseminated)*.

**spring** haru *(season)*; bane *(of machinery)*; onsen *(of hot water)*; izumi *(of cold water)*.

**spring (to)** tobu *(leap)*; shoojiru *(proceed, originate)*.

**sprinkle (to)** maku *(with water)*; furikakeru *(with powder, etc.)*.

**sprout (to)** me o fuku *(put forth shoots)*; haete kuru *(spring up)*.

**spry** subashikoi.

**spur (to)** hakusha o kakeru *(a horse)*.

**spurn (to)** hanetsukeru.

**spy** supai, kanchoo.

**spy (to)** saguru.

**squadron** kantai.

**squander (to)** mudazukai suru.

**square** seihookei *(geom.)*; hiroba *(in a town)*.

**squeeze (to)** hasamu *(between two things)*; nigiri shimeru *(in one's hand)*; shiboru *(press out liquids)*.

**squirrel** risu.

**stable** *n.* umagoya. *-adj.* shikkari shita *(firm)*; antei shita *(steady)*; kyooko na *(steadfast)*.

**stack** shoka *(library)*.

**stack (to)** tsumi kasaneru.

**stadium** kyoogijoo, sutajiamu.

**staff** sao *(pole)*; boo *(rod)*; shokuin *(of a business)*.

**staff (to)** shokuin o soroeru.

**stage** butai, suteeji *(theatrical)*; endan *(elevated platform)*.

**stain** shimi, yogore.

**stain (to)** *v.t.* yogosu; *v.i.* yogoreru *(get stained)*.

**stair(s)** dan, kaidan.

**stammer (to)** domoru.

**stamp** kitte *(postage stamp)*; han *(rubber stamp, etc.)*; keshiin *(postmark)*.

**stamp (to)** sutanpu o osu.

**stand** dai *(to set things on)*; hankoo *(resistance)*; boogyo *(defense)*; uriba *(booth)*.

**stand (to)** tatsu *(get up)*; tachitsuzukeru *(remain standing)*; tatte iru *(be in a standing position)*; oite aru *(be placed; speaking of an inanimate thing)*; aru *(be located)*; tachiagaru *(stand up)*; tateru *(erect)*.

**star** hoshi *(celestial)*; sutaa, hanagata *(theatrical)*.

**stare (to)** -o mitsumeru.

**start** hajime *(beginning)*; shuppatsuten *(starting point)*; odoroki *(shock)*.

**start (to)** *v.t.* hajimeru *(begin)*; *v.i.* hajimaru *(begin)*; shuppatsu suru *(depart)*; deru *(of trains, etc.)*.

**starve (to)** ueru.

**state** kokka *(political body)*; jootai *(condition)*.

**state (to)** iu *(say)*; hanasu *(tell)*; noberu *(express in speech)*; chinjutsu suru *(express in writing)*.

**stately** doodoo to shita.

**statement** seimei.

**station** eki.

**statistic** tookei.

**statue** zoo.

    **bronze statue** doozoo.

**statute** kisoku *(rule, regulation)*.

**stay** taizai.

**stay (to)** *v.t.* tomaru *(stop)*; *v.i.* okuraseru *(delay)*.

**steady** shikkari shita.

**steak** bifuteki.

**steal** nusumu.

**steam** jooki, suchiimu.

**steam (to)** musu.

**steamer** kisen *(steamship)*.

**steel** hagane, kootetsu.

**steep** *adj.* kyuu na, kewashii *(precipitous)*; kyuukoobai no *(high-pitched)*.

**steer (to)** kaji o toru.

**stem** kuki.

**stenographer** sokkisha.

**stenography** sokki.

**step** dan *(of a staircase)*; ashi oto *(sound of a footstep)*; ashi ato *(footprint)*; dankai *(successive stage)*.

**step (to)** aruku *(walk)*; fumu *(tread on)*.

**sterile** ko o umanai *(barren)*; fumoo no *(not fertile)*; minori no nai *(unproductive)*.

**stern** *adj.* genkaku na *(severe)*; kakoku na *(harsh)*.

**stew** shichuu.

**stew (to)** torobi de niru.

**stick** boo.

**stick (to)** sasu *(pierce)*; tsuku *(adhere)*.

**stiff** kowabatta *(rigid)*; katai *(hard)*; ugokanai *(not moving freely)*.

**stiffen (to)** kowabaru.

**still** *adj.* shizuka na *(quiet)*. *-adv.* mada *(more)*; yahari *(after all)*; sore demo *(nevertheless)*; ima made *(yet)*.

    **Keep still!** Jitto shite! Ugokanaide!

**stimulate (to)** shigeki suru.

**stimulus** shigeki.

**sting** hari *(of an animal)*; toge *(of a plant)*.

**sting (to)** sasu, piri piri suru.

**stinginess** kechi.

**stingy** kechi na.

**stir (to)** ugokasu *(move, shake)*; kakimawasu *(liquids)*.

**stitch (to)** nuu *(sew)*; kagaru *(darn)*.

**stock** zaikohin *(goods)*; shihon *(capital)*; kabuken *(shares)*.

**stock (to)** takuwaeru.

**stock exchange** kabushiki torihikisho.

**stocking** kutsushita.

**stomach** i, onaka.

**stone** ishi.

**stool** koshikake.

**stop** teiryuujo *(stopping place for buses, etc.)*; shuushi *(end)*.

**stop (to)** yameru *(discontinue)*; tomeru *(cause to cease)*; teishi suru *(suspend)*; jama suru *(interrupt)*; yokusei suru *(restrain)*; soshi suru *(prevent)*; owaraseru *(put an end to)*; fusagu *(block)*; tomaru *(come to rest)*.

**store** mise.

    **department store** depaato.

**stork** koonotori.

**storm** arashi.

**story** hanashi *(speech)*; uwasa *(gossip)*; monogatari *(tale)*; itsuwa *(anecdote)*; densetsu *(legend)*.

**stove** sutoobu.

**straight** massugu na *(opp. of crooked)*; itchokusen no *(in a straight line)*.

**straighten (to)** massugu ni suru.

**strain** kinchoo *(tension)*; hijoo na doryoku *(excessive effort)*; karoo *(overexertion)*.

**strain (to)** muri o suru.

**strange** mezurashii *(rare)*; fushigi na *(wondrous)*; kimyoo na *(odd)*.

**stranger** shiranai hito *(unknown person)*; yoso no hito *(outsider)*.

**strap** himo.

**straw** wara.

**strawberry** ichigo.

**stream** nagare *(current)*; ogawa *(small river)*.

**stream (to)** nagareru.

**street** machi *(with houses, etc.)*; michi *(road, way)*.

**strength** tsuyosa *(vigor)*; tairyoku *(bodily)*.

**strengthen (to)** tsuyoku suru *(make stronger)*; zookyoo suru *(reinforce)*; tsuyoku naru *(become stronger)*.

**strenuous** hone no oreru.

**stress** kyoochoo *(emphasis)*; appaku *(pressure)*; kinpaku *(strain)*.

**stress (to)** kyoochoo suru.

**stretch (to)** nobasu *(extend in length)*; hirogeru *(extend in breadth)*; dasu *(reach out)*; nobiru *(lengthen)*.

**strict** kibishii.

**stride** kappo.

**stride (to)** kappo suru.

**strife** arasoi *(conflict)*.

**strike** sutoraiki, higyoo, suto *(work)*; storaiku *(baseball)*.

**strike (to)** butsu *(beat)*; tataku *(rap, knock)*; shoototsu suru *(collide)*; sutoraiki o suru, higyoo suru *(quit work)*; kokoro o utsu *(impress)*.

**string** himo.

**strip (to)** hadaka ni suru *(lay bare)*; toriharau *(divest)*; kimono o nugu *(undress)*.

**stripe** shima.

**strive (to)** honeoru *(try hard)*; doryoku suru *(endeavor)*; funtoo suru *(struggle vigorously)*.

**stroke** dageki *(blow)*; suji *(line)*; kaku *(of a Japanese character)*.

**stroll** sanpo.

**stroll (to)** sanpo suru.

**strong** tsuyoi *(having strength)*; joobu na *(not easily broken)*; kenkoo na *(healthy)*; daijoobu na *(reliable)*.

**structure** koosei *(construction)*; kumitate *(framework)*; kenchiku *(building)*; soshiki *(organization)*.

**struggle** kumiuchi *(body to body)*; arasoi *(strife)*; honeori *(violent effort)*.

**struggle (to)** doryoku suru *(make great efforts)*; mogaku *(writhe)*; tatakau *(fight)*; arasou *(contend)*.

**stubborn** ganko na *(hardheaded)*; goojoo na *(obstinate)*; shibutoi *(perverse)*; te ni oenai *(intractable)*; fukutsu no *(unyielding)*.

**student** seito, gakusei.

**studious** yoku benkyoo suru *(assiduous in study)*; gakumonzuki no *(given to study)*; nesshin na *(zealous)*.

**study** benkyoo *(application of the mind)*; kenkyuu *(research, investigation, etc.)*.

**study (to)** benkyoo suru, narau *(learn)*.

**stuff** shina *(material, goods)*; mono *(substance, matter)*; garakuta *(rubbish)*; tawagoto *(nonsense)*.

**stuff (to)** tsumekomu *(fill with something)*; tsumemono o suru *(cooking)*.

**stumble (to)** tsumazuku *(trip up)*; yoromeku *(miss one's footing)*; yoro yoro aruku *(walk unsteadily)*.

**stump** kirikabu.

**stun (to)** me o mawasaseru.

**stunt** kyokugei *(tricks)*.

**stupendous** tohoo mo nai.

**stupid** oroka na, baka na.

**stupidity** baka sa, oroka sa.

**stupor** mahi.

**sturdy** shikkari shita.

**stutter (to)** domoru.

**style** ryuukoo, sutairu *(mode of fashion)*; hanashiburi *(mode of speaking)*.

**subdue (to)** seifuku suru *(conquer)*; uchikatsu *(overcome)*; iatsu suru *(render submissive)*; yokusei suru *(repress)*.

**subject** shinmin *(of a country)*; mondai *(theme of discussion)*; gakka *(of study)*.

**subject (to)** shitagaeru *(subdue)*.

**subjective** shukanteki.

**subjugate (to)** seifuku suru *(subdue)*.

**sublime** suukoo na.

**submission** fukujuu *(subjection)*; koofuku *(surrender)*.

**submissive** juujun na.

**submit (to)** teishutsu suru *(turn in)*; shitagawaseru *(yield)*.

**subordinate** buka, haika.

**subordinate (to)** shita ni oku.

**subscribe (to)** yoyaku suru *(to newspapers, etc.)*; sansei suru *(give assent)*.

**subscription** yoyaku.

**subside (to)** shizumaru *(become tranquil)*; hekomu *(dent)*.

**subsidy** hojokin *(grant of money)*.

**subsist (to)** kurashite iku.

**substance** honshitsu, hontai.

**substantial** jitsuzai suru *(actual)*; hontoo no *(real)*; oohaba no *(major)*.

**substantiate (to)** shoomei suru.

**substitute** kawari *(a person)*; daiyoohin *(a thing representing another)*.

**substitute (to)** dairi suru *(person)*; daiyoo suru *(thing)*.

**substitution** daiyoo.

**subtle** bimyoo na.

**subtract (to)** hiku *(take out or away)*.

**subtraction** hikizan.

**suburb** koogai.

**succeed (to)** ato o tsugu *(be a successor to)*; seikoo suru *(effect one's purpose)*.

**success** seikoo *(favorable termination)*; kooun *(good fortune)*.

**successful** seikoo shita.

**succession** renzoku *(sequence)*; keishoo *(to a position, throne, etc.)*.

**successor** soozokusha.

**such** konna *(like this, of this sort)*; sonna *(like that, of that sort)*.

**sudden** kyuu na.

**suddenly** kyuu ni *(abruptly)*; fui ni *(unexpectedly)*.

**sue (to)** soshoo o okosu *(take legal action)*; uttaeru *(bring suit)*.

**suffer (to)** kurushimu *(be in pain)*; gaman suru *(endure patiently)*; songai o koomuru *(a loss)*.

**suffering** kurushimi *(pain)*; songai *(loss)*.

**sufficient** takusan no *(plenty)*; juubun na *(enough)*.

**sugar** satoo, osatoo.

**suggest (to)** omoidasaseru *(hint)*; iidasu *(propose)*.

**suggestion** kangae; anji, hinto *(hint)*; teigi *(proposal)*.

**suicide** jisatsu.

    **to commit suicide** jisatsu suru.

**suit** yoofuku, suutsu *(of clothes);* kokuso *(legal proceedings).*

**suit (to)** niau *(fit);* tsugoo ga ii *(be convenient).*

**suitable** choodo ii *(fitting, proper);* niau *(becoming).*

**sulk (to)** mutto suru *(be offended);* suneru *(pout).*

**sullen** fukigen na *(in a bad mood);* inki na *(gloomy).*

**sum** gaku *(quantity);* gookei *(total amount);* kingaku *(amount of money).*

**summary** tekiyoo sho *(brief account);* gaiyoo *(synopsis).*

**summer** natsu.

**summit** choojoo *(top).*

**summon (to)** shookan suru.

**summons** shookanjoo.

**sumptuous** zeitaku na.

**sum up (to)** gaikatsu suru.

**sun** hi, taiyoo.
    **rising sun** asahi.
    **setting sun** yuuhi.

**sunbeam** nikkoo.

**sunburn** hiyake.

**Sunday** Nichiyoobi.

**sundry** iroiro no.
    **sundry expenses** zappi.
    **sundry goods** zakka.

**sunny** urarakana.

**sunrise** hi no de.

**sunset** hi no iri.

**sunshine** hinata.

**superb** subarashii.

**superconductor** choo dendoo tai.

**superficial** uwabe dake no *(outward);* senpaku na *(shallow; said of persons).*

**superfluous** yokei na.

**superintendent** kantoku *(supervisor);* kanrisha *(manager);* koochoo *(of school).*

**superior** sugureta *(better);* jootoo no *(of great excellence);* yuusei na *(larger);* kookyuu no *(of higher rank).*
    **to be superior** sugurete iru.

**superiority** yuushuu.

**superstition** meishin.

**supervise (to)** kantoku suru.

**supper** yuuhan.

**supplement** bessatsu *(of a book);* furoku *(of a magazine).*

**supplement (to)** oginau.

**supplementary** furoku no.

**supply** kyookyuu *(process of supplying);* kyookyuuhin *(thing supplied).*

**supply (to)** kyookyuu suru.

**support** sasaemono *(prop);* shiji *(moral support);* fuyoo *(maintenance).*

**support (to)** shiji suru *(hold up);* motaseru *(maintain);* genkizukeru *(encourage);* tasukeru *(assist).*

**suppose (to)** soozoo suru *(imagine);* omou *(think);* katei suru *(assume tentatively);* suitei suru *(presume).*

**suppress** shizumeru *(subdue);* kinshi suru *(stop);* osaeru *(restrain);* kamikorosu *(smother).*

**supreme** saikoo no.

**sure** tashika na *(certain);* ate ni naru *(reliable);* hontoo no *(true);* joobu na *(stable).*

**surely** tashika ni.

**surety** tanpo *(pledge);* hoshoonin *(sponsor).*

**surf** yose nami *(on the shore);* uchinami *(on rocks).*

**surface** hyoomen.

**surgeon** gekai.

**surgery** geka *(treatment);* shujutsu *(operation).*

**surmount (to)** noboru *(climb);* uchikatsu *(overcome).*

**surname** myooji.

**surpass (to)** sugureru *(be better than);* shinogu *(outdo);* sugiru *(exceed);* amaru *(be beyond).*

**surplus** yojoo *(the remainder);* amari *(the rest).*

**surprise** odoroki *(amazement);* omoigakenai koto *(something unexpected).*

**surprise (to)** bikkuri saseru *(strike with wonder);* odorokasu *(cause surprise);* fui uchi suru *(take unawares).*

**surrender** hikiwatashi *(of a thing);* koosan *(of a person);* koofuku *(of an army).*

**surrender (to)** tewatasu *(hand over);* hooki suru *(give up something);* koofuku suru *(submit).*

**surround (to)** torimaku.

**surroundings** kankyoo.

**survey** sokuryoo *(land measurement);* kenchi *(land surveying);* tsuuran *(comprehensive view).*

**survey (to)** miwatasu *(look over);* ippanteki ni miru *(take a general view);* kenbun suru *(inspect);* choosa suru *(examine).*

**survive (to)** ikinokoru *(pertaining to people);* nokoru *(pertaining to other cases).*

**susceptibility** kanjusei.

**susceptible** takan na, kanjooteki na.

**suspect** utagawashii hito *(suspected person).*

**suspect (to)** kanzuku *(have an inkling);* -de wa nai ka to omou *(half-believe);* soozoo suru *(surmise);* utagau *(doubt).*

**suspense** fuan *(feeling of);* mitei.

**suspension** chuuburarin.

**suspicion** kengi *(distrust);* utagai *(doubt).*

**suspicious** utagai bukai *(distrustful)*; ayashii *(doubtful)*.

**sustain (to)** sasaeru.

**swallow** tsubame *(bird)*.

**swallow (to)** nomikomu.

**swamp** numa.

**swan** hakuchoo, suwan.

**sway (to)** yureru.

**swear (to)** chikau *(take an oath)*; akutai o tsuku *(curse)*.

**sweat** ase.

**sweat (to)** ase ga deru.

**sweep (to)** haku *(with a broom)*; sooji suru *(clean up)*.

**sweet** amai *(of taste)*; kawairashii *(of face)*; yasashii *(of disposition)*.

**sweetness** airashisa *(of person)*; amasa *(of food)*.

**swell (to)** fukureru *(bulge out)*; hareru *(become swollen)*; ookiku naru *(expand)*.

**swift** hayai.

**swim (to)** oyogu.

**swindler** sagishi.

**swing (to)** yureru, bura-bura ugoku *(as a pendulum)*; fureru *(use as a swing)*.

**switch** *n.* suitchi *(electric)*
   **to switch on** suitchi o ireru.
   **to switch off** suitchi o kiru.

**sword** katana.

**syllable** onsetsu.

**symbol** shoochoo *(emblem)*; fugoo *(mark, sign)*.

**symbolic** shoochooteki.

**symbolize (to)** shoochoo suru *(be a symbol of)*; fugoo de arawasu *(represent by symbols)*.

**symmetrical** tsuriai no toreta.

**symmetry** tsuriai, kinsei.

**sympathetic** omoiyari no aru *(compassionate)*; ki no atta *(congenial)*.

**sympathize (to)** ki no doku ni omou *(feel sympathy)*; sansei suru *(agree with)*; nagusameru *(condole)*.

**sympathy** doojoo.

**symptom** chookoo.

**syrup** shiroppu.

**system** shoshiki *(organization)*; hoohoo *(method)*; chitsujo *(order)*.

# T

**table** teeburu *(European)*; chabudai *(Japanese low table)*.

**tablecloth** teeburukurosu, teeburukake.

**tablespoon** teeburu supuun; oosaji.

**tacit** anmoku no.

**tacitly** soreto naku, anmoku ni.

**taciturn** mukuchi na.

**tack (to)** byoo de tomeru.

**tact** josai nasa, kiten.

**tactfully** josai naku, umaku.

**tag** fuda.

**tail** o, shippo.

**tailor** yoofukuya *(for Western clothes)*; shitateya *(for Japanese clothes)*.

**take (to)** toru *(get, lay hold of)*; motte iku *(carry or take to)*; tsukamu *(grasp)*; uketoru *(receive)*; tsurete iku *(take to, lead to)*.

**tale** hanashi; monogatari *(old story)*.

**talent** sainoo *(special faculty)*; shuwan *(natural ability)*.

**talk** hanashi; oshaberi *(chattering)*; danwa *(conversation)*.

**talk (to)** hanasu.

**talkative** oshaberi na.

**tall** takai.
   **She is tall.** Se ga takai desu.

**tame** nareta *(domesticated)*; sunao na *(docile)*; juujun na *(submissive)*; mukiryoku na *(dull)*.

**tangerine** mikan.

**tangle (to)** motsuresaseru *(entangle)*; karamaseru *(confuse)*.

**tank** suisoo, tanku *(for water, etc.)*; tanku, sensha *(vehicle of war)*.

**tape** teepu.
   **tape recorder** teepu rekoodaa.
   **videotape** bideo teepu.

**tar** koorutaaru.

**tardy** guzuguzu shita, jikan ni okureru.

**target** mato.

**tarnish** henshoku.
   **to be tarnished** kumotte iru.

**tarry (to)** nagai suru.

**task** shigoto *(piece of work)*; hone no oreru shigoto *(toil)*; tsutome *(duty)*.

**taste** aji *(of food)*; shumi *(for art)*.

**taste (to)** aji o miru.

**tax** zei, zeikin.
   **export tax** yushutsu hin zei.
   **import tax** yunyuu hin zei.
   **sales tax** uriage zei.
   **tax allowance** zei koojo.
   **taxation** kazei.
   **tax base** kazei hyoojun.
   **tax deduction** zei koojo.
   **tax evasion** datsu zei.
   **tax-free income** hibazei shotoku.
   **tax shelter** zeikin hinan shudan.

**taxi** takushii.

**tea** ocha *(Japanese)*; koocha *(black tea)*.

**teach** oshieru *(give instruction)*; shitsukeru *(train)*.

**teacher** sensei.

**team** chiimu.

**tear** namida *(teardrop);* kagizaki *(a rip in clothing).*

**tear (to)** yaburu *(rip);* mushiri toru *(pull violently away);* yabureru *(become torn);* hagasu *(tear off).*

**tease (to)** nayamasu *(annoy);* ijimeru *(torment).*

**teaspoon** chasaji.

**technical** gijutsuteki no.

**technique** gijutsu, tekunikku.

**tedious** kudoi, nagatarashii.

**telecommunications** denki tsuushin.

**telegram** denpoo.

**telegraph** denshin.

**telegraph (to)** denpoo o utsu.

**telephone** denwa.
    **car phone** jidoosha denwa.
    **cordless phone** koodoresu hon.

**telephone (to)** denwa o kakeru.

**telex** terekkusu.

**tell (to)** hanasu *(relate);* iu *(say);* oshieru *(instruct).*

**temper** umare tsuki *(disposition);* seishitsu *(temperament);* kidate *(personality);* kigen *(mood).*

**temperance** sessei, kinshu *(moderation).*

**temperate** odayaka na *(mild);* tekido no *(moderate).*

**temperature** ondo *(of the air);* taion *(of the body).*

**tempest** ooarashi.

**temple** miya, omiya *(Shinto);* tera, otera *(Buddhist);* komekami *(of the forehead).*

**temporary** hakanai *(transient);* kari no.

**tempt (to)** yuuwaku suru *(seduce);* sosoru *(incite);* izanau *(induce);* unagasu *(persuade).*

**temptation** yuuwaku *(seduction);* tameshi *(trial).*

**ten** too, juu.
    **ten days** tooka.
    **ten o'clock** juuji.

**tenacious** shinboozuyoi *(unyielding);* nebarizuyoi *(tough).*

**tenacity** kyoojin-sei, gankyoo.

**tenant** shakuyanin *(of a house);* shakuchinin *(of land).*

**tend (to)** mukau *(be directed toward);* keikoo ga aru *(have a tendency);* kooken suru *(serve);* ki o tsukeru *(attend to);* kaihoo suru *(watch over).*

**tendency** keikoo *(trend);* seiheki *(inclination);* fuuchoo *(drift).*

**tender** *adj.* yawarakai.

**tennis** tenisu, teikyuu.

**tense** katakurushii *(stiff);* jisei *(grammar).*
    **future tense** mirai.
    **past tense** kako.
    **present tense** genzai.

**tension** kinchoo.

**tent** tento.

**tenth** dai juu, juu banme, juu ban.
    **tenth of the month** tooka.

**tepid** nurui.

**term** kigen *(limited period);* jooken *(condition);* gakki *(of school).*

**terrace** takadai *(raised ground);* terasu *(of a house).*

**terrible** osoroshii *(dreadful);* hidoi *(awful);* hisan na *(wretched).*

**terrify (to)** odorokasu.
    **be terrified at** -ni odoroku.

**territory** ryoodo *(as a colony);* ryoochi *(possession of a state or individual).*

**terror** kyoofu.

**test** tameshi *(experiment);* shiken *(probe);* shikinseki *(touchstone).*

**test (to)** kensa suru.

**testify (to)** shoogen suru *(give evidence);* shookodateru *(attest).*

**testimony** shoomei *(law);* shooko *(evidence).*

**text** shudai; tekisuto *(of a document).*

**textbook** kyookasho.

**than** yori, yorimo.
    **less than** ika.
    **more than** ijoo.

**thank (to)** rei o iu.
    **Thank you.** Arigatoo.
    **Thank you very much.** Doomo arigatoo gozaimasu.

**thanks** kansha *(gratitude).*

**that** *adj.* sono, ano. *-pron.* sore, are.
    **that person** ano hito.
    **That's it!** Soo da!

**thaw** yukidoke.

**theater** gekijoo.

**their, theirs** karerano, ano katagata no, ano katatachi no, ano hitotachi no.

**theme** daimoku, shudai *(subject);* wadai *(topic).*

**themselves** ano katagata jishin.

**then** sono toki, sono toki ni *(at that time);* sore kara *(after that);* sore de *(at that point);* sono baai *(in that case).*

**theoretical** rironteki.

**theoretically** rironjoo.

**theory** gakuri *(scientific principle);* riron *(opp. of practice);* gakusetsu *(doctrine).*

**there** asoko, achira *(places outside of immediate reach);* soko, sochira *(places near the conversation partner).*

**thereafter** sore irai.

**therefore** sore desu kara.

**there is (are)** iru *(for animate beings);* aru *(for inanimate beings).*

**thereupon** sokode.

**thermometer** kandankei *(weather);* taionkei *(clinical).*

**these** kono, kore.

**thesis** ronbun.

**they** karera, ano katagata, ano katatachi, ano hitotachi *(pertaining to people);* are *(pertaining to things).*

**thick** atsui *(flat things);* futoi *(approximately cylindrical things);* koi *(liquids, hair, etc.).*

**thicken (to)** atsuku suru, koku suru.

**thickness** atsusa; kosa.

**thief** doroboo.

**thigh** momo.

**thimble** yubinuki.

**thin** usui *(flat things, liquids);* hosoi *(approximately cylindrical things);* yaseta *(persons).*

**thing** mono *(in concrete sense);* koto *(abstract).*

**think** kangaeru *(conceive);* omou *(suppose);* jukkoo suru *(ponder);* soozoo suru *(imagine);* shian suru *(meditate).*

**third** *n.* dai san, sanbanme. *-adj.* dai san no, sanbanme no.

   **third of the month** mikka.

**thirst** nodo no kawaki.

   **to quench one's thirst** nodo no kawaki o iyasu.

**thirsty (be)** nodo ga kawaite iru.

**thirteen** juusan.

**thirty** sanjuu.

**this** *adj.* kono. *-pron.* kore.

   **this one** kore.

**thorn** toge.

**thorough** kanzen na *(complete);* tetteiteki na *(utter);* mattaku no *(out and out).*

**though** ga *(but, however).*

   **Though it was raining . . .** Ame ga futte ita ga . . .

**thought** kangae, shisoo *(that which is thought);* shisaku *(cogitation);* shian *(meditation);* an *(idea).*

**thoughtful** shinsetsu na *(kind).*

**thoughtless** karuhazumi na *(careless);* fushinsetsu na *(inconsiderate).*

**thousand** sen.

   **ten thousand** man, ichiman.

   **three thousand** sanzen.

**thrash (to)** muchiutsu.

**thread** ito.

**thread (to)** ito o toosu.

   **thread a needle** hari ni ito o toosu.

**threat** kyoohaku.

**threaten (to)** kyoohaku suru.

**three** mittsu, san.

**threshold** iriguchi *(entrance);* shikii *(door sill).*

**thrift** ken'yaku.

**thrifty** ken'yaku na.

**thrill** suriru, senritsu.

**thrill (to)** kandoo suru; suriru o kanjiru.

**thrilling** wakuwaku saseru yoo na.

**thrive (to)** hanjoo suru.

**thriving** hanjoo shite iru.

**throat** nodo.

**throb (to)** dooki ga suru, doki doki suru.

**throne** gyokuza.

**throng** gunshuu.

**through** *prep.* -o tooshite *(by the medium of);* tsuranuite *(across);* -no naka ni *(in the midst of);* -juu *(during the whole period).* *-adv.* hajime kara owari made *(from beginning to end);* zutto *(all the way).*

**throughout** *prep.* -juu *(periods of time).* *-adv.* sukkari, doko mo ka mo *(everywhere).*

**throw (to)** nageru *(fling);* hooru *(hurl).*

**thumb** oyayubi.

**thunder (to)** kaminari ga naru.

**thunderbolt** kaminari.

**Thursday** Mokuyoobi.

**thus** kono yoo ni, koo iu fuu ni *(in this manner);* desu kara *(so, therefore);* shitagatte *(accordingly).*

**thwart (to)** jama suru.

**ticket** kippu, ken.

   **ticket of admission** nyuujooken.

   **ticket window** kippu uriba.

**tickle (to)** kusuguru.

**ticklish** kusuguttai.

**tide** shio, chooryuu.

**tidy** kichin to shita *(arranged in good order);* kogirei na *(neat).*

**tie** musubime *(knot);* tsunagari *(connection).*

**tie (to)** shibaru *(tie roughly);* yuwaeru *(tie up).*

   **tie a knot** musubu.

**tiger** tora.

**tight** katai *(close);* kataku musunda *(compact);* harikitta *(taut);* kitchiri atta *(close-fitting).*

**tile** kawara, tairu.

**till** made.

   **till now** ima made.

   **till then** sono toki made.

**tilt (to)** katamuku.

**timber** zaimoku.

**time** toki, jiki *(opportunity);* jikan *(hour);* kikan *(period);* jidai *(era).*

   **from time to time** tokidoki.

   **in time** ma ni au yoo ni.

   **time sharing** taimu shearingu.

   **time zone** jikan tai.

   **What time is it?** Nanji desu ka?

**timid** uchiki na.

**timidity** uchiki.

**tin** suzu.

   **tin can** kan, kanzume no kan.

**tinkle (to)** chirin chirin naru.

**tiny** chiisana.

**tip** saki *(end);* kokorozuke, chippu *(gratuity);* chadai *(gratuity given in Japanese inns).*

**tip over (to)** hikkurikaesu.

**tire** taiya *(for wheels)*.

**tire (to)** *v.t.* tsukaresaseru; *v.i.* tsukareru *(get tired)*.

**tired** tsukareta.

**tireless** tsukare o shiranai.

**tiresome** taikutsu na.

**title** dai, taitoru, daimoku; shomei *(of a book)*; katagaki *(rank)*; kengen *(business)*.

**to** e *(toward)*; made *(until, up to)*.
   **Tell him to come.** Kuru yoo ni itte kudasai.
   **I went to buy.** Kai ni ikimashita.
   **to him** sono hito ni.

**toad** hikigaeru.

**toast** toosuto *(bread)*; kanpai *(proposing a health)*.

**toast (to) (bread)** pan o yaku.

**tobacco** tabako.

**today** kyoo.

**toe** ashi no yubi.

**together** issho ni, minna de *(all together)*.

**toil** honeori.

**toil (to)** roodoo suru; kuroo suru.

**toilet** toire, otearai, benjo *(washroom)*.

**token** shirushi *(sign)*; kinenhin *(souvenir)*; katami *(keepsake)*.

**tolerable** gaman dekiru.

**tolerance** kandai.

**tolerant** kandai na.

**tolerate (to)** oome ni miru *(permit)*; gaman suru *(endure)*; kandai ni toriatsukau *(be broad-minded)*.

**toll** zeikin *(tax)*; tsuukooryoo *(passage money)*; shishoosha no kazu *(casualties)*.

**tomato** tomato.

**tomb** haka *(grave)*; nookotsujo *(vault)*.

**tomorrow** ashita, myoonichi.

**ton** ton.

**tone** oto; kuchoo *(of speech)*; iroai *(color)*.

**tongs** hibashi.

**tongue** shita.

**tonight** kon'ya.

**too** mo *(also)*; -sugiru *(excessively)*.
   **too expensive** takasugiru.

**tool** doogu.

**tooth** ha.

**toothache** haita.

**toothbrush** haburashi.

**toothpaste** hamigaki.

**toothpick** tsumayooji.

**tooth powder** hamigakiko.

**top** ue *(summit)*; koma *(toy)*.

**top (to)** ue ni naru.

**topic** topikku; shudai *(subject)*; wadai *(of conversation)*.

**torch** taimatsu.

**torment** kashaku *(torture)*.

**torment (to)** kurushimeru.

**torture** *n.* goomon *(for forced confession)*; kurushimi *(anguish)*.

**toss (to)** nageru.

**total** *adj.* sookei no *(entire)*; kanzen na *(complete)*. -*n.* gookei *(total amount)*.

**totally** kanzen ni.

**touch (to)** sawaru.

**touching** aware na.

**touchy** shinkei kabin na.

**tough** tsuyoi *(strong)*; ganjoo na *(robust)*; goojoo na *(stubborn)*; hidoi *(laborious)*; katai *(hard)*.

**tour** ryokoo, tabi *(travel)*; kankooryokoo *(pleasure trip)*.

**tour (to)** ryokoo suru.

**tourist** kankookyaku, yuuransha, tsuurisuto.
   **Tourist Agency** Ryokooannaijo.

**tournament** shiai.

**toward** -no hoo e *(direction)*; goro *(about: in point of time)*.

**towel** tenugui *(Japanese)*; taoru *(Western)*.

**tower** too.

**town** machi, tokai *(city)*.

**toy** omocha.

**trace** ato *(remains)*; keiseki *(vestige)*; kekka *(evidence)*.

**trace (to)** toosha suru *(through paper)*; tsuiseki suru *(track down)*.

**track** senro *(railroad)*.

**trade** shoobai *(domestic)*; booeki *(with foreign countries)*.
   **trade union** roodoo kumiai.

**tradition** shikitari, dentoo.

**traditional** dentooteki na.

**traffic** torihiki *(commerce)*; kootsuu *(movement of people, vehicles, etc.)*.

**tragedy** higeki *(opp. of comedy)*; kanashii dekigoto *(sad event)*.

**tragic** higekiteki na.

**trail** komichi *(mountain path)*; ato *(trace)*.

**trail (to)** ato o tsukeru *(pursue)*.

**train** kisha *(steam- or diesel-powered)*; densha *(electric)*.

**train (to)** kyooiku suru *(educate)*; shikomu *(animals)*.

**training** kunren.

**traitor** uragirimono *(betrayer)*; kokuzoku *(rebel)*.

**trample (to)** fumiarasu.

**tranquil** shizuka na.

**tranquility** heian.

**tranquilizer** chinseizai, seishin'anteizai, torankiraizaa.

**transaction** torihiki.
   **business transaction** shoogyoo torihiki.

**transfer** norikae kippu *(ticket)*.

**transfer (to)** norikaeru *(change cars)*; utsusu *(shift)*; ugokasu *(move)*; yuzuru *(hand over)*.

**transformer** hengatsu ki.

**transistor** toranjisutaa.

    **portable transistor radio** keitai yoo toranjisutaa rajio.

**transition** hensen, suii *(change).*

**translate (to)** hon'yaku suru.

**translation** hon'yaku, yaku.

**translator** hon'yakusha.

**transmission** dentatsu.

**transmit (to)** watasu *(hand over);* tsutaeru *(pass on).*

**transparent** sukitootta.

**transport** *n.* unsoo.

**transport (to)** unpan suru *(carry);* unsoo suru *(by ship or railroad).*

**transportation** yusoo *(conveyance);* unsoo *(shipping);* kootsuu no ben *(means of travel).*

**trap** wana.

**trap (to)** wana de toru.

**trash** gomi, kuzu *(rubbish);* garakuta *(odds and ends).*

**travel** ryokoo, tabi.

**travel (to)** ryokoo suru.

**traveler** ryokoosha.

**tray** bon, obon.

**treacherous** uragiru yoo na, fuchuujitsu no *(disloyal).*

**treachery** uragiri.

**treason** muhon.

**treasure** takara.

**treasure (to)** daiji ni suru.

**treasurer** kaikeigakari.

**treasury** shikin.

**treat** gochisoo.

**treat (to)** motenasu *(entertain);* atsukau *(deal with);* chiryoo suru *(give medical treatment);* ogoru *(treat a person to).*

**treatment** toriatsukai *(conduct toward);* chiryoo *(medical).*

**treaty** jooyaku.

    **commercial treaty** tsuushoo jooyaku.

**tree** ki.

    **evergreen** tokiwagi.

**tremble (to)** furueru.

**trembling** *adj.* furuete iru. *-n.* miburui.

**tremendous** taihen na.

**trench** mizo *(ditch);* zangoo *(military).*

**trend** keikoo *(general tendency);* hookoo, muki *(general direction).*

**trial** saiban *(law);* shiren *(hardship);* kokoromi *(experiment).*

**triangle** sankaku.

**tribe** shuzoku.

**tribulation** kannan.

**tribunal** saibansho *(a court of justice);* saiban *(that which judges).*

**trick** itazura, torikku *(mischief);* sakuryaku *(stratagem).*

**trick (to)** damasu.

**trifle** tsumaranai mono *(negligible thing);* kudaranai koto *(insignificant matter).*

**trifle (to)** tsumaranai koto ni jikan o tsubusu.

**trifling** tsumaranai *(uninteresting);* kudaranai *(trivial).*

**trim (to)** karikomu.

**trimming** kazari.

**trip** ryokoo.

    **to take a trip** ryokoo ni iku.

**trip (to)** tsumazuku *(take a false step);* tsumazukaseru *(trip up).*

**triple** sanbai no.

**triumph** shoori *(victory);* daiseikoo *(success).*

**triumph (to)** shoori o eru.

**triumphant** shoori o eta.

**trivial** kudaranai.

**troop** guntai.

**trophy** kappu, torofii.

**trot (to)** hayaashi de kakeru.

**trouble** konnan *(difficulty);* mendoo *(bother);* shinpai *(anxiety);* nangi *(distress).*

**trouble (to)** mendoo o kakeru *(put to inconvenience);* komaraseru *(perplex);* jama suru *(disturb).*

    **Don't trouble yourself!** Shinpai shinai de kudasai.

**trousers** zubon.

**truck** torakku.

**true** hontoo no *(opp. of false);* makoto no *(true-hearted);* shin no *(real);* jijitsu no *(actual);* seikaku na *(exact).*

**truly** hontoo ni *(correctly);* chuujitsu ni *(faithfully);* jitsu ni *(really);* mattaku *(indeed).*

**trump** kirifuda.

**trumpet** toranpetto.

**trunk** miki *(of tree);* toranku *(baggage).*

**trust** shin'yoo *(faith);* gimu *(responsibility);* shinrai *(reliance);* kakushin *(confidence).*

**trust (to)** shin'yoo suru *(give credit to);* shinrai suru *(rely on).*

**trusting** shinzuru.

**trustworthy** ate ni naru.

**truth** hontoo no koto *(correspondence to reality);* jijitsu *(fact).*

**truthful** shoojiki na *(veracious);* jitchoku na *(upright).*

**truthfully** shoojiki ni.

**truthfulness** seijitsu, seikakusa.

**try (to)** tamesu, kokoromiru *(prove by experiment);* yatte miru *(attempt).*

    **to try to go** ikoo to suru.

**tube** kuda, chuubu.

**Tuesday** Kayoobi.

**tumble (to)** korobu *(of persons);* taoreru *(of things);* ochiru *(roll over).*

**tumult** oosawagi *(uproar).*

**tune** senritsu, shirabe, fushi *(melody)*.
**tune (to)** chooshi o awaseru *(adjust);* choowa suru *(be in harmony)*.
**tunnel** tonneru.
**turf** shiba, shibafu.
**turkey** shichimenchoo.
**turmoil** soodoo.
**turn** junban *(place in line, order, etc.);* kaiten *(rotation);* kaabu *(curve);* hookoo tenkan *(change in direction)*.
**turn (to)** mawasu *(cause to revolve);* mawaru *(revolve);* magaru *(swerve)*.
 **Turn left.** Hidari e magatte kudasai.
 **turn on a light** tsukeru.
**turnip** kabu.
**twelfth** dai juuni.
 **twelfth of the month** juuninichi.
**twelve** juuni.
**twentieth** dai nijuu.
 **twentieth of the month** hatsuka.
**twenty** nijuu.
 **twenty years of age** hatachi.
**twice** nido.
**twilight** yuugata, tasogare *(poetic)*.
**twin** futago.
**twist (to)** nejiru *(distort);* yoriawaseru *(intertwine);* orikomu *(interweave)*.
**two** futatsu, ni.
**type** kata *(specimen);* moderu *(model);* tenkei *(pattern);* taipu, katsuji *(printing)*.
**type (to)** taipu suru.
**typewriter** taipuraitaa.
**tyranny** ooboo, gyakusei.
**tyrant** hookun.

**ugliness** migurushii koto.
**ugly** mittomonai.
**ulcer** kaiyoo.
**ulterior** hyoomen no, sotogawa no.
**ultimate** saigo no.
**ultimately** saigo ni.
**umbrella** kasa.
**umpire** shinpankan, anpaiya.
**umpire (to)** shinpan suru.
**unable** dekinai.
 **I'm unable to do it.** Suru koto ga dekimasen.
**unanimity** manjoo itchi.
**unanimous** onaji kangae no *(agreeing in opinion);* manjoo itchi no *(consent of all)*.
**unanimously** iku doon ni *(with one voice);* manjoo itchi de *(with a unanimous voice)*.
**unaware** kizukanai.

**unbearable** tamaranai *(unendurable);* gaman dekinai *(not able to be borne)*.
**unbelievable** shinjirarenai.
**unbutton** botan o hazusu.
**uncertain** fukakutei na *(undecided);* gura gura shita *(unsteady);* tashika de nai *(not sure);* abunai *(risky);* hakkiri shinai *(not settled)*.
**uncertainty** hakkiri shinai koto.
**unchangeable** fuhen no.
**uncle** oji, ojisan.
**uncomfortable** kokochi no warui, raku de nai.
**uncommon** metta ni nai *(infrequent);* hijoo na *(extraordinary);* mezurashii *(rare);* fushigi na *(strange)*.
**unconscious** kizetsu shita *(having lost consciousness);* kizukanai *(unaware)*.
**unconsciously** shirazu ni.
**uncover (to)** futa o toru *(take off a lid);* ooi o toru *(take off a covering)*.
**undecided** kimatte inai.
**undeniable** hitei dekinai, mooshibun no nai.
**under** -no shita ni, -no shita de, -no shita no.
**underdeveloped country** teikaihatsukoku.
**undergo** ukeru; shujutsu o ukeru *(undergo an operation)*.
**underground** chika *(subterranean);* himitsu no *(secret)*.
**underline (to)** shita ni sen o hiku *(underscore);* kyoochoo suru *(emphasize)*.
**underneath** -no shita ni, -no shita de, -no shita no.
**understand (to)** wakaru; rikai suru.
**understanding** *adj.* wakari no yoi. *-n.* rikai.
**undertake (to)** hikiukeru *(take upon oneself);* kuwadateru *(attempt)*.
**undertaking** shigoto *(task);* jigyoo *(enterprise)*.
**undesirable** nozomashikunai.
**undignified** omomi no nai, hin no nai, fukinshin na.
**undo (to)** moto ni kaesu *(reverse);* torikesu *(annul);* hazusu *(unfasten);* toku *(a knot);* akeru *(open, as a parcel);* nugu *(take off);* muda ni suru *(bring to naught);* tokeru *(come undone)*.
**undress (to)** kimono o nugu *(oneself);* kimono o nugaseru *(make someone else undress)*.
**uneasiness** fuan.
**uneasy** fuan na; ochitsukanai *(restless)*.
**unemployed** shigoto no nai *(out of work);* shitsugyooshita.
**unequal** fukoohei na, fubyoodoo na.
**uneven** fusoroi na *(not in line);* deko boko na *(rough)*.
**uneventful** buji heion na.
**unexpected** omoigakenai *(not expected);* yoki

shinai *(unforeseen);* totsuzen na *(sudden);* igai na *(surprising).*
**unexpectedly** igai ni, fui ni *(abruptly).*
**unfailing** tsukinai *(inexhaustible);* shinrai no dekiru *(sure).*
**unfair** fukoohei na *(biased);* tadashiku nai *(not right).*
**unfaithful** fuchuujitsu na.
**unfamiliar** yoku shiranai *(not well known);* shirarenai *(unknown);* keiken ga nai *(inexperienced).*
**unfavorable** yoku nai *(not good);* furi na *(not satisfactory);* tsugoo no warui *(inconvenient).*
**unfit** tekishinai *(unsuitable);* funiai na *(unbecoming).*
**unfold (to)** hirogeru.
**unforeseen** fui no, omoigakenai.
**unforgettable** wasurerarenai.
**unfortunate** fukoo na.
**unfortunately** ainiku *(unluckily);* zannen nagara *(regrettably).*
**ungrateful** arigataku omotte inai.
**unhappily** fushiawase ni.
**unhappiness** fushiawase.
**unhappy** fushiawase na.
**unharmed** buji na.
**unhealthy** karada no yowai *(sickly);* doku ni naru *(harmful to the health).*
**unheard of** mada kiita koto no nai.
**unhesitatingly** chuucho sezu ni.
**unhoped for** boogai no, kitai shinakatta.
**unhurt** kega no nai.
**uniform** *adj.* onaji yoo na *(about the same);* soroi no *(of the same pattern).* *-n.* yunifoomu, seifuku.
**uniformity** kin'itsu, kakuitsu.
**uniformly** dooyoo ni.
**unify (to)** tooitsu suru.
**unimportant** daiji de nai, tsumaranai *(worthless).*
**unintentional** koi de nai.
**unintentionally** koi de naku, muishiki ni.
**uninviting** ki no susumanai.
**union** kumiai *(association);* gappei *(combination);* engumi *(marriage).* **labor union** roodoo kumiai.
**unique** hitotsu kiri no *(single, sole);* dokutoku no *(peerless);* subarashii *(wonderful).*
**union** itchi, kyoodoo.
**unit** tan'i. **unit price** tanka.
**unite (to)** awaseru *(join into one);* ketsugoo suru *(combine);* gappei suru *(amalgamate);* gattai suru *(coalesce).*
**united** rengoo shita.
**United Nations** Kokuren.
**United States** Amerika Gasshuukoku.
**unity** tooitsu, itchi.

**universal** zen sekai no *(covering all the world);* ippan ni okonawareru *(widely practiced).*
**universe** uchuu.
**university** daigaku.
**unjust** fukoohei na.
**unjustifiable** iiwake no tatanai, too o enai.
**unkempt** darashi no nai.
**unkind** fushinsetsu na.
**unknown** shirarete inai.
**unlawful** fuhoo no, hooritsu ni hansuru.
**unless** -nakereba *(if not).* **Unless you come . . .** Anata ga konakereba . . .
**unlikely** arisoo de nai, hontoorashiku nai.
**unlimited** saigen no nai, seigen no nai.
**unload (to)** tsumini o ageru *(a ship's cargo);* ni o orosu *(take down from a truck or train).*
**unlucky** un no warui.
**unmask (to)** bakuro suru.
**unmistakably** machigai naku.
**unnecessary** yokei na *(superfluous);* mueki na *(useless);* muda na *(of no use);* fuhitsuyoo na *(not necessary).*
**unoccupied** aite iru *(untenanted);* yooji ga nai *(disengaged).*
**unofficial** hikooshiki no *(informal).*
**unpack (to)** ni o toku, nimotsu o hiraku.
**unpleasant** fuyukai na *(disagreeable);* iya na *(offensive).*
**unpublished** shuppan sarete inai.
**unquestionably** tashika ni.
**unravel (to)** toku, hodoku *(disentangle);* kaiketsu suru *(solve).*
**unreal** higenjitsuteki na.
**unreasonable** wake no wakaranai *(not governed by reason);* hoogai na *(exorbitant).*
**unrecognizable** wakari kaneru, mitomegatai.
**unreliable** ate ni naranai.
**unrest** fuon, fuanjootai.
**unrestrained** kimama na, yokusei no nai.
**unrestricted** museigen no.
**unroll (to)** toku, hirogeru.
**unsafe** abunai *(dangerous);* anzen de nai *(not safe).*
**unsatisfactory** fumanzoku na *(not satisfactory);* fujuubun na *(inadequate).*
**unsatisfied** fumanzoku na, manzoku shite inai.
**unscrupulous** buenryo na, mukoo mizu no.
**unseemly** mittomonai.
**unseen** kakurete iru, mienai.
**unselfish** rikoteki de nai, jibun o wasureta.
**unspeakable** iiyoo no nai.
**unstable** fuantei na.
**unsteady** shikkari shinai.
**unsuccessful** seikoo shinai, fuseikoo no.

**unsuitable** futekitoo na *(inappropriate);* niawanai *(not becoming).*

**unthinkable** kangaerarenai.

**untidy** darashi ga nai.

**untie (to)** hodoku.

**until** made.

    **until now** ima made.

**untiring** tsukarenai.

**untrue** uso no, hontoo de nai.

**untrustworthy** ate ni naranai.

**untruth** uso.

**unusual** ijoo na *(uncommon);* mare na *(rare);* metta ni nai *(not frequent);* narete inai *(unfamiliar);* mezurashii *(strange);* reigai no *(exceptional).*

**unwarranted** hoshoo no nai, fukakujitsu na.

**unwell** guai ga warui.

**unwholesome** kenkoo ni yoku nai, kenzen de nai.

**unwilling** fuhon'i no *(disinclined);* ki ga susumanai *(reluctant).*

**unwise** oroka na, kashikoku nai.

**unworthy** kudaranai *(wanting merit);* fusawashiku nai *(unsuitable).*

**unyielding** ganko na.

**up** ue, ue ni.

    **eat up** tabete shimau.

    **give up** akirameru.

**upheaval** dooran.

**uphold (to)** saseru, shiji suru *(support);* kakunin suru *(court decision).*

**upkeep** ijihi *(expense);* iji *(maintenance).*

**upon** -no ue ni, -no ue de, -no ue no.

**upper** ue no.

**upright** tatte iru *(erect);* shoojiki na *(honest).*

**uprising** boodoo *(revolt);* ikki *(riot).*

**uproar** oosawagi *(disturbance);* soozooshii koe *(clamor).*

**upset (to)** kutsugaesu *(overturn);* taosu *(overthrow);* shippai saseru *(frustrate);* awatesaseru *(make nervous).*

    **to be upset** roobai suru.

**upside down** sakasama *(topsy turvy);* abekobe *(reverse).*

**upstairs** nikai.

**upward** uwamuki no.

**uranium** uranyuumu.

**urge (to)** susumeru *(incite);* isogaseru *(hasten);* karitateru *(press);* hagemasu *(exhort).*

**urgency** seppaku, kinkyuu.

**urgent** isogi no, kinkyuu no.

**urinate (to)** shooyoo o suru, shooben suru.

**us** watashitachi.

**U.S.A.** Amerika Gasshuukoku.

**use** tsukaikata *(manner of using).*

    **to be of use** yaku ni tatsu.

**use (to)** tsukau.

**used to** -mono da *(habitual in the past);* -ni narete iru *(accustomed).*

    **I am used to dangerous places.** Abunai basho ni narete iru.

    **She used to go there every day.** Mainichi itta mono da.

**useful** yaku ni tatsu *(serviceable);* choohoo na *(handy);* yuuyoo na *(good for something).*

**useless** muyoo na *(of no service);* dame na *(fruitless);* muda na *(futile).*

**usher** annai, annainin.

**usher (to)** annai suru.

**usual** futsuu no *(commonplace);* itsu mo no *(habitual).*

**usually** itsu mo, taitei.

**usurp (to)** ooryoo suru, shingai suru.

**utensil** doogu.

**utility** jitsuyoo, yuuyoo *(usefulness);* kooeki jigyoo *(public utility).*

    **The rent includes utilities.** Yachin ni wa suidoo-gasu-denki ga haitte imasu.

**utilize** riyoo suru.

**utmost** *adj.* sei ippai no *(maximum effort);* kyokudo no *(extreme).*

**utter** tetteiteki na *(total);* kanzen na *(complete);* mattaku no *(entire);* mujooken no *(unconditional).*

**utter (to)** iu *(say);* hanasu *(speak);* iiarawasu *(express).*

**utterly** zenzen *(absolutely);* mattaku *(totally);* sukkari *(completely).*

# V

**vacant** kara no *(empty);* aite iru *(unoccupied);* karite no nai *(untenanted).*

**vacation** yasumi.

**vague** hakkirai shinai *(indefinite);* aimai na *(ambiguous).*

**vain** yaku ni tatanai *(useless);* muda na *(fruitless);* unubore no tsuyoi, kyoeishin no tsuyoi *(conceited).*

    **in vain** muda ni.

**valiant** isamashii *(brave);* yuuki no aru *(courageous).*

**valid** tashika na *(well founded);* yuukoo na *(effective).*

**validity** seitoo sa, kakujitsu sa.

**valley** tani.

**valuable** kooka na *(precious);* neuchi no aru *(in terms of money, materially).*

    **valuables** kichoohin.

**value** neuchi *(worth);* atai *(cost).*

**value (to)** nebumi suru *(appraise);* sonchoo suru *(rate highly);* daiji ni suru *(think important).*

**valued** kichoo na.

**valve** ben, barubu.

**vanilla** banira.

**vanish (to)** kieuseru *(disappear)*; usureru *(fade away)*; nakunaru *(cease to exist)*.

**vanity** kyoeishin, unubore *(conceit)*.

**vanquish** seifuku suru *(conquer)*; makasu *(defeat)*.

**vapor** yuge *(of water)*; kitai *(gaseous state of liquid or solid)*.

**variable** kawariyasui.

**variance** fuwa *(antagonism)*; hendoo *(deviation, discord)*; fuitchi, chigai *(divergence)*.

**variation** henka, chigai *(modification, change)*.

**varied** samazama no.

**variety** henka ni tomu koto *(diversity)*; kuichigai *(difference)*; shurui *(kinds)*.

**various** iroiro no.

**varnish (to)** urushi o nuru.

**vary (to)** kaeru, chigaeru *(alter)*; henka o soeru *(diversity)*.

**vase** tsubo.

    **flower vase** kabin.

**vast** hiroi.

**vault** kinko *(safe)*.

**veal** koushi no niku.

**vegetable** yasai.

**vehemence** hageshisa.

**vehement** hageshii, nesshin na.

**vehicle** norimono.

**veil** maku *(curtain)*; beeru *(for face)*.

**veil (to)** beeru o kakeru.

**vein** joomyaku *(blood vessel)*.

**velocity** sokuryoku, hayasa *(speed)*.

**velvet** biroodo, berubetto.

**venerable** sonkei subeki, rippa na *(respected)*.

**venerate (to)** uyamau.

**veneration** sonkei.

**vengeance** fukushuu.

**venom** doku *(poison)*; urami *(ill will)*.

**venomous** doku no aru.

**ventilation** kazetooshi, tsuufuu.

**ventilator** tsuufuuki.

**venture** kiken na kuwadate.

**venture (to)** kiken ni sarasu *(risk)*; omoikitte yaru *(brave danger)*.

**verb** dooshi.

**verdict** hyooketsu *(of law)*; handan *(judgment)*; kettei *(decision)*.

**verge** hashi *(edge)*; heri *(brink)*; kyookai *(borderline)*.

    **on the verge of** -ni hinsuru.

**verge (to)** chikazuku.

**verification** kakunin.

**verify (to)** shoomei suru *(prove)*; tashikameru *(ascertain)*.

**versatile** tagei no, bannoo no.

**verse** shi *(poem)*; ku *(line of a poem)*.

**version** hanashi *(of a story)*; hon'yaku *(translation)*; iken *(opinion)*.

**vertical** suichoku no, tate no *(perpendicular)*.

**very** taihen, taisoo, hijoo ni, hanahadashiku, totemo.

**vessel** fune *(ship)*; iremono *(receptacle)*.

**vest** chokki.

**vex (to)** urusagaraseru *(annoy)*; okoraseru *(provoke)*; nayamasu *(distress)*.

**via** -keiyu.

**vibrate (to)** yureru *(oscillate)*; furueru *(quiver)*.

**vice** fudootoku *(depravity)*; akuheki *(evil habit)*.

**vice president** fuku daitooryoo *(of a country)*; fuku kaichoo *(of a society)*; fuku shachoo *(of a firm)*.

**vice versa** abekobe, hantai.

**vicinity** kinjo *(neighborhood)*; chikai koto *(nearness)*.

**victim** higaisha *(injured one)*; soonansha *(sufferer)*; giseisha *(one who is a sacrifice)*.

**victor** shoorisha.

**victorious** shoori o eta, katta.

**victory** shoori

**video** bideo.

    **VCR** bii-sii-aaru.

    **video camera** bideo kamera.

    **video disc** bideo disuku.

    **video game** bideo geemu.

**vie (with) (to)** kisou.

**view** keshiki *(prospect)*; iken *(opinion)*.

**view (to)** miru; yuuran suru *(sightseeing)*.

**vigor** seiryoku *(vitality)*; genki *(energy)*.

**vigorous** genki na *(energetic)*; tsuyoi *(strong)*; kappatsu na *(active)*.

**vile** katoo na.

**village** mura.

**villain** warumono.

**vindicate (to)** bengo suru.

**vindictive** shuunen bukai.

**vine** tsuru.

**vinegar** su.

**violence** bookoo *(outrage)*; booryoku *(exertion of physical force)*.

**violent** hageshii, hidoi *(wild)*.

**violet** *n.* sumire *(flower)*; murasaki iro *(color)*.

**violin** baiorin.

**virtue** toku *(moral excellence)*; zenkoo *(opp. of vice)*; misao *(chastity)*; kooketsu *(uprightness)*.

**virtuous** dootoku no takai *(morally good)*; kooketsu na *(honorable)*; dootokuteki na *(moral)*.

**visibility** shikai.

**visible** me ni mieru.

**visibly** me ni miete.

**vision** shiryoku *(eyesight).*

**visit** hoomon *(call on someone);* omimai *(to sick people).*

**visit (to)** tazuneru, hoomon suru *(a person);* kenbutsu suru *(museums, etc.).*

**visitor** okyakusama *(guest).*

**visual** shikaku no.

    **visual education** shikaku kyooiku.

**visualize (to)** kokoro ni egaku.

**vital** seimei no *(of life);* hijoo ni juudai na *(very important);* kan'yoo na *(indispensable).*

**vitality** tairyoku.

**vivacious** kaikatsu na *(jovial);* yooki na *(lively);* genki na *(spirited).*

**vivid** hakkiri shita.

**vocabulary** tango *(individual words);* goi *(list of words).*

**vocal** koe no.

**vocation** shokugyoo *(profession);* shoobai *(business);* teishoku *(regular employment).*

**vogue** hayari, ryuukoo.

**voice** koe.

**voice (to)** koe o dasu *(utter);* iken o haku *(give expression to).*

**void** kooryoku no nai *(not binding);* mukoo no *(nullified).*

**void (to)** dasu *(throw, send out, empty).*

**volume** yooseki *(of a solid);* ryoo *(quantity);* -kan, -satsu *(counter for books and magazines).*

    **one volume** issatsu.

**voluminous** kasabaru.

**voluntary** jihatsuteki.

**volunteer** shiboosha.

**vomit (to)** haku.

**vote** hyoo.

**vote (to)** toohyoo suru.

**voucher** uketori *(receipt).*

**vouch for (to)** hoshoo suru *(guarantee);* hoshoonin ni naru *(stand sponsor for).*

**vow** seiyaku *(promise);* chikai *(oath).*

**vow (to)** seiyaku suru *(promise);* dangen suru *(assert);* chikau *(pledge).*

**vowel** boin.

**voyage** kookai.

**vulgar** gehin na.

**vulnerable** yowami no aru.

**wade (to)** wataru.

**waffle** waffuru.

**wag (to)** furu.

**wage** chingin.

**wager** kakegoto *(act of betting);* kake *(bet).*

**wager (to)** kakegoto o suru.

**wages** chingin *(pay);* kyuuryoo *(salary, payroll).*

**wagon** kuruma.

**waist** koshi.

**wait** matsu koto *(act of waiting).*

**wait (to)** matsu.

**waiter** weetaa.

**wake (to)** okosu.

    **be awakened** okosareru.

**walk** sanpo.

    **Go for a walk (take a walk).** Sanpo suru.

**walk (to)** aruku.

**wall** kabe.

**wallet** saifu *(purse);* satsu-ire *(for paper money).*

**walnut** kurumi.

**waltz** warutsu.

**wander (to)** aruki mawaru.

**want** ketsuboo.

**want (to)** iru *(need);* hoshii desu *(want to have a thing).*

    **want to go** ikitai.

**war** sensoo.

**war (to)** sensoo o suru.

**warble (to)** saezuru.

**ward** boogo *(guard);* mihari *(watch);* kyoodoo byooshitsu *(in a hospital);* ku *(division of a city, borough).*

**wardrobe** tansu.

**ware, wares** shinamono; saikumono *(handicraft);* toojiki *(chinaware).*

**warehouse** sooko.

**warfare** sensoo *(war).*

**warm** atatakai.

**warm (to)** atatakaku suru *(keep warm).*

**warmth** atatakasa.

**warn (to)** chuui suru *(caution);* imashimeru *(admonish).*

**warning** chuui, kunkai *(admonition);* yokoku *(notice).*

**warrant** hoshoo *(guarantee);* shoomeisho *(certificate).*

**warrant (to)** hoshoo suru.

**warrior** heishi *(soldier);* yuushi *(distinguished soldier).*

**wary** yoojinbukai.

**wash** sentaku *(washing).*

**wash (to)** arau.

**washroom** otearai, toire.

**waste** amarimono *(waste material);* kuzu *(refuse).*

    **wastepaper** kamikuzu.

**waste (to)** muda ni suru.

**watch** tokei *(timepiece).*

    **wristwatch** udedokei.

**watch (to)** ban o suru *(guard);* ki o tsukeru *(pay attention).*

**watchful** yoojinbukai *(cautious).*

**water** mizu.

**water (to)** mizu o yaru *(plants)*.

**waterfall** taki.

**waterproof** *adj.* mizu no tooranai. *-n.* boosui, taisui.

**watt** watto.

**wave** nami.

**wave (to)** yureru *(sway)*; hirugaeru *(flutter)*; furimawasu *(brandish)*.

**waver (to)** tamerau *(hesitate)*.

**wax** roo, wakkusu.

**way** michi *(road)*; toori *(street)*; hoohoo *(method)*.

**we** watashitachi, watakushidomo.

**weak** yowai.

**weaken (to)** yowaku suru *(make weak)*; yowaku naru *(get weak)*.

**weakly** yowayowashii, byooshin na *(sickly)*.

**weakness** ketten *(weak points)*.

**wealth** zaisan *(riches)*; tomi *(fortune)*.

**wealthy** kanemochi no *(rich)*; yutaka na *(well off)*.

**weapon** buki.

**wear (to)** kiru *(coat, dress)*; haku *(pants, shoes)*; shimeru *(girdle)*; kaburu *(hat)*; hameru *(ring, gloves)*; kakeru *(spectacles)*.

**weariness** hiroo *(fatigue)*; taikutsu *(tedium)*.

**weary** tsukareta *(tired)*; akita *(bored)*; taikutsu na *(tedious)*.

**weather** tenki.

   **rainy weather** ame, uten.

   **cloudy weather** kumori.

**weave (to)** oru.

**wedding** kekkonshiki *(ceremony)*.

**wedge** kusabi.

**Wednesday** Suiyoobi.

**weed** zassoo.

**weed (to)** zassoo o nuku.

**week** shuu *(counter for weeks)*.

   **next week** raishuu.

   **this week** konshuu.

   **two weeks** nishuukan.

**weekend** *n.* shuumatsu, wiikuendo.

**weekly** shuukan zasshi *(periodical)*.

**weep (to)** naku.

**weigh (to)** mekata o hakaru.

**weight** mekata.

**welcome** kangei.

   **You're welcome.** Yoku irasshaimashita. *(Glad that you've come.)* Doo itashimashite. *(It was nothing. Don't mention it.)*

**welfare** fukushi *(well-being)*; han'ei *(prosperity)*.

**well** ido *(for water)*.

**west** nishi.

**western** nishi no.

**wet** nureta, nurete iru.

**wet (to)** nurasu.

**whale** kujira.

**what** *pron.* nan, nani. *-adj.* dono *(which)*.

   **what he said** itta koto *(that which he said)*.

   **What is it?** Nan desu ka?

**whatever** nan de mo.

   **whatever he heard** nan de mo kiita koto.

   **whatever he saw** nan de mo mita mono.

**wheat** komugi.

**wheel** kuruma, wa.

**when** itsu *(interrogative)*; -toki, toki ni *(at the particular time that)*; -tara *(if, when)*; -to *(whenever)*.

   **When I asked Mr. Yamada** . . . Yamada-san ni kiitara . . .

   **When I have a headache** . . . Atama ga itai to . . .

   **When I went to Kyoto** . . . Kyooto e itta toki . . .

**whenever** -to, tabi ni *(every time)*; itsu mo *(always)*; itsu de mo *(at all times)*.

**where** doko ni, doko de, doko e *(in what place)*; dochira *(polite, used like doko)*; doko e *(whither)*.

**wherever** doko—demo; doko—temo.

   **Wherever we go, there are many people.** Doko e itte mo hito ga ooi.

**whether** ka, ka doo ka. -mo -mo.

   **I don't know whether the library is open today.** Toshokan wa kyoo aite iru ka doo ka shiranai.

   **I intend to go whether it rains or snows.** Ame ga futtemo, yuki ga futtemo iku tsumori desu.

**which** *pron.* dore *(of several)*; dochira *(of two)*. *-adj.* dono.

**while** -uchi ni; -aida ni.

   **Wait a while.** Chotto matte kudasai.

**whim** kimagure.

**whimper (to)** shikushiku naku.

**whine (to)** nakigoe o dasu.

**whip** muchi.

**whip (to)** muchi de utsu *(lash)*; sekkan suru *(flog)*.

**whisper** sasayaki.

**whisper (to)** sasayaku *(speak softly or under the breath)*; naisho banashi o suru *(speak in secret)*.

**whistle** fue *(instrument)*; kuchibue *(made with the mouth)*.

**whistle (to)** kuchibue o fuku.

**white** *adj.* shiroi. *-n.* shiro.

**who** *n.* donata, dare *(interrogative)*.

**whoever** dare de mo.

**whole** *adj.* zen- *(prefix)*; -juu *(suffix)*; zenbu no. *-n.* zenbu.

**wholesale** oroshi, oroshiuri.

**wholesome** kenkoo ni yoi *(salubrious)*; kenzen na *(sound)*.

**whom** dare ni, donata ni *(as indirect object);* dare o, donata o *(as direct object).*

**whose** donata no, dare no.

**why** naze, doo shite.

**wicked** warui *(bad);* yokoshima na *(sinful);* ijiwaru na *(ill-tempered).*

**wide** hiroi.

**widen** *v.t.* hirogeru; *v.i.* hirogaru.

**widow** miboojin.

**widower** otoko yamome.

**width** haba.

**wife** tsuma; okusama *(your wife);* kanai *(my wife).*

**wig** katsura.

**wild** yasei no *(opp. of domestic);* arehateta *(uncultivated);* arai *(untamed);* ranboo na *(lawless);* kyooki no *(frantic).*

**wilderness** arano.

**wildness** ranboo sa.

**will** ishi *(the faculty);* ishi no chikara *(willpower);* ketsui *(determination);* negai *(wish);* kiboo *(desire);* yuigonjoo *(testament).*

**will (to)** yuigon o nokosu *(bequeath).*

**willful** koi no.

**willing** yorokonde . . . suru.

**I'm willing to go.** Yorokonde ikimasu.

**willingly** yorokonde.

**win** shoori, kachi.

**win (to)** toru *(prizes);* katsu *(races);* hakusuru *(fame, etc.).*

**wind** kaze.

**wind (to)** maku.

**window** mado.

**windy** kaze ga fuku.

**wine** budooshu, wain *(grape);* sake *(Japanese; made from rice).*

**wing** hane *(of birds);* yoku *(airplane).*

**wink** mekubase, mabataki *(blink);* isshunkan *(instant).*

**winner** shoorisha *(victory);* jushoosha *(recipient of an award).*

**winter** fuyu.

**wipe (to)** fuku.

**wire** harigane *(metal);* denpoo *(telegram).*

**wire (to)** denpoo o utsu *(send a telegram).*

**wisdom** funbetsu *(prudence);* chie *(intelligence).*

**wise** kashikoi *(sagacious);* shiryo no aru *(sensible);* hakushiki na *(learned).*

**wish** negai *(longing);* nozomi *(hope).*

**wish (to)** -ga hoshii *(wish for something);* nozomu *(hope).*

**wit** kichi *(smart utterance);* richi *(intelligence);* funbetsu *(sense).*

**witch** miko, majo.

**with** -to, -to issho ni *(together with);* de *(by means of).*

**withdraw (to)** hikisageru *(take back);* saru *(remove);* hikiageru *(evacuate).*

**withdrawal** hikisage, tekkai; hikidashi *(bank).*

**wither (to)** kareru.

**within** -no uchi ni, naka ni *(internally);* ie no naka ni *(in the house);* okunai ni *(indoors).*

**without** -nashi *(not with);* -nai de *(without -ing).*

**I went out without any money.** Okane nashi de gaishutsu shita.

**I went to school without having breakfast.** Asagohan o tabenai de gakkoo e itta.

**witness** shooko *(testimony);* shoogen *(verbal evidence);* mokugekisha *(eyewitness);* shoonin *(legal).*

**witness (to)** mokugeki suru *(be a spectator);* shimesu *(show);* shoonin to shite shomei suru *(sign as a witness).*

**witty** ki no kiita, kashikoi *(clever).*

**woe** kunoo *(affliction).*

**wolf** ookami.

**woman** onna, onna no hito, fujin *(lady).*

**wonder** odoroki *(feeling);* fushigi *(cause of);* kiseki *(miracle).*

**wonder (to)** odoroku *(be surprised);* fushigi ni omou *(take as strange).*

**wonderful** fushigi na *(strange);* subarashii *(splendid).*

**wood** ki; zaimoku *(lumber).*

**woods** hayashi.

**woodwork** kizaiku.

**wool** yoomoo *(coat of sheep);* keito *(yarn);* ke *(material).*

**woolen** keori no.

**word** kotoba *(speech);* yakusoku *(promise);* tayori *(news).*

**word for word** ichiji ichiji.

**word processor** waapuro.

**work** roodoo *(manual labor);* shigoto *(mission, job);* shoku *(employment, occupation);* chosaku *(literary work).*

**work (to)** shigoto o suru, hataraku.

**worker** roodoosha *(wage earner);* shokunin *(craftsman).*

**work of art** geijutsu sakuhin.

**workshop** shigotoba, seisakujo.

**world** sekai *(earth);* chikyuu *(the globe);* seken *(society).*

**worldliness** zokushuu.

**worldly** kono yo teki na.

**worm** mushi.

**worry** shinpai *(care);* kuroo *(trouble);* mendoo *(difficulty).*

**worry (to)** *v.i.* shinpai suru; *v.t.* shinpai saseru *(make one worry).*

**Don't worry!** Shinpai shinaide kudasai.

**worse** -yori mo warui, sara ni warui.

**worship** reihai *(religion);* suuhai *(admiration).*

**worship (to)** reihai suru, ogamu.
**worst** ichiban warui.
**worth** *adj.* neuchi ga aru, kai ga aru *(worthwhile)*. *-n.* kachi, neuchi.
**worthless** neuchi no nai.
**worthy** kachi no aru *(good enough for)*; -ni fusawashii *(deserving)*.
**wound** kega *(injury)*; kizu *(scratch)*.
**wound (to)** kizutsukeru *(injure)*; kega o saseru *(hurt)*.
**get wounded** kega o suru.
**wounded** kega o shita.
**wrap (to)** tsutsumu.
**wrathful** ikidootte iru.
**wreath** hanawa.
**wreck** nanpa *(of a ship)*.
**a wrecked ship** nanpasen.
**wreck (to)** hakai suru *(demolish)*; kowasu *(bring disaster on)*.
**to be shipwrecked** nanpa suru.
**wrestle (to)** sumoo o toru *(Japanese-style)*; resuringu o suru *(Western-style)*; kutoo suru *(struggle with)*.
**wrestler** sumootori *(Japanese-style)*; resuraa *(Western-style)*.
**wrestling** sumoo *(Japanese-style)*; resuringu *(Western-style)*.
**wretched** mijime na.
**wring** shiboru.
**wrinkle** shiwa.
**wrinkle (to)** hitai ni shiwa o yoseru *(one's forehead)*.
**to wrinkle with age** toshi o totte shiwa ga yoru.
**wrist** tekubi.
**wristband** udewa.
**write (to)** kaku.
**writer** chosha *(author)*; sakka *(novelist)*; shoki *(clerk)*; kaita hito *(one who wrote)*.
**writing** hisseki *(handwriting)*; kaita mono *(that which is written)*.
**to state it in writing** kaita mono de noberu.
**to put in writing** shomen ni suru.
**written** kaite aru, kakareta.
**wrong** *adj.* warui, yoku nai *(bad)*; ayamatta, machigatta *(mistaken)*; fusei na *(not moral)*. *-n.* fusei, fugi.
**wrong (to)** fusei o okonau.

# Y

**yacht** yotto.
**Yankee** yankii.

**yard** niwa *(garden)*; yaado, yaaru *(measure)*.
**yarn** ito.
**wool yarn** keito.
**yawn** akubi.
**yawn (to)** akubi o suru.
**year** toshi, -nen.
**per year** nen ni.
**ten years** junnen.
**this year** konne, kotoshi.
**yearly** mainen no *(every year)*; nen ni ichido no *(once a year)*.
**yearn for (to)** -ni kogareru.
**yearning** akogare.
**yeast** iisuto, kooji.
**yell** sakebigoe.
**yell (to)** sakebu.
**yellow** *n.* kiiro. *-adj.* kiiroi.
**yen** en *(Japanese currency)*.
**yes** hai, ee, soo de gozaimasu *(extra polite)*.
**yesterday** kinoo, sakujitsu.
**yet** mada *(still)*; soredemo *(nevertheless)*.
**and yet** sore na noni.
**yield (to)** sansuru *(produce)*; yurusu *(grant)*; ataeru *(give over)*; shitagau *(follow)*.
**yielding** juujun na *(compliant)*.
**yoke** kubiki.
**yolk** tamago no kimi.
**you** anata *(sing.)*; anatagata *(pl.)*; kimi *(used by men to close male friends)*.
**young** wakai.
**your** anata no *(sing.)*; anatagata no *(pl.)*.
**yours** anata no, anata no mono *(sing.)*, anatatachi no, anatatachi no mono *(pl.)*.
**yourself** jishin, jibun.
**youth** wakai toki *(the period)*; wakai otoko *(young man)*.
**youthful** wakawakashii.
**youthfulness** wakawakashisa.

# Z

**zeal** nesshin.
**zealous** nesshin na.
**zero** zero, rei.
**zipper** zippaa, jippaa.
**zone** chitai, chiiki *(area)*; -tai *(in compounds)*.
**safety zone** anzen chitai.
**temperate zone** ontai.
**zone (to)** chiiki o kugiru.
**zoo** doobutsuen.
**zoology** doobutsugaku.

# GLOSSARY OF
# GEOGRAPHICAL NAMES

**Africa** Afurika.
**Alaska** Arasuka.
**Algeria** Arujeria.
**Alps** Arupusu.
**America** Amerika, Beikoku.
   **Central America** Chuuoo Amerika, Chuubei.
   **North America** Kita Amerika, Hokubei.
   **South America** Minami Amerika, Nanbei.
**Argentina** Aruzenchin.
**Asia** Ajia.
**Atlantic Ocean** Taiseiyoo.
**Australia** Oosutorariya.
**Austria** Oosutoria.
**Beijing** Pekin.
**Bombay** Bonbei.
**Brazil** Burajiru.
**Burma** Biruma.
**Canada** Kanada.
**Chile** Chiri.
**China** Chuugoku.
**Cuba** Kyuuba.
**Denmark** Denmaaku.
**Egypt** Ejiputo.
**England** Igirisu, Eikoku.
**Europe** Yooroppa, Ooshuu.
**France** Furansu.
**Geneva** Juneebu.
**Germany** Doitsu.
**Great Britain** Igirisu.
**Greece** Girisha.
**Hawaii** Hawai.
**Hokkaido** Hokkaidoo.
**Hong Kong** Honkon.
**Hungary** Hangarii.
**Iceland** Aisurando.
**India** Indo.
**Indochina** Indo shina.
**Indonesia** Indoneshia.
**Iran** Iran.

**Iraq** Iraku.
**Ireland** Airurando.
**Israel** Isuraeru.
**Italy** Itaria.
**Japan** Nippon, Nihon.
   **Japan Sea** Nihonkai.
**Kobe** Koobe.
**Korea** Kankoku *(South);* Kita Choosen *(North).*
**Kyoto** Kyooto.
**Kyushu** Kyuushuu.
**London** Rondon.
**Malaya** Maree.
**Manila** Manira.
**Mexico** Mekishiko.
**Moscow** Mosukuwa.
**Netherlands** Oranda.
**New York** Nyuu Yooku.
**New Zealand** Nyuu Jiirando.
**Norway** Noruuee.
**Osaka** Oosaka.
**Pacific Ocean** Taiheiyoo.
**Pakistan** Pakisutan.
**Persian Gulf** Perusha wan.
**Philippines** Firipin.
**Poland** Poorando.
**Portugal** Porutogaru.
**Russia** Roshia.
**San Francisco** San Furanshisuko.
**Siberia** Shiberia.
**Singapore** Shingapooru.
**South Africa** Minami Afurika.
**Southeast Asia** Toonan-Ajia.
**Spain** Supein.
**Sri Lanka** Suriranka.
**Sweden** Sueeden.
**Switzerland** Suisu.
**Taipei** Taipee.
**Taiwan** Taiwan.
**Thailand** Tai.
**Tokyo** Tookyoo.
**Turkey** Toruko.
**United States** Gasshuukoku.
   **U.S.A.** Amerika Gasshuukoku, Beikoku.
**Washington D.C.** Washinton.

# The **best-selling** language course
## Completely revised and updated!

Words, phrases, sentences, conversations: speak a new language with confidence right from the start with our simple four-step building block approach. Designed to be effective in a short period of time, these comprehensive courses have everything you need—pronunciation, vocabulary, grammar, culture, and practice.

Each course package includes:

- A coursebook with 40 step-by-step lessons
- 4 audio CDs with all the essential course content
- An extensive grammar reference section
- Supplemental sections on e-mail and internet resources
- A learner's dictionary or a reading and writing guide

## Available In:

**4 CDs/Coursebook/**
**Reading and Writing Guide**
$29.95/$34.00 Can.

Arabic: 978-1-4000-2408-7

**Reading and Writing Guide**
$8.99/$9.99 Can.

Arabic Script: 978-1-4000-0924-4

**4 CDs/Coursebook/Dictionary**
$29.95/$34.00 Can.

| | |
|---|---|
| Chinese: | 978-1-4000-2426-1 |
| [Mandarin] | |
| French: | 978-1-4000-2410-0 |
| German: | 978-1-4000-2412-4 |
| Inglés: | 978-1-4000-2414-8 |
| Italian: | 978-1-4000-2416-2 |
| Japanese: | 978-1-4000-2418-6 |
| Portuguese: | 978-1-4000-2420-9 |
| Russian: | 978-1-4000-2422-3 |
| Spanish: | 978-1-4000-2424-7 |

**Coursebook Only**
$10.95/$12.50 Can.

| | |
|---|---|
| Arabic: | 978-1-4000-1992-2 |
| Chinese: | 978-1-4000-2525-4 |
| [Mandarin] | |
| French: | 978-1-4000-2409-4 |
| German: | 978-1-4000-2411-7 |
| Inglés: | 978-1-4000-2413-1 |
| Italian: | 978-1-4000-2415-5 |
| Japanese: | 978-1-4000-2417-9 |
| Portuguese: | 978-1-4000-2419-3 |
| Russian: | 978-1-4000-2421-6 |
| Spanish: | 978-1-4000-2423-0 |

**Dictionary Only**
$7.95/$9.95 Can.

| | |
|---|---|
| Chinese: | 978-1-4000-2452-0 |
| [Mandarin] | |
| French: | 978-1-4000-2444-5 |
| German: | 978-1-4000-2445-2 |
| Inglés: | 978-1-4000-2446-9 |
| Italian: | 978-1-4000-2447-6 |
| Japanese: | 978-1-4000-2448-3 |
| Portuguese: | 978-1-4000-2449-0 |
| Russian: | 978-1-4000-2450-6 |
| Spanish: | 978-1-4000-2451-3 |

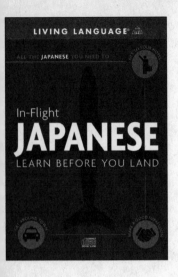

## In-Flight Japanese

Wondering how to make use of all that spare time on the plane? Between your in-flight meal and in-flight movie, brush up on your Japanese! This 60-minute program covers just enough Japanese to get by in every travel situation.

CD Program
978-0-609-81072-9 • $13.95/$21.00 Can.

## Ultimate Japanese Beginner-Intermediate

Equivalent to two years of college-level study, this comprehensive program covers reading, writing, grammar, conversation, and culture. This package includes a coursebook and eight 60-minute CDs.

CD Program
978-1-4000-2113-0 • $79.95/$110.00 Can.

Coursebook Only
978-1-4000-2112-3 • $18.00/$26.00 Can.

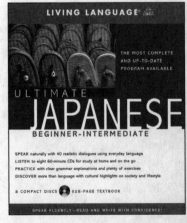